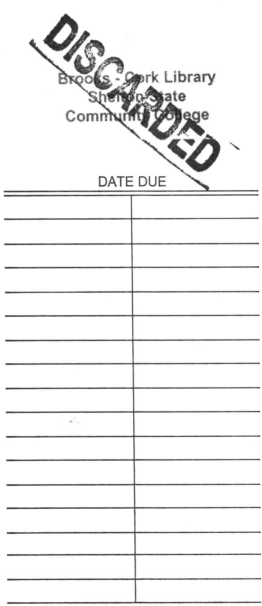

DATE DUE

THE PROVINCE OF PIETY

THE

PROVINCE

OF

PIETY

MORAL HISTORY
IN HAWTHORNE'S
EARLY TALES

Michael J. Colacurcio

DUKE UNIVERSITY PRESS
Durham and London
1995

© 1995 Duke University Press
All rights reserved
Printed in the United States of America
on acid-free paper ∞
The Province of Piety was originally published by
Harvard University Press in 1984.

Library of Congress Cataloging-in-Publication Data
Colacurcio, Michael J. The province of piety : moral history in
Hawthorne's early tales / Michael J. Colacurcio. Originally published:
Cambridge, Mass. : Harvard University Press, 1984. Includes
bibliographical references and index.
ISBN 0-8223-1572-6 (paper)
1. Hawthorne, Nathaniel, 1804–1864—Knowledge—History.
2. Historical fiction, American—History and criticism.
3. Hawthorne, Nathaniel, 1804–1864—Ethics.
4. Moral conditions in literature. 5. Ethics in literature.
I. Title.
PS1892.H5C6   1995
813'.3—dc20   94-42365 CIP

FOR MY FATHER
who insisted on science

AND MY MOTHER
who loved to play with words

ACKNOWLEDGMENTS

I HOPE it will be obvious, from my notes and otherwise, that I have tried to read most of what previous scholars have written on the works discussed in this volume and that I have learned from them most of what I know. Yet some are more equal. David Levin, Roy Harvey Pearce, and Hyatt Waggoner have exercised a special influence: the first two, obviously, on the historicist logic of my argument; the last (scarcely the least), on my estimate of Hawthorne's religious sensibility and my regard for the texture of his fiction. I have, I trust, my own Hawthorne recipe. And I hope I have not offended any of those from whom I have taken important ingredients.

A fair number of professional colleagues have, at different times and for a variety of occasions, read and made encouraging remarks about the manuscript of this book. My special thanks to Sacvan Bercovitch, R. W. B. Lewis, Frederick Newberry, Forrest Robinson, and (among my fellow Cornellians) Jonathan Bishop, Robert Elias, Michael Kammen, Cushing Strout, and Walter Slatoff. Phil Marcus read less of the manuscript than some others, but he endured more coffee-break rehearsals of my arguments than most Yeatsians would have found professionally useful; he must be my friend. So was the late Bill Sale, chairman of the department when I first came to Cornell; his kindness and support I remember as an epitome of the friendliness to my project of my department and college.

Everyone with an electric typewriter, it now seems, has typed a portion of some draft of this manuscript. In the early stages, my wife, Mary—competent and generous in *all* things—was my typist too. More recently, Jane Solomon, Rita Bryant, Valorie Eamer, and Phillis Molock have had to deal with my awkward compositional habits. Meridith Randall and Nancy Shaw helped me, indefatigably, with the laborious task of reading proof, catching some of my most vulgar errors; those that remain are my own, of course. Other graduate students, of an earlier generation, bore a heavy burden of my intellectual trial and error. Many have published essays which smoothed the path of my own argument, so that names like Altschuler, Daly, Duban, Jorgensen, Samson, and Williams show up for (inadequate) acknowledgment in my notes. Others did even more: Allan Emery listened, David Van Leer questioned, Carol Bensick believed. All established Americanists in their own right, they stand for my ideal audience.

Formal thanks to the *Essex Institute Historical Collections* and to *Prospects* for permission to reprint—as chapters 5 and 6—adapted versions of essays first appearing there. And to the Ohio State University Press for permission to quote rather liberally from their now standard edition of Hawthorne's complete works.

PREFACE TO THE PAPERBACK EDITION

I F I HAD BEEN TRYING, in my original Acknowledgments, to curry favor with powerful persons likely to review this long and somewhat specialized book, I could scarcely have failed more completely. Of the precursors most handsomely recognized, one nervously declined to review the book at all, pleading too personal an interest in the premises and conclusions of my study; a second conceded that the work would have to be read by future students of Hawthorne but could not say precisely *why*, and seemed in fact a little put out by my insistent preference for historical readings; and a third went out of his way not only to correct my rather painstaking account of certain historical circumstances but also to inoculate my potential audience against a dangerous infection of Irony. No doubt I had, at the time, something I wished to reply to these troubled evaluators, particularly to the third, whose stone-deafness to tone made my own tin ear seem a sensitive instrument indeed. But life goes on, and newer histories threaten to fold us all theory-drunken in.

From this less personal point of view, the most telling criticism of *The Province of Piety* came from the reviewer who noticed that it was written in several different and perhaps incompatible idioms. Indeed, for by my own account the chapters written last understand quite well the prefatorial observation that "some *text* always comes between" the observer and his historical subject; and in those cases the interest involves Hawthorne's conscious dialogue with some earlier writer on the history of New England or on the theo-political matters which made up their ideology. The best that can be done by history in this mode is negative: what "really" happened could not have been anything like the story told by politicians or by the folk. Other chapters, however, the earliest to be written, seem to imply, a little less critically, that Hawthorne's intuitive genius had somehow managed to recover the fundamental *reality* of moral experience in the proto-American provinces. Another rewrite might have resolved this problem of epistemological self-education. But that delay would surely have brought the near-sighted archivalist face to face with the emerging New Historicism—forcing, among other things, an earnest but in the end banal confession of his own investment in the Hawthorne-and-history project and a more determined account of the political forces acting on Hawthorne in the 1820s and 1830s. And life was starting to look short.

And yet—quarreling as it does with the logic of all those venerable studies which prove a "source" of historical information and then honor the process by which all the facts are changed in the name of "imagination"—the Historicism of *Province* is not altogether "old." If it does not attempt to locate, everywhere, a presentist motive for Hawthorne's interest in the provincial past, or seek to derive, more knowingly, some encompassing theory of his political unconscious, it certainly offers a sense of what it would look like to regard Hawthorne as a reader whose response to the discourse of Puritan and Whig history is quite as sophisticated as our own. And it recovers a fair number of the historical tales which Hawthorne had the wit to identify and put into question by his own ironic retelling. Without which, it appears, his politics become no less a symptom than his uneasy refractions of family romance.

The motive, then, was to look for signs of ironic intelligence wherever they might appear in Hawthorne's text and to credit myself (or language) only as a last resort. No doubt I trusted that uniform intention to underwrite, if not quite to organize, the unruly contest of discursive idioms I recognized but did not quite control. And in this regard, a single anecdote will serve as the last line of self-defense.

Standing in front of a fair sample of the English Department of UCLA in 1984—hoping for an offer but not repressing much for that reason—I found myself trying to connect my study of Hawthorne to the rationale of an "American Studies" which had resisted first the holy ecstasis of formalism and then the dizzy regression of linguistics, but turned instead outward to the public being and social function of the texts that went by the name of literature. An embattled position, surely, in that dark age before the invention of Cultural Studies. But terror is a wonderful substitute for courage, and so, determined to do my worst, I invoked the shade of the departed Perry Miller: "Come again, O Prophet of Reality, and establish us, thy children, in our very own Departments." The audience seemed, for the most part, mildly puzzled; except for one alert young Americanist, who turned in agitation to whisper to the Theorist nearby: "I wonder what he means by Reality."

What indeed?—in a world where the question could arise at all. Not much more, I suppose, than the discovery that something else always brackets the text of present attention. Not beyond the condition of textuality, perhaps; and likely to bleed, or be bled upon, in both directions; yet fairly distinguishable, in the order of both writing and reading, into the founding phenomenology of before and after. And if more than that, then just the primitive faith, well preserved in idioms other than Theory—which we *do* all use from time to time—that writers and the lives they led enjoyed about as much being and explanatory power as we ourselves do now; and that it is not beyond the capacity of their text to remind us why we need that faith. (I wonder what they thought I meant.)

The Province of Piety looks steadily to the "before" of the Hawthorne text; and, within that domain, to the remote religious more methodically than to the proximate political prediction of Hawthorne's early tales. Accordingly, the task of reconstructing their exact relation to the Age of Jackson remains open and inviting.

Sherman Oaks
July 1994

CONTENTS

CONTENTS

THE PROVINCE OF PIETY

❧ PROLOGUE ❧

I F I WERE MYSELF TO REVIEW, in my own astringent manner, the present volume of criticism, I should almost certainly think to suggest that its author seems to have got Nathaniel Hawthorne all mixed up with Perry Miller; that a rather shy writer of strange, imaginative tales has been rationalized, by an obvious academic, into an aggressive historical ideologue. And there would be, I fear, a certain truth in the charge. For this book, despite its history of revision and rewriting, probably did have its real beginning when, too many years ago, I happened to be reading Hawthorne and studying "The New England Mind" in the same fateful graduate semester. What to make of all those lucky correspondences, I wondered. Why "The Gray Champion" is itself, I thought, its own dramatic and diminutive "Profile of a Provincial Mentality." And I recall quite vividly the enthusiasm which indited itself in the margin of some now discarded anthology: "My God—Hawthorne *is* Perry Miller."

Well he is and he isn't, as I've surely had sufficient time to reflect. Like Miller, it may be suggested, Hawthorne carried on a life-long dialectic with the historical "thesis" of American Puritanism; it was his "flood subject," exercising a tyranny that bent the mind and baffled choice. And like Miller, as I will be arguing, Hawthorne had a nearly flawless sense of the way some *text* always comes between the observer and the origins he would observe, making the historian's own tale twice-told at its very most original. But if Hawthorne indeed possessed the critical *mind* of a modern intellectual historian, he nevertheless had a significantly different sense of his *craft.* Obviously: he wrote tales and romances, not monographs and treatises. And even when the modern epistemologists of method shall have made the historian's own craft appear entirely literary,[1] still the ordinary critic will have to notice that Hawthorne often worked in the apparently credulous mode of the allegory, and that his peculiar sensibility often expressed itself in the altogether quaint idiom of the gothic romancer. So that if Hawthorne is

I

Miller, he is also—if only ironically—Spenser, Bunyan, and Milton; Godwin, Radcliffe, and Tieck.

If I everywhere stress the first of these "identities," at the expense of the latter two, the intention is thus merely strategic—to redress an uneven critical balance, not to oversimplify the actual literary case. Because we have never had a really full-scale historical analysis of Hawthorne, I am quite willing to risk hyperbole. But I do not at all wish to neutralize the intriguing psychobiographic or generic problems disclosed by Hawthorne's precise mixture of intellectual style and rhetorical manner. Indeed I try to offer, by the way, some reflections on Hawthorne's actual relation to the problem of "allegory," particularly in its political manifestation, which I believe can be understood better with than without my own (Milleresque) discoveries. But I have taken as my primary task, my own specific province, to make as much historical sense as I can out of such Hawthorne tales as do indeed call attention to themselves as "historical." Recognizing Hawthorne's familiar interest in a fairly wide variety of American colonial texts, I "privilege" his historical allusions. I "valorize" the names, dates, places, events, and views the tales themselves appear to take for granted or "defamiliarize" by their apparent disregard of the obvious. I approach these historical meanings as more constitutive than our old-fashioned source studies have customarily assumed—an intellectual *telos* rather than an imaginative *point d'appui*. Or, at very least, as the metaphors Hawthorne himself deemed appropriate for the meaning he meditated.

As the result of this procedure is not really a source study, so the method is not at all innocent, nor is the documentation primarily positivistic. Indeed, both are at times extremely speculative, as the literary meanings one attempts to determine turn out to depend on other meanings, also entirely literary; and also, in themselves, indeterminate. But as two heads are better than one, so the very *relationship* has seemed to help. So much so that it comes to seem an essential feature of the writer's historic design: we seem to recognize Hawthorne's own complex intendings in the very moment when he verges toward and then differs from a text he would apparently recapitulate. And as I have come to regard "the hermeneutic circle" as simply the ring to which all interpreters belong, I am perfectly willing to live with the unscientific character of even my best documented discoveries.[2]

It is not as if I had not been sufficiently warned of the risks inherent in the project here attempted. The whole "universalist" tendency of the classic Hawthorne criticism everywhere implies that as literature is more philosophical than history, so the best chance at critical significance lies with an investigation of the permanent rather than the transient references of any text. And even scholars friendly to the historical project have avoided, at last, too complete an immersion in the particularities of Hawthorne's altogether provincial New England pre-texts. Neal Frank Doubleday's valuable compendium of the historical materials that went into "Hawthorne's Early Tales" everywhere reminds the reader that such sources tell only a part of the Hawthorne tale. And Michael Davitt Bell's more ambitious exploration of "Hawthorne and the Historical Romance of New England" exists to restrain the enthusiastic student of New England's literary culture from claiming too much material uniqueness for Hawthorne's use of the past. The responses to Bell's book were themselves full of sober instruction: one reviewer detected "the shadow of Perry Miller" (if only the Miller of "The Romance and the Novel") lying too prominently across its pages; and the more representative judgment pronounced that the person who reads Hawthorne with the "broader focus" will find "the emphasis on historical theme . . . distracting"—as if we all knew that, of course, abiding interest could reside only in what James called "the deeper psychology."[3] And even my own best friends and advisers, watching me dig myself in deeper and deeper, have offered a word of wary caution: Hawthorne was simply not *that* subtle an historian. Or again: beware of making Hawthorne's historical themes sound too much like our own current academic interest in the colonial past.

Yet I have decided to take my chances. To me it has not been clear just how, apart from the sort of analysis I have undertaken, we could ever know just how subtle an historian Hawthorne may have been. A firm believer in "intentionality," I do not happen to believe that the thematic ambition of "Young Goodman Brown" is more clearly revealed in the sayings of *Grandfather's Chair* than in the speculative drama of the tale itself. And if I have been guided "backwards" in some of my expositions by the example of Miller—or, as our own historical plot has unfolded itself, of Edmund Morgan, or Bernard Bailyn, or Sacvan Bercovitch—the fact is that I have merely been emboldened by such modern commentary to notice that the texts Hawthorne read really do have the most fascinating social and psychological implications, and that it is not at all absurd, therefore, to imagine Hawthorne as entering into significant dialogue with them.

I usually do work my way back to the "sources." But modern historians have freed me to suppose that, rather than "borrowing" from his historical sources (as if he lacked imaginative capital) or taking here and there a "prod" to his imagination (considered as creative but somehow lazy), Hawthorne may have wished fully to "re-cognize" the sense of his sources as significant expressions of intellectual culture, and thence to speculate about the Influence of Puritan Literature on American Life. And it is my considered conclusion that Hawthorne is indeed, among other things, our first significant intellectual historian; that he is more profitably compared with Perry Miller than with George Bancroft or Catharine Sedgwick; that

3

his historical prescience may well surpass his Freudian acumen. And so I will argue.

One final note, painfully personal yet "methodological" enough in its implications to warrant inclusion. Though this is an unusually long book, it is, in my opinion, just as long as it needs to be: only so could I explain the purport of Hawthorne's historical pre-texts and argue the complexity of their allusive interweaving. Yet it should not have taken nearly so long to complete. No "poor student" (as Thoreau might say) should suppose it requires half an academic career to assemble a few guesses about the thematic significance of the historical allusions in a small assortment of tales. If that were everywhere so, let structuralism reign—as intimations of life are, everywhere, more credible than rumors of method. Illness, distraction, laziness, and compulsion count for much. So does the lack of an appropriate historical education. So too the biases inherited from a previous critical paradigm: it may take a New Critic *years* to realize that "The Minister's Black Veil" actually enjoins its reader to acquaint himself with certain election sermons preached "during Belcher's Administration." But eventually one does learn. And though I have concluded it might take me forever to make all the chapters of this book perfectly self-consistent, still its sequel—a volume on the tales of Hawthorne's "Old Manse Period"—might actually be assembled in a finite stretch of time by anyone willing to read up on "the Age of Swedenborg."[4] All it would require, really, is a firm enough belief in the relevance of historical knowledge to the critical task.

One's sins are one's own. And finally, of course, the astringent reviewer will do as he must: it took all this time to inform us that Hawthorne is a sort of Perry Miller? But perhaps the faithful reader may be persuaded to take the book in terms of Hawthorne's history rather than its own; even if this means forgetting—Oh, Lord!—how long.

❦ POLEMICAL INTRODUCTION ❧
DEPRAVITY, HISTORY, AND THE HAWTHORNE PROBLEM

WHEN HERMAN MELVILLE referred to Hawthorne's peculiar "power of blackness" as a Puritan trait, he touched a problem that has plagued his successors in Hawthorne criticism with nagging consistency. No major critic since Melville has been able to define the terms and the conditions of Hawthorne's special talent without trying to estimate the distance between the apparent intellectual poise of the blue-eyed Nathaniel and the obvious religious intensities of his Quaker-whipping and witch-hunting ancestors. No doubt this is as it should be, given Hawthorne's characteristic subject. But it is also fair to say that only recently have the extent and the significance of the Hawthornean "distance" become at all clear.

In creating the problem of Hawthorne's "Puritanism," Melville actually began in a fairly careful way. In the strategy of "Hawthorne and His Mosses," the dramatic persona of the "Virginian Spending July in Vermont" is more than a tactic of anonymity: it limits Melville to an outside view of the Hawthorne Problem. Thus it proves impossible to decide—at the outset, at least—whether or not Hawthorne's own personality is somehow involved in that "Puritanic Gloom" which was supposed to be a lasting legacy of New England's stern old religion; perhaps Hawthorne had merely "availed himself" of some "mystical blackness" as a literary means. What seemed abundantly clear, however, was that Hawthorne's "great power of blackness . . . derives its force from its appeals to that Calvinistic sense of Innate Depravity and Original Sin, from whose visitations, in some shape or other, no deeply thinking man is always and wholly free." Eschewing psychoanalysis and trying not to be overly technical, Melville's Virginian is merely insisting that Hawthorne's literary vision be taken seriously in a religious way. We are sure to misapprehend Hawthorne, he thinks, unless we notice that, like Plato before (and Newman or the neo-orthodoxy after), he seemed unable to "weigh this world without throwing in something, somehow like Original Sin, to strike the uneven balance."[1]

5

The extent to which Melville may "really" be talking about himself here—anticipating his own Ishmaelian observations on those "untrue" or "undeveloped" men who are unfit to "break the green damp mould with unfathomably wondrous Solomon"—is at least partially beside the point. Melville is thinking of Hawthorne surely enough: the crucial metaphor about "visitations" by "shapes" points directly to "Young Goodman Brown," which the Virginian is not yet supposed to have read.[2] And about the mysterious author of that story Melville wishes to say something simple but fundamental: his vision of depravity arises out of a necessary view of the moral world adequately considered. The religious language points to questions of Truth rather than of Art. For that purpose, perhaps, the language need not have been Calvinist, but we are hardly surprised that it is: the Virginian knows that Hawthorne's essential subject has *something* to do with New England's heritage of Puritanism; and Melville himself knows that such language is, amidst the mild liberalisms of the nineteenth century, the most emphatic. Melville refrains from saying Hawthorne *is* a Calvinistic Puritan; only that he seems so by most available comparisons, or that he evinces a certain relentless quality of spiritual seriousness grown rare in these latter days. To read him is to be challenged at the level of ultimate concern: perhaps that is Puritan enough for most of us.

Hawthorne's other great nineteenth-century critic, however, judged otherwise. Although there is no evidence that Henry James had ever read Melville's review, he seems to oppose its argument almost diametrically.[3] It is precisely the religious Hawthorne with the quasi-Puritan sense of evil that James rejects. On the one hand he is far readier than Melville to accept in Hawthorne some inevitable "inheritance" of the Puritan mentality. His conscience, according to James, "lay under the shadow of the sense of *sin.*" But on the other hand James found it impossible to imagine that the sense of sin in Hawthorne was anything but an inheritance—automatic and unquestioned, a cultural given and a literary *donnée*, which Hawthorne had wisely put to fair imaginative use.

Thus for James the power of blackness was less a vision than an esthetic stance:

Nothing is more curious and interesting than this almost exclusively *imported* character of the sense of sin in Hawthorne's mind; it seems to exist there merely for an artistic or literary purpose. He had ample cognizance of the Puritan conscience; it was his natural heritage; it was reproduced in him; looking into his soul, he found it there. But his relation to it was only, as one may say, intellectual; it was not moral and theological. He played with it, and used it as a pigment; he treated it, as the metaphysicians say, objectively.[4]

6

Again, it is not to the purpose to speculate about the significance of this interpretation for James himself. What we need to notice is that James's Hawthorne is primarily an artist and not a theologian or a philosophical moralist. Hawthorne's undoubted "Puritanism" interested James not as a hard-won insight into the human situation but rather as a condition affecting the exercise of literary imagination. Somehow "this capital son of the old Puritans" had managed to take "the grim precinct of the Puritan morality for [his] play-ground"; and somehow, "exquisitely," he had "contrived" to make it all "evaporate in the light and charming fumes of artistic production." There is more of just such faery language, but the point is abundantly clear: Hawthorne had obviously inherited the Puritan outlook; but such views never became, in the best Puritan sense, any part of his own spiritual inlook.

Nowhere does the Melville/James discord fall more painfully on the ear than in their comments on "Young Goodman Brown." Melville's Virginian goes on to discover that the tale is "as deep as Dante"; and his reservations about the possibly hypothetical character of the Hawthornean vision drop away as he is personally moved to exclaim to the author in the author's own words: "It shall be yours to penetrate, in every bosom, the deep mystery of sin." To be sure, the extravagance of this may betray more than a little of the persona's excitable Southern imagination; but Melville himself seems now to feel in touch with the essential Hawthorne. And he eagerly accepts (and even internalizes) "Young Goodman Brown" as the very apotheosis of the "Calvinist" vision—the imagination of depravity, with a vengeance.[5] James, by contrast, is exceedingly cool, detached, philosophical. He finds the tale rich in genuine invention, better indeed than many others which betray "a small kind of ingenuity, a taste for conceits and analogies"; but he cannot believe that Hawthorne expressed in it anything of his own moral self. The tale "evidently means nothing as regards Hawthorne's own state of mind, his conviction of human depravity and his consequent melancholy; for the simple reason that, if it meant anything, it would mean too much."[6] If Hawthorne were perfectly serious, then his own authentic self would indeed be Puritanical, in the gloomiest sense. The proposition was unthinkable.

Thus early did one crucial aspect of the Hawthorne Problem formulate itself. Was Hawthorne powerfully endorsing, at least metaphorically, some neo-Calvinist view of the world, the classic American expression of which we identify as "Puritanism"? Or was his imagination merely doing the best it could with what it had inherited—"objectively," and *faute de mieux?* More generally, was Hawthorne's essence "religious," or was it rather "artistic," according to some problematic definition which seemed to separate the "play" of art from the vital center of personal belief? And the problem has proved nearly as long-lived as it was early. Without quite indulging ourselves in the academic luxury of a "review" of classic Hawthorne criticism,

7

it may be well to remind ourselves how representative—and yet how philosophically imperfect—is the seemingly inevitable dichotomy between Melville and James, and how lasting have been its consequences.

1

In one sense, most generally, we have seen only the predictable differences between a moral and an esthetic response. And probably it is inevitable that where some critics will follow Melville to emphasize by "interpretation" or elaborate by "commentary" the moral vision behind the works, others will respond to James's gift of "analysis"—whether of the fictions themselves or of the imaginative conditions of their making.[7] But, more concretely, we have also witnessed the beginning of something like two factitious and overspecified schools of Hawthorne criticism, which have, until fairly recently, divided the field with a fair show of mutual exclusion and exhaustiveness. On the one side have been the critics who, like Melville, respond at least metaphorically to the Calvinist language and overtones in Hawthorne; who judge that Hawthorne in some sense really believed in the ideas which order (or disrupt) the lives of his characters; and who see his fictions, therefore, as meaningful adumbrations of their author's own brand of Puritan protest. On the other side are those who, like James, cannot quite take seventeenth-century theology seriously and who, as a consequence, interpret Hawthorne's "play" with Puritanism as a sign of the divorce between literature and reality or belief. Thus two rather different Hawthornes have competed for critical empire: the moralist of high seriousness, offering us penetrating and often shattering insights into the essential blackness of things; and the writer who merely toyed (though often "exquisitely") with the outmoded conceptions of his provincial ancestors and a second-rate (though often "charming") form called allegory. That opposition had to be resolved before one knew which "Hawthorne" one was studying.

Fortunately for Hawthorne's reputation, the Jameseans lost—but not before some rather formidable twentieth-century critics had drawn out the negative implications of James's polite but often condescending pronouncements. William Crary Brownell found "refinement," "taste," and "elevation" in Hawthorne's stories; but he judged that their "informing purpose" lay completely aside from the "sublunary" world and concluded that Hawthorne had wasted his talent on the "vaporings of his infatuated fancy." Van Wyck Brooks was somewhat more poetic, but his verdict was essentially the same: Hawthorne's art was unreal. He was a fanciful or allegorical Puritan in an age which required some more relevant moral guidance to re-

8

place the desperate inadequacies of Puritanism. Accordingly, "the Puritan conscience in Hawthorne is like some useful Roman vessel of glass which has been buried for centuries in the earth and which comes forth at last fragile as a dragon-fly's wing, shot through with all the most exquisite colors . . . Could anything be more exquisite? Could anything more utterly fail to connect with reality in a practical Yankee world?" Even less, as one may imagine, does this "exquisite" Hawthorne connect with Vernon Parrington's idea of liberal democracy. In Parrington's view a skeptical and dilettantish Hawthorne had retreated to a private world of Puritan fancy. As a result of his prolonged dissociation from ideas that matter, he epitomized "the extreme and finest example of that refined alienation from reality that in the end palsied the creative mind of New England. Having consumed its fancies, what remained to feed on?"[8]

Serious as these "political" allegations became, however, it remained for Yvor Winters to press, within the limits of the Jamesean logic of imaginative free-play, the most damning charge of all. To that arch-rationalist, Hawthorne seemed not only to be saying nothing relevant, but indeed to be saying nothing at all. Of the romances only *The Scarlet Letter* escaped the charge of being "impure" allegory. And the stories were at best "slight performances; either they lack meaning . . . or they lack reality of embodiment . . . or having a measure of both, they seem incapable of justifying the intensity of method." Winters thus saw Hawthorne as anti-intellectual to the point of obscurantism. In the Romantic Period, in a clearly post-Puritan America, Hawthorne seemed entirely cut off from the main stream of Western intellectual culture and entirely incapable of compensating this lack out of native wit. Unable to deal with his own times, he turned back in imagination to an age "more congenial to his nature" and wrote in terms of the "exceedingly simple conceptions of his ancestors." When, occasionally, he groped toward more significance, he "was met everywhere he moved by the smooth and impassive surface of the intense inane."[9]

Such charges now seem astonishing, unfounded, wrong-headed. We can scarcely believe James's own bland formulations could take so hostile a form. And yet if one sets aside James's appreciation for the "deeper psychology" in Hawthorne and stresses only the fanciful or hypothetical character of his relation to Puritanism, something like Parrington or Winters would seem to result. For there is no denying that Hawthorne's fictions are lacking in concrete embodiment, firm and convincing ("realistic") social location, the low-mimetic illusion of reality; his own prefaces repeatedly make that very self-criticism—hoping to provoke a different sort of literary expectation, but more or less resigned to the lapse of an older epistemology.[10] And so the criticism was perhaps inevitable: if Hawthorne was not *really* the Puritan redivivus, what on earth *was* he? Would not that strange literary identity

9

have been better than *none?* Thus the way to establish Hawthorne's significance seemed for a long time the way of Melville. The Jamesean note might
continue to be struck by Marius Bewley, or Martin Green, or even (on occasion) by Lionel Trilling;[11] but the majority of modern critics have been
more and more willing to grant Hawthorne's lack of concrete "embodiment" and dwell on the reality of his "spiritual" qualities, his penetrating
insights as religious thinker, a sort of Secular Puritan.

Even before the Melville revival, there were critics to uphold Melville's
Puritan view as against James's exquisite estheticism. Paul Elmer More saw
in Hawthorne's writings the authentic "old supernaturalism" of New
England reasserting itself after the temporary interruptions of rationalism
and revolution. Hawthorne's romances mattered (as *The Castle of Otranto*
did not) because they were organically related to the conscience of their author and that of the country which nurtured him. The line from Cotton
Mather and Jonathan Edwards to Hawthorne is, according to More, clear
and direct: the sectarian conscience had passed away, but "the awful voice of
the old faith still reverberates in his stories of New England life and gives
them their depth of consciousness." Nor was the view of the Puritan authenticity of Hawthorne's conscience limited to academic critics making a
show of historical connection. D. H. Lawrence reproduces the Melvillean
insight as well as anyone. Without losing any love over what he called Puritanism, Lawrence had his own sense of a radical human dis-ease, and he
sensed that Hawthorne also "knew disagreeable things in his soul." To understand him properly one had to attend to "the inner diabolism of the symbolic meaning" of seemingly placid and controlled works. This blue-eyed
darling was no "Goody Two-shoes" and no Jamesean esthete.[12]

But the proof of the power of the Melvillean position is that it could unite
D. H. Lawrence with Austin Warren as well as with Paul Elmer More. Actually, a good deal of Warren's famous "Introduction" to the American
Writers Series *Hawthorne* is devoted to answering heretical readings of *The
Scarlet Letter* such as the one advanced by the pagan spiritism of Lawrence
himself. And yet Warren also wanted to talk about Hawthorne's subjective
knowledge of things puritanically "disagreeable." Aware that Hawthorne
was born, brought up, and educated in an increasingly liberal Salem, Warren is careful to make Hawthorne's Puritanism something fairly conscious
and explicit, less an inheritance and more a decision against the religious
theories of his own day. In doing so he offered a more flat-footed statement
about Hawthorne's literal Calvinism than any other critic before or since.
Warren's Hawthorne was not a theologian, to be sure; "his Calvinism was
nameless and undisputatious." But he was spiritually at home in the older
religion. And, significantly, his "religion had its facts as well as its values."
Sin unpalliated and absolute, theism, some sort of Christology, a future life,

and predestination in the Calvinist sense—these constitute the "facts." Warren cites the infamous "five points" of the Calvinist Synod of Dort and then proceeds to identify them all in Hawthorne's works—even as a Hawthorne conceit had once proposed to locate them in a geographical sketch. Above all, however, looms Hawthorne's overriding preoccupation with sin and guilt, a distinctively latter-day Puritan habit, and a theology which "stops at law and does not go on to grace."[13] Blackness indeed.

This, of course, is much more than Melville's Virginian had said. Arguably, it was much more than Melville himself ever meant to imply. And though one senses that it too is a logical outcome—the last result of a consistent appeal to "Puritan" categories for an explanation of Hawthorne's visionary power—Warren's suggestion was not particularly well received. For most critics it was too logical and too consistent. The problem, after all, was to preserve a Hawthorne present in his fictions in a morally serious way and yet avoid the embarrassing (and finally not quite tenable) conclusion that deep down Hawthorne had in fact been the complete Puritan malgré lui.

Accordingly, Herbert Schneider's formulation, equally consistent with Melville's excited recognition, seemed altogether more satisfactory. Hawthorne had been what one might venture to call an "existential Puritan": he "saw the truth behind the Calvinist symbols; he recovered what Puritans professed but seldom practised—the spirit of piety, humility, and tragedy in the face of the inscrutable ways of God." F. O. Matthiessen solidly endorsed that view. And, in suggesting that Hawthorne and Melville together constituted a sort of tragic counterstatement to the optimism of the Transcendentalists, he referred his readers to Perry Miller's famous justification for studying Puritans, existential or otherwise: "The impossibility of accepting their explanation of the universe should not blind us . . . to the accuracy of their observations of man." It would be a tendentious oversimplification to suggest that Matthiessen closed the case, though clearly his views carried great authority throughout "the Golden Age" of Hawthorne criticism. And thus the recapitulatory gesture of Harry Levin seems all too recognizable. Writing in a book called *The Power of Blackness*, he provides a sort of last refinement of the Schneider-Matthiessen formula: "Hawthorne remained a Calvinist in psychology, if not in theology."[14] Perhaps this is all the excited Virginian had meant in the first place.

But before we celebrate the success of a long and careful attempt to vindicate Melville's insight and rescue Hawthorne's reputation, we ought to notice that not all of the possibilities were being considered—not in logic, certainly, and not even on the phenomenological basis of the works themselves. What if Hawthorne had not been very much involved in Calvinistic Puritanism at all? What if a story like "Young Goodman Brown" were neither a shock of Calvinist recognition nor yet the only form of play permitted to the puritanically entrapped imagination? What if, finally, Hawthorne's primary relation to his Puritan ancestors had been in a significant sense "historical"? What if he had had to get them up as a quasi-academic subject, as part of a quasi-historical attempt to "re-cognize" the authorial intentions of writers like John Winthrop and Cotton Mather, or to "re-enact" the primal American scene on the native grounds of the Puritan conscience itself?[15]

The notion sounds strange in the context provided by traditions of Melville and James. But then that is the point. The idea of "Hawthorne as Historian" is perfectly thinkable, and it even accords pretty well with the prima facie evidences of text and canon; but it has had to swim upstream. None of the Jamesean critics could possibly imagine that Hawthorne possessed the objective distance necessary for the task: either he inherited Puritanism as a given, a myth he could not get outside, or, what amounts to the same thing, he employed it as an inevitable background of coherence into which he could always repair for literary safety when reality threatened. And the Melvilleans, for their part, seemed always to feel that defending the basic authenticity or truth of Hawthorne's vision was task enough: Hawthorne intuitively divined the true spiritual essence of Puritanism; the Devil himself might take all the other facts of the case. Oddly, perhaps, Melville himself came as close as any other classic Hawthorne critic to making the appropriate historical suggestion. The story of the Virginian's having put down his copy of "Dwight's Travels in New England" in order to take up Hawthorne's *Mosses from an Old Manse* might well be strategic; and it could easily suggest that Hawthorne's were the "truer" travels—mental, to be sure, but spread out in time and space nevertheless, so as to comprehend, critically, the essential conditions of "the New England Mind."[16] But if Melville had meant any such thing, no Melvillean took up the suggestion. And, indeed, the full case for Hawthorne's historicity has made painfully slow progress against the current.

But even as Levin was putting the capstone on the impressive critical monument to Hawthorne's "psychological Puritanism," other, more subversive suggestions were beginning to be made. For one thing, Randall Stewart and other "New Biographers" were filling out the Hawthorne portrait in "normalizing" ways that made it progressively harder to think of Hawthorne's "Puritan" writings as either faery playthings or fierce broodings: Hawthorne lived in *nineteenth*-century Salem; he only *studied* the seventeenth-century version; and he may have learned something.[17] Beyond this, certain critics (both old-fashioned and New) were seriously proposing that Hawthorne could be read in a profoundly Christian way without his having been a Puritan in any sense: Hyatt Waggoner suggested, by way of introduction, that Hawthorne's theology was "classically Christian" rather than narrowly Puritan; Leonard Fick argued that his psychology and his scheme of salvation were both "Arminian" rather than Calvinist; and Henry Fairbanks even discerned in Hawthorne a significantly "Catholic" sense of life.[18] If any of this were true, then Hawthorne might well have enjoyed a certain doctrinal distance from his Puritan ancestors and have managed a certain esthetic distance from his Calvinist subject. And it is one of the purposes of this present study to suggest that all of those non-Puritan theological suggestions are indeed part of the truth about Hawthorne's peculiar faith, already established if not quite codified.

But in the end, as it seems to me, such theological codification no longer answers our deepest critical need. For even if we were to succeed in evoking, from some ideal combination of life and works, some normative version of Hawthorne's religion which we could all admire if not believe or practice, we would as yet have left untouched his major achievement as "moral historian"—his extraordinary power critically to discern and dramatically to re-create the moral conditions under which earlier generations of Americans had lived and, in one way or another, sought salvation.

Not that the primarily "religious" task is itself insignificant or simple: one would have to validate George Lathrop's early suggestion that Hawthorne was "one of the great believers of his generation" without quite verifying Edward Wagenknecht's definition of Hawthorne as "God's Child"; one would have to notice in Hawthorne the significance of a certain salutary interpersonalism without making too much of his "saving grace of marriage"; and one would surely have to certify Hawthorne's attractive differences from both Manichean Puritanism and Pelagian Transcendentalism without quite pronouncing him some "Champion of the Middle Way." Any partial or too-comforting effort in this direction will always call forth the Melvillean judgment one more time. Anyone who creates, out of Hawthorne's assortment of strange and often disturbing works, a creed that shall "satisfy the professors of every religion, but shock none" has to answer to D. H. Lawrence for the presence of "disagreeable things." And anyone who makes Hawthorne's religion too ready a solution to the ambiguities of modernism has to face Frederick Crews: do we really believe Hawthorne thought the ego *was* "master in its own house"?[19]

But suppose the Melvilleanism of Lawrence and Crews might be answered—methodologically, by some adequate hermeneutics of "the symbolic and the symptomatic" in Hawthorne, the absence of which short-circuits so much psychoanalytic criticism; and, substantially, by an extended meditation on the skeptical "fideism" of Hawthorne's religious temperament, the subtlety of which baffled even Melville in the end. Or, closer to the actual case, suppose Crews had repented of all of his reductionist *Sins.*[20] Could we, under those circumstances, declare that the Hawthorne Problem had for all purposes of public disputation been solved? Could we, then, simply explicate to our wits' end and our hearts' content? I think not. For as the structure of Crews's own (powerful) argument implies, the relation between religion and psychology in Hawthorne's vision is only the first part of the problem. The other part is history. What does Hawthorne's "Sense of the Past" have to do with his imagination of depravity? Crews is false to the subtlety of some of the more sophisticated sorts of religious speculation that went before his chapter on "Psychological Romance" (though he is surprisingly cogent in relation to many that have appeared since). But he is even more intolerant of the possibility of a genuinely historical understanding of Hawthorne. And that is where the fundamental problem still lies.

The history of Hawthorne criticism clearly suggests that psychology gets along better with religion than it does with history. The psychoanalytic need not absolutely reduce the theological; it only wishes to appropriate it according to some higher law of "Natural Supernaturalism."[21] One idiom retranslates another, already a translation. Only reality resists the process. Accordingly, the most appropriate point of departure for an adequately modern study of Hawthorne is from those few isolated voices who were, even in the early 1950's, beginning to suggest that Hawthorne's most original insights were more empirically historical than speculatively moral or theological. Or, more subtly perhaps, that the key adjustment to be made is not between Hawthorne's theology and his psychology (or his metaphysics, ethics, esthetics, or even his *theory* of history), but between his theology and his understanding of the actual history of New England—always more or less Puritan, and always more Puritan than he himself ever was.

Thus Hawthorne's theology can take care of itself, incidentally and negatively, along the way: what would Hawthorne himself have to believe in order to expose precisely what he does expose? For the important point about Hawthorne is less what he "believed" or what his theology "taught" than what his own special sort of religious vision enabled him to *see* about the distinctive continuity of moral experience in America. Hawthorne's sense of depravity—his power of blackness—is rightly apprehended only as a consciously historical re-cognition of the Puritan "Way" in which America had begun.

2

On the face of it nothing would seem more self-evident than the fact that Hawthorne is in some primary way an historical writer. And, at one or another elementary level, few critics are without some awareness of this fact. To speak of Hawthorne's "Puritanism" at all is to involve him in a problem with a long and complicated history and to express his values in terms of a creed which flourished in centuries before his own point of literary departure. Even more obviously, to take account of the vogue of Scott, Cooper, and William Gilmore Simmes is to notice that certain historical tactics are as vital to a definition of "the Hawthornesque" as is the machinery of the gothic. Nor has it been possible to ignore the historical bias of "Hawthorne's Reading," especially at his outset in the late 1820's and early 1830's.[22] And yet in the bulk of serious Hawthorne criticism, denials of significant historicity have been much more prominent than affirmations. Indeed the psychologists and the moralists have often seemed to vie with each other for the right to publish the discovery that history was no very significant part of Hawthorne's essential subject.

One has given up counting, but no formulation of the Hawthorne Problem seems quite so representative of the 1950's and 1960's as the much-quoted formulation of Seymour Gross: to grasp either the true import or the representative significance of a tale like "My Kinsman, Major Molineux," one had to realize that *"history as history* had very little meaning for Hawthorne artistically." Earlier Gross had found "The Gentle Boy" less about Puritans and Quakers than about the universal reality of the "Evil Principle."[23] And many subsequent readings—of these tales and others, which might seem historical—have followed this lead. Edward Wagenknecht perfectly internalized Gross's judgment: "As an artist Hawthorne was not interested in history for history's sake." Crews also cited Gross with favor. And out of a hostility to the Hawthorne of "American Studies" at least as great as his scorn for Wagenknecht's own pious version of Hawthorne as "dispenser of moral advice," he constructed a whole introductory chapter to tell us that Hawthorne's only vital concern in his "evocations of Puritan times" was intensely and anxiously personal: his repressive and sadistic ancestors "gave him a *guilty identity which was better than none."* A storm of protest followed, of course; but the point was hardly to defend the interests which Hawthorne shared with John Winthrop or Perry Miller.[24]

The really surprising fact about Crews's strategic attempt to discredit the "American Studies" Hawthorne is that there was actually so little in that way to credit. Admirers might count his instincts prophetic, as he sought to save the world from a flood of petty informations about source and situation; but anyone could see that his gesture was largely proleptic. One might have expected that the 1951 article by Q. D. Leavis which started the rush of interest in "My Kinsman, Major Molineux" would have struck a responsive chord in many other ways as well; but her primary contention—that the "essential Hawthorne," easily distinguishable from the larger bulk of his less interesting writings, is the work of a "critic and interpreter of American cultural history"—had not found very general acceptance or critical re-application. The chapters on Hawthorne in Daniel Hoffman's *Form and Fable in American Fiction* look promising, but in fact Hoffman turns as quickly from history to myth as others do to psychology, esthetics, or moral theology. A. N. Kaul's general definition of Hawthorne as an "Heir and Critic of the Puritans" who was "preoccupied with the very origin of things, and repeatedly saw the present in terms of the past" followed Leavis' historical lead very respectfully, but at the respectable distance of twelve years; it hardly represented a groundswell, and Crews did not even take notice of it.[25] Source studies continued to appear, of course, but most of these ended up stressing Hawthorne's imaginative "transformations" of his historical materials; the "spate of articles concern[ing] Hawthorne's attitudes towards American history as they are revealed in specific works" began only as Crews's own book was being published; and books on Hawthorne's sense or use of history would not appear until the 1970's. The critical domain was anything but awash with data; no one was drowning in sociological trivialities. Gross seemed to have answered Leavis to most people's satisfaction. The only really dangerous historicisms to be prevented were those of David Levin and Roy Harvey Pearce. And they knew themselves to be embattled.[26]

Surveying the long-disputed territory of "Young Goodman Brown," Levin had made the modestly empirical suggestion that the tale was actually based on the Puritans' own doctrine of "Specter Evidence" and that readers need to notice this, whatever their ultimate style of interpretation. One had to start with "the literal," with "terms that were available to Hawthorne"; one could always then go on, as Levin himself noticeably does, to explicate or celebrate the psychological value of Hawthorne's "remarkable variety of insights into human experience." Pearce's historicism was only a little less cautious. Generalizing (for the occasion of the *Hawthorne Centenary Essays*) his earlier claims for the historicity of "Molineux" and the importance of Hawthorne's "Sense of the Past," he ventured to suggest that, although "the image of Hawthorne as symbolic romancer [had] been marvellously elucidated, verified, and expounded," perhaps we had come too far too fast: "we have tended to rush on, identifying and collocating his symbols and their forms, and then pursuing them out of space—out of time, too often beyond the consciousness of those whose life in art they make possible." Aware that Hawthorne's tales are highly dream-like and that his longer fictions are symbolic romances rather than realistic novels, "we have hesitated to place them in this world"; instead we have "allegorized, mythologized, psychoanalyzed, theologized."[27] To me this still seems a cogent assessment of the main tendency of Hawthorne's scholarship—even though much profitably historical criticism has appeared since, and in spite of the critical banalities which always seem to take refuge or comfort under the sign of historicism.

As Pearce goes on to imply, the failure to deal adequately with the question of history in Hawthorne may be more serious than in almost any other American writer—though the failure to re-cognize the literal always raises serious methodological questions. Out of the confusion of the post-Puritan American situation, with its party of millennial hope and its party of typological memory, only Hawthorne refused to look "beyond history, towards something larger than the human situation as given in the past and in the present."[28] Perhaps that is an overstatement: certainly the Melville of Milton Stern felt the crucial importance of secular development and historical relativity; and it may be false to imply that Hawthorne's view never passes beyond the historical. But it is well to remind ourselves—as Robert Lowell was moved to do, somewhat bitterly, in *The Old Glory*—that a constantly "transcendental" explication of Hawthorne runs the risk of overlooking a very important and probably fundamental dimension of his meaning. Hawthorne himself repeatedly reminds us that "idealist" solutions are only too available. We ought to let reality resist, as long as it can.[29]

It is easy, apparently, to misunderstand the historicist interest in Hawthorne at just this point. The trauma of "Young Goodman Brown" is not born of Hawthorne's own literal interest in the theological basis of the doctrine of specters. The ambiguities of "My Kinsman, Major Molineux" do not exist solely to reduce the American Revolution to the dimensions of a rum riot in the 1730's. The compulsions of "Roger Malvin's Burial" outrun any conceivable interest in setting straight either the factual or the mythic record of Lovewell's Fight. Even the explicitly deconstructive "May-Pole of Merry Mount" takes for granted that anybody can see more than a jurisdictional dispute or a police action in the Puritan intrusion into the pastoral world of Mount Wollaston. In all these famous instances we are exposed to modes of figuration and ranges of meaning that are in fact unavailable in the pages of Cotton Mather, or Thomas Hutchinson, or the *Collections . . . Relating Principally to New Hampshire*, or indeed in all "the grave pages of our New England Annalists" put together. And not even the simplest sort of historical intentions can change the fact that readers respond differently to twice-told "tales" than to "True Stories from History and Biography." But then everyone already *knows* that poetry is more philosophical than history. It seems dreary to repeat the obvious.[30]

No one wishes to ignore the problems and the pleasures of form in Hawthorne. And the tendency to smooth out or literalize his psychological and theological complexity may reveal not some fatal flaw in historicist methodology but rather the flat failure of significant historical intelligence as such. Individual taste might prefer a redundancy of articles on Hawthorne's imagery to a few discoveries of his sources, especially if the imagery studies pointed to significant questions of theme and the source studies did not; but it probably requires an excess of methodology to prefer them to the primary thematic recoveries of Leavis. Hawthorne's early historical tales may not be, except in a very special sense, "about" their sources; but they are even less about their imagery. And they very definitely are about the moral gains and life losses of Puritan culture in America. As indeed they are also about certain "Rituals of Origin"—so that the essays of Peter Shaw, depending directly on the insights of Leavis, represent some of the most useful work recently done on Hawthorne and demonstrate that historicism need not be mindless or banal.[31]

Nor do we consign away our valid philosophical interest in "just representations of general nature" by admitting, with Professor Pearce, that each of Hawthorne's various adolescent protagonists is given to us amidst the anxieties peculiar to his proper historical world rather than in the hypnagogic state as imagined by Edgar Poe or on our own analyst's couch.[32] Reuben Bourne, Robin Molineux, and Goodman Brown do indeed share a powerful structure of experience in common; it is obtuse to overlook and perverse to minimize the importance of this fact. But only a decent respect to the historical *difference* of each can prevent a structuralist collapse which is on the literal surface problematic and in the symbolic outcome boring. Can we not imagine that Hawthorne noticed certain *varieties* of Oedipal experience? Is it not a mark of his subtle intelligence and a sign of his supple skill if he has in fact deployed an inevitable psychological theme over a certain span of contingent historical variance?

And what, in the abstract, is lost by placing Hawthorne firmly within the context of some perfectly recognizable and altogether plausible attempt to write, in the midst of a bustling Yankee world of stagecoaches and mercantile industry, "The Historical Romance of New England"? To be sure, Hawthorne has clearly differentiated his own aims from those of William Gilmore Simmes and John Greenleaf Whittier—from the superficial manipulation of "lights and shades" of the one, and from the rationalistic condescension of the other.[33] But this may mean only that Hawthorne was committed to expressing, in fiction, a particular sort of historical intention, and to realizing it extraordinarily well. And indeed Michael Bell has found it perfectly possible to distinguish his achievements from those of a long list of lesser writers in the same genre: not only do Hawthorne's historical representations enjoy a significantly greater range of psychological complexity, but even more importantly Hawthorne's own attitudes and methods are consistently more ironic. In Hawthorne's version, the "Romance" of New

England is altogether less "Romantic," everywhere more darkly tinged with Melvillean discoveries.[34]

Surely no theory exists to prevent the possibility of Hawthorne's having been what Pearce calls the "symbolist as historian." And surely the case deserves to be fully argued on its own merits. The critical verdict is virtually unanimous that, out of the large bulk of Hawthorne's early tales, at least, the most satisfying and successful are those which touch the historical matter of America in some way.[35] Perhaps the obvious explanation of this case is the true one: perhaps Hawthorne's deepest interest and intentions really were in some fundamental way historical. Thus my own view of Hawthorne as "moral historian."

"Historian" not in any sense so literalistic as to suggest that his primary concern was to re-tell or to re-discover the actual events of some memorable or significant but forgotten occasion—even though Hawthorne himself turns out to have been astonishingly learned in exactly this literal way, and even though the properly disposed reader is often forced to make himself knowledgeable in order to appreciate some of Hawthorne's most telling ironies. (The deconstructive point of "The May-Pole of Merry Mount" reveals itself precisely as a function of the discrepancy between an actual set of events and the "historical" or mythic record which the reader is presumed to know.) But "historian" primarily in the sense that the intention which reveals itself in the best of the early tales is the wish to recover the affective quality of human lives lived under conditions or assumptions different from those which prevailed in his own later and more liberal age. Or, alternatively, the desire to re-enact the subtle process by which a solid but often unlovely past had thrown its long and often darkening shadow upon an equally solid and apparently sunnier present. Others may argue whether or not such intentions discover an interest in "history *as history.*" What Hawthorne tells us, however, enough times for us to consider believing him, is that imaginative literature is properly competent and perhaps ideally suited to assist us in just such a civilizing and humanizing procedure.

And "moral" not in the sense of that moralism which always wants to substitute itself for vital piety on the one hand or for speculative theology on the other, even though "The Minister's Black Veil" makes us aware of just such problems within the history of Puritanism itself. And not in the sense of some perfectly rational and regular ethics which tries to disguise the psychological problems of real human motivation, even though the moral dilemma of a tale like "Roger Malvin's Burial" is placed in just such a precise and old-fashioned "casuistic" framework. But "moral" in the epistemological sense which opposes itself to "positivistic"—signifying not that verifiable certitude which the sciences require, but only the sort of probable assurance we ordinarily have in matters of practical intentionality. As history itself seemed to Hawthorne always a matter of perception, affection, motivation, and choice, so the reader is never to look for more certainty in the representation than might be supposed to exist in the reality.

A more theoretical book on Hawthorne's "Moral History" is certainly possible. And it might well take its title from my own second chapter: "Moral Dilemma as History." For what the best of Hawthorne's early tales offer us, again and again, is some explicitly fictional moment of conflict or choice, derived from and referable back to some actuality, but generalized and dramatized in such a way as to stand for the limits of perception or experience at a certain critical moment in the historical past. Almost always the moment is one over which Puritanism has cast its shadow. The implications of such an historical procedure might well be compared to the assumptions about history and fiction in Hawthorne's own day, or tested against the practice of historiography prevailing at the present time.[36] But such an effort can afford to wait until the individual texts have had ample opportunity to discover their own historicity. Embarrassments of theory have inhibited that pragmatic testing for too long already.

3

Ultimately, however, it was probably a biographical rather than a critical a priori which prevented both Melville and James, and the "classic" critics who felt their authority, from imagining that the Hawthorne Problem might demand an historical solution above all others—that Hawthorne might be, primarily, an analyst of the social and psychological side-effects of Puritanism. The difficulty resided in the murky problem of "inheritance." A man for whom Puritanism was simply "there," as part of the inevitable heredity or environment, could scarcely be thought to possess the distance or detachment necessary to an objective or critical view of the ancestral faith and morals. One describes the limits of a system only from the outside of that same system—although one certainly has to re-enter it by imagination to understand anything true about it at all.

Now the last thing Melville had meant to suggest was that Hawthorne had, remarkably, worked his faith free from the power of the Puritan creed and then had, even more remarkably, worked his imagination back inside it again. Whatever he meant, it was surely more simple than that. And, as we have seen, his unsuppressed suspicion that there really did lurk in Hawthorne, "perhaps unknown to himself, a touch of Puritanic Gloom" became, in a slightly altered form, the Jamesian dogma: Puritanism was simply given to the conscience of this "capital son of the old Puritans."[37] And there we were. Dissenting biography might insist on Hawthorne as a "Rebellious Puritan," and careful intellectual history could validate no stricter creed than that of an "Ungodly Puritan"; but revisionist criticism itself could scarcely posit a distance greater than that of "Heir *and* Critic." And it would require still more "New Biographies" quite to undo the imaginatively entrapping effects of the old: the family history was just too fascinating to be ignored; "Ancestral Salem" was just too filled with gloomy possibilities to be resisted.[38] Unfortunately, however, it was also just too literary to be true. Perhaps our own attempt to define the Hawthorne Problem—to tell the history of his history—can begin by unraveling a most tangled example of the offensive assumptions and procedures.

A disproportionately influential book on Hawthorne and his ancestors defines the problem of Puritan inheritance as follows:

If the bride and groom [Hawthorne's parents-to-be] observed a custom which was then popular in Salem, they appeared in their wedding finery at meeting in the groom's church—the conservative First Church—the Lord's day following their marriage. The historic old congregation now had an organ, and the hymns were sung in tune. But the theology preached by the minister, the Reverend John Prince, differed little from that which the Reverend Francis Higginson had taught in a mud-and-log hut on the same site in 1629. Since coming to Salem, Betsy had joined her parents in worshipping at the East Church and was accustomed to Dr. Bentley's radicalism. But in taking Nathaniel as her husband she took also his creed. Under the Reverend Prince's guidance, she was soon to be an old-fashioned Congregationalist, qualified to acquaint her children with the doctrines of original sin, total depravity, divine election, and a Providence working wonders.[39]

There are, in this remarkable passage, enough speculations depending on the initial "if" to keep biographers and historians busy for quite some time. Without going too far afield, however, we may examine some of the implications here which are typical of the lingering view that Hawthorne somehow drank in Puritanism with his mother's milk or drew it up through roots sent deep into the soil of Old Salem.

The primary contention—that Elizabeth Manning left Bentley's East Church for Prince's First Church when she married Captain Nathaniel Hawthorne—is undoubtedly true: Bentley's copious diary makes no mention of the Hawthorne-Manning alliance until several years after the fact, and Nathaniel and his older sister Elizabeth were both baptized at Prince's First Church; moreover, it is the old First Church which Hawthorne's son-in-law (and official biographer), George Lathrop, mentions in telling us that Hawthorne did not regularly attend services after college. On the other hand, however, it is quite likely that when, after her husband's death in 1808, Mrs. Hawthorne moved her family over to Herbert Street to live with her own Manning family, she once again attended Bentley's East Church. But the whole question of Mrs. Hawthorne's "conversion" or "reversion" is quite beside the point.[40] The important consideration here is the plain historical fact that, despite the seventeenth-century presences evoked by the specter of the venerable First Church of Salem, the theological difference between it and Bentley's East Church were, in the years around 1800, largely insignificant. Both were liberal, that is, "Arminian"—teaching a theology of sin and salvation which contradicted the very essence of seventeenth-century Puritan Calvinism and which Edwards and his eighteenth-century followers had been relentlessly trying to demolish as a scandalous defection and a treacherous heresy.

Bentley and Prince, the two pastors, were mutual friends, members of the same intellectual circles, colleagues of all the famous "liberal Christians" of Boston; both denied the older premise of a totally depraved human race of whom only a limited number had been predestined to be saved by a grace whose operations would be irresistible and "inamissable." Bentley's liberalism attracted more attention because he was more outspoken in his doubts about Trinitarianism. But even though the conservatives would choose to make "Unitarianism" the hot issue, modern historians have been unable to feel that this is the crucial question in the evolving New England theology; certainly it is not vital in regard to Hawthorne's inheritance. And on the absolutely vital question of "the economy of salvation"—what was the nature of man and what terms of salvation was he on with what kind of a God?— the Hawthorne family church had been liberal at least since the accession of Prince's predecessor in 1755. This fact, in turn, may serve to remind us that the "free and catholic" spirit had been current in Salem for quite some time before Hawthorne was born and that Salem had in fact become something like a center of religious liberalism. Outside of Boston it was the only New England community with a predominance of Arminian churches in 1800: the Reverend Thomas Barnard, Jr. of the North Church brought to three the number of liberal pastors in the five Congregational churches; the minority view was being upheld by one neo-Edwardsean "New Divinity" man and one more traditional "federal" Calvinist, between whom there was less unity on essential points than between Bentley and Prince.[41]

Thus when one finds Hawthorne's implied theology of sin and salvation described as "Arminian rather than Calvinistic" and "in contrast to [that of] the recognized teachers of Puritanism," the description ought to seem perfectly cogent, exactly what we would expect historically.[42] As long as

Hawthorne did go to church in Salem or learn Christian doctrine at his mother's knee, what he heard were the doctrines of man's nature and possibilities which would receive their culminating expression in William Ellery Channing's famous "Baltimore Sermon" of 1819, the doctrinally and culturally definitive "Unitarian Christianity." In one sense, of course, modern criticism has been instinctively correct in ignoring Hawthorne's religious debt to Unitarianism and concentrating on his imaginative transactions with Puritanism; eventually, at least, Hawthorne himself will make "The Celestial Rail-road" and "The Old Manse" seem definitive on that score. But in another important sense it has been wrong: in thinking of the liberal religion of New England as the sterile Lockeanism rejected by Emerson and Ripley, or as the "mere" moralism discredited by the neo-orthodoxy, or even as that tepid form of adult education demolished by Hawthorne himself in the 1840's, we have passed over a necessary way of considering Hawthorne's actual origins. And our metaphorical oversight has even taught us how to miss much that is vital and powerful in some of the early tales. For if Hawthorne eventually offers us, in "The Celestial Rail-road," a definitive view of the religious deficiencies of the Newness, an earlier (and much more powerful) story like "The Minister's Black Veil" confronts us with the good and the bad of the Old Way all inextricably mixed in together; and a very early story like "The Gentle Boy" presents us with a version of what Channing called "The Moral Argument Against Calvinism."[43]

Or if we do indeed find it useful to say that Hawthorne's implicit Christianity is "classic" rather than simply "Calvinist" on the one hand or elegantly "neo-orthodox" on the other, then very likely the liberalization of the New England theology has to be counted in.[44] For Channing is scarcely further from the classic norm than is Edwards or Samuel Hopkins. And if a stream of Congregationalism can be thought to have passed through, on its way from Puritanism to Transcendentalism, a center of orthodoxy on questions of reason and revelation, depravity and virtue, then surely that center has to be located somewhere between 1780 and 1820. After New England religion had ceased to be what we, in our tolerance, would call "narrow" or "harsh," but before it became what we, in spite of our liberalism, would think of as entirely too "free and easy," it seems to have been possible to try to believe the medieval doctrine of Original Sin as (principally) an opposable bias toward actual sin, and to think of divine grace as (chiefly) a resistible aid to a weakened but not entirely ruined nature which *could* not always love or act as it would; one might accept the Pauline formulation without benefit of the Edwardsean correction. It would not be too difficult, I think, to reverse the traditional polarities and sketch out an argument called "Pietism Versus Morality," showing that much of what is called "liberalism" in latter-day New England is scarcely more than the righting of a doctrinal bal-

23

ance so badly upset that not even Covenant could compensate for Calvin, and where only some "Romantic" theology seemed to promise amends for the slander of nature. One might even "re-discover Channing," one more time.[45]

Fortunately, as I have suggested, such a task is as needless here as it would be thankless. If such questions of orthodoxy raise themselves along the way, it is only because some of the early tales do indeed invite us to infer the religious standard of Hawthorne's historical judgments; some version of Christianity—out of the English "Puritans" Spenser and Milton, but also out of the Anglican Jeremy Taylor—occasionally makes us aware of itself. For the moment our conclusion is simple, and negative: so far as we can learn from the primary materials of biography, Hawthorne's natal mind and early sympathies were formed at a considerable distance from the various Calvinisms of his remote Puritan ancestors. In order to write meaningfully about what he would come to call their "miserable distortions of the moral nature,"[46] he would have to recover rather than transcend their essential spirit and beliefs.

Obviously the Hawthorne family preserved a sense of its own past, in fact and legend. And observably, as Hawthorne began (in the late 1820s and early 1830's) to investigate the dark corners of colonial history, he became more and more aware of ancestral gloom and guilt. But too many biographies have devoted too much of their early chapters to the doctrinal peculiarities and social sins of Hawthorne's metaphorical fathers. We have to begin by admitting that literally, at least, Hawthorne's own Salem was liberal, commercial, and banal; and that, at whatever affront to the language of the imagination, he was a "capital son" of a family of established "proto-Unitarians."

Other evidence from Hawthorne's earlier years suggests the same conclusion—of distance from aboriginal Puritan bias. So far as it can be reconstructed, the story of Hawthorne's pre-college days reads more like a late-eighteenth-century novel of enlightened education than a seventeenth-century tract on the nurture of a Puritan Saint. The extended periods of permissive solitariness, the wide and precocious but essentially unplanned reading, the comparatively indulgent training with a succession of mild-mannered tutors—all this contrasts strikingly with Horace Mann's personal recollections of the more usual school-education he set about to reform; once again Hawthorne seems to have escaped a youthful introduction to "all the doctrines of total depravity, election, and reprobation, and not only the eternity, but also extremity, of hell-torments, unflinchingly and in their most terrible significance."[47] One is tempted at first to think of Salem and Raymond, the poles of Hawthorne's axis of experience, as representing restraint and freedom, a less complicated version of Henry Adams' Boston and Quincy—except that there were no Presidents at either place. And although Hawthorne much preferred the wild and nearly idyllic conditions of the Maine woods, it is difficult to imagine that his life among the women of the Hawthorne-Manning household at Salem was much constrained by Puritanical discipline. According to his sister Elizabeth, Hawthorne was "petted." In later years Hawthorne came to think of himself as potentially "Sybaritic"; and it appears that nurture had as much to do with that as nature.[48]

If there was a quasi-Freudian villain of the Hawthorne piece, it was certainly Uncle Robert Manning—who pressed and paid for Hawthorne's education when everyone else seemed prepared to let it slide, and from whom Hawthorne sought to hide his early-formed interest in becoming a man of letters. Indeed it seems likely that Hawthorne's first sense of the ancestral disapproval of "a writer of story-books" came to him from this most practical and most-nearly-Puritan member of the immediate family. But even this repressive theme seems slight in comparison with the other indulgences: Hawthorne treats it serio-comically in "The Story Teller"; and it is easy to overestimate the element of anxiety in the complex strategy of the ever-ironic "Custom House." "Strong traits" of the "nature" of William and John Hathorne were present in his own, but they were mixed in with much else; and no one seemed concerned to foster them by any deliberate education.[49]

There is no evidence, for example, that Uncle Robert selected Hawthorne's early tutors because of their religious bias. And if he decided on Bowdoin because of its reputation as a bastion of evangelical religion (against the always-growing liberalism of Harvard, but without the innovative New Divinity of Yale), he did not get his money's worth. Jesse Appleton, the intense Old-Light conservative who had come to Bowdoin in 1808 after being turned down for the Hollis Professorship of Divinity at Harvard, died in 1820; and no successor appeared to test the conversion and supervise the orthodoxy of the undergraduates. Instead there was only the enforced attendance at the Sunday services of some local church—the Old-Light Congregational being recommended but not dictated.[50] In marked contrast to the painful case of Emily Dickinson, no one seems to have been expecting Hawthorne to undergo a conversion experience; and none of the churches with which he was associated would have taken him into any fuller communion if he actually had been led to witness the Application of Redemption in his own spiritual life. His education was hardly what one would call "secular," but his spiritual life was clearly "once-born."[51]

The academic training at Bowdoin was decidedly Christian but otherwise fairly innocent of sectarian bias: Locke on the mind, and the restatement of his realist and representationalist arguments against Hume by the Scottish common-sense philosopher Dugald Stewart; the anti-deist arguments of Paley's *Evidences* and Butler's *Analogy;* the careful and continuous study of Scripture. These were the common property of the Christian apologetics of the day and could be used, as the example of Harvard proves, to support an advanced Arminian liberalism as well as the older Calvin-Ames-Cotton form of Congregationalism. Thomas Upham, the expounder of Reid and Stewart who came to Bowdoin in Hawthorne's senior year (and who was to write a particularly meretricious ballad about Lovewell's fight), was apparently more interested in refuting such new infidelities as might base themselves on Kant than in shoring up the intellectual foundations of federal Calvinism.[52]

What effect any of this had on Hawthorne's intensely anti-rationalist mind, or on any faith he may have acquired as a very young man, is a subject for speculation only. Certainly Norman Holmes Pearson was exactly right in suggesting that whatever religious doubts or questionings Hawthorne felt he kept to himself, out of a deep natural reticence.[53] Nothing comes through more clearly from the sum of Hawthorne's letters and notebooks than the impression of a man who felt an intense need for privacy on certain subjects and—though it seems paradoxical to say this about a professional writer—a fundamental distrust of the power of language to express deep conviction or formulate general truth. At very least there is a positive intellectual embarrassment with the "disembodied" formulations of philosophy, so that Hyatt Waggoner is absolutely correct to observe that Hawthorne did virtually all of his interesting thinking in the dramatic and symbolic form of fiction. At most there is a recognizably "fideistic" preference for the "heart's reasons" and a nearly mystical regard for the religious value, if not of silence, then at least for the reverent lapse from theological "chatter." Criticism must recognize this bias of mind and respect its emphasis whenever it can, though it must also grasp the religious import of symbolic action when it is clearly present. Hawthorne stopped listening to the banal sermons of the New England churches as soon as he returned from Bowdoin, surely enough; but he never quite passed beyond the limits of a Christian imagination.[54]

Probably Hawthorne found very little at Bowdoin he did not already recognize or that challenged him seriously in a religious way. The family had already lived through "the religious controversies that ended in changing all the old Puritan churches of Boston and Salem from Calvinism to Liberal and Unitarian Christianity" well before Hawthorne went off to college;[55] and the difference between Salem and Bowdoin was finally not that great. At most there was a certain rearrangement of emphasis: at Salem the Old-Light Congregationalism had been failing to beat back the liberal advance for quite some time; at Bowdoin it was still holding its own, but its defense seems to have been neither spiritually vigorous nor intellectually unified. No doubt a young man used to the liberalism of either Prince or Bentley would dislike the more conservative evangelism of the Brunswick minister at least as heartily as did some of the other students; but Hawthorne reacted neither by joining the Unitarian Society nor by helping to burn the Reverend Mr. Mead in effigy. He might lament—in a letter to a pious aunt to whom he never could, by his own admission, find anything meaningful to say—that religion at Bowdoin was "less regarded than could be desired"; but he did not join the evangelical Missionary Society founded to encourage an "Awakening."[56]

It would lack seriousness, on the basis of a few humorous letters, to picture a "Rabelaisian" Hawthorne drinking and playing cards while New England's deep religious struggle went on in little at Bowdoin College. But his playful references to the "Sunday sickness"[57] which frequently kept him away from the preaching of the Converting Word suggest that he was experiencing no profound revulsion from his unconverted state: unlike the youthful Augustine, no one inspired Hawthorne with a magical *"tolle, lege"*; unlike the scholastic Thomas Shepard, no painful preacher broke his rebellious heart. The collegiate outlook of *Fanshawe* is largely satiric, if not deliberately parodic. If one had to oversimplify the problem of Hawthorne's religion in these years, in the way he would come to feel the most intense of his ancestors had repeatedly oversimplified such questions, one would have to say that young Hawthorne was far more nearly the natural man—and the would-be Story Teller—than the Puritan.[58]

It is risky to decide, in advance of the actual career, that Hawthorne was simply not religious. One may argue that "Sunday at Home" is entirely conventional, based as it is on a sentimental poem by Charles Lamb. Or one could more earnestly protest that its defensive assertion of an *"inner* man [who] goes constantly to church" is somehow the wrong moral for a writer whose more strenuous fictions repeatedly express the compelling need to "open an intercourse with the world" and to accept the saving grace of communion with other people.[59] But all such complexities have to wait the evidence of their own embodiment. Probably it is safest merely to conclude that the young man who avoided all the manifestations of conservative religion at Bowdoin, and then declined to return to his own liberalized church in Salem, was thinking more about the condition of his imagination than the state of his soul.

The works Hawthorne seems to have begun at Bowdoin, including those set in some American past, reveal a literary rather than a religious bias. The question of "calling" was no doubt as important to this shy and self-concealing young student as ever it had been to his intensely aggressive seventeenth-century ancestors; but so it was to most other young men of his generation, and it had lost much of its theological significance. Hawthorne might yet prove himself what his family and friends all later proclaimed him, a man of "deep and reverent religious faith"; but there is no firm biographical evidence for any such early identity.[60] He might yet reveal what Melville's Virginian primarily discovered, a serious "vision" of all the less smiling aspects of life; but one looks in vain for evidences to confirm the more specific Jamesean assumption of an inherited Puritan conscience. Clearly Hawthorne would come to write more than one powerful story about the Puritan "Faith." But evidently he was not prepared to write any such tale in 1825.

The ability to imagine the career of Goodman Brown might well depend on some serious religious development in the late 1820's, on some Melvillean insight hidden from our psychobiographic researches. But it would certainly require—as *Fanshawe*, or "The Hollow of the Three Hills," or "The Wives of the Dead" would not—a profoundly intellectual grasp of Puritanism's own historic world. Such a grasp could not be inherited. Puritans are born, if only in that secondary or metaphorical sense of "the new birth." But historians are made by the new vision or second sight acquired through study, whether methodical or merely "desultory." We cannot prove, I think, that Hawthorne was ever born the one. And we can strongly suggest, in the course of this study, that he made himself into the other.

By way of conclusion to this Introduction, therefore, let us briefly consider the Hawthorne Problem in its own sequence of development. Before actually entering the properly historical "Province" of Hawthorne's most significant tales of the 1820's and 1830's, let us imagine what it would be like to regard his whole career as a plausibly unfolding attempt to discover the moral significance of America's Puritan exceptionalism. Without entering, prematurely, into a separate polemic on "The Shape of Hawthorne's Career," we can at least outline his sense of "The Progress of Piety" in America. Without quite "Rediscovering Hawthorne," and without yet redefining the proper sources and legitimate uses of his "Poetics of Enchantment," we can at least suggest the remarkably coherent structure of his career as moral historian.[61]

4

Although there are still some major ambiguities, the sense that Hawthorne's career divides itself, almost inevitably, into several distinct periods or phases is now pretty firmly established. But even this elementary form of literary-historical distinction was painfully slow in getting itself made. The major critical studies of Hawthorne all treat his four completed romances in unvarying chronological order, with some account of the progress of ideas or the lapse of form; but most of them are exceedingly casual about the chronology and the biographical provenance of his hundred-plus stories and sketches, spread out over some twenty-five years. These all seem to have proceeded from some timeless imaginative moment called "Hawthorne's Tales."[62] Whether written from the "dismal chamber" in Herbert Street where "fame was won," out of Puritan materials stored up in the Salem Athenaeum, or from that "most delightful nook of a study" in the Old Manse where "Emerson wrote Nature," out of his own lively observations of the men and ideas of Transcendental Concord, Hawthorne's various stories and sketches often have seemed to proceed from all the same personal concerns and to embody the same range of thematic ideas. These latter might be moral, or psychological, or even in a certain sense "mythic"; they might be trivial and quaint or profound and prescient; but they often sound abstract and hypothetical. The triumph of Hawthornean imagination has seemed to be its really uncanny ability to make the real world go away.

Thus R. P. Adams' definition of "Hawthorne's Old Manse Period" was distinctly a step in the right direction. And the implications of his insight have, finally, begun to be drawn out—not only by John McDonald and Nina Baym, but also by other, younger scholars whose major work is yet to be published.[63] In any event, we now recognize that there is more than a biographical period of idyllic personal happiness to be studied in connection with Hawthorne's first residence in Concord. It is now apparent that almost all of the tales and sketches Hawthorne published between May 1842 and April 1845 arise directly out of the remarkable, indeed the unique experience of a man who, having just managed to open *some* intercourse with what he hoped might be the Real World, abruptly discovered himself, instead, in that gratuitous, unpredictable, and often dizzy sphere of Intellectual Boston and Concord.[64] The man accustomed to spending his days and nights with Cotton Mather suddenly became the "man who had known Alcott." The student who had pondered over certain Puritanical "distortions of the moral nature" suddenly discovered that the rare character of Jones Very "more than realized the conception of entire subjectiveness he had tried to describe" in Eliakim Abbot, the preacher of his early "Story Teller" project. This and other partial recognitions must have been more than a little shocking. Searching, above all else, for the sanative power of the ordinary, Hawthorne found himself set loose among "the true madmen of this nineteenth century."[65] Such a discovery could hardly fail to have significant literary consequences.

Having just emerged from an extended and rather lonely period of studying and writing about Puritanism—which extends as far as the completion in 1838 of the "Legends of the Province House"[66]—Hawthorne suddenly found himself being escorted, reluctantly, to Transcendental lectures and conversations. He might not approve what he heard, but he could scarcely ignore its implications. Having completed a series of major meditations on the alienating effects of Puritan separatism, he suddenly found himself all spectral and alone in the midst of the Transcendental community at Brook Farm. Turning to literature to stay his mind, he found only "Mr. Emerson's Essays, the Dial, Carlyle's works, George Sand's romances and other books" which, agreeing in little else, all seemed "like the cry of some solitary sentinel whose station was on the outposts of the advance-guard of human progression." Evidently the Transcendentalists had, "under one name or another," a principal share "in all the current literature of the world." The thing would be scanned. And then, having rejected Ripley's illusion of spiritual domicile at Brook Farm (where two might live Transcendentally as One), and settling down at last to Real Life at the Old Manse, Hawthorne discovered he had Emerson for a philosophic neighbor, Thoreau for a naturalistic instructor, Ellery Channing for a poetic companion, and the accumulated religious books of ministerial predecessors for a library.[67] There it all was, the newspaper of the age. Like taking candy from one of Alcott's Platonic pupils. How could Hawthorne resist?

The surprise would be if Hawthorne had *not*, under the circumstances, put aside his Puritan researches and fallen upon this contemporaneous material with renewed literary vigor. How could the man who had pronounced that "All philosophy that would abstract mankind from the present is no more than words" have failed, at just this time, to take up the project of writing—in his own Romantic-allegoric way—the History of His Own Times?[68] Who but his contemporaries could possibly be the subject of "The Hall of Fantasy," or "The New Adam and Eve," or "Earth's Holocaust"? What does "The Birth-mark" symbolize more essentially than the Swedenborgian-Transcendental problem of "spiritualizing the material"? When should we locate the timely explorations of the "Egotisms" of Roderick Elliston and Gervayse Hastings but in the radically subjectivist age of Emerson, Very, and Poe? Where do we imagine Hawthorne's "Artist of the Beautiful" lives more really than amidst the art-life conflicts of Platonic-Yankee New England? And why should the redundant theological allusions of "Rappaccini's Daughter" not resolve themselves into "The Transcendental Problem of Faith and Spirit"?[69]

It might turn out to be too much to insist that Emerson is somehow the master key to the rich intellectual treasures of Hawthorne's Old Manse Period or to claim that the last three chapters of *Nature* set out the thesis of a neo-Platonic idealism against which Hawthorne's own antithetic premise of Christian naturalism could develop and clarify itself. That tendentious case would have to be argued separately, in its own terms and on its own merits.[70] But this much at least seems obvious and necessary: from 1842 on, the intellectual and moral dilemmas of mid-nineteenth-century America would never be far from the thematic center of Hawthorne's adult "histories." This capital son of modern Salem, who all but began his career by working his way back into the mind of Puritanism, had embraced the identity of the man who lived among the Transcendentalists.

Thus at some moment in the 1840's, Hawthorne's spiritual development might well be judged complete, even as his outward life and reputation became settled in the normal way. He would continue to read and respond to—even, occasionally, to quarrel with—all that contemporary literature would offer his own reverently omnivorous capacities; but he would be working from a position of established intellectual poise. He would meet, inspire, baffle, and perhaps even repulse Melville; but the literary influence would work all one way. "The Three American Novels" would deeply involve him in the artistic problems peculiar to the "continuous prose forms"; but the leading moral ideas were already there in the Puritan-Transcendental mix. And certainly Europe would challenge both Hawthorne's religious sympathies and his literary imagination; but the "myth" of *The Marble Faun* would turn out to be, after all, a version of the "fable" of "The May-Pole of Merry Mount."[71]

Hawthorne's third period of accelerated creativity, extending from 1849 to 1852 and including "Ethan Brand," "Main Street," *The Scarlet Letter, The House of the Seven Gables,* and *The Blithedale Romance,* may well be called "the Major Phase" for its successful resolutions of "the Pursuit of Form" and especially as a strategic counter to the widespread tendency to see Hawthorne's career as running steadily down from some intense moment of precocious imagination in the early 1830's. But it is as misleading to suggest any really sharp distinction between the intentions of the major romances and those of the tales as it is to merge the real-life concerns of the various tales into a single imaginative moment.[72] Mastering the formal problems of the full-scale romance (which were fairly predicted by the narrative failures of a long story like "The Gentle Boy"), Hawthorne essentially went on with his fictional project of investigating America's self-created moral peculiarities. Under the aspect of "moral history" his career reveals a remarkable unity. Indeed the third period might almost be thought to recapitulate the first two. But rather than merely repeating his Puritan or Transcendental themes, Hawthorne would write them in mutual relation, even in philosophical interpenetration.

The "abortive" experiment of "Ethan Brand" reveals Hawthorne back at his Romantic beginning. Having forsworn the form of the tale, in which he could not surpass himself, he tries again with the Faustian materials of *Fanshawe*—this time seriously but once again without entire success. All the major texts of negative Romanticism can be brought allusively to bear on the quintessentially Puritan problem of the "unpardonable sin," as no Thomas Hooker or Cotton Mather appears to "pluck" the despairing Brand "from the burning"; but Hawthorne knows the limits of this way of negative transcendence even better than those of the positive, and the thing cannot sustain itself to the length of a proper romance.[73] Once again the original problems of America's early history come to his literary rescue— even as the Puritanism of "Alice Doane's Appeal" had redeemed the Gothicism of *Fanshawe*. The matter of "Main Street" reads like a table of contents of Hawthorne's Puritan tales of the 1830's, and it actually serves him as a sort of finger exercise in preparation for the symphonic form of *The Scarlet Letter*.[74]

The leitmotifs of *The Scarlet Letter* are indeed modern, or at least Victorian-feminist, as Hawthorne makes good his promise that the moral of "Mrs. Hutchinson" might easily find nineteenth-century application; but its theme is surely as Puritan as the antinomian sources it re-enacts and vivifies. And its variations adumbrate Hawthorne's sense of the theological failures of classical Puritanism with a virtually exhaustive completeness belied by their brevity.[75] In a remarkable telescoping of history which has never been properly understood, Hawthorne daringly compresses into a seven-year span in the critical 1640's a process of relentless theological self-criticism and of expanding moral insight which would require nearly two centuries of actual New England experience to unfold. A confused and self-divided Dimmesdale finally suffers his way to a position that can only be called "neonomian." And if the plot leaves Hester Prynne suspended between the repressive but obsolescent world of Ann Hutchinson and the dangerous new freedoms of the world of Margaret Fuller, the theme of the romance takes us very surely from the high noon of the Puritan theocracy to the dawn of the Romantic Protest in the nineteenth century. "Past and Present" in New England were related far more subtly than the new typologists were letting on.

Accordingly, *The House of the Seven Gables* telescopes history from the other end. From the vantage of his own novelistic present, Hawthorne emplots a romance that literally begins amidst the spiritual fantasies and the territorial delusions of 1692—which is also, for Hawthorne, the literal "year one" of post-theocratic New England.[76] And the metaphorical roots go back even further, to some more original moment when the "House" of Puritanism muddied the "spring" of life (and politics) in New England. Clearly Puritanism had failed: its controlling theory of an inherited, root-and-branch depravity had evidently given way to the bustling presentism of New England commerce, or the rampant futurism of an "Apocalyptic Whiggism," or to the psychologic and historic innocence of his own dear Phoebe (who embodies an altogether more attractive version of the "girlish" audience of "Alice Doane"). And yet something was clearly wrong. Plainly Jefferson and Emerson did not cover the whole case. Why should the effects of depravity—or of Puritanism—be still so plainly discoverable? What, in fact, was the curse on the House of Puritan Tradition and what, if anything, would be its salvation? Would the altogether Pelagian personality of Phoebe be equal to that redemptive task, even if it were successfully educated by the light-and-shadow portraits or the Romantic histories of Holgrave? The answer scarcely came clear; but the posing of the question represents Hawthorne's most ambitious attempt to deal with the continuity of the New England "years between."[77]

Nor is there any significant break of historical-thematic continuity with *The Blithedale Romance*. The nature of Hawthorne's technical experimentation with "point of view" seems to have eluded (even as it influenced) Henry James; and many critics still seem unsure of the purpose or even doubtful about the reality of Coverdale's status as "unreliable narrator."[78] But the vitality of Hawthorne's enduring interest in the peculiar moral shapes of his own post-Puritan generation continues to be clear enough. In fact, this climactic American romance manages to see double. If the *Seven Gables* traces dark legacies, *Blithedale* studies an ironic repetition: the confident assurance of America's new fraternity of social projectors is superimposed on the classic New England errand of reform by separated, tribalist example. Thus the hopes of Blithedale are mocked by echoes not only from Spenser, Bunyan, and Milton but also, and more crucially, from the records of America's own earlier lapses from social grace—the pitiful breakup of the original "Pilgrim" experiment at Plymouth and the more exemplary failure of the Christian Commonwealth of Massachusetts considered as a holy city set upon a hill. And, by Hawthorne's own brilliant stroke of literary invention, we get this tragic story of historic inevitability from two points of view at once: explicitly we get the tepid remembrances of Coverdale, the feckless minor poet who never does see enough to understand what is involved; but implicitly, and with firm and ironic control, we also get (in spite of Coverdale, as it were) Hawthorne's own terrible sense of Inferno masquerading as Arcadia. In a world which has forgotten its history and sought to bracket the question of depravity, conscience becomes the prisoner of passion, and imagination can do nothing to help.[79]

To follow the inner consistency of the historical progress of Hawthorne's career this far is to have less trouble placing and estimating the significance of *The Marble Faun* amidst the literary wreckage of Hawthorne's "Last Phase." In one sense, of course, this unique last achievement in fiction was somewhat fortuitous: when Hawthorne moved to Italy—and saw the Faun of Praxiteles—he put aside the "Ancestral" romance whose outline he was trying to discover amidst the masses of material in the *English Notebooks* and worked up something else instead.[80] But in another sense *The Marble Faun* followed naturally from the progression established in the early 1850's: the impulse behind the historic romances of post-Puritan America led straight on, if not to the "international novel," then surely to the attempt to place America itself in historical (or perhaps in meta-historical) perspective. The *Seven Gables* had tried "to connect a by-gone time with the very present that [was] flitting away"; "The Ancestral Footstep" continued that attempt, at one more historical remove; and then, as this definitive, Hawthornean search for origins gathered momentum, the storied places and gothic legends of an Old England simply gave way to the more compelling sites and myths of an even Older Italy. And once Hawthorne arrived at that point, his problem became clear at once—to measure the contingent historicity of the neo-Puritan character of America against the threefold antiquity of Etruscan Innocence, Imperial Paganism, and Roman Catholicism.[81]

In the deepest sense, perhaps, the controlling conceptions of *The Marble Faun* went back even further. In Hyatt Waggoner's memorable formulation, "Hawthorne's whole career prepared him to write . . . his 'story of the fall of man.' "[82] And as I have already suggested, Hawthorne's last romance amounts to a sort of "May-Pole of Merry Mount" writ large: a factitious American fable of innocence, guilt, and partial redemption was recast as a structural myth of all possible experience. The result was, philosophically speaking, only too successful. For once in his life Hawthorne really did work through the historic back to the essential. But when he did, his own literary project seemed to collapse. What had begun in the Puritan 1620's seemed to end—despite the gesture of Hilda and Kenyon's enforced return to the sunny banalities of America—in the abstract. Clearly Hawthorne had proved too much, and he may well have foreshortened his own career.[83] For where might he now turn to find a literary subject? From his peculiar moral perspective, what other history was still to be told?

Such, then, is the "career" I imagine as properly begun by the moral histories among Hawthorne's early tales. I do not suppose that all or even most of what he wrote between 1825 and 1838 can be shown to obey the literary-historical laws I am proposing: Hawthorne's beginnings, cloudy as they are, show him experimenting with a variety of forms and styles; and the roughly seventy-five tales and sketches which survive from his early period reveal more than one sort of literary intention. But the problems which this actual variety creates for the ideal of a single, unified, literary "period" can well be reserved for a synthetic conclusion.[84] And thus the primary argument running throughout the manifold details of the particular historical analyses which follow can be perfectly simple and empirical: nearly all of the tales we have long regarded as the most powerful and significant of Hawthorne's early productions do indeed function as moral history. Often, though not always, that history involves the imaginative re-enactment of some pitfall of the Puritan piety. Characteristically, it is a matter of freeing the moral actuality of the past from its popular or political use in the present. The history is at once evidently fictional and arguably deconstructive.

An implied, secondary argument is more complex, tendentious, derivative, and extreme: the moral histories in question constitute the "essential Hawthorne" for the first period; and they reveal the symbolist as historian creating his own definitive version of a life-long project of historical romance. But I am obviously in no position to elaborate this in the present volume. At the other extreme, however, I will insist on taking the historicity of the Hawthorne vehicle as seriously as I can; I do not mean to lapse into the tenor of philosophy or psychology any sooner than is absolutely necessary. For if we would read Hawthorne to say that "the haunted mind" (or even "the mind itself") is like the moral predicament of some old-time Puritan, then we had better know what old-time predicament he has in mind. We miss not only the poetry but also the *sense* of comparing "my love" to a "red, red rose" if we think "rose" means something like "onion."[85] But finally, and somewhere in between, I hope to persuade a fair number of well-disposed readers that Hawthorne is *significantly* addressed as moral historian: the best of his early stories intend to let some dramatized moral dilemma epitomize a whole complex of historically conditioned and historically representative choices or problems; and their intention is often so fully and brilliantly realized as to guarantee Hawthorne a place among our most speculative and daring intellectual and cultural historians.

I wish very much not to ignore James's discovery of Hawthorne's "fine" interest in the "deeper psychology"; and I shall do what I can to validate his sense of Hawthorne's imagination as a rare form of "play." I feel, at the same time, a strong loyalty to the Melvillean vision of the "something, somehow like Original Sin"; and I shall try to define both the power and the limits of this vision in Hawthorne himself. But what I wish to suggest above all is that Hawthorne's serious literary inventions are never free from the pressures of history; and that, in the finest of his early tales, characters like Young Goodman Brown suffer the psychological consequences of the moral assumptions peculiar to their own historic world. Far from explaining away the burden of depravity, the Hawthornean histories precisely locate that univeral problem in a particular American time and space. Hawthorne's researches into "the depths of our common nature" seem to have begun as a form of burrowing into books about the American past; and his discoveries of "the truth of the human heart" are given, characteristically, a New England habitation and a name.[86] In my view that literary activity is philosophical enough to meet the demands of theory, and Puritan enough to fit the facts of the case.

I

The Matter of America

❦ One ❧
NATIVE LAND
FROM CONVENTION TO CRUCIBLE

T O CLAIM that Hawthorne is significantly regarded as moral historian—as one of our earliest and most nearly adequate critics of the
effects of Puritan culture in America—is not to imply that he possessed,
full-formed at the outset, either a completely reflective consciousness of historiographical purpose or an aggressive dissatisfaction with the national
identity. Indeed the premise that an American writer should "use American
materials" may well have come to him as a truism. To be sure, one had to
choose between the cosmopolitan Peucinian and the nativist Athenean literary societies of Bowdoin; and perhaps that choice did somehow make all the
difference between Longfellow's career and Hawthorne's.[1] Still, nobody on
either side could escape stylistic instruction by the example of Washington
Irving. And once the choice of an American subject had been made, one discovered that the various "matters" of an indigenous literature had already
been prescribed, given in advance, while one was still lisping Spenser. They
all lay within that curious realm known as "the past"; and as various American disciples of Scott were demonstrating, the specifically American past
might obey the same laws of light and shadow as any other. Surely an
American writer might begin here as easily, as conventionally, as anywhere
else.[2]

Thus the major instance of development (or even of significant literary
variety) in Hawthorne's early career may *not* involve the difference between
the genial and sketchy character of Hawthorne's earliest "Sights from a
Steeple" on the one hand and the more somber and dream-like qualities of
"The Hollow of the Three Hills" and "The Old Woman's Tale" on the
other. The latter are clearly more suggestive of a certain historicist interest
in Hawthorne. But it probably is a serious mistake to make too close an association between these tonal evocations of some "sense of the past" and
Hawthorne's major experiments with moral history, which began a few
years later. Perhaps we need to hold in mind some proleptic sense of where

39

Hawthorne's historical interest was "going" in order to understand where his literary talent originally "was."[3]

By the time Hawthorne came to write what James called "The Three American Novels," he surely possessed a full and critical habit of cultural consciousness. And in "Main Street," which serves as virtual "Introduction" to the fictional meditations of "the Major Phase," Hawthorne goes out of his way to dramatize his own embattled position: ironically reviewing his earlier career as analytic historian of Puritanism's "miserable distortions of the moral nature," and ambivalently thanking the Deity for his being "one step further from [the Puritans] in the march of ages," he imagines himself accused of preaching a "sermon." Mocking himself, by feigning simple embarrassment at the charge, he begs "the pardon of the audience." But then he drives straight ahead with the same fictional instruction: still apologetic, but still determined, his awkward showman knowingly reviews the bitterness of the Quaker persecutions, the ugly passions of the holy war against King Philip's Indians, and finally that ultimate form of "Universal Madness Riot in the Main Street," the faithless hysteria of the Witchcraft. All of this takes place in despite of objections concerning both glaring formal ineptitude and patent lapses from "biographical exactness." And all of it seems carried out in illustration of the multitude of sins covered by the all-purpose "progressive" doctrine of "Anglo-Saxon energy—as the phrase now goes."[4]

Humorously executed, "Main Street" is nevertheless one of the most destructive attacks on mainstream American ideology ever written. Ironically conceived, it is yet Hawthorne's fullest defense of his own historicist method and doctrine.[5] But it is also well in the future. And we can hardly pretend that any such historical vision is demonstrably at work in or noticeably foreshadowed by Hawthorne's earliest, minor-Romantic fantasies of spiritualized prying or dreaming.

But if it is tendentious and uncritical to portray the original Hawthorne as young-man artist striving to uncreate the Puritan conscience in the smithy of his own soul, still it is no more than fair to observe that he acquired, very early in his developing career, a highly sophisticated perspective on the various "matters" which American history offered up as literary. The treatment of Indian Warfare in "Roger Malvin's Burial," of the Revolution in "My Kinsman, Major Molineux," and of Puritan Piety in "The Gentle Boy" all come fairly soon after Hawthorne's "conventional" beginnings; and they constitute an achievement of a higher order than either "Sights" or "The Hollow."[6] The movement toward "The Gentle Boy" is a movement away from the neutral territory of gothic or otherwise "outré" evocation and squarely into the province of moral history. The introductory paragraph of "Sir William Phips" announces that movement; the self-editing structure of

"Alice Doane's Appeal" self-consciously enacts it; and the odd, semi-detachable conclusion of "The Man of Adamant" satirizes those who refuse to notice that it has occurred. Hence the historical directions and critical instructions of "Main Street" are by no means the earliest Hawthorne himself has provided.

Hawthorne may well have found his way into the domain of his truest talent by trial and error, by experimenting with the various ways in which a writer might "use American materials." And no doubt he continued to work in certain less demanding genres which cannot by any sleight of mind be identified with moral history. *Fanshawe,* for example, can scarcely be considered in that light, and "Sights from a Steeple" points ahead to "The Toll-Gatherer's Day" and many other quotidian observations. But the series of stories beginning with those "Provincial Tales" noticed by Samuel Goodrich in 1829 show that for Hawthorne history quickly became a very necessary subject for art, and that it evidently involved more than convention or costume, more than the local color of the long ago.[7] His province might include that, as it would include dusky legend of vanished ancestral importance and inherited family guilt. But it would include much more. For Hawthorne came quite early to his own unique sense that America required much more from a national literature than the perpetuation of national legend or the creation of national mythology. He seems to have sensed that the substitution of Whig myth and Thanksgiving platitude for an understanding of the complicated set of beliefs and principles which actually regulated the attitudes and behavior of two centuries of Americans might constitute a fundamental error of origins, not to say an original historical sin, and that the first task of a national literature might well be to provide Americans with a truer sense of their own identity in relation to the Puritan past.

Thus the crucial moment in the midst of Hawthorne's plural and experimental literary beginnings may well be his discovery of the contradictions and ambiguities that were inherent in the moral experience of a not-always-so-picturesque Puritanism.[8] The crucial development would be, accordingly, the movement away from "the past" as tone and into the substance of moral history. The matter is important enough that we can afford to look at it in some detail. It may even be worth the risk of pointing to a single direction of development where more than one actually exists.

1

Prior to all questions of development, the interest of adequate description alone should prevent us from seizing on the witchcraft in "The Hollow of the Three Hills" and concluding—by way of hasty comparison with "Young Goodman Brown"—that Hawthorne found his true métier at once. For the one brief story which seems to have survived unaltered from Hawthorne's first "projected" collection ("Seven Tales of My Native Land")[9] reveals intentions and yields interpretations considerably less sophisticated than those of the historical tales which come slightly later. It is fairly arguable, of course, that Hawthorne's initial invocation of "those strange old times when fantastic dreams and madmen's reveries were realized among the actual circumstances of life" (199) announces the convention that will continue to serve him as a way of making weird psychic happenings seem normative, or at least common enough to warrant literary investigation.[10] But there are distinctions to be made. The more clearly historical tales employ this relatively simple convention in order to make judgments about the quality of moral experience in some real time past, which it is possible and meaningful to locate. Once we put aside our ordinary demands for superficial verisimilitude or ordinary (literalistic) historicity, the traumatic adventure of Goodman Brown reveals something essential about The Puritan Mind; the convention of mad reverie turns into the reality of moral history. But apparently "The Hollow of the Three Hills" is more simple. It may be too little to say that "strange old times" are invoked here for their own sake, to create a "romantic" sense of the morally strange and the psychologically lurid. But surely it would be too much to claim that we are dealing the historic witchcraft of colonial New England.[11]

As Poe seemed to recognize, the tale works to create a single, unified impression or effect.[12] From the first description of the "hollow basin, almost mathematically circular" (199), or at very least from the early mention of some "impious baptismal rite," we know we are in the realm of the corrupted sacred. And not much happens to qualify or deepen our sense of the "gothic" evil of that. Our first impression, which we may need to adjust only slightly, is that tone threatens to predominate over theme, not only historical but psychological as well. The tale readily admits of analysis, but of interpretation hardly at all: the surface seems too predictable and too perfect; it offers scarcely any place to cut in.[13]

Certain thematic possibilities seem richly available, but they are not developed. We may actually feel embarrassed in framing propositions about the problem of severed connections and tragic despair because we are not clearly instructed to make them by the tale itself. It might sound impressive to say that Hawthorne's "narrator" does not *underline* his psychological or moral meaning as he so obviously does elsewhere; but the simpler truth is that we never get near enough to the feelings of the erring young lady who visits the old witch-woman to become interested in the precise quality of her own experience. She is desperately unhappy about the way her life has turned out, but this is not surprising. She seems to have strayed beyond the bounds of the eighteenth-century sentimental novel of seduction and to have arrived, all unpredictably, in some weird world we know only as American gothic. But without some telling allusion or other clear literary signal, we hardly know what to make of that fact.[14] Whose plot is Hawthorne imitating, or parodying, or deconstructing? The technique and the conventions are obvious everywhere. The point of it all tends to elude us.

Our grasp of the old crone, who serves as the young lady's medium of privileged information about the unhappy fate of the loved ones she has deserted, is a good deal less tentative; but our moral or psychological interest in her is only a little more vital. We know she is lost to ordinary human feelings almost at once, as she refers to the pre-arranged conference, amid gloomy surroundings, for impious ends, as a "pleasant meeting" (200); and her editorial comments on her black-magical revelations become progressively less human. What the young lady suffers, even unto death, the old crone positively relishes. After revealing the shame and woe of the lost lady's parents, she smiles in the face of this mere novice in evil and grotesquely understates the emotional case: "A weary and lonesome time yonder old couple have of it" (202). The "ghastly" situation of the grief-crazed husband she characterizes as "merry times in a Mad House" (203). And after unveiling the death of the lady's deserted child, she summarizes the entire death-dealing apocalypse as a "sweet hour's sport" (204). She is a bad woman, this unlovely old witch. But then we are not much instructed to learn this. We seem always to have known that witchcraft involves the perversion of the holy.[15] And we can hardly be surprised if an American tale of the 1820's associates the holy with the domestic. The usable truth of this evocative yet strangely objective, intriguing yet intellectually baffling little tale is still to be sought.

If any fact or feature of "The Hollow" really does cry out for serious commentary, it would have to be the brief moment when the young lady herself learns something unexpected about the old witch. In a fictional world this small, where so much of what occurs is so tightly controlled by and so easily predictable from existing convention, any moment of original discovery is apt to loom very large. It might well take us to "the point."

Clearly the young woman is *not* surprised to learn that her family affairs back across the ocean are as bad as they are revealed to be. This is exactly what she expects or foreknows. Indeed, an "elegant" interpretation would argue that the old witch's spiritualistic power amounts to nothing more than the ability to lend a spectral reality to the lady's worst fears. Perhaps her husband is not really in a madhouse, her child not yet buried; we never really know. But as the young lady herself is innocent of the technicalities of Puritan epistemology, she never manages to have this (perhaps) more painful thought, that she has really learned nothing. And neither are we (otherwise) encouraged to pursue the wonderful ambiguities of the invisible world.[16] Nor is our young postulant to evil more than momentarily revulsed to hear "the withered hag" pour forth "the monotonous words of a prayer not meant to be acceptable in heaven" (202). The attentive reader may well be struck by the economy of plurisignation accomplished by the simple word "monotonous"—as if the old hag's terrible words had been tunelessly intoned from the beginning of time. But the lady herself is not a New Critic. Though she may be both telling and hearing her own tale, she is not reading the narrator's "literary" account of it. And in the end she does not care precisely what words are used, so long as they accomplish the desired result. If she does not know from the outset whose power she has arranged to summon, still the recklessness of her own ineffectual remorse quickly overcomes her horror at the thought of a bargain with the Devil himself.

What surprises the young lady, disturbing the otherwise placid surface of an otherwise predictable tale of ultimate woe, what turns her "agony and fear" to "intolerable humiliation" and thus very likely destroys her in the end, is her discovery that the old witch is learning the facts of her desperate case (or the fears of her despairing mind) even as she herself learns (or projects) them: "And did you also hear them?" (202). Having got over the essentially scrupulous thought that some "last crime" might somehow redouble her already damnable guilt, she cannot quite deal with the realization that someone else has plumbed the depths of her sinful heart. Apparently she had thought of the witch as a sort of transparent medium, through whom revelations might pass without let or hindrance and without leaving the slightest trace on her own subjectivity. But evidently the matter is not so simple, for the witch did also hear. And while we argue whether she "heard" authentic voices or only lent voice to guilty mental projections, the young lady apparently dies of shame, her head in the lap and her soul in the power of the old witch. The verdict seems severe, but there is no appeal from it: this guilt-branded woman cannot be plucked from the burning.[17]

Why should this be so? Why should there seem *no way* for this most conventional female sinner to be saved? What unforgiving law of reality has been unpardonably violated?[18] The answer might well have something to do with the idea of "privileged communication." For this is what the young lady has been reduced to seeking. And this is what the old witch offers and then only partially, ironically, mockingly provides.

According to this hypothesis, the last crime of the lost lady consists not so much in seeking black-magical confirmation of her own self-punishing fears as in requesting meta-natural revelations about persons with whom she has severed all natural ties. Such information is morally "privileged" because she has now no natural right to know the fates of those with whom she has been intimate. Of course it is understandable that she wishes such information: she still cares; she still concerns herself, in love and dread, with those whose threads of life have become entangled with her own and whom she left to gather up the broken ends. If this were not so, she would be in the same condition of inhumane depravity as the witch herself; and we would no longer sympathize or find her moral condition relevant. But she is not entitled to know. The desire for knowledge in excess of commitment may not strike us as a positively diabolical form of the *libido sciendi,* but it may be guilty nevertheless. It may be, in some form, the Devil's own knowledge.

The really unpardonable form of this sin is expressed, of course, in the witch's own perverse (rather than merely illicit) participation in the privileged knowledge. Whether she luridly rejoices in the tragic consequences of sin (like the horrible specters in "Alice Doane's Appeal"), or whether she "only" knows the depths of a single erring heart without love or pity, she shows herself beyond the pale of mercy and the power of redemption. If knowledge without commitment is somehow forbidden, knowledge without sympathy is utterly debased. And well might the young lady be surprised to discover how much of evil is revealed in the "pleasant meeting" she had "desired" to arrange. Her useless though pitiable remorse turns to self-devastating shame as she learns that the witch's own hideous knowledge is "also" involved in the guilty process of privileged communication. And she may literally die of the despairing recognition that the last result of her original domestic sin has been to summon this vision of perverted affection. We never come to think of her as, objectively, the Devil's child; she remains, for us, sympathetic to the end. But she experiences herself, finally, as given over to the powers of evil. And such self-knowledge may well be subjectively insupportable.

But even if we accept the presence of some such moral demonstration as the severe thematic substance of this early, experimental tale, we can scarcely claim to have turned up the beginnings of the "Hawthornesque." We may decipher the moral logic by which the tale first associates the young lady with and then distinguishes her from the old hag without discovering any element of historicity. We may even make the witchcraft of the tale morally intelligible—specifying the otherwise vague ultimacy of its evil and thus rescuing it from the realm of the "mere gothic" considered simply as the mode of extreme literary stimuli—without yet discovering any firm connection with the New England past. Unless we can place the action more than nominally within Hawthorne's "native land" and follow the logic by which the moral situation is related to one or another aspect of the historic problem of "the Devil in Massachusetts," we seem forced to admit that Hawthorne has not yet discovered his mature historical method, that he was not yet ready to write "Young Goodman Brown" or to re-write "Alice Doane."[19]

We might hypothesize that the "hollow" space among the "three hills" was meant to suggest the "tri-montane" setting of original Boston. But we hardly know what to make of this possibility, especially as other "settings" are much more firmly suggested: the young lady passes all too easily from the sentimental world of domestic lapse into the gothic region of shrieks, wild laughter, sobs, groans, threats, curses, rattling chains, and funeral hymns. No doubt Hawthorne had already "thrown away much time listening to [superstitious] traditions," but he seems to have spent even more time reading the various literatures we call "pre-Romantic."[20] And though he certainly meant to associate this tale with his "native land," he does not seem to have shaped his legendary sources into the fictional equivalent of any recognizably historical experience. His "witchcraft" may be more than the gothic machinery with which it is associated, but his "past" seems largely a literary convention. The terror of the tale may be more "of the mind" than "of Germany," but it is hard to feel that it belongs to the Main Street of Salem in New England. In general, "The Hollow of the Three Hills" suggests the tentative conclusion that a significant historicism was no more a given for Hawthorne than was any sort of vital familiarity with Puritan faith and experience.[21]

2

Neither "An Old Woman's Tale" (published only a month after "The Hollow" and certainly to be associated with it in some ways) nor *Fanshawe* (representing another sort of "beginning" to Hawthorne's career as the Artist of the Past) can be made to yield a sense of deepening historicity. Both offer far more clues to their own interpretation than does "The Hollow." And though both were in a sense rejected by Hawthorne, either could be made to introduce, or even to stand for, much that comes later. Indeed *Fanshawe* was first apprehended as a "promising of greatness" in dealing with the theme of isolation and as forecasting the entire "future of a style" called the moral gothic. And if one's primary concern were Hawthorne's spectral or dream-like theory of the imagination, "An Old Woman's Tale" might easily figure as a crucial and neglected document.[22] But neither serves to move us away from Hawthorne's earliest "Sights" or toward his mature historical vision.

Intriguingly, "An Old Woman's Tale" appears to concern itself with a past Hawthorne may have actually sensed as real, a personal-ancestral past, perhaps. The basic plot-connection between dreaming and searching for treasure is embodied in a family legend that goes back to the Hawthornes of "the village of Bray in the English shire of Berks," a legend which mingles the questions of love and discovery and which raises questions concerning the sources and reliability of dream visions.[23] And it is hard to avoid the feeling that many of the visionary characters in the tale—especially the "youth in a sailor's dress and a pale slender maiden" (245)[24]—are somehow "parental." Once again, however, the pervasive presence of literary convention and literary exercise ought to give us pause. On the one hand, Hawthorne is not simply unburdening himself of a heavy accumulation of (guilty) ancestral lore. And on the other, nothing in the tale quite prepares us for either the cultural critique or the literary self-deconstruction of "Alice Doane's Appeal." In the end we seem faced with an accomplished piece of writing that does not quite know what it wants to say. Or, if that is too harsh, a tale concerned with "writing about the past" which understands more about writing than about the past, more about its Romantic procedures than its ancestral subject.

We are obviously not supposed to believe in the literal existence of an old woman who, from her long but anachronistic memory, filled the "corners and byplaces" of Hawthorne's mind with "a thousand of her traditions" (240). A frank literary convention, she merely embodies the spirit of what Hawthorne would later call "the fireside narrative," as simple and credulous as "the babble of an old woman to her grandchild, as they sit in the smoky glow of a deep chimney corner." We can easily imagine how a tale that begins by invoking such a legendary "source" might have been intended to serve as an introductory frame for a number of ghostly or spectral adventures, perhaps for the "Seven Tales" project itself.[25] But it is hard to believe she is supposed to preside over some rite of passage, either personal or historical; she calls our attention, rather, to the timelessness of imagination as such.

We begin to get some sense of a real local and temporal happening when the scenery in the dream of David and Esther comes to include a meetinghouse "with an enormously disproportioned steeple sticking up straight into heaven, as high as the Tower of Babel." For a moment we seem on the verge of a potentially recognizable moment of history: this after-thought of a steeple seems to have "excited a vehement quarrel, and almost a schism in the church, some fifty years before" (243). But the rest of the tale suggests it would be wrong-headed to go searching "in history" for the "real" moment—when the apostolic simplicity represented by the unadorned meeting-house was violated by some new spirit of ornament or aspiration. The point of the visionary revival of this ancient quarrel is not to stress its historic importance. Quite the reverse: its true quality is its *in*significance; it cannot be made to seem other than dream-like and vain. We spend our days in foolishness until, at last, sleep comes to us all. And so with the other "colorful" but mysterious and incomplete actions in this "quaint and motley semblance" (246) of a scene: pomposity, avarice, intrigue, like all the petty strivings of the human kind, strut their hour and lapse from reality. Permanence and continuity are all a function of the mind.

If anything pulls (gently) against this essentially anti-historical "philosophy," it can only be a faintly Romantic sense of the power of the dreaming mind itself.[26] With its moonlight-strangeness playing on the homely and familiar, the tale is obviously concerned with the magical power of imagination to recreate scenes of the past and possibly, thereby, to participate in some reality beyond the law of vanity. Thus the teasing suggestion that the strange old woman digging for treasure and the mildly ludicrous Justice who embraces her, the "youth in the sailor's dress" and the "pale slender maiden" who meet to embrace after fifty years of non-existence, and the two young lovers who dream the vision are all somehow the same. Without causal power, the past merely repeats itself in every generation and in the present. And only the power of imagination admits us to this discovery of discrete sameness. It may even be fair to suggest that when David and Esther awake and repeat the old woman's act of digging, they are performing some sort of mythic action. And that dream-inspired act may be itself enough to put them in touch with the pastness or permanence of their own identity.

If they discover any other, more historic "secret," the tale declines to say what it is. David's final, unexplained "Oho!—what have we here?" (250) seems less Hawthorne's discovery of some treasure or skeleton in the Puritan character or closet than the conventional stopping-point of the romancer-as-magician who does not quite know what to do next. If what lies buried is the evidence of some crime, either national or familiar, neither the tone nor the referential tactics of the tale suggest that we ought to find out what it is. And even if the power to make any and all such discoveries participates in potencies once ascribed to the Devil, the significance of this fact hardly comes clear. The self-thwarted positivism of the ending seems in fact to distract our attention away from the process of imaginative discovery itself. Hawthorne seems to suspect that the past hides some secret and that the "dubious" epistemology of the dream may be the only available method of research. But his own imagination seems as yet unable to make any significantly historical discovery of its own.

Nor will *Fanshawe* provide the missing link between Hawthorne's minor-Romantic experiments and his major historical achievements. For one thing, we cannot be sure if this first extended fiction comes before or after the "Seven Tales," which seem to have been completed at (or very soon after) the time Hawthorne left Bowdoin. But for our introductory and still largely "negative" purposes, the precise chronology does not matter that much. *Fanshawe*'s use of "the past" is certainly different from that exhibited in either of the tales so far observed, and that use is arguably even less complex and sophisticated. But the matter is not so clear as to encourage inferences about "positive" matters—especially in view of the possibility of parody in *Fanshawe*.[27] Ideally, for the sake of genetic and etiological completeness, we should very much like to know whether Hawthorne began with the past as a magical place where the imagination could have everything its own way or as a protected precinct in which themes of biographical interest could be set without risk of personal self-exposure. But since neither of these uses is more definitively "Hawthornean" than the other, it seems unnecessary to decide.

Early critics were much exercised to discover the extent to which Bowdoin College had served as a direct model for the locale of *Fanshawe*. Probably it was the starting point for much of the obvious collegiate satire, though even here other secluded seminaries of learning might also be found "peculiarly favorable to the moral, if not to the literary, habits of its students" (334).[28] But the more vital point is surely that the physical setting of the action does not matter that much in *Fanshawe,* even though the work is, by comparison, noticeably more "realistic" than "The Hollow" or "The Old Woman's Tale." It seems naive to worry about the precise location of this "retired corner of one of the New England States" because the book offers us, on the one hand, a perfectly conventional (if sometimes mocking) Happy Valley with all of its appropriate "nowhere" woods, gardens, and streams and, on the other, the equally expected storm, cave, and precipice of the gothic. Whose woods these are—we scarcely care, except perhaps in the literary sense of source and influence. Certain narrative techniques of Walter Scott seem given; a plot from among the many in *Melmoth the Wanderer* is scarcely further to seek; and other, lesser literary *topoi* suggest themselves as Hawthorne's would-be New England is invaded by a "lost che-ild" turned seducer. Like so much else that passed itself off as the "native" literature of America between the 1770's and the 1820's, *Fanshawe* is old grape juice in a new bottle.[29]

Nor does the "eighty-years-since" aspect of *Fanshawe* appear to matter that much, unless we should care to prove that provincial manners were even more absurd in the 1740's than in the 1820's. It would obviously be foolish to argue that, since Bowdoin did not exist prior to 1808, the action must take place at Dartmouth and that, therefore, the outline of Gorham Deane is irrelevant to the figure of Fanshawe.[30] Such factual questions seem entirely aside from the search for any significant literary point. Real time-and-place settings almost never matter to the pastoral, the gothic, or the sentimental, even when they are being parodied. And, at a slightly higher level of critical concern, the idea of naming a "learned and orthodox divine" of the 1740's "Dr. Melmoth" seems mere undergraduate whimsy, an academic joke without an apparent point: what sense would it make for "The Wanderer" to be let loose among the other itinerants of New England's Great Awakening?

Psychological subtlety—in its usual sense of character motivation—seems only slightly more interesting than setting in this pseudo-historical performance. Some critics will certainly want to remark the way fathers and lovers and saviors get all mixed up for Ellen Langton, but the problems of the young virgin are not at the center of our concern. The fact that the situation is sexually more complicated than in many other "popular" novels of seduction serves only to suggest that the real issue may be the meaning of sexuality in some more general way. At this level we may well be dealing with meanings that got into Hawthorne's narrative in a psychostructural or otherwise not-fully-conscious way. But they are there nevertheless, and in a way that would seem to evade self-parody. For Fanshawe and Edward Walcott, whatever else they may be, are fictive versions of the young Hawthorne-self, clearly enough. Trial identities are being explored by a young-man artist who is not sure who else he is, especially in relation to women. The point is significant enough to risk the commission of some biographical fallacy: *Fanshawe* stops being conventional only when we regard it as the work of the young collegian who bet his chum he would not be married within ten years.[31]

After we get past the introductory clichés of chapter 1, we find Ellen and Edward out riding; obviously they are courting. Edward wants to lead Ellen to the "hidden wonders, of rock, and precipice, and cave, in that dark forest" (345). He has in mind, of course, the precise spot where (amidst gothic landscape turned sexually symbolic) the seducer Butler will lead Ellen to make trial of her virtue, and where Edward will find his own initials indelibly engraved. As Ellen is ambivalently declining to "try the adventure," fearing Mrs. Melmoth's rebuke, the lonely scholar Fanshawe intrudes, thwarting Edward's at least indirect (and probably long-ranged) sexual intentions. And this becomes the book's repeated pattern: men try to lead Ellen into sexuality, licit or otherwise, but Fanshawe prevents such initiation.

Again, even more obviously, in chapter 3, Ellen is walking beside a stream with both Edward and Fanshawe. There is some mild sense of sexual competition, but Fanshawe is not really courting Ellen; he has already resigned himself to the hopelessness of his new-found passion. Butler enters the scene as a fisherman, angling to hook not only the fish but also the young Ellen, who immediately identifies with the fish and its fate. The plot suddenly thickens. Who wants what of Ellen? How are these three young men in the story alike? How different? Although the seducer is clearly a professional angler—one who has "learned the art" and "loves to practice it" (356)—Edward himself does not seem so very different: after Butler has drawn Ellen aside, Edward looks for him but can discover "only his own image in the water." Both suitor and seducer intend the same thing, finally, though Edward certainly has no intention of leaving Ellen in the condition of the fish, which the angler has captured and then abandoned "yet alive, on the bank, gasping" (358). But it is Fanshawe and not Edward who saves Ellen at this moment: before Butler can insinuate the lying suggestion designed to catch Ellen, Fanshawe again intrudes and (with a preventing command as powerful as the "Hold!" of Brockden Brown's Carwin) bids the seducer "Retire" (363).[32]

And of course it is Fanshawe who ultimately saves Ellen's virtue from violation. In a sense Edward assists in her virtual abduction because his pride and sexual jealousy cause him to misunderstand the events of chapter 5: he foolishly accuses Fanshawe of being "the deceiver" (393) and misses his chance to learn Ellen's real situation and help her. Hence she *must* be saved by Fanshawe, this time from the very brink of disaster in the now familiar cave. But he does not save her for himself; he is destined to remain a solitary student who has never known the real world. Ellen will eventually marry the noticeably less sensitive Edward Walcott, even though he is made to seem clearly unworthy of her. Fanshawe dies an early death, but lives on in the title of Hawthorne's first clearly sexual fiction.[33]

And thus—stripped of its easy satire on country colleges, its sentimental indulgences at the cottage of a dying mother, and its inflated philosophizings about the "One" who sees and punishes all injustices—*Fanshawe* seems to express a young man's sense that the sexual relation is somehow inconsistent with intellectual sensitivity and moral delicacy. For the moment, at least, Hawthorne would seem to prefer the Fanshawe to the Walcott identity. We may have difficulty believing that the relentlessly ironic Hawthorne ever took the self-abnegating heroism of Fanshawe quite seriously; but it is hard to see that the text makes any serious attempt to revalue the ordinariness of the all-too-ordinary Edward Walcott. To be sure, Edward is not despicable; we might even take him as a fairly engaging type of the average sensual man. But at the level of sensibility he is rather crude and even clumsy. And the book really does seem to prefer the man who remains aloof from normal life in the world, who cannot violate his deepest nature by forsaking his own lonely selfhood, and who does not lead women into the path of sexual experience at all. Evidently Sophia Amelia Peabody would have her saving work cut out for her.[34]

Our only consolation, perhaps—both literary and psychological—is that Hawthorne's appreciation of Fanshawe's extreme sensibility and capacity for self-abnegation is not nearly so delicious or pathetic as it might be. Still, if *Fanshawe* were not the work of a fairly young man, we might worry that Hawthorne had read too much in the sentimental novel or lived too long with mother, aunts, sisters, and female cousins ever to achieve a healthy view of sex and society. But we know there will be a Sophia. And, more important, we know that Hawthorne will soon learn to convict Richard Digby and Parson Hooper for failing to recognize that salvation lies outside the isolated self, with some adequate "other"—that sex is, accordingly, a type of grace. If Hawthorne began by preferring the more "romantic" of two possible selves, it may well be because he had inherited, along with a simple set of literary conventions, a simplistic psychology of personality traits. The dichotomy of isolated sensitivity as against some grosser extroversion and sexual need may have come to him full-formed. If he lacked the insight to reject it out of hand, he had at least the judgment to discover the imperfection of its terms and the wisdom to withdraw from it his own authorial sponsorship.[35]

In the short range, however, the point about *Fanshawe* is similar to the one we have been stressing so far: in ideas as in art, Hawthorne began very much as a man of his own nineteenth century or, given a certain cultural lag, very much as a man of the end of the eighteenth century. His personal attitudes and literary interests are arguably "gloomy," as might befit a man taking up imaginative residence in a "dismal chamber" or walking alone to enjoy his own "pleasures of melancholy," darkening at evening into his own brand of "night thoughts." But such is not the moral gloom inspired and perpetuated by Calvinistic Puritanism—as indeed Hawthorne's first literary efforts have scarcely more to do with the ancestral faith of New England than do the first efforts of Irving or Poe.[36] Hawthorne's use of legendary material may seem a bit more "haunted" than that of *Knickerbocker's History,* and his fictive selves may all be less sensationally Byronic than Poe's Tamurlaine-self; but the differences seem those of degree and not of kind. The minor romanticism of Hawthorne's beginnings is much more easily located than any supposable Puritanism. And Hawthorne's "past" seems largely a convention: in the more sober of the early tales it is cultivated as a literary effect; in *Fanshawe* it affords a protected opportunity for disguised self-analysis and hypothetical self-choice. Neither of these uses of the past is without literary precedent, and each may be thought to have its own literary justification. Both have a history in Hawthorne's later writings, within as well as aside from his major historical tales. But neither adequately embodies the foundation or expresses the essence of Hawthorne's mature historical vision. The origins of the essential Hawthorne are still to be sought.

3

As long as our concern is with origins, and not with intellectual completions or literary perfections, there is little permanent danger of overstating the exemplary importance of Hawthorne's early sketches of three figures from New England history. "Sir William Phips," "Mrs. Hutchinson," and "Dr. Bullivant" were all published in the *Salem Gazette* at about the same time as "The Hollow of the Three Hills" and "An Old Woman's Tale"; but these much more recognizably historical pieces were almost certainly conceived and written later than the "Seven Tales" or *Fanshawe.* Indeed they seem to owe their existence to the course of historical readings Hawthorne began to pursue, in earnest, sometime in 1827.[37] Without quite being "better" than Hawthorne's other early experiments with materials associated with the American past, they yet seem more indicative of the direction his mature talent would take. Here, at all events, is an historicism *tout craché.* And here, accordingly, we can begin to notice Hawthorne's movement away from the conventions of pre-Romantic "sensibility" and toward the more rigorous demands of moral history.

The sketch of Phips—the first governor under the New Charter of Massachusetts—deserves special attention. For one thing, it is the best realized of the three historical sketches; its own inherent procedures manage to suggest a sort of lower limit of success in the task of doing history in fiction. Furthermore, it begins with a prefatorial first paragraph on purpose and method which not only explains what is going on in all three of the sketches but also serves us as Hawthorne's first explicit historical self-justification. Though one or two of Hawthorne's implied suggestions seem elegant and uniquely his own, his more general rationale of "History as Romantic Art" is not particularly revolutionary or original. But for us, surely, that might almost be the main point: the idea of a basically Romantic art which not only "used the past" but actually "did history" in some responsible but non-literalistic way was hardly a shocking departure from the regnant literary theory of the first half of the nineteenth century. Indeed, one might make that experiment almost as easily as any other, in the tentative process of trying to discover a voice that would suit and a purpose that would serve. Nevertheless, since almost any sort of recognizably historical intention amounts to a disputed question in Hawthorne, we ought to quote this first apologia in full and examine it with some care.

Few of the personages of past times (except such as have gained re-nown in fireside legend as well as in written history) are anything more than mere names to their successors. They seldom stand up in our imaginations like men. The knowledge communicated by the historian and biographer is analogous to that which we acquire of a country by the map,—minute, perhaps, and accurate, and available for all neces-sary purposes, but cold and naked, and wholly destitute of the mimic charm produced by landscape painting. These defects are partly reme-diable, and even without an absolute violation of literal truth, although by methods rightfully interdicted to professors of biographical exact-ness. A license must be assumed in brightening the materials which time has rusted, and in tracing out half-obliterated inscriptions on the columns of antiquity: Fancy must throw her reviving light on the faded incidents that indicate character, whence a ray will be reflected, more or less vividly, on the person to be described.[38]

The first thing to be noticed about this formulation of purpose and method is its frank and relatively simple commitment to the values of his-tory *as history*. Negatively, Hawthorne would assure us he intends no viola-tion of the "literal truth" of the events of the past, even though he means to rely on methods "rightfully interdicted to professors of biographical exact-ness." Romantic historiography often claimed much more than this—the right to contrive dramatic confrontations that never actually occurred, so long as they were expressive of genuine and relevant points of view; or to invent speeches that were never actually given, so long as they voiced senti-ments otherwise known to be those of real historical speakers.[39] And in other places Hawthorne himself makes liberal use of such techniques, often to the bewilderment of "source critics," who have a habit of concluding (with more rhetorical flair than theoretical precision) that in such cases Hawthorne has obviously "adapted history to suit his own imaginative pur-poses." We shall have to examine the strategic import of some of those cru-cial instances later, especially the astonishingly revelatory one in "The May-Pole of Merry Mount." But for now it is enough to notice that Hawthorne does not excuse himself from a due regard for the recoverable facts of any given historical case.

More important, however, is the positive doctrine: Hawthorne announces that his primary purpose is the re-creation of some historical reality (here an historical "character") as living and true, not merely as factual and accurate.

Beneath a tone of what may seem special pleading or even self-deprecation, Hawthorne insinuates that he is writing history as in some sense it should always be written, as an act of the sympathetic imagination and not of research alone; the difference, according to his geographical analogy, is the difference between "being there" and looking at a map. There must be some knowledge of history, Hawthorne suggests, at once more trustworthy than the colorful and vivid distortions of "fireside legend" and yet more subjectively affecting than the chronological record of the events in the life of an individual or a society. Anyone might read in the antiquarian researches of Cotton Mather or Thomas Hutchinson or Daniel Neal—as Hawthorne himself had just read—the publicly significant facts of the career of Governor Phips, mid-life convert from the values of the Frontier to the ideals of Puritanism, Soldier of Fortune raised up to Christian Magistracy.[40] But for a thoroughly human understanding of history, somewhat more might be required. And literature, fortunately, stands ready and competent to fill that requirement. Patient research gives the facts. Sympathetic re-enactment gives the life. Far more clearly than the conclusion of "An Old Woman's Tale," the beginning of "Phips" suggests that the really miraculous thing about imagination is its power to re-create the human significance of past lives. The result might be regarded, all simply, as nothing more than *good* history.

Other implications are less simple, however, and they indicate that Hawthorne is proposing somewhat more than the historian's intention as such. The language Hawthorne uses to express his sense of the precise quality of the imaginative contribution is of special importance. Perhaps one should say "languages," for there turns out to be a mixture or competition of idioms. The more obvious, of course, is the now-familiar language of "pre-Romanticism": "Fancy" is the obvious instance; but the references to an interest in "personages of past times," to the unique appeal of "fireside legend," to the effect of the "mimic charm produced by landscape painting," and even to the "license" assumed in "brightening the materials" all suggest that same curious and shaky world of pre-Coleridgean mistrust of the *absolutely* truthful power of the imagination alone. Countering this uneasiness, but also participating in its own conceptual self-limitation, is the secondary, more negative (or at least ironic) meaning we sense in the reference to certain "professors of biographical exactness"—positivists who know what they know too well ever to be denied but who yet deprive us of the rich and colorful world we desire. A recognizable ambivalence, in Hawthorne and elsewhere: wishing to create meaning, but forced to conform to the shape of an accomplished reality, the mind responds by blaming all excess of imitative acumen.[41] A common response, and yet paralyzing to the moral historian. And unless we can discover some principle which transcends this division of feeling, we can never feel any real force in Hawthorne's claims for his own style of moral history, which is also, always, imaginative in construction and symbolic in reference.

The resolution, as it turns out, is also contained in this one brief paragraph. And whatever we feel about the sketch of Phips, the terms of resolution remain operative in all of Hawthorne's major fiction. Surprisingly, perhaps, those terms are more "theological" than literary or historiographical, and more Puritan than Romantic. Even as Hawthorne gets into the significant (and critical) study of the seventeenth century for the first time, he makes his most cogent methodological self-defense in terms of that century's own religious epistemology. It is almost as if a Puritan historicism were aiding in the deconstruction of Puritan theology itself.

Hawthorne's ultimate charge against the map-knowledge of history is that, however "minute" and "accurate" and "available for all necessary purposes," it is "cold and naked." We are tempted to take this for minor romanticism still: such knowledge is true but not pleasing, adequate but not lovely. This reading takes "all necessary purposes" to mean all truly useful ends as opposed to certain merely artistic opportunities, thus conceding the redundancy of the esthetic. But another interpretation is also possible. Hawthorne may well mean to suggest that minute factual accuracy serves only the interest of the operational as opposed to the affective and, ultimately, the human. Certainly this reading is strengthened if we recall that "cold and naked" can be a high theological as well as a low literary formula. In the proper language of radical Protestantism, moralistic good works are "cold and naked" when performed by man (or considered by God) as apart from grace. As such they are, quite simply, insignificant to salvation. Similarly, all knowledge of God, or the Scriptural economy of salvation, or of the properly subjective self is "cold and naked" when unclothed by the robe of faith. Indeed, such an understanding of the Christian Truth was called—and continued to be called, down to the various New-Light revivals of Hawthorne's own day—a "mere historical" faith: one was aware, "notionally," of all the relevant facts of the Christian story, all the pertinent doctrines of the approved creed, but one had no sense of their personal significance; in full possession of all the facts, one necessarily confessed the historic actuality of the birth, suffering, death, and resurrection of Christ, but could not profess their saving "application" to one's own life. The result could hardly be admired: like works without grace, accurate historical knowledge without lively subjective faith signified nothing.[42]

Thus Hawthorne could well be making a fairly drastic suggestion about the nature of historical knowledge: antiquarian information without appropriating insight might be just as dead as the body without the soul. The high-Romantic distinction between the Understanding and the Reason would, after all, drive toward a very similar epistemological point. And who but Continental post-structuralists could ever praise the letter without the Spirit?[43]

What clinches the case for this "theological" understanding of Hawthorne's historicism, I believe, is the figure of the map itself. Fairly common in the "experimental" tradition of Protestant subjectivity, it provides that original American evangelical preacher Thomas Hooker his most famous and telling way to talk about the difference between truly affecting and merely notional knowledge in the cause of spiritual discernment: "There is great ods betwixt the knowledg of a Traveller, that in his own person hath taken a view of many Coasts, past through many Countries, and hath there taken up his abode some time, and by Experience hath been an Eye-witness . . . and another that sits by his fire side, and happily reads the story of these in a Book, or views the proportion of these in a Map."[44] Even if we set aside the reference to "fireside" knowledge, which Hawthorne's paragraph rejects almost as firmly as Hooker's, the intellectual point about the map is too close to be quite accidental: real knowledge is experience—not second-hand reception, however minute; and not speculative appreciation, however colorful, but the primary experience of "being there."

For Hooker, of course, this is a saving knowledge. But so, in a certain sense, and granting a certain ironic change of object, may it be for Hawthorne himself. For the ultimate suggestion of the harmless-looking little prologue to "Sir William Phips" is that, in Hawthorne, the true sight of historical reality stands in for "the true sight of sin" in the process which takes the reflective person from speculation to engagement. Or perhaps it would be truer to say that the two were part of some one larger-than-Puritan process: the same *reductio* that had led Jonathan Edwards—"backwards," as it were—from operational choice to elective preference, and finally to some original bias of will, could easily have led Hawthorne beyond the personal self entirely and into that long foreground of psychological preparation we ordinarily think of, colorfully, as the cultural past, even though we sometimes recognize it as the source and basis of our own moral being.[45] If we may trust our own Melvillean instincts at all, Hawthorne really did believe in "something, somehow like Original Sin." Clearly he saw that no one could be, outside the limits of myth, Adamic; the human world being a form of continuous existence, the sinful choices of the past created powerful influences of limitation on the moral freedom of the present. Even the notoriously naive Phoebe Pyncheon will eventually be required to face up to that lesson. And those near relations of hers who are about to show up as the unwary and somewhat giddy audience of "Alice Doane" will be given this instruction with a vengeance.

Surely we can imagine that a Hawthorne could discover, as easily as an

Edwards, that the realm of moral reality extends back well beyond the personal memory of some original moral choice. And surely it might be traced back into History as readily as into Nature. When this happens, "moral history" defines itself as the affective knowledge of the relevant context of one's own volitional being. Its realm is theoretically limitless, of course, especially if one rejects the Edwardsean (or otherwise Calvinist) appeal to corrupted nature.[46] And yet the task might not be entirely hopeless: for the New Englandish America of the early nineteenth century, the powerful prejudice of Puritanism might well constitute both a significant portion and an apt epitome of that whole field. One had to make a beginning somewhere. Hawthorne seems to have begun—plausibly, though not quite inevitably—with a sketch of the first governor of Puritanism's new order, and of the most famous heretic within the old, and of an embodiment of the only cultural alternative to either. In all of these sketches, as in so much to follow, the historical imagination is not only recreating the life (as well as remembering the facts) of the past; it is also initiating some expanded vision of moral reality. What is increasingly at stake, thematically, is some true (historical) sense of the Puritan (theological) sight of sin and grace.

After his compact advertisement of principles, Hawthorne proceeds in a way we will be able to recognize again and again, with only slight changes of emphasis: first a brief account of the historical setting and then a representative scene (or series of scenes). Here the preliminary material emphasizes the highly un-Puritanical character of Phips's early life. His frontier surroundings in Maine and New Hampshire were quite unlike those of Congregational Massachusetts, where "no depth nor solitude of wilderness could exclude youth from all the common opportunities of moral, and far more than common ones of religious education" (228). Given this original world of settlement for "carnal motives," weak or lawlessly adventuresome governments, a clergy "often destitute of religious fervor" and guilty of "lamentable lapses," it is no wonder that the young Phips seems a mere natural man—mariner, treasure hunter, knight of King James. In spite of this total lack of Puritan nurture, however, he returned to New England, saw fit to confess his (no doubt) considerable accumulation of sins, "was baptized, and, on the accession of the Prince of Orange to the throne, became the first governor under the second charter" (229). A remarkable seachange indeed. And now a day in the life of this Puritan convert and magistrate.

We see a stout man dressed in embroidered purple velvet, wearing a sword and carrying a cane adorned with gold. He confers with Increase Mather (who had secured his royal appointment) on the question of "the dealings of Satan in the town of Salem"; Mather transmits the "doubtful

58

opinion" of the "principal ministers" in favor of "speedy and vigorous measures," and the superstitious Phips seems "well inclined to listen" (230). Then these two worthy representatives of Moses and Aaron, along with a deputation of ministers, walk down the street, watched with interest by the "prim faces of little Puritan damsels." They are almost upstaged by the figure of a man "clad in a hunting shirt and Indian stockings and armed with a long gun"; but the governor recognizes the "grim old heathen" as a "playmate of his youth," asks about the affairs of their common birthplace, and gives the man a coin. All the people duly remark the "humility and bountifulness" (231) of this great man who has not forgot the friends of his lowly beginnings, though the reader may begin to wonder what sameness of character may be concealed by their difference in costume and station. Moving on, he is accosted by a certain sea captain, and the two revive a dispute of long standing; "the affair grows hot," and presently the governor beats the captain with his cane. "Having thus avenged himself by manual force, as befits a woodsman and a mariner, he vindicates the insulted majesty of the governor by committing his antagonist to prison" (232). A few oaths, a wiping away of perspiration, and things subside. But by now it is clear that the natural man in Phips may be "stand[ing] up in our imaginations" a little too straight.

The group proceeds to the governor's dinner table, "where the party is completed by a few Old Charter senators,—men reared at the feet of the Pilgrims." And now, as "the grape-juice slides warm into the ventricles of his heart," the governor "overflows with tales of the forecastle and of his father's hut" (233). The dismay of the august assemblage is understated, but its true proportions are easy to picture. Then, fortunately, the noise of fife and drum interrupts: time to inspect the trainband; now Phips will be in something more nearly his own element. The whole town looks on at the martial exercise, including a few "Indians in their blankets, dull spectators of the strength that has swept away their race." Sir William himself assumes command until, with the weariness of evening, he leans on his sword and piously "closes the exercises of the day with prayer" (234). A various world, to be sure, but nothing so secular as to escape the consecration of Puritan purpose.

As soon as we address this sketch seriously, all of its curious contrasts reveal that its basic spirit is one of irony; that it is, in fact, a highly stylized and "literary" presentation of Phips's character.[47] But it may not be immediately evident where the main emphasis is supposed to fall. First off, we might suppose that a principal irony resides in the bare fact that a treasure hunter became the supreme magistrate in Godly Massachusetts at all: real politics, even of a Puritan sort, might well prefer him to the "tyrant" Andros who was ousted in the revolution of 1689; yet he can hardly be made to look attractive in the line of pious rulers that runs from the vigorous Godliness of Winthrop down to the antique sanctity of Bradstreet. In a society erected on the principle that the primary duty of the ("separated") civil magistracy is to cooperate with the churches in fostering the social equivalent of holiness, and at a time when election-day Jeremiads more and more identified New England's salvation with obedience to "Godly magistrates" (as if that phrase were one word), surely the secular character and career of Phips comes to seem inherently ironical.[48] An unlooked-for "Nehemiah," surely.

This irony is only generalized when we realize how very lucky—and happy—Increase Mather actually was to secure his appointment: failing to get the old "democratic" charter reinstated, and having been forced to accept some royal appointee, he could have done much worse. For Phips *does* confess and take baptism (if not orders) from the crumbling theocratic establishment, whose ministerial representatives take him in tow and escort him about in Hawthorne's sketch. He proves more than considerate of the clerical consensus in the prosecution not only of the witchcraft cases but in many other godly endeavors proper to New England's peculiar "errand." Of course he is a loutish vulgarian from the wild woods of the wicked world north of Boston, but that fact hardly matters, except at state dinners. God works in strange ways. And what Puritan ever confused grace with *ton et gout?* And thus Cotton Mather's long and outrageously celebrative biography of Phips (in and out of the *Magnalia*) is no more absurd than so much else produced by that wonder-working quill of his: if Mather could succeed at the journeyman's task of magically transforming current events into prophecy, the metamorphosis of the sow's ear was work for the sorcerer's apprentice. Mere romance. The thing almost deconstructs itself, as Hawthorne's sketch easily demonstrates.

Thus the concluding irony of Phips's prayer with "his hands upon his sword-hilt" is neither so simple nor yet so devastatingly conclusive as we might first imagine. His prayer closes *all* the day's exercises, not just the military maneuvers; and it subsumes and sanctifies holy warfare against the heathen Indians, or against the Catholic French, as easily as Puritan hermeneutics had justified (and would continue to justify) resistance to "Babylonian" or "Egyptian" interference from England—as easily as Cotton Mather's expanding "American" vision could justify the meta-political and specially providential significance of Phips himself. As we will learn from the image of Endicott and from the sword-and-Bible portrait of the original Pyncheon, Hawthorne never got over his fascination with the mix of pure Spirit and naked power in the Puritan attempt to establish a promised land in the wilderness. This he shared with many other historical romancers of New England. But where the liberal mind pointed out intolerable contradictions, the ironist noticed powerful but unstable resolutions: the Puritan *concors* really did harmonize all *discordia.*[49]

Finally, however, the emphasis seems centered on the character of Phips himself, even as the title and the introductory paragraph suggest. His own is the outline to be brightened into sharp relief. And looking at him we observe only the figure of the natural man, early and late. The "theme" of his life, so to speak, is simply the persistence of the original woodsman in the converted ruler. As we are invited to question the abstract political validity of his alliance with the Mathers, so we may be inclined to suspect that his baptism rests on a conversion and confession of convenience. Grace might be harder to find than other, less spiritual forms of treasure; but baptisms may always be had at a discount, and the rate of exchange was far more favorable in 1691 than it had been in the beginning. But probably this response is too easy, cynical even. Hawthorne's own point is one degree more sympathetic: granted that the conversion and baptism were real enough in terms of Phips's own development, how enduringly real also were the drives given by nature and the traits impressed by early circumstance. Puritan rhetoric might always produce a silk purse, but the results of Puritan conversion were sometimes less predictable.

It is not, for Hawthorne, a question of Phips's "depravity," in the Puritan sense, as against Cotton Mather's case for his converted sainthood. Nor does the sketch quite attack the integrity of his theopolitics: the point is neither to brand him as a tool of the Mathers in the witchcraft nor to blame him for Massachusetts' increasingly militaristic "foreign policy."[50] It is merely that the self-seeking adventurer who found some treasure and the Commonwealth-serving governor who discovered the will of God are so decidedly the same man. Nature has remained emphatically nature, even after the operation of grace—so that the chief executor of the theocracy's holy laws is not essentially changed from the young man who grew up amidst the excesses of New Hampshire's moral wasteland. Ordinary history can never verify the inspired idea that this new governor ever became an entirely New Man. His life may indeed justify the invention of "the New World success story," but it cannot validate either Protestant theology or Puritan hermeneutics.[51] Massachusetts, or at least the party of the Mathers, was indeed lucky to get a royal governor who was willing to be, also, a Visible Saint, just as Phips himself was remarkably fortunate to have found his way up from the Frontier to Knighthood. But none of this forces an appeal to New Birth or to Holy History.

Thus Hawthorne contends that Phips is best understood in his naturalistic ordinariness, a strong and versatile but volatile and not overly sensitive or "gracious" frontiersman. Neither fanatic and diabolical on the one hand, nor zealous and saintly on the other, the head of state in Massachusetts, in what was perhaps her most critical hour, was basically a woodsman and a mariner who achieved wealth, rank, and ultimately political power largely by accident: he found some treasure; and he found himself in the right place at the right time. The rest is not history but ideology. He was certainly no better than the ministers whose consensus gave him power, more truly than the Prince of Orange ever did. But probably he was no worse, either; only less cultivated. Indeed the Mathers may have made better use of Phips than they would of some more refined or authentically spiritual personality: nobody would try to make a Puritan Saint of the Earl of Bellomont. Hawthorne holds back from any satirical "forever honored be the name of Phips," though he seems to have felt some ironic sense of Sir William's fitness for the tasks at hand. But the grim proportion justified a theory of Special Providence even less than the aptitude of Endicott.[52]

From the very beginning of his treatment of the Puritans, then, Hawthorne goes straight to one of the most important problems of New England's moral history: the problem of discovering and enforcing the will of God with instruments that are invincibly natural; and, more largely, the relation between nature and grace. By the time Hawthorne treats Endicott, he will also be treating Roger Williams and will be implicitly preferring the Wilderness of the latter to the Israel of the former. But not yet. Here—if we may trust the sentence referring to the Old-Charter senators—he may not yet know enough to distinguish "Pilgrim" experience from "Puritan" theory. But already he has his theme. As we will see later, Hawthorne apparently believed in a "grace" of some sort. And his awful regard of some sort of (inscrutable) Providence is well established. What he mistrusted from the outset, apparently, was the notion that grace might detectably change the operating principles of average sensual nature. And what he aboriginally rejected, quite evidently, was the definitive Puritan belief that the composition of governments or the shape of history could be predicated on any such change.

Thus Phips stands up as the natural man, however remarkable. Massachusetts offers itself as a natural society, however unpredictably peculiar or singularly problematic. And American historiography is rescued from the ideology of Cotton Mather. The task could not be accomplished by any superior effort of "biographical exactness," for Mather himself was in control of the relevant facts at their primary source. What was wanted, apparently, was lively apprehension in the service of cultural criticism—another way of defining moral history. And Hawthorne's brief sketch of Phips both announces and activates such an intention at its demonstrable beginning.

4

Hawthorne's other early historical sketches are less precisely wrought than that of Phips. If "The Hollow of the Three Hills" and "An Old Woman's Tale" are clearly literary without being demonstrably historical, "Mrs. Hutchinson" and "Dr. Bullivant" are relentlessly learned without being adequately dramatic. Precisely as such, however, they confirm our suspicion that Hawthorne's study of Puritanism was becoming, in the late 1820's and early 1830's, a fairly serious enterprise, and that the task of freeing the New England past from the hold of Puritan ideology was threatening to establish itself as a major project for the serious American man of letters. Indeed we can almost imagine Hawthorne beginning to suspect that the proper literary "use" of American historical materials was not to *use* them at all, but merely to get a responsible mental hold on them—to see them "clearly" and "convictingly." Following out such a suspicion, one might easily become too learned, or at least too "knowing," to be quite effective. The results might well record the source and predict the theme of future masterpieces; but more important, perhaps, they would reveal in themselves a nearly uncanny ability to go directly to the heart of crucial Puritan dilemmas.

Such is certainly the case with the suggestive sketch of Mistress Ann Hutchinson, whose fascinating character and career made her a partial model for Quaker Catherine, a precise analogue of Hester Prynne, and a typic sister of Zenobia and Miriam. The beginning of her sketch suggests that one could easily be interested in her chiefly as a precursor of nineteenth-century literary feminism; and we may fairly hear in Hawthorne's own anxious reference to the amount and quality of "cisatlantic literature" being written by "gentle fingers" (217), a mild anticipation of his eventual blast at the "damned mob of scribbling women."[53] But Hawthorne explicitly calls us away from the search for any "living resemblance" to his subject. Consciously at least, his own primary concern with this "woman of extraordinary talent and strong imagination" (219) is the way in which her "enthusiastic doctrines" constituted a first and most essential challenge to the Puritan idea of a unified civil and religious society. She claimed that the theology of grace espoused by the vast majority of New England preachers marked them as "unregenerate and uncommissioned" men; and thus her doctrinal objection threatened a whole fabric of social organization. Hawthorne's rhetoric is explicit, suggesting a famous canceled passage in "The Gentle Boy": "Unity of faith was the star that had guided these people over the deep; and a diversity of sects would either have scattered them from the land . . . or, perhaps would have excited a diminutive civil war" (222).[54] Therefore the first synod in New England—it had been hoped such things would not be needed!—declared her banished.

The scene of her judgment is a fascinating one. Mrs. Hutchinson stands out, even as she does in the historical record, as a more able debater than even the "deepest controversialists of that scholastic day." They press her, but she foils them at every point with the apposite texts from Scripture. Then, warming to her task, "she tells them of the long unquietness which she had endured in England, perceiving the corruptions of the Church, and yearning for a purer and more perfect light, and how, in a day of solitary prayer, that light was given." The tension mounts, as the personal narrative becomes somewhat too personal, the religious experience altogether too experimental. John Winthrop, John Endicott, and Nathaniel Ward are not famous among the New Lights: perhaps they smell a Quaker. And yet what Puritan diary—including Winthrop's own—does not record a similar pattern of dissatisfied longing, still and holy waiting, prayer, awakening? Perhaps it is only a matter of semantics, after all. But then, disastrously, she asserts somewhat more than the requisite Puritan "true sight": "She claims for herself the peculiar power of distinguishing between the chosen of man and the sealed of Heaven, and affirms that her gifted eye can see the glory round the foreheads of the saints, sojourning in their mortal state. She declares herself commissioned to separate the true shepherds from the false, and denounces present and future judgments on the land, if she be disturbed in her errand" (224). What further need of witnesses? The accusations against her "are proved from her own mouth." Whatever her logic, her arguments are "dangerous"; the woman must be banished.[55]

With the practical necessity of this decision, Hawthorne seems not to disagree: in general he expresses his Miltonic concern that "woman's intellect should never give the tone to that of man" (217); and in this particular instance his own judgment seems to be that Mrs. Hutchinson "bore trouble in her own bosom" (219). And yet the Puritans who banish her are treated most unsympathetically. Vane having been removed from office, "Mr. Cotton began to have that light in regard to his errors, which will sometimes break in upon the wisest and most pious men, when their opinions are discordant with those of the powers that be" (222).[56] Hugh Peters is full of dangerous zeal, Nathaniel Ward of false and irrelevant wit (221). Endicott is simply a bigot, described in language otherwise reserved for Richard Digby in "The Man of Adamant" (223). Here as elsewhere Winthrop seems a mild and just man, but in the end Hawthorne cannot refrain from explicitly declining to allude to the governor's barbarous account of Mrs. Hutchinson's monstrous miscarriage (225).[57] And where the entire Puritan

Establishment had rejoiced in the massacre of the heretic and her family, and did not scruple to point out that her sole survivor was bred in the faith of the heathen Indians, Hawthorne himself ends with the hope that "the mother and the child have met" (226) in the Christian heaven. Where then is the emphasis supposed to lie? How are we to "balance" the meeting of this intense and rather unwieldy sketch?

Obviously Hawthorne has perceived that social order in the Puritan world depended on a high degree of theological consensus and on a political style inspired by that consensus. Apparently one had to believe that the "chosen of man"—the "visible saints" in the churches, the pastors and teachers duly elected by those saints, and the magistrates who ruled them all—were also, identically, the "sealed of heaven." Not absolutely and in every single case, perhaps, but predictably, normatively, and with an approximation closer than we ordinarily require "for government work." How else could things be? The older, more authoritarian ways had been tried, found wanting, and left behind, in England and in Rome. The only alternative was the way of "enthusiasm," in which the will of an inscrutable God was miraculously revealed to the mind of private individuals (including women!) through the workings of an indwelling Spirit. The proposition was unthinkable. It turned the world upside down. One had to trust the system which permitted the holiest of men to summon godly individuals to rule with divine authority in offices which the deity Himself had instituted.[58]

Thus the fate of the dissenting and rebellious Mrs. Hutchinson is inevitable; and this historic, virtually naturalistic inevitability comes to seem the dominant note of her sketch as surely as ironic contrast dominates the strategy of "Phips." Men have insisted on the public and the rational: they rule the world and call the result Revealed Reason. Rebelling, the woman can only mystify the private and the passional, calling the result Immediate Inspiration. But men *do* rule the world, the Puritan no less than any other. And so the woman must be banished.

Except for the fact that Hawthorne declines to involve himself in the technically theological side of the question (concerning the sense in which the Holy Spirit might be said to "dwell in" the regenerate man or woman, in his own "person"), one can scarcely learn more about the meaning of the Hutchinson affair from Perry Miller than from Hawthorne's sketch. Most obviously, Hawthorne correctly identifies his Puritan ancestors not only as rationalists of the scholastic type (in spite of their voluntaristic "Calvinism") but also as a highly authoritarian sort of seventeenth-century sect; he would not need to be reminded, as would certain professional historians of the Bancroft school, that the Puritans were not among the "founding fathers" of the American democracy. Their quasi-democratic methods of government in both Church and State were motivated largely by their fear of

Royal and Episcopal absolutism. But what they feared even more was a universe in which the divine will would cease to be public and social, discoverable in dialectic and enforceable in common; and this overriding concern made "the freedom of the spirit" (or even "freedom of conscience") seem a decidedly secondary matter.[59]

But Hawthorne's insight goes beyond this point of political "revisionism." And we should be slow to separate it from the theology of the situation—even though Hawthorne may have agreed with Winthrop (and with many modern commentators) that only a few persons in the Colony actually understood the nicer dogmatics of the question.[60] When Hawthorne moves into the area of "sexual politics," he may be sharply alert to the relevant theological history. At very least he was (demonstrably) aware that Puritan apologists had themselves reduced the revolutionary power of Mrs. Hutchinson's spiritist doctrines to the misplaced energies of her female sexuality.

Clearly Mrs. Hutchinson's "dark enthusiasm" has some intimate relation to her womanhood—though her mystery is not quite that of sexuality simply, such as less Puritanical religions might easily worship. We might think of Sir Henry Vane as a "young and hot enthusiast" (220), but such language will hardly evoke the mind and the heart of John Cotton; a less likely precursor of D. H. Lawrence could scarcely be imagined, and yet he too has been "deceived by the strange fire now laid upon the altar" (221). John Endicott is not known to have influenced Henry Adams' view of "The Dynamo and the Virgin," but even he is aroused to the threat. Everyone in fact feels the presence of some rare power as, at the climax of the sketch, "in the center of all eyes, we see *the woman*" (224, my italics). The flash of pride "half hidden in her eye" is indeed "carnal," but the word carries only a small portion of its modern meaning: no one fears any literal seductions. And yet sexual tensions are running high indeed; apparently there is reason to fear *some* untoward release of libidinal energy.

Hawthorne declines to reproduce Winthrop's sexist questions (and Mrs. Hutchinson's reasonable answers) about women's rights as religious teachers.[61] Political sociology is not the point; sexuality most emphatically is, but only as it touches questions of theology, freely defined. What Hawthorne does stress, accordingly, is the power of the individual, drawing on deep and newly discovered sources of competence, to withstand, challenge, defy, and threaten to overthrow received doctrine and established folkways, masquerading as the revealed will of God. The oblique personal testimony of Mrs. Hutchinson is perfectly clear as theological prophecy: the Spirit of God is immediately manifest in the deepest recesses of the affective Self, and only atavistically so (if at all) in reasons of State. The figure of this powerful (and dangerous) truth is—inevitably, as it comes to seem—the singular, aroused, female Rebel standing against the assembled, anxious, male Establishment.

The Quakers are coming: call out the National Guard.[62] Meanwhile, *this* woman must be silenced; or if not, banished to the unruly margins of Rhode Island and recommended to the tender mercies of scourging Indians. For God is Reason. And He rules the Puritan State with the mailed fist of an Endicott.

In picturing Ann Hutchinson as a serious threat to the stability of the Puritan State, Hawthorne is only following the primary evidence. In making her a prototype of spiritual (or at least of "individualistic") rebellion against the monolithic Puritan Way, he is merely agreeing with the interpretation of liberal commentators, then and now.[63] But in suggesting that her radical protest might be reduced to some form of frustrated "feminism," he is, far more subtly, imitating the Puritans' own partial and tendentious accounts of her doctrines and career: from Winthrop's original version of her "short story," to Edward Johnson's brief but vivid embellishment in *The Wonder-Working Providence*, to Cotton Mather's near-standard account in the *Magnalia*, Puritan apologists tried to discredit her ideas by appealing to the side-issue of her sex. They never really answered her doctrines, though John Cotton did eventually allow himself to be worn down by Shepard and Hooker. Obscuring the extent to which sexual politics was indeed *part* of the issue ("I permit not a woman to teach"—so Winthrop quoted *Timothy*), they allowed their fear of her "woman's wit" to become confused with their anxiety about "Revelations full of . . . ravishing joy"; and from there sexual metaphor spread out to take over the whole field. By 1700 one could scarcely tell her "monstrous [biological] birth" from her "false [theological] conceptions"; and her threat seemed as literally sexual as that of any Hester Prynne. She was an unsatisfied woman turned "seducer." And that was that.[64]

Ultimately, therefore, the irony in Hawthorne's sketch of Mrs. Hutchinson is subtler and more difficult than that in his sketch of Phips. In the simpler case he merely "reduced" his subject by rescuing him from the inflations of Cotton Mather's rhetoric. With Mrs. Hutchinson the rhetorical plot was thicker. Since she had already been (unfairly) reduced by the Puritans themselves, the task of historical rescue was more complicated: the problem was to suggest a serious religious and political protest which drew psychological strength from feelings of female repression, or which might be symbolized by a male-female conflict, but which did not quite reduce to a case of spilt sexuality. And this seems to be what "Mrs. Hutchinson" *almost* accomplishes. Historically learned, it may also be theologically precise: it lets awakened female sexuality *stand for* spiritual liberty without suggesting the two are quite the same. The procedure is probably too complicated and indirect to be judged successful here; but it holds the key to the metaphoric construction of *The Scarlet Letter*. And it shows the sort of remorseless learning out of which Hawthorne would eventually be able to make great literature. For "The Gentle Boy" and *The Scarlet Letter* proceed from the same sources of moral insight as "Mrs. Hutchinson"; and neither of those works purchases its literary success by sacrificing just this sort of intense historicism.

"Dr. Bullivant" concerns itself with a far less fascinating and crucial figure in New England history. In fact Hawthorne begins by admitting that Bullivant "was not eminent enough, either by nature or circumstances, to deserve a public memorial simply for his own sake, after a lapse of a century and a half from the era in which he flourished." The literary attempt, accordingly, is merely to use the "character" of Bullivant to make a point about "the tone and composition of New England society, modified as it became by the new ingredients from the eastern world, and by the attrition of sixty or seventy years over the peculiarities of the original settlers" (78).[65] The problem, however, is that the presentation of Bullivant's character is so wrapped up in attendant sociological matters that the reader is likely to miss all "literary" sense of his personal reality. In this one case, at least, the passion for accuracy seems to have blunted the instinct for dramatic conflict or ironic contrast. Lacking a subjective correlative, we may not care for a whole world of scholarly objectivity. And yet the point of the effort is clear: "Bullivant" represents a serious, even bookish attempt to understand the course or "progress" of Puritan experience.

The mark of the analysis which surrounds (and all but overwhelms) the two brief scenes involving Bullivant himself is its extreme carefulness, its refusal to oversimplify or to be put off by handy clichés. Thus—in anticipation of the precise sociology of *The Scarlet Letter*—we are warned against the tendency "to employ too sombre a pencil in picturing the earlier times among the Puritans"; customarily "we form our ideas from their severest features."[66] We look, so to speak, at the stern and forbidding mountain peaks and not at the green and pleasant valleys. (Subliminally, of course, we are told that a look at "the hollow of the hills" might upset our "picturesque" view altogether.) And yet there is some truth in even the most available of popular clichés; in the end one has to admit that "a prevailing characteristic of that age" was something somehow like "gloom" (78). Spiritual joy there most assuredly was; and poetry too, if the argument comes to that; but where was the "play"? "Without material detriment to a deep and solid happiness, the frolic of mind was so habitually chastened, that persons have gained a nook in history by the mere possession of animal spirits, too exuberant to be confined within the established bounds" (78–79). In a world where "wit" meant the tortuous analytic of the Puritan sermon, relieved

68

only by the tortured punning of Nathaniel Ward, "a gay apothecary, such as Dr. Bullivant, must have been a phenomenon" (79).

But almost before we get a chance to savor the scene of Bullivant dispensing, with his pills, "an equal number of hard, round, dry jokes" (80), or to measure the curative effect of this unwonted amusement on the Puritanic clientele, Hawthorne resumes his sociological analysis in literalistic earnest. For the relevant standard by which to measure the cultural oddity of Bullivant is not, as it turns out, "the earlier times among the Puritans" at all; for this Anglican and Royalist had practiced his double profession of satirist and apothecary during the period of the "declension." And so we must distinguish between the original immigrants and their descendants:

> The early settlers were able to keep within the narrowest limits of their rigid principles, because they had adopted them in mature life, and from their own deep conviction, and were strengthened in them by that species of enthusiasm, which is as sober and enduring as reason itself. But if their immediate successors followed the same line of conduct, they were confined to it, in a great degree, by habits forced on them, and by the severe rule under which they were educated, and, in short, more by restraint than by the free exercise of the imagination and understanding. (81)

Furthermore, Hawthorne dutifully reminds us, we must also allow for the difference between the tone of life in the commercial centers and that of the interior of New England: in the former (where, according to the reforming Synod of 1679, "the iniquity of the times had drawn down judgments from Heaven") the existence of a mixed society was already a fact of life; in the latter, "the degeneracy of the times had made far less progress than in the seaports" (83–84). And thus the historical plot becomes almost too dense to permit any literary theme to rise.[67]

And yet we can just make out Hawthorne's intention, which is not simply to attack (or to bury us in facts about) the "gloom" of latter-day Puritanism. In the end—in a second scene, which takes place just after the moment of "the Glorious Revolution in America"—the Puritans get their own chance to be humorous. Bullivant is now in jail, along with the other principal members of that uncongenial party of Royalists and Anglicans which ruled New England and New York together, as a single "Dominion," from 1686 to 1689. During that time Bullivant has evidently learned to taunt the grimly loyal Puritans for their grimly humorless ways. Certainly the Mathers must have been stung more than once, for Cotton's life of his father would speak with "bitter and angry scorn of 'Pothecary Bullivant,' " (84) nearly forty years afterwards.[68] And Hawthorne assures us that, one by one, all of Bullivant's old victims pass by his prison to retaliate in some appropriately satirical way. None of their efforts at "stinging sarcasm" has been recorded; possibly none of them was all that funny out of context. But clearly some sort of native Puritanism is asserting the reality of its victory by claiming the last laugh.

It would be too much to interpret this local victory as forecasting the emergence or predominance of American Humor, the triumph of the vernacular over some imported art-speech. But neither is the outcome entirely negligible from a cultural point of view; Hawthorne will take it up again, in various ways, in "The Gray Champion," "The May-Pole of Merry Mount," and "Howe's Masquerade." The issue is something like this: in thinking about the meaning of America, it is a mistake to take Puritanism too lightly. One can make jokes with Bullivant, or with General Howe and Mather Byles later, or indeed with H. L. Mencken and the *New Yorker;* but the jokes may eventually fly up in one's face. For in America—down to Hawthorne's nineteenth century, at least—the Puritan Way was the way of reality for most people. When the laughter dies down, the Puritans go on about their business, earnestly.

Hawthorne formulates the political significance of this fact in rhetoric as explicit as that of "The Gray Champion": only a series of "uncontrollable events" could ever grant even "temporary ascendancy" to persons of the stamp of Andros and Randolph; and surely the atavistic Puritanism of New England could be counted on to re-assert its loyalty to "those upright men who had so long possessed [the people's] confidence" (84). Surely an essential Patriarch like Bradstreet will succeed an epiphenomenal Appointee like Andros. Or, of political events continue to prove altogether "uncontrollable," if one is indeed forced to accept a Phips, then surely the power of rhetoric will be sufficient to the occasion. Phips will be *declared* an august and godly ruler, according to the ancient model. One way or another, the Puritans *will* be ruled by godly magistrates.

The cultural implications of the indestructible survivability of Puritanism are also suggested, in the scenes between the rhetoric and the meaning between the lines. And they are at least equally significant: not Bullivant, and not a whole world of minor Augustan satirists can ever laugh Every Puritan out of his Humor. For the mentality of Endicott—if not ordinary "gloom," then "something which cannot be more accurately expressed than by that term"—has left "its long shadow, falling over all the intervening years"; and it is still "visible, though not too distinctly, upon ourselves" (78). Bullivant may not quite express or represent all the values which Leavis discovered the Puritans rejecting in "The May-Pole of Merry Mount"; and he is, admittedly, "not eminent enough" to merit his own independent memorial.

And yet Hawthorne fairly uses him to express one of his most significant ideas about the nature and influence of Puritanism in America: gloomy or not, that historic creed had chastened "frolic" and exiled "freeplay"; both its enthusiastic original and its repressive progress had successfully resisted laughter and survived satire. Hawthorne's deepest fear, perhaps, was that it might yet escape the devastation of his own literary irony.

Most generally, then, "Dr. Bullivant" is also about the fate of "nature" in the Puritan world: covered over with the cloak of saintliness in the hagiographical after-career of Phips, elevated to the status of Spirit by Ann Hutchinson, and then reduced to mere sexuality by her theological antagonists, it is rejected in one of its most elementary forms in the exemplary career of Bullivant. And there, once again, Hawthorne sought to restore it to its proper place and perspective. Drastic as the first two instances of displacement are clearly made to seem, and blurred as the literary technique of "Bullivant" renders its own instance, this last may yet be the most significant for later history. For "The May-Pole of Merry Mount" will be written to suggest that the rejection of a theology of "play" amounts to a sort of original intellectual sin of the Puritan world. And the entire "Story Teller" project seems designed to dramatize the literary and cultural impoverishment that might be expected to follow—that indeed had followed—a mistake so fundamental.[69]

Thus even the (relative) literary failure of "Bullivant" reveals the extent and the depth of Hawthorne's new-found historicism. And it clearly points to some of his major efforts in the literary criticism of American culture. We will continue to see much of what we can already observe: Hawthorne is not only drawing "material" from important historical sources but he is also, and much more importantly, turning his feelings and judgments about the cultural significance of those sources into themes for literature. That is to say, Hawthorne is not merely "using" history; by now he is writing it. He is not—yet—writing great literature as well. But that will come. And though his most dazzling experiments in historical dramatization and allegory will leave the literalism of "Bullivant" far behind, they will share its passion for accuracy and expand its interest in the moral quality of Puritan experience in America.

5

Few scholars, I suppose, would now think to challenge F. O. Matthiessen's conclusion that somehow Hawthorne managed to acquire an "intensive knowledge of the central problems confronted by the history of the

[Massachusetts] colony"; but many literary interpreters still proceed as if practical criticism need not concern itself with this fact very essentially. Some critics still resist too close an association between literature and history for ideological reasons; they evidently fear that Hawthorne's status as an artist would be reduced if he really did concern himself with history *as history*. Others have trouble believing that Hawthorne could ever have been so unwise as to risk his intelligibility on meanings which, being historically contingent, could be lost; they tend to discount the difference between our own awareness of New England history and that of Hawthorne's original audience; and they firmly resist the idea that Hawthorne may have been, in some sense and at some level, an esoteric writer, more interested in the meaning of texts than in the appearances of naked nature or the states of the wordless mind. And still others, genuinely hearing Romantic tonalities with Hawthorne and accurately recognizing the persistence of Romantic themes of withdrawal and alienation, conclude too hastily that this recognizable literary configuration must constitute the true or even the only Hawthorne.[70] But all of these critics, it seems to me, have trouble making adequate sense of the simple fact that, between 1826 and 1838, and in the midst of other readings we cannot systematically verify, Hawthorne borrowed over a thousand books from the Salem Athenaeum; and that a significant percentage bear very directly on the moral history of New England; and that references to this reading show up, again and again, as strategic allusions in the very best of his early works.[71] Perhaps it is time to suspect that Hawthorne meant something significant by calling his tales "twice-told." Perhaps he thought of himself as re-telling, for ironic effect, stories everyone was already supposed to know.

It has been all too easy to assume that Hawthorne's historical knowledge came to him without any very intense or systematic application on his own part—by way of inherited lore or as the result of some dilettantish and promiscuous reading of random materials relating to "Old Salem" considered as a tonality or as a psychological locus; and this supposed lack of concentrated effort on Hawthorne's part has seemed to justify a corresponding attitude on our part. To cite a personal example: it took me twelve years to realize that, against all my inherited literary prejudices, "The Minister's Black Veil" does indeed wish the serious reader to estimate the sort of election sermon Parson Hooper might have delivered "during Governor Belcher's administration." Once the idea occurred, there was only one response: to *read* the twelve election sermons so delivered. The result was very instructive. One experiment proved more useful than a large number of hypotheses of interpretation—as I hope to show in chapter 6.[72]

Hawthorne's own characteristic understatements are, of course, at least partly to blame for the existing critical laxity. Responding to Longfellow's considered judgment that the 1837 *Twice-told Tales* (which, incidentally, did not include such learned pieces as "Roger Malvin's Burial," "My Kinsman, Major Molineux," or "Young Goodman Brown") were obviously the result of a "studious life," Hawthorne modestly replied that he had indeed "turned over a good many books, but in so desultory a way that it cannot be called study, nor has it left me with the fruits of study."[73] Clearly it is a mistake to overinvest in this sort of self-deprecation. At one level we must recognize it as thoroughly "dramatic": what else does "the obscurest man of letters in America" say to the former classmate who has gone on to become The Professor of Modern Languages in Harvard University? And deeper still, perhaps, we must recognize that the Hawthorne who makes light of his own "study" is the same Hawthorne-persona who will, from this very moment of emergence into life, continually deprecate all of his own best art as "shadowy stuff" concocted out of "thin air" and repeatedly lament that his many years of "seclusion" had carried him, purposelessly and without reward, "apart from the main current of life."[74]

Hawthorne's self-criticisms are by no means insincere, but we should beware of reading them too literally. Everywhere he turned, his irony mocked his earnestness; and for the most part his habits survived repentance and confession. He might come to wish he were Trollope, but the three American romances show him continuing to be very much his own sort of writer. He might judge the active, outgoing "common life" to be healthier than a studious or literary seclusion, but reading and writing continued to be his main occupations. And, evidently, the author of *Fanshawe* was beginning to devote much of his time to a fairly conscious program of historical investigation and criticism. As always, it is necessary to trust the tales, which abound in historical allusions every bit as telling as imagery.[75]

To trust the evidence of Hawthorne's early historical sketches is to be convinced that, whatever the spirit in which Hawthorne first began his "studies" in New England history, he soon came to take that enterprise very seriously. In a literary climate that was to produce, in 1831, both Whittier's *Legends of New England* and Delia Bacon's *Tales of the Puritans*, and which had already produced, in the 1820's, something like a spate of historical romances about colonial New England, it is not necessary to think of Hawthorne as sitting down to "do scholarship" before setting an historical pen to a literary paper. One might be, like Cooper in *The Wept of Wish-Ton-Wish*, a fairly serious disciple of Scott without benefit of a self-taught program in American Studies. One might be competent, as are Lydia Maria Child and John Neal, with very little of the arcane or the recherché. Or one might be an opportunistic hack like James McHenry or Ezechiel Sanford with almost nothing at all. For "the past" was alive and well and living in the popular literature of nineteenth-century New

England.[76] But it should not be too surprising if someone actually learned to take seriously this particular project of historical literature.

Most likely, Hawthorne was being largely experimental—rather than critical or revisionist—at the beginning. Given an early, almost instinctive bias toward authorship, and having introjected the cultural dictum that one should "use American materials," the young writer may predictably begin turning over the pages of some compendious but patriotic history of Massachusetts like that of Alden Bradford. Less probably, but still plausibly, he might even seek to "balance" this account of colonial affairs with the loyal, then troubled, then finally Tory views of the judicious (and dull) Thomas Hutchinson, or to establish some "comparative" sense by consulting Benjamin Trumbull's *Compleat History of Connecticut.* But the stakes suddenly seem higher when he also consults Bradford's edition of *The Speeches of the Governors of Massachusetts, from 1765 to 1772,* or when he borrows and then re-borrows Hutchinson's *Collection of Original Papers Relative to the History of the Colony of Massachusetts.* And the experimental artist has, as such, very little need for either the *Acts and Laws Of His Majesty's Province of the Massachusetts-Bay in New England* or the *Proceedings of the Council, and the House of Representatives* for that same political entity.[77] Psychological Romance and Historical Massachusetts are not necessarily the same province. Perhaps things had taken a turn for the real.

Should the youthful romancer have a taste for the gothic or otherwise outré, he may well find himself compelled by Cotton Mather's *Wonders of the Invisible World* or, more generally, by that summa of American wonders, the *Magnalia;* he may, on this same premise, even find his way to Increase Mather's *Essay for the Recording of Illustrious Providences.* But surely the case alters when his reading list comes to include major works by less "romantic" analysts of the latter-day Puritan world such as Nathaniel Morton, William Hubbard, and Samuel Willard. Ordinary cultural responsibility might guarantee a close reading of Winthrop's famous *Journals,* and unusual literary curiosity justify an amused acquaintance with Ward's *Simple Cobbler.* But what motivates the consultation of Peter Force's compilation of *Tracts and other Papers Relating principally to the Origin, Settlement, and Progress of the Colonies of North America?* Or the repeated borrowing of the extant volumes of the *Collections of the Massachusetts Historical Society?* Or of various Boston papers full of "old news"? Or of a wide assortment of artillery, lecture, election, funeral, ordination, and other "occasional" sermons, together with miscellaneous political pamphlets and tracts?[78]

A fascination with family reputation might suggest the indispensable necessity of a book like Felt's *Annals of Salem;* and an obsession with ancestral guilt might require Snow's *History of Boston,* by the same principle of extended (guilty) association which operates in *The Scarlet Letter.* But what of

Felt's *Ipswich,* or the local histories of Lynn, Scituate, Plymouth, Nantucket, or *The Natural and Civil History of Vermont,* or the three volumes of Farmer and Moore's *Collections Topographical, Historical and Biographical, Relating Principally to New Hampshire?* What connections had the Hathornes with Yale College or with its most famous president, Ezra Stiles? Had any Manning ever taken classes at King's College or attended Unitarian services at King's Chapel? And what family connection was illuminated by the works of Franklin of Philadelphia or Jefferson of Virginia?[79] Perhaps we ought to begin to accept the obvious explanation: Hawthorne wanted to know about American origins—because he wanted to write about them accurately and well.

That principle, if we will entertain it seriously, actually takes us well beyond the obvious "Americana" on Marion Kesselring's famous list of Hawthorne's borrowings. For Hawthorne seems also to have read rather widely in that period of British history most relevant to the earlier years of the American colonies. Besides a dozen or so general histories of Britain, one is especially arrested by the Earl of Clarendon's *History of the Rebellion and Civil Wars in England* and by Bishop Burnet's *History of his own Time;* and one also takes note of works on the Tudors and Stuarts, on the Puritan Revolution, and on Hugh Peters and Oliver Cromwell. Milton might almost be taken for granted, except that Hawthorne did borrow at least the first volume of his *Prose Works,* as he also looked into the polemical writings of Andrew Marvell; nor did the neo-Puritan politics of "True Whigs" like John Hampden and Algernon Sidney escape his curious notice. And—as we widen the circle of works pertinent to the "Protestant" foundation and meaning of America—we discover the relevance of Paolo Sarpi's *History of the Council of Trent,* Geeraert Brandt's *History of the Reformation in the Low Countries,* and Bernard Picart's *Religious Ceremonies and Customs.* All of these bear on the problems treated by the English Puritan William Ames in his *Fresh Suit Against Human Ceremonies in God's Worship,* which had a crucial influence on the problem of form and style in American religion. And Hawthorne's concern with the Puritan esthetic turns out to have been as enduring as his fascination with Puritan politics and piety.[80]

We falsely reassure ourselves and too readily flatter our own modes of ahistorical criticism by repeating that Hawthorne *could* not have been interested in any sort of history as such. The objective case is almost overwhelming, prima facie. Besides Bancroft, who else in his generation of Americans began by reading and ended by realizing more of American history than Hawthorne himself? We do not ordinarily suppose Bancroft was interested in history *as opposed to* humane, psychological, or even literary values. And if we now find Bancroft's theory of history a little naive and self-serving, it does not therefore follow that the only alternative to the procedures of a mindless antiquarianism was the ideology of "Apocalyptic Whiggism." Whatever our embarrassments with mere factuality, we need to keep reminding ourselves that Clio was, in the nineteenth century, a grown-up goddess, and that our most trustworthy extrinsic evidence points to the conclusion that Hawthorne's literary impulse very early became involved with the reality and the legacy of America's moral past.

We might also profitably remind ourselves that the history in which Hawthorne so deeply immersed himself was a significantly religious, even theological, history. To be sure, Thomas Hutchinson does not tell his story this way; but Benjamin Trumbull most decidedly does, and Cotton Mather goes without saying. Daniel Neal's *History of New England* merely edited and extended Mather's venture in *heilsgeschichte;* and his more voluminous and general *History of the Puritans* led straight back into the religious world of Brandt and Sarpi. The implications of Thomas McCrie's *Life of John Knox* might be as much political as theological, but the writings of Owen Feltham and Thomas Fuller are strictly devotional; and the casuistical writings of Jeremy Taylor provide their own solid theological bases. William Sewel's *History of the Rise, Increase and Progress of the Christian People called Quakers* is as polemic and "situational" as most Quaker propaganda, but Robert Barclay's *Apology for the true Christian* [that is, Quaker] *Divinity* is very adequately doctrinal; and the writings of Richard Baxter take us directly to the heart of the Quaker problem—"the Holy Spirit in Puritan Faith and Experience," which is so clearly the relevant matter of "The Gentle Boy." Even William Hone's *Everlasting Calendar* and Joseph Strutt's *Book of Sports* have religious implications; and "The May-Pole of Merry Mount" shows that Hawthorne knew exactly what they were.[81]

Clearly Hawthorne doubted that the great life-questions were to be solved by theological speculation or clarified by doctrinal controversy. But only the most stultifying form of "obtuse secularism" could fail to perceive that such things constituted the essential stuff of Puritan history: without which, why all the fuss? Even if Hawthorne had paid absolutely no attention to the Calvinist-Unitarian controversy in the Salem of his young manhood, or to his carefully structured course in Christian philosophy and apologetics at Bowdoin, almost any one of the histories he consulted would have alerted him to the reality of the issues which exercised the best minds of the seventeenth and early eighteenth centuries. He himself would conclude that those issues had been addressed warmly and in earnest. Thus it is very dangerous to confuse Hawthorne's anti-rationalist distrust of religious speculation with the obscurantism of the anti-intellectual who condemns what he will not trouble himself to understand. To imply that Hawthorne did not know enough theology to tell the moral history of Puritanism is not only to ignore the redundant evidence of his early sketches; it is also to picture him as a dull reader indeed.

From the surface, then—and even before we have encountered a single significant historical-theological allusion in any major tale of the first period—we must suspect the possibility of some deep intellectual seriousness. Some romancers might go a-reading in search of plots merely, or of timeless human experiences that happened to happen when they did merely by cosmic coincidence; others, even less rigorous, might be seeking rare tonalities, or costumes in which to dress up the psychological concerns of their own historic moment. And Hawthorne may well have begun this way. But a strong body of evidence indicates that he did not long continue in any such lax literary condition. By the end of the 1820's he seems consciously embarked on a program of "studies" designed to bring the psychological word into strict (if often metaphorical) accordance with the historical thing. It might be too much to suggest that his twelve years of Salem seclusion amount to his own version of Milton's "Horton Period," a self-imposed time of scholarly moratorium in preparation for some great intellectual work.[82] And yet he did, in any case, read an enormous number of books precisely relevant to his unfolding literary project. And of such reading, Hawthorne's writing almost always leaves significant traces.

When the historical allusions begin to appear, they prove that "Hawthorne's Reading" cannot be set to the side as a sort of rare scholarly curiosity, fascinating to the "source critic" and perhaps to the psychobiographer, but largely irrelevant to the garden-variety literary interpreter. More is at stake than the criss-cross of Shandean Cowpaths that lead to any literary Xanadu. And—though the Johnsonian maxim holds—more is at issue than the principle that to know an author's mind one needs to "read the books he read." For the fact is that, again and again, Hawthorne's major tales absolutely turn on a precise allusion the serious reader is supposed to get. Rarely does Hawthorne walk in another man's way and then cover his tracks. To follow the direction of Hawthorne's primary meaning we must try to keep track of his traces. Nor does the reason for this lie hidden in the obscurities of modern literary (or psycholinguistic) theory.

We need only suppose that as Hawthorne became more and more aware of his own extended moral history, he came to sense not only the literary possibilities in the psychological and moral conflicts of the actual American past, but also, at the same time, the difference between this recoverable reality and its currently available "story." For not only popular romances but also practicing politicians and professional historians had been busy transforming the complex reality of the past into colorful, patriotic, or heroic myth. We noted Mather's canonization of Phips and the more widespread feminization of Ann Hutchinson, less edifying but equally useful. But the problem was ultimately as wide as the Puritan world.[83] And it was also current: the memorial celebrations of 1826 had made the American Revolution seem one of the most profoundly significant events in human history, related to and hardly overshadowed by the birth of Christ and the Protestant Reformation; the lesser but still surprisingly noticeable remembrances of the hundredth anniversary of Lovewell's Fight had made a dirty little bounty-hunting expedition sound like a page out of high chivalry; and everywhere the new typology, which was political without really being secular, was reinterpreting the Puritans' special brand of religious liberty as a program of human rights, even as it transformed an uncertain errand into a Manifest Destiny.[84] Eventually even a mere romancer might wish to resist these upward rhetorical tendencies, if he happened to know the facts and reverence the truth. And if he did, his tales of adolescent anxiety and guilty compulsion and fearful repression might suddenly take on a new and significant temporal dimension. Evoking some actual event and alluding to some too flagrantly literary manifestation of that event, they might well mean to measure the difference between historic reality and mythic appearance.

Nor is it quite necessary to let this complex inference stand as a merely plausible hypothesis about the nature of Hawthorne's early development. Although it will, I think, easily pass that essential, pragmatic test of application to the major tales, there is yet a preliminary way to measure its probability; one which Hawthorne himself seems to have provided, though he left so much else about his literary beginnings obscure. For besides the suggestive contrast between, say, "The Hollow" and "Dr. Bullivant," and beyond the probable implications of Hawthorne's historical reading, there remains the question of "Alice Doane" and its revisions. The final version of this original member of the "Seven Tales" clearly suggests a mature doctrine of the literary use of history *as history,* its power as well as its ultimate limitations. A brief analysis of that vexing tale may serve to complete our sense of Hawthorne's development away from the "conventional" use of "the past" as hypothetical locus of extreme psychic phenomena and toward the primary reality of moral history. It may also help to prepare us for all those difficult cases in which Hawthorne's historical "sources" become an integral part of his own text and (hence) a necessary element in their interpretation.

6

It seems safe to begin by imagining the *ur* "Alice Doane" as a fuller, more extreme, and more frankly psychological exploration of the sort of gothic or unnatural "evil" hinted at in "The Hollow." Its original form might well have rivaled Poe's "Fall of the House of Usher" as the definitive American exemplar of "psychological gothic"; it might even have offended the more timid sensibilities among its original reading public, as Melville's *Pierre* did much later. Preserved partly in its own innocent form but more largely in the critical summary of a narrative persona who tells about the original tale and, chiefly, about one particularly dramatic reading of it, the primary fiction is itself lurid and complex enough to justify the sort of psychoanalytic acumen required by "Roger Malvin's Burial." Leonard Doane, the victim of his own diseased feelings, does indeed "murder his personified incest wish." And yet it is possible to be taken in by a rejected, or at least a transcended intention at just this point: the older fiction of a wizard's grisly "sport" with murder, threatened incest, and psychological doubles is certainly no more important than the newer framework of a narrator addressing a giddy audience at Salem's Gallows Hill on the subject of specter evidence. Indeed it may require an excess of ideology to emphasize the older, more gothic broodings at the expense of the newer, more epistemological speculations. But however our critical responses should balance the original and the revisionist emphases, it remains fair and pertinent to regard the *extant* "Alice Doane's Appeal" as a significant "experiment in the direct communication" of an affecting sense of an actual (and guilty) past.[85]

Certainly this is a major part of the explicit purpose of the narrative persona: deliberately avoiding all picturesque and romantic places, he has led his "audience" of two young ladies to the precise spot where the Salem witchcraft executions occurred. He insists on this: the real place, despite its misleading appearance. The "deceitful verdure" of the "plentiful crop of 'wood-wax' " which grows there may look like common grass or, at a certain season, like "gold" or "a glory of sunshine," just as the story of the past it symbolizes seems to vary only from the pleasantly normal to the heroic. But this delusion will be exposed. The narrator, who confesses that he has often "courted the historic influence" of this very spot, is dismayed that so "few come on pilgrimage to this famous hill"; he even seems a little angry with his two auditors, in advance. The girls might seem merely innocent: nurtured on a soft but steady diet of gift books and other ladies' magazines, what could they know of gloomy ancestral wrong? And yet they are made to seem typical of an entire American generation or national character—a "people of the present" who cannot tell "within half a century, so much as the date of witchcraft delusion"; who build lurid but meaningless bonfires "every fifth of November, in commemoration of they know not what." And so he will try to impress these "girlish spirits" with a more soberly accurate sense of their local heritage. For "guilt and frenzy" are, in his view, as proper to this New England locale as the more familiar prospect, all around, of "prosperity and riches, healthfully distributed" (266–267).[86] He means to threaten their ignorance; and their bliss.

He begins his experiment by reading them a "wondrous tale of those old times" which he had written "years ago." He seems somewhat ambivalent about his youthful production, proud of its passionate power yet also vaguely uneasy about some of its extravagances. He will insist that it is perfectly true to the spirit of that age when "fantastic dreams were realized," and yet he continues to stress its fictional or artful contrivance; in fact he seems a little embarrassed by some of its own more outrageously fictitious aspects. And eventually—in a move which is not nearly so innocent as it seems—he will lay aside his manuscript and try to evoke a simpler terror from a more literalistic story. The results of both experiments are curious and revealing in the extreme.

Though the narrator says he "dare not" tell us everything he once read the girls, "except in a very brief epitome" (277), still we have no trouble sensing the character of his story or of estimating the response of its one-time audience. The young girls are positively caught up in all of its manic excess: Leonard Doane has murdered a recently arrived "double" (a literal but unrecognized twin, as it turns out) who has taunted him with what seemed "indubitable proofs" that his strangely beloved sister is the guilty lover of the double. We notice at once that the original tale bears a marked similarity to Brockden Brown's *Wieland*, which also concerns a stranger who "had actually sought the love" of the sister of a nobly educated gentleman, and the sister's "undefinable, but powerful interest in the unknown youth" (272).[87] We readily suppose that the young girls know how to respond to this, even if the narrator himself seems a bit embarrassed by the extravagance of his youthful fantasy.

And indeed the narrator does hold their utterly rapt attention, through a long series of highly improbable revelations and extreme gothic stimuli: they accept as given the premise that, except for the "superficial difference" of circumstance and education, Leonard Doane and Walter Brome are morally identical; they suspend their disbelief in the idea of a wizard who, controlling the destiny of all, has the power to make false proofs seem "indubitable"; their sense of literary verisimilitude silently accepts a scene of frozen time-lessness in which damned souls and "fiends counterfeiting the likeness of departed saints" have come together "on a holiday, to revel in the discovery of a complicated crime"; and neither their faith nor yet their skepticism thinks to question the final revelation, from the shade of the depraved Walter Brome, that Alice Doane was (like Clara Wieland) "stainless" after all. It is almost too good to be true; the girls seem a romancer's ideal audience. The narrator keeps checking their responses, to see if he may "venture to proceed," but there really is no reason to worry: "their bright eyes

[are] fixed on [him]; their lips apart" (275). Surely he may work upon them his entire imaginative will.

And yet in the end they balk. In fact they laugh; and this at the precise moment of the narrator's master-stroke. For them the entire illusion is shattered as soon as the romancer ventures to suggest that "the wizard's grave [is] close beside us, and that the [cursed] wood-wax has sprouted from his unhallowed bones" (277). Once again the narrator is angry; and now it is pretty easy to understand his reaction. For his punch-line is more than a way of saying "Boo" at the end of a ghost story. And it has flatly failed.

Evidently it is all as he had expected: his audience can accept anything but an "application" of his tale to their own location and circumstances. As long as the narrative is purely hypothetical—merely "literary," as we might say, in a now outmoded usage—the girls can accept even its most fantastic appurtenances. Fantasy as such they find endlessly fascinating, the more implausible the better; Yankee positivism is scarcely *their* problem. But when the narrator tries to bring the story home, to make it touch nearby, the effect is entirely lost. Imagination is one thing, his listeners seem to feel, and moral application quite another. Apparently a story teller would try to mix them at his own considerable risk. And so the narrator, ironic as his self-indulgent confessions and self-doubting worries make him appear, seems fairly angered, though he confesses to being only "a little piqued." His youthful tale had its own sort of truth: it had "good authority in our ancient superstition," and once it "would have brought even a church deacon to Gallows Hill." That is to say, once the narrator would have been taken as seriously as the wizard himself; but now his tale seems, from a moral point of view, "too grotesque and extravagant for timid maids to tremble at" (278).

Still he does not give up. Feeling a little vengeful, but also realizing, perhaps, that he must take the reduced seriousness of his audience pretty much as he finds it, he begins to improvise a new tale, making a "trial whether truth were more powerful than fiction." The world, as he looks at it again, is in fact "no longer arrayed in that icy splendor" which had made it seem "the very home of visions in visionary streets." The world is, perhaps, really changed from "those strange old times" when life itself seemed peopled with "madmen's fantasies"; and if so, then fact *may* be more affecting than fiction. And more appropriate.[88] Still, there is twilight, "congenial to the obscurity of time"; and in just such a zone or atmosphere the narrator summons all his powers of spectral visualization in a final attempt "to realize and faintly communicate the deep, unutterable loathing and horror, the indignation, the affrighted wonder, that wrinkled every brow, and filled the universal heart" (278) in the terrible days of 1692. Perhaps sympathetic recreation will work precisely where metaphoric substitution had failed.

What follows, then, is a lurid and extravagant evocation of a "feverish" procession to Gallows Hill at the height of the Salem delusion. "An ancient multitude of people [are] congregated on [a] hillside," and their "universal madness" is no laughing matter. They witness a parade of innocent but distracted victims, who almost believe in their own guilt. Behind the victims come those whom their witchcraft is supposed to have "afflicted," a mixed lot of vengeful "villains," raving "lunatics," and darkly playful "children" whom "the imps of darkness might have envied." And behind them all, a sort of master-villain: "In the rear of the procession rode a figure on horseback, so darkly conspicuous, so sternly triumphant that any hearers mistook him for the fiend himself; but it was only his good friend, Cotton Mather, proud of his well-won dignity, as the representative of all the hateful features of his time; the one blood-thirsty man, in whom were concentrated those vices of spirit and errors of opinion that suffered to madden the whole surrounding multitude" (279). To us this must seem a bit excessive, especially in the light of Hawthorne's more charitable view of Mather elsewhere.[89] Surely it is no less extreme than anything in the parade of horrors in the story of Leonard Doane and Walter Brome. But the narrator is not now embarrassed, evidently feeling that his imagination is safely confined within the range of permissible interpretation of established fact. Neither are his auditors provoked to laughter by any of this extremity: as the narrator plunges "into [his] imagination for a blacker horror, and a deeper woe" (279), preparing to picture the scaffold, the girls break off his second, supposedly "true" story, by seizing his arm in terror and breaking into pitiful tears. They are affected. They have realized a guilty past.

For this girlish audience, then, "the past had done all it could." Having "found the well-spring of their tears," the story teller is content to lead the young ladies back to the "lights as they twinkled gradually through the town" and to the "mirth of boys at play." And yet there is, for some audience, a further moralistic turn. The more literalistic story of guilty projection and murder leads to a very solemn public conclusion: "We build the sacred column on the height which our fathers made sacred with their blood, poured out in a holy cause. And here, in dark, funereal stone, should rise another monument, sadly commemorative of the errors of an earlier race, and not to be cast down, while the human heart has one infirmity which may result in crime" (280). This is indeed sobering. And it seems intended in full seriousness, whatever one might decide about the personal villainy of Cotton Mather. In an age which did love to build various sorts of triumphal monuments—in stone on Bunker Hill, in the rhetoric on the Fourth of July and Thanksgiving Day, and in the form of antiquarian collections—Hawthorne really does seem to want to stress the other side of the case. Evidently we are not *entirely*, or *in every sense*, "a people of the present"; perhaps we should not try, therefore, to have our past all one way. If glory, then guilt. If we can participate in the heroism of the past and apply its typological revelations to ourselves, then we must also take up its burden of shame. Or, just less metaphysically, if our nature is such that our lives and sacred honor can be morally advanced by the great deeds of our ancestors, then perhaps it is also capable of the same or similar aberrations. A point well taken, in America as elsewhere.

And yet there is reason to suspect that the problem of "the burden of the past" in "Alice Doane's Appeal" is not to be stated quite so simply or solved with such (relative) moral clarity. If there are already two rather different versions of its moral "affect," one for "girlish" readers of romance and another for the more masculine builders of bonfires and monuments, how many others might there be? Somehow, the old story of guilty projection and murder has seemed to represent more than Bunker Hill turned inside out. How soberly are we to take the narrator's angry defense of its serious, even dangerous implications in terms of the world of 1692? And what are we ultimately to make of his ready substitution of an available slander on Cotton Mather for his own arcane creation? That is to ask, what is the real relation between his two experiments? Perhaps the allusive texture of "Alice Doane's Appeal" will explain the significance of its substitutionary structure.

The first thing we need to observe about the narrator's two efforts is their ideological identity: both concern the Puritan problem of "specter evidence." We know, of course, that this was the root issue in Salem's official rush to judgment, with which the enthusiasm of Cotton Mather had at least something to do; and from the narrator's swift but telling reference to the guilt of "the afflicted," we safely infer that he has learned about this problem from that "historian" who has recently "treated the subject in a manner that will keep his name alive" (267).[90] And, oddly enough, the issue is clearer in the inner tale than anywhere else, though the widespread failure to grasp this point once threatened to make the "incoherence" of "Alice Doane's Appeal" into a major critical industry. Once the point is taken, however, much of what is clumsily experimental or obsessive becomes controlled almost to the point of cliché: the narrator is so familiar with his old-time technicalities that he merely *names* them, without explanation and almost with embarrassment. A word to the historical critic is supposed to be sufficient.[91]

Thus the famous "contradiction" in the graveyard revel: "All, in short, were there . . . Yet none but souls accursed were there, and fiends counterfeiting the likeness of departed saints" (276). What—in a gothic epiphany of something somehow like universal reprobation—could possibly be simpler? We see the ghostly shades of persons really lost to goodness but

83

also the false representations of good men gone to glory. Has any reader of Cotton Mather ever supposed the Devil could simulate living saints but not dead ones? The whole nightmarish scene of groaning and gnashing is utterly simple, if technical: the "unreal throng" is luridly composed of "sinful souls and false specters of good men" (276); the tone is the tone of "The Hollow of the Three Hills" but the haunts are the haunts of Goodman Brown. What else do we expect the faithless eyes of Leonard Doane to see?[92]

The case of the much-disputed wizard is almost equally simple, and indeed the narrator breezes by it even more quickly. The problem seems tangled enough at the moment of Leonard Doane's confession: after listening to an account of what he already knows, the wizard laughs; and the tormented young man decides that he has been somehow "deceived" by the seemingly "indubitable proofs of the shame of Alice" (272). But before we can fairly get caught up in the question of how all this credibly came about (or of how it might relate to other gothic cases of mistaken identity, such as that of Clara Wieland),[93] the narrator brusquely covers it all with the veil of a general statement: "In the course of the tale, the reader had been permitted to discover that all the incidents were the results of the machinations of the wizard, who had cunningly devised that Walter Brome should tempt his unknown sister to guilt and shame, and himself perish by the hand of his twin-brother" (277). Not to worry. The Devil and his disciples are very subtle and very powerful; their destructive experiments often greatly prosper. And in the present case, the principal illusion is really not that taxing: all that is really required is that Leonard Doane should become convinced, in a flood of bad faith, that Walter Brome has *actually* performed, with Alice, the sexual deeds that have occurred to his own fantasy. Not much of a trick, as the classic case of Archimago and the Red Cross Knight will demonstrate.[94]

The point, of course, is *not at all* to absolve or to convict the wizard, who scarcely exists apart from Leonard Doane's "diseased imagination and morbid feelings." When has it ever closed the moral case to say that "the Devil made me do it"?—even though that claim may be universally true in its own terms. The relevant question, always, is what one might mean by such a statement. What "the Devil" are we talking about? To what psychic resources of self-disguise or moral powers of self-deception does that diabolic arch-magician correspond?[95]

The answer in the present instance is almost too obvious to require explanation, as indeed it calls forth no elaboration from the narrator, who assumes its moral self-evidence. The Devil's deception of Leonard Doane, his power to make Walter Brome's tauntings seem like "indubitable proofs" of moral perfidy all around, is not different from Leonard's own guilty imagination. As with the Red Cross Knight before and Goodman Brown after, Leonard Doane has obscured his own guilt by projecting it onto others: offered some ambiguous opportunity, he has leapt to the ready conclusion that Walter Brome and Alice are guilty lovers. But that conclusion is (formally) unjustified and (materially) very probably false; it tells us far more about the uneasy conscience or the "giltie sight" of Leonard than about the moral depravity of his familiar but strangely beloved sister or his estranged but all-too-familiar, all-too-cordially-hated twin brother. Leonard fixes in others, as a fact, a feeling he cannot face in himself: he murders his personified incest wish. For this terrible fact the diabolical deception of the wizard is indeed to blame: he has permitted Leonard Doane to see or to hear things that are not to be believed. But such spectral evidence can only adumbrate the psychic law of guilty projection.[96]

And thus the historicity, as well as the unity, of "Alice Doane's Appeal." The Devil, as everyone knows, has often appeared as an Angel of Light. But he also has, according to Cotton Mather, the correlative power, as well, to assume the spectral shape of an innocent person; and this quaint Puritanic belief is literally enacted in the story's most gothic scene. The spectral epiphany, however, is no mere tour de force; whatever witchcraft may mean in "The Hollow of the Three Hills," in "Alice Doane's Appeal" it signifies the precise problems of historic Salem. The terrifying display of "false specters of good men" points to the moral identity of the older, fictional with the newer, "truer" story. Leonard Doane himself and Cotton Mather (as an official representative of Old Salem) are alike taken in by the Devil's powers of spectral deception; and in both cases the charges of diabolical evil probably reveals more about the accuser than the accused.[97]

Ultimately, therefore, the function of the narrator's second effort is not simply to move to tears some clearly inadequate audience; it is, rather, to suggest the extent to which his original story was itself already adequate—in spite of its rather wild indulgences—to the essential history of Salem Witchcraft. Without methodological fanfare, the older story had simply *enacted* the truth of specter evidence as guilty projection: the moral facts were there before the technical language was inserted. Beyond this, the original story contains at least one absolutely telling, allusive clue to its own essential historicity, locating itself in ideological time and validating the narrator's claim to dangerous relevance. Significantly, the historical trace appears in the very first paragraph of the original story; and though the unwary may miss it, its interpretive significance looms as large as the open invocation of the recent historian's "honorable monument."

The older tale, we are told, "opened darkly with the discovery of a murder." Evidently the desperate criminal had tried to hack a hole in the ice on a frozen lake, so as to "conceal his victim in a chill and watery grave"; but the solidity of the ice was "too stubborn for the patience of a man with blood upon his hand," and so the corpse had remained unburied. It *would* not bury, we critically surmise, any more than the moral guilt which Samuel Sewall found himself confessing five years after the legal fact.[98] But then the snow comes to cover the corpse, "as if nature were shocked at the deed, and strove to hide it with her frozen tears"; but even her cleanly concerns can only partly bury the body, so that a traveler soon makes an "affrighted" discovery (270). The corpse *will* not bury, we easily convince ourselves, any more than the remorse of the murderer will ever be forced down into unconsciousness: murder will out; nobody will hear heartbeats from inside a wall or crypt, but we will not be surprised to find the guilty party confessing the whole affair to his local wizard.

And yet somewhat more is at stake here than dramatic irony and depth psychology; there is a learned as well as an obvious significance to the incomplete burial of Walter Brome. For by it we are also put in touch with the most devastating attack on the logic and tactics of Cotton Mather drafted by any of his contemporaries. At something like the emotional climax of his case against the witchcraft proceedings, Robert Calef describes the final "appeal" and death—and partial burial—of Mather's most troublesome and anxious-making victim, George Burroughs. Burroughs appeals to the spectators, with a "Speech for the clearing of his Innocency," and with a prayer (concluded by a precise and perfect repetition of the Lord's Prayer) which was "so well worded," fervent, and affecting "that it seemed to some, that the Spectators would hinder the Execution." But Mather interposes with a résumé of fact and theory: Burroughs is "no ordained minister," there is a legal case against him, and (besides) "the Devil has often been transformed into an Angel of Light." Thus "the People" are "somewhat appeased," and his execution is carried out. And then this: "When he was cut down, he was dragged by the Halter to a Hole . . . about two feet deep . . . he was so put in . . . [that] one of his Hands and his Chin . . . [were] left uncovered."[99] Apparently even contemporaneous observers wished to suggest, in a symbolic way, that the thing could not quite be covered over.

It might be too much to argue that Hawthorne's original tale had been intended as an "allegory" of the last-hour appeal of George Burroughs. But it can only be Burroughs who offers, in the narrator's "true" story, a "petition [not] for himself alone, but embracing all his fellow-sufferers and the frenzied multitude" (279); no other clergyman was counted among the accused; the reference to him as an "ordained pastor" is only Hawthorne's way of taking sides with Calef, against Mather, on the unhappily attendant question of the disputed validity of Burroughs' ordination. And, most clearly and cogently, the detail of incomplete burial is too meaningful to be accidental. Calef goes well beyond the limits of his argument about the legitimate use of evidence in including it. For him it is utterly gratuitous, "literary"; and thus it becomes a sort of "signature" of his own anti-Establishment treatment of the witchcraft prosecutions.[100] Hawthorne, accordingly, can scarcely incorporate it without intending to invoke the meanings, and the considerable moral authority, of Calef himself. Hence the extreme danger of the *ur* "Alice Doane"—were it read aloud or published in 1692. Quite deliberately (if unobtrusively) and quite precisely (if metaphorically) it takes up and extends Calef's worried reflections on the projective temptations involved in dealing with the diabolical. It *already* asks us to discern the historical specters of Cotton Mather and George Burroughs behind the fictional careers of Leonard Doane and Walter Brome. It might almost have been titled *"Still* More Wonders of the Invisible World."

Once the identical historicity of the two experiments is understood, other nagging problems of interpretation tend to solve themselves. The narrator is not so much substituting a true story for a wild romance as he is merely literalizing psychohistory for an audience which obviously lacks the literary sophistication to discern the historical truth of a metaphorical fiction—an audience which insists on regarding all fantasy as *mere* fantasy. And this helps us with his angry tone, which is otherwise very troublesome indeed. Far from conceding the superior affect of historical fact over historical fiction, he is actually protesting the necessity of proceeding in so flat-footed a fashion in order to be taken seriously, truthfully, and in full faith. When the audience proves that it cannot accept moral history as it is given, adequately, to the imagination, he forcefully responds with the only thing he imagines they *can* take—a procession of horrors and a rather simplistic attack on the diabolical villainy of Cotton Mather. In this regard his second experiment is not so much an epistemological concession as it is a moral protest: if you cannot tremble for the potential treachery of your own faithless hearts, you may at least weep for the superstitious errors and violent crimes of your national past; if you will not meditate on the human will to evil, you may at least visit a shrine of national shame.

However we should ultimately estimate the literary distance between the passionate young author who could not find a publisher for "Alice Doane" and the disillusioned persona who takes a sort of vengeance on the audience those publishers imagined they were protecting, it seems clear that the narrator's concluding "trial" to discover "whether truth were more powerful than fiction" does not represent Hawthorne's own deepest view of the significance of the Salem Witchcraft. Unless we wish to concede that Hawthorne's tone really is, for once, entirely out of control, or unless we are willing to suppose that Hawthorne's view of the matter greatly changed between "Alice Doane's Appeal" and *Grandfather's Chair*, it seems necessary to conclude that the final vision of Cotton Mather is strategically overwrought.[101] Nor is our critical decision entirely free. Once again, a precise and telling allusion forces our decision.

At the outset, the reference to the professional "historian" of the witchcraft may seem either gratuitous learning or dutiful citation. In retrospect, it seems much more. The "antiquarian" scholar in question is almost certainly Charles W. Upham, that budding authority on the events of 1692 whose *Lectures on Witchcraft* were published in 1831 and had been originally delivered in Salem the year before; and it is clearly his view that is offered when the narrator shifts from what the girls take as mere romantic fiction to what they are willing to accept as historical fact. In Upham's opinion, Cotton Mather had "got up" the matter of witchcraft for his own bigoted purposes; and the image of Mather as concentrating in himself all the "vices of spirit and errors of opinion" of a hopelessly unenlightened past is essentially Upham's "liberal" view of the matter.[102] Hence the real import of the second experiment: when the narrator has failed to move his audience with a gothic fiction which was (nevertheless) essentially true to the moral history of 1692, he retaliates with an accepted, even an official version of the "facts" that is, ironically, less adequate to the deeper significance of the case. His second experiment is more successful not because it is truer but because it is simpler. And probably because it is less personally challenging, involving as it does a convenient scapegoat.

Thus the moralistic conclusion has to be taken very carefully. It is not exactly false, but it may be slightly beside the main point. Clearly it is not irrelevant to meditate on the sins of Cotton Mather. He certainly did, as Perry Miller has shown, betray an excess of ideological interest in the proposition that the Devil was making a subtle last stand against the Millennial Kingdom in Massachusetts: he helped to keep alive a keen expectation of an invasion of witches, and "he prostituted a magnificent conception of New England's destiny to saving the face of a bigoted court." Moreover, if Calef's account is at all trustworthy, he was all too ready to play upon the ambiguous relation between the Devil and certain angels of light: reversing the intention of the official *Return of the Several Ministers Consulted,* he employed the Biblical warning not to counsel legal caution and epistemological "charity" but in fact to ensure the execution of a fellow minister. The case is full of melancholy instruction, whatever adequate psychobiography may conclude about his complicated motives.[103] Similarly, it would not be a *bad* idea to build a dark, funereal monument on Gallows Hill: the witchcraft executions were in fact illegal, and a "universal madness" really was "riot in the main street"; and for this we are all no less responsible than for the glorious deeds of 1776.

But moral history may touch the soul as well as the citizen, the private self as well as the public scapegoat. And at this level the figure of Walter Brome is more instructive than the example of Cotton Mather. It would be useful to build the negative monument. It is not wrong to weep for the injustices Cotton Mather helped to perpetrate. But better to weep for oneself. Better to begin with a sober meditation, in pity and fear, on the linked fatality of Leonard Doane and Walter Brome, the dark problem of "the same devil in each bosom" (272). And best to end with a sore application, in fear and trembling, of the deep mystery of the wizard buried "here," in one's own faithless heart—always ready for some wicked fantasy, always able to witness a "corresponding" guilt, and always all too eager to imagine its own fleeting thought as the accomplished deed of another.

Thus the historicity of "Alice Doane's Appeal" is actually a fairly complicated proposition. First of all, the tale refuses to make any absolute distinction between the events of 1692 and the fantasies of the story teller, adequately conceived and aptly applied. Furthermore, it suggests a way in which a certain moral psychology might be used to verify the reality of the quaint conceptions at issue between Mather and Calef, in their struggle for ideological possession of "the invisible world"—providing a way to be serious about such matters without quite believing in them. And in doing so, finally, it actually supplants the apparently authoritative but really condescending and ahistorical liberalism of the Upham interpretation. If the *ur* "Alice Doane" had merely re-enacted an essentially "Spenserian" interpretation of the Salem Witchcraft, the extant "Alice Doane's Appeal" insists that such an interpretation remains as valid as any other so far proposed.[104]

In order to say something at all useful about the matter of 1692, one had to make some adequate psychological sense of the fact that otherwise reliable persons were reporting certain odd supra-natural sightings: the "specters" or bodiless shapes of otherwise reputable citizens and church members could be "witnessed" in the performance of actions that suggested an advanced and concentrated depravity, as if they had given themselves over to the Devil. The original arguments about this distressing state of affairs all turned on the Devil's debatable power to simulate the appearance of saintly men in order to tempt their fellow-saints to doubt their holiness—"to lead astray, if possible, even the elect." Was it or was it not reasonable to suppose God might permit the Devil any such power? The infamous court of Oyer and Terminer supposed the thing was *not* reasonable, that God would permit spectral simulation *only* in the case of a person who had sworn formal allegiance to the Prince of Darkness. Others thought otherwise, for what seemed good and sufficient (Biblical) reasons. While the abstruse theological case was being debated, however, a certain number of persons were executed on the basis of testimony about what their "specters" had been seen to do. Contemporary critics (like Calef) argued that an abuse of evidence had occurred: two reliable witnesses had to swear they saw the *person,* not merely the *specter,* performing the actions proper to witchcraft. Yet how could one tell the difference? And so the argument reached an epistemologi-cal stalemate, even as a sort of moral revulsion set in. Never solved, the problem of specters passed into "history," for the "modern" mind to con-sider. But what could the modern mind (of which the "liberal" mind of the nineteenth century is a fair type) possibly make of the categories of this whole incredible episode?

To critics like Upham the case seemed clear: the overstimulated imagina-tion of a gothic age had induced "visions," had caused people to "see" things that never really existed; and in this situation of "frenzy," a fanatical clergy had seized an opportunity to advance its own failing cause, even at the price of judicial murder. Sexually repressed teen-agers and bloodthirsty Puritans produced a witchcraft "hysteria"; a plausible account, that is still being written.[105] But another view was also possible—more subtle, less self-congratulatory, and also more historical, for all of its literary basis in Spenser. Its fundamental assumption was that specter evidence names the local manifestation of a phenomenon that is real and permanent, not merely "superstitious" or "unenlightened." From this it followed that one does not weep for the past alone.

Clearly Hawthorne came to his reading of Mather and Calef (and of so much else related to the events of 1692, including Upham) with Book I of *The Faerie Queene* already fixed in his mind, a permanent feature of his moral imagination. And from there he already seemed to know about the problem of diabolical simulation. In the overt tactics of Spenserian psycho-machia, of course, everything occurs in a sort of dream, but aids to inter-pretation are liberally provided. Freud is close to the point, though well after the fact.[106]

In the famous Spenserian *mythos*, Archimago fashions a false specter of the ever-chaste Una, to abuse the fantasy of a formidable Knight of Holiness and tempt his own commitment to sexual virtue. Redcrosse resists the spec-tral blandishments but awakes in doubt and distress. And then he "dreams" again: this time Archimago permits him to "witness" a spectral Una dis-porting herself in lewd amours with a lusty (but equally spectral) young squire. And this time Redcrosse wakes in a "jealous" rage—"zealous" for her virtue, no doubt, but also simply "envious" of a missed sexual opportu-nity; and, above all, firmly convinced of Una's guilt. He goes his own faith-less way. For the moment, at least, the Devil has won. And how easily. He seems to have, on his side, some universal law of traumatic bad faith: we dream of guilt and anxiously repress; we dream again and find our dreams come true outside ourselves. What haunts our guilty sight of others, there-fore, is largely the specter of our own desire.[107]

A psychological romancer who had meditated on the application of some such law would not come to the matter of Salem Village in ideological innocence. He could scarcely be surprised, for example, to discover that a man once testified in court against the "specter" of the "village Circe" who kept appearing to his night-visions, tempting him to licentious sexuality.[108] Nothing new under the moon. Or, at very least, life imitating art. And though it would certainly be irresponsible to suggest that erotic dreams explain the entire historic problem of "the Devil in Massachusetts," it may yet be necessary to keep some generalized form of the Spenserian law pretty firmly in mind. Certainly Hawthorne thought so.

Amidst the evident intellectual and alleged moral disarray of 1691–92, guilt feelings seem to have been running higher than usual, even in a "Puritan" world: Cotton Mather was warning his religious audiences that every human being is—by nature, apart from grace—no better than the veriest witch or wizard; and there was widespread and anxious uncertainty about exactly whose guilt had blasted New England's fair hopes, including the expectation of the return of the Old Charter.[109] In such a world, a man who lacked "assurance" of his own spiritual destiny might well consider throwing in his lot with the Devil: perhaps a guilty identity really *was* better than none; if one were indeed "the Devil's child," why *not* "live from the Devil." The numbers are still being debated, of course, but (meanwhile) it is the part of Faith (and of a decent historical skepticism) to doubt that very many godly Puritans really did go over to the Enemy. And yet the thing was perfectly thinkable. Christ himself was that way tempted. What wonder if some lesser mortal actually fall? Not "me," of course, but "somebody." Most men *are* lost, are they not? And surely *somebody* must be responsible for the way our Errand has been going. It was a world ripe for projection, ripe for scapegoats.[110]

Of such a world the fictional Leonard Doane must always seem a more adequate figure than the biographical Cotton Mather. Not so satisfactory as Goodman Brown, to be sure, since that not-very-gothic personage is much more easily referable to the full social world of 1692, and since the presentation of his career is totally unembarrassed by an author's epistemological quarrel with his audience. But fair enough to be insisted upon: better to apply the lesson of Leonard Doane than dishonor the memory of Cotton Mather. For behind Hawthorne's fascination with the technicalities and the terror of 1692 lay an interest not in "whose guilt?" but in "what law?" Here, as elsewhere in his relentlessly historical fiction, his intention was not to blame persons but to understand our "common nature."[111]

It follows, accordingly, that the problem behind "Alice Doane" was not the romancer's question of "how to use witchcraft in some effective literary way," nor yet the allegorist's question of "what 'specters' might be used to symbolize." His deepest problem was, rather, essentially historical: "What Happened in Salem?" According to his own romantic mode of inquiry, however, this question immediately translated itself into the terms of philosophical psychology: what does "specter evidence" really mean? If "the evil eye" might forecast mesmerism, and if even the crassly literal belief in stomach-snakes were not without moral meaning, then surely there might also be an interpretative word to say about bodiless shapes portending evil.[112] Ideologues were violently at odds over the matter and, in the disputed territory between their premises, persons were being executed. Probably something serious was at issue. And just possibly something more subtle than superstitious frenzy and political opportunism. These too might constitute permanent conditions of social life; but they lay at several removes from the heart of human being, where the "spectral" temptation to bad faith lay buried.

Thus "Alice Doane" had re-told a rather famous episode from Spenser in order to throw psychological light on the morale of 1692. For whatever collection this early story may have been intended, it was already, in several significant senses, a "twice-told tale." Almost certainly Hawthorne meant his "source" and "debt" to be apparent: he was deliberately applying the clear moral intelligence of Spenser to the murky problem debated by Mather and Calef. And yet no one seemed to recognize: serious publishers demurred and demure females laughed out loud. Stung, as one may easily imagine, Hawthorne retaliated in kind: employing a narrative persona (who cannot quite be taken as a mere author-surrogate) he tries another story out of the same material. Really it is the same story in another form—apparently more true, but actually only more literal and, arguably, more reductive for that reason. Essentially it is Upham's version of the "history" of Salem Witchcraft. And though the unstable narrator will settle for the emotional victory of tears and a chance to moralize the national shame, the author himself is still playing his old game, still hoping somebody will recognize the strategic import of his crucial allusion to Calef and his wholesale borrowing from Spenser; and still holding out for this style of interpretation, as against an apparent concession to the literalism (and liberalism) of Upham. The author will *accept* a Day of Atonement, but he still *prefers* a moment of meditation. And he thinks of the latter as itself an historical act.

Like any other complicated event in the past, Salem Witchcraft had to be understood in all its temporal remoteness, tonal strangeness, and ideological difference. To be useful, however, such understanding also had to be applied. If the past did not introduce us to some essential condition of nature, it would be quite simply meaningless. Or so Hawthorne seems to have thought. For him, history did not cease to be history when made to touch the moral present. It only ceased to be irrelevant. We, for our part, might yet debate the precise point at which one leaves off from history *as history* and begins to engage some other activity or discipline; but Hawthorne is hardly the proper ground for that argument. Hawthorne knew, from

Mather among others, the ontology and the theology of specters; from Calef he learned all about their difficulties for legal epistemology. But he also knew, from Spenser at least, their most probable moral psychology. Without imagining that all these explanations were entirely opposed, he nevertheless apprehended that some sorts of explanations possessed ongoing applications which others noticeably lacked. And these he almost always chose to emphasize. One had to understand the technicalities to grasp any genuine meaning. But one was scarcely forbidden to interpret.

Just so with "specters." More enlightened than Cotton Mather's generation, the nineteenth century did not quite believe in the power of diabolical simulation; it worried about ghosts and speculated about other forms of "spiritualistic" survivability, but it no longer debated the Devil's ability to manipulate a person's separated shape. For this "step further . . . in the march of ages" one might well "thank God."[113] But one might beware of taking too much human pride in this sort of inevitable illumination; for habits of bad faith had not necessarily lapsed with the doctrine of the Devil's magical ability to induce it. As long as men were at all given to projecting their own guilty wishes, of "seeing" their own desires manifested in the behavior of others, one might do worse than to think on the mysteries concealed in the antique doctrine of specter evidence. Even in so gothic a metaphor as the morbid and murderous career of Leonard Doane.

7

By the time Hawthorne finally published "Alice Doane's Appeal" (in *The Token* for the new year of 1835), he had certainly come into full possession of his powers as a writer of significantly historical tales. "Provincial" masterpieces such as "Malvin" and "Molineux" were well behind him. The impulse to estimate the quality of Puritan piety had already flowered into "The Gentle Boy." And, most to the point, "Young Goodman Brown" was already on Hawthorne's own personal record; though not published until April 1835, amidst the general wreckage of "The Story Teller," this definitive treatment of specter evidence was almost certainly composed even as "Alice Doane" was being re-viewed and revised.[114] And so if we discover the Hawthorne of 1834 insisting on the historical validity of his early handling of this same material, we ought to respect his judgment so far as we can.

And yet, as must be evident to everyone, "Alice Doane's Appeal" is not nearly so good a tale as "Young Goodman Brown." For all that critical patience can do to answer the charge of incoherence or lack of control, it remains obvious that the admixture of argumentation is scarcely a beauty; historical critics may find it a godsend, but ordinary readers can hardly learn to love it. "Alice Doane's Appeal" may expose, or permit us to expose, more of the process, but "Young Goodman Brown" is clearly the better product. Furthermore—in ways that may be a bit less obvious, and which will have to be more fully explored at the appropriate point—"Young Goodman Brown" is also more fully historical. In spite of the best efforts of historical contextualism, "Alice Doane's Appeal" must be judged a less satisfactory answer to the question of "What Happened in Salem?" The far more "realistic" texture of Goodman Brown's forest-venture more clearly suggests that a certain sort of social reality might also be important to the specifics of Salem Witchcraft; and in fact the tale both presupposes and comments on an entire sociology of latter-day (third-generation) Puritanism in America. The gothic ambience of Leonard Doane's story contains no such suggestions; and apparently this early tale was intended to address only "deep" psychological questions.[115]

In the end, therefore, we may need to forgive Hawthorne's girlish audience just a little: considered as history, the original "Alice Doane" must have been a rather stiff dose; and it may not have been labeled clearly enough. Audiences do tend to take fictions "only as directed," and the gothic signals must surely have been more clear than the historical. Even in the chastened form, tonal and imagistic extravagances abound; and it is hardly obvious that they are supposed to satirize themselves, any more than the rattling chains and maniacal laughter of "The Hollow of the Three Hills."[116] Neither could it have been *absolutely* clear that witchcraft was supposed to signify very much more than in that other early gothic evocation: an image borrowed from Calef is harder to identify than the explicit mention of Goody Cloyse, Deacon Gookin, and Martha Carrier, the "rampant hag" who had received "the devil's promise to be the queen of hell," all in the context of fathers who lashed Quakers and set fire to Indian villages; and it has taken professional historians of literature a fairly long time to fix the precise Spenserian locus of Leonard Doane's moral aberrations. In the end we are likely to conclude that Hawthorne's exasperated and vengeful persona protests a little too much, that Hawthorne was himself admitting that the historical import of "Alice Doane" had been a little too far to seek.

And even in the strategic re-telling, things do not turn out all that splendidly. The narrative machinery works far less perfectly than it does in "Main Street," where a similar argument about metaphorical history and a related quarrel with the audience find a semi-dramatic form that is elegant by comparison. Almost instantly we know how to take the later showman-narrator—as some ironically self-effacing version of Hawthorne the "mere" chronicler, mocking the mechanical side of his art, even as he scores the aggressive reductionism of his hypothetical audience. Here, however, the precise strategy of the ironic narration is far more difficult to apprehend and may be, after all, just a little blurred. Granted that "Alice Doane" was supposed to be historical, and that a liberal attack on Cotton Mather is no substitute for a metaphor, still we may find ourselves wondering exactly how pleased or embarrassed Hawthorne himself really was by his early indulgences in passionate gothicism.

The best answer to that question comes not from "Alice Doane's Appeal" but from a consideration of the works that came "next"—that is to say, of the works that had come between the earlier and later versions of the Doane material. For if the Hawthorne of 1835 had not yet achieved the ironic self-distance necessary to satirize himself and his audience together, even as he attacked the governing premises of America's "Main Street," he had already produced (by 1829, at the latest) some of his most sophisticated achievements in his own unique mode of moral history. Gothicism had not been entirely left behind, but it certainly had been chastened and in a sense transcended. "Fantastic dreams and madmen's reveries" remain, and they continue to define some portion of the literary territory we regard as "Hawthornesque"; but it will require an ideological investment well beyond the meager means of the girls who once listened to "Alice Doane" to take these aberrations for the whole story. A firm sense of social setting and a surrounding texture of ordinary life plainly bespeak a respect for the pressure of reality at least as strong as for the power of the dream. Thus conceived, the texts speak for themselves: no teller harangues us from in or around the tales because no one needs to; they wear their historicity on their face.

To be sure, readers then may have had almost as much trouble as readers now have in grasping the extent of the motive to historical revisionism in "Malvin" or "Molineux," or in estimating the depth of Hawthorne's encounter with the theology of Puritanism in "The Gentle Boy"; and certainly the case for their status as major achievements in the area of cultural criticism still needs to be made. But distractions based on rampant or grotesque fantasy have been almost entirely eliminated; and critics are forced to look elsewhere to validate their methodological arrogance or to justify their historical bad faith. All the major stories intended for the "Provincial Tales" provide perfectly sufficient (and necessary) clues to their own historical interpretation. And even a minor masterpiece like "The Wives of the Dead" reveals a clear difference from, if not necessarily a traceable development beyond, the world of idea and technique elaborated in "The Hollow of the Three Hills" and "An Old Woman's Tale." Without quite embodying that difference, "Alice Doane's Appeal" at least announces it, or points to the fact that it has occurred.

If there is a significant development within the limited and bibliographically treacherous world of Hawthorne's earliest fiction, it is a very simple one indeed. The young Hawthorne seems to have begun with "the past" as a gothic or otherwise luridly tonal convention. He may then have experimented with it, only partly comically, as a protected precinct for psychological self-exploration and personal identity-trial. But because this indulgent young Romantic was also—*malgré lui*, as it may have oddly seemed to himself—a rather determined and careful antiquarian, he soon began to find himself in undisputed possession of a number of important historical facts, just as they lay before him in those original books we now awkwardly regard as "sources." And the growing power of this gradually developing fact seems to have made a considerable difference to his range of literary capacities, and finally to his intentions. He may well have begun to read dutifully: one should "use American material." Or compulsively: what else was there to do in a "dismal chamber"? Or in search of tones, or plots; or merely in search of *some* sort of stimulus or prod to his own imaginative workings. But the literary remains of "Alice Doane" reveal that somewhat more than all of this had somehow come to be at stake. And the narrator of "Alice Doane's Appeal" insists that we address ourselves to that "somewhat," if not to that "somehow."

The works that come after "Alice Doane's Appeal" make a rather different sort of insistence. Hawthorne seems well beyond the "flat" historicism of "Phips" and "Hutchinson," but the texture of the new tales confidently insists on its own irreducible minimum of faithfulness to social reality. Moreover, the strategic headnotes to the major "Provincial Tales" are as factual and careful as the craft of historiography can make them; they are also shot through with ironies, of course, but it requires an essentially historical perspective to perceive this fact. And the tales themselves are replete with allusions which cry out to be identified, repetitions which beg the reader to ask whose story is being re-told, and why. Nor, once this deconstruction has been performed, do the dramatic confrontations disappear; properly explicated, they linger on the mind as available and compelling figures for what, at some level of motive or experience, may really have happened. Most simply: it is as if the drastically metaphorical ontology of "Alice Doane," chastened of its gothic excess, had gone on to ally itself with the relentless historicism of "Bullivant," itself purified of a certain dutiful literalness. In biographical terms, the minor Romantic as antiquarian had become a major metaphorical artist working in the area of moral history. The result is a whole new literary "kind"—for Hawthorne, certainly, and quite possibly for literature as well.[117]

Except that "Alice Doane's Appeal" is clearly after the fact of this crucial ("Hawthornesque") development, it might well be regarded as a transitional work. Apparently "Alice Doane" had meant to move beyond the conventional domain of the fantastic and ghostly past and into the problematic territory in which the faith of New Englanders had actually been tested; but evidently it had not entirely succeeded. "Alice Doane's Appeal" tries to say why this should have been so. The original tale had worked with a powerful historical metaphor, self-consciously alluding to its own sources and to the class of instances that give it determinate meaning; and its revisions explicitly insist on the seriousness of those strategies. At the same time, however, the revisions concede that complicated literary procedures can easily be misapprehended: in certain literary contexts, a gothic stimulus may be well nigh irresistible; a literary appearance *can* get in the way of an historical reality. Perhaps a change of artistic strategy was indeed appropriate.

That change, when it occurred, would amount to much less than a radical concession to the literalism of the liberals, who wanted all historical guilt to be localized in past individuals. Hawthornesque moral history would remain true to its original, metaphorical method: it would continue to employ figures; and it would go on applying Spenser (or Milton, or Bunyan, or Jeremy Taylor) to experience everywhere. But it would begin to emphasize a complementary point as well: all moral experience is in a significant sense historical; the spiritual quality of every age is, accordingly, tried in the crucible of its own categories. In this sense the "Provincial Tales" would be indeed provincial. Unlike the gothic trappings of "Alice Doane," the new historical vehicle will insist on itself: the concrete embodiment will significantly determine the informing moral idea. Figures abound, but they inhabit real (political) space and actual (ideological) time. Even the "fantastic dreams" of Goodman Brown occur to a mind that went to sleep in a real world, the moral world of Puritanism's troubled third generation. His mad reveries will generalize no less than those of Leonard Doane; and Spenser will again assist in their generalization. But the whole story of Goodman Brown insists on the inevitability of its own location—and on the integrity of its own form—as that of Leonard Doane does not.

In the last analysis, therefore, "Alice Doane's Appeal" indirectly suggests the artistic distance Hawthorne has "yet" to travel as clearly as it calls our attention to the historic ground already occupied. Insisting that "Alice Doane" was not *quite* the indulgent gothicism it may have appeared, it nevertheless concedes that *some* step in the direction of actuality remains to be taken. The "Provincial Tales" take that step—from history moralized to "moral history." Without epistemological compromise, they manage to demonstrate that the flagrantly metaphorical method of "Alice Doane" is not at all inconsistent with intense factuality of "Bullivant." Each will modify and intensify the reality of the other. The result will significantly illuminate those major "matters" of colonial history: Indian Warfare, Revolution, and Puritanism. And when, eventually, the endlessly fascinating subject of witchcraft reappears, it will signify the historic witchcraft of colonial New England. Unavoidably. And with a vengeance that has become integral to its own literary conception.

❦ Two ❦
PROVINCIAL TALES
MORAL DILEMMA AS HISTORY

W E CANNOT BE CERTAIN exactly which of Hawthorne's early works
were intended for the "Provincial Tales." We know that Samuel
Goodrich, a would-be publisher of the collection Hawthorne was "projecting" in 1829–30, "made liberal use of the privilege" Hawthorne (eventually) granted him by inserting four of his tales into *The Token* for 1832:
"The Wives of the Dead," "My Kinsman, Major Molineux," "Roger Malvin's Burial," and "The Gentle Boy." Of these four, scholars have long
agreed that the latter three were almost certainly written for Hawthorne's
second projected collection. Beyond this datum of bibliographical certainty
and minimum of critical consensus, however, much remains in doubt. The
letters to and from Goodrich also mention "Alice Doane": assuming that it
really was an original member of the "Seven Tales," and that it really did
survive some non-fictional holocaust, perhaps it also presented itself, still
unrevised, for inclusion in yet another ill-starred collection. And it has
seemed equally plausible to imagine that some of the tales which did not see
print until after the wreck of "The Story Teller" (1834–35) had themselves
been originally conceived and written for the "Provincial Tales": perhaps
"The Gray Champion" or "Young Goodman Brown" or even "The May-
Pole of Merry Mount" is somehow to be thought of as "provincial." But we
cannot know with certainty. As with the "Seven Tales" before, all we really
have to go on is a somewhat suggestive title, a few stories associated with
that title more or less authoritatively, and our own suspicions and conjectures.[1]

Accordingly, our scholarly arguments about the probable contents and
the likely thematic interrelations of the "Provincial Tales" have tended to
be a bit circular: inventing a principle of unity based on a partial (and somewhat uncertain) list of tales, we go on to fill out that list according to that
principle; the part predicts the whole, even though the whole—if we really
had it—might reveal some other principle entirely. Perhaps it is, under the

99

circumstances, the best we can do. The idea of publishing a collection of tales was clearly important to Hawthorne; and probably we honor that intention (as well as gratifying our own natural passion for larger literary unities) by our efforts at reconstruction.[2]

But surely another approach is also possible. If we cannot quite support a perfect skepticism of mind, we can at least maintain a decent empiricism of method, just a little longer. If we admit that we cannot quite reconstruct the teleology of Hawthorne's early career, we may free ourselves to give a scrupulous account of the various stories we individually value. For we would, presumably, continue to judge "My Kinsman, Major Molineux" a masterful tale even if it bore no "historical" relation to "Roger Malvin's Burial" and shared no "psychoanalytic" theme with "Young Goodman Brown."[3] And thus, before closing our argument on just where Hawthorne's literary impulse was significantly headed, or on what finally makes early Hawthorne both self-identical and uniquely valuable, we might merely continue to investigate what comes "next," in something like the minimum order of survival and publication: "The Wives," "Malvin," "Molineux," and then (in a separate chapter) "The Gentle Boy." Only then, perhaps, will we be in a fair position to judge the relative significance and the mutual relation of psychological moralism and cultural history in Hawthorne's collective achievement.

1

"The Wives of the Dead" has provoked far less critical discussion than its companions in the 1832 *Token,* and the significance of this fact seems, at first glance, easy enough to grasp. Surely the tale is, on its surface, a good deal less challenging than the richly allusive masterpieces in whose company it first appeared; as such, it can doubtless be spared the laborious process of scholarly rediscovery and revaluation which "Malvin" and "Molineux" have had to undergo.[4] One almost feels that it should be set to one side, in a special category of its own—the minor masterpiece: brief, evocative, haunting, ambiguous, inexplicable. And yet the very specialness of its status makes it a crucial piece of evidence in any argument about the range of Hawthorne's literary intentions.

Manifestly simpler, "The Wives" seems also (somehow) "earlier" than the other tales Goodrich inserted in his "Christmas and New Year's Present" for the season of 1831–32. Without more positive evidence to go on, one stops short of concluding that it was left over from, or revised out of, materials intended for the "Seven Tales"; but the possibility is not unthinkable. Hawthorne's sister remembered that the early collection was all about "witchcraft and the sea." Perhaps "The Wives" belonged to that latter interest: involving (in part) a sailor lost at sea, and set "in a principal seaport of the Bay Province" (192), it surely evokes "the sea" as efficiently as "An Old Woman's Tale" evokes "witchcraft."[5] It seems just possible, therefore, that "The Wives of the Dead" takes us back to the very earliest conditions of Hawthorne's "Use of the Past" and does not at all introduce us to the quality of his later, more learned imagination.

But neither simplicity *nor* earliness is quite the distinguishing mark of "The Wives," considered among the Hawthornean contents of *The Token* for 1832. Nor, as it turns out, are these quite the reasons why criticism has tended both to neglect the tale on its own merits and to exclude it from the probable contents of the "Provincial Tales." That reason clearly has something to do with the basically ahistorical character of its literary epistemology: though "the simple and domestic incidents" which inspired the tale are said to have occurred "a hundred years ago," neither methodical scholarship nor intuitive intelligence has been able to make much of this fact. "Domesticity" has, of course, a history like everything else. But its implications are more often synchronic and generic rather than diachronic and temporal. And certainly this is the case in "The Wives," where the homely incidents dramatized are meant to evoke images of the way "the mind" works rather than the ways Americans have thought about the unique conditions of their own experience.[6] Whatever their final literary intention, "Malvin," "Molineux," and "The Gentle Boy" are all unthinkable without a considerable specific density of allusion to certain precise events and to the general tenor of moral life in America. "The Wives of the Dead," by contrast, makes its way almost entirely on conditions of its own devising; and it applies to a world, if not "elsewhere," then surely almost "anywhere."

Critical perception of this fact has meant, first of all, that the tale has not presented itself as an object for the standard "source study": nobody has bothered to determine whether the events behind Hawthorne's narrative "had indeed awakened some degree of interest" in the Salem (or Boston) papers of 1730. And, far more significantly, nobody has thought to argue that the informing idea or the significant achievement of the "Provincial Tales" can be defined by isolating the precise element which is identically shared by "The Wives" and the other tales which appeared at the same time, in the same place. This means, of course, that some elementary form of historicist perception has already operated, however problematically. All sorts of critics who do not believe that "The Gentle Boy" is *ultimately* about Puritans and Quakers in New England have no trouble discerning that "The Wives" is *even less* concerned with the problems of warfaring and seafaring (or with domestic arrangements) in provincial Massachusetts.[7]

Nor is it the latter half of this judgment one would wish to challenge. The point is merely to make one's historicism perfectly self-conscious, and to be as explicit as possible about what actually is at issue in "The Wives of the Dead." Only thus can one measure the precise extent of its generic *difference* from its more famous companions.

What "The Wives of the Dead" insists on, from first to last, is some complex and paradoxical sense of identity and differentiation in the lives and fates of the two young women who believe they have lost their young husbands. At first glance, accordingly, Hawthorne's interest seems "psychological" in a fairly simple sense: the objective situations of Mary and Margaret are very nearly identical, and yet their personal responses to this common "structure" of experience are markedly individual. Married to brothers, they seem "sisters" in more than "law." They live together in "one household," they share a common "hearth," and (we presume) they have learned to rely on one another in the absence of husbands whose occupations are not at all domestic. And when we first encounter them, they have both experienced, but newly, a most untimely stroke of the common doom: both their husbands have been lost, separately, but on a single day. Surely this double tragedy will only strengthen the tie that binds their separate lives together. And so at first it seems, as the two stand together, both sensibly accepting the best and the worst of that "universal sympathy" offered by their "numerous condoling guests," each deeply yearning "to be left alone" (192)[8] for that special sort of solace which each can uniquely offer the other. But after a single brief "indulgence" of joined hearts and silent weeping together, the bonds of their union—profound in life, and made sacred in death—begin to fray and pull apart. The two "sisters" are really very different "persons," and what follows seems to argue that all is fracture and isolation.

Recollecting "the precepts of resignation and endurance which piety had taught her," Mary turns to the practical aspects of their common life and begs her "dearest sister" to keep up her strength by taking a "frugal meal" and (equally) by asking heaven's "blessing on that which has been provided." But her "sister-in-law" (as the narrative now insists on calling her) is of a different mind altogether: "of a lively and irritable temperament," Margaret shrinks from Mary's words as if they had been meant to wound. Moreover, she counters her pious theology with "rebellious expressions" which frighten even herself. The Lord giveth and the Lord taketh away, to be sure, but need He try a woman beyond her strength? "Would it were His will that I might never taste food more" (193). The violence of this certainly anticipates the painful "protest" of Quaker Catherine, if it does not quite predict the more famous "quarrel" of Herman Melville; but the orthodoxy of suffering and evil is clearly not the main point.[9] Rather, the clashing of responses effectively defines the reality of the tale as less a matter of event than of reaction. Evidently an identical world—including an identically cruel act of God or chance—makes greatly different impressions on different characters or temperaments. *Tot feminae, tot sententiae.*

In the very next moment, the narrative provides us with a telling image of the spiritual meaning of the tale so far.[10] After Mary eventually succeeds in "bringing her sister's mind nearer to the situation of her own," the two women retire from the common hearth, each to her respective sleeping room. For we are not to suppose that their domestic union was ever quite complete: "The brothers and their brides, entering the married state with no more than the slender means that then sanctioned such a step, had confederated themselves in one household, with equal rights to the parlor, and claiming exclusive privileges in two sleeping-rooms contiguous to it" (193). The image is so revealing that we are tempted to find it "definitive": some things can be shared and others not; conjugal union may or may not amount to a form or a sign of human incorporation, but everything else is surely a form of "federation" merely. We think ahead to the painful "subjectiveness" expressed in Emerson's "Experience": "souls never touch their objects"; and "spiritual" marriage is impossible because not even the sincerest form of loving sympathy can "make consciousness and aspiration equal in force." And, more cogently perhaps, we think back to a peculiar sentence at the beginning of the tale: "Two young and comely women sat together by the fireside, nursing their mutual and peculiar sorrows" (192). There it *all* is, we now assume: "mutual and peculiar" is offered as a central and powerful oxymoron rather than as some lax and additive effect in the diction of description. It means not "strangely shared together by these two alone," but "shared in common and yet (at the same time) absolutely particular to each, according to her very own mode of psychic reception."

Already the meaning is a little more philosophical than (in the ordinary sense) psychological. But the story does not end here. Nor, as it moves along, does it merely specify its opening paradox or intensify its apparently definitive oxymoron. For one thing, there is narrative rather than image or schema merely. And for another, it eventually discovers a new principle of identity which is altogether unlooked-for at the beginning, and which threatens to take us beyond the world of romantic "sorrow" altogether. If we are following this line of developing meaning, we will probably be spared the troublesome (unresolvable) suspicion that everything which follows is only a dream, or a dream within a dream.[11]

Both women, we are told, do eventually fall asleep: Mary first, experiencing "the effect often consequent upon grief quietly borne"; Margaret much later, and only after becoming "more disturbed and feverish"

(194). And both women are given, eventually, each in her own proper moment of wakefulness, but with the same lantern in hand, the same identical news by one or another "honest man": the lost bridegroom is alive and well, and will be returning after all. Of course we should not be surprised if, somewhere, the troubled souls of numberless bereft sisters were actually only dreaming of such miraculous preservations; and no doubt this fact would indeed figure the terrible fulfillment of all sorts of vain (Melvillean) salvation wishes. Furthermore, the personal differences of *some* Margaret and Mary might easily recall the more significant spiritual differentiation of the Biblical *Martha* and Mary, who pay such different attentions to the earthly advent of their Heavenly Bridegroom; and according to the cruel irony of some other law of predestination, *both* would fail of redemption. Or, invoking a related Biblical "place," we can easily imagine numberless Wise and Foolish Virgins *all* taking up their well-trimmed lanterns, receiving their midnight revelations, and all being entirely self-deceived about the objective reality of that longed-for second coming.[12] It would not make a bad story. But "The Wives of the Dead" does not appear to be that story: there are too many "realistic" clues to the contrary; and the hypothesis ultimately creates more "narrative" problems than it solves. Above all, perhaps, such a reading interferes with another meaning far more congruent with the story's initial issue and imagery.

The real story here continues to involve the utter inability of two legal, situational, and "structural" sisters to share anything, even though their deepest and most sympathetic feelings turn out to be as identical as their fates. For their individual discoveries of "joy" turn out to be as painfully isolating as their "mutual and peculiar sorrows." Pressing its own logic of sameness and difference, the story's doubly paradoxical conclusion suggests that the only thing which separates the two sisters is, in the end, their very "identity."

Well prepared as to the temperamental differences between Mary and Margaret, we are yet not at all surprised to discover that they both receive their good news in pretty much the same joyful-troublesome way. Both are, at first, simply overjoyed at the stroke of blessed fortune. Each considers waking the other, to share—or at least to express—her spontaneous overflow of powerful emotion. But both hold back. Each in her own proper and inevitable turn very keenly imagines the subtle effect her own joy will have on the affections of the other. The contrast will be too great: the expression will seem mean-spirited or, at very least, inconsiderately selfish. How can the joyful rejoice in the face of sorrow? How can the sorrowful ever unite with the rejoicing? Or how, at any rate, can the joyful ones expect that they should? And what, in the last painful analysis, can the triumphant, from their blessed point of view, ever say to the afflicted or the despairing? There is a distinct theological overtone here (if not actually an anti-Calvinist allegory), but it is founded on an acute observation of human difference; and it fulfills (even as it annuls) the original psychological terms of the story. We need to look at it closely.

Approaching Mary's early and apparently contented sleep, Margaret shrinks "from disturbing her sister-in-law" with the news of her own good news; she feels, somehow inevitably, "as if her own better fortune had rendered her involuntarily unfaithful, and as if altered and diminished affection must be the consequence of the disclosure she had to make." She turns away, to sleep, and to her own "delightful thoughts," which sleep will transform to "visions" (196). With Mary, the case is essentially the same, despite her more sensitive and delicate character, and despite her more explicit Christianity. Remembering, perhaps, the way Margaret had "shrunk" from her earlier expressions of solicitude, she stifles her initial "impulse to rouse her sister-in-law, and communicate the new-born gladness." Her motives, we may be sure, are humanly unimpeachable, and yet she too "remembers": "Margaret would awake to thoughts of death and woe, rendered not the less bitter by their contrast with her own felicity" (198). She well knows, we have no doubt, that pious Christians are everywhere bidden to be of one mind, to share everything, to mourn with those who mourn and to rejoice with those who rejoice. But she demurs. How can human love join together what cosmic fate has put asunder?

At that very moment, however, she inadvertently wakes her beloved "sister-in-law" (as we now conclude her bosom friend and fellow mortal can *only* be) with the tears of her own balked and ineffectual sympathy. And the story ends—abruptly, blankly—where it must. What may at first seem like some immature lapse from artistic duty and moral courage, reminiscent of the ending of "An Old Woman's Tale," or what in the second thought of a desperate (grammatical) hypothesis may present itself as some magical resolution of human ambivalence into the all-involving ambiguity (and cliché) of a dream, appears at last as the only possible form of suspended conclusion, a triumph of strategic omission.[13] Of course the "story" goes on, painfully, but the "tale" wisely stops short of its own needless and grotesque elongation. For how could any brief fiction ever hope to give an account of what must now follow, in all of its slow and uncertain inevitability? What narrative—short of the perfect and instantaneous revelation of the Last Judgment—could ever be adequate to the scene which will necessarily follow? We must imagine it for ourselves. The logic being forced, the details assemble themselves.

How will Mary and Margaret *ever* manage to reveal to one another the blessed identity they secretly share in common? Who will speak first? In what tones of prevention and concern? With what self-protective strategies of delay, indirection, evasion? Common sense might solve the matter at a stroke, effectively foreclosing the possibility of all that false delicacy and needless heroism which generate the matter of popular romance. But where is the stern realist who will blame Mary and Margaret if their approaches to confession should be careful and tentative?[14] "You mean . . . you too? I thought that only I . . . I mean I thought that you would think that I . . . Oh, how *could* I simply declare without seeming to wound?" There is, of course, a clear "reason" in the matter: facts are facts, and no one is really responsible for his own blessed fortune. But in a world where so many appear to be lost, how can the solitary saint avoid feeling something somehow like guilt?

In the "end," therefore, "The Wives of the Dead" clearly suggests (though it stops just short of dramatizing) some essential fact about the inherently precarious and unavoidably risky nature of all significant revelations about the self, and about the desperately straitened possibilities of human communion that are the inevitable result. Its basic perception is psychological, but its ultimate attempt is to raise its "given" of insight to the status of a general law rather than to adumbrate itself in the manifold creation of fictional "varieties." Theological overtones are audible everywhere, most especially in the language of "woe," "felicity," and a gladness "newborn"; with them comes the clear possibility of historical application—to that problematic half-world of provincial New England, where the unlovely facts of life, not entirely uncovered by some "stark" Calvinist proposition, were just giving way to the softening influences of religious civility and literary sentiment. But the narrative only hints at this dimension of meaning. Romantic epistemology outweighs Calvinist doctrine; and, as in the case of "The Hollow of the Three Hills," Puritan history remains an aura of possibility rather than an elaborated network of controlled allusion. That is to say, "The Wives of the Dead," whenever it was written, remains in some clear sense "minimum Hawthorne."

Clearly the tale is, as I have suggested, much better than we usually allow. Arguably, it is as precise and well formed a short piece as Hawthorne ever wrote. And, as we shall see, the psychology peculiar to all of Hawthorne's early tales is always more or less as we see it here, precise and "regulative" rather than expansive and "empirical." It will be twenty years before Hawthorne risks experiment with any of the "extended prose forms," and even his major romances might be thought "fine" (in James's sense) because they deal in a psychology "deeper" than the one required for novelistic verisimilitude.[15] Meanwhile, at the beginning of Hawthorne's development, "The Wives of the Dead" remains a "minor masterpiece." Its "minority" is clearly marked by the divergence between the moral psychology of its conception and the possible historicity of its application—or, at very least, by its failure systematically to insist on the facticity of its own datum.

"Malvin" and "Molineux" are, in this regard, rather different. They differ not so much in psychological style or subtlety as in situation and setting. And in literary epistemology. Like all the famous "historical" tales to follow, they wear their determined historicity on their own ingenuous face. They insist on it, advertise it; as if to forestall modern "psychoanalytic formalism," they even flaunt it.[16] These tales do not, of course, exist univocally to explain the nature of Indian Warfare or the cause of the American Revolution, but they do insist that certain contingent conditions of those events are necessary to their own valid interpretation. We *can* read "The Wives of the Dead" without reliance on the Calvinistic doctrine of predestinating decree, even though the tale may be read as a gloss on the solipsistic problems of solitary sainthood. We *cannot* read "Roger Malvin's Burial" without specific reference to "Lovewell's Fight"; or "My Kinsman, Major Molineux" without a keen awareness of what happened "after the kings of England had assumed the right of appointing the colonial governors," as we are instructed in this by "the annals of Massachusetts Bay." "Malvin" and "Molineux" thus insist on some necessary "pre-text" in a way "The Wives" does not. And that is the difference which, in Hawthorne's early tales, makes all the difference.

2

To say that "Roger Malvin's Burial" flaunts its own historicity is not at all to suggest that the tale openly "discusses" some problem well known to historical scholarship; or that it dutifully provides all of the historical information necessary to its own interpretation; or that it reveals its nuances of historical meaning without irony or indirection. Indeed, the very reverse is the case, as the critical history of the tale obviously suggests. Clearly there is *some* problem: unless the modern reader is a "colonialist," or unless he has consulted a certain body of "source" articles first, he will probably never have heard of "Lovewell's Fight" before he encounters the words in the first (introductory) paragraph of Hawthorne's tale; and without some extra-textual information—to illuminate the words of the text itself—he will cer-

tainly miss the nice criss-cross of irony in that otherwise rambling and pro-
saic introduction. And thus he may miss an important clue about how to
begin.[17]

He may accept as authoritative, on ordinary literary faith, the report that
"history and tradition [have been] unusually minute in their memorials of
[the Lovewell] affair"; but he will hardly see the ironic point of calling this
minor touchstone of nineteenth-century memorial history "well-remembered" (337)[18] unless he is aware that the Lovewell episode also represents a
high point in American literary "lying for the right." If any further, less
isolated meanings come to depend on this preliminary notification, the unprepared reader will certainly miss them as well; if these meanings turn out
to be crucial in the story's overall rhetorical design, our unprepared reader
may end up reading (that is to say "writing") a "text" pretty much of his
own devising. That possibility will probably excite some critics more than
others, but surely its theoretical basis must always seem precarious: it really
is necessary to know the meaning of *all* the words; and some words—like
"Lovewell's Fight"—have *no* significance apart from some singular historical particular. The story's famous "images" of graven rock and blasted oak
may or may not be entirely "natural symbols," but its opening "allusion" is
surely as little innocent as *The Scarlet Letter*'s inceptive reference to Ann
Hutchinson. We may or may not possess a general theory of "Beginnings,"
but ignorance is *always* a bad place to start.

What the "modern" (but otherwise unprepared) reader is least likely to
miss is the painful complexity of the moral conflict in which Reuben Bourne
involves himself at the outset of the dramatic action proper.[19] His decision
to leave his wounded companion seems, in itself, entirely justifiable, even if
the companion is dying, and even if he is a sort of "father." And yet this
decision somehow involves him in a web of deception and doubleness, and
then a compulsive self-destruction from which he seems morally unable to
break free. The "morality" of the tale seems somehow to get out of hand,
leaving the reader as baffled as Reuben himself about the exact place where
something went wrong. Desperate, and yet not without resources unavailable to Reuben, he may well repair to psychoanalysis for critical aid and
comfort. And at first the step seems well taken: once the thought has occurred, nothing is easier to verify than the virtually psychoanalytic complexity of Reuben's "case"; for it depends on Hawthorne's own insistent
analysis rather than on uncensored revelations which must be teased out of
the text.[20] Historical problems will surely develop, but perhaps it is fair to
begin here—with the "facts" of Reuben's own "story." Perhaps it is even
proper, at the outset, to "bracket" the question of history, even though
Hawthorne's own first paragraph obscurely flaunts it. Once we know, with
precision, what actually "happens" to Reuben Bourne, we ought to be in a

better position to speculate about the quality and effect of his historical figuration.

Reuben's behavior in the not-quite-primal scene of his parting from the fatherly Roger Malvin is a veritable casebook of rationalizations, disguised motives, and wish fulfillments. Whether or not his eventual killing of his son functions as some obscure but terribly purposeful form of sacrificial self-punishment, his decline in business and general prosperity is precisely self-thwarting; and his magical return to the exact spot where he left Malvin is explicitly compulsive. But while no one can or should wish to refute the powerful "logic of compulsion" in "Roger Malvin's Burial," it blurs several important issues to suggest that all moral and religious issues are reduced to psychological ones. No such thing happened in "The Wives of the Dead," despite the discovery of some powerful law of separation and identity underlying a superficial moral delicacy; nor will it quite occur in that most famous "case" of Goodman Brown. And "Roger Malvin's Burial" turns out to be, in its own right, an elaborate "case of conscience" in the precise and classic sense of Jeremy Taylor, if not of William Ames or Cotton Mather. Indeed "Malvin" is probably the earliest of the extant tales (certainly it is the most significant) to depend on the subtle moral analyses of that Anglican "casuist" whose writings Hawthorne repeatedly borrowed between 1826 and 1834. There may be no provable allusions. And probably the casuistical experiment breaks down in failure—there being, apparently, no (medieval) way to doubt Reuben Bourne out of his (modern) doubts. Nevertheless, "Roger Malvin's Burial" tests the method of Taylor far more cogently than it anticipates the system of Freud.[21]

Considered most simply, then—not quite "in itself" and yet entirely apart from the tangled question of New England's early "local" or later "memorial" history—"Roger Malvin's Burial" dramatizes a particularly difficult or ambiguous problem in practical morality. Its casuistical assumption is that general rules cover only the more obvious (philosophical) half of the moral life, and that all the really difficult problems arise in the (psychological) area of specific application. Its interest, accordingly, is not in the abstract or normative possibility but in the concrete and (in a sense) "peculiar" case, as every actual moral decision turns out to be relatively "situational" if not positively *sui generis.* It asks about subjective choices rather than objective propositions, motives rather than actions. Accordingly, Hawthorne tightens all the screws, balances all the scales, creates as much ambiguity as the rational mind can bear, and still demands that his exemplary character make some meaningful moral decision in minimum good faith. Further, like any serious, humanistic and non-satiric writer, he requires a certain "charitable" judgment from the reader, even if the character appears to have made the wrong choice. As in all casuistry, the point is precisely that the regulative idea of obligation and the empirical particulars of motive psychology always come together in the crisis of choice, which constitutes, for anyone who believes in any sort of freedom, the essence of the moral life. Neither consideration obliterates the other.

This much should be obvious. What makes Reuben's case particularly difficult (and in a sense "modern") is the apparent absence of *any* general rule to apply, well or ill, to his precise situation. His life is threatened, and his decision is thus, in the philosophical sense, "forced"; but for once the matter seems almost *entirely* one of motive or intention. He must decide; and he knows that, either way, his decision is fraught with most serious and painful consequences; but there appears to be no single, compelling "reason" to which he can, before the fact, appeal. He must discover his own moral reason, create his own standard of value, project his own idea of moral adequacy in terms of nothing other than his sense of the kind of moral person he wants to be(come). It is all, somehow, not quite a matter of right and wrong in the traditional sense. For him, at least, to apply a moral principle is also to invent it.[22]

To leave Malvin and so to save himself is clearly a justifiable alternative: throughout all his later doubts and self-tortures, Reuben never once questions his judgment that "for leaving Malvin he deserved no censure" (349). But to say that Reuben *may* desert Malvin is not to say that he *must* do so, for he may also stay (and die) with him. Indeed this permissible course of action threatens to seem like the part of heroic virtue: surely a man may always decide to lay down his life for his friend—not to save his mortal life, perhaps, but to comfort and assure his lonely death amidst the terrors of a howling wilderness. So strongly does Reuben feel the attraction of this heroic possibility that his first response is clearly to prefer it as an ideal, as opposed to a merely ordinary (though justifiable) alternative. "I will remain and watch by you," he boldly declares; "I will receive your parting words. I will dig a grave here by the rock, in which, if my weakness overcome me, we will rest together" (340). Of course there is a certain amount of bravado in this, but clearly Reuben wishes he could make these motives prevail; or that, even more blessedly, they were his only motives. Self-sacrifice attracts him. He would like to be a hero, in his own eyes and in the eyes of others as well.

Unfortunately, however, Reuben feels "many another motive" just as strongly. Doubtless he knows that a self-sacrificial decision to remain with Malvin would be, like many other acts of heroic virtue, subject to a number of legitimate and telling criticisms: self-preservation, the greatest good of the greatest number, the practical "uselessness" of the action. Hawthorne raises self-interest to a theological level by suggesting that Reuben's moral scruples might hold out against the bitterness of death and the wilderness of despair even less well than Malvin's rugged but superstitious courage. But there are also, of course, all the ordinary "selfish" motives as well: as Reuben's young life passes in summary view before his eyes, he finds he very much wants to get back to civilization and to enjoy life—and Dorcas. And it is at this point that his motives get tangled, or confused, or "mixed" in a way the traditional casuist would find very dangerous.

What will Dorcas think of him? Will not his "desertion" of her father, however justifiable by any moral principle one might wish to make normative, look to her like simple cowardice? Can he face her with a personal narrative which smacks of self-interest in any way? "She will ask the fate of her father, whose life I vowed to defend with my own. Must I tell her that . . . I left him to perish in the wilderness? Were it not better to lie down and die . . . than to return safe and say this to Dorcas?" (341). Better? Not ultimately, perhaps, for we can scarcely imagine that Dorcas would rationally wish them *both* dead instead of just one; but we easily see what Reuben means nevertheless.

There will be no way, he correctly sees, to make her understand *exactly* how things were. Malvin's rude moral sense only half grasps the problem, even though he is himself at the scene; what moral experience can possibly have prepared Dorcas? In the end, one's private understanding of circumstances, and of the "casuistical" quality of the choices they offer, can never be perfectly understood from the outside; and Reuben is clearly afraid to face her "objective" judgment of his unheroic decision. Malvin—who really does wish Reuben well, but who pities his scrupulous weakness and has thus been "helping" him reason aloud—assures him that everything will all be right in time, that Dorcas will eventually come around and agree to marry him after a period of "mourning." But the old Indian-fighter's pragmatic logic is quite beside the nicety of Reuben's moral qualm. Reuben knows there will be that moment, however brief, when, before he can *at all* explain the situation and his motives in detail, Dorcas' eyes will convict him of cowardice. From such a judgment he plainly recoils: "better to lie down and die."

At this impasse, while Reuben is tending toward an heroic action based on an un-self-reliant motive, Malvin ruefully tips the scales in the other direction with his irrelevant story about a rescue made in a "similar" situation. His "mournful smile" and his "sighing" (342) signal his tough-minded recognition that Reuben's tender character is incapable of the sort of courage needed to save himself and live with the judgmental consequences of that action. Again "helping" Reuben to settle his conscience, but again acting, unwittingly, the part of the tempter, Malvin offers him a construction of the case and a set of motives which will allow him to satisfy his deep (and obviously legitimate) wish for self-preservation and yet enable him to preserve his equally deep (but certainly problematical) wish to think of himself as heroic. The suggestion is clearly made in a spirit of benevolence. And we have no trouble understanding why Reuben should seize it. But the rigorous moralist immediately notices that things now go desperately wrong.[23]

In a situation where almost *any* action honestly taken, *any* deed truly done, *any* choice honestly made will be morally justifiable, Reuben makes virtually the only moral mistake available: refusing to be completely honest about his own motives (to "settle his intention," as the casuist would say), he lets the issue be decided for him in terms of a specious rationalization offered him by another person. Of course Malvin's suggestion—that he save himself and then come back to save his "father" as well, that he have life and heroism too—is really his own deepest wish. But Reuben can scarcely admit this contradictory desire to have it both ways as his own conflicted motive. And the fact that the explicit proposal comes from outside himself only points to the spurious "objectivity" of its moral status.

Accordingly, Reuben has the worst of both worlds. On the verge of heroism by moral default, he is diverted into a path of self-interest with a false touch of heroism about it. Malvin thinks he is saving Reuben by offering his generous but weak nature the moral solution it is searching for, but he innocently offers Reuben only the opportunity to imitate his Biblical counterpart, in abusing his conscience and temporizing with truth. And we already sense not only Reuben's "instability" but also his desperate moral dis-ease when we see him scrambling around the scene of Malvin's "burial," collecting "a useless supply" of "roots and herbs," only "half convinced that he was acting rightly" (343).[24] By the time he actually takes leave of Malvin, he has become "internally convinced that he should see Malvin's living face no more" (345). Thus the "wild and painful curiosity" which then impells him to creep back and take one last look can hardly strike us as other than a deep moral symptom. And we are not surprised to learn that "conscience, or something in its similitude," is still strongly pleading with him "to return and lie down again by the rock." We may decline the rhetorically proffered opportunity to "impute blame" to Reuben for "shrink[ing] from so useless a sacrifice" (346). But we can hardly take Reuben's temporizing rationalizations as anything but a dangerous "similitude" of conscience.[25] And we predict no untroubled future.

In fact, we now have no trouble establishing a perfectly unbroken law of moral connection beween this initial scene and the subsequent one, in which Reuben first confronts Dorcas. For according to this "casuistical" analysis, there are not two simple moral events in the story—the decision to leave Malvin *and* the virtual lie to Dorcas about that action. There is only a single complex moral history—the constant refusal to admit one's motives, "settle one's intention," and face the moral consequences courageously. The same psychology which operates in the forest continues to operate in the chamber where Dorcas watches Reuben regain consciousness (but not conscience). Actually, we now realize, the first episode has been merely proleptic or prefigurative, for once again Reuben is afraid to admit that he chose the "unheroic" way.[26] He gets himself hopelessly trapped into deceiving Dorcas about what really happened because his first speech, in defense of a decision he has never honestly faced and estimated, begins to be as extended and circuitous as Dimmesdale's balcony address to Hester. His dazed effort to explain and qualify, to anticipate and prevent, is doomed to failure because Dorcas is understandably impatient and immediately draws her own conclusions. The circumstances and motives so crucial to Reuben's own uneasy casuistry are quite secondary to her: she is interested in the fate of her father and hence in simple facts and overt actions. She suspects that her father is dead, but it has never occurred to her tender mind to suppose that Reuben has left him to die alone in the howling wilderness. Reuben realizes all this only too well; and adding the artifice of a mental reservation to his initial deceptive evasiveness, he willfully allows Dorcas to believe that he gave her father the rites of civilized burial he so earnestly desired.[27]

Of course it is a terrible moment. And it requires a pretty stern moral principle to begin convicting Reuben now as, still only half alive, he wakes up to the inquisitorial objectivity of Dorcas' "filial anxiety" (347). But the reader who has noticed how Reuben got himself started down the road of ambivalence and indecision takes his own gloomy instruction from the turn things have taken. Reuben Bourne is to be pitied; but purity of heart is to will one thing. We know where we are.

Nor, given this much in the history of Reuben's doubleness, do we find that his failure to return to the original site and bury Malvin requires separate moral consideration. It adds, as a moral theologian might say, "nothing essential" to the original case of unsettled intention. In one very severe sense Reuben's vow merely expresses his radical self-division: of a piece with his ritualistic collection of roots and herbs, its chief function is to make his initial decision to desert seem more tolerable to himself. But even if we take it at face value, its meaning still tends to collapse back into the significance of the original motive-situation. Clearly Reuben lives with the feeling that he has bound himself to return, and in as serious a manner as he knows—by a vow on his own blood. And, just as clearly, it is the failure to keep this explicit and sacred promise which spoils all his joy in life and drives him to compulsively self-destructive behavior. But all this gothic guiltiness is, from a moral point of view, secondary, harking back to his original failure to admit to himself his own deep preference for the less heroic of two justifiable moral alternatives. Obviously, Reuben cannot go back because he has denied (to Dorcas and others) that there is any reason to do so; and he has denied this because he cannot face the charge of ordinariness. Thus, as much as we may sympathize with Reuben Bourne, we are forced to recognize that before his actions became "compulsive" (which is to say, "psychotic"), they all proceeded from a set of dangerous rationalizations which bordered on the "voluntary" (which is to say, the "human" or "moral").

Some analysts may be satisfied to characterize all of Reuben's behavior as "semi-deliberate."[28] But such a verdict would scarcely satisfy the moral rigor of a casuist like Jeremy Taylor. In his sober view, men need to be reminded that (in the words of Seneca) "the same things are honest and dishonest; the manner of doing them, and the end of the design, makes the separation." In theory, at least, Hawthorne seems to have agreed. In his "classically Christian" system, guilt is always incurred at the level of motive or intention. And the case of Reuben Bourne seems to dramatize the relevance of the first of Taylor's basic "Rules for Our Intentions": "In every action reflect upon the end; and in your undertaking it, consider why you do it, and what you propound to yourself for a reward, and to your action as its end."[29] Clearly Reuben might have learned from that maxim. Or, if that verdict is too rationalistic and harsh, surely *we* may yet learn from his failure to take instruction. If Reuben cannot redeem his vow, the cause has ultimately to do with his original confusion of intention. And if his "concealment" eventually imparts "to a justifiable act much of the secret effect of guilt" (349), the reason is that his primary and essential concealment is of his own motives from himself. Since intention stands to action as "the soul to the body . . . or the root to the tree," then no wonder if it turns out that Reuben's moral "body is a dead trunk."[30]

All this, then, counts for something in the overall interpretation of "Roger Malvin's Burial"—and in the more general attempt to classify and account for the various elements that combine in the subtle mixture we recognize as "Hawthornesque." If it is arrant "psychologism" to imply that the moral drama in the tale reduces to the psychoanalytic, it is nevertheless perfectly true to say that Hawthorne's psychological analysis of the case of Reuben Bourne is as sophisticated as anything he ever accomplished in his short fiction. Only with Dimmesdale, perhaps, and then only in places, is Hawthorne as relentless in exposing the subtle shifts and wily subterfuges which moral theology must regard as a dangerous "similitude" of effective moral reason. And with Dimmesdale, the drama is almost entirely a matter of what theologians call "consequent conscience": *The Scarlet Letter* is, after all, Hawthorne's classic study of what critics call "the *effects* of sin." "Roger Malvin's Burial," by contrast, is very largely concerned with the central fact of the guilt-inducing choice itself, and with what most moralists (with the towering exception of Jonathan Edwards) would consider relevant moral conditions before the fact.[31]

And yet we should hesitate to propose that "Roger Malvin's Burial" offers itself as a perfect epitome of Hawthorne's achieved method. Certainly we must hold back on the strength of the evidence so far presented. To be sure, its psychological advance over "The Wives of the Dead" is perfectly apparent—despite certain characteristic similarities, and whatever the chronology. The feckless delicacy of Reuben's original moral feelings seems recognizable as a terribly advanced instance of that useless tenderness which prevents Margaret and Mary from facing their own less desperate situation head-on. And, though Reuben's case is given with much greater and more analytic precision, Hawthorne is still more interested in regulative ideas than in empirical details. The chastened and brutal brevity of the tale effectively prevents all possibility of sentimental (or even "novelistic") sympathy with the particularities of Reuben's "personality." However unique or casuistical may be the precise nature of his crucial choice, he remains a figure or a moral exemplum rather than a "character." The same will be true of Robin Molineux, Goodman Brown, and Parson Hooper. And even more so, as if Hawthorne had turned "back" from the elaborate casuistry of "Roger Malvin's Burial." So far, at least, it is safe to say only that "Malvin" seems the most thoroughly psychological tale Hawthorne ever developed out of his readings in the provincial history of New England.[32]

The argument begins to advance only when we raise the always difficult (and in this instance almost bewildering) question of history itself. How could any moral career as thoroughly elaborated as that of Reuben Bourne possibly function as an historical figure without becoming hopelessly overspecified and hence reductive? Or, to look at the question from the other end, what sufficiently general interest could Hawthorne possibly have taken in so banal an affair as "Lovewell's Fight," or indeed in the whole tedious and depressing history of frontier skirmishes of which it was so pathetically a part? Even those who find Hawthorne's interest in "history *as history*" a credible literary possibility must be slow to suppose that his art (like the scholarship of some modern "colonialists") concerned itself with certain details just because they were there. We might get used to the idea that Cotton Mather is Hawthorne's necessary "pre-text." But can we ever be quite comfortable with William Hubbard?

The second historical question—concerning the larger cultural significance of "Lovewell's Fight"—is by far the easier to answer. We must begin by reminding ourselves that more than national desperation about the impoverished possibilities of a native literature lies behind the elevation of "Indian Warfare" to parity with Puritanism and the Revolution among the trinity of American literary "matters." Much nearer than we are to the literal problems of physical (and cultural) survival in a newly occupied (and still alien) country, the last century's sense of its tenuous territorial grasp was far more lively than our own; only since then (if at all) has the land truly become "ours." The *territorial* destiny of America was, in the late 1820's, not yet "manifest"; and, in the first years of Jackson's policy of "Indian Removal," the tragical farce of "supplantation" was still going on. Accordingly, narratives of Indian warfare and captivity flourished well into the nineteenth century as a major American genre. Indeed, by some accounts, this is where American literature truly begins, making the "Entertaining Passages" of Benjamin Church a more significant and influential work than either the "Faithful" or the "Personal Narrative" of Jonathan Edwards, and D. H. Lawrence a more penetrating critic than Perry Miller. In any case, as Hawthorne would make painfully clear in "Main Street," the original Americans did not simply "vanish"; they had to be killed.[33]

Thus the history of Indian warfare is by no means so "local"—to the "colonial" period, or to the cultural margins of some vague "frontier"—as we might tend to imagine. The problem itself is major, at least as significant as that of the Revolution; and the earliest American literature (such as it was) rightly recognized that this was so. It may have misunderstood the meaning, as it surely lied about its own motives; but it could hardly fail to identify at least the name of one of its own most fundamental problems.

Hence we should not be too surprised to learn that the sovereign states of Massachusetts, New Hampshire, and Maine all carefully planned and carried out, in 1825, a lively and visible celebration of the "centennial" of "Lovewell's Fight." One of Hawthorne's more intellectual teachers at Bowdoin executed a ballad on the local subject, which was entirely to the national purpose; and the same Longfellow who would later recognize the colonialism of "Molineux" forced his own rude fingers to produce a timely piece of unmemorable memorial verse. Many other writers responded as well, and none placed the name of the event in self-protective quotation marks; and probably no reader thought to bracket the question of history while reading the poetry. The subject was too important to be reserved for the sake of art alone. It might be too much to suggest that little children in the streets were all singing the epic and nation-making deeds of Lovewell's brave and chivalric heroes, but the celebrations (and the literature) figured prominently enough in the *Salem Gazette;* thus Hawthorne's irony can touch only the precision or the honesty of the collective memory when he refers to the events of 1725 as "well-remembered." For all one could tell in 1825, "Lovewell's Fight" was seriously competing for an honored place in the newly (but rapidly) forming national mythology.[34]

The problem, therefore, is not that one *could* not be concerned about the true meaning of "Lovewell's Fight," for in fact almost everybody was: *ab esse ad posse*. The difficulty is, rather, that "Roger Malvin's Burial" does not itself seem, on its own elaborately casuistical surface, to be very significantly so concerned. In spite of its initial invocation, and even after the determined efforts of a fair number of serious source studies, many critics and (one imagines) most ordinary readers do not feel compelled by any grown-up historical point.[35] Thus we must take the first of our two historical questions a little more carefully: granted that "Roger Malvin's Burial" may have been inspired by the celebrations of 1825, and granted also that Hawthorne's all-transforming imagination did indeed "borrow" certain suggestive details from original sources, how can the "case" of Reuben Bourne possibly function as a valid historical figure?

Our first clue to the determined and astonishingly complex historicism of the tale clearly comes from the elusive but insistent ironies of the first paragraph. Like the openings of "Molineux," "The Gentle Boy," and "The May-Pole," that innocent-seeming little "preface" appears perfectly nominal and perfunctory, almost self-nullifying: here is a little authentic history for the antiquarians in our audience; sensitive literary types will go right on to the psychosis and the symbols. Actually, however, and (again) just as in those other cases, the rhetoric is designed to alert the initiated and baffle the invincibly ignorant: colonialists will suspect they know where they are and proceed with caution; others must be expected to pause and wonder. Only those already overcommitted to some marvelously serviceable premise of the meta-historical truth of "romance" will sail blithely on; and they, unhappily, will be in danger of committing the same sort of historical sin which the story exists to dramatize. Ignorance of the facts is no excuse, even if we should know all the hermeneutical laws in the world: truth is not a method.

At first glance, the historical facts which guarantee the literary ironies of Hawthorne's first paragraph—and which thus establish the essential historicity of the whole—seem dishearteningly complicated. And yet Hawthorne clearly knew them, and he may fairly have expected some more literate segment of his original audience to know them, or else to stop and be baffled. Fortunately for us, scholarly detection and historical criticism have already succeeded in recovering and publicizing many of the essential facts, thus appreciably narrowing the gap of knowledge between ourselves and Hawthorne's "own" (or perhaps only his "ideal") audience. The task is possible. To some it will seem like a hard saying, but it remains true that we must advert to the difference between the "facts" and the "story" of "Lovewell's Fight" to be at all certain we are not guilty of re-writing "Roger Malvin's

Burial" in one of our own more or less exciting, more or less transitory idioms.[36]

Most obviously, Hawthorne's introductory remarks intend to remind us that "Lovewell's Fight" has not been in *every* way "well-remembered." The quotation marks around the event in question call our attention to the fact that it already has a literary status: as in most such cases, a chance skirmish has had to acquire a definite denomination, even as it was retrospectively judged to possess some definitive significance. And in this instance, even the level of diction suggested by "Fight" gives the case away. We know that literature has operated, and we suspect that myth may be involved as well, even before we advert to the dismal facts of the historical situation. Once we remember these facts, we instantly know how to proceed.

Having set out on an officially sponsored (if personally motivated) scalp-hunting expedition, Captain Lovewell's irregular troops began by slaughtering a party of Indians in their sleep. So much for vengeance. In the aftermath of this lucky (and profitable—for they were to receive a bounty of 100 pounds for each scalp) raid, they went on to bungle their own mercenary strategy by the tactic of pursuing a lone Indian in such a manner as to get themselves ambushed; and in the bloody "Fight" that followed they were to suffer great (and needless) losses from among their own number. Worst of all, according to the excessively nice morality of the time and place, they had engaged in this ill-advised piece of heroism on the Sabbath, when Divine Service recommended itself as a more fitting occupation than Search and Destroy. Possibly some of the men who survived (either the battle or the temptation to desert), and who managed to straggle back to civilization, actually had some sense that their enterprise would not bear much looking into; nevertheless, some of them seem to have told the truth. Other, more decorous observers saw at once the obvious advantages of turning the affair into a ballad. At least one such "historian" seems to have had the quite local motives of small-town friendship and family ties. But presumably anybody might perceive, in this instance at least, the superiority of some chivalric myth over the altogether unlovely facts of the case.[37]

And so a "story" about daring, loyalty, and personal heroism came into existence (and print) almost at once. Lovewell's men ceased to be bounty hunters and became selfless patriots and courageous heroes. Furthermore—in a small move that has the most astonishing significance for the interpretation of "Roger Malvin's Burial"—the date of the bloody "Fight" was moved back from Sunday (May 9) to Saturday (May 8). Many people knew better, but apparently no one protested; thus the matter passed into the folklore of the region. And thus the "story" was still being re-told as the "event" was ceremoniously memorialized in 1825. Small wonder, perhaps, if the same writer who (half-seriously) proposed building a monument on Gallows Hill (to balance the one at Bunker's) should have his own word to say about the one gradually taking substance at "Lovewell's Pond."[38]

Accordingly, "imagination" would indeed have to cast "certain circumstances judicially into the shade" before seeing "much to admire in the heroism of a little band who gave battle to twice their number in the heart of the enemy's country" (337); what seems a conventional enough justification of the tedious claim of "romance" to some "neutral territory" is actually a rather fierce (if obvious) attack on the most debased form of literary lying. If "chivalry itself might not blush to record the deeds of one or two individuals," the reason is only partly that one or two individuals probably did act bravely in a basically depraved situation; the other and more telling reason is that "chivalry itself"—as it was taught in the textbooks of the day, and as it went on from there to influence the standards of heroism operative in the pages of contemporary romance—seemed to possess a fairly high threshold of shame and could be made to countenance similar acts of moral desperation.[39] And finally, as we slide from the airy realm of heroic ideals into the real world of might-politics, everybody can at least confess some minimum pragmatic justification of the "end" of "Lovewell's Fight," whatever the mean-ness of its motives: "The battle, though so fatal to those who fought, was *not unfortunate* [my italics] in its consequences to the country; for it broke the strength of a tribe and conduced to the peace which subsisted during *several* [again, mine] years" (337). The irony reeks: the ballads we read, from then and now, ask us to renew our national purpose at the shrine of an event which purchased a few years of freedom for imperialistic expansion at the price of a carnage originally inspired by intentions equally materialistic and altogether less grand.[40] Perhaps we should examine our national conscience—or, if our own intentions are pure, re-examine the facts on which we hope to base a national literature.

Thus we easily understand the general fitness of Hawthorne's wish to associate the not-quite-heroic career of Reuben Bourne with the "occasion" (and with the "matter") of "Lovewell's Fight": on its surface a story of noble wishes and unlovely facts, it aptly reminds us of the tendency to confuse, and even to lie about, such matters in our national past. But much more than this is at issue. For many of the structural and thematic details of Reuben's story actually mock the situation of event and official report as it originally existed in 1725. Not *all*, to be sure, for Hawthornean "romance" everywhere aspires to the condition of historical deconstruction rather than that of *roman à clef*; and though its literary mode is never typological in the established American-Puritan sense, its epistemology is always figurative rather than allegorical. Accordingly, we are to look for less than identity but more than fitness. And certainly, in this instance, Hawthorne's historicism amounts to much more than a borrowed handkerchief become the occasion of casuistical freeplay.

The burden of Hawthorne's historical intention becomes clear as soon as we realize the extent to which Reuben Bourne functions as an "historian": he has, after all, lived through an event in which the whole community is interested; and he is their only available source of vital information. Thus we need to re-examine the dynamics of his own manifest failure to tell the whole truth in the context of the relation between the historian and the community whose image and identity he necessarily serves. And even his own drastically personal self-destruction may enact—or predict—some dire public consequence which may be expected to follow from a lie about origins.[41]

Reuben's own deep division of motive, based on a fundamental conflict of values, may or may not reflect the sort of self-division experienced by any of the actual survivors of the Lovewell farce; but his manipulation of the truth, in accordance with the conventionally heroic expectations of his "audience," perfectly recapitulates the process by which a trivial and ugly (if also, in some sense, a necessary) event had been transformed into an heroic story. We have seen how, by one account, Reuben lies to Dorcas *exactly as* he had lied to himself. We have also noticed how the "second" event seems to infect the "first," rendering the two not-different from a moral point of view. We are now in a position to see the full implication of this fact. Reuben lies to himself because of Dorcas and the community whose standards she embodies. He lies to himself precisely *because* he knows he will be unable to face her, and them, with a faithful narrative of the grisly realities of Love and Death in the American Wilderness: it was Malvin alone or Malvin and me too—just as it had been, at the outset, them (the Indians) or us (the White Provincials). The situation is inherently objectionable; no concept and no language can redeem it, though the utilitarian realism of Malvin seems closer to the mark than the sentimental idealism of Dorcas. Malvin is dying, however, and it is to Dorcas that Reuben must report. And in this case, unfortunately, the expectation of the audience infects the veracity of the reporter. He tells her exactly what he knows she wants to believe: that everybody in question acted with story-book bravery and that (therefore) things came out cleanly and for the best, if not quite happily.

And that, in general, is what every historical audience always wants to believe. So the inhabitants of Maine and Massachusetts preferred their story in 1725 and so, on a larger and more dangerous scale, did the vast majority of Americans continue to prefer it a century later, even as a significant number of them celebrated the making and the maintenance of a lie. Possibly American magazine readers of the 1820's were even more corrupted than their ancestors by conventional notions of "heroism," like those to be derived from Charles Mills's *History of Chivalry;* and certainly they had not yet learned (as Robert Daly has cogently argued) the sobering point of Thomas Hutchinson who, in writing about a colonist named "Bourne," suggests that true heroism lies not in combat and conquest but in the foundation of flourishing towns and colonies.[42] But above all they had not yet learned to tell the unlovely truth about their national experience. Caught up in the exhilarating momentum of an advancing destiny, they were still refusing to face the implications of the existence of America as an ordinary (that is to say, a "guilty") country. For neither Cotton Mather's *More Wonders of the Invisible World* nor yet Thomas Symmes's *Historical Memoirs of the Late Fight at Pigwacket* would be the last instance in which some patriotic American "prostituted a magnificent conception" to save something or other.[43]

Possibly it is overly ingenious (as it certainly is melodramatic) to "allegorize" Reuben's slaughter of Cyrus as a prophecy of some bloody purgation from national guilt. "Roger Malvin's Burial" may be, in fact, a sort of secular Jeremiad, but Reuben's sin is presented as psychological or literary; he is guilty of nothing more "positive" than a sort of semi-tacit (or semi-deliberate) dishonesty. As such, his actions imply not so much the crime of genocidal "supplantation" as the failure to face the brutal facts of American survival, from colony to province; they figure less the Original Sin of American "geopolitics" than the besetting vice of American "hermeneutics."[44] And they do, very clearly, figure at least this much. Reuben is obviously guilty of *something.* Hawthorne plainly associates that guilt with a "celebrated" historical incident. And thus it is necessary to notice his fear that representative sins will *somehow* be visited on representative children.

Nowhere is Reuben a more precise figure of provincial America than in "the enthusiasm of [the] daydream" which carries him from a settled home into "the tangled and gloomy forest" (352). We readily understand Reuben's own personal wish for a "world elsewhere," away from the seaboard scenes of his guilt-ridden failure; and we may readily respond to the narrator's lyrical suggestion that Reuben's dream is really that of Everyman. But what may seem obvious delusion or gratuitous pastoral turns out to be a perfect epitome of the territorial "esthetic" of post-Puritan New England:

Oh, who ... has not wished that he were a wanderer in a world of summer wilderness, with one fair and gentle being hanging lightly on his arm? In youth his free and exulting step would know no barrier but the rolling ocean or the snow-topped mountains; calmer manhood would choose a home where Nature had strewn a double wealth in the vale of some transparent stream; and when hoary age, after long, long

years of that pure life, stole on and found him there, it would find him
the father of a race, the patriarch of a people, the founder of a mighty
nation yet to be. (352)

The passage continues and grows even more extravagant, suggesting that
"future generations" might reverence the "mysterious attributes" of this
"godlike" founder. Surely some readers will not find this last fantasy among
their own wishes. Clearly we are involved in the peculiarities of some myth;
but, just as clearly, the application of that myth is not quite universal. The
answer to the narrator's rampantly rhetorical question—all but lapsed in the
last extremity of poetic diction—is supposed to be "not quite everybody."
   Captain John Smith has dreamed this dream. So have most of the writers
of the scores of wilderness narratives that lead up to and come down from
"The Adventures of Col. Daniel Boon." Hector St. John de Crevecoeur has
dreamed it, and so has D. H. Lawrence, dreaming over the seductive pages
of Crevecoeur's *Letters*. So have certain dreamy *philosophes*. Probably every
adolescent who has ever wished that Cooper somehow could have fashioned
"one fair and gentle being" for Leatherstocking can be said to have
dreamed this dream. But surely they are not Everyman. Some literary soci-
ologists would have us believe that this is the dream of Every True American. But John Winthrop did not dream it, despite his intense interest in
American real estate. Jonathan Edwards did not, not in quarrelsome Northampton and not in ragged Stockbridge. Jefferson may have dreamed it,
while absorbing the totality of the Enlightenment; but Franklin and Hamilton did not. Neither did Edgar Poe. And neither, it should go without saying, did Nathaniel Hawthorne, who seems to have known, more clearly than
any of these others, about that marvelous process by which the Indian
Fighter is apotheosized as Pastoral Poet and Founding Patriarch.[45]
   Hawthorne's literary economy is, here, at least as concise and dazzling as
that in "My Kinsman, Major Molineux"; and his historical insight is, if anything, even more precise and prescient. If Robin Molineux brilliantly evokes
the political activities of a Rising and then a Revolutionary people by conflating the first protests of the 1730's with the determined resistance of the
1770's, Reuben Bourne embodies most of what is left over from any such
account of post-Puritan New England or, for that matter, of non-Puritan
America. We are just now learning to re-write Hawthorne's "poetic" law in
sociological prose: whenever the Exemplary City fails, there is always the
Frontier; or, even more generally, wherever Puritanism is not, there is the
irresistible lure of the Wildwood.[46] But Hawthorne's point is not so much
that provincial Americans vainly sought to escape the guilty memories of
colonizing an inhabited country by desperately plunging yet further into
conquered territories, recently made safe by protective retaliation; as that

action is, from a moral point of view, grotesque rather than casuistical, so its story could be only melodramatic. Hawthorne's point, rather, is that American "literature" repeatedly mis-defines—lies about—the nature of frontier experience.

In a sense one began killing Indians because, granted colonization, one has had to kill or be killed: certain Indians really were "readier to fill [our] sides full of arrows than otherwise."[47] But it is probably not necessary to define such self-defense as an heroic or chivalric activity, whatever the "demands" of inherited literary forms. Similarly, and more to the point of the latter half of "Roger Malvin's Burial," it seems utterly meretricious to re-define each new territory as the next available locus of an innocence that never was, especially if the myth in question perverts the mores of the people being "supplanted" as obviously as it misrepresents one's own motives. One *continues* to kill natives not so much for survival as for empire; and, "Indian" religion not being recognizable as *any* version of Renaissance pastoral, no native American ever defined his place or his mode of being as a "middle landscape." Such a definition expresses chiefly the "wish" of transplanted Englishmen who are moving into the places where native Americans have been killed. They lie about the nature of the place even as they lied about their intentions. And of this generalized case the specifics of Reuben Bourne's moral career provide a fair enough epitome.

But it is not only the dream which leads him on that marks Reuben as a consciously contrived provincial *figura:* the social world he most immediately abandons seems as strategically representative as the vision which ultimately draws him beyond it. Reuben's failure to "profit by the altered condition of the country" may place him in an unhappy minority, since many people's agricultural enterprises seem to have prospered from the removal of the "savage" threat to their fields and barns; but it takes two to make a court case. His own dis-eased irritability explains his "frequent quarrels . . . with the neighboring settlers"; but to understand his involvement in "innumerable lawsuits" we need to remember that "the people of New England, in the earliest stages and wildest circumstances of the country, adopted, wherever attainable, the legal mode of deciding their differences" (350). And never more so than in those expansive but troubled generations that lie between the Half-Way Synod and the Awakening. This litigious spirit, deep down, is what a very large proportion of American Jeremiads are all about: it provides the sociological context for Perry Miller's masterful study of the transition of New England society "from colony to province"; and it has become the weary substance of many later, less ideological and more "local" accounts of the same process.[48] A Whole People who once enjoyed, in Covenant, the Divine Right to appropriate the Lord's Waste have fallen to legalistic wrangling about personal claims to specific lands stolen from a native population. William Bradford may have foreseen it all in the 1640's—the Devil would insinuate himself into the New World "under fair pretences" of the necessity of more land; but the prescience of his prediction did not lessen the shock of recognition that attended its fulfilment. "Bulkeley, Hunt, Willard, Hosmer, Meriam, Flint" might all manage to forget the way they came to possess the land that "lies fairly" around Musketaquit; but apparently even good Congregationalists require good fences.

But what gives certainty, and even primacy, to some such anti-mythic reading of Reuben's case is, finally, our sense of the glaring historicity of the story's major symbols. Critics have long suspected that the "gigantic rock" which serves as the "gravestone" for both Roger Malvin and Cyrus Bourne has, in its latter-day New England setting, some explicitly "covenantal" significance, and that the veins on its face, which seem "to form an inscription in forgotten characters" (338), record some promise or condition beyond Reuben's unredeemed vow to bury his fellow-survivor.[49] And it turns out that the oak tree which towers over the final scene and (otherwise) organizes so much of the story is actually a rather famous symbol of the terms according to which New Englanders held their own land of promise. Together, the rock and the oak tell virtually the whole story of the National Covenant.

As Reuben, Cyrus, and Dorcas set out into the American Wilderness, in search of some Earthly Paradise, they are explicitly called "pilgrims"; and the mood of their departure recalls an earlier pilgrimage which, for specifically *American* experience, may well be regarded as archetypal. Very like William Bradford's original congregation, this "little family snapped asunder whatever tendrils of affection had clung to inanimate objects, and bade farewell to the few who . . . called themselves their friends" (351).[50] Accordingly, the gigantic rock upon which they stumble can hardly fail to remind us of that most immemorial Rock at Plymouth which, well prior to the monumental Bicentennial of 1820, rampant filiopietism had caused to be dragged from the rocky coast to the town square (and which—though such Special Providences are little noted nor long remembered—had been broken apart in the patriotic process). If it has, so far, failed to put us in mind of a whole race of kindred monuments erected in stone, perhaps our ignorance is somewhat more forgivable than that of Hawthorne's original readers; for fewer of us, proportionately, have recently made a pilgrimage to worship at some shrine of ancestral heroism. If we cannot quite make out the "inscription in forgotten characters" on the face of the great stone monument, the reason is partly that we ourselves have not been quite so directly involved in the process of obscuring the particular truth and transmitting the general falsehood about what really happened at "Lovewell's Rock." And yet Hawthorne's story exists to conquer the invincibility of even *our* ignorance.[51]

Perhaps the inscription is very simply Biblical: "Thou shalt not kill"—
serving Reuben as a subliminal reminder that his *original* forest-expedition
was far from innocent, however the casuistry of motive and circumstance
might seek to "condition" the categorical nature of the divine imperative,
and consciously alerting us to the likelihood that, in the end, Reuben's murderous guilt feelings are rooted in the (irrational, ironical) conviction of his
responsibility for the death of *Malvin*. But if the inscription says this much,
it probably says "Honor thy father" as well, underscoring the fact that
Reuben's original division of mind is a virtual paradigm of "filial anxiety."
On the one hand he loyally desires to give up his own life in perfect devotion
to the values of an heroic past; and on the other he selfishly wishes to be
about his own business in the ordinary affairs of a reduced present. Obviously his suggestively Oedipal situation is not without close Biblical precedent: as if to predict the Christ-ian *difference,* Old Testament sons seem only
too anxious to enjoy their patrimony, to come into their *own* kingdom. But
it is also, by no very great accident or coincidence, an *almost* perfect epitome
of "generational strife" in latter-day New England. Some of the proper
names seem strange, or at least distinctive to the New World; but when was
that ever a bar to the ever-advancing habit of typology? With the rare exception of that relentlessly historicist Roger Williams, who in New England
ever held that mere metonomy could alter the inexorable metaphors of the
Covenant?

If the ancient Hebrews keep the commandments written on their two
stony tablets, those twin rocks of their national covenant, they will come to
possess their own land; or, as their own moral science evolved toward its
(casuistical) perfection, if they can learn to *love* those laws in their fleshly
hearts, they will inherit a *good* land, beyond Jordan, flowing with milk and
honey, and overflowing with progeny more numerous than stars. They
must pass through some desert, of course, but if their hearts be faithful,
saving waters will gush like tears of repentance from yet another covenantal
rock. Some hapless Amalek will have to be "supplanted"; but God's ways
(and means) are not our own, as even the experiences of Abraham, Isaac,
and Ishmael clearly suggest. God's last ends often suspend the ordinary
logic of life, territory, and destiny: natural ethics is one thing, but Holy History is quite another. And just so in New England—where it is the pastoral
and dynastic ("trans-Jordanian") lands of the supplanted Amalek which
Reuben hopes to inherit, though somewhat desperately, in the light of his
self-convicted disloyalty to (even his Oedipal hatred of) Malvin.

Except of course that it will not all work out. Some brutal fact or other
keeps spoiling the perfection of typology, insisting on the crazy details of its
own too-literal story. The principle of that exegetical disruption, however,
is rooted at least as deeply in Hawthorne's passionate concern over the de-

terminate course of America's actual history as in the necessary elaboration of some psychoanalytic (or casuistical) hypothesis occasionally invented for the chauvinistic enrichment of a National Literature using provincial themes. Accordingly, just when the American Israel is about to be transplanted to the good lands beyond Jordan, Abraham spoils the whole plan by killing Isaac (instead of some sacrificial animal providentially tangled in some fortuitous bush) only to force tears from his otherwise hardened (Mosaic) heart. The Divine Masterplot will *not* repeat, for reasons that have to do with the ultimate Marplot of American history. God Himself not intervening, there will be no pastoral and dynastic future, only a repetition of the terrible ritual of blood already shed and lies already told. Surely a nation somehow blights its future by seeking to cover the ugly realities of its origin with either the heroics of chivalry or the pieties of typology.[52]

Evidently the "beautiful young hunter" whom Dorcas imagines to have "slain a deer" (358) will not really live to fill the moccasins or legitimately grow to fill up the mythic outlines of Cooper's leather-stockinged hero; and the story may well predict the agency of his typic destruction.[53] For we sadly note that, within the story's own explicit eighteen-year chronology, the year of Cyrus' death is the very year when Indian warfare began again, wasting once more the budding vigor of New England's young manhood. Literally, if one insists on insisting, a guilt-maddened Reuben Bourne guns down his only-begotten son in an outburst of blood-lust that seems psychotic rather than symbolic; and yet his action really does function as a grotesque and elemental parody of the Old Testament's paradigm of Covenantal Faith. And even more aptly, in a figurative move we must be willing to follow, in spite of the evident failure of New England's own meretricious hermeneutics, his actions clearly suggest that the heroic lies of American historians and the pastoral delusions of American mythologists have "blasted" the scion of destiny and blighted what might have been, in some cold prose, a fair enough hope for some modest new beginning. Transcendent Vision has predicted a New Israel beyond Jordan. But its murderous deceptions have precipitated only the French and Indian War.[54]

And so the "gigantic rock" looms up to remind all who can read the signs of the times, with a warning that balances and answers the patriotic pieties inscribed on "Lovewell's Rock": "Thou shalt not kill," not even Indians. Or if, somehow, in the rough course of ordinary providence, thou dost shed the blood of thy natural brother, do not "bear false witness" about this sinful fact. Above all, perhaps, do not do so in the name of thy Founders. "Honor thy father," to be sure, but do not reverence the folkways of thy ancestors above the Divine Commandments. "I am the Lord thy God"; thou shalt not make a graven idol—or a green and golden idyll—of America.

And if the "gravestone" of the "near kindred" of Dorcas Bourne is plainly a sort of Rock of the Covenant, reminding New England of the Divine Law which must always guide and restrict the national purpose of any just people, the familiar oak tree which sheds its "withered topmost bough" at the moment of Reuben's tearful recognition is flagrantly a sign of New England's deeply problematic attempts not only to extend or enlarge the terms of the paradigmatic National Covenant but also to cast "certain circumstances" of national expansion, "judicially," into the shade or covering shadow of the more-than-secular symbolism of civil religion. As John Samson has noticed, Hawthorne's description of the oak tree which seems to shed a final benediction on the weeping stone that is Reuben Bourne is based on the appearance of the famous "Charter Oak" of Connecticut—in which ark were safely hid the "liberties" of that colony when they were being viciously sought by the villainous Governor Andros. According to a brief memorial in Farmer and Moore's *Collections* (where Hawthorne is known to have learned so much about the primary matter of Lovewell), the "historic" tree "appears to have lost its upper trunk," but its foliage remains "remarkably rich and exuberant"; in Hawthorne's more judgmental representation, "the middle and lower branches were in luxuriant life . . . but a blight had apparently stricken the upper part of the oak" (357).[55] Hawthorne adds, of course, that "the very topmost bough"—where his own Reuben had, eighteen years since, tied the vow of his own bloody handkerchief—was "withered, sapless, and utterly dead"; thus his own story, with its own appropriate (and fairly obvious) natural symbolism, retains, as it must, its own symbolic integrity. But a structuralist criticism which tiresomely locates the placement of natural images within the visual shape of the spatial text but resists examination of the historical semantics by which a hole in a tree becomes a cardinal fact of Holy History may be diseased at its own root.[56]

According to that logic, the "Charter Oak" is a glorious symbol of the land rights and other sacred immunities of the Israel in the Canaan of *New* England, as against the Babylonish interventions and usurpations of the *Old;* and in Farmer and Moore its story is mixed in among accounts of "the landing of the Fathers at Plymouth" (celebrated now as *"Forefathers' Rock"*) on the one side and of "Lovewell's Fight" on the other, with no sense of historical variety.[57] According to the (deconstructive) logic of "Roger Malvin's Burial," however, the tree stands in the midst of a field of blood, a bloody flag waving from its "topmost bough," serving (all but unconsciously) as a guilty reminder of a dream and a habit of expansion which not only "added ridge to valley, brook to pond" but also, in the making of "America," annexed Hartford to Boston, Connecticut Valley to Massachusetts Bay, wooded frontier to fertile seacoast. Weirdly transplanted from Hartford (the very first wilderness offshoot of Puritanism's original plantation "on the hille" at Boston) to Pigwackett (the current site of discontent and migration), it stunningly reminds the historical reader not of the organic unity of God's covenantal plan for salvation throughout all history but of the similarity of all of New England's ventures into Indian territory, and of the ready availability of noble rationalizations. Standing (as Hawthorne twice reminds us) in the midst of "other hard-wood trees [that] had supplied the place of the pines, which were the usual growth of the land" (338, 355), this oddly misplaced historical remembrancer marks the fact that the various American dreams—Puritan Israel, Yankee Liberty, and Romantic Nature—all take place on a ground no longer virgin, and in the mode of supplantation.

Dorcas weeps for Deerslayer, but we never hear what the Indian women think. Reuben weeps for himself, for Malvin, for his son, and for a promised future his own progeny will never see. And weeping, he sends "up to Heaven" a prayer from the bottom of his guilty heart, from the depths of his confused mind. But while Christians dispute Freudians within a territory bounded by the Decree of Predestination on the one side and the Logic of compulsion on the other, the historical reader prays that the Great Father may not show a red face. For if He should, then the "forgotten characters" on Malvin's rock must surely carry a message of American doom.[58]

One other bit of evidence supports this hypothesis in favor of a radically historical reading of "Roger Malvin's Burial"—an odd coincidence not entirely "textual" in the ordinary sense, and yet too wickedly relevant to be ignored. At the fatal moment just prior to Reuben's sacrificial slaughter of Cyrus, and breaking the tension of Reuben's madly teleological wanderings, Hawthorne shows us Dorcas perusing "the current year's Massachusetts Almanac, which, with the exception of an old black-letter Bible, comprised all the literary wealth of the family." A small bibliographic detail, this: strangely out of keeping with the texture of the tale everywhere else; and more proper to the social realism of Howells than the psychological romance of Hawthorne. One necessary explanation for this mixing of modes is very close at hand: Reuben needs to be instructed that "it was now the twelfth of May" (354), *that very day* when, eighteen years ago, he abandoned Malvin and cursed his own life. And as if to apologize for the excessive clumsiness of this highly "literary" coincidence, Hawthorne waxes sententious: "None pay greater regard to arbitrary divisions of time than those who are excluded from society." But another fact is needed to account for this awkward inclusion which is, within the "logic of compulsion," at least as objectionable as the magical falling branch.[59]

If Hawthorne has any other "pretext" for this inclusion, it certainly reveals itself in an article about the Centenary Celebrations of Lovewell's

Fight which appeared on the front page of a Salem newspaper in April 1825. The article begins and ends in what (by now) we recognize as the predictable and provoking manner—with rich praise for the gallantry of Lovewell's men and a ringing commendation of their anniversary as the fit occasion for renewing national values and purpose. But if there were no substantive doubts about how to memorialize Lovewell's Fight, there was a very considerable uncertainty about precisely *when* to do so. For, as a learned writer solemnly explains, in three long columns of great scientific density, the calendar had changed between 1725 and 1825; and unless one were a very meticulous student of the high astronomical sciences that lie behind the penny-wisdom of the almanacs, one was in danger of dishonoring the past by celebrating one of its most memorable events on the wrong day![60]

The first irony here is casual enough: much intellectual labor is being expended on behalf of a cause which is in fact not heroic but shabby. If this were all, we might well suspect blatant historical accident rather than oblique authorial intention. Beyond this, however, and beginning to stir our suspicions that Hawthorne's own ironic intelligence is strategically at play behind his seemingly clumsy reference to Dorcas' curiosity, is our perception that in Hawthorne's own world the antiquarian motive has allied itself with appearance rather than reality: masquerading as chronological science, historicism expends itself in a game of numbers that leaves the question of motives (and even of actual events) entirely out of revisionary account. And finally, confirming our most drastic suspicions about the potentially esoteric nature of Hawthorne's contextualism, is our astonished recovery of Hawthorne's ultimate (contextual) irony: unless the almanacs of New England are indeed adjusted by one day, then reverential sons may, by some wild secular accident or wicked providential wonder, inadvertently celebrate the bloody deeds of their unknown fathers on the correct but concealed date after all. Unless their historical science is excruciatingly careful, they will restore the real, Sabbath-breaking chronology which lie and then legend had worked so effectively to conceal.[61]

To be sure, any very strict doctrine of literary internalism will reject the hermeneutic necessity of these ironies as extraneous, or at best peripheral, to Hawthorne's *own text*. But if we should find ourselves thus resisting them, clinging to literary autonomy and historical innocence, then we may well want to question the relevance of this prevailing (strict) critical method to the developing Hawthornean mode. For we have arrived at a pretty fair model of how that mode distinctively works.

If there is not always an external *occasion* quite so explicit and notorious as the Lovewell Centenary, still there is, always, an implied *audience* whose historical beliefs are so well known to the writer that they must be considered "internal," if not to the text, then certainly to the rhetorical system which completes the circuit of the text's intention and (alone) gives it full personal meaning. Always these implied historical beliefs are wrong, often disastrously so. And thus the penalty for not informing ourselves about them—as the text itself almost always suggests we should—is double: not only will we miss the distinctive *difference* of Hawthorne's own intended meaning, which is always a function of his subtle but devastating play with prevailing opinion, but we also will stubbornly though unwittingly call down upon our own heads the sins of such American Fathers Hawthorne's stories exist to identify, confess, and repent. Surely literary hardness of heart can go no further.

And surely some alternative sort of critical procedure is eminently thinkable, with or without that "New Historicism," the rumor of whose fame still runs before us. For the purposes of the practical criticism of the various colonialist tales of Hawthorne's "first period," the "theory" could hardly be simpler. Hawthorne's texts everywhere present us with historical names and facts (or versions of facts) which are, to the perfectly unhistorical reader, perfectly meaningless. To learn the meaning of these words, from whatever source, is to study history. To study the relevant history is to learn to construe the text. To construe the text is to be instructed in the difference between the events of the past and their legend or "story," as solemnly celebrated in occasional poems or as soberly editorialized in the newspapers. Thus in the end contextual criticism and valid interpretation become the same thing. Or so we will have to argue, again and again, in stories whose "history" is, like that of "Malvin" and unlike that of "The Wives," more and more strategic, less and less evocative. Surely we cannot imagine Hawthorne himself objecting to the notion of his readers learning the facts of American history in order to understand his fictions. And we should at least entertain the notion that to interpret his tales is to deconstruct, one by one, the various chapters of an emergent American mythology.

3

"My Kinsman, Major Molineux" is, by almost all accounts, the masterpiece of the "Provincial Tales," however short or long the table of contents of that "projected" collection is imagined to be. And doubtless it presents us with an unavoidable test of the style of interpretation we have been imagining. On the one hand, its historical locus is unarguably more obvious than that of "Roger Malvin's Burial": to recover the tale at all—from among those which Hawthorne did not reprint in his famous collections of 1837,

1842, and 1846, and which the ongoing tradition of moralistic appreciation did not know how to value—was in fact to observe the evidence of its ("proleptic") relation to the American Revolution. And at some level this fact has always seemed fair enough, for that "event" (along with its fifty-year anniversary celebration in 1826) was altogether more famous than the original doings (or memorial sayings) at Lovewell's Rock. On the other hand, however, its distinctively literary merit has continued to seem more obvious and unflawed; so that ever *since* the initial moment of re-discovery and re-valuation, the critical history of this tale can fairly be described as the dialogue created by a series of more or less elegant attempts to set it free from its historical moorings. Critics have found themselves repeatedly insisting that the perfection of "Molineux" is (to change the figure) its ability to ride on its own superb melting.[62]

Evidently it can do so very well. Few sensitive readers have trouble responding, in a vital and elementary way, to the literal details of Robin's anxious progress. And most tend at once to associate the private results of his strange misadventures with their own experience of adolescent disillusion and adult choice, spontaneously and without the mediation of history. One readily sees why. We watch Robin taking, all innocently, a long and crucial first step into psychic independence. We sense, almost immediately, that he is stepping in over his head, involving himself in a process which, having a structure of its own, he cannot entirely control; we worry that he may get somewhat more than he shrewdly bargains for. When he does, we sympathize with his child-like wish to turn around and go home, even as we conclude, in our own adult wisdom, that "you can't." And we sadly imagine that he too will soon internalize this inevitable conclusion of experience. In all of this the "philosophical" perfection of Hawthorne's plot seems too general and complete to admit the slightest adulteration of historical particularity. The sequence of Robin's night-time confrontations, rendered in a superb modulation of tones—from callow confidence, to violent frustration, to honest uncertainty, and on to the verge of some mature toleration of self-contradiction—seems regulated by some absolutely universal law of growing up. It is as if the entire genre of *bildungsroman* could be epitomized in the single evening of ambiguity and weariness of some Provincial Everyman.[63]

Accordingly, we do not much resist the translation of this inevitable human plot into the appropriate clinical terms. In seeking the economic and social assistance of a worldly uncle, Robin is, truly enough, searching out some more tolerant surrogate for the loving but strict, ministerial father he has left behind. He evidently desires an extension of his sphere of personal freedom, without the loss of social identity which complete self-reliance inevitably entails; indeed, since Major Molineux is a famous and successful relative, Robin is evidently seeking the best of both worlds. It is, therefore, no more ironic than it is appropriate that every male figure he meets turns out to represent a more absolute version of paternal inhibition than the one he left behind: evidently it is even harder to hang between than it is to go back. And though some relatively innocent readers may resist the inference that Robin never did "really" want to locate Molineux, few who know about "Oedipal violence" (from Freud or from his mythic sources) will find Robin's hysterical response to their eventual meeting either gratuitously cruel or outrageously unmotivated. Edifying or not, the process of maturation has a logic of its own. The Unconscious has a reason which the political commitments and even the family sentiments do not know. And it has wrecked more than one enlightened critical system.[64]

Thus the problem of "Molineux" is different from that of "Malvin." And more crucial. With "Malvin" the task has been to suggest that *only* some fairly sophisticated form of historicism can fairly comprehend all the tale's arcane references and adequately unify its fictional logic. With "Molineux," however, the problem is evidently to show that *any* form of historicism is supple enough to avoid reduction. The "Hutchinson Mob" episode of *Grandfather's Chair* throws an astonishingly useful light on the moderate politics of "My Kinsman, Major Molineux"; but the static moralism of the one will never replace the dramatic irony of the other. And not even the strongest evidence in favor of the developing historicity of Hawthorne's imagination can justify a criticism which enlists symbolic richness and psychoanalytic acumen in the aid of a high-school history lesson.

Nevertheless, there is ample reason to imagine that the historical setting does very intensely matter. Even the staunchist "myth critic" will have to concede that the "vehicle" of "Molineux" is as pointedly particular as its "tenor" is timelessly general. To be sure, Hawthorne's prosy headnote seems to call us off from too detailed an investigation of the local history of Boston in the earlier eighteenth century, begging to be excused from the obligation to provide "an account of the train of circumstances that had caused [the] temporary inflammation of the popular mind" (209); but surely the anti-historical signal may be entirely ironic, as are the similar gestures at the beginning of "Malvin." Perhaps the tale itself will stand in for those events, in a general way, and by some acceptable law of literary substitution. Or quite possibly the "historical" interest touches matters far more significant than the precipitating causes of some unpleasant but forgettable rum riot. Or, most wickedly—as Roy Harvey Pearce long ago suggested—possibly Hawthorne means to alert the reader to the sort of language or habits of perception that have erased all real ugliness from the historical memory.[65] Ugliness there certainly is, in the tale's final parade of horribles; it all seems, somehow, *very* historical; and it must mean *something*, even in a story about the absurdities of growing up.

With or without the gloss from *Grandfather's Chair,* the orchestrated cacophony of the Molineux procession evokes a great deal of the night-time activity of the pre-revolutionary 1760's and early 1770's. The lord of this misrule recalls the notorious revolutionary mobster Joyce, Jr., as unmistakably as the name "Molineux" reminded Longfellow, however oddly, of that somewhat more polite Bostonian who was known to sponsor and organize such purposive festivities.[66] Even the name "Robin" (as we shall presently observe) is not without an astonishingly apt significance in the lexicon of eighteenth-century politics, the language of which is elsewhere strewn all over the tale. And surely some sense of history pervades the story's primary "literary" realities, lower down the cognitive scale: tone, attitude, and gesture everywhere bespeak a rising and unruly people, if not quite a revolutionary populace.

We can say, of course, that the tale has to be set "somewhere"; and where *better* than in the Age of Revolution? What better backdrop for a rite of personal passage than a nation's own problematic and, yes, ultimately violent transition? Or we can suggest, somewhat more pointedly, that the political ambiguities of eighteenth-century Boston provide, for Hawthorne, precisely the sort of "neutral territory" he needed for such a tale: following Scott (and perhaps Cooper), he learned to let disputed or non-aligned real estate stand for those neutral times when the bewildered psyche does not know if it is "here or there." Or we might propose—in some ultimate gesture of reconciliation, designed to incorporate both the preceding suggestions and to "split the difference" between the political Historicist and the psychoanalytic Myth Critic—that Hawthorne means *both* his matters, public and private; that he means both *equally;* that in this one instance, at least, he has made it impossible to tell tenor from vehicle or to decide what reality is being studied in terms of what image.[67] In this view, the process of personal maturation and the dynamics of political independence go round and round in our mind forever, in the aftermath of Hawthorne's tale, like equilibrists; or, not unlike "My love" and "a red, red rose," Robin and Revolution now exist in that sort of indissoluble union which only literature can create. What Art has joined together, let no man deconstruct.

And yet certain nice questions would always remain, evading solution by such a large, easy, genial, and tolerant view. For example, why should Robin's experience be regarded as the personal equivalent of *both* the 1730's and the 1760's or 1770's? It might well be seen as inseparably like one or the other, depending on whether Hawthorne thought the rite of passage occurred most perfectly in the psychic context of benign neglect or of threatened enslavement; but probably not both, without the plot's coming to seem a little too thick. As in fact it does, for surely one major effect of the story is to leave the reader wondering, uncertainly, whether he is "here" in a minor episode of provincial unruliness or "there" in the glory and chaos of full revolt. Taken seriously, the question can become fairly unsettling: what if this cardinal ambiguity of setting, which amounts to something between a redundancy of plot and a contradiction of theme, were somehow the clue to an interpretation altogether less conciliatory than the one we have imagined?

What if Hawthorne's main purpose were to suggest that the fit between the private-personal and the public-political is hardly ever so perfect as literature can make it seem? Arguably, the major result of *any* such too-perfect identification would be to obscure important differences, to blur certain distinguishing features of each. And thinkably, that effect might be, in certain cases, somebody's deliberate and meretricious intention. What if Hawthorne were perceiving that the American Revolution were *not,* or did not *necessarily* enfigure itself as, some inevitable rite of national passage? If so, then the tale of Robin Molineux is more ironic than we have yet supposed, its patriotism more bitter than anything in Robert Lowell.

What we need to imagine, then, in order to test for the ultimate thematic relevance of the history on the face of "My Kinsman, Major Molineux" is the possibility that the literary identity we are invited to experience as the heart of the tale is less the creation of Hawthorne's own esemplastic imagination than it is a cultural *donnée;* not a last philosophical insight but only another popular story, obscuring the problem it pretends to solve and creating others along the way. And if this is so, then the task of criticism is not to admire but to criticize. It is, in fact, to tear asunder a fabric whose one seam calls critical attention to its evident fabrication. But we may well begin, less drastically, by noticing certain surprising colorations in the historical weave.

At something like the climax of "The Boston Massacre" section of *Grandfather's Chair,* the most sensitive of the youthful listeners painfully protests that he is learning more than he had wished to know about the way things really were back in the 1770's: " 'The Revolution,' observed Lawrence, who had said but little during the evening, 'was not such a calm, majestic movement as I supposed. I do not love to hear of mobs and broils in the street. These things were unworthy of the people, when they had such a great object to accomplish.' "[68] Grandfather is moved at once to soften the effect of his "true story." Everywhere on his guard against the danger of tainting the pure springs of youthful patriotism with some premature admixture of irony, he hastens to reassure Lawrence that "our Revolution" was indeed a grand movement, full of "great and noble sentiment," whatever fault the historian could find with its mode of expression. Lawrence takes the instruction, and yet we sense that his innocent pain survives the consolations of political philosophy, and that it is supposed to. Somehow his response, and even his language, has seemed truer and more convincing than Grandfather's own. Probably it is the word "majestic" that gives away Hawthorne's deepest and most adult case. We are surprised to find a youthful observer discover so absolutely just a word to characterize the half truth by which the Revolutionary Fathers have sought to socialize their revolt from authority—and their Sons.[69] We may even remember the word as an echo of the conclusion of "Molineux" where, surprisingly, it characterizes the calm of the deposed ruler, in myth-shattering contrast to the "counterfeit pomp," "senseless uproar," and "frenzied merriment" (230) of the deposing mob which broils in the street.

Majestic indeed had the Revolution come to seem by the time Hawthorne began (in the late 1820's) to write "My Kinsman, Major Molineux"; or by that moment, slightly earlier, when he began to borrow such "annals of Massachusetts Bay" (208) as underwrite whatever history the tale contains. Nowhere, in fact, have the convulsive events of the American 1760's and 1770's been made to appear more simply and calmly majestic than in the public oratory which marked the semi-centennial celebrations of 1826. Probably these festivities have to be set down as at least the remote rhetorical occasion of "Molineux"; and arguably they were the immediate and impelling psychological cause.[70] For the appropriately placed observer could hardly fail to mark the drastic difference between the way the events had got themselves recorded and interpreted in the sober pages of Thomas Hutchinson's *History of Massachusetts Bay* and the way they reappeared, miraculously transfigured, in the altogether more occasional productions of democratic visionaries who rejected Hutchinson's theory of history as absolutely as their fathers had anathematized his political commitments.

For Hutchinson, a fatal constitutional error had launched a slow but perceptible drift toward criminal violence. The rumor of the royal governor "driven from the province by the whizzing of a musket ball" (208) really does set the stage, though unintentionally, for his own bitter experience with the tender mercies of his fellow Bostonians—in an historical episode which, in Grandfather's re-telling, would also teach Lawrence more than he wanted to know. And yet what had interested Hutchinson most was not the threat of violence lurking within the slumbering "Puritanism" of the secularized New England populace but rather the cumulative (and evidently wearing) effect of a determined (and apparently ideological) "Resistance" to the "six governors" who ruled Massachusetts after "the surrender of the old charter, under James II." Little of majesty here, in their "continual bickerings with the House of Representatives" (208). And yet, as more than one historian of historians has ironically noted, Hutchinson's endlessly patient

135

and tediously "legitimist" constitutional *History* quickly came to serve as the standard sourcebook for past greatness and less directly as a ready textbook for "rising glory."[71]

Latter-day Puritan Jeremiahs used it for their fast- and election-day sermons through more than a decade before Lexington and Concord, as naturally as if it had been but an updated version of Mather's ancient "Wonderbook." And incipient American Republicans continued to draw on its riches in a lengthening series of Fourth of July orations designed to inculcate the lessons of Apocalyptic Whiggism, in spite of the fact that Hutchinson himself was regarded as a malicious traitor to the American cause. That Hutchinson's work tended, in itself, strenuously to resist enlistment in *any* version of the dominant American teleology seemed scarcely to matter. Bancroft's hour having not yet come, one had to make do with what there was; or, rather, make what there was do what one wanted.[72] What one wanted, evidently, was "majesty." *No one* loved to hear of mobs or broils in the street. And nearly everyone wanted to hear that the Revolution had been a major event in Holy History. It would overstate the case only slightly to say that in 1826 (Hutchinson himself to the contrary notwithstanding) all one could discover about the Revolution was that, in the Cosmic Progress toward a Universal Salvation in Holy Liberty, it figured as only slightly less important than the Birth of Christ and the Protestant Reformation, whose libertarian meaning it essentially fulfilled. And this astonishing fact of public attitude and political rhetoric probably explains the basic literary strategy of "Molineux."[73]

Only in this context of outrageous typological inflation does Hawthorne's deliberate running-together of two rather markedly different moments in the political life of the colonial eighteenth century reveal any plausible motivation or express anything like satifactory sense, historical or literary. Some drastic reduction is being made, clearly enough, but its *raison* is neither factual ignorance nor that imaginative gratuity supposed by suggestions that Hawthorne altered history to suit his literary purposes.[74] Evidently Hawthorne is striking back at the flagrant idolatries of America's pseudo-Puritan civil religion: in the face of a nearly overwhelming national consensus in favor of the holy-historical significance of 1776, Hawthorne is studying the majestic Revolution in terms of a minor outbreak of provincial unruliness, a mob scene.

Such, apparently, is the strategy of irony and insult of the historical headnote: abandon all critical discrimination you who enter here. Do not inquire too exactly into the local details of the "here or there" in your Great Chain of Becoming, and you can easily discover not only pre-figuration but even pre-enactment everywhere; but beware lest the ordinariness of the type destroy the majesty of its fulfillment. Proceed into this fiction as if safe in a world so politically insignificant *in itself* that only an obsessive legitimist like Thomas Hutchinson (or an unreconstructed romancer like Freud) could love it. Then encounter not only certain historic identities (the mobster Joyce, Jr., and, by association, the scoundrel William Molineux) but also a famous metaphorical logic (coming of age) that cannot *but* imply the Revolution. Then wonder: *am* I here or there? Which is to ask: just what sort of "event" was the Revolution, anyhow? The completion of the Divine Plot so long preparing, the final unveiling of God's own historico-literary *majestas?* Or just another local anxiety, one more utterly "temporary inflammation of the popular mind"—predictably violent and relentlessly ordinary?

The epistemology of the tale is still remotely "typological," if one insists, but only in some negative or ironic mode. And the motive is much more obviously "critical" in the eighteenth-century and modern historiographical sense. Nothing that happens in this midsummer nightmare is elevated or transfigured by its reference forward to the Revolution; not the piteous and terrible tarring of Major Molineux, and not the traumatic hazing of his kinsman. The red-and-black-faced Joyce, Jr., evidently means to claim descent from one of the Regicides of Charles I; and his having exchanged his ancestor's patient ass for an apocalyptic horse seems to express somebody's belief that some last revolution of human affairs is at hand.[75] But as a violence of rhetoric gives way to a violence of fact, the reader is more effectively reminded that the Boston Tea Party would, like any other tactic of resistance, have to be *led,* and by someone willing (at least temporarily) to invoke the powers of darkness. Similarly, the implication of the historic Molineux insinuates (among many other things) that even *American* protests need to be sponsored, organized, planned, and managed as well as led; and that often enough they were paid for by the very rum the British have made an issue "here," in 1733.[76] So that the unlovely but subtle idea of conspiracy is added to the ugly but obvious idea of violence: not only do revolutionary passions express themselves in ways that seldom accomplish God's justice, but they proceed far more intelligibly from somebody's ordinary political design than from God's special providence.

As a matter of distressing fact, Hawthorne has come much closer to dignifying the "Tory" cause with religious significance than he has to endorsing the familiar typological argument which explains "How the Puritans won the American Revolution." For as the tale moves toward its violent and hysterical revelation of Robin's Royalist kinsman, Hawthorne suggests that Major Molineux might recall somewhat more than the Scapegoat King who organizes pagan politics and presides, in "pity and terror" (229), over the birth of tragedy. Borne along by a torch-light procession, he reminds us not a little of a Christ betrayed by an apostle from Gethsemane to Calvary. This, surely, is the view being prepared for when Robin is instructed, all

Biblically, to "Watch here an hour" (220) and when, earlier, someone in authority is bold to declare "I know not the man" (211). We need no crowing cock to remind us that, whoever may be the Judas of the piece, it is finally Robin who fills up the role of the faithless Peter by refusing to come forward and own the man he had taken for a political savior.

But all of this, of course, is also in the mode of irony. It is simply the *other* religious view of the American Revolution—the Tory view, barely hinted at in the scrupulously secular pages of Hutchinson's *History*, but rampantly revealed in all the other conservative critics of 1776 (or 1649) that Hawthorne had likely read.[77] According to this very traditional and august view, *any* form of resistance to established authority not only violates the divine command to "honor thy father" but essentially re-enacts mankind's Original Rebellion; and violence against the person of *any* of God's vicarious agents of saving order re-commits the crucifixion of Christ. Not a Tory but an Ironist, Hawthorne is as far from endorsing this patriarchal and sacramental, essentially Anglican view of history as he is from precipitating an idolatrous extension of Puritan typology. No doubt a fair number of "Lawrences" in Hawthorne's audience could take useful adult instruction from the Tory view: notably deficient on the score of comparative religion, they needed reminding that God's politics are too much disputed to serve as nationalistic creed. And yet the main purpose of Hawthorne's impressively dramatic "Toryism" is simply to strike the uneven balance.[78]

For, finally, it is the idea of ordinary human conspiracy rather than high theologic violence which organizes most of Hawthorne's pre-diction of the revolution. The Tory view does not at all reduce the cosmic implications of this provincial ouster of authority; it merely turns them inside out.[79] Hawthorne's own strategy is far different: as he relentlessly reduces Apocalypse to rum riot, he keeps rubbing our nose in the painfully plotted quality of the action in which Robin has got himself involved. And it is in reading the tale from this point of view that we grasp the truly re-visionary quality of Hawthorne's provincial imagination.

The "Robin Molineux" who enters the "little metropolis of a New England colony" as eagerly "as if he were entering London city" (210) is more aptly named than we have supposed. His problematic surname reminds us, first of all, that he is very nearly related to somebody who will turn out to be on "the other side"—as soon as it shall have become clear that there *are* sides, in a strife which can be made to appear every bit as "civil" as a later one so named. And, somewhat more teasingly, it serves to remind us that neither we nor Robin himself can be entirely certain which side he himself is going to be on. He may back up from the brink to which he is approaching so near. Or, as seems more likely, he may indeed decide to throw in his lot with the faction his friendly observer refers to, conspiratorially, as "us"; if so, he may yet grow up to be the Molineux of history recognized by Longfellow, and by Professor Pearce, as that "organizer and leader of anti-Loyalist mobs," deemed a "martyr" to the cause or a "Pest to Society," depending on one's side.[80]

Beyond this, however, his name surely recalls another Molineux who also figures in the pages of Hutchinson's account of the ordeal of legitimacy in Massachusetts. Way back in Volume I (in the 1670's), the men of Massachusetts had protested the difficulty of conforming to Parliament's "acts of trade," which they apprehended as "an invasion of the rights, liberties, and properties of the subjects of his Majesty in the colony, they not being represented in parliament." This, of course, is a classic statement of the classic problem, so that Hutchinson can scarcely let it pass: thus early, he remarks, did the colonists betray "the wrong sense they had of the relation they stood in to England." Furthermore, the colony's error was so serious that it rightly became "one great article of charge against it" in the proceedings against their original charter. And yet, unforgivable as their error must certainly be judged, it is at least understandable: "The people of Ireland, about this same time, were under the same mistake"; and certainly "they had not greater color for an exemption from English acts of parliament, than a colony of natural born subjects, departing the kingdom with the leave of the prince." Still as loyal and loving a Massachusetts man as any, Hutchinson is actually "glad [to] have the instance of Ireland, and that so sensible a gentleman as Mr. Molineux, the friend of Mr. Locke, engaged in the cause; for it may serve as some excuse for our ancestors, that they were not alone in their mistaken apprehensions of the nature of their subjection."[81]

Much is at stake here, obviously. When the theory of Locke is added to the Molinesque premise of a plurality of "parliamentary" bodies, all equal under the headship of the King (not to mention "taxation without representation"), we have a nearly perfect epitome of the legal and constitutional question of the Revolution as we used to understand it. Very likely, "Molineux" does not mean to address itself to the problem at this technical level. But we know where we are: the colonists conspiring to oust Robin's kinsman and, eventually, to enlist Robin himself in their own partisan cause, are still laboring under the same "wrong sense" of their relation to England. The rum tax lies directly between those difficult-to-obey "acts of trade" England began to pass (and to try to enforce) in the years following the Restoration, and the Stamp Act, which would undo the career of Hutchinson himself. And the local response is as clear as ever: no such act can possibly be legal in Massachusetts; so that those who forcefully oppose it are no more outside the law than those who would forcefully execute it. Thus, if our Young Man Molineux does indeed grow up to be a version of the "well-to-do radical Boston trader" Molineux, he will only be moving into the political space originally occupied by his Irish-patriot namesake, his "Uncle Molineux."[82]

Before we decide this is a little too "much" to be other than gratuitous— some half-conscious echo of the effect of chance reading desultorily done— we should note that "Robin" itself is scarcely an innocent name in the lexicon of eighteenth-century political conspiracy. In the still Biblical New England, it sounds strangely unlike a given or "Christian" name. Almost certainly it means to put us in mind of "Robin" Walpole, so nick-named, in mock-affection, by the long list of his true-blue political enemies in England's own neo-Puritan Country Party, and of the "Robinocracy" he was accused of creating in order to stabilize the modern nation and/or to subvert the ancient constitution.[83] The "Robinarch," as the "gloomy" Bolingbroke famously explained, "is *nominally* a minister only . . . but in reality he is a sovereign, as despotic, arbitrary a sovereign as this part of the world affords." And more particularly: "The *Robinarch* . . . hath unjustly engrossed the whole power of a nation into his own hands . . . [and] admits no person to any considerable post or trust or power under him who is not either a *relation*, or *creature*, or a *thorough-paced tool* whom he can lead into any dirty work without being able to discover his designs or the consequences of them."[84] Now obviously Robin is not—and may indeed never grow up to be—that sort of wily usurper and pernicious corruptor. And yet he is, from his very outset, on his way to join what somebody's politics might easily identify as a Robinocracy.

Robin may think of himself, all innocently, as merely seeking to "profit by his kinsman's generous intentions" (225), but what his wealthy and politically influential relative has in mind, apparently, is patronage. Unless he has been *utterly* deceived by Uncle Molineux, he is on his way to some "place" or "post" in a local Royalist "establishment" (224)[85] which clearly predicts the network of interrelated appointments by which Thomas Hutchinson himself would seek to manage the political process in Massachusetts, and for which he would be accused of deeper plotting than Walpole himself. No one has mentioned those "*bribes* which are called *pensions* in these countries." And, as things turn out, Robin never will get himself "tied down with *honors, titles,* and *preferments.*" He can scarcely be said to have "sacrificed [his] principles and conscience to a set of *party names,* without any meaning, or the vanity of appearing in favor at *court.*" But none of the night-time Revolutionaries Robin encounters has any trouble recognizing him as someone "persuaded to prostitute [himself] for the lean reward of *hopes* and *promises.*"[86]

Of course this political "style" is far less proper to provincial Massachusetts than to Hanoverian England. One of the American problems, in fact—as Hutchinson himself would learn, to his dismay—was that there was not nearly *enough* patronage to make the thing work: two posts for yourself and a single place for your brother-in-law, and the local resources were pretty well exhausted; and so the native political process, with its own peculiar "genius," seemed destined to go its own ragged and illegitimate way.[87] But this fact did not prevent the local Jeremiahs, in a marvelously successful imitation of their transatlantic counterparts, from creating the impression that innocent New England was becoming as deeply mired in "corruption" as Old England at its "Egyptian" worst; or (to change the figure) that Boston was a city hellishly like London. From a sheerly rhetorical point of view, Robin might indeed be entering the one as well as the other. And apparently the outline of the problem could be discerned even at the distance of the 1730's, when the secular (and essentially alien) idea of political "parties" was only just beginning to take shape in the land founded on a myth of holy consensus.[88]

For there it all is in the story of Robin's painful initiation into the politics of conspiracy. Before this political innocent has proceeded very far in his insufficiently shrewd attempt to place himself under the patronage of his royal kinsman, he runs directly up against an impressive display of that sort of transplanted "courtliness" which lent social credence to the imported political style. "Promenading on the pavement" are a number of "gay and gallant figures" who seem on transatlantic loan from Vauxhall Gardens: "Embroidered garments of showy colors, enormous periwigs, gold-laced hats, and silver-hilted swords glided past him and dazzled his optics. Travelled youths, imitators of the European fine gentlemen of the period, trod jauntily along, half dancing to the fashionable tunes which they hummed, and making poor Robin ashamed of his quiet and natural gait" (215). It hardly matters whether these "figures" are *really* the local specimens of those "Anglicized" New Englanders already corrupted by "luxury," or whether this is all, also, part of the evening's ritual *en costume*—any more than it matters whether one is "here" in the 1730's (or Boston) or "there" in the 1770's (or London). Social reality or literary satire, the operative point is the same: an Old English Court Party has insinuated itself into the provincial life in countrified New England.[89]

The point is extended and emphasized as Robin makes "many pauses to examine the gorgeous display of goods in the shop windows" (215). Already "ashamed," the American Jonathan is now being tempted by those imported manufactures which are the social (and economic) counterpart of the political establishment he is already on his way, half-wittingly, to join. Of course Robin cannot afford to *buy* any of these luxuries: after satisfying the ferryman's demand, his "little province bill of five shillings" has returned him only a "sexangular piece of parchment, valued at three pence" (209), scarcely enough to cover the cost of a couple of "great puffy rolls." Clearly the province is suffering a serious "depreciation in [Robin's] sort of currency," and everywhere the balance of more than trade seems to be running against New England. British taxes on rum, an American "Good Creature" (212), handsomely supports a mercantile empire, which sells its gorgeous manufactures back to the provinces at prices which only those who have sold themselves to the system can afford. It may or may not be all part of some deep-dyed conspiracy of economic, then social, and then religious "enslavement," but one would scarcely be surprised to discover the existence of some local counterplot. Or, at very least, to learn that the values of the Puritanic "Country" will be resisting those of the Aristocratic "Court" in some fairly self-conscious way.[90]

Thus the second, and altogether more telling, *political* irony of Robin's reference to the man with "authority"—he of the "two sepulchral hems"—as "some country representative" (211). Robin is himself, quite obviously, the country bumpkin; but almost certainly the authoritative gentleman he encounters is a "Representative" in the intransigent local "Parliament," of the values and interests of the resistance, the "Country Party." Quite probably he is the Speaker of the Massachusetts House of Representatives: some such function is comically suggested by his continual hem-hem clearing of the throat, as if to deliver a speech; and only that position would seem to justify his reappearing, at the climax of Robin's political initiation, on the balcony of the building where that body was accustomed to hold its Molinesque deliberations. The joke is pretty broad, even though everybody seems to have missed it so far: the first man of whom Robin demands the whereabouts of his courtly kinsman turns out to be the leader of the Country Opposition, Molineux's deepest official enemy and (it seems likely) one of the principal organizers of the evening's political festivities.[91]

Everywhere, clearly, Robin locates himself in the most ironic and dangerous relation to a highly contrived and carefully orchestrated political demonstration. Indeed he seems the only person in the story who is *not* in on the plot. The reader has to learn fast or lapse himself into the psychology of adolescence.

In effect the French Protestant innkeeper tests Robin's political sympathies when he inquires, "From the country, I presume, sir?" And he anticipates the conspiratorial conclusion of Robin's guide later, when he also presumes that Robin "intend[s] a long stay with *us*" (213, my italics). But Robin knows only one magic name, "Molineux"—at the mere mention of which "there was a sudden and general movement in the room," expressing not "the eagerness of each individual to become his guide" (214) but rather the general hostility, based on the common suspicion that the well-known plan is being exposed, or satirized. No more does Robin know the local words and ways when he encounters "little parties of men . . . in outlandish attire": "They paused to address him, [but] such intercourse did not at all enlighten his perplexity. They did but utter a few words in some language of which Robin knew nothing, and perceiving his inability to answer, bestowed a curse on him in plain English and hastened away" (219). In well over his head, Robin simply does not know the password to the evening's plans and arrangements. And so, again and again, his innocent blundering comes dangerously close to provoking violent retaliation.

His situation is especially perilous just when, cudgel visibly in hand, he rudely accosts the figure with the "infernal visage." Absurdly addressing him as the philosopher's "honest man," he blatantly demands the "whereabouts [of] the dwelling of [his] kinsman, Major Molineux." At first the confrontation seems fated: "Keep your tongue between your teeth, fool, and let me pass," says the "deep, gruff voice," confident of its own power to wield the cudgel. "Let me pass, or I'll strike you to the earth." But Robin, issuing his own violent but pre-political "Don't tread on me," boldly repeats his preposterous demand; and for this repeated impertinence he receives, strangely, not a thrashing but rather the instruction to watch for an hour, when "Major Molineux will pass by" (219–220). What saves Robin is hardly the threat of his own main strength. Possibly it is his very innocence, provoking the mob leader to reveal his political role, though not his personal identity, by unmuffling what the narrator wickedly calls his "unprecedented physiognomy"—so "strange" to youthful travelers but so familiar to students of political typology. Ultimately, however, Robin is spared out of the mobster's own conspiratorial confidence, and out of that political restraint which the perpetrators of "controlled violence" can so generously afford. Apparently the movement is too well disciplined to lose its temper and waste its force on chance objects awkwardly thrown in its way.[92]

And thus the story's structural irony is never more dramatic and telling than when, at the end, the whole horrible procession comes "rolling towards the church" (227) where Robin has stationed himself. The conclusion seems preordained, as Robin uncomfortably concludes that "the double-faced fellow has his eye on me" (228). Literally, of course, Robin's perception is true enough: the mobster will indeed fix "his glance full upon the country youth," enforcing his earlier revelation, as his horse moves slowly by. But the psychoanalytic reader's nearly irresistible feeling that in some symbolic sense Robin's initiation is the goal or informing *telos* toward which the whole elaborate action tends is as critically partial as it would be politically naive.

For in a deeper sense Robin has merely bungled his way to the center of an action entirely independent of his personal anxieties, with which he has only accidentally (and perhaps proleptically) to do. The procession of political events simply moves on, as unconcerned about Robin's maturity as it is unthreatened by his politics.

Explaining Robin's instinctive sense of his own centrality and, at the same time, highlighting some more critical grasp of his relation to the events as late-come and epiphenomenal is our gradual discovery that he has in fact blundered his way to a sort of "reviewing station," past which everyone knows the well-made pageant is scheduled to pass, and from which it is being essentially (though "secretly") controlled. The procession is coming straight "at" Robin's dazed and vibrating consciousness only because he just *happens* to be standing in the place where its organizers wait to watch its dramatic progress and judge its political effect. The authoritative man with the sepulchral hem-hem is, as we have suggested, very likely the Speaker of the House of Representatives; and he appears on the balcony of the Town House to observe the public embarrassment and personal pain of his political enemy, the confirmed Royalist and would-be Robinarch Molineux.[93] He laughs cruelly enough, but not primarily at Robin; the fact that this innocent has been making political enemies thick and fast does not excuse his paranoia or justify our psychologism.

Nor are we at all safe in assuming that the apparently friendly man who stands with Robin on the steps of the church, witnessing his meeting with Uncle Molineux, is himself anything but an *arch*-conspirator. Only a species of critical wish-fulfillment will assume that he is meant to function, mythically, as some kindly superintendent of Robin's initiation. And only some extreme of textual (and political) credulity will conclude that he is actually very concerned about Robin's own best interests.[94] True, he first accosts Robin in "a tone of real kindness, which had become strange to Robin's ears" (224); but in a tale which explicitly "teaches" that a "man [may] have several voices . . . as well as two complexions" (226), we have to be alert to other tones as well. At least as alert as Robin himself, who does, in the end, finally recognize the motives of his interest in watching him watch the rites of Molineux's "passage."

Surely there is something other than simple kindness in this stranger's "singular curiosity to witness [Robin's] meeting" (225) with his much-sought kinsman. And though there is a strong hint of voyeurism, some political motive is even more obvious. Accidentally, but not in the end unusefully, Robin lends himself as an almost perfect "experiment" or test case: a leader of the rebels can observe first-hand the impact of the evening's demonstration on the political sensibilities of the rising generation. He might well wish that Robin were not *quite* so naive about the ways of the political world in the metropolis of Boston, but perhaps someone even this untutored will prove "shrewd" enough to take the point about the real path to power in the provinces. And, whatever may be true of the future, clearly this stranger knows exactly what is going on here and now.

The irony of his answers to Robin's astonishingly innocent questions is broad enough to be called sarcastic. It may even strike us as a little cruel. And certainly it gives away his own conspiratorial identity. He does indeed know the "ill-favored fellow" with the face "of two colors"; "not intimately," to be sure, but well enough to have "chanced to meet him a little time previous" and well enough to "trust his word . . . that Molineux will shortly pass through this street" (225). The principal irony here is obvious: their meeting was not at all by "chance" but by careful, conspiratorial design. Except for Robin, everyone in the story knows everyone else, and all have been conferring about the progress of the plot; everyone knows very well the established route of the procession, and only just a moment ago has the rough and visible leader made it clear to the smooth and secret organizer, by way of some final report, that everything will go off as planned. But a second, somewhat nastier irony is also discernible: *of course* this polite planner does not know his lieutenant very "intimately"; revolutionary politics may indeed make strange streetfellows, but ultimately one knows one's place.

The stranger's ironies continue broad, and only a little less cruel, in answer to Robin's inquiry about "the meaning of this uproar," as the demonstration begins in earnest: "Why, indeed, friend Robin, there do appear to be three or four riotous fellows abroad to-night" (226). Robin is temporarily distracted from the insult-value of this alien sort of rhetoric by the altogether more vital question of whether a woman may have several voices as well as a man. But ultimately he learns to use just such grown-up talk himself. At last beholding his kinsman, in all his "tar-and-feathery dignity" (228), he finally seizes the political outline of what has happened; and when he does his ironic maturity confirms our cynic suspicion.

No, Robin has *not* been "dreaming," as he bitterly realizes.[95] And "Why, yes," he is now able to reflect, "rather dryly," he *can* now be said in some manner to have "adopted a new subject of inquiry." And then, with devastating insight and not a little of that wit by which the eighteenth century knew to turn personal bitterness and political gloom into literary satire, this: "Thanks to you, and to my other friends, I have at last met my kinsman, and he will scarce desire to see my face again. I begin to grow weary of a town life, Sir. Will you show me the way to the ferry?" (230–231). Denouement indeed: to mark Robin's passage from the single-mindedness of childhood to the fallen wisdom of adult duplicity, nothing could be finer than his pose of urban weariness, worthy of the London coffee-house wag or the

Parisian *roué;* and to prove his newly acquired political intelligence (and to instruct ours), nothing could be clearer than his ironic identification of the friendly stranger as no better and no worse than all the "other friends" he has met this weary evening. He may or may not decide to "prefer to remain with us" (231), but he now knows perfectly well who "us" is.[96]

Evidently, therefore, a man may smile and smile and be, in despite of a narrator, a conspirator still. Even if that man should turn out to be a Congregationalist minister. For surely we must agree at least this far with Robert Lowell's poetically licentious identification of the man who watches Robin watch his kinsman fall from royal grace.[97] Robin has come to be on the steps of Boston's own First Church, directly across the street from the home of Massachusetts' own local "parliament," only by the sheerest and most bewildering of pre-historic accidents; but surely this calm, restrained, polite, decorous, knowing, and (yes) even friendly gentleman is exactly where he is expected to be, at his own proper reviewing post, watching a political demonstration in which the "Black Regiment" has had as deeply conspiratorial a hand as the merchant class and its political representatives.[98] There stands (so to speak) the recognized head of the local church, across from—that is to say, separate from but at least equal to—his secular counterpart, the elected head of the local government. Alike they judge the impressive result of their common machinations: not even the arrest of Andros, way back in the "miraculous" Revolution of 1689, had come off more smoothly.

It is, apparently, the "religious" significance of the evening's not entirely Puritanical sort of "merriment" which Hawthorne means to suggest in the scene of Robin's lonely reverie at the deserted church, just before its proper minister arrives to "watch." Robin begins by fondly imagining that the "large square mansion" across the street is actually Molineux's residence (and not that of the rebellious legislature). He ends by supposing, even more vainly, that this deserted church can somehow put him in touch with the values of the pious, ministerial home he has left behind. And in between, his wayward fancy feeds on even less substantial visions, involving "moon beams" as these come "trembling" in the church, falling "down upon the deserted pews," and extending themselves "along the quiet aisles." Haunted mind, indeed. Unless we are tone deaf, or unless we have *already* overinvested in the pseudo-Wordsworthian significance of "moonlight on a child's shoe," we will surely conclude that the narrator's sentimental diction gives away the author's ironic game:

A fainter yet more awful radiance was hovering around the pulpit, and one solitary ray had dared to rest upon the open page of the great Bible. Had Nature, in that deep hour, become a worshiper in the house which man had builded? Or was that heavenly light the visible sanctity of the place,—visible because no earthly and impure feet were within the walls? (222)

The scene makes "Robin's heart shiver with a sensation of loneliness," but it is supposed to make our skin—and our suspicion—itch just a bit: what *are* we to make of an empty church? And why *should* we speculate about the idea of "visible sanctity" (that strict and definitive mark of Puritan ecclesiology) so oddly warped and romanticized? Here's the church. And here, presumably, is the steeple. Climb (absurdly) up "a window-frame"; and—*where are all the people!*

In the street, one readily concludes. Marching "towards the church" in apocalyptic procession, led by a "single horseman, clad in military dress and bearing a drawn sword," a man whose "variegated countenance" caused him to appear like "war personified" (227). The majestic calm of "visible sanctity" has given way to the "counterfeited pomp," the "senseless uproar," and the "frenzied merriment" of that ungodly mob which christened itself "the Boston Saints." So that this totally unwonted merriment can, under the aspect of the problem of "Puritanism and Revolution," be referred to quite fairly and technically as *"congregated* mirth" (230, my italics).[99]

Evidently these riotous saints are not coming to rest at Robin's particular church. Almost certainly the procession turns the corner and continues on, slowly and by design, to the Old South Church, across from the Province House, the official residence of the royal governor. For there, most usually, were revolutionary meetings most notoriously held, in order to obtain maximum visibility and intimidation.[100] It might take these Boston Saints several more decades to get there, in literal political fact. But given the story's own wickedly figural chronology, we know very well where events are tending—as new taxes breed new riots, and deeper fears of enslavement spawn subtler conspiracies of resistance.

Robin, of course, cares very little about where next the Revolutionary Procession may pause. His own story ends on a very distinctive note of ironic insight and political suspense: a light having gone out of his world, he scarcely concerns himself with the Tendency of Great Events. He may yet grow up to help speed the cause of the American Revolution, but he will hardly think to view the whole affair as "majestic." He has watched the beginners of the process end by "trampling all on an old man's heart" (230), and he may have noticed, in the process, that contrivance is not the same thing as Design. He may even be about to suspect that man's providences are but accidental to the Universal Plan. Other Americans might yet learn the lesson.

*   *   *

Perhaps the last word in "My Kinsman, Major Molineux" *will* always concern Robin himself, the meaning of his own youthful dis-illusion, the nature and extent of his own initiation. Whatever the audience of 1826 needed to learn, few modern readers (I suppose) will be convinced that Robin's presence on the "reviewing stand" of the Molineux procession is in every sense accidental; or that the political enrichment achieved by locating the tale, subtly, amidst "the Ideological Origins of the American Revolution" can quite account for its full fascination. Clearly, by now, Robin's growing pains cannot be taken for the whole of Hawthorne's plot; and yet they are, just as clearly, an integral part. In contrast to certain of Hawthorne's later political stories, the evident fact is that here some anxious adolescent does indeed get his first hint of the relative unsimplicity of things-in-general upon the occasion of a chance encounter with some ironic and wildly overspecified political prefiguration. Probably we need to conclude by explaining why this should be so.

And yet we must learn to do this very carefully. We need to recognize, first of all, that it is no longer fair to conclude that within the terms of historical analysis "the great bulk of the tale, Robin's quest, remains sheer Gothic mystification."[101] For at every step the tale deepens its political irony in direct relation to Robin's enduring naiveté. Probably most readers will feel defrauded if, in the end, Robin proves nothing more than a literary device, a figure off of which the tale repeatedly scores its dramatic ironies. But surely this dynamic accounts for very much of the tale's conscious strategy. And we need to imagine that the gap between historical reach and literary grasp might be narrowed still further, by anyone unorthodox enough to pursue the lead of teasing allusion and to resist, temporarily, the nearly irresistible lure of *passage.*

The obvious example would be Robin's encounter with the "pretty mistress" who shows him a "strip of scarlet petticoat." Conceding that sexual experience is, nowadays at least, everywhere a more vital and interesting subject than ecclesiological or even apocalyptic theory, one may still want to insist that this "lady of the scarlet petticoat" (217), who claims to reside in Major Molineux's own house, probably has a figural-political as well as a literal-sexual identity. No ordinary prostitute set out to lure the farm boys, she is easily recognizable as a figure of that Scarlet woman, the "Whore of Babylon," whose Romish outline American Puritans always seemed to discern behind the shape of the Anglican Church, and whose fatal charms seemed to have been spread abroad, from Babylonish England, as part of some total strategy of slavish entrapment. Apparently a *variety* of "hopes and promises" invite Robin to "prostitute" himself.[102]

And, beyond this classic contest of sexual surface with political symbol, it

is absolutely essential to notice how the single most improbable and astonishing formal detail in the entire story—the view the "Man in the Moon"
takes of the whole riotous affair—actually confirms our critical sense of the
large-scale irrelevance of Robin's painful anxieties. Quite obviously and deliberately, Hawthorne's tale does whatever it can to upset our ordinary
range of assumption and response. Ultimately, our psychological empathy
must stand against some really *cosmic* view or lapse into the somewhat pathetic fallacy of misplaced sentiment.

Just when the "contagion"[103] of cruel and barbarous laughter has engulfed Robin himself, so that now everyone (except of course Major Molineux) seems united in sending a "congregated mirth . . . roaring up to the
sky"; just at the moment when Molineux's abasement seems most piteously
and terribly complete and when, accordingly, Robin's own anxious passage
from innocent separation to guilty participation seems most painfully accomplished; just when, that is, our primary human sympathies seem most
powerfully and primally engaged, the scene (or at least the point of view)
suddenly shifts. Suddenly, and just before the human pain lapses into some
myth in which "fiends . . . throng in mockery around some dead potentate,"
everything waxes calm, cosmic, and even jolly. Apparently the "Man in the
Moon" can be thought to have "heard the far below," and to have a view
sufficiently disinterested to be worth considering; and the rare detachment
of this ultimate structuralist threatens to embarrass our moral earnestness
even more seriously than the ironies of the "friendly" stranger satirize
Robin: " 'Oho,' quoth he, 'the old earth is frolicsome to-night!' " (230).
Frolicsome indeed, under the aspect of eternity: one more night of rowdy
misrule, one more "temporary inflammation of the popular mind," one
more "revolution" among the numberless and continual turnings of sublunary events. One more anxious adolescent, it may be; it scarcely matters
what—those earthly fellows are at it *again.*

Here, then, would be the ultimate insult which the deflationist strategy of
"My Kinsman, Major Molineux" offers to the vaunted claims of American
typological historiography: so far from being a unique and climactic event in
the unfolding of Divine Purpose, the "majestic" Revolution is no more remarkable, "structurally," than any other local resistance to local authority;
and no more distinctive, "psychoanalytically," than the anxious overflow of
Oedipal emotion. Compared, from the outset, to a rum riot in the 1730's,
and discovered, throughout, to be a thoroughly plotted and stage-managed
affair, the entire episode is revealed, at the end, to amount to nothing more
than one or another form of utterly local unruliness.

The same deliberately "reductionist" insight will, not incidentally, put
into immediate and perfect perspective all of Hawthorne's famous anticipations of Sir James Frazer. Here, as in "The May-Pole" later, pagan myth

149

spreads out to surround the swelling pretensions of Puritanic vision until, at the limits of coherence, we are forced to recognize *nothing* new under the moon. For if the long-ranged definition of Major Molineux as "dead potentate" seriously threatens his more parochial identity as conspiratorial Robinocrat, still that relatively timeless definition is itself first embarrassed by and then subsumed into the absolutely "secular" view of the Man in the Moon. The ritual of the "Scapegoat King" is far older and more venerable than the night-time activities of the Boston Saints or the civil-millennial vision of "Apocalyptic Whiggism"; but the lunar theory of "frolic" comprehends them both. They are at it again. Thus does time, in the midst of some midworld evening's trauma, "fold us music-drunken in."[104]

We respond, of course, by reformulating the political significance and re-emphasizing the human pain from our own, equally valid, sublunary point of view. Governments are not *entirely* like streetcars, as mortal men structure their common life; and crises of loyalty and relation are the very substance of our identity, as sexual energy erupts into consciousness. And it is in just such a philosophical mood that we think to *answer* the moon (and solve the critical ambiguity) with a "compromise" theory of the relation between politics and analysis in "Molineux." Without denying the lunar view that political revolutions are just as inevitable (and almost as common) as Oedipal strife, we may want to add that they are, as well, equally violent and painful, as even Grandfather's youthful auditors had to learn. And, reversing our sense of sign and signified, we may want to insist that the passage from adolescence to adulthood is just as definitively significant for the life of the human individual as any political revolution ever was (or was claimed to be) for the life of a nation. We confidently imagine that Hawthorne could well have been interested in the significance of *both*, separately and at once. And, with growing literary confidence, we think to propose that perhaps it has been Hawthorne's intention so to join tenor and vehicle that we cannot assign primacy to either the individual or the social passage. Each one illuminates the other.[105]

Perhaps. And yet another, far more ironic interpretation also suggests itself, especially to anyone who has followed the "progress" of American ideology from provincial Jeremiad to national myth. Such a person might want to suggest that, in the name of literary reconciliation, it is all too easy to pass from one "story" to another, without ever facing the issue of reality. For if the dominant view of the American Revolution was, in 1826, still some survival of that pseudo-Puritan "propaganda" of Holy History used by the participants to justify their revolt, nevertheless that view was even then being challenged by a proto-Freudian "literature" of growing up; and if the new explanation were in many ways opposite to the old one, it was nevertheless at least equal in its power to neutralize the guilty memories of violent rebellion. A culture critic of Hawthorne's severity could easily have noticed that the new, more literary "history," obscuring as much as it clarified, was at least as objectionable as the old one.

Of course the older ideology of Protestant Destiny never really died, susceptible as it was of ever more subtle (and idolatrous) translation; and yet it was, in Hawthorne's Jacksonian Age, beginning to fail as a single persuasive account of the events of 1776. But even as it began to lapse, it was all too easily supplanted by an explanation which, equally large, also refused to face head-on the crucial questions of contingent local conspiracy and voluntary local violence. If the Revolution were not, clearly, the crowning denouement of God's Plot, then surely it was, inevitably, an irresistible part of Nature's Plan. Jefferson had declared it in the quaint idiom of the Enlightened *Philosophe:* evidently there comes a time, "in the course of human events," when nations, just like individuals, need to assume that "separate and equal station to which the laws of Nature and Nature's God entitle them." And then a whole chorus of literary nationalists translated the political insight into its inevitable literary form, the Romantic *bildungsroman:* the American Revolution was *just like* growing up.[106]

The problem, of course, was that human time and ordinary sublunary change continued to drag their slow length along, with the same unapocalyptic insignificance in Republican America as they had in plodding and provincial Massachusetts or in merry and monarchical England. And so what could *not* be rationalized in Divine Teleology needed some justification in human process. All things grow and change, even America. The process is continuous, for the most part; and yet there are moments when national identity undergoes the temporary though painful and confusing process of changing relations. The temporary disorientation is regrettable, in a sense; but not ultimately so, for in the long run maturation is inevitable and necessary. In the vast number of cases, the adolescent comes through. And so— as Robin's features begin to lose their troubled distinction—did we.

And yet that famous psychopolitical story will not *quite* tell itself here, in the midst of the weird moment when Robin's divided consciousness vibrates back and forth between the pastoral pursuits of the rural countryside and the political policies of the Country Party, and when our own doubled vision watches the Revolution pre-enact itself as a rum riot. Surely the particular complexities of Hawthorne's historical emplotment embarrass the simplicity of the new myth, at the outset, as clearly as they reduce the majesty of the old one in the moment of its eclipse. For the two stories Hawthorne is telling are in fact quite different. Neither is anything like a perfect recapitulation of the other. That, ultimately, is the point of insisting on the redundant overspecification of the political world into which Robin has wandered: it has a contingent and even, in a sense, a factitious life of its own. Robin's moment of passage may be scientifically predetermined by "the course of human events," but rum riots and tea parties require local plans and private invitations.

None of the conspirators in the story cares at all about Robin's stage along life's way. And surely all of them are absolutely convinced that *they* (and not he) represent "Young America."[107] He may just happen to start to grow up in the midst of their political demonstration; the thing always happens somewhere; and if he does, then he is welcome enough to join in. But *only* the moon could fail to notice all the differences. Only some excessively simplistic will-to-structure will ever confuse the subtle and necessary pain endured in the natural process of growing up to manhood with the gross and (in a sense) gratuitous suffering inflicted by the political actions required to throw off an alien government.[108]

Accordingly, therefore, we are left with two stories, unreconciled—as Hawthorne resists the conflations of America's political psychologism at the outset. Robin Molineux grows up *just when* his Royalist uncle is being tarred and feathered for Robinocracy; he passes beyond his own "Season of Youth" *just when* America is beginning to exercise its conspiratorial imagination. But his experiences are not *just like* anything else, unless they be like *all other* transitions under the moon. But at that level of generality all political discrimination, like all human intelligence, lapses into cosmic indistinction. Such a view might serve well enough as a sort of religion; indeed the utter secularity of its insistence on "vanity" usefully counteracts the cosmic teleology of Puritan politics. Or it might serve as some new "ideology" of the American Revolution—as anxious to minimize questions of local causation and local guilt, in the name of literary form, as the older theory had been, in the name of God. But it is a poor way to study life in the provinces.

Here, as elsewhere, Hawthorne's revisionist strategy validates all sorts of conflationist tactics. To emphasize the altogether unabstract suffering of the Revolution, he allows the figurative torture of Major Molineux to mingle with our memory of the real-life hazing of Governor Hutchinson.[109] To increase our sense of the undeniable evil being perpetrated (in whatever cause, toward whatever end), he momentarily permits the tragic view of this event to merge with the Tory theology of rebellion. To remind us—at the same time, but on the other hand—of the un-majesty of political resistance, he structures the whole event as a local riot; and he even comes to the verge of conflating the revolutionary beginnings of the American republic with an Oedipal itch. But there his ironies stop and even begin to reverse themselves. He plainly resists the all-too-reassuring view that revolutionary politics recaptitulates adolescent psychology: maturation is painful but it knows nothing of conspiracy.

And so we are left, deliberately, with Robin's *difference*. He has finally entered into an adult world, but he remains very little representative of its historic complexity. He has finally learned what the reader has had to know all along—that, politically as otherwise, grown-ups have a story which boys do not know. But his "moral adventure" is quite different from their historical plot. *His* story is not *theirs*. *His* story is, quite simply, the discovery that they do indeed have one. The reader must know *their* story to appreciate Robin's own (for Robin discovers far more than scarlet petticoats and ambiguity); but he may not, without political naiveté, pretend they are the same. He can decide to choose between the two stories, but any such "reading" must always seem selective and and willful, the result of his own literary bias or preferred style of interpretation rather than of Hawthorne's controlling intention. For in the ironic structure of Hawthorne's complex and even deconstructive tale, the two stories are as inseparable as they are different: everybody grows up somewhere, but Robin passes out of adolescence in the process of discovering, first-hand, the distressing secrets of a provincial politics already rather shrewdly adult. In this tale, at least, the formal purity of universal *bildungsroman* will not quite subsume the ragged matter of local conspiracy.

Evidently Robin gets a rather heavy dose of reality—heavier, obviously, than that prescribed for Lawrence and his friends by Grandfather, who really *does* exist to supervise their passage from chauvinism to charity, even as he mediates their experience of political history through a form of personal literature.[110] Accordingly, therefore, we are not unduly surprised to learn that Robin would like to "go back." But we must avoid imitating him, even momentarily; for we have, after all, the advantage of *his* mediation. If his first experience of real politics is significantly stark and not a little cruel, still his own drastic experience is designed to ease the reader's political transition from righteousness to irony. The "old-style" (or Puritanic) reader is supposed to be reminded that as the ways of Special Providence are often a little rough, so America's revolutionary origins can seem relentlessly ordinary and noticeably guilty. And the "new-style" (or psychologistic) reader is tempted but forbidden to reduce politics to *passage*. If he does so reduce the complexity of one of Hawthorne's most perfectly crafted tales, he will surely involve himself in a moral regression far worse than Robin's own last-stated wish. For after the lapse of innocence, natural or theologic, nothing protects us from the ugly facts of political life quite so well and comfortably as that literary miracle in which brutal psychic law achieves its formal redemption as national myth.

4

 器 器

We are often tempted to think of Hawthorne's age as "Adamic," populated by a race of perfectly self-reliant men and women who disavowed ancestry and scorned tradition—as if Every American were, in those days, some version of Daniel Boone about to be apotheosized as Leatherstocking or, alternately, some walled-in Transcendentalist about to break forth into a "Song of the Open Road." Surely this is a drastically partial view of the case, especially in the 1820's and 1830's, when certain "provincial" reminiscences seemed to Hawthorne a meaningful project. For one thing, it omits at least half of the participants in R. W. B. Lewis' most famous version of this emerging national myth: not a few American writers, it seems, explicitly *denied* that American experience was a journey on which the Soul accomplished "nothing save the journey . . . accomplishing herself by the way." And even the Adamic prophets had no sense of speaking for a spiritual independence already achieved. On the contrary: the Transcendental gospel of liberation from the past is almost always delivered as inspired prediction rather than accomplished fact; the saving power of the "original relation" is, evidently, still to be discovered by a deeply conservative and inhibited majority.[111]

Furthermore, certain ordinary evidences not always considered by our more intellectual anthropologists tend to suggest that the power of the Party of the Past was firmly entrenched indeed. The popularity of the genre of the historical romance is itself an indication of this fact; and the tendency of the popular romancers to hallow rather than to criticize certain already famous chapters in the American "story" only increased their power—and its.[112] The flourishing institution of the historico-patriotic sermon points to the same conclusion: on the Fourth of July, on the newly regularized Thanksgiving Day, and on all sorts of local and national election days, the American citizen reverentially recalled the past before thinking to project himself ahead. He well knew the glorious future was not to be separated from the heroic past. Indeed, he might even wonder whether he himself were quite *worthy* of that future, *de*-scended as he knew himself to be from "such ancestors," those august and accomplished forebears he reverenced at Bunker's or at Lovewell's or at Plymouth's monument. He might or might not be less committed to ordinary Puritanic or Republican virtue, but the bare moral fact scarcely seemed to matter. For one thing, all the great deeds seemed already done. And for another, that was the way "the American Jeremiad" worked: typic heroism lay behind; anti-typic glory stretched ahead; but in between, in the urgent now of self-examination, anxiety alone sufficed.[113]

Nor is it irrelevant to recall, in this context, that the years of Hawthorne's "provincial" beginnings were also the golden years of American antiquarianism. To be sure, the Massachusetts Historical Society had come into existence before the Spirit of 1776 was itself quite extinct—as if, in Massachusetts at least, ideological self-perpetuation were part of the great revolutionary deed itself. But all of New England's own local institutions developed at a later moment, which extends down to the precise point of Hawthorne's emergence into literary manhood. And they all seem to evince a slightly different spirit: bent on preserving absolutely *everything* that pertained to America's colonial birth and provincial adolescence, they seemed to affirm that it was the part of patriotism to reverence everything *American*, if not as some "magnalium," then simply as such. Clearly they meant to bind Americans to their local as well as their national past.[114] And thus the very institutions that made possible "Hawthorne's Reading" served also to give it intellectual focus and thematic point.

To be sure, a growing number of ambitious literary men had already issued an impressive series of declarations of literary independence. But in repudiating the corrupting models of Europe, they did not at all forswear the influence of *all* human history. Indeed the cause of American literary independence regularly identified itself with the value of the particular American past, however barren it might seem to eyes of foreigners and other jaded men. This is precisely what it meant to propose certain specific "matters" for an American literature: the source of our transcendent glory lies hidden in the local records of the local heroism of our Puritan, Indian-Fighting, and Revolutionary ancestors.[115] Only in Emerson, apparently, was the issue of literary independence nearly allied with the more radical (and potentially Oedipal) cause of "the plain old Adam, the simple genuine self."

It seems only proper, therefore, to imagine Hawthorne's primary and original audience as still a fit subject of Solomon Stoddard's anti-Jeremiad teachings "Concerning Ancestors." Only a sectarian minority might still remain so literalistically loyal to Puritanic folkways as to experience Congregational "Sacrament Days" as "Days of Torment"; and to them a newly liberated Emerson would go on to direct his infamous and patricidal "Divinity School Address." But surely a fledgling disciple of Scott might observe that a much more significant portion of the American populace still required a lower-case reminder of Stoddard's larger concern: "It may possibly be a fault and an aggravation of a fault to depart from the ways of our fathers; but it may also be a virtue and an eminent act of obedience to depart from them in some things."[116] Politically, Hawthorne's Jacksonian America might well know that "the earth belongs always to the living generation"—

though by 1851 Hawthorne's *House of the Seven Gables* would still be struggling with the ambiguities of that definitive Jeffersonian proposition. And, however that may be, surely the author of "The Provincial Tales" must be thought of as meditating on Stoddard's general observation that "the mistakes of one generation many times become the calamity of succeeding generations."[117]

Not that Hawthorne thought of America as *itself* an ancestral "mistake," to be repented in prefaces and atoned through the symbolic acts of fiction. Though a good deal of evidence suggests that Hawthorne regarded all of America's various theories of its own "exceptionalism" as theologically misguided and politically dangerous, he was in fact emotionally content to have had "such ancestors" as the Puritans, and intellectually satisfied that the "hearts and minds" of America's Revolutionaries were ruled, for the most part, by "honorable motives." And not even the bitter ironies of Indian supplantation in "Main Street" quite cancel out Hawthorne's sense that the ugly realities of Indian Warfare—strategically obscured by the "chivalry" of "Roger Malvin's Burial"—were somehow inevitable.[118] The point was not at all to repudiate America, any more than it was in any simple sense to liberate and empower the Natural Man. Not until the second half of the 1850's did Hawthorne ever seriously consider the possibility of renouncing New England to become a "citizen of someplace else." And even then he only proved, in *The Marble Faun*, that as an artist he could never escape the conscience of Puritan America.

Even less meaningful, therefore, would be the project of learning to *hate* America, as if to prove the mature finality of one's intellectual separation from its dominant ideology. The point was simply to *understand* it. Or, if that were too naive, as either historical purpose or literary project, one could at least learn to see, and in fiction to show, where the available and growing national "story" was dangerously wrong. Where many others solemnly memorialized and made monuments, and a few free spirits made bold to repudiate, Hawthorne sought to criticize and deconstruct. But even this complex and ironic procedure might yield certain political and psychological benefits.

It is just possible to imagine that many of Hawthorne's most apparently historical fictions—once judged to be the product of an imagination so alienated from the present as simply to have fled to the past for refuge—were actually written *on behalf of* the rising generation. And quite deliberately so. Clearly Hawthorne's more famous narrators share the obvious problems of that generation. The ironic protagonist of "The Story Teller" will (very shortly) be trying to get away from the inhibiting influence of the Puritanic Parson Thumpcushion too far and too fast; but surely his creator does not want him simply to go *back*. And the more nearly autobiographical (but *still* ironic) narrator of "The Custom House" would like nothing better than to pay his hereditary debts to the familiar past, discharge his literary obligations to his ghostly predecessor Pue, and get on with the business of Jacksonian democracy and Trollopian realism. To be sure, the implied author of "Malvin" and "Molineux" seems as angry concerning certain mythic misinformations about Indian Warfare and the Revolution as the explicit narrator of "Alice Doane" is about the general ignorance of "What Happened in Salem." But the point, evidently, is not simply to disabuse the innocence of the audience with a stiff dose of past ugliness. It might also be, apparently, to free up the present generation for meaningful political and moral action of its own by placing the past in a more critical or realistic perspective.

It is not, after all, only "guilt" that is "most tellingly imputed to us through our history." And if Professor Pearce's special sense of imputed "righteousness" seems a little in excess of Hawthorne's ironic case, then there is still Lewis' sense of "irony" itself. For surely Hawthorne did belong to that distinct third party, the Party of Irony.[119] From that vantage, the point about America's past was not that it was ugly and depraved rather than holy and heroic; only that it was so predictably *provincial*, which is to say *ordinary* from a moral point of view. Of course Indians were ignobly killed in securing the frontier; how could anyone have imagined frontier killings as pure and chivalric? Of course the Revolutionaries conspired in taverns to embarrass local officials; when did the Spirit of an Age ever express itself spontaneously and without political organization? And perhaps even the witchcraft—to return to what seemed the blackest colonial case— was itself a natural and political rather than a mysterious and diabolical episode in the curiously mixed pre-history of the American Republic; certainly it did not require hysterical interpretations of the character of Cotton Mather.

The point of this reduced and ironic re-cognition of the past would be double, as irony is always double. On the one hand, nobody should think to flatter himself by rehearsing the American past as one long and unbroken train of *magnalia*. Error, infirmity, and crime there abundantly were; not so much as to rival Imperial Rome, perhaps; nor even, as it turned out, sufficient to sponsor a full-length American gothic romance; but quite enough, surely, to dot the landscape of historical imagination, here and there, with a fair number of negative monuments in "dark funeral stone." Here the "persecution" of the witches (or Mrs. Hutchinson, or Roger Williams, or the Quakers); there the hazing of "Loyalists," from Dr. Bullivant to Thomas Hutchinson; and just beyond, where gigantic rocks still lodged amidst unfelled trees, the repeated tactics of a continuous strategy of supplantation.[120] But on the other hand, the very recognition of these facts, in all their depressing inevitability (without which, no America) might somehow *enable* the present generation—not by liberating it altogether from the "measles and mumps" of history, or fully empowering any supposed natural innocence, but rather by reducing the exemplary or typological binding power of the past to realistic (and psychologically manageable) proportions. If the American past were, after all, simply provincial in its manners and barely ordinary in its moral sense, then surely the present might feel qualified enough to interpret its meaning without misplaced awe and then to pursue its own moral projects without misplaced and futile guilt. It might yet feel "reduced"; but it would no longer need to measure itself by a standard "elevated" to the point of mystification.

It may thus be useful, at least momentarily, to associate Hawthorne's historical projects not only with the theological presentism of Stoddard, but also with the moral realism of a fair number of other "latter-day" Puritans who had earlier sought to alleviate the Oedipal anxieties of several generations of Puritan sons without at the same time flattering their moral vanity. No more than Samuel Willard (or William Hubbard or Urian Oakes) did Hawthorne wish to say that I, you, and America are all "OK," free to do our own things (or pull our own strings) without let or hindrance.[121] Without *at all* licensing natural energy unchecked, Hawthorne does seem to have sworn enmity to every sort of ancestor worship, including the tyranny of typology.

The point seems abundantly clear in "Malvin" and "Molineux," where ancestral heroism is first reduced to crime and then leveled out to the provincial ordinariness of democratic guilt as such. The moral vision of "Alice Doane's Appeal" seems, at first blush, a little more hysterical—even as, in some strong way, the crimes (of a few) against the accused witches had come to seem much blacker than the crimes (of the many) against Tories and Indians. But then the inception of that fable has indeed seemed earlier than that of the various "Provincial Tales." And in the re-telling we can see that the author is himself blushing a bit, realizing how he may have permitted his audience their gothic simplification of his more elegant moral and historical point. And even "The Wives of the Dead," which had seemed so innocent of historical irony at first glance, may yet share in this complex revision of the American past as merely "provincial." Read off from its own records, which include newspaper narratives *at least* as cogently as Thanksgiving Day ideologies, the happy accidents of the past can seem just that. And perhaps it is not overly tendentious for the moral historian to imagine that perfect Christian community, devoid of sentimental false delicacy and energized instead by some perfect benevolence to Being in General, was probably as hard to achieve "then" as it is "now."

Certainly we must suppose that some such re-visionist attitude and deconstructive habit were pretty fully developed in Hawthorne by the time he turned his attention to the Problem of the Puritans. Quite probably Hawthorne took up this subject not by ancestral or even by theological compulsion but, much more innocently, as one of the three major "matters" which everyone seemed to argue were inevitable for the writer who did *not* want to be Irving or Longfellow. But quite evidently it becomes, almost immediately, the "flood subject"—not only, literally, of his first and most *simply* historical phase but also, metaphorically, of his entire source-haunted career. Hawthorne became and remained compelled not so much by "origins" as by stories *about* origins; and, whoever *actually* invented America, the Puritans had evidently got the drop on the American imagination. So that without some sense of "the Hawthornesque" as something like Historical Irony, we would be doomed to wander forever among the pleasing vagaries of "Hawthorne's Ambivalence Toward Puritanism."[122]

With this sense, however, we are ready to confront the complexities of "The Gentle Boy," the longest and in many ways the most ambitious of the tales we can certainly identify as "provincial." With this sense we become at least as aware of precise thematic meanings controlled by apt historical allusions as we have always been of formal difficulties generated by ultimate theological uncertainty or by youthful artistic overreach. With this sense, that the moral investigations of the "The Gentle Boy" are as determinedly provincial as they are inevitably cosmic, we can begin to measure the historical slant of Hawthorne's decidedly oblique approach to the most enduring problems which Calvinistic literature had bequeathed to an age of democratic liberalism.

❧ Three ❧

THE PURITAN BIAS

NATURE, VIRTUE, AND "THE GENTLE BOY"

I F "My Kinsman, Major Molineux" and "Roger Malvin's Burial" treat, in Hawthorne's own peculiar way, the matter of the Revolution and the matter of the Indians, "The Gentle Boy" brings us to his extended and penetrating consideration of the matter of Puritanism. Given the ambiguities of "The Hollow of the Three Hills" and of the original "Alice Doane," it seems proper to regard "The Gentle Boy" as something of a beginning: it is the first Hawthorne tale which clearly and in its original form deals with the nature and effects of Puritan piety. And, contrary to a rather widely received opinion, Hawthorne's later revisions of the story did not materially affect its essentially historical character.[1] Thus if we are interested in the original impulse or "bias" of Hawthorne's treatment of the Puritans (whether of method or of doctrine), we have to begin with "The Gentle Boy." This consideration alone should encourage us to give the tale a fuller and fairer reading than it has so far received. But there is more: even as Hawthorne deals with what William Ellery Channing had called the "tendencies" of Puritan piety, he reveals something about his own deepest convictions, his "theology," as we should not scruple to call it. Only at this level is "The Gentle Boy" in fact a "very fine story" which we "need to reread."[2]

To be sure, the tale is flawed: one major difficulty is, as many critics have recognized, a certain profusion of invention and, consequently, a diffusion of emphasis and even a blurring of focus. The tale contains far more material than Hawthorne could possibly exploit within the limits he set himself—enough, probably, for a romance as long as *The Scarlet Letter*. Some of Hawthorne's famous revisions try to sharpen his emphasis. They are, it must be admitted, not entirely successful: the best one can claim is that there is, in the tortured religious careers of Quaker Catherine and Failed-Puritan Tobias Pearson, a certain large, emotional, "romantic unity." But even as we criticize the author's disposition of his material, something about his basic invention refuses to be dismissed; indeed the very scope of the tale's discovery or *donnée* is part of its power. Hawthorne's troubled partiality toward this story is well known: "Nature," he explained, had "here led him deeper into the universal heart than art [had] been able to follow." This might sound like a defensive cliché; and of course it is possible that his judgment may have been affected, retrospectively, by that of Sophia Peabody. But it seems otherwise credible that he did genuinely sense that he had come, in "The Gentle Boy," closer to his own most important realities than in any of his other early tales.[3] Here, we can legitimately feel, he was not only working in his proper historical mode, but he was also bearing down on his truest subject, those "miserable distortions of the moral nature" which he always felt Puritanism tended to produce. Perhaps something of his own natural self was indeed too much called forth.

The other problem concerns the literalness we may sense in parts of the tale. Certain portions of the 1832 version, particularly, may remind us more of the discursive factuality of the sketches of "Governor Phips," "Mrs. Hutchinson," and "Dr. Bullivant" than of the dramatic fictionality (and ironic compression) of "Malvin" and "Molineux." And even where the tale seems most daringly figurative, it is still clear that Hawthorne is not quite ready for the metaphoric speculations of "Young Goodman Brown" or the allegoric deconstructions of "The May-Pole of Merry Mount." But perhaps a close examination may reveal that the differences are more in degree than in kind. It is true, of course, that the tale's most important revisions were aimed at relieving something of the sense of literal historicity. But only a radical misunderstanding of Hawthorne's historical intentions and methods has led critics to argue that the revisions show him moving away from cultural specificity and into psychological generality. Ultimately "The Gentle Boy" does not become less historical for being made less literal. We must learn to deal with that method, in a Puritan context, as elsewhere.

1

Considered as history, the "method" of "The Gentle Boy" is simple enough: Hawthorne attempts to make a single and essentially fictional tale of moral crisis and conflict stand as somehow the imaginative equivalent of a complex set of historical occurrences or conditions. We start with a "fact," that painful sectarian conflict which resulted in the persecution and execution of Quakers. The fact has considerable interest in itself: we would like to know about the moral climate which surrounded such an historical circumstance. But since the method of fiction is neither analytical nor cumulatively factual, we get a scene or several scenes of dramatic conflict which are controlled by and hence reveal similar moral conditions. In every case the purpose is double—to expose the moral premises which shaped the experience of the past and to discover how it might have felt to live in such a moral climate. The method presupposes that the writer has already grasped, from an acquaintance with the more usual sources of historical study, a familiarity with certain conditions of the past, an interest in exploring them further, and (on the assumption that he has read more or thought more than his imagined readers) a wish to communicate to them his own lively (if troubled) sense of the past. And, as we are finally beginning to appreciate, it is reactionary to deny that Hawthorne possessed all of these qualifications, interests, and motives.[4]

As a way of "doing" history, Hawthorne's method is theoretically compatible with any period of time, governed by any set of moral premises; and it may be used in conjunction with almost any number of "literary" techniques. Thus, at one level, "The Gentle Boy," "My Kinsman, Major Molineux," and "Roger Malvin's Burial" all employ the same method. Its fundamental assumptions are epistemological; and they are "realist" rather than "nominalist." This method is a species of "History as Romantic Art" not because it is limited essentially to a non-rational tonality or moral atmosphere but because it is affective rather than positivist in basic intention and because, accordingly, it claims an extraordinary latitude in the creation of poetic figures to stand as historic types. It asserts, implicitly but on every page, that fiction's tendency to create a figure to embody or representatively characterize a whole complex of historical persons or conditions or assumptions is not incompatible with a very serious attempt to understand the literal past as in some sense it "was." Hawthorne was, evidently, pledged to the principle of Scott and Manzoni: "to represent by means of an invented action, the state of mankind in a past, historic epoch." Accordingly, "The Gentle Boy" offers us Tobias and Catherine as figures of humankind in that seventeenth-century epoch we call "Puritan." This historical provenance is clear from the outset.[5]

Thus the sketch with which "The Gentle Boy" begins is the longest and most detailed in any of Hawthorne's historical tales. Even with the substantial deletions of 1837, Hawthorne gives us a full and firm location in a precise, historically recognizable situation: "In the course of the year 1656, several of the people called Quakers, led, as they professed, by the inward movement of the spirit, made their appearance in New England." They knew enough to expect martyrdom for their doctrines which, in their stress on the spiritual autonomy of the inner light and the integrity of the private conscience, were considered "mystic and pernicious" in Massachusetts; but they came for that very reason, all too "eager to testify against the oppression which they hoped to share." They came *to be* persecuted. The resulting clash between the enthusiastic individual's right to dissent and the theocratic community's demand for conformity is not pleasant to recall: the Puritans "liberally" granted the Quakers ample opportunity to bleed for a cause. But however unpleasant, the passions of the clash were real and may be studied in the historians of either side.[6] One finds them even in the eighteenth-century Quaker historian Sewell; he takes bitter satisfaction in the "death by rottenness" of the governor of Massachusetts who brought affairs to the historical climax of a double martyrdom in 1659—when, on an autumn evening, the fictive action about to be introduced is said to begin.

The reader immediately grasps that there is guilt on both sides. With or without Hawthorne's overly cautious (and eventually deleted) qualifications concerning the extent of Quaker provocation and the importance of the Puritan unity which was being challenged, and despite his explicit reference to the "indelible stain of blood . . . upon the hands of all who consented to this act" of persecution and martyrdom, the guilt is clearly seen as not simple or one-sided.[7] If the point of the tale were to fix responsibilities, Hawthorne would plainly be entitled to praise for the adult and undeceived character of his judgments. The reader further sees that, in some sense, this is the way things always are: sectarian warfare never seems to advance the cause of true religion, and yet it continues unabated; evidently it rests on principles of human nature that are not easily eradicated. And finally the acute reader senses that the whole episode is susceptible of a psychoanalytic analysis, as masochists confront sadists. All of these ideas are firmly rooted in Hawthorne's historical sources; they are clearly implied in the rippling ironies of his introductory remarks; and all reappear as part of the surface of the story itself. None of them needs to be extracted from the tale as an inner or symbolic meaning because all are part of the literal vehicle itself, a story of persecution in seventeenth-century New England.[8]

The most striking fact about the introduction, then, is not the range of "deep" meanings its historicism struggles to express, but rather the intensity with which it centers a number of relatively sophisticated considerations on a circumstance of history. The tale proper—the story of Tobias and Dorothy Pearson, of Quaker Catherine and gentle Ilbrahim—is quite evidently offered as a fictional series of events expressly contrived to enable us to understand the passions and problems of a real historical situation, which always was for Hawthorne the true locus of "Evil." It is in this large, figurative way that the story as a whole is symbolic. As readers we are asked primarily to consider the moral significance of the conflict between two dogmatic, seemingly opposed and yet strangely similar (or symbiotic), and radically incomplete life-philosophies called seventeenth-century Puritanism and Quakerism. Beyond this we are directed to notice how the events in question become typical of "the agonizing difficulty of finding an integrated, fruitful religious experience in America."[9] But to isolate out of this complex historical situation a set of moral or psychological doctrines as a theme independent of circumstance is to read the tale in reverse: it is to mistake means for ends, to hypostatize the sort of general truths necessary to understand any concrete situation into abstract essences which are humanly obvious and threaten to become thematic doggerel.

Purposefully, "The Gentle Boy" reaches out to touch and explain persons and events, motives and actions that seem to epitomize a given and recognizable historical time. Only indirectly does it suggest archetypal images of what is always true. We will persist in reading for this latter pseudo-content only so long as we are inclined not to care for versions of the world that are primarily diachronic, and only on the assumption that our experience of reality is already sufficient to recognize any general truth we might ever come across. This way we never learn anything outside our own synchronic present. And this way we misconstrue Hawthorne's imaginative relation to his proper audience, whom he takes to be historically less aware and badly in need of historical information and awakening. If we imagine we are a more privileged audience, we flatter ourselves. With these "methodological" considerations in mind, then, we should bend our efforts (and categories) to inquire what the dramatic construct called "The Gentle Boy" asks us to recognize about the quality of Puritan moral experience.

2

The tale proper begins with a not-very-flattering image of Puritan piety. As Tobias Pearson (the kindest and most sensitive of the Puritan men in the story) is passing the place which had just a few hours before been the site of Quaker executions, he hears a mournful sound like the wailing of a child. His first response is "superstitious," but he struggles against the "fears which belonged to the age, and compelled himself to pause and listen." Reasoning coolly with himself, he wins another victory: "For the ease of my conscience I must search this matter out" (71). The point, of course, is that Tobias' charity is cold and slow indeed. One can scarcely imagine his words in the mouth of the Good Samaritan of the New Testament, whose motive we must suppose is love of neighbor rather than "ease of conscience." Nor did the Samaritan of the Gospel trouble himself to see if the man he stopped to help were an "apparition" which must "stand the test of a short mental prayer." By New Testament standards, the Puritan Tobias seems less than a model of Christian charity; he seems, in fact, rather tightly bound by legalistic formulae.[10]

Nor does Tobias grow in our estimation when we see him discover that the outlandishly named Ilbrahim is the son of an executed Quaker: "The Puritan, who had laid hold of little Ilbrahim's hand, relinquished it as if he were touching a loathesome reptile." We think of Edwards, perhaps, but the image is older than that; and it is not supposed to be reassuring. Nevertheless, Hawthorne protests, Tobias Pearson "possessed a compassionate heart, which not even religious prejudice could turn to stone" (73); a trifle cold, perhaps, yet this one Puritan at least will escape the fate of the Man of Adamant. As proof that Tobias is not really an uncharitable man, Hawthorne offers us the mental process by which he decides to take the boy into his own home: "God forbid that I should leave this child to perish, though he comes of the accursed sect ... Do we not all spring from an evil root? Are we not all in darkness till the light shine upon us? He shall not perish, neither in body, nor if prayer and instruction may avail for him, in soul." At first this may sound a little better: authentically "Puritan," it is touched by that sort of moral democracy for which Puritanism has often been praised. It may, in fact, sound *very good* if we recognize it as a deliberate echo of Roger Williams' warning to Englishmen about the "natural" equality of all men, including Indians:

> By nature, wrath's his portion, thine, no more
> Till Grace his soul and thine in Christ restore.[11]

But still there are problems. Eventually the insistent allusions to Williams force us to make clarifications which undo any positive impressions made by Tobias' theological rationalizations; and from the first we are troubled by his moral tone.

From the first, I think, we can see amply verified the truth of Matthiessen's suggestion that Hawthorne's chief stricture against New England was that "its feelings were less well developed than its mind." The historical point has not passed without debate in modern scholarship. But Hawthorne's own view is perfectly clear. He notices a certain rationalism in the Puritan worthies of "Mrs. Hutchinson," and there is ample evidence of it here. Only after a series of complicated intellectual maneuvers is Tobias Pearson able to accomplish the simplest act of Christian charity, the spontaneous performance of which would seem to define primitive and authentic Christian virtue.[12]

And the "reasoning" which leads Tobias Pearson to perform that act of charity is, ironically, an evident rationalization. He wants to help Ilbrahim, but something deeply ingrained holds him back. And so the good he *would* do he *cannot* do until he has proven to himself that there are, after all, good theological and even Puritan reasons for doing so. His conflicted mind must think of a text before his whole personality can get into Christian action.

As Tobias arrives home with Ilbrahim, Hawthorne presses his analysis of the sources of Christian charity. Dorothy Pearson—who strikes us more as a Mother than as a Puritan, and makes us wonder about the Ramist "relation" of those terms—naively imagines that Ilbrahim's parents have been killed by Indians. But Tobias, already being softened by Ilbrahim's strangely mollifying influence, must sadly inform her otherwise: "No, Dorothy, this poor child is no captive from the wilderness . . . The Heathen savage would have given him to eat of his scanty morsel, and to drink of his birchen cup; but Christian men, alas, had cast him out to die" (75). This is risky, almost sentimental. But fortunately somewhat more is at stake than the obvious, vaguely Romantic irony of savages being more Christian than Christians, although this "comparative" theme is present in Hawthorne as well as in Melville. What Hawthorne is questioning, ultimately, is the essential "civility" of the Puritans; and this in a very precise historical sense. Again it is hard not to feel the strong pressure of Roger Williams behind Hawthorne's own analysis. Not only are all men made "Of one blood," but

> The courteous Pagan shall condemn
> Uncourteous Englishmen,
> Who live like foxes, bears and wolves,
> Or lion in his den.

The risk, then, is well taken. Hawthorne is not the first to notice that those claiming a rather exclusive title to grace within the covenant did not, in ordinary ethical practice, come up to the standard of "The wild Barbarians with no more / Than nature . . ." The echoes of Roger Williams may serve to suggest that we are involved with more than a nineteenth-century "liberal" critique of seventeenth-century bigotry.[13]

One scarcely needs the deleted phrase about the Puritans' "original bond of union" to see that Hawthorne is talking about the covenant as a "tribalist" and self-serving form of religious exclusiveness.[14] Separated out of "the world" and united into a highly cohesive and intensely special form of religious and social organism, the covenanted community of the Puritan was no ordinary civil compact. That union was God's explicit determination for the saving remnant of saints on earth. Within their covenant the Puritans said they enjoyed "liberty"; to Hawthorne they seemed to be shutting themselves up in an "iron cage." But the chief effect of their voluntary and exceptional communion, Hawthorne seems to be suggesting, is to make the Puritan behave like a "natural man," and even on occasion like a savage, toward those supposed to be outside the covenant. Behind the easier ironies is the clear implication that the idea of a divine covenant which includes less than all of humanity is at its roots pernicious. Again the intended comparison with the story of the Good Samaritan is telling: as Jews are instructed that the new covenant will apply to and be perfectly fulfilled even by outcasts, religious enemies, and failed-Jews like the Samaritan, so Hawthorne suggests that Puritan, Quaker, and Indian are, depending on their charity, equally members of the only covenant there is—that of sinful humanity trying to realize the love of God in the love of man.

Thus the "separatist" principle of a national covenant, which prevents the Puritan community and *almost* prevents Tobias from ministering to Ilbrahim, is measured by the classically Christian principle of the universal salvific will. And "Ilbrahim," accordingly, is no casually chosen pagan name: at very least its linguistic similarity to "Abraham" serves to remind us who are and who are not, for the Puritans, the legitimate children of "Our Father in Faith."[15]

Once the effects of Puritanism are seen in this light—as contributing to the artificial, sectarian, and even clannish separation of some specially elected men from the rest of natural humanity—the most important fact about the first section becomes the sense in which "Puritan Tobias" is not really an authentic Puritan. His wife, Dorothy, completely free from explicit doctrinal encumbrances and acting out of simply natural or maternal benevolence, agrees to care for Ilbrahim spontaneously and unquestioningly; in doing so, she points up again the "Puritan" slowness of her husband's sympathies with general humanity. But Tobias' sympathies have, finally, been stirred, in direct proportion to his ability to shed the encumbrances of his exclusive, sectarian prejudice. And he is able to do this at all, Hawthorne suggests, because he has been pretty much of a failed-Puritan all along, acting out of basically "unregenerate" motives. "Not among the earliest emigrants from the old country," he came to Massachusetts chiefly as a place of refuge from the degenerating Civil War in England; and he was not without a sense of the "advantages" New England offered "to men of unprosperous fortunes" (76). Not basically a "dissatisfied religionist," Tobias Pearson is a Puritan more by historical circumstance than by personal propensity. Fortunately, his own natural-fatherly propensities have not entirely disappeared. The portrait that emerges from the first section of "The Gentle Boy" is basically that of a well-disposed natural man whose natural sympathies have been impaired, though not wholly thwarted, by the covenant principle.

The Puritans at large have not been slow to notice Tobias' "impurity of motive." At worst they would have branded such concerns as "carnal"; and at best merely those of the "civil, honest man." They have, in fact, seen the death of his children as proper retribution for his "overthoughtful" concern for their prosperity and earthly welfare. Nor does his latest act of human

solicitude for "the body" as well as "the soul" of Ilbrahim escape their notice. "Those expounders of the ways of Providence, who had judged their
brother, and attributed his domestic sorrows to his sin, were not more charitable when they saw him and Dorothy endeavoring to fill up the void in
their hearts by the adoption of an infant of the accursed sect." If gentle Ilbrahim can soften even their hard hearts for a brief and occasional moment,
they think him an agent of the Devil: "no merely natural cause could have
worked on them" (76–77). And their antipathy only increases when "divers
theological discussions" fail to change the religion "strong as instinct in
him." Their frustration, in turn, further redounds on the all-too-natural
Tobias: the Puritan community—which is the "antagonist" in the story, to
Tobias as well as to Catherine—is ever on the alert for those failings among
the brethren which may adversely affect the standing of the whole community in its special relation with God; accordingly, Tobias is threatened with
the scourge, and his "tolerance" of Ilbrahim (it is really "love") is branded
as "backsliding."

Given this, we scarcely need to consult one of the deleted passages to
know that one of Hawthorne's Puritan sources for "The Gentle Boy" has
been Nathaniel Ward's *Simple Cobbler of Aggawam*, as famous for its arguments against sentimentally misguided toleration as for its false wit. We
begin to sense that certain submerged Puritan sources for his tale are at least
as important as the announced Quaker ones—that his subject is more distinctively Puritan than Quaker.[16] And we readily see that Hawthorne's primary concern is not with fallenness or even sectarianism generally, but with
the specific and monumental sectarianism implied by the Puritan version of
the covenant.

3

And so before we have reached the second of the story's major fictional
sections, we have already seen Hawthorne define and judge an important
impulse within American Puritanism. And at the same time we have witnessed the first working out of some very crucial "Hawthornean" ideas.
Before going any further, it might be well to advert to some of these and to
recognize the significance of the fact that these important themes see their
first light of day in connection with the Puritans.

First of all, quite obviously, is that set of ideas which Hawthorne critics
were once inclined to call by the cliché of "the head and the heart." But
ideas that may seem sentimental or Romantic reactions against the rationalism of the Enlightenment take on a rather different coloring when we see

that their primary relation is to Puritanism. "The Gentle Boy" makes clear what "Mrs. Hutchinson" only suggests: Hawthorne regarded the Puritans as, essentially, rationalists of the scholastic sort. It is probable that the vaguely anti-intellectualist doctrines of his Bowdoin education and of his nineteenth-century ambience became meaningful to him only when he seemed to see their truth demonstrated by negative example in the seventeenth century. The head—considered as the rationally held dogmas uniting a peculiar people in the Truth—might indeed get in the way of the heart's call to universal charity. And in the context of "The Gentle Boy" it is possible to recognize the precise significance of "head" and "heart" far more accurately than in later formulations related to "evil scientists" like Aylmer or Rappaccini, or psychic meddlers like Ethan Brand and Westervelt. To be sure, the "heart" held as good against scientific as against theological rationalism, but it took its initial definition and felt religious quality as against the theological variety. What Hawthorne opposes to the desire to be in possession of the Truth, for its own religious sake and in spite of ordinary social considerations, is the ability to sympathize with, trust, and act charitably toward human beings, naturally and equally.

The head and the heart, then, are for Hawthorne basically Christian conceptions. Granted Hawthorne's reading of the major Romantics, and granted the wish of thinkers after Hume to discover and define a universally valid knowing power distinct from and independent of Lockean sensation and/or Cartesian reason, still the heart in Hawthorne, which is always in danger of becoming separated from the head, does not mean "imagination" or "intuition." Hawthorne's *method* as historian is epistemological, but his *doctrine* is theological.

Hawthorne's reading of Puritan sermons and polemical tracts had evidently progressed far enough by the time of "The Gentle Boy" to convince him that the Puritans were indeed rationalists: not in the sense that they preferred a discursive to an intuitive knowing power; and still less, obviously, in the survey-book sense of preferring "reason" to "revelation"; but in the sense that they trusted the results of a fairly elaborate typological and eschatological reading of Scripture far more than they trusted its simpler message of Samaritan brotherhood. Given the choice, in the terms in which the nineteenth century would have seen it, between the New Testament's definition of religion as "taking care of widows and orphans" and the stricter view that the two testaments together offered a complete prescriptive definition and an accurate historical description of "the people of God" (past, present, and future), the Puritans unswervingly chose the latter. For Hawthorne, Puritan rationalism consisted in the fairly un-self-conscious trust that the human mind could extract from Scripture that one way of life and worship which God had willed for those whom his selecting decrees had chosen.[17] To him this seemed a highly dangerous assumption. When a society became convinced that it alone, out of all the world, had perceived the ideal pattern, one grew suspicious; when it inferred from this conviction that it was an Elect Nation, one's suspicions grew to alarm; and when one discovered that this double conclusion had led to the judicial murder of Quakers (and to the persecution of widows and orphans), one evidently wrote "The Gentle Boy."

Clearly, then, part of Hawthorne's head-and-heart intention in the story is to remind a people with a disputatious tendency that their history contains at least one clear though complicated example of religious men using the best intellectual tools at their disposal to work out of sacred Scripture a complicated social and religious system which systematically violated the essential spirit of their Scripture's most crucial documents. If Hawthorne's idealistic scientists choose Science over persons, his Puritans choose Holy History over persons.

Obviously Hawthorne's feelings about a "magnetic chain of humanity" are bound up in the same historical recognitions. Not only might the doctrine of election "tend," as Channing had argued, to degenerate into a holier-than-thou religious presumption, but the idea of a limited group of men in a special social convenant with God ran counter to the very spirit and tone of the New Testament, which Hawthorne (like Melville) regarded as fundamentally democratic. It has often been suggested that Hawthorne's Jacksonian sympathies were founded, paradoxically, on the rather conservative religious doctrine of a universal fall; and in support of this, of course, we have seen Tobias Pearson reason that before the "light shines on us" we are "all in darkness." But we are eventually led to view this as a rather clumsy, overintellectualized, and finally misleading way of getting at a truth that is far more simple: whatever we are, we are all that together, without the distinctions of *before, after,* or *until.* Any separation of mankind except by the Last Judgment, as the parable of the weeds and wheat doubtlessly taught Hawthorne, would be premature, presumptuous. There might be such a thing as "Providence," Hawthorne thought; indeed formal investigations of his theology have insisted that such a belief was his most fundamental and unshakable. But there was no such thing as Calvinistic predestination; and Providence was not to be expounded by men at all. To decide where favor and disfavor lay—whether in the matter of Tobias and his children or in the larger question of special social dispensations—was to begin by presuming on an uncommunicated divine privilege and to end by denying one's moral identity with all other men.[18]

The other important consideration which "The Gentle Boy" has touched so far is, although absolutely crucial to any adequate understanding of Hawthorne, almost never discussed. I refer to the radically Puritan problem of the "dialectical," Ramistic, either/or relation between Nature and Grace.[19] As I have been implicitly suggesting, Hawthorne wished to regard their relation differently: to make a strong (even risky) case for the validity (even graciousness) of certain natural impulses. We have seen that Hawthorne evidently intends more than an easy sentimentalism. We are not likely to be much impressed by the noble impulses indirectly ascribed to the "wilderness folk" with their "birchen cups": neither disciple Freneau nor master Rousseau will quite take us to the moral center of "The Gentle Boy." Hawthorne's insistent emphasis on the salutary instincts or impulses of Dorothy Pearson, and the retarded but not entirely inoperative ones of her husband, leads us straight to that intense and long-lasting, quintessentially Puritan debate about whether a person could perform any virtuous actions without the special aid of divine grace. And of the "sources" so far proposed, Roger Williams brings us closest to the heart of that matter.

Like Williams, Hawthorne was a Seeker and not a Finder of the New Jerusalem. Like Williams, he believed that its true "place" was interior only; that no "Christian" commonwealth, no exemplary "city," and (more radically) no visible church could claim special status as a group elect of God. And like Williams, Hawthorne seems to accuse the regnant New England Puritans of living, essentially, according to an Old Dispensation still, as if Christ had never entered and altered salvation history once and for all. This accusation—that the Puritan really preferred Moses to Christ—would imply more than the easy charge of an anachronistic loyalty to the outmoded values of legalism, rigor, and retributive justice (though it includes this, and we shall see its importance when we come to examine Quaker values). The accusation would also mean that the Puritans' ecclesiological disputes had blinded them to the potentially "universalist" import of a parable like that of the Good Samaritan, as if Love were not the *summa* of the New Law. And it would mean that although the parable of the wheat and the tares might fairly be given a Calvinist (predestinarian) exegesis, it could be made to reinforce the values of separatist societies and gathered churches only with severe logical strain, as if the New Covenant were not infinitely wider and more gracious than the Old.[20]

Hawthorne has all this in "The Gentle Boy," but he is also beyond it. Hawthorne reinforces Williams' denial that grace can be discovered and made the basis of church, town, and state; he underlines Williams' pointed discovery that those who claim to embody and organize the gracious life in this way very often betray themselves by behavior that is ungentle, discourteous, uncivil, and even inhumane. But beyond this is Hawthorne's own suggestion that grace is, after all, a possibility of nature or it is nothing.

The dominant Puritan attempt had been to discover an Order of Grace and try to reshape all other orders in correspondence: converted saints, acting out of regenerate and hence unselfish motives, would control a theocratic state; that state would uphold orthodox belief and enforce godly behavior. Williams, witnessing the all too predictably human results, and convinced of the ineluctably interior and marvelously precious character of grace, demanded that it should not be polluted by an adulterous union with the civil order. And with these very telling criticisms of the New England Way, Hawthorne wholeheartedly agreed. Evidently, then, Williams and Hawthorne can both testify against sins against humanity committed in the name of grace; both can tendentiously suggest that many of the covenanted activities of the Puritans seem not so much gracious as simply anti-natural; both suggest that the pagans of the piece seem to be acting in a more gracious or Christian manner than the Christians.

But this is as far as Williams can go. His rhetoric *seems* to deconstruct the Puritan logic of Nature and Grace, but it does so only polemically; or, at best, it severs the ordinary Puritan connection between Grace and the State.[21] Hawthorne goes much further. When Williams suggests that the Indians seem more Christian than the Christians, his point is chiefly negative: the civilized Puritans had better examine their own spiritual estates very carefully; it would be embarrassing to hold that uncivil or even savage behavior was a distinguishing mark of grace. Hawthorne's suggestion, obviously, is far more radical: since the New Covenant is really open to all men, and since nature is, observably, the only order of reality in which all men share, then one had better posit an order of grace *within* and not *opposed to* the order of nature.

The root question, once again, concerns the "truly virtuous" action: could such a thing ever be ascribed, in any part, to nature? If the question lurked only around the edges of Williams' polemics, and if it was for him more rhetorical than real, still it seemed to be everywhere else in Puritan intellectual history. It was at the heart of the antinomian controversy—as Shepard and Cotton seem finally to have realized. Salvation was, by unquestioned Protestant axiom, totally gratuitous. And yet there were good Scriptural and practical reasons to believe that men had to "prepare" for the grace of saving faith. Such preparation might be considered, positively, as the strenuous effort to live morally; or, negatively, as the bare realization of one's own hopeless moral bankruptcy; but either way the logic remained intractable. Preparatory actions were either virtuous or they were not. If not, then (by Ramist necessity) they were sinful; and if they were sinful, how could faithful shepherds fairly call upon their flocks to prepare? Or if preparatory acts were not sinful, then were they not the result of grace already present? And under such an assumption, how were they genuinely preparatory? Either way, the Calvinist logic of the natural man's *total* inability to posit a non-sinful act apart from the special influence of grace seemed incapable of a coherent solution.

And so the problem of Nature and Grace had vexed the Puritan divines from the beginning; and those divines had, however inadvertently, vexed their congregations. Massive and repeated sermons did not really help. The more explication, one comes to feel, the less clarity. Contrary to most accounts, the logical situation cannot be shown to have changed very much between the 1630's and the time Edwards came to face it head on. The case seems, rather, that by Edwards' day the leading exponents of the doctrine of natural "striving" were somewhat readier to admit that they might, in some sense, be Arminians after all. And eventually, by Hawthorne's day, the problem had been given over rather than solved.[22]

In any event, the argument between those who were quietly, perhaps unconsciously, and one way or another "expanding the limits of natural ability" and those anxious or intellectually determined to hew the hard line of a more consistent Calvinism reaches its climax with Edwards' *Nature of True Virtue*. This treatise more than any other single Puritan work defines the peculiarly Puritan emphasis on *true* virtue. And it is difficult to imagine that Hawthorne could have written "The Gentle Boy" without having carefully read and been powerfully moved to answer, or at least to worry over, what Edwards has to say in his sixth and seventh chapters about "Particular Instincts of Nature, which in Some Respects Resemble Virtue" and about "The Reasons Why Those Things . . . Which Have not the Essence of Virtue, Have Yet by Many Been Mistaken for True Virtue." It seems certain that "The Gentle Boy" makes its initial ironic points about Grace and Nature by boldly appropriating the polemics of Roger Williams. And I should have to guess that it derives its depth, its power, and its final affirmative overbelief from Hawthorne's encounter with Jonathan Edwards.[23]

In Edwards' classic statement, the so-called benevolent instincts—such as parental love, marital love, and pity—are seen as radically limited: not only are they directed at an object less than Being-in-General, but they are in fact an aspect of self-love; they "consent to being" only as that being is considered as an extension or an imaginative version of oneself. As such they are *merely* human or natural. Not precisely evil in themselves, they are yet the root of evil because they are incomplete. Edwards prefers to think of these instincts primarily in a negative way, as not "truly" virtuous. But it is clear that he regards them as fallen since he sees how easily loving a wife or child too much can be a form of idolatry; or worse, one suspects, how easily a "sentimental" pity of sinners can swallow up the virtuous hatred of that negativity called sin, an intense hatred which can and indeed must consist with a benevolence to Being-in-General.[24]

Edwards' emphasis is obviously different from that of an earlier Puritan like Cotton. His analysis is less doctrinally technical, more psychological, potentially more literary. And under this literary aspect it stands as the culmination of still another tradition of the anti-natural bias of Puritan salvation theory. One thinks of Thomas Shepard at his wife's deathbed: he is trying *very* hard not to be jealous when his wife's thoughts stray from him to the Heavenly Bridegroom who is coming to consummate a heavenly marriage with her soul. Or of Anne Bradstreet who, for all the love her early poems lavish on her fleshly husband, is, at the last, all too eager for that same Heavenly Bridegroom. Or of Edward Taylor, carefully "weaning" his affections from those children whom a Heavenly Hand untimely plucked from his earthly garden. Or, most painfully and least sympathetically, one thinks of thousands of readers of Wigglesworth's *Day of Doom* striving mightily, at the end of his poem, to believe that on the last day they will indeed be capable of complacency or even joy at seeing a beloved but reprobated husband or wife, parent or child, cast off into the lake of fire. The Puritan was *always* being reminded that, as spouse or parent, he could love his relations too much; or, as true believer, he could pity the heretic or the sinner to the point of insubordination. All Edwards did was show why the Puritan sociology had to be true in Augustinian logic.

For the most part Hawthorne's generation could only rebel. And it would be hard to show that Hawthorne—any more than Channing—ever satisfactorily "answered" Edwards. Certainly "The Gentle Boy" does not consistently develop a logic by which Edwards might be disproven. But just as certainly a strenuous disagreement with the Edwardsean position defines the story's center of feeling. It is precisely pity and the familial affections which are on trial here. And critics who love to find "the fall" everywhere in Hawthorne have never been further from the mark than in their analyses of this tale which, in its heart-inspired recoil from the logic of Edwards, *almost* tumbles over into Rousseauvian sentimentality. It stops short of that; and, as the story progresses, we see that Hawthorne does have a profound doctrinal "overbelief," even if he does not have a fully articulated theological position.

So far we have seen only the negative side: if all the best impulses of human nature are in some way fundamentally corrupt, based on the radically partial principle of self-love, then our common sense of the meaning of all normal human communion—that is, of every intercourse outside of a divinely established covenant—is radically undercut. One could say too much, Hawthorne evidently felt, about the dangers of pity and love. One might prefer *agape*, but one might have to settle for *eros*.[25] One might wish for a marriage-covenant with God, but perhaps a certain "intercourse with the world" ought not to be set aside too lightly. Perhaps, in short, nature was already a sort of grace. But what strengthened those ideas, and what motivates a story like "The Gentle Boy," is not so much a fully articulated countertheory of Nature and Grace as the painful counterexample of the Puritans. If one discovered, among the significant actions of covenanted saints, the judicial murder of Quakers-as-Samaritans, and if one could link the logic of this action with a logic that pervaded all of Puritan moral theory, then one's moral suspicions might be said to be fairly aroused.

But what "The Gentle Boy" goes on to suggest is an idea we can see repeated over and over in Hawthorne's attempt to take the measure of Puritanism: whatever human nature is, it is not to be transformed utterly. If there is no capacity for virtue in human nature as nature—or in nature as grace—then there is simply no virtue. The negative example of Hawthorne's Puritans embodies a lesson which neither his Shakers nor his Radical Reformers nor his neo-Platonic scientists could quite learn: human nature is a constant. In one meaning grace might aid what is already there; or it might, in another meaning, validate limited human actions, making love of man pass for love of God. But it could not in any operative sense provide entirely "new principles" of action. This conviction constitutes the basis of Hawthorne's non-Puritan economy of salvation. And it is to the question of the naturally gracious meaning of love and pity that the heart of "The Gentle Boy" tries to speak.

4

Even though Tobias and Dorothy Pearson are being accused of having endangered New England's religious and social solidarity by harboring a willfully recalcitrant and possibly diabolical heretic (with no better motive than the manifest self-love involved in the satisfaction of frustrated parental instincts), they attend Sabbath meeting with Ilbrahim. Hawthorne continues to emphasize, with a series of sharp ironies, the rigorously anti-natural bent of Puritan piety. The drums which sound the "martial call to the place of holy and quiet thoughts" are obvious enough. A trifle more subtle are Hawthorne's suggestions about the naked interior of the meeting-house, offering "nothing to excite the devotion, which, without external aids, often remains latent in the heart" (78); decorations and ceremonials may be merely human contrivances rather than divine prescriptions, but without them the human heart may remain permanently barren of gracious affections; as always, one stamps out the "merely" human only at considerable expense.

The third clue to the meaning of Hawthorne's meeting-house image of Puritan religion in its proper Sabbath surroundings is his merest mention of the "broad-aisle [which] formed a sexual division, impassable except by children beneath a certain age" (79). The temptation is great, perhaps, to leap ahead to Henry Adams and the problem of stunted American sexuality—discovering that Hawthorne too lays the blame on a "Puritanical" mentality which confused sex with sin. But Hawthorne's cryptic suggestions, like the perfectly explicit ones in "The Man of Adamant" and "The Minister's Black Veil," do not work quite that simply; more is at stake, evidently, than what Henry James called "the decline of the sentiment of sex."[26] The question of the meaning of sexuality, like the related one of stable and broken homes, is a modern rather than a Puritan concern. Hawthorne was well aware that the record of large Puritan families and of vigorous men of God who wore out three or four wives with conception and childbirth gives fair indication that the Puritans did not suffer from excessive sexual delicacy or fastidiousness. The dominant tone of Puritan life was, Hawthorne says in more than one place, "coarse." Hawthorne is evidently using a nineteenth-century humanistic metaphor (synecdoche) for a seventeenth-century religious problem. The sexual division of the Puritan congregation clearly stands as an image of the way rational doctrine (the male) and human feeling (the female) have come apart. In such a divided condition it is no wonder that nature does not seem to suffice.

Tobias Pearson, on whom the story tries again and again to establish focus, is "separated at the door of the meeting-house" from Dorothy and Ilbrahim; his problem, as we have seen it, is precisely the difficulty of integrating, within the confines of a relentlessly dichotomizing Puritan religion, his natural-instinctual life with the prescriptions of his consciously held doctrines. Significantly, of course, Ilbrahim goes with Dorothy: if the heart and the head come apart, if the life of nature must be separated from the life of the legal community, then "the sweet infant of the skies" properly belongs on the side of nature and the heart. This is not, we should notice, an optimistic or romantically simplistic solution. Hawthorne is quite sorry to see the division and the consequent reduction made: theologically its proper result is pure naturalism; sociologically it leads to matriarchy. Elsewhere he has been anxious to warn us that woman's "morality is not exactly the material for masculine virtue." But despite these evident dangers Hawthorne felt that, if the basic division were made, then nature and the heart would have to be trusted with the religious sentiment.

What follows is a vivid dramatic realization of the natural and inevitable consequences which proceed from the division of life into radically incomplete dichotomies or "logical" opposites. The Puritan minister, who in earlier times "had practically learned the meaning of religious persecution from Archbishop Laud" and was "not now disposed to forget the lesson against which he had murmured then" (79–80), delivers an aridly intellectual, unsympathetic, and finally erroneous sermon on the history and tenets of the Quaker sect. His harangue—stretching out toward the end of a second hour, echoing Nathaniel Wards's *Simple Cobbler of Aggawam* on toleration and John Norton's *Heart of New-England Rent* on Quakers, and unconsciously grotesquing the Sermon on the Mount—ends with pointed remarks on "the danger of pity," especially to heretics.[27] Scarcely has he completed his instructions on how those who have the hope of salvation are to deport themselves toward those incorrigibly lost, when the antithesis of his deracinated scholasticism arises in the form of a "muffled female" dressed in a "shapeless robe of sackcloth" and evidently "wild with enthusiasm." She does not long remain "muffled": "Her discourse gave evidence of an imagination hopelessly entangled with her reason; it was a vague and incomprehensible rhapsody, which, however, seemed to spread its own atmosphere round the hearer's soul" (80–81). Her hopelessly self-involved rhapsody soon leads, inevitably, to her own peculiar sorrows; and as her own "hatred and revenge now wrapped themselves in the garb of piety, the character of her speech was changed, her images became distinct though wild, and her denunciations had an almost hellish bitterness" (81). The immediate point of the contrast is obvious: the harsh Puritan dogmas (public, intellectual, and held in common within the covenant) and the self-indulgent Quaker enthusiasm (private, passionate, inspired) are, respectively, mind and instinct pursued in separation. A world has come apart.

Ilbrahim's mother, as we soon discover the "woman of mighty passions" to be, is characterized quite technically. In language used by Arminian opponents of revivalism, in common with urbane religious thinkers of the eighteenth century and with anti-pietists generally, she is technically defined as an "enthusiast." And as a seventeenth-century embodiment of the Quaker Spirit, her voice is neither "still" nor "small." Her speech, we know, has a plurality of sources in the literature of Quaker protest that Hawthorne has read; and her excesses are only partly the results of persecution.[28] She charges that the Puritans have not only "slain the husband" but have also "cast forth the child, the tender infant, to wander homeless and hungry and cold, till he die" (82). The latter charge, however, redounds ironically on herself. She, as well as the Puritans, has cast Ilbrahim out to die. In doing so both she and the Puritans are quite clearly rejecting the grace of salvation in the figure of Christ. And in a one very troublesome but important sense Quaker Catherine is guiltier than the Puritans. Whereas they have cast out only a "neighbor," she has rejected her own natural child. The balance is delicate and suggestive: the Puritan, having begun it all with a cardinal error of some sort, seems locked into the rigor and the letter of his rationally held but humanly pernicious convictions; but the Quaker, responding, seems caught up in some "opposite" version of the same Puritan error. The pro-

177

test has not succeeded in changing the terms of the argument. And the theological story is, evidently, rather convoluted.

Catherine almost gives over her crusade against organized and rationalistic Puritan intolerance when Ilbrahim calls out to her, as if "the indulgence of *natural love* had given her a momentary sense of [her] errors" (84, my italics). But her enthusiastic need to testify against persecution by being persecuted remains the strongest motive of her being. Dorothy Pearson asks to keep the child, and the two women confront each other over Ilbrahim. Dorothy, in her "neat matronly attire," is evidently "*blameless, so far as mortal could be so*, in respect to God and man; while the enthusiast, in her robe of sackcloth and girdle of knotted cord, had as evidently violated the duties of the present life and the future, by fixing her attention wholly on the latter" (85). The language, as my italics are meant to suggest, is theologically very careful. And the scene, like one to come later in "The May-Pole of Merry Mount," strikes Hawthorne as a "practical allegory": it was "rational piety and unbridled fanaticism contending for the empire of a young heart." For this one time, at least, rational piety overcomes. Dorothy keeps Ilbrahim. Formerly her motherliness, even her femaleness, has stood simply for the domestic and humane instincts; now, given a new and oxymoronic definition, her rational piety stands out from the extreme, dogmatic rationalism of the Puritan as sharply as it contrasts with the unbridled fanaticism of the Quaker.[29]

And thus Hawthorne raises her instinctive maternal protectiveness to the level of a positive Christian virtue; he defines her action as salutary "in the present life and in the future." He sees in her action what Puritan and Quaker, unequally rational but identically fanatical, fail to see: not only that mind and passional instinct, reason and heart-felt inspiration are coordinate in human nature, but that natural actions are, under the guidance of an adequately social outlook, truly virtuous in themselves. There is, then, at this moment of harmony, not only no opposition but a positive parallelism between the orders of Nature and Grace. It is, within a Puritan context, an extremely poignant moment. And, in any context, it is a difficult position to maintain. Hawthorne himself clearly finds it difficult to maintain because of his own keen appreciation of the meaning of the Fall; and this conflict may be, at bottom, what troubled him most about the story. Perhaps nature had led him deeper than *either* theology or art could follow. *Could* one really answer Jonathan Edwards? When *was* an outlook adequately social? Why did the Family seem a more valid image of community than the Covenant? Was it, after all, only some form of Romantic Naturalism or Victorian Fireside Sentimentality to stress the salutariness of nature as maternal and benevolent?[30]

In any event, the moment stands. And for that moment the Incarnation is true and recognized. Dorothy finds grace in loving a human Son, and Hawthorne sees the love of God finally realized in human love. Human beings touch, and questions of orthodoxy seem to disappear. For a very brief moment, Catherine herself is almost drawn into the harmony. She charges that the Pearsons will not be able to teach Ilbrahim the "enlightened faith" for which his father was martyred. Dorothy readily admits that they can only "do towards him according to the dictates of their own consciences" (86). A Quaker would have said "lights," claiming slightly more spiritual originality. But the delicate irony is clear enough: Dorothy admits the cogency of Catherine's own most sacred (Protestant) principle; Catherine recognizes it and surrenders the child to the ideal of rational piety as realized in the natural, maternal love of Dorothy Pearson. But then the moment ends abruptly and with strident discord. Catherine hears "the voice" bidding her to "break the bonds of natural affection, martyr [her] love, and know that in all things eternal wisdom hath its end." Hawthorne makes it quite clear, however, that it is man and not God who has set up the irreconcilable opposition between the divine and the merely human; for Catherine's call is to become only "the apostle of her own unquiet heart" (87). If she must seek her salvation apart from her natural duties, the reason would seem based on a number of man-made distinctions of reason.[31]

5

The rest of "The Gentle Boy" is noticeably less tight and sharply dramatic than what we have seen thus far. The essential terms of the dichotomy have been dramatized in a series of brilliantly formed images of the varieties of unnatural religiosity in the world of seventeenth-century Puritanism. A stable moral center has been defined by the diametric opposition of contending moral perversions. It is hard for Hawthorne to get beyond this in the static, pictorial form; when he presses on, it is into complexities which only the narrative devices of *The Scarlet Letter* could adequately solve. People and events develop in ways which suggest much more narrative and historical time than either Hawthorne's technique or his facts would quite allow.

The section which follows is undoubtedly the weakest and most diffuse in emphasis. We get, first of all, the betrayal of Ilbrahim by the "sullen and reserved" boy who had been "brought wounded into the cottage" of the tirelessly maternal Dorothy Pearson. The episode serves chiefly to emphasize that Ilbrahim, with his Moorish name and Ishmaelite associations, is indeed the "figure" of Christ. Ilbrahim is Christ primarily in the sense that anyone who appears under the Biblical aspect of "the least of my brethren"—needing to be fed, clothed, sheltered, or ministered to—must be addressed exactly as if he literally were Christ. His proper literary analogues include not only Saint Stephen and all the various child martyrs who descend from him in Catholic hagiography but, even more appropriately, all those legendary Christ-bearers who appear in some distress, call out for gratuitous assistance, and then reward the Samaritan who aids them with a vision of Christ. This, of course, is the relation in which he stands to Dorothy and Tobias Pearson: if they can see God in Ilbrahim, he will in turn reveal God to them. In the ironic mode of Hawthorne's story, however, this Christ whose demands and rewards are so radically human is himself quite human enough to die of the rejections and betrayals which greatly outnumber the charities of his particular historical world. Hawthorne will, of course, invoke his death as eventually redemptive, but the "kiss" planted on his mouth by the staff of his friend who has greeted him in peace is not without its natural effect; Ilbrahim's eventual death-by-rejection is forecast in the depression of spirits which follows the betrayal by this young "friend."

The Judas theme is probably more functional here than the more obvious image of depravity in childhood on which criticism has tended to insist. To be sure, the sight of "baby-fiends" suddenly visited by "the devil of their fathers" is nothing short of "loathesome" (92). But we can scarcely ignore the fact that nurture is more at issue here than nature: on the one hand, Ilbrahim's character shows no such violent propensities, in spite of what he and his family have already suffered; and, on the other, these children of the Puritans are merely imitating the un-Christian cruelty of their saintly elders. Moreover, grown-up Puritans have rejected the theological Ilbrahim long before one of his imperfectly nurtured playmates seals the fact of his literal rejection. So too, for that matter, has his Quaker mother. Indeed only Dorothy and (more slowly) Tobias relieve the impression of a culture that is organized—doctrinally—to destroy the truly religious sentiments. Practically speaking, nearly everyone seems bent on killing a Son of God in the name of some other seemingly religious values. And, theoretically, it seems necessary to keep issuing ourselves the Melvillean reminder that Original Sin is a grown-up doctrine, or nothing.[32]

Hawthorne's other attempt in this relatively lax third section is to restore the emphasis on Tobias—the "civil, honest man," whose religious crisis probably ought to be the center of the tale. Tobias the failed-Puritan, we are told, was at the very time of his finding Ilbrahim searching for a "more fervent faith." Since then, and under the boy's influence, he has been drifting toward Quakerism and its less intellectualistic, more personal, more spiritually or at least instinctually satisfying doctrines. Subconsciously, however, ne recognizes their excesses of individualistic enthusiasm to be quite as un-satisfactory as the Puritans' narrowly rationalistic constraint. And thus he not only continues to hate the enthusiasts, but he begins to hate himself as well. His crisis is acutely psychological, but its source is not completely or even primarily internal: a basically well-disposed, basically religious man, his historical situation seems to offer him no really valid choices and no hope of a complete and genuinely satisfying religious experience.[33]

While his inner struggle goes on in a quiet desperation which Hawthorne hints at but does not dramatize—and which we feel would take longer than the year allotted—the policies of England's Restoration have not yet been made to prevail in New England. The clash of religious oversimplifications goes on, a gross external parody of Tobias' own inner division; Ilbrahim continues to "pine and droop"; Catherine continues "to wander on a mis-taken errand, neglectful of the holiest trust which can be committed to a woman" (95). In short, religious perversions flourish while vital religion and true virtue languish.

In the last section of the tale proper, Hawthorne tries to dramatize once again the dismay and anger he feels at the "religious" displacement of natu-ral virtue. Tobias, impoverished by repeated fines for his dissent and "by his own neglect of temporal affairs," sits by a glowing fire which, in the absence of "cheerful faces," can warm him no more than the cold comforts offered by his Quaker associate who reads him the "consolations" of Scripture. The old visionary rebukes his weakness: "Art thou he that wouldst be content to give all, and endure all, for conscience sake; desiring even peculiar trials, that thy faith might be purified and thy heart weaned from worldly desires?" (96). Evidently not. The fires of supernatural zeal are for Tobias a poor substitute for the warmth of natural ties and the full range of human satis-factions—which are, in the end, symbolized well enough by the clichés of home and fireside. The Quaker errand into the enduring Puritan Wilder-ness, undertaken on behalf of the inviolability of individual conscience, has left him as cold as the original Puritan errand itself. Tobias' nature remains as divided, as incomplete as ever. Once nature is fractured, no experience of grace seems possible.

His companion tells his own story as exemplum, a history of endurance and self-abnegation. But his chief supernatural glory is in reality a horror: led by the sacrosanct inner voice, he was "moved to go forth a wanderer when [his] daughter, the youngest, the dearest of [his] flock, lay on her dying bed, and . . ." Still faintly human, the Quaker saint wishes he could forget "her woeful look" when he left her "journeying through the dark valley alone" (98). But he is glad now that he did not yield, and he has long since beaten down the devilish thought that his action may have been merely

181

that of "an erring Christian and cruel parent." And he is confident that Catherine will also be able to overcome the maternal heart which "may seem to contend mightily with her faith" (99); surely she will accept Ilbrahim's impending death not only with resignation, but with peace and joy. The world-weary Tobias can consent to all this only with an expression of his own death wish. His conversion to Quakerism, Hawthorne makes clear, has not helped solve his psychological or theological dilemma; he has merely drifted from one form of doctrinal sin against life to another.

As Catherine interrupts their musings, Hawthorne brings his protest against the hostility to nature masquerading as the life of grace to a tortured climax. The news of toleration out of England is not what the weary, death-seeking Tobias or his inspired, pain-seeking friend wishes to hear; and the Quaker saint confronts Catherine with another bit of news—this time of God's "love displayed in chastenings." She who would "fain to have looked heavenward continually," but whose affections were repeatedly distracted back to earth by "the cares of that little child," will soon be free: "Sister! Go on rejoicing, for his tottering footsteps shall impede thine no more" (101). The chilling terror implied by the calm fanaticism of this climactic speech is, I think, unsurpassed in American literature.

But we will certainly misread Hawthorne's intention if we feel, as some critics have felt, that Catherine's finally human response ("I am a woman, I am but a woman; will He try me above my strength") is to be read as part of Hawthorne's "quarrel with God."[34] Catherine is indeed at a crisis similar to those of Ahab and Pierre; her experience may even have suggested theirs; but we have seen that the cause of her moment of despair is of man and not of God. God's law, considered as natural, impels parents to love their children; as Biblical, it requires a man to love his neighbor as himself—even if that is, paradoxically, a form of self-love. Christian Scripture, or at least the portions of it to which Hawthorne's tale deliberately and repeatedly alludes, asserts that the "two great Commandments" are analogous: loving neighbor as self is "like unto" loving God above all else. In the historic world of Tobias Pearson and Quaker Catherine, in the "Puritan" world which is, in spite of all sorts of seeming contradictions, also the Quaker world, the two great Commandments have come apart. Human love and human virtue have been, Hawthorne senses, somehow set over against divine duty. The pitiful result for individuals caught in such an historical trap is always some perversion.

The cause of Catherine's final "agonized shriek" is human because it is historical. Man is free to make of his moral history what he will make of it: this is the only "theory of history" implied by "The Gentle Boy." Providence may, in some ultimate sense, bring good out of the evils man exercises himself to perpetrate; but (as we have already seen in "Roger Mal-

vin's Burial") He does not intervene to prevent the psychological consequences which follow, by implacable law, man's perversions of the natural
order. The root of Tobias' and Catherine's confusions lie deep in fallen
man's psychological make-up, to be sure; but the source studied primarily in
"The Gentle Boy" is a specific and recognizable set of theological and moral
premises that found their boldest and most striking expression in Calvinistic
Puritanism. At issue in "The Gentle Boy," and at the root of Hawthorne's
"bias" in dealing with Puritanism, is precisely what C. S. Lewis, reading
history backwards, has called the "Barthianism" of the Puritan mentality—
the habit of distinguishing, radically and at every point, between the human
and the divine, between the order of Nature and the order of Grace.[35] It is
Hawthorne's sense of the dangers of that mentality which gives moral if not
literary unity to the seemingly various concerns of his first major tale of the
Puritan world.

On the surface, of course, Puritanism and Quakerism are hopelessly divided by a series of doctrinal differences and psychological dichotomies
which seem fundamental. But they are not absolutely so. Deeper still is the
separation between Nature and Grace, which we recognize as Puritan in
origin and which, ironically and puzzlingly, makes the responses we identify
as "Puritan" and "Quaker" in some ultimate sense indistinguishable.
Hawthorne's Quakers have revolted against much that seemed objectionable in mainstream Puritanism, its arid "scholastic" intellectuality, for example; and, in America, its inordinate stress on absolute religious
uniformity, based on the totalizing myth of a politically visible chosen people. This last demurrer, as we now understand it, is not to be taken lightly.
But they seem to have accepted—perhaps even have exaggerated—the Puritan dichotomy between nature and the supernatural. For the Quakers too
the separation between the things "of God" and the things "of man" is so
wide as to constitute an opposition. The Puritans locate (and mystify) the
order of grace on the side of a community believing rationally and acting in
articulate unison. The Quakers identify the heartfelt voice of the private
conscience as the only true locus of the divine. But both obviously accept the
premise that God is to be sought and served directly, above and apart from
the mediation of all "merely human" considerations. In the sectarian warfare which results, both sides miss the only human salvation there is.[36]

Both sides are missing, obviously, a certain humanitarian ("Samaritan")
strain within the New Testament. But to say this is not to exhaust Hawthorne's theological meaning. Obviously God is love—just as in the nineteenth century salvation is obviously home and hearth. But both sides, in
their identically "Puritan" slander of the natural, miss what medieval thinkers called "analogy": God may be known and loved in man because, despite
the ontological gulf between Absolute Being and conditioned beings, the re-

ality of "being" is common to both; man is like God, one might say, because being is all there is.[37] More cogently for this story, perhaps, and in the equivalent terms available to Hawthorne, both sides ignore the theological implications of incarnationalism: the appearance of God in Christ means not only that God may no longer be thought of as totally alien; it means also that the highest religious call cannot be away from the world. God-made-Flesh has redeemed the life of the Flesh. God may still be "other" but he has, after all, revealed himself "as man." By the negative examples of Tobias' confused and world-weary search and of Catherine's desperate emotional crisis, "The Gentle Boy" asserts not only that salvation is home and hearth, but also that the human impulses to love and pity constitute the foundation and model of all virtue. And finally it judges that the sectarian warfare of seventeenth-century New England is directly related to a climate of theological opinion dominated by the zealous denigration of the human for the sake of exalting the divine: God Glorified in Man's Irrelevance. In such a climate neither Puritan nor Quaker seems able to recognize God incarnate; in such a climate they vie with each other, equally, in killing the human Christ.[38]

6

And yet there are some lingering problems. Puritans and Quakers are not *exactly* alike, not in the historical record and not in "The Gentle Boy." Their fierce quarrel may have been, as we now say, only a "family dispute"; but quarrel they did, and fiercely. Seventeenth-century Quakerism may have been only a left-wing outcome of a certain sort of "experiential" Puritan logic pushed to its own extreme, but it was an extreme to which not every Puritan went. Only some Puritans would admit to being what others scornfully or maliciously called "Quakers."[39]

At issue, of course, was a certain newly re-discovered doctrine of the "Spirit," which Quakers interpreted far more radically than other Puritans. That Quakerism which Hawthorne read about, in the definitive doctrinal "Apology" of Robert Barclay as well as in the representative historical protests of Bishop and Sewell, went to the point of asserting that the Spirit of God was present in absolutely every man. Perhaps that presence could only be called "potential"; and certainly it was not at all "by nature"; but the Quaker Everyman might discover in himself spiritual possibilities equal to those of the greatest of God's prophets or apostles or saints. George Fox regarded this as his primary "opening," and it was for this principle that Quaker men—and, notably, Quaker women—went off to testify.[40] Surely this "universalist" difference might be thought to matter, especially as against the Puritans' rigidly hierarchical emphasis on election and limited atonement. We can hardly escape the feeling, in spite of all that has been written about the story's careful balance of guilt, that the spiritualism of the Quakers *ought* to be closer to some humanitarian insight of Hawthorne's own than the covenanted legalism of the Puritans. When it turns out they are not, we immediately suspect that there must be some fairly subtle reason why not. And so we may infer that some further theological distinction remains to be made.[41]

The explanation of the "non-difference" of Hawthorne's Quakers may well depend on Hawthorne's own brand of Trinitarianism, and especially on his "doctrine" of the Incarnation. He seems to have seen or sensed that what makes spiritual Quakers so *painfully* like legal Puritans is a common inability to discern the human and ethical meaning in Christianity's distinctive teaching that, in Christ, God is revealed primarily *as man*. Given the tight-lipped secrecy of Hawthorne's own skeptical faith, any such analysis must be frankly speculative. But given the problems raised by "The Gentle Boy," the risk may be worth taking. For where "Molineux" and "Malvin" ironically deconstruct, "The Gentle Boy" fervently overbelieves.[42]

The world of "The Gentle Boy" invites us to imagine the God of the Puritans as "the Father," the Power which created the world and the Authority which imposed the Law. Existing as Objective Transcendence, He would be that Ultimate Other who placed man in a world he never made and dictated conditions of behavior which do not always seem, in all senses, natural. A recognizable figure, surely. The Unitarians of Hawthorne's own day might try to soften the outline by insisting on the ordinary or human-paternal character of the one-and-only divine "person"; but as their views seem based on a prior disposition to discover Benevolence everywhere, they do not always fit the harsh facts of life; and we usually reject them as sentimental. The Puritan "Jehovah," we think, cannot be denied, even if He tends to become the ultimate Freudian parent of Frederick Crews.[43] But as He does not answer to all our experiences of God, perhaps this particular "hypostasis" does not exhaust the divine case.

Clearly Hawthorne's Quakers worship a different God—or, at very least, a different aspect or conception or revelation of God. Perhaps their "Spirit" will serve to strike the uneven balance. Appearing as our own experience of creative freedom, this Spirit exists as Transcendental Subjectivity. He is "in us," but we are not identically Him; or else we would be God instead of the fallen men we so obviously are. Rather, He is the Ultimate Self on whom we safely rely against any mystified and idolatrous claim which threatens our moral or psychological authenticity. (If the Puritans will claim divinity for the New England way, the Quaker Spirit will nullify it all.) In our more conservative or self-critical moments we worry that such a God will make us (or, more usually, others) a little reckless; but we will not entirely give Him up. He too must be counted in, even as Emerson and his Transcendental contemporaries rightly insist.[44]

But neither of these ultimate, unmediated formulations exhausts the possibilities of ultimate commitment: not a priori, not in the actual formulations of Christian theology available to Hawthorne, and not in "The Gentle Boy." There is also—and pre-eminently, Hawthorne's story would seem to be implying—"God the Son," even if no one seems adequately aware of Him. His "Eternal Generation" may be, as various sorts of New England theologians of the 1820's were willing to agree, both a more recent and a less demanding problem than the matter of His earthly appearance;[45] but logically it has its own (prior) place. As Logos, He would figure as that seminal "Reason" by which we relate ourselves intelligibly to Ultimate Being and ethically to all other men. Considered as "co-eternal" with the Father, the Son signifies the tendency of Divinity to express itself in appropriate images, of which our own faculties of intelligence and rational appetite are some evidence. As such, He validates the enterprises of rational theology and natural ethics; he even guarantees that all divine covenants or mutual restipulations will be humanly fit or apt.[46] All this is something. And then, finally, as incarnate in Jesus of Nazareth, this Son of God would constitute the reality and the sign of God's revealed existence as *human other*. The formula holds as good for any Christ-figure as for the historical Jesus. It means not that "I am Christ"—*à la* James Nayler, riding into Bristol on a patient ass, with his followers shouting "Hosannah"[47]—but that "my neighbor is Christ"; or that I am Christ only insofar as I am related, as "neighbor," to any other human being.

As "Father" God tends to be totally other, the *Totaliter Aliter* of scholastic jargon and the Hidden Will of High Calvinism. As Spirit He tends to become identified with the ground of our own selfhood. But as "Incarnate Son" He is a God radically separate from our own ego but not really alien either; radically "other" yet fully human and unequivocally personal. Ultimately, therefore, the paradox of the Incarnation would seem to mean that any human intercourse of good faith, any valid regard for the revelatory Christ that is potential in any other human, any genuine I-Thou relationship is gracious. The literary doctrine recapitulates the theology: any person may be, to any other person, a Christ-figure. Demythicize as we may, this much at least remains. And worry about Hawthorne's anti-speculative temperament as we must, at least this much seems necessary to a full understanding of the history of "The Gentle Boy," where the problem of defective natural virtue leads straight on to the image of unrecognized Incarnation.

Forced ourselves to recognize Ilbrahim as a Christ-figure, and observing that Puritans and Quakers do indeed cooperate to kill that Christ-figure, we can only conclude that Hawthorne has noticed, somewhat in advance of our own best historians, something fundamental about the theological life of provincial America. The overwhelming allegiance of Hawthorne's Puritans is obviously to the Father; of his Quakers, to the Spirit; and both of these allegiances turn out to be held in a way that is, to understate the fictional case, prejudicial to the recognition of the Son. The tale says this, if it says anything of significance. And the sources on which it is based seem largely to confirm the flat historical truth of the tendentious fictional assertion.

The Puritans present the easier case. According to Hawthorne the community which rejects Ilbrahim worships law, authority, obedience, uniformity, rigor, logic, justice—every reader can make his own list of their "Father" values. The portrait is "partial," to be sure. Certainly Hawthorne knows this; his prosy headnote concedes as much. But John Endicott and John Norton were "there": the policies of the one and the polemics of the other stood for something important (perhaps "dominant," by the 1650's) in the New England Way; and no amount of concessive rhetoric could make it go away. Roger Williams had seen it from the first: the Puritans preferred Moses to Christ, History to Persons, and Covenant to Conscience; rather than fulfilling, "spiritually," the types of Jehovah's Chosen, they were merely replaying the pre-Christian past in an odd corner of the world. They were living according to the Old Dispensation still. With this much already on the historical record, the next step seems easy. And Hawthorne took it: because God is now revealed *as man*, because figurative Samaritans fulfill the terms of the New Dispensation as well as figurative Jews, and because every man is now revealed to every *other* man as a type of Christ, love is the only covenant.

Objections occur, of course. Did not Winthrop begin it all with an emphasis on "Christian Charity"? And was there not, within Puritanism, a continuing strain of emotional pietism, "from Edwards to Emerson"? And, most cogently, what about the volumes of importance ascribed to Christ by Puritan theologians of the Covenant of Grace? How is all this to be reconciled with the charge of Father-Worship? The answers, partial and fragmentary, for the most part lie elsewhere in Hawthorne's composite morphology of Puritanism. They can only be stated here. Winthrop's enthusiastic "Model" gave way to his rigorist "Little Speech"; however mystical his original vision, his ultimate definition of "liberty" suggested Hawthorne's "iron cage." Pietistic emotionalism there was, to be sure; but well before the advent of the Quakers, the affair of Ann Hutchinson (which prefigured this later "rent" in the heart of Norton's New England) revealed that this was to be a recessive and not a dominant strain. And whatever the Puritan theologians might say about the graciousness of the New Covenant, the ecclesiology of "visible sanctity" meant that the Christian covenant was always being conflated with public and political contracts which were secular by definition and rigorist in fact.[48]

What Hawthorne nowhere quite "says," but what criticism of "The Gentle Boy" seems constrained to discover, is that even in theory the Puritans do not have a particularly rich theory of the Incarnation. The full historical case would have to be argued elsewhere, especially as it touches the famous question of "the rise of Unitarianism in New England," but a single summary remark by Perry Miller will serve the purpose here. In going "as far as mortals could go in removing intermediaries between God and man," the Puritans "even minimized the role of the Savior in their glorification of the Father."[49] Miller means, of course, that the emphasis on salvation by predestinating decree makes the will of the Father more important than the action of the Son in the drama of man's redemption. And it would be fair to add that the Christ who comes to dominate the theology that triumphed over Ann Hutchinson and then persecuted the Quakers is Himself a "Fatherly" or legal Christ. More than a legal fiction, perhaps, He nevertheless figures more as a man-substitute than *as man*. He it is who suffers in our place, to satisfy the full demands for retributive justice of a punitive Father. And even as a man-substitute, He bears the image of the Father somewhat too plainly; "proceeding from" the Father a little too directly, He is more a projection than a separate "hypostasis" or revelation, a Father's self-image rather than a true Son, a Divine Idea of Perfect Obedience rather than a Word made Flesh.

Nowhere, as it turns out, is this essential Puritan tendency more fully realized than in the famous theological treatise of the notorious archantagonist of the Quakers: *The Orthodox Evangelist* of John Norton. Norton's theology might have some sort of primacy in *any* context, since it expressly undertook to reconcile the contending views of John Cotton on the one side and those of Hooker and Shepard on the other. And given the present question, surely it is more than coincidence that the man who penned the original and definitive anti-Quaker polemic also produced an absolute *summa* of the Puritans' relentlessly "Fatherly" version of the Christian redemption. Even a cursory glance at this "other" book of Norton would have discovered to Hawthorne an epitome of the Puritan tendency to assimilate the Son to the Father.[50]

As the most recent commentator on *The Orthodox Evangelist* has written, Norton's "drive to see everything in the context of divine sovereignty undercut [the] Christocentric image of redemption and located it instead in the realm of the divine decrees . . . The work of Christ was demoted and the cause of redemption was pushed back into the invisible mystery of the divine good pleasure."[51] Though Norton's Christ might be argued to have a separate *function*, He clearly has no separate *identity*. Needful in a certain scheme of atonement, He merely executes Divine Decree; He reveals nothing new about the nature of God. Or of man, who He also needs to be for the (Anselmian) atonement to work. Virtually assimilated to the Father, His redemptive act can only ratify the old values. It can never validate the significance of the fleshly world, or guarantee the sacramental character of self-sacrificial human love, or express the existence of God in every man.[52] Clearly Norton's Christ is not the only *possible* Christ. But it is the dominance of that Christ within the Puritan world which makes Edward Taylor seem "heretical" when he meditates on the shocking *discordia concors* by which "There's run / Thy Godhead, and My Manhood in thy Son"[53]—and which justifies the fictional logic of "The Gentle Boy."

There is room for misunderstanding here. The conservative Puritans evidently felt that they alone were holding on to the one really significant fact about Christ; that, by clinging so tightly and so narrowly to the literal and perfect and divinely decreed atonement, they were—precisely against a certain metaphorical tendency of the Quakers to talk about the "Christ" in us—upholding the true importance and uniqueness of Christ as the watershed of human history. But as Hyatt Waggoner notes (in a rather different context), their theory had a painfully ironic result: its basic aim may have been to "magnify the role of Christ in the atonement," but its ultimate tendency was to deny, at least by implication, "the meaning of another, more central, Christological doctrine, the idea of the Incarnation itself."[54] And so we have to be wary. Arguments between Puritans and Quakers often seem to concern those who allow more and those who allow less "historic" importance to Christ. In reality, however, they involve the difference between assimilating the Son to the Father and assimilating Him to the Spirit.

Which brings us to Hawthorne's Quakers. The historicity (and the doctrinal basis) of their rejection of the Ilbrahim-Christ presents, as we have suspected, a slightly less obvious problem. Simplistically considered, their "enthusiasm" is easy enough to identify and reject: as individualistic seventeenth-century "prophets" rather than communitarian eighteenth-century "Friends," their spiritual "voice" reduces to social frustration, exhibitionism, misplaced sexual energy, and zealous masochism even more readily than the Puritan "covenant" reduces to that sadistic pleasure which the "sociologically competent" always derive from the need to punish misfits.[55] But they also embody, even at their origin, the authentically religious experience of that Spirit of God—that "spiritual Christ," as they said—who is quietly present in every man, provoking, if not precisely justifying, a loud and often lurid witness. And it is only in that form that they would offer a serious challenge to the theology of "The Gentle Boy." It is only toward this sort of experience that we can imagine the noticeably unexcessive Tobias Pearson "drifting," away from Puritan "society" and toward some spiritual "home." And only in this form do they reveal the subtle danger of assimilating the Son to the Spirit.

The outraged majority of Puritans—from Richard Baxter in England, to John Norton in defense of the New World persecution, to Cotton Mather in holy retrospect—accused the Quakers of a perversely "subjective" emphasis on the private revelations and solipsistic guarantees of the Spirit as against the public teachings of Scripture and the historic actions of Christ. To be sure, the operative God of those Puritans was so fundamentally Other that *any* testimony on behalf of Divine Immanence might strike them as self-indulgent, socially dangerous, and even crazy. But it is wrong to think of Hawthorne's Quakers as giving just *any* such testimony: the relationship is too coordinate or symbiotic. Where the Puritans locate (and mystify) the will of God in the meta-personal dictates of the Holy Community, the Quakers discover (and also mystify) it, by simple opposition, in the spontaneous motions of the pre-personal Self. In both systems the personal revelation of the Human Other goes begging. Legalistic Puritanism inspires persecution of the deviant self-expression of others as rigorously as it enforces self-restraint (masquerading as self-transcendence) on itself. Its strength lies in just such unmediated simplicity: there are Revealed Duties based on Otherworldly Loyalties which no "merely human" considerations can contravene; hence the dangers of tolerance, or of pity. But Spiritist Puritans do not, in reaction, seem to solve this problem of mediation at all. The affirmation of the presence of the Divine Light shining from behind or through the soul of every man is hardly to be socialized; it leaves every man searching for and then acting out the leadings of his own not-always-kindly Light. Especially in the face of persecution, the Light comes to signify not the Incarnation of God in every Other Human but rather the immediate duty of the Higher Self prophetically to oppose. The lesson may be read, identically, in literally hundreds of stalemated Puritan-Quaker confrontations. The wonder were if Hawthorne had *not* seen it.[56]

The Puritans repeatedly charged that the Quaker doctrine of the God-within not only pulled down the Father from his rightful, sovereign place, but that it also disrupted the traditional (Anselmian) scheme of substitutionary atonement. If the vivifying Spirit of God were so readily available, moving behind the private experience of every man, then what became of the Father's selecting decree, which created the basis of an objective justification? And what need would there be for a special rescue from total depravity by the direct historical intervention and unique activity of Christ? As Baxter would famously charge, many Quakers seemed to "deny that there [had ever been] any such Person as Jesus Christ who suffered at Jerusalem . . . and only call somewhat within themselves by the Name of Christ." And Roger Williams, for all his own insistence on Conscience over Covenant, essentially agreed: "They preached not Jesus Christ but themselves—yea, preached the Lord Jesus to be themselves."[57]

The Quakers had ready a series of responses that seem, polemically at least, equally serious and cogent. According to Cotton Mather, they "scoffed at our imagined God beyond the stars."[58] As well they might. For where in the world, they wanted to know, was the historic Christ *now?* Was He not more really in the hearts of men than in the Bosom of the Father? And when, according to the Puritan view, had His decidedly limited atonement ever expressed more than a slander on divine justice?[59] Where was there any newness, any grace in *their* covenant? How could they so obviously have missed the point? Was not the principle of spiritual immediacy (of a lively, experimental faith) the crucial re-discovery and cardinal tenet of all valid Reformation thought? Was not a "subjective" knowledge of Christ more important than all the facts of the Christian story and all the notional dogmas of the schoolmen, late and soon? Surely the Christian had to "witness a Christ nearer than Jerusalem."[60] And, as for the Father, the Quaker did not deny or ignore Him; he merely perceived Him correctly, as a kind and loving Father who forgave rather than as a Tyrant who needed to be placated and appeased. Was not Christ Himself, in fact, the figure of our adoption as His sons rather than our suffering surrogate? And so on.

And yet not quite endlessly, as we are wearily tempted to suppose. For it is with the idea of "adoption" that "The Gentle Boy" makes its most explicit contact with the technical (if heretical) categories of Christian theology. The tale's most central concern, after all, is the social fact and the religious meaning of Tobias Pearson's decision to adopt Ilbrahim—the original "Puritan" slowness of that action and the later "Quaker" distraction from it.

Noticing that the adoptionist idiom is somewhat more prominent in and more proper to Quaker than to Puritan theology, a modern historian puts the Hawthornean case quite simply: "an adoptionist Christology . . . would be likely to conceive salvation in terms of communion rather than atonement."[61] Salvation on this model would be more the revealed possibility of available union with God than the magical rescue from an otherwise inevitable and incurable depravity. Thus, in Hawthorne's version, Tobias Pearson's wish to adopt Ilbrahim would be the same as his otherwise puzzling "drift" toward Quakerism. Dimly recognizing the meaning of Ilbrahim, he is moved to adopt this figurative Samaritan just as God the Father is said to have adopted us all, Jew and Gentile alike, all as figuratively present in Christ as in Adam.[62] Mysteriously, Tobias hopes to find his earthly satisfaction and his heavenly salvation together, in human communion rather than in a Covenanted community.

And yet this is only part of the story. Sadly, Tobias finds neither a doctrinal nor a literal home among the Quakers, whom he seems partly to have misconceived. Somehow they are not quite what he had hoped; they are too busy testifying to something within their own unquiet hearts to care very much what happens to Ilbrahim. Indeed we must imagine that the figurative Ilbrahim is dying as much from Quaker disinterest as from Puritan rejection. The "voice" which called on Catherine to desert Ilbrahim has given way to the "light" which leads the Old Quaker to celebrate his approaching death. Evidently something else has caught their attention and drawn them away (literally) from a Scriptural duty and (figuratively) from the source of saving grace. They have rebelled against the Puritan Way—protested and sought elsewhere—without solving the main theological or human problem. If the Puritans are killing Christ in the name of the Father, the Quakers seem to be killing Him, just as efficiently, in the name of the Spirit[63]—and this in despite of their own "adoptionist" tendencies.

Modern historians have not quite worked it all out, from a body of Quaker literature which is more personal than dogmatic, and which is mostly defensive or polemical when doctrinal at all. But one can see in these "dry-bones" formulations the same troubled approach to understanding which Hawthorne seems to have reached from his own "desultory" examination of the original disputes. As it turns out, an adoptionist Christology is only one of many religious idioms struggling for primacy in the welter of seventeenth-century Quaker expression. Finally it does not predominate. More than a rhetorical point against the Puritans, perhaps, it nevertheless gets swallowed up by a simpler and more radical doctrine of the Spirit. Evidently the Puritan criticism was in some sense correct: ultimately the Quaker Spirit *did* displace the Divine Son.

If the Puritans of Perry Miller had, in spite of their own express loyalties, "minimized the role of the Savior in the glorification of the Father," the Quakers of Geoffrey Nuttall had just as clearly allowed their emphasis on the immediate presence of the Spirit to overshadow "the sense of uniqueness in the revelation of God through Christ." If Quakerism had meant *primarily* an adoptionist Christology, then one would expect to notice only that "forgiveness of sin recedes into the background, and . . . is replaced by a direct experience of God and victory over sin." But obviously it meant much more (or less) than this. Its tendency to conflate the historic Incarnation of the Son with the subjective Apocalypse of the Spirit meant that it would inevitably "reduce the significance for redemption of the coming of Christ in history."[64] The "positivist" point of critics like Williams and Baxter and Norton and Mather may well be beside the point: most Quakers (as opposed to certain Ranters) did not *entirely* transmute the historic Christ into a mystic allegory.[65] And surely Hawthorne was in no position to endorse the charge that the Quakers upset the balance of the Anselmian atonement. But there is still plenty of room and reason to imagine that Hawthorne was troubled by the ethical implications of the metaphorical affirmation that "Christ" is, in any sense, something "within ourselves." For here is where we discover that the doctrine of God-within is radically ambiguous.

That doctrine could mean, of course, that since the Spirit of God is within absolutely every man, then every man has to be regarded as a "Christic" revelation of God; and this would make most Spiritist formulations pragmatically interchangeable with most universalist interpretations of the Incarnation. But within Quakerism the doctrine does not usually mean that. More often—as in the fairly representative instances of Catherine and the Old Quaker—the doctrine of the God-within means something much simpler and more consistent with the linguistic formula itself. God-within usually means within *me*, since we obviously do not experience others as "within." What the Quakers offered was thus a theological redundancy: a Christ-within who was not different from a Spirit-within.[66] But what Hawthorne was looking for, and what Tobias sought but did not clearly find, was what the Christ-as-my-neighbor parable of the Good Samaritan so clearly suggests, and what only a steadfast doctrine of the Incarnation will guarantee: a revelation of the God who is without, who is Other, and yet fully human and fully personal.

Repeatedly, the Quaker loyalty turns out to be as simplistic and untroubled by worldly ambiguity as the Puritan: God is *in me*, and my duties accordingly proceed from my own spiritual experiences. The Spirit of God is in other men too, of course; but I discover it there by projection or willful fiat or prophetic confrontation rather than by ethical encounter. And since the Spirit is expected to be the same in all men, He usually authenticates what I already subjectively know, or else He is discerned to be not the True Spirit. One may have to make certain exceptions for the religious genius of George Fox. And the rule will scarcely hold for later generations of quietistic Quakerism. But, in general, historical or personal pluralism is no more the main point of the original Quaker "Awakening" than it is of the more conservative style of Puritanism at the same period.[67] If the latter sacrifices the human Christ in the conservative name of the Father's Justice, the former sacrifices Him in the revolutionary name of the Spirit's Prophecy. And this, as we have seen, is precisely what happens to Ilbrahim, that strange but human Other from outside the covenant, who yet finds no spiritual home within the Quaker protest. The orderly Puritans hate and fear the human difference he embodies. The prophetic Quakers scarcely notice his bodily existence at all.

If Hawthorne may be thought to have noticed any other peculiarity of the short-circuited Christology of the seventeenth-century Quakers, surely that would be their overly divine conception of even that Christ who was "without." One commentator, appealing to the sort of learning that almost certainly did *not* interest Hawthorne, calls their view "docetic," in recognition of their tendency to write "as if Christ had been a divine being who had come down from heaven and [merely] used the earthly body of Jesus." Another, noticing a Quaker injunction to "distinguish . . . between that which is called Christ, and the bodily garment which he wore," remarks that many Quakers "tended to make Jesus' life the ultimate instance of a human life and a human body taken over by the power of God"; and he concedes the (Apollinarian or Eutychean or Nestorian) tendency "to avoid linking too closely the human and the divine in Christ." Leaving all such *names* aside, we can well imagine that Hawthorne may indeed have sensed some *reality* in all of this: not only that seventeenth-century Quakers had the same trouble with the unified "personality" of Christ as they often had with their own, both being schizophrenically divided between a "soul" which was a manifestation of God's own "Spirit" and a "body of flesh [that] was but a veil," but also that no such self-divided Christ could ever reveal the divine *as man*.[68] The Quaker Christ, like the Quaker himself, always seems no more than a Ghost in a dying animal. It is a poor way to redeem a real world: if God is not *fully* incarnate in Christ, then He is surely not more so in Ilbrahim.

Thus at bottom the Quakers are as "Puritanical" as the Puritans. Their assimilative reductions of the Christian Trinity are separate, but in the end they are equal. Assimilating God's Incarnate Son to the Transcendent Father, the Puritans worship "a God beyond the stars" and establish a persecuting Superstate in his idolatrous image. Assimilating that same Son to the Spirit, the Quakers proclaim a God transcendentally "within"; if they care for some worldly salvation, it can only be some ultimate "Joachite" Age of the Spirit. In either case, the body's beauty dies.

In a confrontation between sects making these two different, equal reductions, it might indeed be hard to prefer. The Quakers might seem better but might in fact turn out ironically to be worse. And in the end all senses of difference and opposition might seem insignificant compared with the crucial, painful, "privative" similarity: neither side would have a doctrinal guarantee for the truth that in a fallen and pluralistic wilderness of the historical world the prime ethical imperative is *simply* loving one's neighbor as oneself. It should not be altogether surprising if, in such a world, the worshipers of the Father and the worshipers of the Spirit do indeed vie—or at least symbiotically cooperate—to kill the Son of God. And if we sense that this happens in the drama of "The Gentle Boy," then we probably need at least this much theology in our exegesis. We hear echoes of Williams' critique of legalist Puritanism, and we sense a painful confrontation with Edwards on natural virtue. We see Quakers protesting but ironically reduplicating the Puritan tendency to act out of unswerving loyalty to an unmediated absolute, substituting the ahistorical God-Within-the-Self for the ahistorical God-Beyond-the-World. We come to suspect that deficient theories of the Incarnation explain it all. And, if we can get past the prejudices, we can imagine how Hawthorne's totally historical bias and commitment would have led him inevitably to this discovery.

7

Our instinct for complexity or plurality of literary explanation, our preference for an historiography which is endlessly patient and judgment-reserving, and our *own* embarrassment about the "impertinence" of most theology may all conspire to make us uncomfortable with "The Gentle Boy" as history. If we accept the tale's primarily historical reference, and if we recognize the presence of its theological sophistication and moral severity, we may find ourselves ready to dismiss the tale as a "tract." This is a serious mistake. Those critics who have addressed the tale as "a mature study of bigotry and persecution" have rightly denied that it is a literalistic attack. And those who have sensed that there is more than "pathos" in Hawthorne's theme have rightly encouraged a seriously religious reading.[69] We will certainly be right to feel that a full explanation of the events in the New England of 1656 to 1661 depends on more influences than Hawthorne's fictional construct can possibly reflect. And (on the other hand) it must seem self-evident that all instances of religious persecution may be explained in part by somebody's transcendental overcommitment. But if we begin by turning away from "The Gentle Boy" as history because it implies clear moral judgment based on a more or less traditional theology, then we will end by rejecting the more controlled achievements of "Young Goodman Brown" and "The Minister's Black Veil" as well; for neither psychological ambiguity nor literary deconstructionism ever manages to obscure Hawthorne's own moral earnestness. And surely the major achievement of "The Gentle Boy" itself is the unfailing accuracy with which it identifies the theological sources of false transcendence in the specific world of seventeenth-century Puritanism.

Founded on a theology of the religious irrelevance of the "merely human," the Puritan Problem expressed itself in a relentless and fundamentally parodic attack on the hypothetical natural man and his supposed natural virtue. To be sure, the available natural virtue and the ideal true virtue might be materially the same; they differed only formally, according to the natural or gracious motive or informing spirit. Thus it never was quite wrong—indeed it was always quite appropriate—to love one's spouse, parent, child, or indeed one's "neighbor." But never "as oneself." Just there peeped forth the Devil's claws, for all love founded on the analogy of self-love could never be anything but "selfish." And even this delicate emphasis is everywhere upset by the literary vigor of the Puritan attack upon the entirely fictitious image of the man who endlessly resisted true humiliation and inner conversion, and who ceaselessly pointed to the glorious raiment of his outward works, stupidly unaware or stubbornly unconvinced that they were but filthy rags.

As one twentieth-century historian has summarized this dominant effort of Puritan moral rhetoric,

> There was a type of man whom the Puritans never tired of denouncing. He was a good citizen, a man who obeyed the laws, carried out his social obligations, never injured others. The Puritans called him a "civil man," and admitted that he was "outwardly just, temperate, chaste, careful to follow his worldly business, will not hurt so much as his neighbors dog, payes every man his owne, and lives of his owne; no drunkard, adulterer, or quarreller; loves to live peaceably and quietly among his neighbors." This man, this paragon of social virtue, the Puritans said, was on his way to Hell, and their preachers continually reminded him of it.[70]

Not recognizing the extent to which such rhetoric is in fact parodic, the historian in question is at some pains to explain why, in the moral climate created by virtually thousands of sermons delivering this same message—that mere natural virtue is always not only worthless but hypocritical as well—so many Puritans were yet so moralistic. But evidently Hawthorne responded to the pervasive Puritan attack on human nature and virtue by asking somewhat different questions. As always, what he wanted to know was partly hypothetical. What would "tend" to happen if people really believed such rhetoric and operated accordingly, unchecked by any other beliefs or influences?[71]

What, he wondered, would be the life of ordinary persons who followed the Puritan's ideal logic of Grace and Supernature, unflinchingly, to its logical conclusion? Suppose the natural man were not necessarily the hypocritical man who trusted in his own works *as against* humiliation and regeneration. What if he were simply a person who seemed to remain, despite his very best intentions, ineluctably a natural man? What about the case of a person whose inner consciousness simply did not provide constant testimony of the presence of saving grace? He believed Puritan doctrine,

196

presumably, but he lacked the experience of regeneration. What about the unparodic, and very probably normative case—which William James himself neglects—of the Once-Born Sick Soul? Only an "Arminian," of course, can see that the question has real relevance. In strict Puritan logic such a man has to be either hypocritical about his own moral "striving" or else already in grace, needing only to be enlightened about the true condition of his New Birth.[72] But Arminian temperaments *have* to ask the question in all seriousness. And the best answer ever given in all of American literature is embodied in the more-than-pathetic career of Tobias Pearson.

Though officially within the covenant at the beginning of the tale, he is nevertheless not a completely convinced and assured Puritan. He is, as Hawthorne says rather carefully, in "a state of religious dulness" (94). This might be *merely* psychological, the naturalistic and very familiar "ebb" after some original "flow" of grace; or it might be the fatal sign that his public status never *was* justified by a truly regenerate inner reality. Acutely sensitive to that possibility, and to the community's charge that his excessive concern for mere human good marks him all too clearly as the "backslidden" (that is, deceived or hypocritical) Puritan, Tobias Pearson's troubled psyche executes the simple expedient of "drifting" toward Quakerism. It is a "warmer" religion; perhaps the true experience of grace is to be found there. Or perhaps (in spite of his intellectual hesitations) the Quaker doctrine of the Spirit can provide some sense of self-worth and afford some guarantee for the natural affections. Perhaps the recessive personality of Tobias Pearson can find a religious "home" outside the dominance of Puritan orthodoxy.

But the crushing irony, as we have seen, is that the Quakers are not that different. At one level they are merely a sectarian offshoot of an already sectarian Puritanism; as such they have merely reversed certain polarities in redefining the locus of grace without really providing a place for integrated nature; lacking any satisfactory sense of God's Incarnation, they never really escape the fatal either/or of Puritan logic. And as rebels, primarily, they are worse off than the Puritans: their enthusiastic protest throws off all those restraints which in most cases keep orthodox Puritans well within the limits of the ordinary virtues they scorn. Their own unquiet hearts keep the Quakers worse than homeless. Catherine may not "go naked for a sign," like a number of her real-life counterparts in the sources; but she does strip her spiritual self of all its earthly encumbrances, including her child. Thus the early movement of the story from Tobias to Catherine—from the failed-saint trying to treat a Samaritan as a neighbor to the failed-mother acting as prophetic spiritual nomad—traces the progress of moral and psychological aberration which follows from the slander of the human in the name of the divine. The result of consistent action in accordance with such a logic would be the extinction of life, as we scarcely need the chilling speech of the Old Quaker Saint to remind us.[73]

To deny nature so entirely, even if "strategically," is to sin against life, even if in the name of grace. And so Tobias longs for death because his unregenerate natural life seems spiritually meaningless. So Catherine gives spiritual testimony while her natural child is dying of rejection. And so, by natural extension, Puritans execute Quakers who invite execution. The "heart" of New England is more than "rent"; it seems positively committed to its own self-extinction. And with a pretty full awareness of the values at stake, Hawthorne takes his own once-born stand on "The Absurdity and Blasphemy of Deprecating Natural Virtue."[74]

It does not matter that his judgment is tendentiously incomplete, or that any good Puritan could answer Hawthorne with a clarification or a distinction.[75] If history were to be morally useful—as Hawthorne would later complain Simmes's historical novels were not—one would have to conclude something, take a stand somewhere on the meaning of the moral experience of the past. Permanent openness would lack seriousness. Hawthorne elected to take his first stand on the question of Nature and Grace. Attractive as it might seem as a form of private piety, the premise that God is everything and man absolutely nothing had not stood the "pragmatic test" of application as public dogma in seventeenth-century America.[76] In itself the Puritan position has seemed to produce sadistic sins against nature in the name of a Transcendent Father; by reaction it bred self-expressive but ironically self-destructive sins against nature in the name of an equally un-incarnate Spirit. Something fundamental seemed missing, some guarantee that mutual respect for our common life according to nature is in itself a religious value of the highest significance. And that something would seem to come from a Christology more humane than that implied in the "Puritan" doctrine of substitutionary atonement. If this meant adoptionism in even its heretical form, so be it. It is characteristic of Hawthorne that his fiction points toward theological ideas beyond the range of orthodoxy but does not push out to explore them; this, we may well suspect, is what Melville found so fascinating but ultimately so frustrating. In any event, and with whatever intellectual risk, Hawthorne aligns himself against that "singular Christian" Jonathan Edwards—against that Edwards whose *Nature of True Virtue* epitomized the orthodox position on Nature and Grace.

And possibly against the greater genius of George Fox himself. The problem was, after all, sufficiently evident in one very famous "Puritan" passage from the *Journal:*

I found that there were two thirsts in me, the one after the creatures, to have gotten help and strength there, and the one after the Lord the

Creator and his Son Jesus Christ. And I saw that all the world could do me no good. If I had a king's diet, palace, and attendance, all would have been as nothing . . . But the Lord did stay my desires on himself, from whom my help came, and my care was cast upon him alone.[77]

Obviously, our hearts were made for God alone; neither Augustine of Hippo nor yet Miller of Cambridge could say it better.[78] And yet somewhat too obviously in these latter days, perhaps. One has to be obtuse indeed to confuse God with food, or wealth, or honor; the significant questions all concern the spiritual "use" (if love may ever be so called) of human creatures. And at the theological level they touch the problem of the relation between that "Son Jesus Christ" and that "Lord the Creator"—who is also, obviously, the "Lord" who stays Fox's desires. What might that Son imply about the proper "use" of the human creature? Such questions neither Fox nor his immediate disciples ever quite cleared up, not for themselves and not for Tobias Pearson. Fox left the impression that, because the thirsts of the Spirit are perfectly satiable only in some perfect world beyond, the leadings of the Spirit were always a call to that world alone. "Even Jesus Christ," he thought, spoke primarily to that condition of desire.[79]

Hawthorne, we may safely infer, judged otherwise. We may easily overstate the self-consciousness or the precision of his own (probably demythicized) Christology. And it would be folly to doubt that many of his nineteenth-century readers responded less to the theology of adoptionism than to the sociology of orphanhood. But we must also suspect that "The Gentle Boy" exists to suggest that the problem of "the creatures" may not be as simple in human life as it is in Augustinian logic; that "Christ" exists to remind us to be slow to slander the whole of "carnal" creation. The story "teaches," by negative example, what it might be like to live in a world unredeemed by the Incarnation. It might very well be like the lives of Tobias, Catherine, and the Old Quaker. Its proper results might be sadism, masochism, death-wish, and murder.

Happily, however, the tale's history does not end on quite so grim a note. Toleration—out of England, Hawthorne grimly insists—does finally prevail. In England where a whole array of sects were competing for supremacy or at least for the right to exist, people evidently learned earlier that not even the lust for Godliness could justify the disruption of ordinary patterns of natural life and virtue. Even English Puritans found they could live the common, natural life with other men, as good men if not as visible saints. In America, Hawthorne evidently felt, where Puritan dichotomies continued to be official dogma, the realization that the limits of nature are absolute and not to be transcended in this life was longer in coming. Still, the ending of

"The Gentle Boy" asserts, more as a hope than as a fact, it finally came. Even Catherine, after a period of "fanaticism [that] had become wilder by the sundering of human ties," finally returned "to Pearson's dwelling and made that her home." It was as if Ilbrahim's "gentle spirit came down from heaven to teach his parent a true religion" (104).

And yet there are ironies even in this last section, which seems so hopefully to promise redemption through the "liberalization" of simple historical continuance. "In the process of time," as Hawthorne summarizes, "a more Christian spirit—a spirit of forbearance, though not of cordiality or approbation—began to pervade the land in regard to the persecuted sect." The transformation is, of course, a happy one, but it is incomplete. Things are *almost* back to the level of the expectations of natural virtue. There is no vindictiveness (although Hawthorne is not forgetting the bitterness of Sewel, the eighteenth-century Quaker historian); but neither is there cordiality. Still lacking was that quality which a New England critic of New England Zeal had once called "gentleness."[80] With regard to Catherine specifically "there was that degree of pity which it is pleasant to experience" and "every one was ready to do her the little kindnesses which are not costly, yet manifest good will" (104–105). Mere sentiment, perhaps, yet here is where religion might begin again. True virtue there might yet be; but historically, psychologically, and theologically it would have to come after or in supplement of such natural virtue, not in magical replacement and never in rhetorical opposition. All men might yet come to realize some sort of "Likeness to God," even as William Ellery Channing was promising. But for Hawthorne that process would have to begin with the recognition of Christ as revealed in every man—not as Saint but simply as man; and not as Self but as Other.

The final irony from Hawthorne's historical point of view is that in his own 1820's, New England's religious good will could not be seen to have progressed *very* far beyond the moment of its official "restoration." The orthodox-liberal religious controversy, which (in Sophia Peabody's words) "divided all families," had been raging openly since about 1815. It had come to its most public climax with the legal division of Massachusetts' "Standing Order" in 1820, the year before Hawthorne began his (essentially religious) education at Bowdoin; and the fundamental points of difference were still being openly debated in the years when "The Gentle Boy" was being conceived and written. In those hectic days, when every man was forced to be his own theologian, the relation of natural virtue to saving grace remained the central problem and continued to provoke religious hostility in the pages of religious magazines. Questions concerning the Unity of God and the precise moment and nature of the "generation" of the Son by the Father subsided soon enough, well before Hawthorne began to borrow the *Christian Examiner* from the Salem Athenaeum in 1827. But the more vital questions of Christian "anthropology" and of the "economy of salvation" raged on. And those hot debates may have had as direct a bearing on "The Gentle Boy" as the celebrations of 1825 and 1826 had on "Roger Malvin's Burial" and "My Kinsman, Major Molineux."[81]

To be sure, the angry passions on both sides had not resulted in persecutions or judicial murders; but the whole affair manifestly lacked human tolerance, charity, "gentleness." And though the theological "sides" were by no means precisely what they had been in the 1660's, many of the fundamental propositions being debated were versions of the old unsolved problems. The orthodox were still clinging to their "inhumane" dogma of substitutionary atonement, along with the embarrassingly mechanical account of the divine separation of powers with which it was allied. The replacement of Anselm by Grotius had not helped much: God the Father now demanded full legalistic atonement for "governmental" or pragmatic rather than for "vindictive" reasons; but he still demanded it.[82] He demanded it from a creature whose ontological status meant he never could entirely pay up, and whose post-lapsarian state of total depravity meant he *would* not even do what he *could*. Ergo Christ, the second Adam, the second legal substitute. And ergo the Spirit, enabling an otherwise impotent man to accept Christ as his atoning redeemer and only then, for the very first time, to place a truly virtuous act. Surely it is impossible—without uncritically overvaluing Unitarian liberalism, even in its most attractive (Channingesque) variety—to imagine that Hawthorne was very sympathetic toward such a Trinitarian schema. The impoverished Christology at its center probably has as much to do with "the Beginnings of Unitarianism in America" as some of the other causes more often noticed.[83] And surely it is possible to believe that Hawthorne saw the problem as clearly as Channing.

It goes without saying that there are important differences between the glowing affirmations of Channing's pastoral theology and the darkened implications of Hawthorne's critical fictions. Casual as they often seem, Channing's views can be formulated much more technically than Hawthorne's. And, more specifically, Hawthorne's everywhere-repeated emphasis on the "Christic" significance of the Saving Other is different in tone and theological implication both from Channing's recognizably Arian Christology and from his more original theory of the "essential sameness" of God and man. Probably Hawthorne would have found his view both too literal and too liberal. Quite possibly he would have noticed that Channing's perfectionist anthropology actually neglected the Spirit; certainly the Transcendentalists would see that this was so.[84] But however all that may be, it seems necessary to advert to the Trinitarian controversies of the 1820's to grasp the full historical context and to feel the full historical motivation of "The Gentle Boy."

Like Channing, Hawthorne's attention could not escape a fascination with the intractable dogmatics of New England's own indigenous religious tradition. Like Channing, Hawthorne was deeply concerned about the "tendencies" of Puritan piety. Hawthorne, however, was equally fascinated by the "Romantic" problem of "the Solitary," the basically religious man who somehow failed to find a home anywhere in the human world. Where Channing's investigations would lead him on to the triumphant affirmation of man's nearly univocal "Likeness to God," Hawthorne would find his own distinctive note in the saving grace of genuine intercourse with the Human Other; from the first, his "Christology" would be affected by his overriding fear of religious solipsism. Both men began with a "liberal" bias against the legalistic rigor of the Puritan account of salvation, from which spiritualistic fervor was somehow no relief; both men wished to make greater allowances for "nature" than did the tradition epitomized by Edwards. Channing would go *on*, theologically, to affirm much more about the similarities between the spiritual powers of man himself and those he had always ascribed to God. Hawthorne's essential task remained more historical, even as his essential "bias" disposed him to the problems of Puritanism.

For Hawthorne it remained to go *back*—to examine and to dramatize, again and again—the desperations of Nature and the parodies of Grace which led even self-declared Puritan Saints to end up no less alone and unsatisfied than the baffled Tobias Pearson. For Hawthorne, Godliness alone was never enough to solve the riddle of man's social existence: Elective Redemption rent the heart of humanity, and Universal Perfectibility scarcely fit the facts of any condition short of the eschatological. Liberal theologians and philosophers of good hope might *yet* discover some principle of unity on the affirmative ground of shared "Likeness." Hawthorne would continue to look for salvation from the Other. And he would continue to carry out his researches within the historical province of Puritan Piety. Deconstructing only where political "story" came flagrantly in his way, he remained committed above all else to analyzing the powerful failure of Calvinist logic and Covenant tactics to find or build a home for man in the wilderness of his own world.

II

Tales of the Puritans

✤ Four ✤
PIOUS IMAGE AND POLITICAL MYTH
A RESOLVED AMBIVALENCE

ALL THREE of Hawthorne's early projected collections were deeply involved in the literary business of "using American materials"; to that limited extent all are equally historical in their intention. And yet we can notice a marked increase of historical sophistication from the "Seven" to the "Provincial" tales. Nor will our argument be complete before we have suggested—by way of a Conclusion, still some way off—that "The Story Teller" was intended as a piece of cultural historicism as complicated as anyone in America has ever attempted. For the present, however, it may be enough to remind ourselves of the nature and import of Hawthorne's earliest detectable development.

Largely it is a matter of learning: not only did Hawthorne seem to know much more about the large tensions and local textures of the American past in 1829 than he had in 1825, but also, and more significantly, he had brought far more of that knowledge to bear on stories like "Malvin" and "Molineux" than he had on "The Hollow" or even "The Wives." The reader can learn more history from the later tales than from the earlier ones, and in an important sense he *has* to: the early ones evoke a tone of pastness and (perhaps) propose an image of a certain local and temporal past; but the later ones riddle with irony the process by which popular story has turned "well-remembered" images into national myth. Which is to say that *more* is involved than mere knowledge, crucial as that must always be to the historicist's account of the world, in literature or in criticism. At issue as well is an entirely new literary epistemology—"essentialist" still in its use of character, but "ironic" in its understanding of American politics, "critical" in its historical intentions, and even (in a limited sense) "deconstructionist" in its mimetic strategies.

What might a specifically committed "American" writer do, in the 1830's, with just such a "modern" set of attitudes and procedures? No doubt more than one project might seem available. And clearly it will not do to homogenize Hawthorne's early career by suggesting that, after "The Gentle Boy," the Puritans simply took over; too much else is going on in the tales that ultimately got themselves collected into the 1837 *Twice-told Tales.*[1] But, just as clearly, a series of "Tales of the Puritans" is one thing that did in fact suggest itself. And surely criticism has long recognized that some such series is definitively important for our appreciation of Hawthorne before his experiences in Boston and Concord or at Brook Farm: these are the tales which, as a group, we customarily anthologize and write about; and these are the tales which Hawthorne himself, anticipating one of his modern editors, once thought to collect into a volume to be called something like *"The Scarlet Letter* and Other Tales of the Puritans."[2] Evidently we already understand, at some level, that long before there was an interesting literary unit called "Hawthorne and Melville," there was an absolutely vital one called "Hawthorne and the Puritans."

That problem, as we began this study by suggesting, has always seemed to involve Hawthorne's "attitude toward Puritanism." Was he as hostile as he might seem from the dominant evidence of "The Gentle Boy"? Was he as approving as the overt conclusions of "The Gray Champion" and "Endicott" seem to suggest? Or was he simply ambivalent, as both the strategic dichotomies of "The May-Pole" and certain instructed re-interpretations of those other tales would indicate? And if so, what were the precise terms of that ambivalence? Did he reject the dogmas of that rigidified Puritan religion and yet embrace their psychological equivalents? Or did he eschew their radical piety altogether, while yet endorsing the "tendency" (or perhaps the "typology") of their proto-revolutionary politics?[3] And how would *any* of these formulations of unresolved personal ambivalence help us assess the studied literary ambiguities of masterpieces like "Young Goodman Brown" and "The Minister's Black Veil"?

These questions may seem, by now, a little old-fashioned. But they are honest ones; and probably every interpreter of Hawthorne has some preferred solution, whatever aspect of Hawthorne's work his particular style of analysis means to problematize. Probably they need to be faced explicitly. But probably they need to be related to other sorts of questions as well. For in the end Hawthorne's personal attitude toward Puritanism itself is not to be separated from his historical judgment of the meaning of their myth.

On the more personal or "religious" side, the evidence of "The Gentle Boy" seems trustworthy. Insofar as Puritanism may be defined as that extreme of Augustinian piety which constantly insists that nothing *merely* human can be spiritually salutary or psychologically satisfying, our first impressions of Hawthorne's dogmatic rejection are probably right enough. To be sure, Melville is always there to remind us that Hawthorne continually meditates on the existential truth expressed in the story of the fall of man; so

Melville and Schopenhauer are not alone, in the nineteenth century, in being thus reconciled to the whole of the Old Testament. But like Melville himself, Hawthorne is just as clearly a part of that large and more "liberal" cultural movement which aimed at reaffirming the value of man's ordinary capacities.[4] And neither "Young Goodman Brown" nor "The Minister's Black Veil" finally alters this sense. In fact, the more Hawthorne meditates on "the dark problem of this life" (down to *The Scarlet Letter* itself), the more convinced he becomes of "the moral argument against Calvinism": Puritan theological categories do indeed have gloomy moral consequences. Evidently Hawthorne would continue to feel that, whatever may be required for the "Glory of God," human sanity cannot sustain too radical an opposition between nature and grace.

But (also evidently) this is only part of the problem. For if the majority of intellectual persons in New England shared this "belief" about Puritanism, based on an image that was both readily available and difficult to dispel, still this was not the only image available.[5] Nor was it, in fact, the image which generated the dominant American (political) story. Granted that Puritanism made individuals "gloomy," did it not also make a whole people strong and stern in defense of principle, even fierce in righteous resistance to tyranny? Is not this higher, more social and historical consideration the reason why it is proper to value and even venerate them?—why, in cold prose, we may be so fervently glad to have had "such ancestors"? Did they not lay down their own psychological and moral lives so that later generations of more liberal ("demythological") Christians might enjoy a richer experience of "liberty" than their own gloomy and sectarian minds could ever conceive? Had this not been, after all, their truly Christic function?

Such, at any rate, was the story which George Bancroft essayed to tell in the first volume of his *History of the United States,* published (in 1834) just a few months before Hawthorne's evocation, proscription, and deconstruction of "The Gray Champion." And if anyone *besides* Hawthorne thought to protest, the fact has gone unrecorded. Indeed later historians have been forced to conclude that Bancroft took over almost the entire historical field at once, and held it virtually unchallenged for over fifty years, primarily because he was able to enunciate—with conviction, elegance, and learning— what nearly everyone already believed.[6] Thus, for an "American" writer of the 1830's, the brightening myth of Puritanic liberty was as inescapable as the darkening image of Calvinistic gloom. Deepest down, it could be said, Puritanism fostered "the undying principles of democratic liberty."[7] And wasn't it pretty to think so?

A series of "Tales of the Puritans" would have to notice this question. It might well tempt a moralistic writer to dig up for geologic inspection the stony heart of Puritanism's representative "Man of Adamant." Or, much more seriously, to face again (in spite of the hard-won conclusions of his "Gentle Boy") his own personal relation to that "something, somehow like Original Sin"; and out of that embattled reconsideration might come the astonishingly adult "cases" of Brown and Hooper, conflicting the categories of Calvin, pre-empting the acumen of Freud (and requiring their own separate chapters). But the project would almost certainly force him to consider the "historic" relation between Puritanic virtue and the democratic creed; surely that matter could generate the minor masterpieces of the "Champion" and of "Endicott." And it might even tease him into trying to discover some master image into which the entire gloomy-stern-righteous-democratic myth of Puritan America had already been conflated. If so, then "The May-Pole of Merry Mount" will turn out to be a more dazzling example of historical criticism, and of literary deconstruction, than we have even begun to suspect.

1

Except that the shades of its irony have been so difficult to detect, and except for its suggestive relation to Bancroft, and except that Hawthorne placed it first in (and first thought of making it the title piece of) the first collection of tales he *did* manage to publish, "The Gray Champion" might almost pass with only the briefest notice, even from the most determined historicist.[8] But for all these reasons—and perhaps for one further reason, of "method"—it really does call for more careful treatment than it usually receives.

We need to notice, first of all, that like the sketches of "Phips," "Hutchinson," and "Bullivant," "The Gray Champion" employs the indirection of ironic contrast on its own fairly simple surface, so that even when Hawthorne seems to be going out of his way to say approving things about the stern and independent "spirit" of Puritanism, the literary irony counts for more than the personal patriotism. But there is also a less superficial reason why we are badly deceived if we regard this little tableau sketch as Hawthorne's own "imaginative" contribution to the myth of the Puritans as founding fathers; for when Hawthorne's magic begins to "mobilize" his already legendary "Angel of Hadley" in all sorts of Puritan-Revolutionary causes and occasions (and *only* in these), he actually shows us how a patriotic myth is put together and, in case we care, how we might learn to escape its drastic political oversimplification.[9]

The patriotic rhetoric with which the sketch begins, and which rattles its saber throughout much of the tale's authorial "talk," is recognizable enough, and extreme enough, to make us at least suspect that Hawthorne's use of it is situational and dramatic rather than personal and didactic. There is, of course, no perfect litmus test for detecting irony on the tongue of the speaker; it always exists (or not) pretty much in the ear of the listener. But in the end most of us will think better of Hawthorne's intelligence if he doesn't quite mean *all* that his "narrator" says—if "Hawthorne" is merely invoking the given and conventional definition of all American history as "libertarian" (though often *malgré lui*), and of everything "anti-American" as evil in the extreme. This is how we always decide the question of irony: how plausible—and how admirable—is the literary result?

Accordingly, the elaborate description of the administration of Sir Edmund Andros—who, on behalf of James II, ruled New England and New York together between 1686 and 1689, under the terms of "the Dominion of New England," after the revocation of the original charter and before the New-Charter government of Phips—seems a little excessive.[10] The people of New England are said to have "groaned under the actual pressure of heavier wrongs than those threatened ones which brought on the Revolution"; James II is referred to as "the bigoted successor of Charles the Voluptuous"; Andros himself is called an "unprincipled soldier [sent] to take away our liberties and endanger our religion" (9), his administration a tyranny of taxes and laws without representation.[11] Even so, until this last minute the colonists have remained loyal, out of sheer "filial love," to whatever government has happened to emerge from the political turbulence of England's century of revolution. Of course there are broad "hints" that things can be seen another way as well. This very first paragraph ends by reminding us that, till now, American colonial loyalty has been fairly "nominal": the colonists having "ruled themselves" throughout England's decades of distraction, actually enjoying more "freedom than is yet the privilege of the native subjects of Great Britain" (9–10), filial submission has amounted to the unimpeded power of the colonial government to do exactly as it wished; and even *that* submission, we now back up to notice, was "sullen." And, as our own political instincts and knowledge of the facts of the case begin to restore our sense of proportion, if the "wrongs . . . which brought on the Revolution" were themselves only "threatened," then perhaps those that provoked an after-the-fact ouster of some pompous royal surrogate may have involved somewhat less than the extinction of Saxon Liberty.[12]

But we scarcely need the "hints." The rhetoric itself is extravagant and the political style—here, and in everything that follows—is "paranoid," in just the sense that Perry Miller has taught us to recognize. The narrator of "The Gray Champion," whatever else may be true of him, has been reading too much Cotton Mather.[13] We fully expect his rhetoric to proclaim, if not to precipitate, a Glorious Revolution.

Just so, in the midst of these strained loyalties, the first rumor of the rising fortunes of the Prince of Orange has turned the "sullen submission" to James's vicar into "bold glances." The official response is as predictable as it is unimaginative: "an imposing show of strength" (10). Fatal miscalculation, since what the Puritan spirit lacks in religious toleration or mere political tolerance it more than makes up for in strength of purpose: somber, stern, sober, and severe, this crowd of latter-day Puritans wears a "gloomy but undismayed expression," retaining their "confidence in Heaven's blessing on a righteous cause" (10). The point, clearly, is not to decide whether this oddly proto-revolutionary cause is *in fact* righteous, but merely to grasp that in the view of provincial Puritanism, *all* its causes are righteous, all its wars holy; hence all are espoused alike with religious zeal. Accordingly we glimpse, among the crowd, "veterans of King Philip's War, who had burned villages and slaughtered young and old, with pious fierceness, while the godly souls throughout the land were helping them with prayer" (11). Thus even if we are unfamiliar, historically, with the ugly character of *this* particular Indian "Fight" as Holy War, even if we do not advert to the "devilish" suggestion (made to Goodman Brown) that the torches the Puritans used in this war were lighted in hell, and even if we do not (yet) recall that this is where the prototype of Hawthorne's mythic Champion made his literal appearance, we can read no more politics except under pain of irony.[14]

The comments which ripple through the crowd reveal a combination of unquestioning self-righteousness and political persecutionism which amounts to Cosmic Paranoia indeed, even if the Puritans do have certain enemies, here and at the Court of King James: "Satan will strike his masterstroke presently"; "the Pope of Rome has given orders for a new St. Bartholomew" (11). Somebody burn an effigy; call out the North End Mob, and the South End Mob, to break unjust laws, and heads.[15] Only the "wiser class" sees the distressing pettiness of Andros' real and "somewhat less atrocious" (12) object—to confound the opposition by capturing and holding hostage the Old-Charter governor, the patriarchal Bradstreet. Bradstreet himself cautions against rashness; but violence is not at all out of the question, as events may yet discover (in the words of the departed Endicott) a spirit "wiser than [Bradstreet's,] for the business now in hand."[16]

As the procession of Royal Rulers advances toward the Puritan Populace, Hawthorne offers us his own stunningly perceptive "profile of a provincial mentality":

A double rank of Soldiers made their appearance, occupying the whole breadth of the passage, with shouldered matchlocks, and matches burning, so as to present a row of fires in the dusk. Their steady march was like the progress of a machine, that would roll irresistibly over every thing in its way. Next, moving slowly, with a confused clatter of hoofs on the pavement, rode a party of mounted gentlemen, the central figure being Sir Edmund Andros, elderly, but erect and soldierlike. Those around him were his favorite councillors, and the bitterest foes of New-England. At his right hand rode Edward Randolph, our arch enemy, that "blasted wretch," as Cotton Mather calls him, who achieved the downfall of our ancient government, and was followed with a sensible curse, through life and to his grave. On the other side was Bullivant, scattering jests and mockery as he rode along. Dudley came behind, with a downcast look, dreading, as well he might, to meet the indignant gaze of the people, who beheld him, their only countryman by birth, among the oppressors of his native land. The captain of a frigate in the harbor, and two or three civil officers under the Crown, were also there. But the figure which most attracted the public eye, and stirred up the deepest feeling, was the Episcopal clergyman of King's Chapel, riding haughtily among the magistrates in his priestly vestments, the fitting representative of prelacy and persecution, the union of church and state, and all those abominations which had driven the Puritans to the wilderness. Another guard of soldiers, in double rank, brought up the rear. (12–13)

Evidently Hawthorne has read the psychohistorical meaning of the Jeremiads of the 1680's with perfect inerrancy: the Puritans have believed without effective challenge in the absolutely singular nature of their arch-Protestant mission for so long that conflict of relative political interest seems a direct and even diabolic affront to the will of God. If we cannot grasp the entire performance as an "echo" of Perry Miller, we can surely notice the "borrowing" from Cotton Mather: Edward Randolph, that "arch-enemy" who "achieved the downfall of our ancient government," has become a "blasted wretch"; the minor bureaucratic functionary who thought to get ahead by forcing New England to obey the laws of imperial commerce—and by making America safe for Anglicanism—has become an accursed soul and an apt figure of the Devil himself.[17] The formula has never seemed more clear: discovering themselves in the midst of a Holy War against their ancient Arch-Enemy, the latter-day Puritans recover their original, significant identity. No wonder a Gray Champion appears: he is only the soul they seemed to have lost.

Of course the political situation is not, in all literal fact, a very happy one. The offspring of zealots whom history had once uniquely offered "a wide door of liberty" are watching that door close; a transplanted remnant which has never known the confrontation and the compromise of British politics is finding out what it is like to live under a government which does not grow out of its own express compacts and which cannot therefore be said to flow directly from God. Obviously such a people cannot rejoice at such a prospect: having dared to dream the "Why not?" of a divine covenant, they now find themselves face-to-face with the "Nevermore" of provincial history. Failing some altogether unlooked-for accommodation with reality, there will surely be resistance. And perhaps bloodshed.

But just then, as if miraculously, and in a "moment" which the story seems neither to condense nor expand, the Puritans are saved from both politics and violence by the magical appearance of a "Champion." His voice, "fit either to rule a host in the battle-field or to be raised to God in prayer," orders the advancing oppression to "Stand"; and, holding his own true ground, he further prophesies that, thanks to some marvelous turning in secular affairs beyond the ocean, "there is no longer a Popish tyrant on the throne of England" (16). So as indomitable Puritans prepare to follow their leader into battle, the suddenly-less-confident oppressors nervously retreat. Perhaps even they can recognize an avatar; perhaps they have merely taken a body count. In any case, they leave the field all uncontested; and bloodless.[18]

"And who was [this] Gray Champion?"—the story now challenges us to decide. And, less sententiously, what are we to make of his glorious revelation of Sion's safety? Clearly the ideological stakes are pretty high: if oppression proves the Devil, what might not be inferred from liberation? Challenged so squarely, we can scarcely evade the issue. And yet we also realize, once our historical scholarship has caught up with our own unavoidable involvement in political myth, that to identify the Gray Champion is to meddle in a matter already well developed by the demands of national story. No very simple answer can produce anything less tedious than a twice-told tale. Nor can it heal an irony already so far advanced.

Acting carefully on our behalf, therefore, Hawthorne's own "history" refuses categorical decision. Remote, legendary sources have suggested that we are dealing with an "Angel," a divine emissary sent to intervene on behalf of the Chosen, by way of Special Providence; more proximate, literary sources identify this Champion as General Goffe, one of the regicides of Charles I, fled to New England for safe hiding, but available still for all manner of service in latter-day manifestations of Puritan zeal.[19] And so the tale equivocates. On the one hand the Champion introduces himself as one who has "stayed the march of a King himself, ere now"; and the tale's own rhetoric suggests that perhaps his name might indeed be found "in the records of that stern Court of Justice" which taught such a "humbling lesson to the monarch and [a] high example to the subject." On the other hand, however, the Champion is himself constrained to confess that it has been "vouchsafed" for him "to appear once again on earth, in the good old cause of [God's] saints" (16–17); and his foreknowledge of the overthrow of James I seems to confirm the supernatural origin of his mission. Thus a conflicted text recapitulates an uneasy case of contradictory ontologies and a steady state of historical overdetermination. Resolution seems impossible. Some identification tests baffle even historians.

Failing resolution, then, the text attempts transcendence, again on our own anxious behalf. Perhaps the literal (historic) identity of the Champion is entirely beside the symbolic (political) point. Suffice it to call him "the type of New England's hereditary spirit," which he surely is in either case. In either case he "stands for" that inbred and inveterate resistance to oppression which will (as we know) reappear at the Boston Massacre, at Lexington, and at Bunker's Hill; and which may (as we both trust and dread) materialize yet again, whenever there is darkness, adversity, and peril—whenever "New England sons" need to "vindicate their ancestry" (18). Demon still, if man or Angel.

At the level of *secular* myth, obviously, further distinction merely dulls our wit. And in this regard, the Champion is precisely what Sir Walter Scott surely recognized him to be—even as his own inspired antiquarianism redeemed a story out of the pages of Timothy Dwight's dusty *Travels*—that immemorial "King in the Mountain" who "will not die but is removed to a mountain or a cave and sleeps until some need or danger of his people will call him out . . . to lead them to victory."[20] They have their myths. The people. Yes. So that if Irving can appropriate sleeping German folk tales for the cause of nostalgia and old New Amsterdam, surely Hawthorne can rouse the same interests on behalf of Progress, New England, and the Nation. Unless, of course, New England should turn out to be somehow different—and in a way that Hawthorne was in a position to understand. Perhaps the epistemology of Hawthorne's antiquarianism is *not* precisely Scott's; and perhaps his legendary manipulations differ from those of Irving in more than political loyalty. Once we begin to suspect Hawthorne of understanding that "the Supernaturalism of New England" will not naturalize quite so innocently as other, more famous varieties, we may begin to notice more than metaphysical evasion in his famous devices of multiple choice.[21]

For it turns out that Hawthorne has done far more than naturalize and generalize ("symbolize") his Puritan Champion. First of all, as source critics have long recognized, he has relocated the original epiphany: the legendary "Angel of Hadley," as we are surely supposed to know, intervened (in 1675) to save a small town in New England from the ravages of King Philip's retaliating Indian warriors; here the locus of salvation appears to be the principal metropolis of Massachusetts Bay, on the eve of the Glorious Revolution in America.[22] Already there is, as we have noticed, a significant local irony: the mention of the "pious" slaughter and praying of that Indian War reminds us not only, accidentally, of the Puritans' occasional capacity for holy violence but also, far more essentially, of the unbroken logic of their holy history; fighting Indians or fighting Tyrants, the same People fight the same Enemy. And thus, at a level which is still relatively superficial, the metaphysics of Hawthorne's irony works backwards to embrace barbarism as well as forward to predict freedom: the bloodless coup of 1689 may well "pre-figure" the more glorious events to come, but none of those antitypes quite annuls the provincial paranoia of the originary event.[23]

Deeper down, however, we are dealing with an irony which would utterly destroy rather than merely embarrass the politics of Puritan typology. In translating New England's guardian spirit from Hadley to Boston, Hawthorne is merely following the lead of a movement, both political and literary, which is already well begun and far advanced. Already American story, ill disguised as regional literature, had begun to discover Angels of Hadley everywhere: wherever tyranny threatened the liberty of the people, there appeared America's own King in the Mountain, full-formed and without ontological or political disquietude. Considered as nothing more than a wicked extension of this process, "The Gray Champion" merely insists on certain awkward moral disparities. But if *difference* really is a crucial literary fact, then Hawthorne's intriguing omissions may count for as much as his insistent inclusions: if Hadley reduces Lexington—and embarrasses the logic of the covenant—what might be the effect of Salem Village?

Here we may have to trust Hawthorne's sense of his historical (or else become his ideal) audience. If he could rely on readers to "have heard" of his Champion in Scott's *Peveril of the Peak* (1822), could he not count on at least some of them to have read of his further exploits in James McHenry's *Specter of the Forest* (1823) or James Nelson Barker's *Superstition* (1824)? Certainly we must suppose his own familiarity with these notable uses of American materials. And in both these works, it turns out, Hawthorne had heard that the Angel of New England had got himself involved in witchcraft. In McHenry's version, indeed, he appears just in time to free certain persons imprisoned for being too sympathetic toward accused witches. Speaking on behalf of God, he forcefully and effectively apprises a Puritan community of "the error into which [they] are now fallen." This is clearly, as one scholar has noticed, "a long cry from the military activity at Hadley."[24] And yet a noble salvation, surely. Why then does this curious avatar play no part in Hawthorne's own rendition of New England's ghostly destiny? A specter is a specter.

To entertain the question at all—and to recall that McHenry and Barker are both critics of Puritanic "superstition"—is to see the answer at once; and also, once and for all, to fall out of fascination with the idea that Hawthorne was himself *at all* involved in that idolatrous civil religion which

Jacksonian ideologues were rearing on the foundations of the New England covenant. For the holy war against witchcraft would seem to be that one Puritanic event which Democratic myth never *could* subsume, despite the best efforts of Cotton Mather himself.

Considered in its proper Matherean context, the witchcraft episode was simply that one most cunning effort of Satan to thwart the divine plot unfolding in New England. Accordingly, the prophecy of Mather's *Wonders of the Invisible World* merely extends the logic (and heightens the drama) of his own defense of the political events of 1689 and of his father's explication of the martial ones of 1675. It may have driven Perry Miller's apologetic patience to the breaking point; certainly it disrupted the otherwise inviolable irony of his own historical vision. But it was meant as a promise of continuity and not at all as a threat of disjunction.

I believe that never were more satanical devices used for the unsettling of any people under the sun than what have been employed for the extirpation of the vine which God has here planted, casting out the heathen and preparing a room before it, and causing it to take deep root and fill the land, so that it sent its boughs unto the Atlantic sea eastward, and its branches unto the Connecticut River westward, and the hills were covered with the shadow thereof. But all those attempts of hell have hitherto been abortive. Wherefore the devil is now making one attempt more upon us, an attempt more difficult, more surprising, more snarled with unintelligible circumstances than any that we have hitherto encountered, an attempt so critical that if we get well through, we shall soon enjoy halcyon days with all the vultures of hell trodden under our feet.[25]

Only the untimeliness of Lewis and Clark prevents Mather's vision from reaching out to encompass all that was visible from sea to shining sea. And only the abysmal failure of his theocratic imagination *in fact* to subdue the invisible world prevented the national mythographers from redeeming 1692, along with so much else, from the charge of provincial paranoia.

Not that Mather's territorial prophecy failed. Or even that the fulfillment of his more apocalyptic vision was unduly delayed: evidently we always have been and always will be about to enjoy our glory "soon."[26] The problem, rather, is that our halcyon days had to continue to come on in despite of—or was it merely without reference to?—the events of 1692. Whether or not the audience of "Alice Doane" could ever quite forget What Happened in Salem, still the ideologues of Americanism would little note nor long remember what Cotton Mather would write to save "the face of a bigoted court."[27] Mather's prose might succeed in "blasting" the Indians, or Randolph, or Andros; and, purifying the typographic style even as they refined the typological scheme, others might learn to do the same job on Governor Hutchinson; but against George Burroughs the trick simply did not work. In this one instance, at least, Might seems to have gone with Wrong. And if anyone appeared to "champion" the right, it was only Robert Calef or Thomas Brattle. Perhaps there were indeed *More Wonders of the Invisible World* than were dreamed of in the schizoid phantasm of Dr. Cotton Mather, but their philosophical manifestations were too little and too late. And not even the literary efforts of McHenry and Barker—belated as they were, and too liberal by half—could right the uneven balance.

Of course it must always seem problematic to argue that something left out of a text counts for as much as all the rest that is redundantly there. But in this one instance, at least, we are dealing with an absence that is palpably present. The entire logic of this utterly ironic tale—epitomized by that "blasted" reference to Cotton Mather, and haunted by the hostile specters of McHenry and Barker—points to the witchcraft episode as (at once) provincial America's most fully elaborated instance of Puritanic paranoia and Cotton Mather's most fully articulated prophecy covering the role of Satan in America. Among all the "Ebenezers" published so far, *The Wonders of the Invisible World* made the frankest and most direct connection between the defeat of the Cosmic Conspiracy and the Millennium in America. All the signs agreed: this should have been IT.

Except that it did not work out. In this one crucial instance the future refused, in Hawthorne's single most knowing and devastating anti-typological word, to "vindicate" the past. Colonel John Hathorne does not seem to have repented himself, leaving to his more sensitive descendant the task of adding a letter to the family name, and the names of Alice Doane and Goodman Brown to the literary Custom of Salem's Main Street. But Samuel Sewall, "spite of all the Indian-summer sunlight on the hither side" of *his* comfortable middle-class soul, not only posted an absolutely public profession of personal humiliation, but also nullified all his former legal confidence by inscribing, in the vacant margins of his opulent private *Diary,* a spiritual skepticism to shame whole worlds of Royal Societies: "doleful witchcraft." And even Mather himself, when he came to construct that ultimate Ebenezer he called his *Magnalia,* seems to have known enough to include the witchcraft in his "scientific" chapter on "Remarkables" rather than in his (concluding) prophetic treatise of "The Wars of the Lord."[28]

In that climactic chapter a number of fascinating and (to the modern mind) disparate historical matters are made to lie down together. The antinomians and the Quakers coincide well enough; indeed Mary Dyer always has walked hand-in-hand with Ann Hutchinson. But Roger Williams seems a strange bedfellow, with or without his severing tie to Endicott and the Red

Cross. And all of these must be herded into the same ark with the Indians. The result is not only a veritable *Pequod* of secular politics masquerading as Holy History, but also a nearly irresistible source-book of "matters" for the American mythographer. Each of these historic episodes might require some sort of "vindication" by an age that seemed categorically more "liberal" but was in fact only relatively more secular and more idolatrous of the Progress of Liberty in America. Yet each of them *could* be so vindicated because in each of them the local victory seemed to predict the Ultimate Victor. But *no* later event could possibly perfect and annul the events at Salem Village. In this one really "remarkable" but finally "unintelligible" instance the Devil seems to have won. The only acceptable conclusion was that the matter was not in *any* sense "typical." Sober historians might overlook it, concede it, rationalize it, or explain it away; vindicate it they could not. And tribal mythographers would not touch it with a ten-foot totem.[29]

Thus the glaring omission at the mythic center of "The Gray Champion." One perceptive writer has had the literary sense to ask why there is no typological reference to "the Stamp Act riots in King Street"; and the political sense to answer, on the basis of "My Kinsman, Major Molineux," that Hawthorne apparently saw therein "the worst of the ritual of overthrow." But surely the other question is more vital; for surely "The Gray Champion" is more significantly Hawthorne's critical analysis of the logic of "vindication" than it is his own mythic contribution to the "Ritual Typology of the American Revolution."[30] What Hawthorne's deconstruction of New England's mythic Champion does, most essentially, is beg to be questioned on the question typology always begs: what if it had *not* worked out? Or, more pointedly, what to make of the type that failed? For if—aware of the example of McHenry and Barker, as well as that of Scott—we follow the tale's own logic, we absolutely demand to know the whereabouts of that Absolute Enemy of which all these other local enemies are merely the blasted types; and, concomitantly, where is the Champion to lead the Final Resistance. And once we ask, we know: might is right only when its might *in fact* proves sufficient to the task; and myths can include only the propitious instances. Prophecy may predict a glorious future but, God having absconded to some heavenly mountain, typology must wait upon a happy event. "Man's accidents are God's purposes"—whenever things work to our advantage. The result may not be "history," but the rest is silence.

Thus "The Gray Champion" may be a far more sophisticated tale than we have suspected, its local ironies shaded more toward historical criticism than toward political admiration, and its shape revealing far more of Hawthorne's literary elegance than of his personal uncertainty. It may or may not typify his entire collection of *Twice-told Tales,* but it may stand at the head of his "Tales of the Puritans." And its general implications may be worth noting: it does not praise, nor does it really blame, the Puritan past, though surely it does more than worry it; least of all does it, on its own authority, typologize anything. As history it criticizes that essentially mythic *process* of vindication, and as literature it deconstructs a rather famous *product* of that process.

In order to do so, of course, it must seem to partake of that process itself. For the Gray Champion does not "exist" as a fact for the inspection of the literary naturalist or historical positivist; he must be evoked from the memory of the audience. But as the brevity of the text suggests, and as the density of its context confirms, that act is not, in this instance, itself too difficult. Evidently the Champion *almost* exists: nearly everyone will "have heard," will recognize, and will believe. A few familiar words of worried invocation and, poof!—the Ghost of Paranoia Past is well evoked. Whereupon, politically, the task is very simple: proscribe him (or "warn him out," as New Englanders have learned to say of their itinerant poor); his hour being one of "darkness," "long, *long* may it be, ere he comes again!" (18, my italics).

We can, if we choose, read a penultimate "still may the Gray Champion come" as a terribly direct optative rather than as a conditional terrified into inversion; but even if so, its political syntax must still survive the lingering indirection generated by the mythical grammar of an "I had heard." And if the optative does survive, it does not come through as an option the sane man would happily choose: you can have your Gray Champion if you are willing to take your Crimson Massacre as well. So that if this verbal ambiguity yields up a political statement *at all*, it is surely not the sort on which one might found a "Party" any more partisan than that of "Irony." Indeed, if anyone should ever notice that certain twice-tellings were not merely patriotic re-tellings (or that some figures are antitypical in a simple oppositional sense), then you might even lose your job in the Custom House.[31]

And yet, as Hawthorne was, in some ordinary good faith, a Jacksonian Democrat, so there is a lower-case political theme involved in "The Gray Champion." And so we have to deal, finally, with some other non-typological senses of Hawthorne's verb to "vindicate." When that loaded word stops telling us to perfect and annul the past by might, or by retrospective sleight-of-mind, it begins to suggest that we should try to make up for the blameworthy actions that really have been performed. And this one does as much by dutifully plodding as by romantically confessing in "The Custom House." Whigs (like Zachary Taylor) may still believe that all justice is essentially "vindictive," so that political heads must roll; but Democrats properly hold that, though all atonement must be vicarious, it need not all be literary. And so one did what one could. Perhaps—if that blasted Champion might tarry hence just a little longer—America might yet become safe for honest political difference. But this would require a sort of wisdom learned less well from the prophecy of Cotton Mather than from the analysis of John Wise, whose spirit "The Gray Champion" equally evokes, without at all proscribing, and whose *Vindication of the Government of the New England Churches* does not seem to invite deconstruction.

Wise, we recall, had "championed" certain less-than-typological Rights of British Subjects in America during those years, after 1686, when the well-ordered but finally insensitive and "imperial" mind of Edmund Andros attempted to straighten out New England's hereditary fiscal and legal situation. Minister of the Gospel though he was, Wise nevertheless stirred up the town meeting of Ipswich to resist the imposition of taxes without benefit of an "assembly," for which he was arrested, taken to Boston for trial, convicted, fined £50, relieved of a "surety of £1,000 for . . . future good behavior, and suspended . . . from the ministry during Andros' pleasure"; his response was simply to charge that the jury which convicted him had been "illegal since very few of its members were freeholders."[32] Real-politics, this. As real as warning a frontier town of the approach of Indians. As effective as anything Mather may himself have done, in April 1689, to effect the arrest of Andros. And exemplary enough in its own terms to require no after-the-fact vindication.[33]

What Wise did think it worth the prose to vindicate was the potentially democratic character of New England's Congregational churches; and this at a time when Mather himself had decided that a certain amount of spiritual hierarchy, of the modest Presbyterian sort, might not be such a bad idea after all. The true task, Wise thought, was not to shift with the wind once again, as nearly everyone had done in the case of the Half-Way Synod of 1662, but merely to hold fast to such truth as we seem to have been given and go on to draw out the best we find implicit in that. This is also a sort of vindication, but one which allows for historical development—and even for a certain amount of lower-case enlightenment—rather than the constant reinterpretation of past reality in the name of some arrogant meta-history. And for that reason, surely, Hawthorne's tale is willing to evoke the spirit of Wise, as a clear alternative to the Angel of Hadley and the Specter of Cotton Mather.[34]

We cannot know whether the author of this radical *Vindication* (of even church government) was, obscurely, in the 1710's, a theological "liberal" of the same sort as Chauncy and Mayhew, Hitchcock and Gay, would famously become in the 1750's. But it scarcely matters; for surely the epistemological premises of "supernatural rationalism" and the theological promises of "conditional justification" are quite beside the point of Hawthorne's real-political allusion. And probably it is only slightly more significant to point out that Wise was a more truly *popular* Champion than either Cotton Mather in the 1680's or the so-called liberals of the later date. What matters about Wise's *Vindication* is its utter separation from Puritanic meta-politics on the one hand, and from Whiggish meta-history on the other. Wise defends the institution of the Congregational Way on the ground that its actual (demystified) structure is more just than any other, and not because it advances the world-cause of "visible sanctity." And it defends the maintenance of that Way as a prudential act of literal politics rather than as the typological fulfillment of some spiritual destiny. On that basis alone the *Vindication* might warrant republication in 1772; and on that basis alone would Hawthorne's allusion dare invoke its exemplary authority.[35]

But as it *is* invoked, the redundant verbal ambiguities and dense literary ironies of the conclusion of "The Gray Champion" subside at last into a kind of political prayer. We may be embarrassed to *say* that prayer; but we must at least learn to read the history lesson on which it is based, as the outline of that lesson survives among the deconstructed remains of a twice-told tale.

General Goffe did at least one deed of history: in Old England he sat in judgment on a would-be absolutist. And perhaps he did another, less terrific one as well: in New England he *may* have saved a meeting from the Indians. But the Angel of Hadley, considered as a movable feast, is a pious and deadly fiction. Similarly, Cotton Mather may have organized—certainly he wrote to justify—a local resistance to a higher authority; and as that authority seems to have been careless of certain traditional limitations of power, the resistance seems to have been just. But he "blasted" his political enemies beyond all reason and conscience; and his specters were mere delusions of millennial grandeur. On the other hand, however, the spirit of John Wise may command a much more simple allegiance, for it needs no vindication other than its own domestication. Wherefore, let us pray: let us remember to atone for crimes against both "devilish" Indians and poor "bedeviled" victims of witch trials; let us remember to forswear paranoic historiography as effectively as we have learned to forget a certain episode of historic paranoia; but let us not forget to heed the example of such real-life champions of democratic liberty as we in fact have had, here and there, amidst a distressingly intolerant past. We pray this in the name of . . . well . . . probably not—unless this praying should have dulled our sense of irony—probably not in the "name of Endicott."

2

Blasphemy aside, however, the problem of what historic "honor" may be due that name arises in precisely this context. For if "The Gray Champion" has acquired a companion-piece, in the criticism of Hawthorne's miscellaneous "Tales of the Puritans," that tale would surely be "Endicott and the Red Cross." We probably need to be careful about this companionship, and for reasons much more specific than our generalized anxiety about all canonic unities: the critical linkage here weakens considerably, as soon as close analysis discovers crucial differences in structure and strategy; or as soon as we allow Robert Lowell to remind us that the separatist sword of Endicott links the "Red Cross" more closely with the "May-Pole" than with anything else. And yet the problem of "conclusions" which mix patriotism with irony remains real, forcing us to estimate Hawthorne's precise attitude toward the "championship" of Endicott.[36]

Working backwards from the ringing, oratorical conclusion—"forever honored be the name of Endicott" (441)[37]—we swiftly find ourselves caught up in the embarrassments of dramatic irony. Local sarcasms (of the "pious fierceness," prayer-for-slaughter variety) which only ripple the surface of "The Gray Champion" fairly roil the waters here. In fact they threaten to *become* the surface, of a tale whose morality is as dusky as its image is "highly polished." Newly arrived from a world defined by the persecutions of that "bigoted and haughty primate, Laud" (433), and fearing still his secular intervention into their religious affairs, the Puritans are "resolved" to resist, of course. But at first glance they seem preparing not so much to defend a purified religion as to secure their own historic opportunity to lord it over consciences; in this case, those of a few hapless deviants who lacked the wit to realize, in advance, that all really "great" migrations are covenantal.[38]

Thus "an Episcopalian and suspected Catholic" appears "grotesquely encased" in a pillory while, opposite him, and answering him in secular kind, "a fellow-criminal, who had boisterously quaffed a health to the king" (434), is confined by the legs in the stocks: so much for the separation of the first and second tables of the divine commandments; somewhere in the pseudo-Platonic heaven of Puritan images Moses and Aaron are kissing each other.[39] Moving right along—we can almost imagine the camera of WGBH panning the crowd—we discover not only a "WANTON GOSPELLER" wearing his appropriate identification, but a whole cast of Puritan "extras" with cropped ears and branded cheeks. And then, as Puritan semiology takes its customary turn toward the literal, we notice that famous "young woman . . . whose doom it was to wear the letter A on the breast of her gown" (435); the casual observer may think "Admirable," but doubtless we can count on the true meaning of the letter to insist on itself in the appropriate unconscious. The Puritan leadership thinks of all this as "discipline," a distinguishing mark of a truly reformed church polity, but Roger Williams recognizes it as nothing but Erastian policy as usual. And the reader well realizes, long before Endicott emerges as the scene's prophetic Champion, that the "liberty" exhibited here amounts to little more than the power to protect an enclave of privileged persecution.[40]

Seeming to reverse, but really only deepening somewhat, this more obvious irony, some patient antiquarian narrator warns us not to infer that "the times of the Puritans were more vicious than our own"; the difference is merely that, as Bradford himself observed, it was Puritan policy "to search out even the most secret sins, and expose them to shame, without fear or favor, in the broadest light of the noonday sun" (436).[41] Point well taken, especially by the reader of "Fancy's Show Box." Unless that reader also happens to have read those opening scenes of *The Scarlet Letter* which frankly attack the near identity of "religion and law" in the Puritan world, even as they begin an extended meditation on the problem of "Privacy in Colonial New England." Or unless, even more drastically, he happens to have noticed that, except for some question of "fear or favor," the notoriously out-of-place "Governor" Bellingham would be standing on Hester's popular scaffold of shame instead of his magisterial balcony of judgment. Or unless he reflects, somewhat more solemnly, that all this Puritanic searching—the substance of the Beadle's triumphant boast to Chillingworth—is in fact Hawthorne's most graphic image of the Unpardonable Sin.[42] Perhaps Puritanism does enjoy some sort of primacy, if not of the privately sinful, then possibly of the publicly retributive sort.

Since much of this consciousness is anticipatory, however, perhaps it does not stand as the essence of that Puritan world championed by Endicott. The stronger impression may be the simpler one, of a sort of holy sadism: the purer your religious ideal, the harder you hurt its felons and failures. And on this aspect of the example of Endicott Hawthorne has said it all before, in that prefatory conclusion which the revisions of "The Gentle Boy" never did put under erasure: Endicott was a man of "uncompromising bigotry . . . made hot and mischievous by violent and hasty passions"; his "whole conduct . . . was marked by brutal cruelty." One almost suspects that some biological pun survives from the ecclesiological patriotism of the first paragraph: Endicott is the bigoted "primate."[43] Or if this animalism is only one more equal part of the Swiftian instruction Hawthorne drew from reading the criminal records of the whole coarse and violent "Elizabethan" world,[44] then perhaps *nothing* distinguishes the reign of Endicott from the general rule: the Puritan is a wolf to man, and to the Indian (however Anglo-Saxons should decide the humanoid status of that bewildered primate), and even to the wolf. Endicott may or may not *be*, in some simple sense, Bunyan's *Diabolus;* he may or may not invert all the holiness of Spenser's Red Cross. But he is not at all what Roger Williams would call "courteous"; he even seems a little savage. And thus the reader, alerted by a premonitory plashing of blood on the doorstep of a meeting-house hardly recognizable as a house of prayer, is well warned that any historic honor will have to blink, or cover over, or wash and make white, a multitude of inhumanities.[45]

And yet the climactic vote of honor seems to insist upon itself. Whereas the dangerously condensed and fearfully prayerful ending of "The Gray Champion" merely implies the example of some real-life hero—all but obscured by the not-quite-spiritual tendency of Puritan typology, and scarcely restored by the not-quite-natural force of romantic demythology—the altogether less compressed conclusion of "Endicott and the Red Cross" not only describes a real person but confesses an historic deed. Whereas the ghost of John Wise has to rise up out of the ashes of an exploded myth, the literal action of Endicott is here said to reveal, "through the mist of ages," the "first omen" of a "deliverance" (444) which Hawthorne was probably loath to repudiate. In this later (and less strategically placed) tale, the "spirit" of Puritanism receives a proper historic name: Endicott slashed the (Anglican) "Red Cross from New England's banner," and we are forced to recognize a Revolution therein. So definitive is the example of Endicott that *his* story, unlike that of Goffe-Mather-Wise, can be repeated, carefully, but without the poison of irony, to the youthful auditors of *Grandfather's Chair.* What adult lesson (but "ambivalence") can we draw from the final self-contradiction of "Endicott," so unlike the concluding equivocations of the "Champion"?[46]

One rather drastic and yet not altogether implausible suggestion might be that Hawthorne wished the flat self-contradiction simply to stand, all unmediated, as a clearly *in*appropriate conclusion to the tale he has actually told—to see whether the politically chauvinistic and literarily simplistic reader might be forced to recognize, for once, that the reassuring "conclusions" we demand do not always summarize the complex and often ugly facts which actual experience constrains us to rehearse. Indeed something like that might be the essential strategy of the twice-told tale (political or otherwise) precisely as such: re-tell a story the outlines of which are, to a certain audience at least, all too familiar; but tell that tale with a somewhat unwonted insistence on all the appropriate if unedifying naturalistic details; and then conclude, outrageously, with the *perfectly* customary conclusion.

Would anyone notice? Anyone who did might well discover, in his shock of *un*recognition, something fundamental about the difference between reality and "story," and also about his own expectations as a reader of fictions. Everyman might yet become his own historical critic. Anyone who did *not* notice might well be convicting himself of invincible bias. Could you trust such a person to write the definitive "History of the United States"?[47]

Perhaps all this is, in the end, only an oblique way of saying that Hawthorne was, and wanted his readers to become, more genuinely and deeply ambivalent about the American past than an official historian like Bancroft could quite afford to be. And yet even that conclusion carries with it a significant clarification of Hawthorne's attitudes and of his status as an historian; for it recognizes that Hawthorne is highly self-conscious about his own deep divisions of political feeling, and that he has embodied his own self-division in a series of literary gestures that have explicit designs on the credulities of his readers. Thus the fall into personal ambivalence receives its literary redemption as historical ambiguity: as Endicott was *both* a bigot *and* an exemplary figure of colonial revolt, so we are introduced to Leavis' sense of "what was lost and what gained" in the separation from Old England, to Pearce's theory of "the imputation simultaneously of guilt and righteousness through history," and ultimately (perhaps) to the distressingly mixed story of "How the Puritans Won the American Revolution."[48]

And yet if this is all we learn from the modest proposals of "Endicott and the Red Cross," we will have missed its most complex but least ambivalent historical teaching. For there is something else going on, even in this very brief tale. At first glance the only problem might seem to involve an adequately complex explication of the political image of Endicott as bigot-Revolutionary. But a closer look reveals an element of drama as well as of image, so that a fuller interpretation has to account for the meaning of the interchange between Endicott and Roger Williams. What exactly, we have to ask ourselves, is Williams doing in a story which announces itself as belonging, for all time, to Endicott?

Our first answer to any question about the presence of Williams might well seem definitive enough: he is there for the sake of the truly liberal judgment his mature spirit delivers on all spurious and oratorically elaborated theories of "liberty" and "conscience." Why did we come here?— Endicott recklessly harangues his trainband: "Was it not for liberty to worship God according to our consciences?" To which, the Wanton Gospeller: "Call you this liberty of conscience?" Whereupon, "a sad and quiet smile flitted across the mild visage of Roger Williams" (439), in rueful recognition, surely, of the nice debater's point. Williams is there to endure, so to speak, the bigoted seventeenth century—and to establish against it, on Hawthorne's behalf, the rightful balance of the liberal nineteenth. And even in these simple terms the confrontation is telling indeed. For Endicott has, well prepared, a ready and easy answer, which is not so much *his own* as it is *the standard* answer: John Cotton would use it against the furious "windmill" arguments of Williams himself; Nathaniel Ward would leave off punning just long enough to give it serious expression against his tolerationist brethren in England; even the pragmatic Winthrop, provoked into theory by fifteen years of wearing struggle with the Deputies, would use it against his own Freemen: not natural but Holy liberty; not conscience but Covenant.[49]

I said liberty to worship God, not license to profane and ridicule him . . . As I was saying, we have sacrificed all things, and have come to a land whereof the old world hath scarcely heard, that we might make a new world unto ourselves, and painfully seek a path from hence to heaven. (439)

Clearly Hawthorne wanted to face up to the Puritans' distinctive claim. He struggled to give it full weight in the lengthy original headnote to "The Gentle Boy." And if he finally deleted it there, it was only to bring it up again, here and elsewhere, for full hearing and honest meditation: the Puritans invoked—in fear and trembling, as they thought—a higher rule of liberty than that permitted to the private conscience of the individual seeker, the holy rule of a "higher law" which alone could seem "like love." But he could believe it no more than could Williams; it was but the "holy pretense" one more time, and "how like an iron cage."[50] And so in this regard Williams is there to remind us that Hawthorne always *was*, in some important sense, "a citizen of somewhere else," a troubled wanderer in the wilderness of common providence, and not at all a settled dweller in the holy city of Salem.

And yet this immediate response to Williams really does clarify things too quickly. Breaking through into the nineteenth century at once, it intuits the liberal theology of the teller before it has quite accounted for the orthodox history of the tale. For as inevitable as the case of Endicott "versus" Williams may seem, it has had to be arranged, out of source materials which make matters seem far more ragged and various. The historical Endicott can hardly be recognized, as of 1634, as "typical" of anything at all; and it has not always been so easy to make out the world of difference between him and Williams. For one perilous moment, at least, Endicott himself seemed too radical a Zionist to be anything but a Trouble-maker in the

Modell Citty of the ever cautious Winthrop. And as for Williams, a prophet may smile and smile and be a zealot still.

But the major task of analysis is not simply to observe that the tale's dramatic self-unity has required considerable art. We scarcely need Grandfather's patient concessions to remind us that *any* version of Endicott's "little speech on liberty" will be some historian's own ("Romantic") invention; or that Endicott scarcely thought of his rebellious action in a "political" way.[51] And we should not be too dismayed to learn that no historical evidence places Williams, with or without some dangerous news from Winthrop, at the actual scene of Endicott's famous cross-cutting. Somebody has got to perform the function of the positivist critic of "Main Street," pointing out that in all probability "these historical personages" never "met together" in the precise way our "Showman" has suggested; and for us Neal Frank Doubleday may well play that necessarily inglorious part. But we are not sufficiently instructed until we can fairly surmise what Hawthorne may have *meant* by his outrageous fusion of elements that are, historically, disparate without being in all senses perfectly opposed. The conflationist plot is not quite so thick in "Endicott" as in "The May-Pole," which positively begs for deconstruction; but it scarcely covers the case to observe that Hawthorne has (once more) chosen to manipulate the historical record "for the purposes of his tale." We need an adequate account of those purposes.[52]

What is involved here, apparently, is some wish to discover what will and will not typologize; and more specifically, what events and figures will and will not serve as faithful images of our own (not very radical) Revolution. For it is only the character of later American political history that forces us to look back "through the mist of ages" and see Endicott rather than Williams as our true Father in Liberty. That outcome, though it might be all too predictable, is not to be thought of as perfectly inevitable; for Williams himself had bid fair to establish a tradition of religious revolution in the New World. The problem was simply that he did nothing at all to found a Redeemer Nation.

Hawthorne's sources make perfectly clear, and Grandfather himself openly confesses, that it was Roger Williams who first awakened the separatist conscience in John Endicott; and that, in one sense at least, Endicott was merely enacting one of Williams' own revolutionary theories when he cut the Red Cross out of the banner of the Salem trainband.[53] Strictly speaking, therefore, Williams might well smile a very different sort of smile, at a very different place in the story: "Ah! Well done, my true disciple; now we have indeed cut ourselves off from those mixed assemblies we have left behind in England. For what have the truly reformed to do with the impurities of the parish system?" Why then, according to this logic of history, should we not "honor"—rather than nervously remember, or ruefully reverence—the name of Williams? Should not the very thought count for more than the mere deed? Or if we should decide (following the pragmatism of John Winthrop, perhaps) that it really is the deed which matters most, then it will be hard to tell from the pages of Winthrop's own *Journal* (Hawthorne's "primary" source, surely) why it is Williams and not Endicott who will have to abscond to the wilds of Rhode Island. Cotton Mather knows why, of course, and rejoices in the knowledge; and the whole thing will be painfully clear to Thomas Hutchinson. But then these two (opposing) historical witnesses both have the immense advantage of knowing what the future shall have vindicated.[54]

All we can tell from Winthrop's account is that the whole situation is very fluid and dangerous. The colonists have professed a most profound loyalty to the Established ("Mother") Church in England; but in their original policy of "member franchise" they have enacted religious treason. Nor have these establishments gone unreported in England, so that it is no wonder if there are dire rumors. It may be somewhat paranoid to imagine that Archbishop Laud really will risk an expeditionary force against them, in spite of the rumors. But they *have* been asked to surrender up their precious "patent," so daringly transported across the ocean and so imaginatively transformed into a political constitution; and perhaps the King will indeed decide to send a governor general, to anticipate the meaning (and perhaps the fate) of Andros.[55] The best that can be hoped is that, if nothing further is done to provoke the Erastian Establishment in England, the crisis may yet pass. Thus Orthodoxy in Massachusetts will continue to develop its own unique Way, vindicating by the way its original Errand into the Wilderness, whether anyone ever follows its Light or not.

Of course Williams will have to be reduced to Truth, or at least to silence: when New Princes are contesting Old Princes for the effective sanction of divine will, the last thing they need to read is a Mirror for Magistrates written by Don Quixote. And for one brief moment (in January 1634) it looked as though Williams' peculiar brand of separatism might not in fact be "unleashed." Salem had had to be warned about him in April 1631: could they really mean to call a Teacher who "had refused to join with the congregation at Boston, because they would not make a public declaration of their repentance for having communion with the churches of England, while they lived there," and who had further declared "that the magistrate should not punish the breach of the Sabbath"? But of late he had given evidence of living in the real world after all: "very submissively" he had confessed that his opinions had been written for the eyes of New England leaders alone, that he had not meant to stir up anything; he even offered to submit his offending book for burning. And "at the next court he appeared penitently, and gave satisfaction of his intention and loyalty."

Whereupon "Mr. Cotton and Mr. Wilson . . . found the matters not to be so evil as at first they seemed"; so all "agreed, that, upon his retraction, etc., or taking an oath of allegiance to the king, etc., it should be passed over."[56]

But although this momentary outcome more than justifies Hawthorne's portrait of Williams as calm and politic in contrast to Endicott—"thy words are not meet for a secret chamber, far less a public street" (439)—it is scarcely the conclusion of Winthrop's troubled story of Williams and the Red Cross. For just now the General Court is apprised of a bold symbolic enactment of at least part of Williams' separatist point, the defacing of the "ensign at Salem." As with all symbols, there may be more (or less) there than first meets the eye; but the implications for foreign policy are clear, and certainly they are no less dangerous than those associated with the teachings of Williams. So they first question Richard Davenport, the actual ensign-bearer (and ancestor of the ambivalent Hawthorne); and then they call in Endicott himself, the duly elected commander of the Salem trainband (and somehow the father of us all). And all of this at the precise moment when, amidst the most dire rumors from England, they are quietly deciding to resist if absolutely necessary, but in the meantime to "avoid and protract," hoping to buy time, space, and just enough independence to evolve a "due form of government, civil and ecclesiastical."[57]

Thus Endicott's timing could hardly have been worse. What the Devil could have got into this putative saint? Surely he is not unaware of the content and political import of the Puritans' official *Farewell to the Church of England.* Can he not understand that we may yet wait the Anglicans out? Does this hothead not realize that the American Revolution begins in 1775 and not in 1634?[58]

And yet, as we surely realize, Endicott comes out of it all right. Not exactly unscathed, perhaps, for he is excluded from office-holding for one year; but not suffering any permanent political disability, surely, since he will be there, in 1649, to take over from Winthrop, and to endure long enough to lash and then hang those Quakers whom Williams found so debatable. He cannot be let off entirely, of course, even in "the infancy of a plantation," when (in Winthrop's view) "justice should be administered with more lenity than in a settled state"; for his offenses have been provocative indeed. Not only has his symbolic action been "rash and without discretion, taking upon him more authority than he had"; not only has it had the effect of "laying a blemish . . . upon the rest of his magistrates, as if they would suffer idolatry"; but it has had the most dangerous effect of "giving occasion to the state of England, to think ill of us."[59] And yet the court could somehow judge that *his* heart, unlike that of Williams, had been in the right place all along. Why should this be so?

Partly it is a matter of Endicott's ability to accept canny and politic instruction. For we notice him learning to give "place to the truth" at the very moment when Williams resumes his quixotic crusade against the "antichristian" churches of England; and in the end we find that not even Mr. Hooker is able to "reduce him from any of his errors." Partly it is a matter of relative theological (or semiological) sophistication, as the court concludes that only "tenderness of conscience" had drawn Endicott, over his head, into the abstruse symbolisms of "antichrist."[60] But clearly there is a deeper reason why things came out as they did; and why, accordingly, the American story can be prefigured not by Williams, but only by Endicott, and the Red Cross. And Hawthorne's brief tale exists to reveal—in a single, smiling, dramatic instance—a reason that only patient analysis can discover in the terse and circumspect journalism of John Winthrop, whose account *must* be read if we care about the "pre-text" of Hawthorne's tale *at all.*[61]

Evidently several sorts of separatism are at issue in the arguments and maneuverings of 1634–35. Full political separation from England *might* have been one of them; and though the Tory historians of the Revolution unanimously insisted that it *was*, it is precisely this sort of separation that Winthrop was trying to deny, or prevent, or at least forestall. Nor does Hawthorne's "Grandfather" accept the Tory view: asked by a youthful auditor whether Endicott had "meant to imply that Massachusetts was independent of England," he answers by doubting that Endicott "had given the matter much consideration, except in its religious bearing."[62] Just so the anxious court had carefully decided: though many persons feared that Endicott's action "would be taken as an act of rebellion," the truth seemed to be, rather, that "it was done on the opinion that the red cross was given to the king of England by the pope, as an ensign of victory, and so [was] a superstitious thing, and a relique of antichrist." And this is the view Cotton Mather would "loyally" sponsor—elaborating (while he seemed to criticize) the theological pedantry involved, even as he omitted all mention of Endicott's proper name and transferred the qualities of rashness and indiscretion to Williams.[63]

Thus Endicott himself intended, apparently, only a separation from the trappings of Popery, and not at all a break with the King and Constitution of England. That any such limited separation was in fact impossible seemed less "self-evident" in 1634 than it would later come to appear—in the 1760's, for example, to those zealous patriots who reacted so violently to the prospect of an American bishop; or in the 1950's, say, to somebody like Q. D. Leavis, who seemed to know that the element of Anglo-Catholic paganism is not to be separated from the British Constitution, adequately considered.[64] But all this is hindsight, like the view of the Tory historians. Nor is it necessary to suppose that the type is *ever* quite aware of himself precisely as such. And yet if Endicott is to become a type of the American Revolution, it must be in spite of the fact that his motives were not the sort we ordinarily regard as political. Or unless it should turn out that there is something faulty and even naive in the way we ordinarily regard politics. For granting that Endicott did not himself "intend" a "separate and equal station" for America, we might still ask about the relation between his own (Puritanic) idea of separation from Popery and Williams' (rather more radical) program of separation as such; and about the political implications and consequences of each.

What "Endicott and the Red Cross" dramatizes, from the seventeenth-century point of view, is the painful fact, clearly *there* but scarcely emphasized in Winthrop's *Journal*, that two very different sorts of specifically religious separation have been unleashed on the colony of the Massachusetts in the 1630's. And what Williams' rueful smile recognizes, ultimately, is that the two are utterly distinct and unreconciled; that they are in fact competing with one another; and that the far more conservative sort is about to win out, whatever Laud and the King should decide to do. Where hatred of Popery is concerned, Williams is scarcely less fanatical than Endicott himself; and no doubt he might fairly point to Williams as his official Teacher on that issue. But Williams stands for another sort of separation as well—not only the separation of New England from every last vestige or symbolic memorial of human admixture with the truth of divinely revealed religion but also, and far more significantly, the separation of things spiritual from every possible source of profanation by civil and even concerted ecclesiological power. Not "separatism with uniformity" but the complete separation of the soul from every threat of human coercion. And evidently that distinction will make *all* the difference.[65]

Williams' theory would cut off, at the source, not only every conceivable sort of "civil religion," without which "the idea of America" is utterly absurd, but also every imaginable version of "Manifest Destiny." One might almost propose that here, even more fundamentally than in "The May-Pole of Merry Mount," two opposing ideologies are "contending for an empire." Except that if Williams should prevail, there will be *no empire*, only a wilderness filling up with Seekers. Endicott's Salem and Winthrop's Boston *both* mean to sponsor a program we could call "geo-theo-political"; they even suppose a jealous God will prosper it as opposed to that of Mount Wollaston or Virginia.[66] But Providence in Rhode Island is nothing special.

Surely Hawthorne has deftly dramatized the issue that vexes the early pages of Winthrop's record most deeply, even though its solution occurred so quickly and had taken (otherwise) so long to question—not so much the degree as the purpose of separation. Separation to "establish" or separation to "seek" the Truth of the Spirit? In demanding some complete and public renunciation of the Church of England, Williams and Endicott equally threaten to bring the authority of King James I down on the heads of the newly emigrated Puritans. But Williams alone threatens to pull up, root and branch, an idea of New England's Plantation which Winthrop and Endicott hold in common. For even if James or Laud never gets *any* disturbing word from New England, of either Williams' literal or Endicott's symbolic demand for repudiation of Anglo-Catholic paganism, Winthrop will still have to deal with Williams' "other" teaching: "The magistrate [may] not punish the breach of the Sabbath, nor any other [religious] offence, as it [is] a breach of the first table."[67] For if that be true, then boisterous health-quaffers and Wanton Gospellers never *can* be the subject of a single Biblical constitution or the object of a unified agency of discipline.

If Williams is correct, then there is indeed no such thing as a "Christian Magistrate," and much of Winthrop's own authority, so carefully exercised and so patiently explained to both Dudley and the deputies, is as weirdly spurious as that of King James, or of the Man of Sin himself. And, just as clearly, there never can be any such thing as a "Christian America." Where then would we find our identity, from colony to province? We might even have to purchase our lands from the Indians.[68] No wonder the magisterial Winthrop could reconcile only Endicott. No wonder Cotton and Hooker could agree on Williams as on nothing else. A "Citty on a Hill" is quite a different thing from a separatist outpost in the spiritual wilderness.

And well may Williams smile—though better, in some less ironic story, weep—at the scene before him. His smile suggests somewhat more than the easy (Tory) irony that "zealous partisans never fail to inflict on others what they will not themselves endure."[69] But what it registers much more fundamentally is Williams' realization that a very imperfect sort of separation has got control of the engines of repression; and worse, that in spite of a momentary embarrassment in logic, it is about to seize the powers of ideological control as well. Read proleptically, it hints not only at Williams' own lamentable fate before Winthrop's own Hooker-assisted court, but at the fact that in New England at least he will lose his argument against the essentially mindless propositions of John Cotton; and this in spite of his pious ("Miltonic") trust that Truth will overcome.[70] And in the slightly longer run it may well suggest—Thomas Jefferson to one side, and Isaac Backus to the contrary notwithstanding—that the American Revolution will be, from an ideological point of view, more an affair of reactionary religious loyalty than of liberalizing spiritual influence. Williams smiles to realize that once his own subtle voice is silenced, nothing can stay the tide of overbelief in Endicott's furious rhetoric. The mild, ambiguous smile of Parson Hooper scarcely reveals so much, or so sympathetically.

Of course all of this comes on us pretty fast. But then the whole story of

"Endicott and the Red Cross" is surely supposed to strike us as, like virtually every instance of political typology, too well made by half. And clearly this tight little tale means to discover the significance of its own specious conflations in the very next moment—when Endicott, now unopposed, resumes his incendiary speech in the "public street" of Salem. For there, under the entirely ironic sign of Williams' own "peace," his nearly automatic and altogether predictable rehearsal of Winthrop's "little speech" on Puritanic liberty turns into something larger, more dangerous, and (from a soberly historical point of view) utterly inappropriate, a full-scale oration on the civil-religious meaning of the American Revolution. Are we here or there?

At first glance Endicott's address may seem a plausible invention, as fixities and definites such as "Charles of England," "Laud," and "a governor-general" appear to specify the familiar seventeenth-century locus; and perhaps we may fairly suspect that New England's Puritanic expatriates hated and feared to "kiss the Pope's toe" long before they had begun to build bonfires against that truly paranoid prospect. But his rhetoric is heavy and embarrassing indeed; not at all characteristic of Massachusetts' foreign policy in the seventeenth century, and exactly like the sort we learned to suspect in "The Gray Champion": hardly Endicott's, and better entirely if not at all Hawthorne's own. And we ought to notice that the speech is delivered, from the first, "imperiously" (439), and to suspect that Hawthorne personally intends all the word itself can signify. Evidently we have entered into the argument Endicott himself "scarcely considered," the thesis of independent empire for America. So that if Hawthorne's Grandfather is to be trusted, we have left the literal Endicott far behind and are dealing already with his antitypical perfection, to be adopted or disowned, depending on our politics.

By the next paragraph it is certainly too late to begin holding back: if we have read this far in literary innocence, then historical guilt has already been "imputed"; surprised by violence, our only rational option is to repent, before instinctive rhetorical complicity shall turn to explicit political honor. For the profile offered is now of a mentality not so much provincial as it is furious:

> If this king and this arch-prelate have their will, we shall briefly behold a cross on the spire of this tabernacle which we have builded, and a high altar within its walls, with wax tapers burning round it at noonday. We shall hear the sacring-bell, and the voices of the Romish priests saying the mass. But think ye, Christian men, that these abominations may be suffered without a sword drawn? without a shot fired? without blood spilt, yea, on the very stairs of the pulpit? No,—be ye

strong of hand, and stout of heart! Here we stand on our own soil, which we have bought with our goods, which we have won with our swords, which we have cleared with our axes, which we have tilled with the sweat of our brows, which we have sanctified with our prayers to the God that brought us hither! Who shall enslave us here? What have we to do with this mitred prelate,—with this crowned king? What have we to do with England? (440)

Honor here may well involve blood-lust as well as Anglophobia. We must have taken leave of our senses. As soon eat babies. How have we been led to this conclusion?

Obviously "Endicott's" fantastic execration has less to do with the anxieties of the 1630's than with the paranoia of the 1760's: at worst Endicott seems to have been looking at scurrilous political cartoons; and at best he seems just to have risen up from reading a "Dissertation on the Feudal and Canon Law." But from whatever local sources Hawthorne has drawn his rhetoric, it epitomizes nothing so well as that desperate vision according to which a complex and deep-dyed conspiracy in England seemed plotting to deprive New England of all her hard-won and long-protected immunities, both civil and religious. An "obtuse secularism" will dismiss it as "propaganda" merely; a more sensitive historiography can grasp it as a perfectly authentic response to the threat of "Mitre and Sceptre"; someone might even take it for a paradigm of "Religion and the American Mind."[71] Hawthorne offers it, much more simply, as the way the eighteenth century learned to appropriate the language of the seventeenth: religious typology as political sanction. The identification works not because Endicott was a prophet of political independence, but merely because "Puritan" rhetoric could still be used to "ideological" advantage; and because, from Hawthorne's point of view, the Revolution looked more like the fury of Endicott than the subtlety of Williams.

On this point Hawthorne would seem to challenge Bancroft most directly. For Bancroft had suppressed the Endicott episode in order to claim that ultimately America vindicated Williams.[72] So it might almost appear from the vantage of 1833, with the disestablishment of Congregationalism in Massachusetts. Yet the longer one looked the less clearly one might read, even then, the signs of the halcyon times; indeed too much looking could produce a Melvillean vision of utter racial pluralism and political naturalism as easily as the neo-revivalist and meta-sectarian "nation with the soul of a church." And Hawthorne's own "Main Street" would come along to suggest that the proponents of Manifest Destiny ought to confess Endicott as their very own Father in Faith.[73]

Furthermore, the case of 1776 was really much simpler: granted the "business" of separation for empire—or, just less tendentiously, of a humanly independent but divinely sponsored state of advancing grace—Endicott's "spirit" is indeed "wiser" (439) than Williams'; and not so much because Endicott's personal nature was the more violent as because the project at hand required an ideology of *force*. Under the aspect of Revolution, in fact, what else *was* there to see, in the moment of New England's first crisis of separated existence? Winthrop counseled caution, and Williams offered only the tangled argument of wheat and tares, the dialectical (and turgid) claims of Truth and Peace. As soon go on with constitutional arguments about virtual representation and divided sovereignties. How much easier, surely, to execrate Popery and invoke salvation.

Thus the typology of "Endicott and the Red Cross," the most subtle and dangerous in Hawthorne's entire Puritanic gallery, is entirely ironic. Far from discovering, as if in some dim but authentic origin, some sacred but partial principle of liberty, needing only to be released from the local bigotry that held it captive, it merely adopts the eventual rhetoric of effective revolution and places it in the mouth of a minor disturber of Winthrop's patiently elaborated New-World order. Or, in an equally telling reformulation, it dares turn the arch-rebel of the Tories into the *ur*-type of the Revolutionaries.[74] And then it dares ask why a full-blown "propaganda" speaks more prophetically there than anywhere in the perilous political half-world of a cautious and confused Utopian venture. Better there than in the mouth of Williams, obviously, since his fanatic hatred of popish enslavement was expressly subsumed by a more reasoned opposition to all spiritual dependencies, including New England's own never-quite-separatist Errand; and because the force of his politics was blunted, quite frankly, by the spirit of a kingdom which really is *not* of this world. And better than in the mouth of Winthrop, we are finally required to think, since *his* cautious policy knew too well the value of silence.

Probably the last word on "Endicott and the Red Cross" should indeed concern Winthrop, that nearly archetypal "good Father" among the founders, whose moral presence informs the drama of this deceptively simple tale of the American political story as surely as his historical authority renders that drama politically intelligible. What satisfactory reason can be given for his personal absence here? It is his rule, after all, and hardly Williams' own, which Endicott breaks by publishing the news out of England and by haranguing his trainband on its implications; just as, in real life, it was primarily his magistracy on which Endicott was guilty of "laying a blemish" by implying he "would suffer idolatry."[75] Why not let him speak for himself? Why drag an ironically smiling Williams in by the ears and leave the potently frowning Winthrop unrepresented except by hearsay?

A cautious criticism will suggest that Hawthorne was every bit as regardful of Winthrop's political reputation—here, and analogously in *The Scarlet Letter*—as his contemporary practitioners of "The Historical Romance of New England." A cannier suggestion would have him covering the tracks of his sources, as he is often said to have done with Spenser.[76] Yet a bolder and less politic view can also be advanced, one which gives far more credit to Hawthorne's historical intelligence and literary craft: probably Hawthorne means to represent Winthrop's authority touching complicated matters ambiguously civil and religious exactly as it was most often felt in the early history of Massachusetts itself, powerful but indirect; it may even be supposed that Winthrop's literal silence in this tale stands for the single most voluminous omission in his entire *Journal.* As Hawthorne's exceedingly artful tale begins to make political sense only when we read it against Winthrop's historical account of the contiguous yet conflicting careers of Williams and Endicott, so it leaves us with the nagging question of Winthrop's own deepest view of the whole messy business—which Winthrop himself declines to give us. More than willing to lay aside his *merely* historical role long enough to write a (lengthy) *Short Story of The Rise, Reign, and Ruine of the Antinomians, Familists, and Libertines,* he nevertheless avoids all comment on the altogether less quaint problem of the possibility of theological resolution without political independence.[77]

At one really crucial point, in fact, his silence arrests the critical attention of even a *most* regardful modern editor. The passage begins in utter circumstantiality and with full detail:

There came over a copy of the commission granted to the two archbishops and ten others of the council, to regulate all plantations, and power given them, or any five of them, to call in all patents, to make laws, to raise tythes and portions for ministers, to remove and punish governors, and to hear and determine all causes, and inflict all punishments, even death itself, etc. This being advised from our friends to be intended specially for us, and that there were ships and soldiers provided, given out as for the carrying the new governor, Capt. Woodhouse, to Virginia, but suspected to be against us, to compel us, by force, to receive a new governor, and the discipline of the church of England, and the laws of the commissioners.

All of this, understandably, "occasioned the magistrates and deputies to hasten our fortification" and, with increasing interest, "to discover our minds each to other; which grew to this conclusion, viz.: [a blank space]"— leaving us to wonder just how far Winthrop (and his Boston associates) were willing to go. At fanatical Salem the issue appears to have been idolatry. But in the sobering atmosphere of Boston it may well have been sovereignty. Who knows what would have happened "had not King and Bishops now begun to feel the heat of a back-fire at home"?[78] Maybe the simplistic view of Endicott was the correct one after all.

If any such interpretation of the shadow-presence of Winthrop is at all cogent, then it will follow that Endicott merely stands in for him as the figure of the founding of Puritanic empire, the historic validity and the cosmic value of which there was plenty of reason to doubt; and that we are supposed to suspect this. A famous reputation may seem protected, but only for the reader determined to be uncritical. For "Endicott and the Red Cross" really *does* force us to ask. And surely the relation between Winthrop's death and Hester's escape from "what [he] called liberty" is somewhat more than a literary accident.

Modern historiography may well have to confess that Winthrop more than anyone else shaped the political direction of Puritanic America—transforming, as he did, a clumsy colonial patent into an effectively independent political constitution; assuming, as he did, the power to mediate the inevitable disputes between congregations obviously unable to bind themselves in a presbytery; and supervising, as he did, the trial and expulsion of a plurality of local prophets whose various styles of sectarian spirituality threatened to turn his dominant (and "churchly") New-World "Citty" into a sprawl of recessive (and "sectarian") suburbs.[79] Clearly Hawthorne knew it was the authority of Winthrop which ultimately forgave Endicott, even as it forced Williams to flee from an order of deportation. And the ultimate irony of "Endicott and the Red Cross" very probably depends on our own realization of the reason why Endicott will come out all right: if his act of symbolic separation *were* a political deed, it would certainly have the *most* severe consequences in England; but even so it probably accorded with Winthrop's own deepest instinct, the desire to empower an historic opportunity in a space made vacant to receive it.

Very well, according to this view, might Hawthorne's personal feelings be ambivalent; and more deeply so than we customarily imagine. For there would be, upon this premise, far more at issue than esthetic dismay at the prospect of provincial paranoia, more than quietistic revulsion at revolutionary fury. And the literary problem would require far more (and less) than the manufacture of the sort of romantic-historical plot which invites the reader to reverence the memory of the wisdom of Winthrop, reject the fate of the conscience of Williams, and—in spite of the bigotry—honor the name and the typology of Endicott.[80] Deconstructive or not, any tale based on an adequately informed and decently critical sense of the real politics of New England's actual ideology, organization, and operation in the 1630's would have to question not only the significance of Winthrop but also, and accordingly, "the meaning of America." Without Endicott, the mythology of civil religion might well be the poorer by one or two forceful symbols. Without Winthrop, however, there might well be no "Redeemer Nation." How much more "complex," then, the American Fate? And clearly "Endicott and the Red Cross" does demand to be read in just this way. What else, in general, are we supposed to do with a tale which seems strategically contrived to contradict itself? What, more particularly, are we to make of one where the great majority of spoken lines are put in the mouth of an historical character who never published a single word and who rehearses far more of Winthrop than his "little speech" on the "liberty to obey"? Clearly Endicott's whole sense of the meaning of New England derives from Winthrop's original "Modell" of an enclave of convenanted privilege.[81] And the climax of his outlawed political speech merely exposes to full publicity the essential question raised, but not plainly answered, by the whole checkered pattern of Winthrop's magisterial career, and by the curious alternation of specification and silence in his masterful *Journal:* "What *have* we to do with England?" (440, my italics). Well might Hawthorne wonder. And necessarily must we inquire: whose "imperious" words *are* these, really?

Edmund Wilson has made it popular to blame Lincoln for the creation of American empire: the "Union" was less an Edwardsean transcendental than the political condition necessary for the creation and maintenance of a modern nation-state powerful enough to compete with Germany and Russia; and the Civil War meant Union essentially, Abolition only by military implication.[82] "Man's accidents," indeed. Would it have been any less improbable, in the 1830's, to have implicated Winthrop, without whose vision America might have become not two nations divided as slave and free, and not even two cultures identified as "Puritan and Cavalier" (with Yankee and Yorker struggling to divide the remains of one of these), but a veritable Europe of separately rightful states, except that each of these would be individualized not so much by racial difference or by a long history of feudal alliance as by a series of miscellaneous sectarian preferences all let loose in the Reformation of the sixteenth century and variously empowered to found colonies in the seventeenth? Certainly "Endicott" seems the appropriate occasion for us to think that thought. And how shall we authoritatively deny it as Hawthorne's own?

From the first labored beginnings of "The Gentle Boy," Hawthorne struggled to estimate both the significance and the justice of the Puritans' "original bond of union"; and, like virtually all of his historically minded contemporaries, he had to concede that to destroy that complex bond would have been, in all probability, "to subvert the government, and break up the colony."[83] And yet his judgments on the spiritual effects of that union remain uncompromised and unforgiving, in that tale and in others which will come later. Would it have been so bad to subvert *that* government, break up *that* colony, undo *that* particular religious bond? Perhaps not. The land would scarcely have reverted to the Indians, though in deference to Roger Williams even that thought might prove thinkable. All you would lose, really, is your last, best hope. And if, decades hence, *The Marble Faun* will spoil its own literary integrity by clinging so hard to that embattled option—in opposition to earlier and lesser hopes that are better dramatized, and in defiance of sentiments expressed in the letters and journals of the period—then all we can fairly conclude is that Hawthorne's ambivalence about "the meaning of America" endured in spite of his utterly clear-sighted hatred of every sort of historical absolutism. Returning to the region of homely New England rather than to the ideal of Puritanic America, he was entirely content to surrender the Union.[84]

Perhaps the whole thing had been, from the first, altogether less inevitable than everybody seemed to think. Or if that seems too radical a skepticism to be inferred from "Endicott and the Red Cross," then we can at least suspend our own political disbelief until we fairly confront "The May-Pole of Merry Mount." For there Endicott will stand in for an invention of America even older than Winthrop's marvelous "Modell." And Hawthorne will deconstruct it with literary tools more cunning (and Miltonic) than even Roger Williams could furnish.

3

Meanwhile, however, there is the problem of the Puritan Piety, more properly so called, which we seem to have left behind in "The Gentle Boy," but which will also play a major part in "The May-Pole," not to mention "Young Goodman Brown" and "The Minister's Black Veil." So before concluding our sketch of Hawthorne's quarrel with the political myth of Puritanism, it may be well to take a further look at his manipulation of its pious image. That too may be more deeply problematic than it first appears: if a close and fully historical analysis of "Endicott and the Red Cross" surprises us into a suspicion of everything *except* Williams, another sort of doubtful Hawthorne allegory works to bring even that last hope—temporarily, at least—under a cloud. Or into a cave.

In one sense "The Man of Adamant" seems scarcely to require a "revaluation." Though it is a somewhat more complex and interesting literary performance than we usually allow, we can probably rest in Hawthorne's own value judgment: he "failed in giving shape and substance" to what initially seemed a "fine idea."[85] And further, the "attitude toward Puritanism" expressed there is just as obviously hostile as that of "Endicott" turns out to be subtly so. No surprise there. What makes the tale more than a little intriguing, however, is the extent to which the most adamantine of Hawthorne's Puritans is allowed to appear in the attitude of Roger Williams himself. In the end we may be forced to conclude that the self-burial of Richard Digby recalls nothing so clearly as John Davenport's entrenchment in his own arch-Puritanical outpost at New Haven; but only after he has clearly reminded us of Williams digging in at Providence. This problematic layering of literary meaning might well provoke a major research into the archaeology of Hawthorne's historical knowledge. Our theme requires only the turning over of a stone or two.[86]

Our first impression is that Hawthorne intends Digby as nothing more than a generalized image of "Puritanism itself"; or, just a bit more subtly, one of its (two) leading "tendencies"—"an absurd extreme of a Puritan direction." In contrast to Endicott, who stands for the eventual need to establish and defend a certain "uniformity," Digby embodies the pure and unconflicted drive toward "separation." And this impression of tendentious generality probably explains much of our dissatisfaction with the tale. Compared with Parson Hooper, for example, Digby is an absurdly simplistic character; and compared with the actual record of Puritan attempts to explain the peculiar quality of their "non-separating Congregationalism," he clearly reduces a complex historic effort (to carve out a safe place for pure religion, in a wilderness, if necessary) to some psychotic form of "escapism." If ego-psychology and intellectual history are both to be elided, perhaps the story might just as well be about "genital obsession."[87]

And yet even simplistically considered, Hawthorne's original "vision" of the meaning of Digby has some cogency. If Puritan ecclesiology is indeed somewhat defective on the score of "catholicity," then perhaps Digby's story may well have been worth Hawthorne's writing, and our reading, even in its simplest terms. Digby can stand as merely "the gloomiest and most intolerant" of a group which, taken overall, seems fairly gloomy and intolerant wherever you look, and which can be called a "brotherhood" only by an irony which convicts the whole group of having lost touch with its origins.[88] The Puritans had been a "preaching brotherhood" in England (or in Holland, or in their earlier places of "exile"), but in America they tend everywhere toward their own solipsistic epitome. Considered, plausibly enough, as but a single sect amidst the many surviving from that general shipwreck called "the Reformation," they seem indeed possessed of a "plan of salvation so narrow, that, like a plank in a tempestuous sea, it could avail no sinner[s] but [themselves,] who bestrod it triumphantly, and hurled anathemas against the wretches whom [they] saw struggling with the billows of eternal death" (161).[89] A partial portrait, to be sure, but close enough for the purpose of an "apologue" which functions as the very reverse of an historical "apologie."

From the outset, therefore, the tale evokes not only the limited nature of the Calvinistic atonement, but also (and more pointedly) the whole thrust of the Puritan "movement." Determined to "hold no communion" (161) with the mixed assemblies of the Old England, "the Puritan" (as we now fairly generalize) seeks a more exclusive sense of religion in the New. And if the conditions of "visible sanctity" become, early or late, too lax in the ever more populous regions around Boston, then there will always be further migrations into such "wilderness" as remains—redundantly provided, in the literal, and always typologically the same. Witness Providence, in 1636; or New Haven, in 1639; or indeed any of the holy church-migrations down to the separations of the Great Awakening, and beyond. If the doctrine of "Reformation Without Tarrying for Any" proved too simple to cover the real polity of any Puritan plantation north of Plymouth, still somebody or other was always refusing to "tarry longer in the tents" (161) of some place or other. It may not be quite *the* American experience but, again, close enough for an apologue.[90] Against compromise with the children of "this generation" (162), American Puritans are, all of them, always adamant: "What fellowship hath righteousness with unrighteousness? And what communion hath light with darkness?" If a British Royalist—named "Digby," as it turns out—could plausibly predict that Puritanism would empower "a pope in every parish," then surely an American Ironist can fairly notice the reductive accomplishment of that already reductive prediction: Everyman his own Pope.[91]

Tendentiously considered, therefore, the career of Hawthorne's Digby seems perfectly inevitable: no *donnée* this simple can possibly generate any very complex plot, literary or historical; in this one instance, at least, adequate literary form could only belie the historical premise. "The Minister's Black Veil" would find a way to evade this fallacy of imitative form without falsifying the historical record, but here Hawthorne seems almost perversely to face the Puritans' own dead end. And so we are not surprised when the gloomy sequel predicts an "end" of Puritanism definitive enough to satisfy the most liberal hope, and which deserves to compete with Oliver Wendell Holmes's better-known myth of the "wonderful one-hoss shay": if the Puritan "Church" (coach that it was, in Edward Taylor and others) endured intact for a hundred years and then fell apart in a single day, the Puritanic drive toward a perfectly separated purity drove "the Puritan" to his own stony extinction. Neither Thomas Jefferson nor yet William Ellery Channing would wish to improve the result.[92]

That Digby's private retreat is to a "Cave of Error" is scarcely to be doubted. Retired from the common precincts of his "fellow men," he "read the Bible to himself" and even "prayed to himself" (162). More remarkable, perhaps, but still predictable on premise, is the discovery that he managed to accomplish, all unaided, a perfect reversal of authentic Biblical conversion—changing his own "fleshy heart to stone" (164), against which the "slender grace" of "love and faith united" (165) proved perfectly inefficacious.[93] Perfectly separated at last, he triumphs over all merely natural influences: what has he to do with the sunlight of reason or common grace, any more than with some supposedly sacramental waters? Seeming largely "perverse" (166), sexual love itself need not apply. What had the radical separatism of Endicott to do with the popish sign-systems of England? And "what hast thou"—Mary Goffe—"to do with my prayers?—what with my heaven?" (167). How *can* the righteous unite? So exit you rumors of spiritual merger, and enter you whispers of heavenly death.

Once again, as in "The Gentle Boy," Hawthorne's judgment is perfectly relentless: "the Puritan" hates life. We may (Puritan-fashion) reject the typology of Mary Goffe as *pseudo*sacramental, and therefore sentimental merely. And we may choose to make much or little of the available Spenserian archetypes.[94] But Hawthorne will not let us escape the rigor of his conclusion that even the more primal revelations available in the older of the Christian's two testaments convict Digby of aboriginal un-Godliness. Let Digby's cave remind us of *either* "Elijah's cave at Horeb" *or* "Abraham's sepulchral cave, at Machpelah" (162), and the judgment is equally final and perfect. And destructively ironical in either case.

At Machpelah, Abraham dies a venerable patriarch, in the midst of proper descendants assembled in reverence around. *Consummatum est.* His founding work is done and, potentially at least, the members of his covenantal family are more numerous than stars. But Digby dies alone, Father in Faith (as in the flesh) to no one. This is the way the world ends. Or if we prefer Digby's own less "tribal" association, his case is scarcely improved. Repeatedly rebuffed by the children of "this generation," Elijah repeatedly repairs to his fugitive and cloistered cave at Horeb, abandoning a ragged career of prophecy for the solitary satisfactions of the "one just man." Whereupon God himself, condescending to act the part of Mary Goffe, repeatedly calls him out, repeatedly sends him back to his proper ministry, even to the court of Ahab.[95] But Digby, seduced by the pleasures of purity, and loving too well the text of his own isolated consciousness, can discern in the humanistic call of Mary Goffe—"Come back to thy fellow-men" (166)—no more divinity than in the wiles of some Godless Jezebel. Endicott will scarcely hate his maypole more fiercely than Digby hates the seductive appeal of Mary Goffe. And this common hatred of the flesh defines, at last, the hateful piety of Hawthorne's essential "Puritan": since there is no grace in nature, salvation is to be sought away from the world. No wonder Hawthorne would learn to confess salvation in Sophia.

And yet the obvious biographical consideration need not press in on us, not even in this simplest instance. For reductive of Puritan experience as "The Man of Adamant" undeniably is, it is so by evident design. It plainly suggests why, quite apart from personal wish, someone might well think to make this particular reduction; it even suggests why, given the leading facts of the historical case, the partial portrait of Puritanic separation as solipsist in tendency might be somehow more adequate than any other single view. That is to say, even this simple tale forces us to recognize certain historical facts and then to consider the purposes they might legitimately serve in the hands of the moral historian. Thus we cannot dismiss this strategic reduction of Puritan experience without fairly estimating both its representative status and its paradigmatic function. Accordingly, a word about each of these in turn.

Representatively considered, the rigidly plotted story of Richard Digby can hardly fail to remind us of the historic career of no less a personage than Roger Williams himself. Up to a point, at least—where the ironies begin to reverse themselves—their stories are so perfectly parallel that the facts of the Williams case seem to "have wrought themselves, almost spontaneously, into a sort of allegory." We need to recall, of course, that before Williams worked his way out the other end of the distinctively Puritan problem of "separation with uniformity" (making it all too easy for liberal historians to confuse his brand of spiritual pluralism with the altogether more secular sort of Jefferson), he had been himself something like the purest of the Puritans.[96] But then the smiling irony of "Endicott and the Red Cross" has already forced us to remember precisely this fact, even if Digby's *own* tale did not force our interpretative intelligence back on its own sources.

Winthrop made careful note of Williams' impossible extremism, in political dismay and personal regret; and Mather would emphasize it, as part of his own triumphant but tendentious account of the marvelous reasonableness that had guided the more sober majority of New England men in the discovery and prosecution of their wonderful Middle Way between Episcopacy and Brownism. Even as others were learning to compromise, and to settle, Williams was struggling for a purity that proved well-nigh singular, and that forced him out of the pleasant settlements and into the wilderness. Williams it was who rejected first Boston and then both Salem and Plymouth because they would not reject the mixed multitudes of England; he could not, in Winthrop's account, "communicate with them, except they would refuse communion with the rest." Nor were Winthrop's internal policies found to be any less impure: to "tender an oath to the unregenerate man" was, whatever the political necessity, to accept "communion with a wicked man." Purity, after all, forbade a man even "to *pray* with such, though a wife, child, etc."[97] Thus Digby's own definition of "acceptable prayers" as those in which his own voice would "not be mingled with the sinful supplication of the multitude" (163). The only saving grace, perhaps, is that Digby will never have to face the problem of polluted communion with a merely natural wife or child.

If the career of Roger Williams may fairly be said to reveal one principal "tendency" of the Puritan logic, then the story of Richard Digby simply abstracts, intensifies, and then re-embodies that tendency, with a vengeance against the tendency rather than against any historical persons. Very probably the story's glancing references to "Providence" (161, 163) and "wilderness" (162) are meant to remind us of both the geographical and the typological end of Williams' literal migration and then life-long spiritual pilgrimage. And undoubtedly the central action of the tale does little more than adumbrate Winthrop's (and then Mather's) account of the next-to-last phase of Williams' religious progress, which normal Puritans took to be both insane and self-parodic. Though Williams would famously end by deciding "he would preach to and pray with all comers," the decision came, according to Winthrop, only after he had, one spiritual moment before, "refused communion with all, save his own wife."[98] Separation for the sake of purity can take only one step *beyond* this, of course, and Hawthorne's Digby is simply the figure of the man who has taken even *that* step: everyone is damned but me and thee, and now I begin to suspect . . .

It would be easy enough to object to the tendentious reductionism of Hawthorne's procedure, from the historical point of view no less than from the literary, since its result is no more a "balanced" history, in the ordinary sense, than it is a fascinating characterization. If even the Puritans themselves saw the potential madness in Williams' position, why bother (especially at this late date) to single him out for special ridicule? Or, more cogently—since the story really does insist on its own representative generality—why slander all of Puritanism by reducing it to the semblance of one quixotic figure and then reducing *him* to the absurdity he courted but finally resisted? Since it really is true that only particulars exist, why risk "essentialism" in so deeply problematic a form?

Again, one answer might well come from Hawthorne's own "psychobiography," from his own *feelings* about the moral consequence (or equivalent) of Puritan separatism. But a more ready explanation surely comes from the observable quality of Puritan experience itself. For if the Puritans saw the absurdity of Williams, they did not always so clearly see their own; or, more cogently, they did not seem to realize that his could be seen as only a heightened form of their own. Winthrop, for example, regards Williams' ultimate decision, to "preach to and pray with all comers," as no *less* absurd than his penultimate one, to "refuse communion with all." And Mather will positively satirize the waywardness of Williams' logic while yet struggling to rationalize the half-way remnants of a convenantal church-system which threatened to exclude his and everybody else's own children.[99] What Hawthorne's reduction is designed to reveal, accordingly, is precisely what the Puritans never *did* recognize—that Williams was merely driving their own logic to its own mad terminus; and that when its essential absurdity did (finally) begin to appear, he left off at once, so that the intellectual history of Rhode Island will be *far* different from that of Massachusetts and Connecticut. Thus Hawthorne's Digby stands as the end toward which they were *all* headed, and from which only Williams made a significant or noticeable "retreat," back toward the world. And neither Miller nor Morgan has said it more deftly or fairly.[100]

But to realize this adequacy in "The Man of Adamant," and to notice that all of its significant drama arises from the tension between its own literary formulations and the actual historical case, is already to sense that the tale manages to invoke more than the notorious example of Williams; that crucial doctrines and representative attitudes may be as important as a single eccentric career; and that other figures may also play their own silent, eloquent, allusive part. Coming back to the story from even the necessary pretext of Winthrop, for example, one can scarcely avoid the suspicion that the problem of baptism looms quite as large as that of "communion," in either its specific sacramental or general moral sense. According to Winthrop, Williams had barely broken communion with Massachusetts when he began to question his own infant baptism; straightaway he got himself "in all haste rebaptized," and then "was come to question [even] his own second baptism."[101] Evidently the Puritan logic of "communion" leads in that direction, though our own scholarship has not always been perfectly clear on this point. And though Mary Goffe invites Digby out of his cave to drink rather than to be immersed, it is, after all, only water that she offers. The wine appears in Digby's other story, "The Minister's Black Veil."[102]

Pursuing still the still-Puritan example of Williams, we find a man who first questions and then rejects the originary Christian sacrament because, once he has crossed back over Jordan into the territories of Rhode Island, he cannot locate John the Baptist—unless, as Winthrop wickedly implies, the man be Williams himself. Rather like the scholar who declines the doctorate because there is no adequate examiner. We could perhaps discover the man who *circumcized* the prophet in the Wilderness; but if we look for his baptizer we may be forced to conclude that such spiritual origins as are not lost really are original. Somewhere, somehow, somebody had seemed willing to make it up as he went along and to call the result a new and more spiritual dispensation. No wonder Williams changed his style: if a man has to endure the desolation of secular history without the prior guarantee of the sort of covenant in which magical christenings *do* make Christians, then he had better pray with as many of his fellows as he can, in all civility, assemble in one place. So out of your cave, Digby, and back to the settlements. Have you not heard? God has made all men of one blood. Or come at least to the "bubbling fountain" (163). Even savage men think to offer a cup of water to an alien; for we all do drink the same natural drink.[103]

And yet the problem of baptism remains, even after we have invoked and dispelled the specter of Williams. Once it has been fairly raised, in fact, we suddenly realize just how much definitive Puritan history this little tale actually has compressed into itself and how much naturalized theology it might be struggling, against its own (sentimental) tendency, effectively to contain. Surely Digby has a model nearer home than Providence. And we may even have passed over the most telling point in the very first paragraph.

Clearly baptism originates all but the most radically Puritan forms of Christian "brotherhood." And in this sacramental context Digby's exclusivist "plank" (161) refers most precisely to the particular plank in the 1648 "Platform" of the Synod of Cambridge which drastically limited the availability of that sacrament to the "seed" of the "saints"—to the children, that is, of such men and women who possessed the spiritual fervor or discernment or assurance or arrogance to confess some specifically Christian "experience." That plank, as we are now all in a position to realize, was the self-defining, self-enclosing, and in the end self-defeating proposition framed by the founding generation. Struggles over strict or lax administration of the communion supper would come much later, in time as well as in logic; and too late, it could be argued, to make any real difference. If baptism were, in its own way, a seal of rather than a means to the special graces of the covenant, then its administration could hardly become "promiscuous," after the manner of ordinary generation. Nor would there ever be enough "true" Christians to fill up the churches; scarcely enough, by some accounts and standards, to constitute a self-respecting sect. So why *not* represent the entire experiment as nothing but a childless, misogynist, misanthropical Old Badman digging his own grave in a nightmarish womb full of phallic excrescences? Close enough for an apologue.[104]

Especially when the decisions of the notorious "Half-Way Synod" of 1662—designed, as we should now judge, to lead the Puritan "Church" back to the real "world"—succeeded only in transferring the ontological (and the biological) problem from one sacramental occasion to another; or, by even the friendliest account, in saving the entire enterprise from solipsistic extinction only at the expense of a tribalism so "spiritual" as to be undreamed of in the Old Testament. And this because certain Digby-like

Puritans remained fixed in their defense of the original logic of sacramental exclusion. If an eventual rebirth of the spirit were *that* much more significant than the original one according to nature, and if a virtual "test-tube experiment" proved that the number of the one always approaches zero even as the other increases by Malthusian multiples, then Richard Digby perfectly embodies the essence of American Puritanism.[105] Biblically considered, he is a failed-Abraham masquerading as a pseudo-Elijah, not quite prepared to bite the bullet and call himself Ishmael. Historically considered, we may as well identify him as John Davenport, the seeker of purity who never *did* turn back.

Cotton Mather remembers Davenport as the man who came out of Holland, even as he had earlier come out of England, for the express purpose of witnessing against the "promiscuous baptism" of children who did not seem to have chosen truly "Christian parents." The Presbyterian exiles, as it turned out, were very nearly as flagrant in their "profanation of [this] holy institution" as the native Anglicans had been. And so Davenport was drawn to New England by the utopian report of John Cotton: the order of the churches established there was so purely perfect as to put one in mind of "the new heaven and new earth, wherein dwells righteousness." Yet Davenport remained in Massachusetts only long enough to take part in the "blessed work" of silencing Ann Hutchinson. Thereupon, he and his friends "chose to go farther westward," to begin a new plantation in the name of "a yet stricter conformity to the word of God." Even Cotton's city fell short, apparently, of the City of God.[106]

The experience in Holland had already convinced Davenport of the virtual impossibility of getting any reformed people to take a single step "beyond the first remove of the first reformers": "as easily might the ark have been removed from the mountains of Ararat."[107] And so it proved even in Massachusetts. Cotton, after all, had compromised, and sooner or later Boston would be baptizing children of parents whose interest in Christ came to nothing more than such preparatory motions as any moderately self-conscious pagan might experience. But as Davenport's eye was fixed on eternity, he pressed on to his own new heaven at New Haven, by all accounts the single most exclusive church known to seventeenth-century Puritanism and at the same time, in most interpretations, the very essence, epitome, and *reductio* of the distinctive New England Way.[108]

Mather's own account tries hard to be friendly; but no defender of the Half-Way Covenant could ever really approve the length to which the desire for utopian purity had driven this arch-Puritan:

He used a more than ordinary exactness in trying those that were admitted unto the communion of the church: indeed, so very thoroughly, and I had almost said, severely strict, were the terms of his communion, and so much, I had well nigh said, overmuch, were the golden snuffers of the sanctuary employed by him in his exercise of discipline towards those that were admitted, that he did all that was possible to render the renowned church of New-Haven like the New-Jerusalem.

Mather saves Davenport for his own purposes by emphasizing a concession that absolutely no one else could possibly take as the meaning of his radical example—that even *he* had to concede the practical impossibility of an earthly church "where there 'enters nothing which defiles.' "[109] So odd is Mather's special plea, so late and so reluctant is Davenport's own appeal to the principle of "charitable discretion," that we can easily imagine Hawthorne's story as taking off from precisely this point and merely denying this obvious limit to Davenport's *almost* perfect exclusionist tendency. And directly behind Digby's tendentious refusal to "tarry longer in the tents of Kedar" (161) lies Mather's already suggestive characterization of Davenport as "more fit for Zebulon's ports than for Issachar's tents." Some men, Mather clearly implies, simply cannot bear the heat of the plain.[110]

But Hawthorne's Digby adumbrates somewhat more than Davenport's archetypal (if multiple) withdrawal from the mixed multitudes of the dusty midworld unwatered by Jordan. There is also the matter of his steadfast refusals to come back to his fellow-men in need—to England, in the 1630's, though envoys were sent out to Holland; to the *classes* of Amsterdam, though his independent religious exercises were taken as scandal; to the Westminster Assembly of Divines in 1642, though he was sent for sincerely and by name. Most famously, of course (though the matter is omitted by Cotton Mather), there is his refusal to come back from New Haven to Boston to attend the deliberations of 1656–57, or of 1661–62—his refusal, that is, even to *discuss* the possibility of some compromise which would permit the grandchildren of the founders to remain within the church *at all*. To remain so, of course, they would have to be baptized, whether or not their parents, the sons and daughters of the original Saints, had experienced conversion and professed a "saving faith." And this possibility remained unthinkable to Davenport. Better to declare those "civil-honest" child-parents *felos de se* than to risk further "profanation" of baptism. Hartford might continue its steady, pragmatic drift toward the Presbyterianism of Saybrook. Boston might compromise and call the *Result* a clarification of the mind of the fathers. But Davenport would remain, in the accidental but telling phrase of New England's most competent sacramental historian, "adamant against any relaxation of New England's standards."[111] What had they all "to do with [his] Bible?—what with [his] prayers?—what with [his] Heaven?"(167).

Of course Davenport would *finally* come back to Boston, in 1667, to take over the pulpit of the First Church; but his motives were scarcely those of rational charity, loving reconciliation, mutual help, or even of compromise with the ways of the settled world: "he wanted to mount the throne of Cotton and denounce from it the Synod of 1662." Which he did. And the arch-Puritanical policies he followed upon his return served only to split that ancient church immediately and irreconcilably in two; and that bitter split, in the judgment of Perry Miller, "nearly destroyed New England."[112] So that Hawthorne has in fact protected Davenport's reputation by leaving his own Digby decently buried in a cave, leaving our history to dig him up if it will.

In the end, however, Hawthorne's last word on Digby parodies Mather more nearly than it anticipates Miller. For Mather, the last thing to remember about Davenport—and doubtless this discovers the deepest motive of his refusal to compromise the definition of the Church with the needs of the world—is that he continued to expect, right up to his own apoplectic end, "a personal, visible, powerful, and glorious coming of the Lord Jesus Christ unto *judgment*, long before the end of the world." Others might trim sail for the long voyage of history, but Davenport wanted only (to change the figure) to keep the lamp of his own virgin church in perfect good trim. And thus we are asked to leave him, "resting in his hope to *stand in his lot* at that end."[113] But as that coming is long, long delayed, it remains for Hawthorne's children, baptized or not, to discover his rigidified remains; and for his narrator to twist the moral as he changes the posture:

> There still *sits*, and, unless an earthquake crumble down the roof upon his head, shall *sit* forever, the shape of Richard Digby, in the attitude of repelling the whole race of mortals—not from heaven—but from the horrible loneliness of his dark, cold sepulchre. (169, my italics)

Expecting to stand firm until the awaited end, Digby merely sits rigid, Pope in his own singular parish—less able than Judge Pyncheon, even, to rise ex cathedra. Forever, like Hooper behind his veil. Or else, more literally, like some ironic Lot turned to stone for *not* looking back. This is the way the Church ends. World without end. Amen.

Which ought to be the last word on the representative character of so slight and, superficially at least, so sentimental a tale. Except as it might be necessary to remind the literary positivist, nervous about "sources" and about "proof," that one of the envoys sent out from England to negotiate with Davenport in Holland, in the midst of his notorious controversy with the Church of the Reverend Mr. Paget, was named Goffe, in ironic anticipation of the angelic Mary Goffe of our own legendary tale.[114] And to assure the historical nominalist, anxious about any representation of the historical many by the literary one, that the same story which tendentiously evokes some hypothetical end to uncompromised Congregationalism also alludes most knowingly to the signal example of its actual founding. For we can always take the idea of shipwreck implied by the first paragraph literally—as referring, obviously, to the most real and dire disaster which threatened the ocean-crossing of every one of New England's holy migrants. And if we do, we can scarcely help recalling the original gesture of John Cotton, the archfounder whose glowing report had lured Davenport out of Holland in the first place.

Surely it were forgivable if the prospect of some untimely death by water had provoked or frightened even some moderately reformed Christians into baptizing their children at sea, fondly hoping that straight up from that ocean-perishing might leap their Christian apotheosis. Could it have seemed altogether foolish, or "profane," to imagine that such children might somehow be redeemed by this seal or promise of membership in some truly "catholic" (as opposed to "Roman") Church? And yet Cotton was the man who knew better; and who, wishing to teach others by his own disciplined example, steadfastly and self-consciously chose to defer the baptism of his own "Seaborn" son until the saintly parent had himself made profession unto and been accepted of some truly reformed and duly instituted "particular" church in New England. This same John Cotton was, by all accounts, a charitable Christian and even a kind man; no one has ever thought him the sort of Badman who would throw Elizabeth Horrocks out of his cave for drinking water. But a church is a church is a church. And no one has ever "bestrode" the narrow plank of Congregationalism more "triumphantly" (161) than, in that moment, the man Cotton Mather would credit with providing the sense of "exactness" to the gathered churches of New England.[115] No wonder Davenport would wish to denounce 1662 from his very throne.

All Davenport had ever wanted, apparently, was to get Cotton's logic exactly right, for once, once and for all, in one final and perfect removal of the ark, just before the end. Just like Digby—whose only "parody" consists in the faithfulness of his imitation of Davenport's faithfulness to Cotton; and who thus remains historical until literature is forbidden to imitate life.

But if "The Man of Adamant" functions as a near-perfect epitome of the non-catholic tendency of the Puritan piety, it also presents itself, pretty self-consciously, as a paradigm of Hawthorne's practice as a moral historian. This is to say that, like the beginning of "Sir William Phips" and the conclusion of "Alice Doane's Appeal" (and far more directly than the famous headnotes to "Malvin," "Molineux," and "The Gentle Boy"), the conclusion of this tale means to comment on its own status and procedure as historical recovery. There may actually be some sort of "allegory" involved—depending on our ability yet to discover some public event which corresponds to the childish episode which is said to occur "above a century" (168) after Digby's stony self-interment. But even in the least specific case, Hawthorne has once again left us a model of his own literary-historical activity, according to which, significantly, the "guilt" is not at all that of "the artist."

Perhaps the inadvertent discovery of the Digby remains by "a little boy and girl" is meant to suggest the youthful (and at first innocent) researches of Hawthorne and one of his sisters, even as both those sisters may be invoked by the bio-historical frame of "Alice Doane's Appeal." Perhaps at some level of association there lingers also a trace of adolescent sexual curiosity, not only in the suggestive details of this exploration of caves and shady places but even in the indecorous outcome—as, in immemorial imitation of Jack and Jill, the children all come "tumbl[ing] headlong down the hill" (168). But surely a public issue arises when we recall that the children have been playing hide-and-seek: like Digby himself they have been retiring away from their fellows; but unlike him they have been shouting "at intervals" so that their "party of pursuers" will indeed find them out. Like the children in a poem by Robert Frost (or in a monograph by Edmund Morgan), they seek to cultivate specialness without quite courting solipsism.[116] But they are playing at a deeper game than they realize; perhaps they require the image of Digby to frighten them back to the full society of all their fellows.

For they are, quite literally, those children of the Puritans of whom Nature has taken fuller and fairer account than had the founders—and whose ironic triumph it is to stumble upon the cardinal fact of a history which refused to allow for the facts of life. This, apparently, is the way the world does *not* end. Someone might yet grow up to espouse the proposition that Society truly *is* the Redeemed Form of Man; but already we are supposed to know that (in a more modern idiom) "Love will never do / What you want it to."

What can occur, at this moment, when some truly significant discovery seems to have been made? What might New Englandish America yet learn about the archaeology of its own solitary moral knowledge? As the moral attitude and posture of Puritanical separatism really is just as repulsive as the physical aspect of Digby is "frightful," it is hardly surprising that some attempt at concealment will be made. Historians, one readily supposes, have often exercised the same tender concern for the sensibilities of their audiences as parents for their children. And for roughly the same reason: some facts, it always seems, will not bear much looking into; we find them out for ourselves, in privacy, or not at all. So the historically innocent are left with only that paradigm of filiopiety which parodies the more seriously historical process. Digby is so perfectly reburied that "all traces of the discovery were obliterated, leaving only a marvellous legend, which grew wilder from one generation to another . . . till few believed that there had ever been a cavern or a statue, where now they saw but a grassy path on the shadowy hill-side"(169). *History* refusing to end at its appointed term, the process of *Story* continues to fill its customary place—tempting Goodman Brown (and Melville's Pierre) to "live from the Devil," and forcing the historian into the Party of Irony.

For even in New England, as it turns out, some children will "want to know why." Even there someone might think to retrace the moral steps along that "shadowy hillside," to discover what lay buried. Especially if he had, more melodramatically, already gone to stand on "Gallows Hill." Natural process has a way of turning the entire setting of the ordinary past into the same "grassy path," but the moral historian could discover more than one patch of "deceitful verdure."[117] And well before there had been those (far too many) witches, there had been those (far too few) visible saints.

Who deserve—and in this otherwise slender little apologue actually get—their own negative monument. Morally, of course, Hawthorne's highly moralistic conclusion perfectly agrees with the judgment of the filiopietists: no one can lament the fact that "grown people avoid the spot, nor do children play" any longer in the vicinity of Digby's sepulchral cave; for it seems only proper that "Friendship, and Love, and Piety and all human and celestial sympathies should keep aloof from" (109) the motives that led the Puritanic church so far from the real world. And yet the same voice which "draws the moral" also very explicitly "tells the tale": how can we dismiss the example of Digby until we have first reconstructed it? So that, as always, the ethical instruction is perfectly meaningless apart from the precise facts of the case, even as the story has forced us to dig them up. Perhaps we should remember the method as well as the moral when, momentarily, we come to confront Hawthorne's major explorations of the doctrinal source and psychological significance of Puritan piety.

4

"The May-Pole of Merry Mount" is, I should judge, a major tale, but not quite in that full "psychological" sense. It is one of Hawthorne's most richly learned and ironically manipulated stories; and it does mean to speculate, seriously enough, about the relation between original Puritanism and "the future complexion of New England" (62).[118] But its mode is severely mythical; or, rather, demythical. Unlike "Young Goodman Brown" and "The Minister's Black Veil," it cares very little for the personal trauma of its youthful protagonists, who seem more like prescriptive definitions than like "characters." Nobody in the tale is given more than one original thought, to differentiate him (or her) from some archetypal norm; and when that thought does come, almost no attempt is made to make it seem "consistent." This is all quite deliberate, the tale's own law and specific difference; and it requires a certain determined misprision to discover that the Lord and Lady of the May are flat and even a little boring.[119]

What makes "The May-Pole" work so brilliantly is precisely its ability to manipulate our expectations; to make us almost believe that we could have written this pat and patent little "allegory" ourselves—out of our own fund of moral wisdom, if that is what we usually rely on in matters of literary interpretation; or even out of certain "authentic passages from history" (62), if we happen indeed to have read the relevant matter "recorded on the grave pages of our New England annalists" (54). But the tale is absolutely booby-trapped with twice-told ironies, as just a little *more* attention to the quality and condition of the original tellings makes absolutely clear. So that it works to embarrass our more-or-less Puritanic moralism, in even its historicist variety, as thoroughly as it balks our psychologism, itself always more or less Puritanic.

"Puritanism overcomes," we seem to learn, even as in literal fact it once did overcome the only credible challenge to a local hegemony aspiring to become totalized. But how do we know this? Or, supposing we really do *learn* it, why are we so easy to convince? Someone must have our number. But whose vision is this, really? And whose "allegory"? Bradford's, Nathaniel Morton's, Joseph Felt's, Catherine Sedgwick's, Hawthorne's, our own? And who, at this late date, would still be trying to convince us that things were, are, and always will be so? The story itself begs us to ask. It also provides all the clues we need to find the answer. To heed them is to dismantle an entirely factitious (though obviously fairly cogent) allegory of someone else's making and thereby to disarm a moralism that proves as arbitrary as it once was powerful.[120]

And yet, as deconstruction is never the whole story in Hawthorne, a certain burden of thematic meaning survives—moral without being "Puritanic," in the sense in which the example of Endicott teaches us to define that notion; and also political, as we come to realize the fusion of politics and piety in the Puritan world. And that latter point may yet serve as conclusion to both the discussion of this tale and to our whole eclectic chapter. For if

Digby has represented, from a political or worldly point of view, the recessive strain of Puritanism, Endicott stands for the dominant. If his excision of a popish symbol from a military banner might be made to symbolize a certain Puritanic nicety of conscience which an otherwise bourgeois revolution seemed yet to require, then perhaps the conditions of honest citizenship demanded the honor of ambivalence. But if his hacking down of the maypole were taken to signify the castration of Nature considered as moral norm, of if his arrest of Blackstone were interpreted as a token of some final triumph over the values of Anglo-Catholic tradition, or if the induction of Edith and Edgar into the pious armies of the Puritan Israel were read as the crucial episode in some anti-Miltonic masterplot, then probably simple protest was much more in order. For unless you could deconstruct those allegories, there might be no more stories to tell.

We can scarcely pass from "The Man of Adamant" to "The May-Pole of Merry Mount" without observing certain crucial differences of literary manner as well as of historical material. Both are, loosely speaking, "allegories" of Puritan moral experience; and both evidently wish to locate some deep and even fundamental fact or condition. But otherwise the dissimilarities are so great as to suggest some basic difference in literary kind. The textures are different, and so are the epistemologies. Inviting historical suspicion, "The Man of Adamant" yet manages to survive analysis; it stands as the enduring image of Puritan piety as it might operate "essentially"—if the One True Puritan were to follow the lead of his own moral logic, without significant opposition and hence without compromise; unopposed, that is, by such historical considerations as seem always to call for half-way concessions. It thus proposes a "timeless" definition of Puritanism: the separating and even solitary search for the divine, untainted by human or natural circumstances. And it does so by means of an allegory of its own tendentious making; we resolve the tale's thematic conflict as soon as we concede that Digby really *does* embody essential Puritanism.

But the convention of "The May-Pole" is significantly different. Its allegorical claim is not so much to the essential as to the originary; and, even so, it introduces us to a Puritanism already firmly located in time and place.[121] At one level this means only that we have to take account of politics as well as of piety: Endicott has designs on Edith and Edgar, whereas Digby has absolutely none on Mary Goffe. But at another level it may suggest that the allegorical terms involved are not quite of the story's own making. How could one story be at once both original and allegorical without calling attention to itself? If real existence is to abstract essence as dialectical contradiction is to monolithic tendency, then perhaps origins themselves are debatable. Perhaps we have not got back to first things so much as to first words.[122]

Possibly the story's apparently innocent little headnote means to alert us to precisely this unsettling possibility: the allegory here may be thought to have occurred "almost spontaneously," but perhaps this metamorphosis had taken place long before "the obscurest man of letters in America" ever thought to shut himself up in his famous "dismal chamber," to force his own rude fingers in the production of certain "blasted allegories" of his very own; possibly "the facts recorded in the grave pages of our New England annalists" had long since "wrought themselves" just so. If this should indeed turn out to be the case, then it may well follow that the ponderous and prolific moral choice offered—Puritan or Reveller, Gloom or Jollity, even (in a slightly more demanding idiom) Grace or Nature—is entirely spurious, the product not of moral reality, adequately considered, but of somebody's antique prejudice. A Puritanic reduction masquerading as a perfect dichotomy.

Surely this is what the plot itself, in its own lowly and moralistic way, would lead us to discover. Endicott (except perhaps in one illogical moment) can see no grounds of truce or compromise with the Revellers; but the reader is supposed to be able to discern, in the figures of Edith and Edgar, after they have quite fallen from their high places as Lord and Lady of the May, but quite apart from the Israelite identities Endicott is busy imagining for them, some possibility which the Puritan cannot as such conceive. We may or may not wish to erect, on the basis of a literary figure so slender, an entire orthodoxy of "the middle way"; but we cannot clearly deconstruct the allegory until we have fairly construed the moral action.[123]

The first fact we have to notice, accordingly, is that, as a group, the Revellers are awarded a rather sobering judgment long before Endicott thrusts his prying and prurient nose into the story at all; and that the judgment is more naturalistic than Puritanical. We may indeed require Endicott's very own allegorical intelligence to learn (or to suspect) that what we are witnessing is in fact a cultic paganism of a rather flagrantly phallic sort, but the narrator, mere "Story Teller" though he may be, clearly knows enough to suggest that, in the latitudes of New England at least, May Day is scarcely a movable feast. Everything *looks* perfectly innocent and appealing: the gaily decked maypole, the silken banner, the splash of brilliant color all tempt us to conclude that the Revellers are indeed a "people of a Golden Age" exulting in a world of natural beauty, naturally innocent of anything like "ultimate concern." But even before we are told that "May, or her mirthful spirit, dwelt all the year round at Merry Mount," we already know that the true name of today's bright day is "Midsummer Eve" (54–55). Surely joy is the condition of life!—except that always at our back we hear Andrew

Marvell or Anne Bradstreet, if not Satchel Paige: something may be gaining.[124]

Possessed of his own elementary theory of history, the narrator hastens to warn us that "the wild throng that stood hand-in-hand about the May-pole" could not be "that of Fauns and Nymphs" translated from classic fable to western woods. These "Gothic Monsters" are not at all merely natural; they are, rather, men (and perhaps women) of quite another condition and stage of history. Northerners, and late arrivals on the poor scene of the chilly and fallen world, they are merely playing at the altogether more southerly and original myth of sunny innocence. In fact they are men imitating animals— not only the "stag" and the "wolf" but also, as their determined sexuality begins to insist upon itself, the "venerable he-goat" and the "bear erect" (55). Perhaps, if they are not *merely* playing, they are degenerating, even as a soberly scientific "dispute of the new world" predicted they would.[125] At best they are affecting the primitive: "the Salvage man, well known in heraldry"; and beside him the Indian hunter, "a nobler figure but still a counterfeit" (56). The narrator has seen it all before, authentically; the colorful simulacrum seems merely pale.

The Puritans who live nearby will inevitably label it all diabolical: the very idea that human beings should forsake civility in pursuit of their lower nature. Some "bewildered" forest wanderer, anticipating Coverdale, and with or without benefit of Milton, would likely fancy them the "Crew of Comus": "some already transformed to brutes, some midway between man and beast; and others rioting in the flow of tipsey jollity that foreran the change" (56). The Dionysian, indeed; too poetical by half. The narrator merely finds it out of place: inappropriate because removed from its proper natural phase, and faintly indecorous therefore. Affronted in some simple historic sense rather than outraged in any very complex theology, he merely assumes that we are all, by now, supposed to know better. Sobriety and decorum having occurred, human life is scarcely, in these latter days, any longer to be so defined or arranged. To say more were Puritanical.[126]

If he does indeed venture just a bit more, it is only after he has, in his own self-consciously inserted discussion of the relevant historical conditions, taken account of that "one stern band" who voyaged to the west "to pray" (59). And even then his judgment is noticeably more chaste than that of Endicott; it takes the tone of a wise refusal, and not at all of a categorical exclusion. The reader is well prepared to conclude that the Revellers are perfectly debased, having reduced man to the state of nature considered as an animal state, thus to relieve themselves of the burden of prudential reflection and existential choice; that, as they are not truly animals whose only law is an instinct in harmony with natural process, nor truly primitives who may be somehow innocent of consciousness in its moral dimension, they are

255

in fact the very basest of men. But the narrator accuses them only of falling prey to some age-old illusion which, though clearly errant, has yet misled many before and might even now deceive the not truly wary:

The young deemed themselves happy. The elder spirits, if they knew that mirth was but the counterfeit of happiness, yet followed the false shadow wilfully, because at least her garments glittered brightest. Sworn triflers of a lifetime, they would not venture among the sober truth of life, not even to be truly blest. (59–60)

Thus the Revellers come to seem not so much debased as simply deceived, even if self-deceived. Their "wild philosophy of pleasure" (in the narrator's most severely judgmental characterization) is not so much idolatrous as it is merely idle. And in no case will it defraud our own moral maturity, any more than will the tyrannical sectarianism of Endicott and his Puritans. This is, after all, the nineteenth century.

What positive philosophy of life this "sober" refusal may imply is a nice moral question indeed. And how it might serve an orphaned "Story Teller" in flight from a Puritanical guardian is a risky, ticklish, and speculative matter we must postpone for the present.[127] But clearly *even this* narrator knows we do not need the help of Endicott in rejecting the Mount Wollaston Way. Whence we are led to suspect that the clash of categories Endicott introduces may afford more heat than light: allegorical oppositions are made in sectarian conflict, not born of historical reflection.

The same undialectical point is suggested by the moral career of the Lord and the Lady of the Revellers themselves. Long before Endicott bursts in to place their fragile young consciences under permanent Puritanic arrest, and utterly without benefit of the narrator's own elementary historical wisdom, Edith and Edgar have already begun to suspect the vanity of their mirthful young lives. Especially Edith, in whose eyes there appears, at the very climax of the wedding ceremony—itself a kind of sacramental epitome of Mount Wollaston's religion of nature—an "almost pensive glance" (58). Oh, dear: what can the matter be? Has she stayed too long at the fair? Has she even, somehow, in spite of her garland of roses, weirdly remembered death? Edgar is no *penseroso*, but he knows enough to ask. Ah, yes, and not only death, dear Edgar, but what they will be calling appearance and reality: "I struggle as with a dream, and fancy that the shapes of our jovial friends are visionary, and their mirth unreal, and that we are no true Lord and Lady of the May. What is the mystery in my heart?"(58). No philosopher, Edgar is lucky to be spared his reply; for "just then, as if a spell had loosened them, down came a little shower of roses from the May-Pole" (58). The fairy tale is over: this is your life. What follows now can only be that other fall we call the fall. And whether the spell were on the leaves or on the lovers, it is *Margaret* they mourn for.

After such pathos, presumably, all comment were fallacious. You see life this way or you don't. If you do, you don't need Endicott to crop your hair "in the true pumpkin-shell fashion" (66). And if you don't, all it means is that you shouldn't major in English: the cherries get only so ripe, and the Cavalier Poets get only one day in the Survey. But as fools do rush in, the narrator cannot forbear the insertion of his own thematic doggerel: "From the moment they truly loved" they had waked up, kissed the good life goodbye; nor would they ever waste "one regretful thought." A few fragments shored against ruin, and then some "authentic passages from history."

Which is not to say that serious moral commentary is not possible, or even absolutely demanded: why *is* there an Ecclesiastes? and does his "un-Christian wisdom" require Augustinian conversion or not? and even if so, where does this leave the problem of Calvin and the Covenants? It is only to suggest that the narrator hardly provides us with a model of what such commentary would sound like.[128] Not only sex but the whole natural world for which it stands may be an unworkable arrangement; that were vanity with a vengeance, and it might well provoke the idea of depravity. Still the narrator can tell us only what we already recognize in the experience of Edith and Edgar: you don't need Endicott to spoil your fun. Nor, we might add, Mencken or Heffner to define your Puritanism.

What all this further implies, pretty clearly, is that it requires a certain intellectual naiveté—a love of dialectical opposition for its own sake, or an infatuation with literary propositionality, or at the least a certain deafness to tone—to get very excited about the tale's famous "ambivalence." How can we find the endlessly subtle and self-protective Hawthorne hung up on the supposedly unmakable choice between Reveller and Puritan when a narrator this clearly overspecified can easily sense that Edith and Edgar represent a distinct enough moral "third"? They outgrow Merry Mount before they even hear of Endicott's "Israel." Nor does it appear that they ever are really converted to his "way." In "softening" that "iron man" (66) at last, they may be said to convert him as effectively as he them. It is just that he has the guns, and there is now no place else to go.

In fact, Edith and Edgar have their very own symbol, itself a distinct third, a fact which surely counts for much in a tale so carefully overwrought. The Revellers have their maypole, Endicott his iron "head-piece and breast-plate" (63), and the lovers their "flowery garland" (67), *unwithered,* as it heretically appears. Conceptually, we might be tempted to conclude that there is a certain splitting of the symbolic difference: the roses have originated in the symbol system of Merry Mount, and yet they have been thrown "over the heads of the Lord and Lady of the May" (66) by the same "gauntleted hand" which wielded the sword which hacked the maypole which Blackstone built. Except that the paired conceptions with which we have been dealing are not supposed to admit of this sort of compromise or synthesis. We readily understand how the altogether unsystematic narrator can evade the sharp edge of Endicott's either/or; but it comes as something of a shock when Endicott himself appears to surrender his own categorical sovereignty. Perhaps—though the narrator can scarcely tell us this—it is the imperious exclusiveness of those very categories which we are supposed to be considering. Not whether, or (if so) in what way, we can make some definitional TWO generate an existential third, but how we came to be dealing with that peculiarly idealized dichotomy in the first place.[129]

If Puritans succeed in arresting the spread of a pagan cult in New England, or if they manage to place certain strayed and reveling Anglicans or other "dissenters" from the New England Way under house arrest to await deportation, or if they merely manage to arrest the development of plain people's natural conscience, the event will indeed possess a certain historic significance. If lovers have to live in Salem because there is no place else *to* live (not even, any longer, Naumkeag), the fact must not escape our anthropological notice. And, as the author of "Dr. Bullivant" did not require the narrator of "Main Street" to tell him that Puritanism really is, on the whole, gloomier than most other things, we can safely imagine that, whatever is really going on, affairs will be less colorful and poetic if there turns out to be no effective appeal from Puritan conviction. But perhaps Jollity and Gloom may contend for empire without telling us anything at all about the ideal relation between the moral condition of primitive nature and the theological guarantee of a Puritanic state. And as that turns out to be the dichotomy Endicott holds in his perfectly binary mind, we find ourselves well warned, even by the soft distinctions of sobriety and sentiment.

It is easy enough, of course, to eschew Endicott's "morality" of power and sadistic cruelty: "bind the heathen crew, and bestow on them a small matter of stripes apiece, as earnest of our future justice"; "set some . . . in the stocks to rest themselves" for further penalties, "such as branding and cropping of ears"; and "shoot [the dancing bear] through the head" (64). Regular historians may argue the facts, and psychobiographers may debate the reason; but Hawthorne had hated Endicott since the 1829 headnote to "The Gentle Boy," and it were irrelevant now to struggle with a given. Nor is it especially difficult to reject either Endicott's own "esthetics" of iron or the more generalized Puritan "liturgy" and even "culture" of prayer and work and sermon and psalm. "A writer of story books" would rue it in 1849 no less than a Story Teller in 1835: having managed to "establish their jurisdiction" at the outset, the "spirits" of the "grizzled saints" would continue to "darken all the clime" of New England for many years to come; it might be "forever" (62). As Henry James observed, you had to deal with it, one way or another.[130]

What is harder to escape is Endicott's "allegory." Harder, because it is so difficult to recognize precisely as such, either *as* an allegory or as *his*. So inevitable have his attitudes come to seem that we continue to look elsewhere for the vision that raises the ragged realities of pre-colonial *realpolitik* to the status of an ontology—to the thinly abstractive mind of an author rather than to the densely symbolic activity of a protagonist. And yet the text really does insist that the allegory is, all "spontaneously," Endicott's own. And all the various pre-texts, in the "grave pages of our New England annalists," force the same ironic conclusion: the only problem facing the adequately critical writer of the nineteenth century was what to make of an allegory which, composed long since, seemed quite to have imposed itself.

By the time we hear Endicott speak of "Israel" (66) or even, much earlier, of a "wilderness" which "the Lord hath sanctified . . . for his peculiar people" (63), the ideological overdetermination is already pretty far advanced. It is, already, too late to protest, for a certain highly articulated form of piety is merely receiving its appropriate civil-religious implementation. One can hardly object to Puritanism's idolatrous definition of America if one has already granted its Puritanic definition of England. The moment to be astonished, therefore, is the very first one, when Endicott boldly identifies Blackstone as the high-priest of an arch-pagan fertility cult.[131]

Endicott enters the story late, and only after his appearance has been largely prepared for by the narrator's learned yet graceful little essay into the sociology of American colonization. Some adventurers to New England, who do not appear in the tale, have come three thousand miles "to barter glass beads"; others, whom we have already seen and soberly judged, have seized some rare opportunity to force Philosophy "to put on masques and play the fool"; and still others, about to appear for the first time in their own proper persons, have come "to pray" (59). Their appropriate persona is, of course, "Endicott himself," the "Puritan of Puritans." And yet nothing in the weary and demystified historiography of the narrator has quite prepared us for Endicott's first outrageous and typologically definitive words: "Stand off, priest of Baal!" (63). Suddenly, the metaphysical stakes are raised well beyond what we took to be the house limit. Expecting a stern enough moralist, we encounter in addition a Prophet, one who judges not by the ordinary, timely social or moral appearances but by the absolute names of God's own totalized and synchronous revelation.

And even at the historic level, this one appears to know exactly what he is talking about, as if he had already read his Cotton Mather: "I know thee,

Blackstone! Thou art the man, who couldst not abide the rule even of thine own corrupted church, and hast come hither to preach iniquity, and to give example of it in thy own life" (63). Of course this will not be tolerated. For "now shall it be seen that the Lord hath sanctified this wilderness" for you know who.[132] But by now it is, as I have suggested, already too late.

By now all the dislocated reader can do—which he certainly *ought* to do—is notice the sober but curious footnote which suggests that, despite his bold religious confidence, Endicott seems to have made some awkward historical misidentification: "Did Governor Endicott speak less positively, we should suspect a mistake here. The Rev. Mr. Blackstone, though an eccentric, is not known to have been an immoral man. We rather doubt his identity with the priest of Merry Mount" (63). If this bizarre literary tactic does not arouse our historical suspicion, then I suppose nothing will. But if it does, we will instantly recall (or poke about to discover) that Blackstone, whatever his moral character, cannot be placed within many miles of Merry Mount on the day Endicott felled "the only May-Pole in New England" (63). Whether or not he was, that day, "seated on the back of a bull," he was almost certainly tending his own garden on the crest of that "beacon hill" which dominates the peninsula of the bay of the Massachusetts. We can always say, of course, that Hawthorne has (once again) "altered history to suit his literary purposes." But the case scarcely ends there, for evidently that funny footnote means to require of us a pretty severe and exacting inquiry into the explicitly relative (or "intertextual") nature of those purposes. And this may involve both historical research on and thematic speculation about the significance of Blackstone.[133]

Yet even the most sophisticated effort of historical criticism will come too late unless we have already noticed what it is about Blackstone that so offends the prophetic sense of John Endicott. When Endicott identifies his unwitting antagonist as a "priest of Baal," he is not for the moment attending to his ceremonial maypole—in either its immemorial pagan or its too well remembered English significance. Nor is he concentrating primarily on the flowers and streamers into which it seems to have blossomed forth. Nor yet on the band of worshipers who surround it, either as sexually interested and therefore idolatrous or as gaily deluded and therefore merely idle. When he first speaks, he is, in fact, "laying no reverent hand upon the surplice" (63) in which Blackstone, this "figure of an English priest," is quite "canonically dressed" (57). Here, evidently, is where Endicott's own allegory properly begins.

It begins with a category and a symbol which antedate the scrubby events of 1628 by many years; which can survive all possible defense of Blackstone's moral character; and which by themselves, it almost seems, might well justify the dragging of Blackstone before a bar of judgment he did not, in literal fact, ever happen to have faced. Priestly vestments, indeed. As well dress yourself up in the fantastic regalia of the King of Christmas. Or sacramentalize a perfectly natural and (in another sense) entirely civil arrangement like marriage. If Blackstone were not at Merry Mount, well then he *should* have been. That is where he really *belongs*. Phallic maypole, flowers on the altar, surplice on the priest: things equal to the same thing all tell the same Holy History. More than this were pedantry, mere antiquarianism, of Germany and not of the Soul.

Except that a complicated history of "source and influence" does also hang hereby—and one we would do well to pursue; for to identify an allegory is not necessarily to deconstruct it. Therein lies not only the fun of a literary afterplay that is not quite "free" but also the power to free ourselves from the bonds of a semiological union made well but not wisely. Yes, Children, there really *is* a Santa Claus, despite Endicott. And quite possibly—though it will require more than the sketchy researches of Geoffrey Crayon to discover it—there may even be a Virginia lurking somewhere beneath the Puritan idea of America. But even if not, we need to be absolutely certain that Hawthorne's own wizard hand has not involved itself in Endicott's myth *at all;* that it was not Hawthorne himself who allegorized Endicott as that "Puritan of Puritans" who allegorized the historic opposition between Anglican and Puritan by raising it to the level of a theological dichotomy. For if that were so, then Endicott's appropriation of Edith and Edgar would yet, as Henry James might say, "mean too much." And all the elaborate Catholicism of *The Marble Faun* would turn out to mean just nothing at all.

Fortunately, the story of the story is not that difficult to reconstruct, even at this distance. Though Blackstone's fame remains, as it was in Hawthorne's own day, far less widespread than Endicott's own, his essential fact is not particularly far to seek. And though our prevailing version of literary history makes rather more of Milton and his *Comus* than of Strutt and his *Book of Sports,* the accidents of intellectual fashion have not rendered the significance of that once oddly relevant book entirely obscure. Moreover, as everyone is supposed to know, the entire maypole affair has something, however oblique, to do with those various "annalists" who gravely repeated an episode out of some *ur* and nearly eyewitness account; and, quite possibly, with that one most ungrave response an actual (and principal) participant is known to have written, as if in deliberate aid of our own deconstructive purposes. A bit of a jigsaw puzzle, no doubt; but then many of the pieces have already been identified for us. All we have to do is pull them out of their pat little places.

Of course Blackstone was not leading the Anglo-pagan services at Merry Mount the day Endicott cut down the maypole. But then, for all anyone paying strict attention to the available sources could ever learn, neither was anybody else. And that, surely, is what Hawthorne's outrageous footnote means to force us to discover: the entire event is a flagrant fiction, scarcely more so in his story than on the allegorical pages of those otherwise grave annalists. Except in the allegory of somebody else's rampant theological imagination, nothing even remotely like the events of "The May-Pole of Merry Mount" had ever in fact occurred. All you have to do is read the available sources—without which the story itself is well nigh insignificant—closely.[134] What they reveal is the prime fact that by the time Endicott arrived on the New England scene at all (as late in the political reality as he appears in the symbolic fiction), all the *real* action was over.

Our suspicion that Blackstone is merely a convenient (clerical) stand-in for Thomas Morton, in a tale which centers on the obviously fictional career (and marriage) of Edith and Edgar anyway, falls to the ground the moment we recall that by the time Endicott appeared at Merry Mount, Morton was already on a ship back for England. Whatever his alleged penchant for paganism, or his self-confessed relish for bawdy poems, that worthy had long since been arrested and deported on charges of serious political misconduct, selling guns to the Indian braves and abusing their women. He would never be convicted of these grave charges, of course; and he would eventually return to cause yet further trouble, not only for pious New Englanders who never could get him convicted, but also for sober historians who are still fussing about the plausibility of all their various accusations.[135] But the point here is very much simpler: Captain Miles Standish having already made his mock-heroic arrest (with a single bloody nose the only casualty on either side), *nobody* of any significance was at Merry Mount the day Endicott cut down the maypole. And thus the only action left for him was purely symbolic.

What?! You arrested the Master of those Revels and left his May-Pole standing? We'll fix that: hack, hack. And, lest anyone miss the *act* of symbolism, let the *name* of this place henceforth be called "Mount Dagon," even as Naumkeag must be known as Salem. By just such miracles of transignification, apparently, does the Lord sanctify a "wilderness for his peculiar people."

At one utterly fundamental level, all Hawthorne's footnote about Endicott's mis-identification of Blackstone forces us to do is inquire about "What Happened at Mount Wollaston?" (Every man his own David Levin.) And when we do, everything else falls out of place. What happened there was much or little, depending not only upon your (allegorical or real-political) point of view, but also—and very radically—on when you happen to be looking in on that sportive little unsettlement. Nobody *ever* was married there, so far as we can discover, by an Anglican priest or anybody else; but then everybody knows enough about the liberties of fiction to guess that. Somebody was indeed arrested there, but not by Endicott; he comes later. He did indeed cut down their maypole; but by the time he did, that mystic symbol of such powerful Anglo-pagan potency had subsided, for all the powers of natural observation could discover, to the altogether more banal status of a common pine tree; one among many, even as Hawthorne's Peter Palfrey forces Endicott to concede.[136] To view it otherwise were to engage in a pursuit of signs that can only be called Puritanical. And yet, not to know about the real existence of some such allegorical pursuit, or to fail to notice its present relevance, is to beg for someone to revoke your history license. Ironical if that person were a mere romancer.

The problem, of course, lies precisely in the way Bradford elected to tell his original and, to his otherwise modest mind, absolutely definitive New-World allegory; and even more so, perhaps, in the way his various redactors—unwittingly, as it seems, and yet with perfect allegorical instinct—followed his allegorical lead. As there are really two issues, the real-politics of Indians with firearms and the mythopolitics of paganism, so there are two different "Merry Mount" occasions, each with its own appropriate story. A hard saying, perhaps, but the footnote forces it.

One day, in 1628, long before any of us straggling planters (of Plymouth and elsewhere) had ever heard the magic name of Endicott, we all agreed that Thomas Morton was a clear and present danger to our common survival. Bead-traders and prayer-mongers achieved a rare meetings of minds: Morton *had* to be stopped; if not, then *nobody* would be contending for empire. So we all agreed to support the military expedition of Captain Standish, whatever the courts will decide about the limits of sovereignty in the midst of a territory so raggedly defined that, unless it all belong to God or Sir Ferdinando Gorges, nobody knows who rules. At all events, the expedition succeeded, and so we present you, Charles of England, with the miscreant Morton. You decide: is Separation a greater threat to your Majesty's American strategy than drunken, cuckolded Indians with firearms?

Just so, in rough paraphrase, would the story have to be told to a most un-Puritanical King, in the letter which accompanied Morton to England, to justify a para-constitutional arrest and deportation; and which was published, in due course, in the grave pages of the *Massachusetts Historical Collections*, to establish the base line of Hawthorne's historical irony.[137] But clearly that was not the only story Bradford felt needed telling. Nor, as it takes only very little literary sensitivity to notice, is it the one which really fired his imagination. Or, as it turns out, that of the *other* Morton—Nathaniel—in whose filiopietistic redaction of Bradford Hawthorne himself found the *real* (that is, the "allegorical") story so faithfully quoted. For an entirely different audience, which is clearly supposed to include our own meta-historical selves, what really mattered was less Morton's irresponsible Indian policy than his flagrant pagan example. And, correspondingly, the real triumph occurs not in Standish's serio-comic arrest of Thomas Morton's physical body, but in Endicott's later (politically irrelevant) destruction of his pseudo-spiritual symbol; and, if we can bear one more turn, in his final (and true!) renaming of the much disputed "Mount" in question.

We have come to regard the Puritan tendency to read Biblical eschatology into current events as very nearly innate. And yet here, for the moment at least, American politics are still politics as usual: whose guns, his territory. But from the very first, it appears, religion is quite another story: whoever has the symbols, he has the minds and hearts of the people. And in Israel, we.

Accordingly, therefore, Bradford's remarkably full account of the Merry Mount episode, in his magisterial history *Of Plymouth Plantation*, does not scruple to attach extreme importance to the issue of Thomas Morton's exemplary paganism. Nor does Nathaniel Morton's later account lift a finger from the scales to right the uneven balance. Following Bradford's allegorical strategy very religiously, the text of *New England's Memorial* (1669), plainly Hawthorne's main "source" for "The May-Pole," awards clear primacy of place to the story of Endicott and the Colorful Maypole, rather than to Standish and the Dangerous Firearms; that latter, we are left to conclude, is "mere history."[138] Nathaniel Morton even abets Bradford's inspired tendency to obscure the actual chronology of events, leaving it to the "grave" but dangerously deconstructive footnote of a later editor to (almost) set the record straight. And yet even a romancer could take the point: you have to read the *whole* text, including the footnotes.

Morton (that is, Nathaniel) patiently quotes Bradford's account of the arrival of Captain Wollaston, of his rather vainglorious naming of his community after his own immodest self (as if Plymouth had been called "Bradford"), and of his somewhat precipitate departure for Virginia, to get rich quick by selling off "a great part of his servants." He faithfully reproduces Bradford's version of the rebellious "good counsel" given the remaining servants by the crafty but unscrupulous Thomas Morton, quondam "petty fogger at Furnival's Inn": stay as you are and be "carried away and sold for slaves with the rest," or join with me and "be free from service, and we will converse, plant, trade and live together as equals." He even adds Bradford's own disclaimer, concerning the "essentialist" nature of his own historiography: "or [words] to the like effect." He omits to quote D. H. Lawrence, of course, though we can scarcely close our ears to his own mode of editorializing: "Henceforth be masterless."[139] But he omits almost nothing from the passage which will make Bradford a Founder and Hawthorne an Ironist.

The rebellious counsel being "easily followed," they all "fell to great licentiousness of life, in all profaneness." And that in no very original manner, as Nathaniel Morton recognizes what Bradford had already recognized as already a twice-told tale:

> The said Morton became lord of misrule, and maintained, as it were, a school of Atheism, and after they had got some goods into their hands, and got much by trading with the Indians, they spent it as vainly in quaffing and drinking both wine and strong liquors in great excess, as some have reported, ten pounds worth in a morning, setting up a maypole, drinking and dancing about it, and frisking about it like so many fairies, or furies rather, yea and worse practices, as if they had anew revived and celebrated the feast of the Romans goddess Flora, or the beastly practices of the mad Bacchanalians. The said Morton likewise, to shew his poetry, composed sundry rhymes and verses, some tending to lasciviousness, and others to the detraction and scandal of some persons names, which he affixed to his idle or idol may-pole; they changed also the name of their place, and instead of calling it Mount Wollaston, they called it the Merry Mount, as if this jollity would have lasted always.[140]

Without ceasing to be English—even specifically "Anglican," as that capacious concept grew latitudinarian enough to comprehend a *Book of Sports* as well as a Prayer Book—Morton's merry men easily slip into the prepared identities (if not into all the precise practices) of classical pagans. Their maypole may be a cultivated idolatry or merely an unconscionable idleness, but evidently life is too short to waste on distinctions at that level: what *possible* Eden could a scoundrel's *"non serviam"* ever restore? "What is truth?"—a jesting Thomas Morton might inquire; but neither the sober William Bradford nor the pious Nathaniel Morton could wait around for the answer.

Nor, least of all, could John Endicott, as the now fully allegorical narrative races headlong to assure us. Or, rather, the narra*tives*, as they now diverge significantly for the first time. By now Nathaniel Morton has lost all control (either factual or rhetorical) over what actually happened. But even Bradford, sober historian that he is, overleaps everything else to tell his American audience what we really need to know: whatever other, petty or vulgar issues may have been involved, and whatever the military history of the matter, Endicott is the man who taught us all to spot a maypole for what it *really* is, and to act accordingly:

But this continued not long, for after Morton was sent for England (as follows to be declared) shortly after came over that worthy gentleman Mr. John Endecott, who brought over a patent under the broad seal for the government of the Massachusetts. Who, visiting those parts, caused that maypole to be cut down and rebuked them for their profaneness and admonished them to look there should be better walking. So they or others now changed the name of their place again and called it Mount Dagon.[141]

To Endicott, apparently, a maypole expresses the phallic essence of Anglo-Catholic paganism, whether any one's smutty poem is attached to it or not, and whatever one may read in the *Book of Sports.* And, no less significantly— as the practical distinction between idolatry and idleness rushes to its theoretic extinction—a land where such symbols are permitted to grow and flourish is always a land of perfect devil-worship. The Protestant Ethic is one thing; but Puritan Exegesis is quite another.

Actually, of course, Bradford has tried to be careful. Perfectly aware that his unaccustomed rhetoric is making more ideological haste than historical goodspeed, he dutifully inserts that awkward parenthesis: *"as follows to be declared."* At the risk of confusing the meaning with the mere facts, Bradford feels honor-bound to let us know that he knows that he is conflating things, blurring details for the effect of a Truth in capital letters. And indeed the careful reader of his text really *can* figure it out: this did not all happen at the same moment in time; Endicott is not even here yet, in this annal of 1628; he comes over to cut down the maypole (on purpose, as it almost seems) next year, in 1629, as you will see if you read on, as at one level you certainly should; and in the proximate mean time, as you will *very shortly* see, Standish will arrest and we will deport the troublesome supplier of arms.

Even so, however, the course of his allegory is perfectly steady: Paganism is a Maypole, Puritanism an Endicott; and the repulsive appeal of the one attracts the violent dichotomies of the other like a theological magnet. All uncharged particles—like Standish and pieces and shot and powder—are left to be swept up by mere history; even though, rhetorically, the villainy of Thomas Morton's Indian policy (not to mention his disruption of the supply side of the servant economy) does eventually draw forth its own rather vigorous condemnation. But if man cannot live by allegory alone, apparently Puritan historiography cannot live without it. And so, whatever the actualities, the "story" of Merry Mount involved, primarily and from the first, Endicott and the Puritanic response to the Anglo-pagan symbolism of maypoles.[142]

It is hard to imagine just what, if anything, Hawthorne would have made of the entire episode if he had seen Bradford's own account, and that only.

Perhaps that version alone might have inspired *some* critical response, since it certainly does contain the stuff of allegory. But we can scarcely suppose that his tale would have been quite so devastating as in fact it is. For it is in Nathaniel Morton, as I have been suggesting, that things really get out of hand. And into mind. And the problem of Hawthorne's response to *this* text is, if problematic and the subject of a certain critical risk, not at all hypothetical: this is the text Hawthorne took for his text.

Nathaniel Morton changes only a few of Bradford's words, and yet he somehow manages to change everything. All he does is omit Bradford's dutiful, crucial, counterallegorical parenthesis: *"as follows to be declared."* So that the unwary reader of *New England's Memorial* is likely to be entirely deceived about what actually happened. All we can learn from Nathaniel Morton's own text is that Endicott's destruction of New England's only maypole occurred "shortly after" the great instauration of Merry Mount. Possibly this redactor of Bradford was himself a little confused (or, on our behalf, a little bored) by some of the problems created by Bradford's curious mixture of styles and genres.[143] At any rate, he knew Reality when he saw it; and so he moved surely to complete Bradford's allegorical work by eliminating all narrative awkwardness and chronological confusion. In the resulting text, the allegory became the history. The *real meaning* became not only the thing you needed to be concerned with, but in fact the only story that was really at all clear.

But how did Hawthorne know this? Lacking the advantage of our own latter-day (Bercovitchean) suspicion, how was he to avoid simply being taken in, as an unwary and too clear-sighted Nathaniel Morton himself may have been, by the inevitable tendency of the Puritan mind? Or, to put the question less tendentiously, how could Hawthorne be expected to sense— not having access to Bradford's *ur* account—that chronology was getting itself rearranged and that, in the process, Standish and the guns were losing out to Endicott and the maypole? For evidently he did sense just this, or else his funny little footnote is tasteless in the extreme.

Obviously Bradford's original letter would have helped, supposing one had read it carefully and thought to compare its story with that of the *Memorial.* So too would some other accounts of the entire episode, which made more of that political letter than of the theological spirit struggling here to free itself.[144] Most important, however, and serving to clarify those other aids to interpretation, was the footnote supplied by Nathaniel Morton's nineteenth-century editor:

From the order of occurrences in this narrative, relative to Thomas Morton, it would be inferred, that the May-pole was cut down by Mr. Endicot, before Morton was arrested by Capt. Standish; but letters from Plymouth to the Council for New England, and to Sir Ferdinand Gorges, written to be sent to England, with the prisoner, bear the date June 9, 1628, which was more than two months before Mr. Endicot's arrival at Salem.[145]

The note stops just short of offering any criticism of Morton's qualifications as an historian, and yet the entire effect of his account is utterly undone. Filiopiety might motivate antiquarianism, but it could not, in the nineteenth century at least, pervert it from the gravity of its determinedly literalist aims. And so the footnote itself has a footnote, proving its case and suggesting, by the way, just how to go about conceiving "The May-Pole of Merry Mount": "See Gov. Bradford's *Letter Book,* hist. coll., III, 62, 63."[146]

There is no doubt that Hawthorne did indeed *see* that letter.[147] And that it had made all the difference. Providing him with the facts required not only to set straight the chronological record but also to sort out the mix of issues, it showed him that Endicott's real victory had been to get himself into the story *at all.* Having intruded himself into a place where he had no earthly business or historic jurisdiction, and into an affair already (in 1629) concluded in every way except the literary, Endicott had succeeded in warping all other stories into his own. Simply by cutting down the maypole when in fact nothing at all political depended on it, he had won at a stroke a contest of chronologies and even of deep historic issues in the name of Puritan Allegory: *here* is our meaning, don't you see—hack, hack!—and Devil take the view of the King and his Council for New England. Hawthorne never could know the extent to which Endicott's ideological swagger would upset the plain style of William Bradford. But he simply could not miss the fact that Nathaniel Morton had wrought an allegory: it said so, gravely, in a footnote,[148] which Hawthorne is merely imitating in his own inspired footnote about Endicott's mis-identification of Blackstone.

What "The May-Pole of Merry Mount" has done, most simply, is to drag Blackstone into itself by the same allegorical logic which had drawn in Endicott in the first place. And this whether we consider that logic as literal or as literary. At the one level it furnished Endicott with his only real motive for intruding at all: the history of this episode is incomplete until somebody cuts down that maypole. Who actually does so scarcely matters, before the fact; the gesture is what counts. But whosoever shall have the theological wit to do so shall in that very act become, and in aftertimes may well be remembered as, the "Puritan of Puritans"; as always, a representative savior is recognized not a priori and by ontological essence but only in the saving deed. Just so was Endicott recognized by Bradford and the annalists who followed him: endorsing his theologic intrusion, they validated his allegory at the literary level, where it first blurred and then entirely obscured the ordinary process of historical narrative. In the story of guns and Indians, Endicott has (of course) no place; but when it comes to the triumph of Israel over Dagon, he is the man. Surely the mysterious process of historical "re-cognition" can go no further.[149]

Unless it goes all the way, paradoxically, and recognizes Blackstone as well. And why not? If grave annalists may so conflate events as to allegorize reality, what may be forbidden the mere Story Teller?—especially if he furnish the footnote needed to deconstruct his own allegory; and, in the process, theirs. Surely the only (still) unfrocked Anglican priest currently at large in the chartered and about-to-be-encovenanted confines of an England made eschatalogically New by the advance of Holy History *also* belongs.[150] Especially if "the Puritan" were, in reality, about to turn his attention from the maypole at Mount Wollaston to the surplice at Shawmut.

Nobody seems to know where the author of *The Scarlet Letter* encountered the Europa-like image of Blackstone "seated on the back of a bull";[151] but the narrator of "The May-Pole" evidently assumes that his audience, provoked by a single, outrageous footnote, can easily learn a thing or two about Blackstone's "canonical coat"—the Anglican surplice, that is, which he insisted on wearing even as he moved from the care of souls in England to the tending of an American garden. Pastures new, indeed. Nor should that audience be quite shocked to learn the Puritans' response to this astonishing reversion to pastoral type. Dichotomy itself precluded the notion of a "minister" who lacked the proper correlative of a "settled congregation." And even if one waived all such considerations of "science" as inappropriate to some raggedly pragmatic New World, did not that surplice symbolize, as flagrantly as the maypole itself (and far more plainly than a red cross in a militia banner), the entire religious order being rejected? No wonder the new men of the Massachusetts had it in for the coat of this failed-parson who was yet, perversely, no candidate for the brotherhood of Puritanism.[152]

There were, of course, certain embarrassing practical considerations to be got over. Blackstone, after all, had got there first. And not only had he contributed to the fund for the suppression of Merry Mount, but his claim to possession of the entire Shawmut peninsula (then called "Blackstone's Neck") was strong enough to require a financial satisfaction well above the one the Dutch offered the Indians for Manhattan. And had he not, from the first (and with a "courtesy" Roger Williams would find more characteristic of the Indians than of the English), positively invited the newcomers to share in the benefits of the single spring of really decent water in the entire area? If Blackstone were to be displaced from this new "Boston," surely the fact would call for some important historical notice. And if, as it turned out,

it had got far less than it deserved, then it would have to serve as the originary event in Hawthorne's own most complex myth of origins, *The House of
the Seven Gables;* for there we are reminded that, long before anyone's guilty
art had ever mesmerized anyone else, somebody had gained a (clearly unjust) socio-political advantage by beating somebody else out of "a natural
spring of soft and pleasant water—a rare treasure on the sea-girt peninsula."[153] A complex tale, as yet once-told.

Here, however, the story is as distressingly simple as the historical record
is maddeningly incomplete. Endicott's "recognition" of Blackstone as the
man who, unable to "abide the rule of [his] own corrupted church," had
come "hither" to preach and exemplify iniquity seems but a hostile version
of Mather's much-quoted quotation: "I came from England, because I did
not like the *lord-bishops;* but I can't join with you, because I would not be
under the *lord-brethren.*" Though we may fairly detect here a faint hint of
Bradford's own (Lawrentian) suspicion of Thomas Morton ("Henceforth be
masterless"), yet his overall account is surprisingly mild, characterizing
Blackstone as a "Godly Episcopalian" or at least as one "commonly reck-
oned" to be such.[154] Earlier annalists had been far less tolerant. Edward
Johnson had found him singularly unfit for the (true) task of "building the
Temple," despite his flaunting of the "Canonicall Coate." And William
Hubbard, after quoting and amplifying Johnson, sought patiently to put the
problem in its proper perspective: as "Antiquity was always wont to distinguish persons and places by their garb or habit," and as Blackstone *did,* after
all, insist on retaining that "canonical coat" as a "symbol of his former profession," it is no wonder he ran into *some* sort of trouble: "For anyone to
retain only the outward badge of his function, that never could pretend to
any faculty therein, or exercise thereof, is, though no honor to himself, yet a
dishonor and disparagement to the order he would thereby challenge acquaintance with."[155] Apparently an insult was to be taken, whether or not
anybody had meant to give one; things mean what they mean.

That Endicott's—and, by now, Winthrop's—"order" did somehow meet
this "challenge" seems perfectly apparent, even though the original records
are remarkably silent about exactly *how.* Following in Hawthorne's footsteps, we can authoritatively discover that Blackstone was admitted as a
"freeman" of the Massachusetts Bay Company, even though he steadfastly
refused to join the New-World church-order; that he did indeed invite the
new settlers to share the unique benefits of what a nineteenth-century antiquarian characterized, with astonishing innocence, as his "fountains of living
water"; that he was, eventually, compensated for all the land he said he held;
but that he did, before very long, depart Shawmut-turned-Boston for
greener pastures.[156] No one in the seventeenth century will say exactly
when or why he left; and it might be somewhat too poetical to imagine that

the sword of Endicott's own keen faith ever quite cut off the significance of "Blackstone's Neck." And yet one extremely suggestive passage in Caleb Snow's (nineteenth-century) *History of Boston* forces us, as it had forced Hawthorne, to raise the crucial question: what displaced Blackstone?

After a rather full and fair summary of the whole elongated and intriguing Blackstone episode, Snow concludes with the following defensive but damaging summary: "We have no thought 'that [Blackstone] was driven from Boston because he was an Episcopal minister,' but a man may be very ill at ease in a place where he may be allowed to stay by sufferance."[157] Exactly whose (quoted) charge he is dismissing Snow does not tell us; nor have modern researches (including those of the present "sub-sub-librarian") been able to discover this possibly relevant fact. Perhaps Hawthorne would have known—it sounds like the remark of some embittered "Tory" historian. And possibly he himself knew (or thought he knew) whether this obvious, almost inevitable allegation were true (or false). But in any event things had already got close enough for allegory, particularly the sort the Puritan annalists themselves had bent their otherwise grave energies to invent. For, at the very least, the place was now being called "Boston" (rather than "Shawmut," or "Blackstone's Neck"); and, in some relation to this now familiar pattern of Puritan transignification, the original landlord had lapsed to a condition of "sufferance." One way or another, Blackstone was displaced from the fountainhead of New England history for the same (meta-political) reasons that had moved Endicott to destroy the original (meta-historical) symbolism of Merry Mount.[158]

Or, rather, for an a fortiori version of those same reasons. For, given the ascendancy of Endicott's allegorical logic, a surplice at the heart of the Bay will prove altogether less tolerable than a maypole somewhere near the limits of Plymouth. Bradford had to be educated in this logic, to allow himself to be subsumed by it, even as he took pride in the validation it offered. But probably we are to imagine Winthrop and his fellow expatriates as perfectly alert to all manner of symbolic possibilities from the outset. How could they not have been, given their extended Puritanic education in the England of the 1620's? A surplice at the center of their altogether exemplary City on a Hill was more than intolerable: it was precisely "unthinkable," and this is what Johnson and Hubbard were struggling to suggest.[159]

If Blackstone's surplice meant anything at all, it would express some perfectly unacceptable "challenge" to their own purified New-World "order." Springs of pure water to the contrary notwithstanding, how could the Truth come three thousand miles to have fellowship with the very lie it came to escape? And even if it seemed to mean just nothing at all—the aberrant gesture of a perfect "eccentric"—the case against it would be scarcely altered; how could rational men rest easy in the face of a "meaningless" symbol?[160] All men drink the same natural waters, to be sure; but since *things mean,* a surplice in Boston will break the mind—even if the man who wears it prove only a disillusioned though still courteous eccentric personally intent on nothing more political than tending his own private garden.

Of course things mean in different ways. At least part of the problem is that the surplice, like the *Prayer Book* itself, had been *commanded,* by earthly powers who had no divine right to issue any such commands, as a symbol of loyalty to a religious establishment which everywhere substituted its own inventions for the clear and permanent plan of Scripture. And yet its symbolism could scarcely be understood as merely conventional. If the maypole signified the naturalistic substance of all merely human religions, then the surplice expressed the guilty wish to hide or clothe with spurious ("sacramental") dignity all such spiritual nakedness. Surely, deep down, this is why the agents of antichrist have always, not quite unwittingly, commanded the use of supposedly sacred vestments: to dignify or to cover up their obvious pagan connection. Less obviously than the maypole, perhaps, but much more treacherously therefore, the surplice is also "of Baal."[161] Sinful still, whether its wearer be found explicitly idolatrous or merely idle, while others build the Temple.

Well may Hawthorne's Endicott hate the surplice of Blackstone, therefore; more than the maypole itself, as it almost seems. Particularly as it was but the next object to attract (and define) the Puritanic attention. And most especially if, as Hawthorne's footnote forces us to realize, the untold story of Blackstone and the Canonical Coat had, like the bungled story of Standish and the Dangerous Firearms, much more *literally* to do with the future complexion of New England than the much-told tale of Endicott's curious experiment in the harvesting of pine trees.

Or, to come at the problem of meaningfulness from the other direction (and so to preserve the full political significance of Endicott's vaunted act of piety), we can observe that the maypole had itself been in a significant manner *commanded*—by the same pseudoreligious authority which prescribed both the surplice and the *Prayer Book,* and for many of the same not quite spiritual reasons. Nor can we, without some such observation, ever quite explain what Hawthorne's otherwise merely pedantic reference to "Strutt's Book of English Sports and Pastimes" has to do with the matter of Endicott and Blackstone. And, finally, that same observation will alone account for the enduring significance, to Hawthorne's tale, of the arguments expressed in Thomas Morton's notorious *New English Canaan,* despite the strategically footnoted displacement of Morton by Blackstone.

It turns out that Joseph Strutt's compilation of *The Sports and Pastimes of the People of England* (1801) was not the first work in the rich bibliographical history of old England to become known as the *Books of Sports.* As

J. Gary Williams has aptly pointed out, no less a personage than King James I had authored, in 1618, a far briefer document (an edict, actually) that came to be known by that same short title, even as it became the center of a significant controversy within the English Church, one which Strutt himself takes notice of.[162] So that in a story about the origins of the Puritan *difference*, one handles the whole matter with extreme circumspection.

The astonishing (and to the Puritans appalling) fact is that James, in response to popular protest against an increasing strictness of Sunday observance, had actually *commanded* that his edict in favor of "lawful recreations" be read from every pulpit in his realm. No one can prove that he intended, thereby, to elevate the Book of Nature to equal authority with the Book of Sacred Scripture, or to indicate the necessity of supplementing the holy Word of God with the parodic words of man; but neither should anyone be surprised if radical Puritans interpreted his command in just this drastic way. When ministers who could only "read" but not at all "open" the text of Scripture went "dumbly" on to the matter of sports and pastimes, it seems fair to say that theologic insult had been given as well as taken. And then, when that subtle ideologue Archbishop Laud persuaded Charles I to reissue and strengthen his father's edict, the horrible meaning seemed explicit and complete. But even at the outset, the case was sufficiently grave: all surplice-wearing, *Prayer Book*–reading (that is to say, all loyal "Anglican") ministers were required to encourage, from every pulpit, on every Sunday and holy day in the Christian calendar, a fair sample of the Games People Play.

Or at least *English* people, which for the purposes of the present monarch quite covered the relevant case. There will be no "beare or bull-baitings," to be sure; and nothing must distract from "divine service." But:

> It is our will, that after the end of divine service, our good people be not disturbed, letted, or discouraged from any lawful recreation, such as dancing, either for men or women; archery for men, leaping, vaulting, or any other such harmless recreation; nor for having of May-games, Whitsun-ales, and morris-daunces, and the setting up of May-poles, and other sports therewith used.[163]

Blue-nosed Sabbatarianism to the contrary, James wished vividly to suggest, the Sabbath was made for Man. In *my* realm, at least, no "puritanes or precise people" will prevent my people from playing all games in season, including May-games. To forbid which were, even in the name of grace, to denature a people.

On one perfectly plausible and well-promulgated theory, of course, the King's realm extended to New England without interruption; all English laws were to be obeyed there, without exception, and without let or hindrance. Bradford may have been blissfully ignorant of James's unprecedented elevation of a *Book of Sports* to canonical status when, in 1621, he reprimanded some of his New-World workers for playing at "stool-ball and such like sports" on "the day called Christmas Day"; but on certain related matters—like the difference between the civil and the religious observance of marriage—he was clearly (and proudly) aware of departing from the Anglican Way.[164] And certainly Endicott himself was keenly aware, in 1628, that in cutting down "the only Maypole in New England" he was utterly nullifying the spirit (if not *quite* violating the letter) of the royal edict in favor of May Games. An English monarch might well interpret such an action as no less "rebellious" in implication than the defacing of a cross-bearing ensign or, indeed, as the rejection of the symbolism of the surplice. It may all hang together, in sociology as well as in law: no maypole, no King.

Such, in any event, was Thomas Morton's clear understanding of the matter when, in the *New English Canaan*, he defended his own conduct in terms of an express "Anglican" loyalty. Never convicted on the grave charges of gun-running, Morton essentially waves them away, stressing instead his own explicit and unshakable fidelity to the religious folkways of old England. Without at all falling into the terms of the accumulating Puritan allegory, indeed while mocking them rather effectively, Thomas Morton's account of the much-vexed matter of Merry Mount nevertheless agrees with that of the Puritan annalists in one very important way: the really vital issue involved the political implications of religious symbolism.

Deprived of the historical advantages of a Q. D. Leavis, Morton has no sobering reflections about the *mixed* blessing of a Puritan success in America; in his singular view it would be all loss and no gain (and no wonder if the delicious waters of Blackstone's spring should turn brackish). And lacking the theological resilience of a C. S. Lewis, he cannot quite suggest that since this really *is* Merry Middle Earth, we *do* require merry middle things; that a minister in a business suit (and "walking on rubberoid") is a poor substitute for a priest treading a carpeted altar in celebration of a High Mass: *"Io* to Hymen" with a vengeance. But he does manage to suggest that his two English books—the *Book of Sports* and the *Book of Common Prayer*—go together, in a way that everyone can understand, both as commanded and as symbolic. And Hawthorne seems to have understood that the wearing of the surplice implied both understandings.

The *real* source of all these difficulties in New England, Morton specifically argued, was simply that Captain Wollaston and his loyal Anglican comrades at Merry Mount quite openly conducted their religious services according to England's own "Sacred Book of Common Prayer." And similarly, that they, like their royal sovereign, thought it perfectly appropriate to indulge, on the Sabbath, in such "harmless mirth" as will be "made by young men that lived in hope to have wives brought over to them." Their own behavior posing no credible threat to anybody, the problem arose only with the Puritans' absurd but scarcely uncharacteristic response: of course they hated the *Prayer Book*, which their whole migration made bold to reject; and their hostility to "sport" was perfectly in keeping with the well-known tendency of "separatists" to make "much ado . . . about things that are indifferent."[165]

What Morton cannot quite think to add is what the entirety of "The May-Pole of Merry Mount," footnotes and all, exists to remind us: that for the allegorical imagination of Puritanism there cannot really ever be any such thing. Not the traditional maypole of Thomas Morton; and still less, amidst the flood of non-conforming ministers which soon began to fill up the Bay Colony, the canonical coat of the Reverend Mr. Blackstone. The law that links them can well be thought of as "literary," in spite of the political implications which everywhere abound. But it had been discovered by story tellers of a far graver complexion than the nineteenth century could show. The best a modern writer could do was to indicate how that law had operated in the writing of history—wherever, indeed, the history got written at all.

In the end it seems unlikely that the record ever can be set perfectly straight. Probably we never will discover, for example, the precise nature of the "mirthful" activities of Merry Mount; any more than we can hope, at this date and distance, to convict or acquit the absent Thomas Morton of selling guns to the Indians, or of threatening to disrupt New England's needful supply of servants. But for the sake of reading that n^{th}-told tale called "The May-Pole of Merry Mount," it is needless to know. Nor is it quite to the point, though here our own temptation may be somewhat stronger, to speculate about the degree of "pagan" sympathy which the narrative intelligence behind Hawthorne's Story Teller may have felt for the fate of "jollity" at Merry Mount, even amidst the mainstream of a culture committed, on even its supposedly "liberal" side, to the gloomy instructions of works which emphasized the enduring importance of "Christian Sobriety."[166] The present story is not primarily about any of these more or less vital themes.

It is, more nearly, about the cultural significance of the much re-told tale of the symbolic activity of Endicott; and about the largely untold story of Blackstone, which a mock-pedantic but actually quite literally imitative footnote forces us to reconstruct, even as we proceed to deconstruct almost everything else. Most precisely, it is about the allegorical logic according to which *sportif* persons like Blackstone and Morton can be displaced from reality almost as easily as Captain Standish can be left out of a story; and about the light a *Book of Sports* can throw on the significance of both. Accordingly, therefore, it may be more than poetic justice to let Joseph Strutt have the last word on this most astonishingly "provincial" aspect of Hawthorne's tale. Formally, we will merely be explicating the full sense of Hawthorne's "other" footnote (the headnote); and materially we will be completing our own account of the games being played here—by the Puritans and also by Hawthorne himself.

No critic of "The May-Pole" has ever found it very rewarding to read every word of Strutt's entire literary performance; a more laborious book about play can scarcely be imagined. Yes, we are likely to conclude fairly early on, "the masques, mummeries, and festive customs, described in the text" are indeed "in accordance with the manners of the age" (54); once again, for whatever reasons, Hawthorne has done his homework. Or, once we concede that retrospective sociological fidelity really is largely beside the point, we may rightly grasp that it is the earlier, ideological use of "the matter of Strutt" which really counts; that the real games are those of the King and of Endicott, and not those of the richly playful English past at all.[167] And yet there may be one more point which some antiquarian reader of Strutt is supposed to get. And this in the very last words of his very long and (for most audiences) tolerably tedious book.

The last few entries in Strutt's work seem almost a sort of desperate appendix, devoted to the explication of some plates picturing children's games which have no recorded name, and then to a mere listing of a few others of which the author has merely heard reference but which he is, in spite of his own really Herculean labors, absolutely unable to describe. Ideally, at the outset, and admirably, for the better part of 500 pages, he has been able to instruct his readers in the meaning of the suggestive old names and the precise rules for playing all sorts of wonderful, traditional games. But then, in the interest of the sort of completeness which only the antiquarian could love, he produces a mere list of literary references to games for which, we must suppose, the rules are irretrievably lost. At the very end of which, and constituting the ultimate entry in the entire book, the following unexplicated quotation from some "supposed correspondent" to *The Spectator:* "I desire to know if the merry game of *the parson has lost his cloak* is much in vogue amongst the ladies this Christmas, because I see they wear hoods of all colors, which I suppose is for that purpose."[168] One hesitates—even as with the para-textual ironies of newspaper reports on just when to celebrate the anniversary of "Lovewell's Fight." But how is it possible to say, in the latter days of these post-New-Critical years, just when the inter-textual jest has crawled too far?

Every reader of "The May-Pole of Merry Mount" will surely have noticed that Endicott and his Puritans are presented as not without their own grotesque idea of fun and games. The heavy sociology of the narrator— "Woe to the [Puritan] youth or maiden who did but dream of a dance!" (61)—merely prepares us for the heavier irony of Endicott's bitter cruelty: "I could find it in my heart to plant [this maypole] again, and give each of these bestial pagans one other dance around their idol. It would have served rarely for a whipping-post!" (64). A bad game this; and yet the sober truth of a certain sort of history appears to require its mention. And if so, might not an entirely different and more subtle sort permit the final, wry suggestion of another kind of game as well?

Surely there is nothing new or surprising in the unhappy discovery of an ugly strain of moralistic cruelty in the Puritan character, whether or not it amounts to some species of sexually displaced and barely disguised sado-masochism. But can we truly say, amidst so many "authentic passages from history," that games of hurting are those which most distinctively characterize and effectively exhaust the region of Puritan play? Evidently not. Where, for one thing, would this leave their love of allegory?[169] And have we not already seen that Endicott has proven himself a better player at Parsons and Cloaks than Strutt himself? Strutt has recorded the bare notion, but Endicott has actually played the game—"experimentally," as the Puritans might say.

Thus in the end, the Blackstone footnote may be read playfully, as a footnote to Strutt as cogently as it must be identified, gravely, as a note to the Puritan annalists themselves. So construed, it appears to read as follows: "For further instructions on how to play at the game of 'the parson has lost his cloak,' consult the 'works' of John Endicott; he seems to have played *some* such game with the famous 'Canonicall Coate' of a certain (otherwise obscure) Mr. Blackstone, just a short time after Captain Standish had mastered the Revellers at Merry Mount; Endicott must have been an expert player, for he seems to have won the contest and retired the trophy. Without which, where are now those ladies' hoods of many colors? Where, indeed, in our wintry New England at least, is Christmas itself?"

It makes a nice footnote to a story which certainly seems to require one. And, in pointing to the theological basis of the Puritan tendency to subsume all "sports" into its own master game of allegory, it might well point to something like the true history of "The May-Pole of Merry Mount."

5

The readiest "conclusion" we can draw from this miscellany of Puritan tales is that Hawthorne's literary "ironies" are everywhere such that his personal "ambivalences" are nowhere what they seem. "The Gray Champion" and "Endicott" appear to endorse the political "tendency" implicit in the unlovely piety of Puritanism; so that "The Man of Adamant" exists to reject that piety "in itself" (and thus provide a necessary "control" for the otherwise baffling significance of "The Minister's Black Veil"). Leaving "The May-Pole of Merry Mount" to grieve and ponder, if not to waffle and waver, over the eventual recognition that the politics and the piety went inevitably together; that in giving the political sign to England, "Endicott" was also serving moral notice on America, freeing the continent from transatlantic control but liberating nothing so much as a Moral Majority which might yet turn out to be neither. That morphology we can now regard as "naive." It is not quite "wrong," earnestly founded, as it is, in the rhetoric of the texts themselves; but it is simply inadequate to the complex historicity of Hawthorne's play with meaning.

From this conclusion-turned-premise it could be argued that the traditional estimate of these tales has, by overemphasizing the personal elements (of "belief" or even of "attitude"), somewhat overestimated their significance as philosophical humanism while drastically slighting their operation and effect as rhetorical constructs. And from this realization it would seem to follow—in the case of Hawthorne, at least—that history may tell us at least as much about form as about theme; or, to put the matter even more paradoxically, that the historical moralists may have much to learn from the literary deconstructionists. Provided, that is, those deconstructionists are themselves willing to take the self-conscious historicity of Hawthorne's texts into full account and thus let Hawthorne himself in on their own games. And provided they are willing to tolerate, on Hawthorne's own authority, the survival of certain cultural (and perhaps even religious) overbeliefs as something more than "thematic doggerel." For Hawthorne's texts always seem to grant that *we* require to hum our own little tunes, even as *they* march to the drummer of alienating *difference*.[170]

Most conservatively, therefore, it seems proper to conclude that "The Gray Champion" and "Endicott" do hold out some hope of a truly "liberated" politics in America: one built on the possibility of change implicit in a less traditional society, but founded in the clear-sighted recognition of the reactionary import of much that has in fact occurred in our own insufficiently "separatist" past; a hope liberated, that is, from the closed logic of typological vindication. And "similarly," as we can now more comfortably say, with the problem of piety itself. Typology having lapsed, one is glad simply to *have had* such ancestors. So that redemption—supposing there is indeed any to be had, and that it will be sought by Americans no less than by others—is to be pursued not in the caves of solitary egotism, but in communities liberal enough (at least) to extend full membership to all children of the tribe, and gracious enough to imagine that even the law of nature may predict salvation. For in the end the paradigms of piety we call "Endicott" and "Digby" are not *that* different: the iron enforcements of the one are scarcely more truly social than the stony withdrawal of the other.

Now obviously these themes are, though flagrantly general in their moralistic formulation, intensely provincial in their local application. Here, as elsewhere, when Hawthorne stops saying "the head and the heart," he begins to imply the texts and the texture of a history so local as to threaten embarrassment to all but the dyed-in-the-wool "Americanist"; perhaps only the "Colonialist" can truly love a Hawthorne whose literary play depends on pre-texts as uncanonical as John Winthrop, not to mention Nathaniel Morton. And no wonder if citizens of the great critical world (holding that all literary knowledge aspires to the condition of theory) should abandon Hawthorne's "history" for their own meta-theme of "writing itself."[171]

The final answer to these latter-day embarrassments can involve, of course, nothing but the verbal insistence of Hawthorne's texts themselves. They appear to imply that the matter of Winthrop and Morton ought to be somewhat better known than (in fact) it at present is. The close and scrupulous reader repeatedly discovers that to interpret the texts is to learn the history of the twice-told words they quite self-consciously repeat; and to learn that history is to grasp the issues that tortured the texts into their own remarkable shapes. Counterintuitive, perhaps, but the truth of history seems to require it.

Yet it may not be entirely inappropriate to notice that not all of Hawthorne's pre-texts are equally provincial. Spenser and Bunyan do indeed suggest fixed points of significant departure for "Endicott and the Red Cross" and "The Man of Adamant." And, in the extreme case of "The May-Pole of Merry Mount," the example of Milton provides an absolutely necessary standard. By it one measures not the deviation of Hawthorne himself from the great tradition of reference and allusion in British (or "World") Literature so much as the divergence of his thematic subjects— the American Puritans—from a more catholic stream of politics and piety. Thus the repeated allusions to Milton provide Hawthorne's explicit recognition of his own (and perhaps our own) literary and historical plight: provincial is what we are, in or out of "American Studies." Endicott (so to speak) has made us so. Our only real choice is to try to understand our momentous disadvantage, or not.

Probably it is only "humorous" to recognize that Endicott (who is elsewhere conceived as a parodic Red Cross Knight) is here presented as a sort of mock Samson—demolishing some pillar of paganism even as he gives the Philistines themselves a Puritanic haircut. And possibly not every reader will require a full "explication" of the *Comus* allusion: conservative moralists will be heartened to learn that the narrator's disapproval of the Revellers enjoys full Miltonic sanction; but for any criticism basing itself on D. H. Lawrence, it may be enough to be reminded of the Dionysian connection of Merry Mount.[172] Somewhat more to the story's ironic point would be the recognition that the entire morphology of "Jollity" and "Gloom" finds its full naturalistic anticipation in "L'Allegro" and "Il Penseroso": tempted (by the narrator's sobriety) to erect an historic ontology on the basis of some "poetic" translation of Endicott's own dichotomies, the reader may yet be rescued by recalling that somewhere these insatiable opposites signify no more than "the pleasures of the imagination," as these correspond with nothing more than the changing moods of any man. Fear death by allegory.

Absolutely indispensable, however, and every bit as central to the pious political theme of "The May-Pole" as the displacements of Endicott, is the gentle reminder, in the very last paragraph, of the momentous conclusion of *Paradise Lost*. Endicott himself is, to be sure, only a very parodic archangel, turning this newly fallen (yet strangely loving) couple out of their provincial Eden. But the newly conscious pair, Lord and Lady no more, are designed to be every bit as sympathetic as that truly archetypal couple who (alone) give them enduring significance. And yet their own situation is significantly, painfully different: where Milton's Adam and Eve had ("fortunately," we all agree) a whole "world" before them, "where to choose," Edith and Edgar have, literally, *no choice;* only Salem and the enforced definitions of Puritan Sainthood. Worse luck.

Of course we can easily soften our sense of their unhappy fate. On the one hand, they have clearly won their own sort of victory over Endicott, softening that "iron man" till he "almost sighed for the inevitable blight of early hopes" (66). Just so, we could argue, humanity will eventually humanize even the most doctrinaire Puritanism. And, on the other hand, it seems only accurate to notice that Hawthorne's couple draws its best strength, on life's "difficult path," not from the institutions of Endicott's "Israel" so much as from "each other" (67)—which is why they manage to remind us of Milton's Adam and Eve at all. Perhaps it may yet appear that some covenants really are more fundamental than others. And yet, in the near term, some sense of historic misfortune remains: Adam and Eve could work it out for themselves; nobody knowing better was standing right there, just waiting to place their brand-new consciences under Puritanic arrest. Something or other seems unhappily short-circuited.

Or, again, we can even *defend* the present outcome, if we wish to invoke an orthodoxy rather than a humanism. After all, Adam and Even are quintessentially "pre-Christian." Altogether "historical" they may now finally be, so that no romantic myth of pristine simplicity and unrestriction need apply. And bearers of the promise of eventual redemption they now most assuredly are, so that no image of "upright barbarian" will quite cover their case.[173] Still, lacking the advantages of Abraham, of Moses, of the historic Christ (not to mention the Reformation), what more can in honesty be expected or in justice exacted of them? *Of course* they will have to make it up as they go along. We may think of them as long-range candidates for the unique advantages of some Israel "sanctified" for a "peculiar people." But all this is not yet. They must wander. They must both choose and endure all that *mere history* will hold in store. Wise they were, beyond their mere hours of knowledge, to pray for Salem, even as an end of their natural liberty.

Unless, of course, this plot comes to seem a bit too orthodox. Unless Hawthorne—and behind him Milton, as well as Roger Williams—should conclude that, though Christianity might alter and redirect history, not even America could end it.

What Milton's Adam and Eve enter, even as they leave the altogether mythic realm of Eden, is precisely history; at the very beginning of whatever stages or phases it is to have. What follows—Providence superintending, and even perhaps a Redeemer interrupting—is exactly what they shall choose. Inelegant, no doubt, as the argumentative messiness of "Book III" exists to confess. But really there is no other way. If you want a "world" at all, you have to take what you can get. The whole thing may yet be saved. But it cannot be abrogated. Thus history will be, in large measure, a plot that shall write itself.

This same history, we somehow sense, is what Edith and Edgar ought to be entering as well. Or indeed what they *are* entering, beneath the ideological overspecifications (and political usurpations) of Endicott, and despite the latter-day weariness of the narrator. Softened, but not converted, Endicott insists they have been spared to join an enclave of Covenant, an Israel where piety sanctifies politics; all of it divinely granted, in these latter days, as a stay against the ravages of ordinary history and a pre-enactment of the perfect future. If the narrator understands what he has in mind, he does not bother to protest; for him the outcome is justified by some sober (and *pseudo*-Miltonic) sense that gloom always wins. But the Miltonic paradigm survives to give the lie to Endicott's Puritanic meta-history: all history is the same history; the City of God is where Augustine had said it was: elsewhere. Perhaps the progress of study is to the West. Possibly a *new* Boston will make a better "Modell of Christian Charity" than the old; certainly it will bid more fair to become "the hub of the universe" than ever would "Blackstone's Neck." Even Salem might yet become a more humane place to live than Naumkeag ever was. But nothing is gained by insisting on Old Testament names and tribal mores: language itself is historical, not magic. And the Gospel being universal, there are no sanctified places. Fall and Redemption being timely, history is all there is. Thus Milton forbids the existence of "America" no less than Laud.

So we must read the "conclusion" of Hawthorne's extended account of Puritan politics and piety. For failing to waste even "one regretful thought on the vanities of Merry Mount" (66), Edith and Edgar must certainly answer to the commanding authority of R. W. B. Lewis—as one more myth goes by the board, in a world which may have altogether too few. But other authorities insist that the greater failings were our own, were we to do other than first identify and then reject the allegory of Endicott.[174] Or, just less drastically, to fail to take account of the world it created, when we come to consider the inward careers of Goodman Brown and Parson Hooper—about whom Milton himself has no stories.

❦ Five ❧

VISIBLE SANCTITY AND SPECTER EVIDENCE

"THE TRYAL OF G.B."

N ONE OF THE TALES considered thus far has quite the claim to centrality as have "Young Goodman Brown" and (in the next chapter) "The Minister's Black Veil." Without forgetting the ironic achievement of "Malvin" and "Molineux," we may yet sense that we have *now* come to the masterpieces of Hawthorne's "first period." For in these two compelling cases of conscience Hawthorne has made his most ambitious experiments in moral history. Symbolic re-presentations rather than textual deconstructions, these tales mean to dramatize the psychological consequences of Puritanism as an historic creed: what *would* it have been like?[1] And they do so with such a remarkable economy of means that criticism might well take as long with their certainties as with their more famous "ambiguities."

Both tales are plainly speculative, hypothetical. And both are a bit less tied to some specific "event" than those considered so far. Both are indeed intensely psychological, with the interest in political "story" at a minimum. Thus both have yielded a variety of ahistorical interpretations, many of which—depending on the degree of psychological "science" granted by the individual reader—are likely to seem entirely appropriate. Yet as the two stories are *about* New England Puritans, any hesitancy to restrict the relevance of the historical "vehicle" is likely to have rather serious consequences; and any refusal to grant the stories' own terms must seem suspect. On the one hand, thematically, there is the danger of denying the author his best insights into his given subject; for surely Hawthorne is most brilliant when exposing the ways in which eccentric propositions can vex moral weakness into psychological nightmare. And, on the other hand, the familiar psychobiographic trap: neglecting the distance which history adds to that already inherent in literary form, we risk exaggerating Hawthorne's personal involvement with (or unconscious exposure of himself in) the dilemma of his characters. "Young Goodman Brown" may not, as James would have it, "mean nothing" in terms of Hawthorne's own beliefs or anxieties, but it reveals the author's psyche in only an indirect and "artificial" way. And though Brown's blasphemies helped to inspire those of Ahab, other evidence suggests that Hawthorne's literary detachment was steadier and more predictable than Melville's own, and that a grasp of the psychological problems inherent in Puritan piety was firm in his intentional mind.[2]

Accordingly, it seems to me, serious interpretation of "Young Goodman Brown" must somehow take account of David Levin's rather exact rendition of Brown's experience in the actual language (and quaint categories) of 1692. It may well be possible to disagree with his conclusion—that the literal dimension of "Young Goodman Brown" is social—but it seems positively obscurantist to deny that "specter evidence" really is, in some sense, the central issue of the tale. Attempts to answer Levin seem forced. And surely it is now evident that many earlier readings were approximating his own prime insight: the inadvisability of accepting the Devil's word about the constitution of the invisible world.[3]

Evidently this sort of historicism makes us very anxious. We wish to identify, also, some larger (or "deeper") significance. Thus one historicist provides us with a chart purporting to show a deliberately contrived and consistently maintained sexual "level" of allegory, reconciling us, presumably, to the "impudent knowingness" of Frederick Crews. Even more revealing, perhaps, is the fact that our most detailed study of the tale's response to the miscellaneous texts of the latter-day Puritan world enlists its considerable scholarly authority in a fairly nominal argument about Hawthorne's own "guilty" choice of art as a career. Another very particular study of "influence"—the debt to a pamphlet by Deodat Lawson, *Christ's Fidelity*—cannot rest its case with the fixities and definites of this rare and curious encounter, affirming instead "a new and timeless drama about the distortions of the human mind." Nor is Levin himself exempt from this prevailing critical pressure: the Hawthorne who worked up this exquisite case of specter evidence may have dealt with "a narrow range of types and subjects," but he developed from these "a remarkable range of insights into human experience."[4] History first, we seem to say, but last and always the "human mind" itself.

What makes these critical gestures significant is our sense of how accurately they reflect the predilections of the entrenched academic audience. Not then (and perhaps not yet) challenged by the paradigms of linguistics and structuralism, it defers everywhere to the ultimacy of psychological interest and explanation. Without quite canonizing *The Interpretation of Dreams*, it yet clings dogmatically to the belief that literature is everywhere indeed more philosophical than history. And, having substituted psychology for ontology as the first philosophy, its way of being philosophical is to affirm commitment to abstractions like "the human mind" or "human experience," whatever the actual substance of its own explanatory power. If Freud turns out to provide the ultimate structures, so be it. Preferable, perhaps, might be the softer, not-quite-consistent determinism of Erik Erikson. Lacan need not apply. For best of all would be our own gleanings from our favorite humanist authors, seriatim and ad hoc. Ready to face any truth so long as it is a *general* one, we seem willing to take our generalizations wherever we can find them. Even if they seem tacked on.[5]

Yet granting the inevitability of all this—and content to await some future linguistic translation[6]—the historicist point remains: whatever our own terms of last resort, Goodman Brown's experience is somehow "Puritan"; and, further, it takes place in a region Hawthorne has elected to define as "spectral." Bluntly, not only are the proven sources of the tale obsessed with the technical implications of specter evidence, which wracked the official conscience of latter-day Puritanism as almost no other; not only is this mysterious specter evidence the very premise of the tale, determining its meaning as surely as any given signifier its putative signified; but further, from "Alice Doane" straight through his unfinished romances, Hawthorne repeatedly allowed the Puritan language of diabolical simulation and, more generally, of the "invisible world" to control the limits of his own psychological investigations. The very language of dreams, it might be suggested, represented not so much a rational clarification as a phenomenological impoverishment of the older system of reference.[7] So we must psychologize with caution. It would have required a remarkably perverse reading of Cotton and Increase Mather (not to mention Deodat Lawson) to have passed over the specific import of their actual problem; or a notably dilettantish reading to preserve dozens of minute details while ignoring their local significance; or a singularly self-involved reading to translate the entire affair into a version of his own Oedipal (or artistic) anxiety.

In fact, Hawthorne's story faithfully preserves the central Puritan issue of specter evidence in an even more telling way than Professor Levin first suggested. Obviously, as we notice, "Young Goodman Brown" is not "about" the infamous witch trials of 1692—even less, I think, than "The Gentle Boy" is "about" the judicial murder of the Quakers of 1659. Although the tale refers to a number of non-diabolical personages whose names figure prominently in the records of Salem Village, and although the scholarly reader can detect dozens of significant little details disarranged from these, we hear nothing about witch hunts in the tale—so that Arthur Miller will occupy his own historic province quite free from the anxiety of Hawthornean influence. The unhappy Goodman Brown simply lives out his faithless life in quiet and gloomy desperation, with no suggestion that he was ever to know the clash of courtroom controversy. History there unquestionably is. But not this sort.

We can say, if we wish, that the action takes place "near Salem Village, probably in 1692."[8] Probably this is better than suggesting it occurs, all simply, in "the haunted mind." But there really is no need to insist. Far more significant, as we shall see, is the simple fact that Goodman Brown is a traditional, indeed a third-generation Puritan. At issue, accordingly, is something besides that one infamous outbreak of "universal suspicion"—though Hawthorne's later reflections in "Main Street" make it clear that, as the gothic terror of "Alice Doane's Appeal" was not all managed melodrama, so he continued to feel real horror when he thought of that historic episode.[9] In "Young Goodman Brown" an entire habit of the Puritan mind is on trial, the protagonist its unwitting yet not quite unwilling victim. Even as Hawthorne revises "Alice Doane," he recognizes the finality of the problem discovered there: the difficulty of detecting a witch is distressingly similar to the radically Puritan problem of discovering a saint. They stand or fall together. And the whole world depends.

Although the hysteria of 1692 stood out like an ugly blot on the historical page, Hawthorne could not view it as an isolated event, separate from the whole texture of Puritan moral experience. It epitomized something, even as it ended it. And though the faithful reader must carefully test before excusing himself—one really can, it comes to appear, almost always be surprised by almost any sin—it will scarcely do to say it epitomizes everything. Brown behaves like a third-generation Puritan under latter-day duress. We have to deal with that.

As with the Quaker persecutions, customary moral assumptions might not *always* produce their proper psychological effects; as Channing thanked God, moral tendencies are not *always* realized. Yet it was not altogether surprising if occasionally they did. And they did, finally, as Hawthorne ventured to suggest, in the actual events of 1692; and so they do, symbolically, in the fictional experience of Goodman Brown. His story is, like that of Tobias Pearson, Hawthorne's way of inspecting the projected outcome of certain pervasive Puritan attitudes, which are ours only if they are. If Hawthorne will not quite "localize" his response to 1692, neither will he quite "universalize" it. Less is at issue than "the human mind." We will not find Hawthorne implying (with certain modern historians) that, since the belief in witchcraft was once nearly universal, there can be nothing peculiar about the episode at Salem Village; nor suggesting (with certain modern critics) that, since bad faith and projection are well nigh universal, there can be no specifically "Puritan" witchcraft. In Hawthorne's rigorous view, Goodman Brown's forest-education enfigures the ultimate breakdown of the Puritan attempt to define the human form of the Kingdom of God: "specter evidence" turns out to be only the negative test case of the definitive Puritan problem of "visible sanctity." Cotton Mather gave the hint, in his own most troublesome case. Hawthorne merely took it.

1

At the beginning of his fateful excursion into the forest, Goodman Brown is a more than tolerably naive young man. We scarcely need to observe his dismay at hearing (and then seeing) a multitude of communicants and tavern-haunters, saints and sinners mixed together, to sense his initial assumption that the orderly divisions of the Puritan Community embody Moral Reality. More particularly, his initial attitude toward his wife is so naive as to be condescending: "Say thy prayers, dear Faith, and go to bed at dusk, and no harm will come to thee" (75).[10] On the face of things this is too easy; and the reader of "Fancy's Show Box" has been taught to worry that, on the contrary, "in the solitude of a midnight chamber . . . the soul may pollute itself even with those crimes, which we are accustomed to deem altogether carnal."[11] But such naiveté is far from his worst trait. Whatever may be the truth about the moral character of Brown's pink-ribboned wife—and whatever may be our own working assumptions about the relation between faith and salvation—we are expected to worry about this Goodman's belief that "after this one night" he can cling to the skirts of Faith and "follow her to heaven" (75). Even before we get any sense of the sorts of self-indulgence that may become available to Goodman Brown, we know that this sort of temporizing with one's eternal salvation is likely to be risky.

Actually, as it turns out, Goodman Brown is already in a state of "bad faith": there has already been some sort of devilish pre-arrangement concerning his nocturnal outing; he knows at the outset that he has so far "kept covenant" with the Powers of Darkness. His "excellent resolve for the future" may be temporarily successful in allowing him to feel "justified in making more haste on his present evil purpose" (75), but the rationalization is as transparent to the psychologist as the risk is to the theologian; not likely to stand much testing. And, as an external sign of his compromised internal condition, he has *already* begun to be suspicious of others, even those in whose virtue he is most accustomed naively to trust. Accordingly, his wife's understandable plea that he stay with her, to quiet her fears, on this "of all nights of the year," draws a nervously revealing response: "Dost thou doubt me already, and we but three months married?" Now October 31 is a good night for Puritans to stay home,[12] and there is not the slightest evidence to suggest that Faith doubts her husband in any way. Brown's attitude plainly involves some sort of guilty projection: his own will-to-evil is *already* causing him to begin the transfer of his own moral obliquity to others.

Clearly, then, much more is at stake than simple naiveté, the much-discussed innocence of the archetypal American hero. Studied closely, Brown's situation is not *much* like that of Robin Molineux.[13] And well before the analyst has much evidence of Oedipal anxiety to work on, any decent casuist (Puritan or otherwise) is constrained to conclude that Goodman Brown is deeply involved in that particular sort of bad faith which used to be called "presumption." He is assuming his own final perseverance *even as* he deliberately embarks on a journey which he knows is directed diametrically away from the normal pursuit of salvation.[14] The point is not trivial: to understand the "unpardonable" gravity of his initial moral assumptions is to be protected from being more tender-minded about the terrifying results of his experience than Hawthorne's tough and tight-lipped conclusion asks us to be. No especially severe morality is required to see that, from one very significant point of view, Goodman Brown deserves whatever happens. Indeed he asks for it.

Given the unflinching and unpardoning outcome—of a moral career that is already well under way when we first begin to hear about it—we ought to find ourselves wondering how Goodman Brown has got himself *already* so far involved in the "unpardonable sin" of presumption. If everything seems to follow from, or indeed to be contained in, the initial situation of the story, perhaps that initial situation itself deserves very careful attention. We need to proceed with care: on the one hand, it is very easy to distort and make nonsense out of Hawthorne's delicate ethical formulae by going behind the *donnée* of his initial premises; yet on the other hand, his stories are often packed with clues about exactly "where," morally speaking, we really are. And "Young Goodman Brown" does not leave us entirely without such clues.

If Brown is "but three months married" to Faith, then it does seem necessary to regard him as a recent convert to the high mysteries of the Puritan Religion; Thomas Connally was certainly right about this, even if the story is not so consistently "allegorical" as he wanted it to be.[15] But evidently the situation is not quite simple, for we swiftly learn that this good man's father and grandfather have been faithful Puritans before him, and that he himself has been duly catechized, in his youth, by the dutiful Goody Cloyse. At first glance there may seem to be some sort of confusion in the allegory, reminiscent of the more famous one in "Alice Doane's Appeal." Can Goodman Brown be, at once, a new convert *and* an heir to a redoubtable saintly ancestry and a formidable Christian nurture? The solution to this apparent difficulty, as well as the key to Goodman Brown's presumptuous psychology, lies in the implicit but demographically precise Puritan background of the story, in the subtly emphasized fact that Young Goodman Brown is a *third-generation* Puritan.

Thus even before we encounter any enchantments, we are forced to suspect that Hawthorne's reading in Mather's ancestral *Magnalia* has been extremely perceptive and that his use of a particular Puritan world is entirely functional; for Goodman Brown is quite evidently the product (victim, as it turns out) of the Half-Way Covenant, that bold compromise by which the Puritans tried to salvage their theory of "visible sanctity," of a church composed of fully professed saints, in the face of changing historical conditions. Externally, at least, Goodman Brown's status is perfectly standard, indeed inevitable: as a third-generation Puritan he would have been spending the years of his minority in the half-way situation defined by the compromise of 1662. Grandson of an original saint, son of a professing member, he has been reared, like virtually everyone else in his generation, in the half-way condition of presumptive but not yet professed or tested sainthood. Obviously he has had *something* to do with the community of visible saints because the promises of the new covenant are made with "the seed" of saints as well as with the saints themselves; but just as obviously he has not (until very recently) been a full, "communing" member because he had not been capable of that fully voluntary confession of conversion and profession of committed sainthood which alone could redeem the New England Way from the crassest sort of tribalism.[16]

Original Sin might well be transmitted by the simple act of physical generation. So also, as the theological plot unfolded, might something called "federal grace"; or, less technically, a saint might fairly expect baptism for his seed, and baptism ought to have *some* gracious significance. But in the last analysis the New Birth had to be truly "spiritual" in every sense, and thus "sanctifying grace" could come neither biologically nor by infant ritual. And thus, as the New England theology gradually clarified itself, that very troubled third generation of Puritans simply had to *wait:* in the *expectation* of full, visible sainthood *eventually,* they all attended church, were duly catechized and nurtured, and were thoroughly indoctrinated (and threatened) by Jeremiads into the proper respect for the ancestral appearances of saintliness. And eventually some, though pitifully few, were admitted into that most guarded and holy of holies—full, "communing" membership.[17] Into this ultimate earthly state, Goodman Brown has but newly entered. After years of "preparation" and presumptive but not proven sainthood, Goodman Brown has, we must infer, finally received official certification by the public representatives of the Communion of Saints. Quite likely, in all sociological probability, this theologic certification coincided with his marriage:

two covenants in one. Thus adulthood and salvation have blessedly arrived together. And this complex fact can scarcely be unrelated to the terrible ease of his moral premises.

Goodman Brown's assurance is not, one should hasten to stress, orthodox. The expounders of the Puritan system never tired of emphasizing that, despite Calvin's stress on the "comfort" the saint might find in a predestinarian system, one's assurance could never be complete. Indeed too great (or, at any rate, too easy) an assurance should certainly mean that one's experience of gracious regeneration was illusory: decree is certain, but men change their minds. Yet as Hawthorne was no mere "expounder" of the system, so he seems to have sensed that all such warnings would not alter the basic psychology of the situation. Some modern commentators have held that the Half-Way Covenant inevitably cheapened the concept of sainthood by allowing *some* recognizable church-status to persons without—so far as they or anyone else could tell—any specifically "Christian experience."[18] Apparently Hawthorne thought otherwise: whenever one declared oneself a Saint and had that weighty claim accepted by the community, the formal declaration and the social fact might well tend to loom larger, psychologically, than any attendant (fussy) qualifications about continuing uncertainty, or about the sole importance of God's free grace in the process, or about the continuing need for watchfulness and sanctification; and, by providing a formalized schema of waiting or probation out of which most persons never moved, the Half-Way Covenant may well have served to increase this basic psychological tendency. Although the new dispensation served to broaden the base of baptized membership in the Puritan churches, it left the inner circle of full communicants as small as ever, and seemed, if anything, to heighten the significance of that sanctum sanctorum.[19] Safe at last.

When one moved, then, from the lamented and berated coolness of halfway membership into the warmth of full communion, the event could have no small significance. And one perfectly likely (though by no means "approved") meaning of such an experience is implied in the moral posture of Goodman Brown as recent-convert. After all protective distinctions have been made, the doctrine of election—especially in the context of thirdgeneration Puritanism, which Hawthorne so delicately evokes—is likely to imply the sin of presumption. Hawthorne seems to say it all in the first scene when he tells us that "Goodman Brown *felt himself justified.*" To Cotton Mather, no doubt, to Edward Taylor, or to any other approved theorist of latter-day Puritan conversion psychology, Brown would be an example of the bold hypocrite, outrageously presuming on grace: no *really* converted person ever *would* behave in such a manner. We can view him that way if we choose. To Hawthorne himself, however, he is only the enduring natural man whose naturally self-regarding instincts have been treacherously reinforced by the psychological implications of doctrine.

Now all of this is merely the story's background, implied by the setting and compressed context, and helping us to place the sociologically and doctrinally precise point of Goodman Brown's departure. If the analysis seems somewhat technical, we may well recall that as early as the sketch of "Dr. Bullivant" Hawthorne had been intensely interested in the mentality of declining Puritanism; and here he associates the experience of Goodman Brown not only with the specific context of the witchcraft (the most dramatic problem of Puritan third-generation declension) but also with the pervasive moral quality of that mentality.[20] No one can read Hawthorne's known sources without sensing that with the death of the original saints, whose experience in England and in "coming out" to America made their stance of sainthood seem natural and believable, the problem of continuing an order of visible saints became disproportionate, even obsessive. The rest, perhaps, is Hawthorne's own speculation; but surely it is apt. No Arminian critic of Calvinism ever fails to warn that the doctrine of election protects the sovereignty of God only at the risk of human smugness, over-confidence, self-indulgence, antinomianism.[21] The Calvinist doctrine of election looks very much like the traditional sin of presumption. And nowhere, Hawthorne cogently suggests, was the danger greater than in declining New England, in those exasperating days when Puritan ideologues turned nearly all their attention to the continuance of churches constituted of God's visible saints. Obviously Goodman Brown's experience is not to be taken as a model of "Augustinian Piety." And even if his career does not represent any sort of statistical Puritan "average," he is a representative, latter-day Puritan nevertheless, following some highly probable moral logic. The general situation is indeed as Roy Harvey Pearce has suggested: "granting the Puritan faith . . . it is inevitable that Young Goodman Brown should have envisaged his loss of faith as he did and as a consequence have been destroyed as a person."[22]

Accordingly, therefore, his situation will not bear immediate psychoanalytic translation or complete reduction. *Of course* Goodman Brown will prove anxious about his relation to his father, and to "his father before him"; this is an inevitable fact of Puritan life in the 1670's, 1680's, and 1690's—where, as Perry Miller has remarked, the spokesmen for the failing Puritan Way "called for such a veneration of progenitors as is hardly to be matched outside China."[23] It is their reputed level of piety which has (we are to imagine) been repeatedly used to mark the level of Goodman Brown's own declension. In a very real sense it is into the community of *their* putative sanctity that he has so recently been admitted. The perception that the

Puritan world "in declension" was bound to be fraught with Oedipal anxiety belongs to the order of history as surely as to the order of psychoanalysis. And the suspicion that in such a world a son, however naive, might be all too likely to make certain Pierre-like "discoveries" about his venerable progenitors belongs to an order of common sense. Together these insights add up to something like the figure of Young Goodman Brown—the moral adolescent who, after years of spiritual (as well as sexual) anxiety, has newly achieved what his ancestors defined as "Faith," and who is now, from the absolutely "inamissible" safety of that position, about to investigate the reality of the dark world he has escaped. Moral science, in a way. But only for the saved.

2

The moral progress of Young Goodman Brown—from the presumption of his own salvation by Faith, together with a naive but thin confidence in the simple goodness of familiar saints; through a state of melodramatic despair; and on to the enduring suspicion that outside of his own will "there is no good on earth"—represents a triumph of compression unequaled in Hawthorne's art. Robin Molineux's "evening of weariness and ambiguity" is, by comparison, painfully drawn out. Here things happen almost too fast, and only with a sense of the special Puritan character of Brown's beginning can we accurately trace his path.

Brown enters the forest convinced that he can always return to the Bosom of Faith; his nice pink-ribboned little wife *and* his familiar place in a stable and salutary community of saints will always be there. It may be that neither his marriage nor his conversion has, after three months, proved quite so enduringly satisfactory or perpetually climactic as could be hoped; all things do ebb and flow. But both have provided him with the assurance needed by one who would press beyond the limits of socialized sex or religion. Recalling the usual typological value of marital union, we can see the danger of Brown's presumptive confidence. But the full significance of his presumption lies in his feeling that he can now explore the dimension of diabolical evil with impunity. Having joined the ranks of the safe and socially sanctioned, he can, he believes, have a little sight of witchcraft—which is simply, as Cotton Mather says, human depravity par excellence: without the grace of Faith, "we should every one of us be a *Dog* and a *Witch* too."[24] An intriguing proposition. Now that he is finally sure which side he is on, he can afford to see how the other moral half lives.

The most significant fact about Brown's naive acceptance of the appearance of sanctity in his fellow saints is the swiftness with which it disappears. Based on the normal, approved, social, presumably "real" manifestations of goodness, it is destroyed by extraordinary, private, "spectral" intimations of badness. His ancestors have been "a race of honest men" (77); Goody Cloyse taught him his catechism in his youth; the minister and the deacon are the pillars of the religious community, sentries who stand guard at the "wall" which surrounds the "garden" of true grace, models of converted holiness whose experiences are the standard by which those of new applicants for communion are judged. All this is evidentially certain: it is "visible"; it makes the Puritan world go round. But what if these same figures of sanctity are reported, or even "witnessed," to perform other actions? What if a grandfather is reputed to have had devilish motives in lashing a Quaker woman (half-naked) through the streets? or the teacher of catechism is seen to conjure the Devil? or the sternly inhibiting elders are heard to smack their lips over a "goodly young woman" about to be taken into a quite different communion? Surely this contradiction of evidences will prove unsettling to a young man who, the victim of his system in regard to others as to himself, has the habit of believing that the moral world is adequately defined as the mirror-image opposition between the covenants and communions of God and Satan; and that these ultimate differences can be discovered with enough certainty to guarantee the organization of society. Only some very special, as yet undreamed species of faith could rescue him from such a contradiction of evidences.

Ultimately, of course, Goodman Brown passes through a phase of distraught, despairing confusion into a more or less settled state of faithless desolation. But more remarkable, almost, is the equanimity with which he at first accepts the Devil's "revelations." He jokes about the moral secrets of his saintly ancestors: funny he had never heard any such family secrets before; no, on second thought he guesses they *would* keep their forest activities a secret, since we Puritans are "a people of prayer, and good works, to boot, and abide no such wickedness" (77). With the telling and technical pun on "Boot" (a seventeenth-century nickname for the Devil), the joke is a little funnier to us than it consciously is to Goodman Brown. As yet he does not quite wish to define a universal Puritan hypocrisy as the prayers to God of people who actually serve the Devil. But he is still being rather too easily ironical about his worthy forebears. And if he is, in the next moment, truly amazed to hear the Devil claim such an impressively general acquaintance among the important personages of New England, still he responds less by doubting or discounting the Devil's claim to near-sovereignty as by writing it off as irrelevant to *his own* moral condition: "Howbeit, I have nothing to do with the council; they have their own ways, and are no rule for a simple husbandman like me" (77). This social deference might be a species of humility; except that Goody Cloyse, with whom his moral connection *has* been direct and important, whose "rule" has been quite literally his own rule, can be dismissed just as easily: "What if a wretched old woman do choose to go to the devil, when I thought she was going to heaven! Is that any reason why I should quit my dear Faith, and go after her?" (80).

Now clearly all of Goodman Brown's responses are still too easy. Even before the Devil has introduced his most convincing, most visible evidence; even when it is all a matter of mere rumor, Goodman Brown has been quite willing to accept the Devil's "doubtful" informations at something like their face value; he believes their truth and merely denies their relevance. At one level, of course, this mental operation is merely an extension of his initial bad faith in relation to his wife; at another, however, it seems to adumbrate the implications of some sort of belief in "limited atonement." Brown's habitual, doctrinally ingrained sense of the relative fewness of the visibly elect is growing more and more keen. Firmly possessed of the distinction between the inner circle of proven saints and all outer circles of the many "others," he seems willing to reduce the circumference of that inmost circle *almost* to its single-point limit. *I* and *my* Faith: it all comes down to that self-referential center. But since he has already deceived and abandoned his wife (and, in doing so, vitiated his faith through presumption), even this two-term protestation rings false. The Devil really has not very much difficulty with this Easy-Faith of a Young Goodman Brown. "With heaven above, and Faith below, I will yet stand firm against the devil!" (82)—so our self-assured young man roundly declaims, after consigning the rest of his world to perdition. But a murmur of spectral voices and a flutter of spectral ribbons later and his "Faith is gone!" (83). It could hardly have turned out otherwise.

And yet the swiftness and seeming inevitability of Goodman Brown's reduction to despair depend for their believability on more than his naive and presumptuous understanding of faith as a sort of private haven. "Young Goodman Brown" is, no less than "Rappaccini's Daughter," a story about faith and evidence, and so there is also, just as crucially, the question of his evidences to be considered. Explicitly, of course, some narrator raises the question only at the very end of the story, and then in a completely nontechnical way: "Had Young Goodman Brown fallen asleep in the forest, and only dreamed a wild dream of a witch-meeting?" (89). Was his evidence, therefore, only "subjective," a species of that diseased fantasy to which the nineteenth century universally ascribed the witchcraft "delusions"? As David Levin has amply and carefully shown, however, the evidence or "reality" question is built into the story everywhere in a very precise seventeenth-century way. Not only are we warned from the outset that Goodman Brown may be speaking to the Father of Lies, so that scandalous rumor and innuendo may be even *less* trustworthy than usual, even in a notoriously quarrelsome Puritan small town; but everywhere the persons seen by Brown are referred to as "shapes" or "figures" or "appearances." People appear and disappear in the most magical sorts of ways, and no one is substantial enough to cast a shadow. It is all, quite demonstrably, a technical case of specter evidence. And this is precisely why the narrator's seemingly casual answer to the dream-or-not question ("Be it so if you will") is neither a coy evasion nor a profound "ambiguity." It simply does not matter: obviously not in terms of practical consequences, since the psychomoral response is certain and terrible, whatever the nature of the stimulus; and not in terms of epistemological assumptions either, since the choice lies (as Levin put it) "between a dream and a reality that is unquestionably spectral."[25]

Thus it is distressing to encounter the claim that Levin has tried to make all the story's challenging moral problems go away by blaming everything on "infernal powers"; and that, *really*, Goodman Brown's " 'visions' are the product of his suspicion and distrust, not the Devil's wiles."[26] The point is surely that in Hawthorne's psychological scheme Brown's suspicion and distrust and the Devil's wiles are not different. No doubt Hawthorne "believed in" the literal Devil even less than Spenser, who had long before deliberately conflated Archimago's magic powers with the Red Cross Knight's suppressed desires; and as Hawthorne conned the lesson of Spenser's faith-protagonist, and then defined the problem in "Alice Doane's Appeal," specter evidence became *nothing but* the necessary historical "figure" for guilty, projective dreams or fantasies. "Literally," in the seventeenth century, Brown "sees specters" that *seem* to reveal the diabolical commitment of the persons to whom they belong; but this seeming is highly untrustworthy, and Brown's inferences are illegitimate. "Allegorically," as we interpret Brown's twilight or limit-experiences, as we try with Hawthorne to imagine what sort of reality might lie behind the widespread but ultimately superstitious belief that people have detachable specters which may or may not require a pact with the Devil to detach, we can only conclude that specter evidence *is* projective fantasy.

Once again, as so often the case in a Hawthorne "allegory," *history itself* provided the "figurative" term: specter evidence was simply there, a given; Hawthorne had merely to imagine what it really meant. And if we really understand this perfectly historical but almost anti-allegorical process, we can see how fundamentally wrongheaded is the assumption that Hawthorne merely "used history" as costume or as convenient setting for his timeless themes. Hawthorne's problem in "Young Goodman Brown" was *not* to find an appropriate historical delusion which might validly enfigure man's persistent tendency to project his own moral uneasiness onto others; it was, rather, to discover the sorts of reality which made the belief in specter evidence significant at *any* point in human experience. As is the case with "The

Gentle Boy," "Young Goodman Brown" is primarily a moment in which there are brought to bear on an actual, complex historical situation all the imaginative sympathy and psychological acumen at the command of the artist. That, I think, we might well want to call *history as history*. It is *good* history because the artist in question was one who constantly speculated about the pitfalls of inner life.

The doctrine of specters as a specific form of superstition is actually not very complicated—though the story is immeasurably enriched for the reader who is familiar with the witchcraft sources and who can thus sense the full historic reality of Goodman Brown's problem as a classic case of seventeenth-century religious epistemology. Perhaps we need not linger over all the wonderful ramifications of the problem about whether God would or would not permit Satan to manipulate the spectral form of a person who had *not* entered the Devil's own covenant. The arguments are inexhaustibly fascinating.[27] On the one hand, if Satan *can* do such things, would this not constitute a rather drastic lacuna in the providential order? If the observation of someone in diabolical settings or activities *might* or *might not* really indicate his adherence to the Devil's party, would not appearance and reality have come so far apart as to make the whole moral world illusory? What, more especially, would be the significance of that ever-so-watchful moral surveillance so characteristic of the covenanted community? What *could* you believe? Whom *could* you trust? But on the other hand—and Cotton Mather himself said it all—the Scripture doctrine is clear: "the Devil has often been transformed into an Angel of Light." And so, who could assert with assurance that, as some sort of ultimate faith-test for a special people, a royal priesthood set apart, God would *not* permit Satan to impersonate saints so as to lead astray, if possible, even the elect? But if the ramifications are teasing, still the crux is simple. To imagine the epistemological heart of Goodman Brown's problem, Hawthorne probably needed no more than a single interrogative suggestion from Increase Mather's *Illustrious Providences*: "Suppose the devil saith, these people are witches, must the judge, therefore, condemn them?"[28]

Mather is speaking, literally, of vulgar, "white-magic" sorts of witch-detection (such as the water test), which he condemns as using the Devil's own means to detect the Devil; and Brown is not quite the sort of "judge" Mather probably had in mind. Still, his question covers the matter of spectral activity as well: the appearance of a person's specter is, in precise fact, the Devil's ocular claim that the person thus spectrally represented is indeed a member of his own desperate anti-covenant. And it is hard to imagine a clearer posing of the question which faces Goodman Brown. Whether we are thinking of the Devil's verbal slanders, or the spectral sounds and sights of the forests, or those famous now-you-see-them, now-you-don't pink ribbons, the case is essentially the same. For granting that the Devil *is*, from time to time, permitted to impersonate saints without their consent, and granting that in these days of his last desperate assault against the purity of faith in the New World he would do so if ever he could, then, "literally," there is no evidential difference between the Devil's general and urbane innuendoes about all the Great and Holy of New England and Goodman Brown's actually "seeing" Goody Cloyse, or Deacon Gookin, or his parents—or Faith, with or without her ribbons. Nasty, small-town rumor, simplistic tricks of "materialization" such as even Pharaoh's magi could perform, spectral simulation: in all these instances, Goodman Brown's vaunted "insights" into Mankind's Total and Unredeemed Depravity depend on a diabolical communication.

Such informations would be scanned. A less technical case did not turn out well for Young Nobleman Hamlet: things were rotten enough in Denmark, one discovers, but man's ghost-bidden (and Oedipally anxious) revenge did not exactly accomplish God's justice. And the case of Brown's direct spiritual ancestor is even more instructive: the instinctive "jealousy" Spenser's Red Cross Knight feels when he beholds the Spectral Una disporting in lewd amours with a Spectral Squire suggests that even the Arch-Magician's specters embody little more than suppressed suspicion or repressed desire.[29] Hawthorne is too sympathetic a moral historian to imply, flatly, that "he who believes in the Devil, already belongs to Him"; but "Young Goodman Brown" exists to suggest that any "diabolical" account of the moral world represents a culpable degree of credulity. If you want the Devil's views, you must go to meet him. But if you do this, you are already on dubious ground at best; you might well expect the worst. Just so, Goodman Brown's spectral intimations of depravity are merely the seamy psychological underside of his initial naiveté and (even more) of his initial bad faith.[30]

Probably—if we find such "on-premise" speculations interesting—the Devil is telling the truth when he implicates Brown's ancestors in persecution and sadistic cruelty: these are, after all, the sins of Hawthorne's own fathers, and of the fathers of many others among his historically naive generation; doubtless the Father of Lies is well practiced in the meretricious rhetorical art of universalizing the Half-Truth. Probably the Devil exaggerates when he claims that nearly all of the deacons, selectmen, and General Court representatives in New England owe him their formal, covenanted allegiance. (Hawthorne would have been, I imagine, less disturbed than some liberal modern observers to learn that, for all the historian can discover, there *was* indeed some real enough witchcraft at the bottom of the Salem "hysteria"; but his statistical reservations about the size of Satan's consciously enlisted army would have been as wary as his doctrinal reservations about the totality of human depravity.)[31] And presumably the Devil's use of the specific "specters" of Goody Cloyse, Deacon Gookin, and Faith is pure deceit: he conjures their shapes without their contractual permission in order to test (destroy, as it lamentably turns out) the naive and compromised faith of Goodman Brown. A cheap trick, perhaps, but not without a certain diabolical cleverness; and not, in this case, ineffective. Brown may think that Faith is "inamissible," that the final perseverance of the elect is certain. But Satan evidently knows better: even fully communing saints can be had. Or, if the Calvinist Fathers of Dort were correct, if the gracious gift of a true faith *cannot* indeed be lost, then at least there is the diabolical pleasure of hazing the "presumptive" saint whose faith only *seemed* true and whose salvation was all too easily assumed. In any case, the extreme result of this new communicant's presumptive bad faith is his willingness to accept spectral (whether diabolical or traumatic) intimations of evil as more authoritative than the ordinary social appearances of goodness.

3

Once we realize how fundamentally Goodman Brown's moral discoveries depend on the spirit (and the place) in which he asks his questions, we are inevitably led to wonder about the validity of the questions themselves. Clearly it *is* "impertinent" (in Levin's language) to ask whether the people represented to Brown in the forest are "really" evil: questions concerning the nature and extent of human depravity may not, in themselves, lie "beyond the limits of fiction"; but surely the true, ultimate condition of Goody Cloyse is a question whose answer lies beyond the proper limits of *this story,* which is "not about the evil of other people but about Brown's doubt, his discovery of the *possibility* of universal evil."[32] And there is reason to believe, further, that certain forms of the depravity-question are themselves illegitimate. Posed in certain terms, they may be the Devil's own questions.

From Hawthorne's cautiously Arminian point of view, Calvinist Brown is habitually making simple judgments about settled moral realities in a world where only the most flickering sorts of appearances are available as evidence. And he is asking about spiritual "essences" where probably only a process exists. In one very important sense the evidence of the forest is no more "spectral" than was all the previous communal evidence in favor of the saintliness of the now-exposed hypocrites. Hawthorne repeatedly joked about the separation between his own real and spectral selves; and as the author of "The Christmas Banquet" he seemed intrigued with the Emersonian dictum that "souls never touch." Further, he made it unmistakably clear in

"Fancy's Show Box" (which might be read as a gloss on "Young Goodman Brown," suggesting Hawthorne's *own* doctrine of depravity) that "stains upon the soul" are simply not visible. Moral and spiritual status is, accordingly, an invincibly interior and a radically *in*visible quality. Any outward representation of a person's moral intentionality, of his voluntary allegiance to God or Satan, of his "state" with reference to the "grace" of "faith" (even if this is *not* in a process of constant, "ambivalent" fluctuation) is a mere similacrum—a specter.[33] Giving the epistemology of Berkeley or Kant a distinctive moral twist (which Jeremy Taylor could have appreciated better than Emerson), Hawthorne means to suggest that all moral knowledge of others exists in us as phenomenon, or idea, or appearance merely; the moral essence, like the Lockean substance or the Kantian *ding an sich*, remains an *ignotum x*. True, for certain fairly important social uses, we must assume that a person's statements and bodily actions correspond to his own intention, that *he* and not some devil is in control of his bodily form. But this is only a compromise. It should not be taken as an accurate rendition of Reality. Clearly a religious system which would, rejecting the ironic personal lesson and then the powerfully prophetic teaching of Roger Williams, confuse the compromises imposed by the necessities of worldly order based on appearances with the absolute configurations of the invisible moral world would be running a terrible risk.[34]

In a sense, therefore, *any* answer to questions concerning an individual's absolute moral condition will be in terms of specter evidence. Probably the truth lies with the Arminians and pragmatists and existentialists: man makes himself; he has a moral history but no moral essence, not at birth and not by rebirth; his whole life is a journey which may or may not lead to the goal, and a series of choices in which any one may undo the *moral* import (though not, of course, the psychological results) of any other. The "sides" in such a world would be impossible to define. But even if there *were* sides, ineluctably defined by ineffable divine decree, who could ever discover them? Accordingly, Goodman Brown's mental organization (and, by implication, the Puritan ecclesiology) dissolves into moral chaos because in every instance he must choose between the show of social appearance and the specter of diabolical simulation and suggestion. In every case evidence counters evidence—where, Hawthorne implies, only faith can be salutary.

The paradigmatic instance of this dilemma quite properly concerns Brown's wife: the test of faith is Faith. Supposing the worst, let us adopt the improbable view that Hawthorne intends the forest experience of Goodman Brown to have the full authority of a sort of "Melvillean" vision of "blackness," uncomplicated by the epistemological uncertainties inherent in the historical problem of specter evidence or the psychological problem of Brown's bad faith. Even if we should decide that Brown's discoveries are *neither* the troubled, projective dreams of a man in bad faith *nor* their literal seventeenth-century equivalent, a show of black magic put on by the Devil for Brown's private "benefit"; that is, even if everything he sees and hears in the forest is unequivocally asserted by Hawthorne himself to be "true"— his ancestors, his moral preceptors and models, and virtually all other New England saints are consciously and voluntarily in league with the Devil; even granting all this, we are still forced by the logic of the tale to make an exception for Faith. Again, grant that it was *her* literal voice from the cloud which obscured Brown's view of, and seemed to obliterate his belief in, heaven; that her *real* and not spectral ribbons floated down to crush her husband's spirit; that she was really *there,* with Goodman Brown's parents, physically transported to an actual blasphemous witch-meeting; still we come to a cardinal uncertainty ("ambiguity," if you will) which cannot be resolved except by faith, either a gracious and charitable decision to believe the best or, alternately, an extreme of pernicious credulity. We know that Goodman Brown's own protracted dalliance ends in revulsion, expressed in his agonized plea that Faith "look up to heaven, and resist the wicked one" (88). This plea, we must presume, constitutes his own last-second refusal to accept an unholy baptism and communion: in spite of his earlier blasphemies, he seems to draw back at the last moral instant. But "whether Faith obeyed" his plea, we, like Goodman Brown, can never know with certainty. In the structurally climactic, epistemologically paradigmatic, and (for Goodman Brown) emotionally crucial instance, there is, evidentially, only uncertainty.

Ultimately, evidence fails. Finally, in a way Goodman Brown had little expected and is totally unprepared to accept or even comprehend, everything *does* depend on Faith. The individual can judge his own moral case. Imperfectly, no doubt, but with some legitimacy; for besides the Searcher of Hearts only he has access to the evidence of his own intentions, which are (according to Jeremy Taylor) related to his words and actions as the soul to the body. In every other case, moral judgment is irreducibly a species of faith. Morally speaking, we can observe specters flirting with the Devil, but (even if such a thing were possible) we cannot observe a soul fix itself in an evil state.

That certain people in a Puritan world might *wish* so to fix themselves, we can easily imagine: the earlier case recorded by Winthrop, of the woman who murdered her child so that she could now be *"sure* she would be damned" (my italics), is full of terrible instruction; and doubtless there were other cases of persons forcing *"a guilty identity, which was better than none."* Especially in the latter days of Puritanism, when so many people lived out whole lives of spiritual tension in a half-way status, the temptations must have been both strong and various: simply to get the whole business settled;

or authentically to accept the highly probable import of one's unremitting sinfulness (and perhaps to enjoy some sense of true significance in this world); or even to join the Devil's party out of sheer rebellion against such singularly infelicitous figures of covenant authority as Cotton Mather.[35] Thus for every village hag who practiced some crude form of image magic or evil eye to frighten her neighbors into a frenzy of self-destruction, there must have been dozens of more robust souls who saw, in Emersonian terms, their appropriate moral hypothesis quite clearly: "If I am the Devil's child, I will live then from the Devil." Yet obviously such intentions are reversible: above all else the Puritans tried to obtain *repentant* confessions from accused witches, to bring them back from the Deviant to the Normative Covenant.[36] This might strain their predestinarian logic, but not perhaps unduly. One could be as wrong about one's reprobation as about one's election: in either theological case, one "consented" but did not, himself, make the really efficacious choice; and in psychological practice, a wild, desperate, overly willful embracing of unconditional and irrevocable reprobation is probably no easier to protect from doubt or change of mood than the astonished and relieved acceptance of one's election. Even the flood of despair may one day ebb—sensing which, Ethan Brand must slay himself in a moment of cosmic blasphemy. But Goodman Brown draws back.

But this is getting slightly ahead of the immediate question, which concerns the relation of faith and evidence to the serious moral judgment of others. The question put so directly and so unavoidably to the theologically ill-prepared Goodman Brown at the climax of his forest-experience is, quite simply, Hawthorne's own version of the faith-question in its human dimension: in the face of the final breakdown of all reliable evidence concerning the hidden but defining essence of moral decisions or continuing "heart" intentions of others, which are you more prepared to believe in, goodness or badness? Much critical ink has been spilled over the *angst* of Goodman Brown's wracking doubt, his ambivalence, his inability finally to settle his belief one way or the other; and in an ultimate sense, of course, it *is* true that Brown does not hold a fixed and final conviction that his wife is in league with the Devil. But practically there is not much question. Hawthorne did not need the will-to-believe analysis of William James to tell him that theoretical doubts have a way of solving themselves in practice, in accordance with the individual's deepest suspicions; and at this level Brown's ideas are quite clear. He hears an "anthem of sin" when the congregation sings a holy psalm; he scowls while his family prays; he shrinks at midnight from the bosom of Faith; and he dies in an aura which even Puritans recognize as one of inordinate moral gloom.

To be sure, he does not die in precisely the same state of "despair" that sent him raging through the forest, challenging the Devil, burning to meet him on his own ground. At that moment his despair is universal: "there is no good on earth; and sin is but a name." At that moment it includes himself; indeed it applies to himself pre-eminently: "Come witch, come wizard, come Indian powwow, come devil himself, and here comes Goodman Brown. You may as well fear him as he fear you" (99). At that moment only does the element of hesitancy (or as one recent critic rightly insists, "ambivalence") disappear from his mental state; and as it disappears Brown becomes guilty not only of some sort of cosmic blasphemy but also of that personal and technical sort of "despair" which, in its utter abandonment of the possibility of personal redemption, constitutes the second of traditional Christianity's two unpardonable sins—the other, its obverse, being the presumption with which Brown began. But as we have said, this lurid, melodramatic phase subsides: his call upon Faith to "resist" is, in part, his way of taking back his own overly willful self-abandonment.[37] And thus, as he was initially not *entirely* certain he wanted to sneak off into the forest at all, so he is *finally* not convinced that he himself is a lost soul. Nevertheless neither his crucial refusal of baptism nor his returning ambivalence can now save him from some sort of moral gloom for which there may be no neatly prepared theological name, but which the story exists to define. Indeed Goodman Brown's final state may be his worst of all. A "brand" has indeed been "plucked from the burning," but where is the Cotton Mather who will write up the case history as a triumph of casuistry or exorcism?

Having begun by assuming that all visible sanctity was real sanctity and by presuming his own final perseverance in faith, having next despaired of *all* virtue, he ends by doubting the existence of any unblighted goodness but his own. There is simply no other way to account for the way Goodman Brown spends the rest of his life. Evidently he clings to the precious knowledge that he, at least, resisted the wicked one's final invitation to diabolical communion; accordingly, the lurid satisfactions of Satan's anti-covenant are not available to him. But neither are the sweet delights of the Communion of Saints. He knows he resisted the "last, last crime" of witchcraft, but his deepest suspicion seems to be that Faith did not resist. Or if that seems too strong a formulation for tender-minded readers, he cannot make his faith in Faith prevail. Without such a prevailing faith, he is left outside the bounds of all communion: his own unbartered soul is the only certain locus of goodness in a world otherwise altogether blasted.[38]

It would be easy enough to praise Young Goodman Brown for his recovery from the blasphemous nihilism of his mid-forest rage against the universe; for his refusal to translate his cosmic paranoia into an Ahabian plan of counterattack. Or, from another point of view, it would even be possible to suggest that if the Devil's proffered community of evil is the only community possible, perhaps he should have accepted membership instead of protecting the insular sacredness of his own separate and too precious soul. Perhaps salvation is not worth having—perhaps it is meaningless—in a universe where depravity has undone so many. But both of these moral prescriptions miss Hawthorne's principal emphasis, which, as I read the tale, is on the problem of faith and evidence; on that peculiar kind of "doubt" (in epistemological essence, really a kind of negative faith) which follows from a discrediting of evidences formerly trusted. Brown is damned to stony moral isolation because his "evidential" Puritan biases have led him all unprepared into a terrifying betrayal of Faith. He believes the Devil's spectral suggestions not merely because he is naive, though he is that; and not merely because he is incapable of the sort of evidential subtlety by which John Cotton instructed the very first members of those newly purified New England churches in the art of separating sheep and goats, or by which the Mathers sermonized the court of Oyer and Terminer on the occult art of the distinguishing of spirits.[39] Brown believes the Devil because, at one level, the projected guilt of a man in bad faith *is* specter evidence and because, even more fundamentally, absolute moral quality is related to outward appearance as a real person is to his specter.

In short, Hawthorne suggests, one had better not raise such ultimate questions at all: to do so is to risk the appearance-and-reality question in its most pernicious, even "paranoic" form. At best one would be accepting the deceptive appearances of sanctity, as Goodman Brown evidently continued to be accepted at the communion table of a community which never suspected his presumption, despair, blasphemy, and his near approach to witchcraft; or as the representative Mr. Smith of "Fancy's Show Box" is, in later times, accepted as a paragon in spite of his impressive list of sinful intentions. And at worst, if one is already in bad faith, his penetrating glimpses into the "reality" behind the appearances will be no more than spectral projections of his own guilty wishes; such are the evidences Goodman Brown accepts no less clearly than Leonard Doane or Spenser's Red Cross Knight. The truly naive will simply accept the smiling light of daytime, church-day appearances; the already compromised will "see" in others (as irrevocable commitment) what already pre-exists in themselves (as fantasy, wish, desire, or momentary intention). The only alternative would seem to be the acceptance of some ultimate and fundamental equality in a common moral struggle; a healthy skepticism about all moral appearances, firmly wedded to the faith that, whatever men may fantasize, or however they may fall, they generally love the good and hate the evil.

That such standards will suffice for all judgments except perhaps the Last, Roger Williams, Solomon Stoddard, and various Arminians variously tried to suggest—as against the main thrust of the New England Way.[40] What none of them could quite say, but what Hawthorne quite clearly saw the witchcraft "delusion" to prove, is that beyond this sort of moral and epistemological humility lie only varieties of specter evidence. And these, ironically, turn out to be species of perverted faith after all.

For, finally, once Goodman Brown's search for evidences has ended in nightmare, his enduring doubt and suspicion prove to be only an abiding "faith" in the probability of evil. Lacking conclusive evidence, he yet believes the worst of Faith. His doubt of goodness is equally a faith in evil. The Judgment of Charity (which the wariest of the Puritans always insisted was the proper rule in estimating the presence of grace and by which they almost undid their basic premises) might construe even Faith's actual presence in the forest in some lenient way; charity ought to be willing to believe that a wife would refuse a Devil at least as soon as a husband would. But bad faith precludes such charity. What determines Brown's practical disbelief in Faith and in all "other" goodness is the subconscious effect of his own dark (if ambivalent) reasons for being in the forest, reinforced no doubt by the violence of his blasphemous nihilism; the total personality, it turns out, is less supple and flexible than the "will." Brown's initial easy-faith in his own election, which makes everything else possible, is based on the evidence of his acceptance (finally!) into a community of professing, visible saints. His final gloomy-faith in the reprobation of the rest of his world is based on the suppression and outward projection of his own continuing fallenness. Goodman Brown believes the Devil's specter evidence because ultimately it coincides with his own guilty projections; indeed the "levels" of the "allegory" collapse so perfectly that the specter evidence produced by the Devil's most potent magic becomes indistinguishable from the bad dream of a man in bad faith. Goodman Brown's supposedly inadmissible faith has, to paraphrase Poe, indeed "flown away." And whether "In a vision, or in none, / Is it therefore the less *gone?*" The note of finality seems cruel, but so, apparently, are the pitfalls of visible sanctity for a Young Calvinist Saint.

4

Hawthorne will return to the question of faith and evidence, most significantly in "Rappaccini's Daughter" at the climax of his second, or "Old Manse," period. There the "vile empiric" will turn out to be not any scientific experimenter or positivist, but the Brown-like Giovanni Guasconti, who loses his Dantesque Beatrice for many of the same reasons Goodman Brown loses his Spenserian Faith. By then, Hawthorne's fictional arguments will have caught up with contemporaneous religious questions; in the case of

"Rappaccini's Daughter," with the "miracles controversy" raging three-sidedly among Calvinists, Unitarians, and Transcendentalists, and with the universal problem of the fate of "historical Christianity" of which that controversy is a part.[41] But in the early and middle 1830's, Hawthorne is not yet writing "the History of His Own Time." His outlook is still dominated by his wide and perceptive readings in seventeenth-century Puritanism; the subjects of his most penetrating analyses are still Puritans trapped by the moral definitions of their historical world. As with "The Gentle Boy," "Young Goodman Brown" unarguably demonstrates that Hawthorne's most powerful early stories grew directly out of an authentic and creative encounter with the Puritan mind.

The neo-Puritan Calvinism of Hawthorne's own nineteenth-century world was, despite its fairly widespread continuance of the structures begun with the Half-Way Covenant of 1662, not obsessively concerned with the attempt to unite the visible church with the invisible. Most local New England religious communities were still divided into "the church" (of converted saints) and "the congregation" (of hopeful, or interested, or habitual service-attenders); often the line divided families in half, or even into more disproportionate fractions; but the explosive potential seemed to be going out of such divisions. Despite the undeniable effect of successive waves of revival enthusiasm which stressed the saving (and normative) importance of a converting "Christian experience," New England seemed to be on its way to learning the lesson summarized so succinctly, much later, by the heroine of Harold Frederic's most Hawthornean novel: "The sheep and the goats are to be separated on Judgment Day, but not a minute sooner. In other words, as long as human life lasts, good, bad and indifferent are all braided up together in every man's nature, and every woman's too."[42] Hawthorne was, no doubt, helping to teach or to reinforce that lesson—along with everyone else involved in any way with "the moral argument against Calvinism." But it was a lesson already pretty well learned in practice, if not a doctrine settled in theory. And it would be doing Hawthorne no essential service to assert this sort of contemporary "relevance" as one of the chief claims to greatness of "Young Goodman Brown."[43] The past could not explain the present until its own logic were discerned.

"Young Goodman Brown" is a dazzling achievement of the historical imagination as such; and its greatness cannot be accounted for without close and continuous reference to its insight into the psychology of religion in New England, especially in its most "troubled" period. From one point of view, "Young Goodman Brown" may well be "Freud Anticipated"; from another, it unquestionably is "Spenser Applied." But it applies the Spenserian teaching to New England's problems of specter evidence and visible sanctity as precisely as "The May-Pole of Merry Mount" applies the Mil-

305

tonic doctrines of mythic innocence and historic fall to the problem of America's imaginative (and political) state; or, later, as surely as "The Celestial Rail-road" would apply Bunyan; or "Rappaccini's Daughter," Dante; or "Ethan Brand," Goethe—to problems which had a specific American context and quiddity. And if "Young Goodman Brown" is one of Hawthorne's more stunning anticipations of Freudian themes, it *discovers* these themes in the historical record, not only in the painful testimony of men who were lewdly tempted at night by the "specter" of the local prostitute, but also in that distressing record of the moral identity crisis which two generations of saints had inevitably if inadvertently prepared for a third. Granted the "enthusiastic" decision of the 1630's to depart from all previous Reformation practice and require virtual "proof" of sainthood for full membership in Congregations of Visible Saints; and granted the existence of scores of diaries and spiritual autobiographies from the first and second generations of New England saints—documents written "Of Providence, For Posterity," solemnly charging the son "to know and love the great and most high god . . . of his father"; granted these, the piteous and fearful experience of Puritanism's third generation was indeed inevitable.[44] And Hawthorne has enfigured it all, with classic economy and without misplaced romantic sympathy, in the tragic career of Young Goodman Brown.

First of all, Hawthorne has completely elided the sentimental question of "persecuted innocence" which, as Michael Bell has shown, so obsessed the popular romancers who dealt with the episode of 1692. Furthermore, he has got beyond all naive versions of the question of witchcraft "guilt"—individual or collective, unique or commonplace, original or actual, self-limiting or transmitted, which troubled those of his more professionally historical contemporaries who knew or cared enough to consider the problem, and with which he himself wrestled somewhat clumsily (if honestly) in the beginning and end of "Alice Doane's Appeal."[45] In *this*, though not in *every* instance, Hawthorne is a writer of *psychohistorical* fiction; as such, and with the full authority of Scott behind him, he has gone straight to the task of creating a doctrinally adequate and dramatically believable version of "how it might have felt" to live in the moral climate of Puritanism's most troubled years. The imaginative insight which lies behind "Young Goodman Brown" may stand as a significant part of Hawthorne's reasons for being so "fervently" glad to have been born beyond the temporal limits of the Puritan world. Hawthorne was, to be sure, far from unique in preferring the moral climate of the 1830's to that of the 1690's: perhaps only a minority of his readers (in Boston, or Salem, or Concord, at least) *really* felt that America had declined, even from the *best* qualities of the *noblest* figures of the *first* generation of Puritan Fathers; and, less tendentiously, it would imply no very impressive moral or political virtue to prefer the liberal utterances of William Ellery

Channing to the Jeremiad rhetoric of *The Spirit of the Pilgrims.* But no one else in Hawthorne's generation was able to dramatize with such compelling clarity, and with so firm a grasp of the psychological implications of doctrine, what the older system might have meant to a representative individual conscience. And beyond this achievement of history as psychological vivification, there is the brilliant hypothesis by which Hawthorne has offered Goodman Brown's representative encounters with the spectral world as a comment on the meaning of witchcraft in the specific context of latter-day Puritan experience.

Aside from those who have set out to blacken the Puritans by cliché and oversimplification, modern commentators were once at pains to prove that there is no operable or intelligible connection between New England's Puritanism and its problems with witchcraft. The American Puritans, it was tediously reiterated, executed fewer witches and gave over the whole enterprise of witch-hunting sooner than enlightened men and practicing Christians elsewhere. The whole accumulated bulk of such arguments, I think, would not have impressed Hawthorne. He heard the argument, at its source, from Charles Upham in 1831; and while he may have appreciated it as a subtler response than that of the romancers (who kept insisting that the persecution of supposed witches was simply the most horrendous form of Puritanism's hysterical intolerance), he seems to have seen that it conflated two questions which must be kept distinct. For to establish that up to a certain point in human history, everybody believed in and, from time to time, hunted witches is not quite to demonstrate that the belief in witchcraft, or the impulse to become a witch, or the need to expose and punish this form of deviancy has had, in all times and all places, precisely the same meaning.[46] Perhaps we could admit, a priori, that deep down at its psychic source, all witchcraft is the same witchcraft—just as, presumably, all Oedipal strife or all anal fixation reveals a single, "structural" morphology. But, obviously, that is not the only sort of "meaning" witchcraft might have. There remains the question of witchcraft as an event in intellectual history: what do various witches, witch-hunters, and skeptical critics have to *say* about the meaning of their actions? Such declarations might be a species of rationalization, either cheap or elegant; but people *do* put constructions on the most elemental responses; they *do* strive to find names for and thus make intelligible to themselves even those actions to which they are driven by their most unopposable "drives." And in this sense, New England witchcraft has its own fairly unique meaning.

Certainly the everyone-did-it arguments would have astonished those men who wrote about witchcraft in New England between 1684 and 1705, including those who either attacked or defended the proceedings of 1692. Not one of them could doubt that what was happening was directly connected with New England's existence as a covenanted community of proven saints, a saving remnant against whom the powers of darkness were most likely to be arrayed; at very least, what was happening had to do with certain people's *vision* of New England in these terms. In a sense it is our very "enlightenment" which is likely to mislead us here: the fact that "such things happened everywhere," and the discovery that, therefore, the Puritans were by our enlightened standards "no worse" than anyone else, is likely to blind us to the unique meanings witchcraft may have had in a (still) fairly unique Puritan world. Hawthorne is not so blinded. His suggestion is that, whatever might be the meaning of witchcraft elsewhere, in New England in 1692 it is not to be considered apart from the larger problem that Puritan Sons were having in trying to keep the outlines of the moral world as clear as they had been in the minds of those Puritan Fathers who first defined the community's project of salvation. And this, according to Cotton Mather, in despite of the Devil's own devices: after many "abortive" attempts at the "extirpation of the vine which God has here planted," his growing, latter-day desperation has impelled him to make

one attempt more upon us, an attempt more difficult, more surprising, more snarled with unintelligible circumstances than any hither to encountered, an attempt so critical that if we shall get through, we shall soon enjoy halcyon days with all the vultures of hell trodden under our feet.[47]

Thus the witchcraft episode tried the eschatological identity of New England. And thus "Young Goodman Brown" epitomizes its entire faith-experience.

The reader of "Young Goodman Brown" needs to keep constantly in mind the first theological premises and the latter-day ecclesiological practices of the Puritan economy of salvation. For the Puritan, salvation "by faith" was in a sense "voluntary"—God does not save geese; but it was by no means a free option depending critically on the originating impulse of man. Rather, it was an event which the human will might or might not experience, according to the hidden "Pleasure" (or, for the more rationally inclined, the "Wisdom") of God. But if the "Reason" of the Divine Decrees lay hidden in His mysterious and transcendent essence, the results of those decrees were a good deal more clear; no Puritan could understand *why* he was elected *while still* a sinner and *in spite of* his sinfulness, but none was allowed to remain ignorant of what followed if indeed he *were* so elected; and, in the seventeenth century, at least, it was the rare congregation which permitted the spiritually unsure to relax into a state of settled neutrality on the question of regenerating experience. After all sorts of appropriate distinctions had been made and a range of individual differences allowed for, the Puritan system (defined by 1636 and not *essentially* compromised in 1662) depended radically on the Church's fairly sound ability to determine who was and who was not elect of God. On all necessary occasions the Puritan apologist could, of course, argue that "visible sanctity" meant no more than sanctity insofar as that mysterious quality could ever *be* visible—that is, relatively and not absolutely, with human approximation rather than divine certitude. But in the end, as Hawthorne seemed to know, the defining essence of American Puritanism, socially considered, is its rather confident attempt to locate by profession, institutionalize by covenant, and monitor by discipline Christian Experience as such. No modest ambition.

Small wonder, then, if such a group begins its witchcraft investigations with sufficient confidence in its ability to identify witches, those actively hostile anti-saints. If a people is accustomed to sift the relatively delicate evidence that constituted the rainbow-like shadings of the conversion experience—from the inconclusively preparatory to the definitively sanctified—surely the distinguishing of witches would prove a simple matter by comparison. Evidentially speaking, depravity should be far cruder and more obvious than sanctity; the ultimate depravity should immediately expose itself by its very lurid and melodramatic colorings. And, once the problem was fairly raised and widely discussed, the Puritan system seemed to depend as essentially on the institutional identification of witches as of saints: not only psychologically or sociologically, as a certain style of normative behavior may seem to require and create an appropriate deviancy in mirror image of itself, but also as a confirmation of the epistemology which underlay orthodoxy and a guarantee of the logic which confirmed identity.

If the Mathers (and all others who opposed the "un-American" innovations of Solomon Stoddard) were correct, the New Englanders were God's Chosen Saints, or they were nobody. It was precisely *because* they were saints, organized and mobilized as such, that they were now being exposed to an end-time plague of witches. If witch-identity could not be confirmed, then how could their own? Hence the "Several Ministers Consulted" must call for "speedy and vigorous prosecution," in spite of their own clear warnings about the Devil's undoubted ability to appear "in the Shape of an innocent, yea, and a virtuous Man."[48] And hence the sense of intellectual desperation in Cotton Mather's own after-the-fact defense of the tainted procedures of Stoughton's bloody-minded Oyer and Terminer. Failing to impress Robert Calef or Perry Miller, he would yet convince some more evangelical reader that unless witchcraft could *somehow* be detected, "all the rules of understanding human affairs [were] at an end." Grant the Devil all conceivable guile and subtlety, and concede man's own innate capacity for sin and error, still the confession of some final, unresolvable ambiguity about matters thus invisible "threatens no less than a sort of dissolution upon the world."[49] Certain forms of moral skepticism were, quite apparently, altogether inconsistent with the dominant form of the Puritans' ecclesiastical faith.

One had always been warned, of course, about hypocrites in the Church; and one was moderately well prepared to grant and accept the presence within the holy community of a few people who were simply wrong about their conversion. With less equanimity, perhaps, one could even accustom oneself to the bold reprobate who simulated grace for social advantage. Such cases simply indicated the practical "limits" toward which the theory of visible sanctity could only approximate. But what if it should prove utterly impossible to detect a witch? What if, in a given case, all the available evidence made it impossible to decide whether a given person belonged to God's Covenant or to the Devil's Party? Then one had indeed reached the inevitable outer limit of one's world—and, if the question of Saint or Witch seemed vital, the reduction to absurdity of one's fundamental premises. Then, presumably, it was time to give over the whole attempt to make church-exclusions based on "visible" moral distinctions and return, in *some* manner, to a more lax Presbyterian system (not to say "free and catholic spirit") of including everyone who was willing to announce his intention to do good and avoid evil. This *could* mean "Stoddardism," but that was not the only alternative. It *had* to mean a recognition that Augustine was right after all: there is, on earth, no way to identify the invisible church with the visible. And it also created a strong presumption in favor of Williams' rather than Cotton's reading of the parable of the wheat and the tares.[50]

In this ultimate context, what "Young Goodman Brown" dramatizes is the final failure of all "visible" (or any humanly "outerable") moral evidence. To the explicit destruction of Goodman Brown, and to the implicit confounding of the Puritan system, "Young Goodman Brown" takes up where the carefully controlled, even exasperatedly technical definitions of "Alice Doane's Appeal" leave off: it lets us watch a representative latter-day Puritan fail the ultimate test of faith and undergo moral self-destruction precisely when it becomes impossible to tell whether his wife is a saint or a witch.

Brown's enduring suspicion of his whole world, but especially of his wife, gives us a quiet and reduced version of that melodramatic moment of madness Hawthorne describes in "Main Street"—when "among the multitude . . . there is horror, fear, and distrust; and friend looks askance at friend, and the husband at his wife, and even the mother at her little child." There, as Hawthorne tries to be a fairly "regular historian" of the public frenzy of 1692, the problem is that "in every creature God has made, they suspected a witch, or dreaded an accuser."[51] But here, as we have said, the public frenzy and the courtroom accusation are absent; and accordingly, Hawthorne's approach is more radical. No doubt much of the historical record of 1692 is to be explained in terms of spectral deceits not unlike the ones revealed in "Alice Doane's Appeal" and "Young Goodman Brown," but the ultimate question lies deeper. What Hawthorne suggests is that the "real" breakdown of faith in Salem Village and its "enfigured" loss by Goodman Brown are both the result of Puritanism's ecclesiastical positivism, of its definitive attempt to found a Church (and beyond it a State) on the premise that visible sanctity can be made to approximate true sanctity. For Hawthorne, such a system could *only* end in nightmare: it introduced evidence into a system where only faith could be appropriate and salutary.[52]

The witchcraft episode provided the logically necessary (if humanly regrettable) test. When in a spectral epiphany you realized you *could* not tell a saint from a witch, your logical world, by logical necessity, collapsed. When you realized that the Devil's ability to "transform himself into an Angel of Light" could be used one day as an argument against Stoughton's injudicious handling of specter evidence, and another day as a way to discredit an impressive, last-second Gallows Hill protestation by George Burroughs, then someone would surely *see* it had collapsed. Robert Calef saw it: his account of Cotton Mather's behavior at the execution of George Burroughs is extremely revealing. And certainly Hawthorne saw it: when a moving profession of faithfulness (such as ordinarily sufficed for admission into Puritanism's full communion) could be discredited with the same slogan used to caution aggressive witch hunters, then Mather's chosen world had dissolved indeed.[53]

Thus it is scarcely surprising to hear Mather regret the need to mention "so much as the first letters" of the name of "this G. B.," and hardly overreading to notice they are the initials of Goodman Brown as well.[54] For although "Alice Doane's Appeal" evokes the Burroughs episode more directly than does "Young Goodman Brown," still the logical contortions into which this case forced Mather are built into the very structure of this tale as well. Indeed the story may be, in this last, logical sense, about the fall of Cotton Mather, whom it forces us to "identify" in a fairly direct way.

We can pretend, of course, that the reference to Martha Carrier as that "rampant hag" who had "received the devil's promise to be queen of hell" (86) quotes Mather's *Wonders* merely to put us in mind of that lost world when (according to the convention of "The Hollow of the Three Hills") "fantastic dreams and madmen's reveries were realized among the actual circumstances of life." But what are we to make of the more gratuitous observation that the entirely fictive father of the entirely fictive Brown "had an indescribable air of one who knew the world, and who would not have felt abashed at the governor's dinner table or in King William's court, were it possible that affairs should call him thither" (76)? The Devil is a worldly man, no doubt; and well acquainted, too, as he will claim, with "a majority of the Great and General Court" (77); but in fact it is Cotton Mather's own literal father, Increase, who was, at the very moment, away on political business at the court of King William—securing the appointment of the new governor, who would empower the witchcraft court Mather's *Wonders* would elect to defend. The names have been changed, but less to protect the innocent than to expose the logic.

The ultimate irony of "Young Goodman Brown," historically considered, is that Mather's fictional metonym is forced, on his behalf, to endure his own direst prediction. Mather lives, if not happily ever after, yet well and long enough to compose, in the *Magnalia,* the most elaborately contrived and meretriciously rationalized defense of the premise of "visible sanctity" the Puritanic mind could ever imagine. But Goodman Brown is left without defense, without excuse. Recovering from some too willful certainty that we live in what "may too reasonably be called the Devil's World,"[55] his only retreat is to a world dissolved of spiritual certainty, where all the old rules of understanding human affairs are indeed at an end. Too late, we fear, he rudely learns what no paternal guidance ever thought to say: the invisible world is, at last, entirely a matter of faith.

5

In *Grandfather's Chair* Hawthorne offers May 1692 as the end of the "era of the Puritans." The event which marks the break is the death of Old Simon Bradstreet, "the sole representative of [the] departed brotherhood" of Original-Charter governors; after that "Sir William Phips then arrived in Boston with a new charter from King William and a commission to be governor."[56] Such indeed are the political realities, and so indeed might the story be divided for children. But in a far more fundamental sense, "Young Goodman Brown" shows us that witchcraft "ended" the Puritan world. Its logic of evidence could not stand the Devil's own test of faith.

We now know, of course, that it is unhistorical to imagine a massive popular revulsion against a clerical oligarchy which hurried a well-meaning but unsteady populace into a frenzy of suspicion and judicial murder. And yet there may be some reason to believe that the events of 1692 really did accelerate a growing disbelief in human ability to chart the invisible world.[57] To be sure, the New Charter forbade New England to use proven sainthood as the sole requirement for provincial citizenship; but it may not be altogether wishful to believe that the terrible discoveries made in 1692 about the positively diabolical subtleties of spiritual evidence, and about the pre-eminent human need for Faith as a Judgment in Charity, may have hastened the realization that all temporal separations of sheep and goats are premature. If so, then the Puritans' first religious premise would be as intolerable as their first political premise was intolerant. The statistics concerning the desire for full communion just before and just after the events of 1692 are not available. It is clear, however, that the popularity of "Stoddardism" continued to grow, and that the hegemony of the Mathers was about to be challenged, from within their own sphere of influence, by persons who believed in the premises underlying a church of visible saints even less than did Stoddard. It is probably more than coincidence that one of the founders of the Brattle Street Church, which admitted all baptized persons to full communion and discontinued the tests for specific Christian experience, had written, in 1692, a fairly cogent letter against the basic assumptions of the witchcraft proceedings, and that he seems to have furnished Calef with his materials for *More Wonders*. And worlds of skeptical faith might fairly be read into Samuel Sewall's recognition of how the truth had eluded his most judicious search in that matter of "doleful witchcraft."[58]

But whatever should turn out to be the case in statistical or other "regular" history, the moral historian's view is clear: in confusion and with a hopelessly inadequate sense of what faith might require, Goodman Brown has come to the end of the Puritan moral world; his inevitable moral collapse enfigures the logic by which the quest for visible sanctity leads unavoidably into the realm of specter evidence. A more authentic, less institutional form of Puritan piety might yet be "revived"—in the Great Awakening, or "The Minister's Black Veil"; the political dynamism of Puritanism might be "reawakened"—in the various moments which make "The Legends of the Province House" bristle with the hostility of Endicott. But the power of "visible sanctity" to organize the American world ended in 1692. And the credibility of the logic by which it proposed to do so disappeared in doubt when Hawthorne's Goodman Brown discovered that only faith could save his Faith from doubt. Without accepting a fundamental change of premises, Puritanism could, like Goodman Brown, continue to exist only as "gloom."

❦ Six ❦

THE TRUE SIGHT OF SIN
PARSON HOOPER AND THE POWER OF BLACKNESS

THE CASE of Parson Hooper is more difficult than that of Goodman Brown—arguably it is the most difficult of all Hawthorne's cases of Puritan conscience.[1] On the one hand, "intrinsically," the text itself seems to thwart interpretation, as if neither Hooper *nor* Hawthorne quite understood the "ambiguity of sin or sorrow" in which he became enveloped. Rationalists might suspect obscurantism, and theorists discover indeterminacy; but perhaps the old ("New") critics were right, for once, to protest that the tendency to explain everything is simply wrong-headed; that, unlike the Emersonian universe, a Hawthorne text cannot be counted on to answer all the questions it raises.[2] And, on the other hand, "extrinsic" or "contextual" aids to interpretation have been hard to come by. The "fact" that Hooper once preached before Governor Belcher (1730–1741) has been noticed, but it has produced neither a shock of critical recognition nor a flood of historical commentary. To be sure, many critics regard the tale as "historical," but they have been unable to "place" Hooper in any significant stretch of Puritan history.[3]

Perhaps, therefore, "The Minister's Black Veil" should be thought of not only as the most ambiguous but also as the most nominal of Hawthorne's tales of the Puritans, not at all an analysis of motivation and behavior under the pressures of some well-defined historical moment, but only a generalized evocation of some putative psychological essence, such as "Puritan Subjectivity." Or, perhaps, even more radically, it represents the terminus toward which Hawthorne's other fictional researches were all along tending, the point where specific events altogether failed to embody his "deeper" meanings. Or perhaps we missed something.

At the outset, then, the task of interpretation is double: not only to grasp, if we can, some intuition of the approximate depth and drift of Hooper's meaning, but also to inquire whether his career of exacerbated subjectivity contains any clues to a principle of historical representation. Only if we fail in the first should our bottom line read "ambiguity." And only if we fail in the second will we be forced to seek the magical rescue of modernism—whether the personal obsession with sex and solipsism or the more properly authorial compulsion to play with the self-reference of all signs.[4] Both these meta-problems lurk here, of course, at least as ominously as they do in the darkness which surrounds the highlighting of any text. And we can always explore them, whenever we conclude the old laws no longer apply. But if we are patient we may yet discover "The Minister's Black Veil" as a model of Hawthorne's "moral history" at its most complex and demanding.

1
🎔🎔

At first glance Hooper's difficulties appear deep indeed. Though attempts to link him to Dimmesdale in terms of specific guilt are probably misdirected, Hooper does seem a "forestudy" of intense introspection and privateness. And surely Hooper is a more challenging "figure," if not a more fully developed "character," than Goodman Brown, having seen or felt things beyond the range of that Average Sensual Puritan. If we cannot accept the critical judgment that Hooper succeeds just where Brown fails, still it is from Hooper's level of consciousness that we most effectively sound the depths of Brown's shallows.[5] Hooper's tone is, *almost* everywhere, milder, sadder, wiser; his style less declamatory and sophomoric. Surely he is the deepest of Hawthorne's early Puritan figures. For once, it almost seems, Hawthorne has given us an adequately complex, if not entirely sympathetic, presentation of the psychological equivalent of Puritan separatism.

And yet Hooper's career reveals distressing similarities to that of Richard Digby. However complicated, ambiguous, modern, and adequate may be Hooper's understanding, his *fate* seems identical to that of Hawthorne's crudest Puritan *figura*. Indeed it seems likely that "The Man of Adamant" was written after "The Minister's Black Veil," as something of a simple gloss on a meaning that had somehow got too complicated.[6] Perhaps the paradox will bear a little inspection.

The outline of Digby's moral progress is, we recall, very simple: his sense of being unique separates him from the community; the separation is hardened by his refusal of the graces not only of a woman's love but indeed of all natural influences; thus alienated, he damns himself to stony solipsism. Stated thus generally, the outline will also work for the moral career of Hooper. And surely the image of him, at the end of his life, as a "dark old man" who has effectively severed all his former (indeed all natural) ties with the community is an evocation of the Digby syndrome. The clear suggestion about Hooper is that he loses all chance for human communion when his veil prevents the consummation of his marriage to Elizabeth and causes his congregation to suspend their invitations to Sunday dinner. From a "structural" point of view, "The Man of Adamant" and "The Minister's Black Veil" are the same story. Their essential action is identical: a self-regarding protagonist confirms his potentially solipsistic separation by refusing natural graces. The Digby "mytheme." Period.

Still—says the less strict voice of a more semantic (and potentially historical) interpretation—once all this has been observed, a number of important qualifications spring to mind. Granted that in these two stories (as in so many others) Hawthorne is generally at pains to "deplore all attempts to step aside" from "the common highway of life,"[7] nevertheless the particular deployment of meaning is really quite different. Hooper's initial "separating" insight does not seem morally arrogant; indeed nothing could seem further from Digby's belief in the uniqueness of his own salvation than Hooper's sense that *all* men treasure up secret guilt. Further, the "amiable" Mr. Hooper seems far less simply hostile to other people: he tries, in his way, to share his insight with them; and his refusal of the gracious Elizabeth seems infinitely more ambivalent than Digby's hysterical rejection of the angelic Mary Goffe. Indeed one might argue that Hooper is separated because no one else can come up to his standard of honesty or level of moral apprehension; that he merely suffers the fate of any prophet whose message is too profoundly true for the majority of his hearers to accept. And, however complete his isolation, metaphysically considered, he does continue to minister to the community, from behind his veil and smile.

Clearly all these differences are significant. In one sense our response to Hooper may depend on whether we concentrate on the shape of the essential action or choose to immerse ourselves in all the psychological particulars. But however we choose, it would be both sentimental and critically naive to ignore altogether the features of Digby behind the veil of Hooper. Because there is, evidently, something of that "purest" of the Puritans in Hooper, not even his Dimmesdalean sensitivity can save him. Worlds beyond Goodman Brown in point of perception and moral logic, he is still (somehow) not at all beyond the simplistic absolutism of Digby. And not at all beyond Puritanism.

Which brings us to our second preliminary consideration—Hooper's historical meaning, his possible significance as "representative" Puritan. And here, where particularities may be supposed to matter most, details of doctrinal difference may count for more than outlines of structural similarity. If, in the one view, Hooper already seems a relatively complicated case of the Puritan as Separatist, he may yet appear as a particularly subtle example of the imaginative recovery and symbolic representation of the authentically Puritan "true sight" of sin.

Evidently Hooper avoids the vulgar errors of Puritan epistemology. First of all, he does not make the paranoid distinction between his own moral case and that of everybody else. Quite the reverse. If anything, he feels himself (like Jonathan Edwards) the very worst of sinners. More technically, of course, it may be truer to say that, far more than anybody else, he simply sees his own sin "clearly" and "convictingly." Following the explicit instructions of somebody like Thomas Hooker, let us say, he has grasped the root fact of his own pervasive and interior sinfulness "not in the appearance and paint of it but in the power of it; not . . . in the notion and conceit only, but . . . with Application."⁸ Thus Hooper may indeed *be* different. He may, as a sort of Puritan hero of consciousness, *see* more than anyone else about the dark mysteries of the Secret Sinful Self. But ultimately, as he sees things, all men *are* in the same condition of being trapped behind a veil of sinful subjectivity, and all should be able to see themselves in exactly the same terrifying way. Accordingly, therefore, Hooper sees nothing so plainly as the deceptiveness of all moral appearances. To judge by any such appearances is, in his severely Puritan view, to live by social compromises rather than by the knowledge of reality as it stands in the mind of God, the only true Searcher of Hearts. And, Puritan fashion, he evidently refuses to live by any less absolute standard.

Thus Hooper's career can fairly be said to begin where Brown's ends: the sadly smiling minister seems to know there is no human way to tell whether saint or witch lurks behind the veil of human subjectivity. Perhaps he even realizes that in most ways there is *no* difference. Yet the insight does not save him. Having exposed the theory of visible sanctity for the easy presumption it most assuredly is, and having confronted his not-very-Puritan congregation with the laxity of their eighteenth-century premises and perceptions, he seems himself to become obsessed with the very idea of the pervasiveness and ineluctability of human moral secretness. Because all social intercourse is based on some compromise, he effectively rejects it altogether. Or at least he loses it. The man who will accept nothing less than God's truth, and who finds that such truth is embodied in no human institution and validates no human relationship, is evidently doomed to solipsism and rejection of life as utterly as is Goodman Brown. Or as Richard Digby, the separatist paradigm of them both.

This thematic formulation of "The Minister's Black Veil" takes us closer to the provincial heart of American Puritanism than does any other Hawthorne tale. The normal, social assumption of that historic creed, so plainly on trial in "Young Goodman Brown," is that once putative Christians have learned to put aside all moral, theological, and ecclesiological compromises, the result will be a Church of Saints separated out from a World of Sinners; that in grace the ability to distinguish the Kingdom of Light from the Kingdom of Darkness approaches certainty as a sort of asymptotic limit. And this Hawthornean discovery would seem in many ways to be the defining rationale of Puritan experience as we now most usefully understand it. But the case of Parson Hooper reminds us that there is probably a deeper premise still, of which visible sanctity is only one not-quite-necessary application. That far-more-absolutist premise touches the human possibility and religious necessity of discovering, under the aspect of depravity, and of communicating, through the medium of symbol, some fundamental truth about the moral status of the human Self as such. And some such premise is evidently on trial in "The Minister's Black Veil."

Probably it is this very "essential" character of Hooper's experience that has made it seem unnecessary to locate any proximate context for his revealing-and-concealing action of self-veiling. To those critics concerned with the Romantic and modern problem of subjectivity itself, the import has seemed clear enough. On Hawthorne's more historical critics Hooper's words and actions have simply imposed themselves—as an ultimate and paradigmatic Puritan gesture, however unique in literature or absurd under the aspect of Governor Belcher. And for certain purposes it probably is enough to know the moral geography and mythic sequence: beyond Goodman Brown and on his way to being Dimmesdale, Hooper is nevertheless, in his absolutism, still a Digby-figure.

Yet Hooper is not quite an archetype. And the way to discover this is to place his experience in the New England of the 1730's and 1740's. Hooper "flourishes," it turns out, during precisely those crucial years of the "Great Awakening." Once we take this historical fact seriously, everything begins to make a much fuller and firmer sense. Hooper, we are expected to see, is an "awakened Puritan," living in the midst of decent and common-sensical but not spiritually illuminated Yankees. Most simply: Hooper somehow recovers or "revives" an older insight into the problem of sin and the self; thereupon, he forces his hapless congregation to the limits of their slackened, eighteenth-century consciences. In doing so he presents himself to us as the figure of Hawthorne's Puritan par excellence, the prophetic preacher of "the true sight of sin."

What follows as a result of his awakening insight and prophetic gesture is significant indeed. Although Hawthorne never emphasizes sociology, the alienation of Hooper from a significant number of his parishioners provides a classic image of the social dynamics of the phenomenon historians have come to call "Revivalism and Separatism in New England."[9] It also tells us much about the schizophrenic split that seemed to occur in the collective American consciousness in the eighteenth century, with Edwards on one

318

side and Franklin on the other—New England contemporaries who seem to us to have lived in different universes. Startling as it may seem to critics who have thought of Hooper's career primarily as a proof text for Hawthorne's obsessive involvement in Puritan gloom, or Romantic subjectivity, or Victorian sexual fear, or Existentialist absurdity, or Modern artistic alienation, there really is more historically disciplined observation about the exact moral causes of specific social effects in "The Minister's Black Veil" than in "The Gentle Boy" or "Young Goodman Brown." To be sure, we get no shouting or swooning, and very little hint of itinerant preaching and intra-congregational bitterness; just as, elsewhere, we get nothing about accusations, trials, and executions. But we do get an absolutely firm sense of the relation between a heightened spiritual awareness and the disruption of ordinary affairs.

Nevertheless, the emphasis is primarily on the meaning of Hooper's own troubled but instructive career. Puritanism, we are thus permitted to see, *is* awakening: in essence its peculiar style of "piety" is nothing but an expanded consciousness of the self under the aspect of hidden but pervasive "sin." As such it is a far from trivial form of moral intelligence. Indeed it may look like the highest form of Truth itself. In the very next moment, however, or in the order of praxis, all sorts of difficulties begin to appear. A sinful self can be a True Self only For Itself—or in the sight of God. And so the problem of what follows practically, at the level of community, from the Puritan consciousness of sin becomes the source of a whole new range of ambiguities which that consciousness itself has no power to resolve. Sin separates. Absolute sin separates absolutely. Granted that God may forgive any man, still no one else can know for certain that He has; so that this side of the Last Judgment all human communities are compromises. And Hooper is unwilling to compromise his insight.

Hooper is no self-righteous, sectarian "Pope in his own Parish." But it is hard to believe that his arch-Puritan solution to the problem of sin and community is a very happy one. After a long career of mild and indulgent alienation, his final hour is strident as well as gloomy, and Hawthorne is careful to carve "no hopeful verse upon his tombstone." All his honesty and all his insight are not enough, apparently, to save him from the terrible loneliness of solitary sainthood.[10]

2

"The Minister's Black Veil" opens with an image of the integrity of ordinary life—the natural goodness of which only a very strict Puritan would deny, but from which Hooper is about to exile himself. The vision of the sunshine of natural benevolence and illumination falling "peacefully on the cottages and fields" might appall Richard Digby, but it is supposed to appeal to the ordinary reader. And even more reassuring is the human scene this Sabbath morning:

> The sexton stood in the porch of Milford meeting-house, pulling lustily at the bell-rope. The old people of the village came stooping along the street. Children, with bright faces, tripped merrily behind their parents, or mimicked a graver gait, in the conscious dignity of their Sunday clothes. Spruce bachelors looked sidelong at pretty maidens, and fancied that the Sabbath sunshine made them prettier than on weekdays. (37)[11]

As in a well-composed picture, everything is very satisfactory. Everybody is there (except, at this point, Hooper) in a setting that seems solid, suitable, and sufficient to the purpose; it seems good to be alive in God's world, going to an act of common celebration, on the day which the Lord has made. What, in such a world, could possibly be wrong?

Nothing very drastic, surely. Endicott himself might be hard pressed to find a fault. To be sure, this eighteenth-century congregation is not noticeably "Puritan" according to Hawthorne's sense. They seem to treat the Sabbath as something of an innocent holiday, a thing Hawthorne believed it never was in the sterner seventeenth century. But no one will suppose that this dignified and decorous group will move from divine service to an afternoon of "sports and pastimes": Puritan solidarity and bourgeois domesticity have overcome too utterly for anything like that. The people's sense of natural pleasure carries with it no hint of "mirth" or "jollity," and the idea of revelry, debauchery, or conscious debasement is, here, simply incredible. And besides, there is no Endicott-narrator to protest that there is no such thing as natural experience which is "merely innocent," or as a "thing indifferent"; and no holidays that are not really holy days. So what could be wrong?

A strict Sabbatarian might worry about the new clothes and the mild flirtatiousness of the young. Jonathan Edwards, for example, in his *Faithful Narrative of Surprising Conversions*, makes such youthful worldliness almost as telling a sign of a people's unconverted state as a subtle and silent creeping Arminianism.[12] But our narrator is not nearly so scrupulous: he finds the Sabbath being "profaned" only later when, ironically, loud talk and "ostentatious laughter" try to dispel the gloomy shock of Hooper's prophetic gesture and searching sermon (40). And our own first impression is likely to be either personal relief or historical tolerance: by this time (the late 1720's or early 1730's) the strict piety of the original Puritans has simply worn off.

The Puritan Sabbath is still observed, no doubt. But the congregation does not seem to be expecting either a Jeremiad or a stiff, Hooker-like, preparationist sermon on the nature and effects of sin; and their reaction to their minister's veil suggests that they have grown unaccustomed to unwonted displays of deep or eccentric piety. This congregation is, quite clearly, "backslidden"; but who are we to lament that? Or to imagine that Hawthorne himself is not "fervently" thankful for being so many steps "further from them in the march of ages"? Religion in New England, we are likely to conclude, has merely the status of religion anywhere else, and pending some deeper insight we sense nothing particularly wrong with this. God is still in His heaven; but in His world He lets His people be.

If there is any loaded word in the first paragraph, any hint of a meaning that runs subtly counter to the dominant impression of natural integrity, it is of course "conscious." The "conscious dignity" of the children is the only verbal clue we have to the fact that the story is ultimately about kinds and degrees of consciousness. And by the standards implied in Hooper's donning of the symbolic veil, a heightened consciousness is not a distinguishing mark of this particular eighteenth-century congregation.

We are not told what generally occupies the minds of the middle-aged and elderly persons of this unawakened "Milford," but we should not be surprised if they seem determined to take things as they appear in the light of common sense. Perhaps the height of their consciousness will not be far above the child-like awareness of the change of clothes from Saturday to Sunday, or the adolescent sense that the glory of the divine work and week is a certain *je ne sais quoi* enhancement of maidenly charm. One begins to sound like a Puritan to say so, perhaps, but it is not evident that the sacred and the secular stand in quite so simple a relation. And perhaps there are more (terrifying) things in heaven and earth than have been naturally stored up in the provincial mind of Massachusetts and Connecticut.

And so we quickly discover. Although everyone is deeply disturbed by the sudden alteration in Hooper's natural appearance, feeling that by hiding his face "he has changed himself into something awful" (38), still the attempts to deal with his symbolic meaning are primitive indeed. Some hard-headed individuals think him simply mad behind his veil; and the local physician, a "sober-minded man," even puts this *simpliste* verdict in a jargon typical of an easy Enlightenment: "Something must surely be amiss with Mr. Hooper's intellects" (41). The idea that the problem might concern his *soul* has evidently not occurred to him. Others among this group of Yankee interpreters shake their "sagacious" heads and, anticipating the acumen of Edgar Poe, "penetrate the mystery" and solve it in the obvious moralistic way. Still others, perhaps the most hard-headed of all, affirm that "there [is] no mystery"; it is merely that "Mr. Hooper's eyes were so weakened by the midnight lamp, as to require a shade" (40–41). Generalized, the spiritual prescription appropriate to such a diagnosis might translate as follows: when emerging from the Dark Night of the Soul, wear sunglasses. (Isn't that Saint John of the Cross behind those Foster Grants?)

But if there is almost certainly more of deep religious awe concealed and trying to reveal itself behind Hooper's veil-as-symbol, still the hard-heads may not be entirely wrong. As anyone who has ever thought about the problem of "the Light and the Dark" in Hawthorne's fiction can easily understand, Hooper's eyes may indeed have become sensitive to "the light." We simply have to be more careful than anyone in the tale about the difference between cause and effect, and between literal and spiritual-metaphorical statements. This latter is not always easy to do in a world where, as Edwards and Emerson agree, all our words for spiritual realities are drawn from natural appearances. Or in the works of a writer whose subtle play with our opposing tendencies to literalistic reduction and allegorical overextension is such that we often find ourselves constructing spiritual interpretations before ever settling what literally happens. And especially in a tale where the narrator—himself neither speculative mystic nor hermeneutical theorist—does not always know enough to keep things straight.[13]

Literally, of course, the veil does serve "to give a darkened aspect to all living and inanimate things" (38). But this is obviously not the cause of Hooper's problem. His sight of the corporeal world through a veil, darkly, is (we must suppose) only an after-image of his insight into the nature of some spiritual reality. And, obviously, it is this insight, and not the veil, which throws the significant "obscurity between him and the holy page, as he [reads] the Scriptures" (39). So understood, his veil is nothing but the metaphor for his awakened Puritanism which, if truly revived rather than merely inherited, might indeed amount to somewhat more than the "gloom" so easily diagnosed by popular romancers and Unitarians. With them, Hawthorne has recognized that a temperamental bias to the negative might be the significant legacy of Puritanism; and that for a certain number of generations no great harm is done in saying it was. But the case is at least thinkable in which somebody, somehow, by some grace of insight or imagination, actually recovers or revives the authentic thing in all its original power. True revivals are just as possible as valid history. And doubtlessly both of these things are happening here: Hawthorne has re-created a moment in which somebody has become sensitive to the light because he has had a genuine Puritan glimpse of the dark. To come up to Hawthorne's own standard of judgment, we must imagine that Hooper may really know something. Puritans may actually see something which their liberal historians do not.

It is impossible to recover the specificities of Hooper's first veiled sermon: the narrator is in our way. Perhaps he does not know the precise heads of doctrine and application Hooper employed; or perhaps he is uninterested in such details. Possibly he assumes that a theologically literate audience can instantly supply the details from its own experience, either of sermons or of the personal consciousness of sin. Or possibly he assumes the reader will be interested primarily in the domestic sociology of the case and will only be embarrassed by too precise an attention to the gloomy formulations of a gothic theology. Certainly Hawthorne himself must have felt a queer mixture of those last two motives, as he designed a tale which might divide and elect its audience much like a converting sermon itself. But in any case, the reader may clear his own conscience of the charge of obscurantism or reductionism only if he tries to follow Hooper as deep as he may possibly be thought to have gone.

About the affective power of Hooper's performance there is no doubt or disagreement. On this first day no one seems to understand or approve what is being expressed, but no one is left complacent. Just after the event some may try to laugh it off or explain it away, but even our rationalistic physician is eventually led to reflect that men sometimes are "afraid to be alone with [themselves]." And at the sermon itself no one evades the "subtle power [that] was breathed into his words": "Each member of the congregation, the most innocent girl, and the man of hardened breast, felt as if the preacher had crept upon them, behind his awful veil, and discovered their hoarded iniquity of deed or thought. Many spread their clasped hands on their bosom" (40). No one shrieks or swoons or stands up to confess sin and profess repentance, but "more than one woman of delicate nerves was forced to leave the meeting-house" (39); and in every way it is hard to miss the suggestion that this sermon, delivered in the mild manner of a Jonathan Edwards (rather than in the more rampant and inflammatory style of a Whitefield) is in fact a piece of conversion rhetoric.[14]

It is no wonder the congregation does not like it: it is designed to remind them that beneath all their own sunny and smiling Sunday appearances, they are, in their secret deeds, or at least in their silent life of thought, wish, desire, fantasy, and motive, *simply* sinners. And such sin—if the truth of it be told—alienates man from God by smiting at His essence; and from every one of his fellows by making his whole outward appearance of decency, decorum, domesticity, and natural virtue a sham and a lie. The wonder is that, eventually, in the world we are given, it makes any converts at all. Or that the whole congregation does not officially declare Hooper mad (as a whole town later declares a similarly motived Roderick Elliston) and apply to a "council of the churches" or perhaps even a "general synod" (45), not merely to inquire into the meaning of the veil, but to petition his removal from his pastoral office. Or that the majority of them do not simply pick up and remove themselves from Hooper's ministry to another, remoter part of

New England. Such things happened, repeatedly, in just such a world, at just such a time. And for no more serious cause: the revivalist reminder that the radical and pervasive but secret sinfulness of all human beings must be known, in its power, and with application, before individuals or societies can ever be true. That, I take it, is nothing but the Puritan-Evangelical theory of "a Christian America."

The other surprising thing is that our narrator, given his limitations or biases, comes as close as he does to naming and correctly interpreting Hooper's real theme. He seems to approach about as near as a merely "notional" Christian may get; and in a studiedly general way, he is actually quite expansive: "The subject had reference to secret sin, and those sad mysteries which we hide from our nearest and dearest, and would fain conceal from our own consciousness, even forgetting that the Omniscient can detect them" (40). To go any further than this the narrator would have himself to adopt the language and the attitudes of the Evangelical Christian. This he is manifestly unable or unwilling to do: the indirection of his "had reference" utterly betrays the "objectivity" of his approach to the subject.[15] And any further explicit analysis of "the true sight of sin" would turn the story from a species of moral history into a form of preaching. And that function would violate the skepticism required by Hawthorne's historical calling and imposed by his own ironical narration.

We are given just this much, together with a few more hints of precisely the same purport later: Hooper recovers the Puritan sight of a kind of sinfulness so subtle and "original" that only God and the Awakened Self can see it, but so pervasive as to effect a total alienation of the family of man. This is supposed to be enough, even apart from the original context of "The Story Teller," where a Methodist preacher of the "new birth" is struggling with whatever soul may be possessed by an irresponsible man of letters who is running away from his evangelical-Puritan upbringing.[16] If we require more, we may be convicting ourselves of an "obtuse secularism" not much different from the sort displayed in the story itself. Anyone who cannot find that Hawthorne was profoundly interested in Puritan history as such, and particularly (though skeptically) in the problematic effects of the struggle between sin and grace therein revealed, is going to have trouble with Parson Hooper.

3

But granting, for the moment, some such thematic interest, where does this historical placement leave us in the internal attempt to decide between

324

the claims of the self-exiled Hooper and his newly alienated congregation? How are we to evaluate Hooper's newly acquired consciousness of sin? And what can be said on behalf of the congregation's stubborn but not particularly hardened inability (or unwillingness—in classic Puritan theory they are exactly the same thing) to take Hooper's converting insight into their own hearts and lives? Can we locate any significant tipping of the balance between Puritan Consciousness and Ordinary Life? Or, at very least, can we define the limits of Hawthorne's ambivalences and of the story's famous ambiguity with any precision drawn from an historical understanding of the issue?

In fact the balance is fairly delicate. On one side the congregation would obviously prefer to see matters return to normal. They would like to get the mystery cleared up, once and for all. They wish, understandably, to put an end to the upset and go on with their lives in the world; and in the Church. Someone might accuse them of adding willful complacency to their constitutional obtuseness, but probably we should not. We must assume that, left alone, their lives would continue to have the same inherent satisfactoriness suggested by the first paragraph. Surely life in eighteenth-century New England might go on as "unterribly" as Robert Frost says it does in most American times and places. Given adequate moral leisure, somebody might even invent the street light. But, obviously, Hooper's continuing prophecy is effectively designed to prevent any such reassuring outcome. A newly awakened man, Hooper intends what preparationist preachers always intend toward their audience: to keep their "Conscience under an arrest, so that it cannot make an escape from the Evidence and Authority of it, so that there is no way, but either to obey the Rule of it, or else be condemned by it."[17] Between such a minister and his congregation there cannot be the simple peace of ordinariness as usual. And if the danger on the one side is the shallow trap of natural self-satisfaction, on the other looms the deeper pitfall of spiritual self-obsession.

As mild mannered as ever, Hooper's new sermons all get tinged "more darkly than usual." His veil has not blinded him to things as they naturally are; neither does it cause him to hallucinate, like some madly inspired enthusiast. His darkened optic has merely afforded him a vision of the world he lacked before. Natural men and women, bright and healthy as they may continue outwardly to appear, now seem all fallen. "Spruce bachelors" and "pretty maidens" abroad in the natural world on an innocent Sabbath are revealed as the sinners they "truly" are, in the sight of the Calvinist God, even if their conscience should trouble them with no glaringly "actual" sin. And the hopeful Scriptures now seem just as truly a Book of Sorrows.

Some conversion has brought what Thomas Hooker called "a strange and a sudden alteration" into Hooper's world; it has varied "the price and the value of things and persons beyond imagination." He now judges "not by outward appearances as is the guise of men of corrupt minds, but upon experience, that which [he has] found and felt in [his] own heart . . . and cannot but see so and judge so of others." By some process which the story does not explore—but which may indeed have to do with "the midnight lamp" not of eye-straining study but of truly illuminating self-examination—he has come to glimpse not only the vanity of the natural world but the fallenness effectively masked by human appearances. Unlike his abidingly natural congregation, Hooper will not now live by appearances or judge according to nature but will measure existence absolutely. No more than Saint Paul will he judge "humanly." His world may or may not be "well amended," but clearly it is "strangely altered."[18] And his conscious design is to produce the same revolutionary change in the subjective "worlds" of as many of his hearers as possible.

And eventually, as we are told, he is not entirely unsuccessful. Though he immediately alienates Squire Saunders, totally balks and baffles the congregational deputation sent to inquire about the meaning of his strange new prophecy, sadly instructs but does not make a convert (or a wife) of Elizabeth, makes himself generally a "bugbear" to the multitude and alternately a fright or mockery to children, and finally defies the extreme unctuousness of the well-meaning (though clearly obtuse) brother-minister who attends him at his deathbed, his reputation and his record of accomplishment as an occasional cause of conversion experience must be regarded as impressive. And we must take this aspect of Hooper's career somewhat seriously if we are to adjust the balance accurately.

The narrator, as our structural sense ought to inform us, has constructed the story so as to give a whole series of dramatic instances of the humanly unfortunate consequences of Hooper's conversionist calling: amply illustrated are the domestic penalties attendant upon a career of Puritan Prophecy. But he has reduced the "Christian History" of Hooper's achievements to a bare list, compressed into a simple paragraph near the end of the story. Still, the list of specifics is fairly long. And, more cogently, the generalization which introduces it contains one phrase so telling that it must be regarded as an index to the complexity of the author's own ironic estimate: "Among all its bad influences, the black veil had *the one desirable effect*, of making its wearer a very efficient clergyman" (49, my italics). Critics have suggested that "efficient" here is "not very flattering." Perhaps it is not, though it does seem to be a technical term in the official jargon of revivalists, rather like "experimental" in the lexicon of piety associated with the "Application of Redemption."[19] But in any case the more significant irony informs the idea of "the one desirable effect": what is easily taken as a scarcely flattering concession may more literally be read as *somebody's* trenchant assertion that the only good Hooper ever did, amidst so much that seems humanly bad, is the only spiritual good desirable, the only true good there ever could be. Though Hooper may smile ironically at the disruptions and alienations he produces, he himself evidently considers it all a world well lost. And so might anybody else who is completely convinced that salvation lies on the other side of a true sight of sin.

That class of persons includes, pre-eminently, all of Hooper's converts. To "souls that were in agony for sin," as everyone in the way of "preparation for salvation" must always be, according to the orthodoxy of Puritanism, his "awful power" is both necessary and, in the outcome, a positive good. What true religion without "awe"? And, false sympathy and sentiment aside, what "efficient" exposure of human self-deception and pretense without the "power" to destroy self-defense? True, each of Hooper's converts has once regarded him with "a dread peculiar to themselves," but how else will the anxious soul regard an agency intending nothing less than the death of its old consciousness, its old self? What wonder if before Hooper could bring his converts "to celestial light" they must first be with him "behind the black veil"(49)? With authentic Puritanism it is never otherwise: without an awful "conviction" of sin, nothing else follows. Only a flagrant antinomianism or a pathetic liberalism would teach that the good news of salvation comes before (or independent of) the bad news of sin. Spiritually considered, Hooper's "veil" is utterly orthodox; the response of his converts, perfectly according to the established morphology.

Equally intelligible are Hooper's other accomplishments as authentic re-inventor of the Puritan consciousness. He ministers effectively to dying sinners and to all who are overtaken by "dark affections." He profoundly affects many itinerant visitors who have come "long distances to attend services at his church": in Hawthorne's ironic revision of the classic formula, they came to "gaze" and stayed to "quake." And finally—in the detail expressly designed to tell us very literally and precisely where we are, in case the whole spiritual outline of the awakening situation is still unclear to us—he gives an election sermon "during Governor Belcher's administration" (spanning the years of Edwards' first revivals at Northampton and of Whitefield's first great tour of America) which convinces the legislators to enact measures favorable to the "piety of our earliest ancestral sway" (49).

To a certain extent, therefore, what can be said for Hooper is whatever our religious sensitivities tell us must be said on behalf of revivals or awakenings. That they have socially disruptive effects on the daily lives and weekly church-going habits of people of ordinary human decency and virtue is scarcely news: that truism has been perfectly obvious to everyone, at least since Edwards defined "the distinguishing marks of a work of the spirit" and defended its importance in spite of a far more grotesque display of human craziness than has found its way into "The Minister's Black Veil." The true definition of "confusion," Edwards argues, is the disruption of means that are known to lead to man's proper and highest end.[20] And since, on Puritan premise, natural life and ordinary consciousness lead only to the "vanity" of Ecclesiastes, or the "corruption" of Augustine, or the "self-love" of Calvin, then evidently natural life and ordinary consciousness ought to be broken up. Calvinist salvation is not natural life but a New Birth. The New Birth is not natural consciousness but conversion. And conversion begins in the consciousness of the self under the aspect of "sin"—or, rather, that habitual ("Calvinistic") sinfulness which is as "secret" to the natural man himself as it is to the outside view of the casual observer.

To see the question in proper perspective, then, the reader must get beyond the anti-evangelical bias of the narrator and imagine that Hooper's "one desirable effect" *might* be a very important one indeed. To fail of this imaginative recognition is to trivialize the whole case. To call Hooper simply crazy (or pridefully self-deluded, or a false prophet, or an antichrist) would be much like taking the views of Charles Chauncey, at face value, as an adequate account of the whole meaning of the Great Awakening. Even if we should judge that Hooper's way of salvation is ultimately a falsehood and a delusion, we must yet allow for its moral seriousness and psychological power.[21]

But of course we can scarcely stop there; for the story's final judgment does seem to be against Hooper. Even with the narrator unmasked, the story will scarcely read otherwise. And if it did, we should hardly trust our own judgment: given Hawthorne's own clear-enough rejection of Puritan orthodoxy—in both its ancestral, inherited, "gloomy" form at Salem and its more current, revived, "powerful" embodiment at Bowdoin—where should we locate his sudden conversion? Or why should we imagine Hawthorne would sponsor in art what he evaded in life? Or endorse in "The Minister's Black Veil" what he exposed in "The Gentle Boy"? With some assurance, then, we turn to the case against Hooper, still hoping to strike some uneven balance. We must be sensitive enough, both to history and to the terrors of the spiritual life, to "throw in something, somehow like Original Sin." But perhaps we should not throw out everything else.[22]

What tips the balance against Hooper is some sense of his too-powerful partialness. To come to terms with him we need to take seriously the idea (of Hooker and Edwards and other such "formidable Christians") that natural man needs to have his consciousness renewed and his world turned upside down, and that there may indeed be a form of divine wisdom that will always appear as folly to the world. But even as we do, we begin to sense that Hooper himself may have taken these ideas *too* seriously, if that were somehow possible. Or that he has somehow crossed over the fine line which divides the needful "wisdom that is woe" from a more extreme "woe that is madness." Probably it is some such thought which helps us get things back in perspective, and to come to terms with Hawthorne himself.

Surely the balance is not restored by any powerfully positive and dramatically realized counterimage of moral heroism or spiritual insight which close analysis may yet discover in Hooper's congregation. Indeed, to look beneath their explicitly unawakened naiveté for some major revelation of truth or virtue, buried in their collective or "catholic" wisdom, is probably to misconstrue Hawthorne's commitment to the sanative power of the ordinary, precisely as such.[23] It is, by definition, simply ordinary: without categorical understanding, and insusceptible of interpretive revaluation, it simply is whatever it is, savable or damnable in those terms alone. It is once-born. Or, if that generalization seems too wide, at least it would be a thankless task to enter a special plea for the other-than-ordinary character of the persons with whom we see Hooper having to deal. As if by some predestinating decree, they remain simply unawakened. Or, alternately, they may be obeying some romantic law that the plain people should not mean but be. In any case, the really heightened consciousness remains pretty much the sole possession of the minister. Hooper alone has looked on subjectivity bare.

To be sure, Elizabeth seems the sanest intelligence in the story. And in her interview with her "plighted" husband she comes close to meeting Hooper (in our behalf) on his own ground. And her own long life of single devotion to the self-exiled bachelor-minister may well strike us as more truly selfless than Hooper's tormented career as delegated minister to the haunted mind. Still, we see so little of her that only a premature investment in the values of domestic sentiment can cause us to elevate her to the stature of an ideal spiritual role-model. Theologically, and in relation to Hooper, she may figure as a rejected natural grace. But literarily, and to us, she is no "heroine," only the jilted but ever-faithful girl-next-door. And around her, filling up the definition of the community she most sympathetically represents, are ranged only versions of that invincible moral ignorance which simply *cannot* take Hooper's point with the power of subjective application.

Hooper's converts we never directly see. About the efficacy and human satisfactoriness of his cure of those souls "in agony for sin," who become the proper object of his ministry, nothing definitive can be said. Though the "experimental" details of their religious experiences may run to considerable length in the pages of *The Christian History*—the official record of the historic revival with which Hooper's fictional career is associated—they are simply not in this "narrative" in any effective way. Fair or not, all we are given is the sick-soul psychology of Hooper himself, to be measured against the once-born naiveté of persons who seem, by and large, not to sense the presence of disease anywhere but in the "intellects" of their spiritual physician; and in relation to the disruptions produced, in Hooper's own ordinary life and in theirs. But even when we have compensated for this narrative bias, by granting the authentic existence of a significant class of New-Light Hooperites in this incorrigibly Old-Light world, it is hard to feel that what is gained quite compensates for what has been lost.

Obviously we must be wary of resting our case against Hooper solely on the disruptions produced by his doctrine or style of prophecy. On the one hand, emotionally, our personal recoil probably does not spring from that source primarily. And, on the other, our intellectual objections would be vulnerable to Edwards' famous reply that *of course* the Spirit will break up the patterns of the ordinary in favor of the "true." We might yet clear ourselves by rejoining that there are limits of decorum not to be violated by *any* agency; that certain universal folkways, having a sort of sacramental efficacy, can be defended on grounds other than rationalistic prejudice or affective attenuation. But, far more simply, what leads us to the deeper source of our feelings about the tragic failure of Hooper's career, and indeed of his life, is a precisely Edwardsean question about the true nature of his spiritual achievements. What, we should ask ourself, are the "fruits" of Hooper's own conversion?[24]

One obvious and fairly telling "sign" is that Hooper's spiritual life does not seem to grow or advance. From his initial donning of the black veil straight through to his final deathbed speech, his insight bears only repetition. It may deepen, but it does not lead on to anything else. Indeed it seems to trap him. It is as if he were in the *midst* of some very profound and important process but unable to move on to its saving completion. For him at least the fruits of the Puritan consciousness of sin are identically that consciousness. A form of awareness everywhere defined and evaluated as "preparatory" seems here to begin and end with itself.[25] The spectacle is not pleasant, nor is the prospect hopeful. What may, as process, look like a necessary step in a saving progress or as an important stage along life's way comes to appear, as an end in itself, not true spiritual health but a very desperate form of spiritual insanity. So that—to say the least—Hooper's last state may be not better than his first.

The individual reader may or may not believe that man as such is sick in his being and radically in need of a spiritual cure. And critics will no doubt continue to suggest various estimates of Hawthorne's own precise relation to evangelical orthodoxy. But few of us, I suspect, are willing to grant that *any* salvation is exempt from the general rule that a cure must not be worse than its relative disease. And it may prove hard to resist making the appropriate application of that maxim to Hooper, who cannot seem to move beyond the tragic human implications of the true sight of sin.

The other sign that all is not well in the spiritual case of the Reverend Mr. Hooper is at once more obvious and more subtle in its implications. Surely some deep spiritual dis-ease is manifesting itself in his obsession with *the veil itself,* the mere external symbol by which he has sought to express the spiritual import of his insight. His jealous guarding of the outward appearance of a veil which hides his individual face becomes as important to him as the universal fact of a sinfulness which prevents spirits in deepest communion from ever adequately revealing their inmost hearts and minds. Hooper develops a kind of symbolic literalism which actually resembles the congregation's own persistent reduction of his message to its medium, except that theirs is naive and his compulsive. It is almost as if—like certain literary critics who want all symbolic works to be about the function of symbols, or indeed all literary works to be about their own literariness— Hooper has got trapped in the epistemology of his chosen career. Or, more to the story's Puritan point, as if some Jonathan Edwards had suddenly become more interested in the metaphors of his "rhetoric of sensation" than in the moral psychology of sin and grace.[26]

Eventually, of course, we may wish to ask why Hawthorne would have imagined such an exaggeration or mystification of the "merely" literary to occur in the midst of the American eighteenth century, whose common-sense philosophy is not noticeably indebted to Heidegger; just as, indeed, we must eventually face all the widest implications of Hooper's symbolic and subjective self-entrapment. But to leap at once to such considerations is to pass too quickly through the historical surface of Hawthorne's tale of the revival of Puritan consciousness. Almost certainly it is to misread the tale's precise referent; and very likely it is to involve ourselves in yet another species of Hooper's own problem, which the story exists to identify rather than to spread. Much nearer Hawthorne's starting point would be some observation about the Puritan source and moral dimension of Hooper's obsessive self-reference.

In these terms Hooper's insistence on the importance of his own veil is merely the sign of a deeper moral problem still, his perpetual and finally self-convicting insistence on his own exemplariness, in spite of the explicitly universal character of his express doctrine. In his attempt to make a symbolic prophecy about the sinfulness of absolutely *every* person's secret or subjective life, he seems forced to use his own self as exemplum. To the person well acquainted with all the various genres of Puritan writing, Hooper's life-long experiment with "Auto-Machia" may seem simply inevitable, as indeed Hawthorne intends Hooper's effort to be widely representative of a major effort of the Puritan consciousness. And there is no doubt that such a project can often be productive of great literary results: we scarcely need the example of Whitman to remind us that, given adequate standards of genuine personal frankness, usually mixed with at least a modicum of self-mockery, self-reference is the very stuff of modern literature. But neither should we need to be reminded that the first-person exemplum everywhere tends to spread out and take over the whole psychological field; and that when such a thing actually happens, heroic honesty may turn into something much less admirable. If we need any reminder, it is identically the one which "The Minister's Black Veil" exists to give—namely, that such a thing might happen in a Puritan world as easily as anywhere else; or, more perceptively, that it is precisely there that such things predictably began to happen.[27]

Thus the case of Hooper stands primarily as Hawthorne's figure of that potentially exhaustive and incipiently solipsistic sort of self-reference into which a powerfully heightened or Puritan or even "true" sight of sin can be discovered all ironically to lead. And the likelihood appears especially great in a common-sense world whose sociology no longer reflects that level of consciousness and whose established mode of discourse has lost touch with the symbolic idiom on which such a consciousness would seem to depend. In such a world one does not have to be a self-congratulating bigot of the Digby variety to end up utterly alone, irrecoverably lost in the cave of selfhood. Rather the reverse: the more one insists on the absolutely universal application of one's own perfectly subjective discovery of sin, the more isolated one becomes. The irony of such an unlooked-for outcome might well provoke, in an appropriately situated person, a sad smile. And surely an adequately instructed critic might sympathize with such a smile, even if it were tinged with a trace of self-pity. But if the sadly humorous recognition of the penalties of divine wisdom should turn into an hysterical rejection of the compensatory good of all merely relative human palliatives, then one may pardonably decide that salvation is to be sought elsewhere.

And so, even when we grant that Hooper's dark illumination has afforded him—or, more accurately, has been identical with—a revived sight of sinful human subjectivity, we are still required to wonder if he has not stopped short of some other "light beyond."[28] In possessing so absolutely the Truth of the Self, he has somehow lost the Good of the Other. A partial conversion, surely. Or if it should turn out that the "preparatory" insight into the radical alienation of the Self is the ultimate knowledge available to the human point of view, then we may still conclude that such ultimates are too true to be useful.

4
褻褻

Our sense of the passionate power of Hooper's static commitment to his unique standard of self-reference clarifies itself only gradually. With the congregation, we are made aware of Hooper's histrionic eccentricity at once; but our first intimations of stiff and even obsessive behavior come only later, as we acquire a more particular knowledge of the way his new insight and prophetic stance have affected his personality. We may grasp, better than the congregation (or the narrator), what Hooper's first veiled sermon intends; we may feel able to gloss, confidently, that "something" either of objective "sentiment" or subjective "imagination" which makes that sermon "greatly the most powerful they had ever heard from the pastor's lips" (40). We may even approve his symbolic strategy, depending on our approval of his spiritual end as evangelical preacher and on our feelings about the "tactics" of revivalism generally; wearing a "simple black veil, such as any woman might wear on her bonnet" (41), is, after all, rather more refined than sliding into home for Jesus. But we can also sense, much more simply, that the congregation's first in-church, face-to-veil confrontation with their "own Parson" has been a nervously moving experience.

How much more upsetting, therefore, when Hooper continues to wear his prophetic veil outside the church. In the pulpit Hooper's veil had seemed, for all the unwonted anxiety it had produced, not entirely inappropriate, especially given the subject of his sermon. Except for the relentless ordinariness of the congregation's perceptions, it almost seemed an apt way to force everyone to see for himself a universal truth, one which could not *fairly* be associated with Hooper alone. But somehow the veil seems far less decorous on the face of a pastor out among his flock. We have no trouble understanding why, after the service of the divine word and outside the church, on what we and they think of as normal social terms, the congregation finds the veil simply intolerable. And perhaps we do not entirely blame them if they take it personally: Pastor Hooper knows his own, but his own do not know him. Whatever might be happening to their spiritual consciousness, their ordinary world is being upset in a drastic way.

Our first indication of some fairly deep disturbance comes, ironically, from the perfectly ordinary and placid manner in which Hooper greets the predictable uneasiness outside the church: he elects not to apologize, not to explain; indeed he does not even seem to take notice of the anxious stir he has created:

Turning his veiled face from one group to another, he paid due reverence to the hoary heads, saluted the middle aged with kind dignity as
their friend and spiritual guide, greeted the young with mingled authority and love, and laid his hands on the little children's heads to bless
them. Such was always his custom on the Sabbath day. (41)

It is as if he believed that everything *ordinary* could go on precisely as before, even though everything *real* has, by some absolute shift in perception,
been changed utterly. This might just be possible if the subjective change
had already occurred identically in all, if "good Parson Hooper" and
"Goodman Gray" were equally converted. But obviously this is not the case.
And so what we witness is the rather lamentable spectacle of the divine subjectivist moving through the ordinary world of unreconstructed objectivity
as if nothing had happened, evidently wishing most affairs to proceed as
usual.

Of course they do not. And the results are, on the one side at least, predictable enough: "strange and bewildered looks" repay Hooper "for his
courtesy" (41); no one walks by his side, and Squire Saunders neglects to
invite Hooper to bless and to partake of his Sunday dinner in the long-accustomed manner. Prophetically Hooper may still be dramatizing that essential separateness which, according to the "doctrine" of his sermon,
results from the sinful secrecy of the inner life; but humanly he is destroying
all those accidental communions which ease (though they may not heal) that
separateness. A symbolic gesture intended to reveal an essential fact about
the moral condition of all and which, accordingly, might conceivably become the basis of some sort of spiritual unity turns instead into the impelling
cause for a whole series of painful separations according to the flesh. If this
outcome owes something to the unawakened naiveté of the congregation, it
may be no less the result of Hooper's absolutist intransigence. Hooper, as
we later learn, has taken a vow to wear the veil continuously; and his interview with the Reverend Mr. Clark finally reveals why this is so. But as
long as the prophet must bear the sign of his function everywhere in the ordinary world, the ordinary world will always react pretty much as we see it
here.

That Hooper at least partly understands what is happening seems clear
from his first "sad smile," which continues to "flicker" and "glimmer" un-
changed through the tale, up to the very moment of his deathbed self-ex-
culpation. Why, he must already be wondering, should anyone tremble and
shrink back, when the sad mystery which the veil obscurely typifies is one in
which everyone is involved? Does not our general identity as sinfully alienated humanity constitute the only approach to unity there can be until the
Last Judgment shall draw aside the private veil from the peculiar sinfulness
of each? How simple this agitated response! And yet the people do shrink

back. Nor does the determined minister do anything to clarify his meaning or mitigate their reaction. Ironically, he seems satisfied that their response is as inevitable as it is simplistic. Evidently ordinary affairs will not go on as before. But that does not alter the Truth of his insight and the nature of his calling. It only makes both harder to bear. But what of that? Was prophecy ever promised otherwise?

And so he drives straight ahead—through the afternoon's funeral, the nuptials of the evening, and through a whole undeviating career of unswerving loyalty to the truth of secret sin and the sorrowful alienation which results. Granted the first dramatic gesture, and the firm resolve to live with all of its consequences, the rest of his life seems as fixed and fated as that of Wakefield, the Outcast of the Universe. And, by contrast, it makes that of Richard Digby appear a "short, happy life" indeed. Only two brief interviews relieve the impression that Hooper's unsettling career is itself so settled that it can be told rather than shown, and swiftly. Although the educable reader is supposed to go on learning about Hooper's psychological situation, Hooper's own spiritual development seems as arrested as that of his hard-headed congregation. And for the most part the results are now predictable on both sides.

The two remaining services on Hooper's first veiled Sabbath amplify, with somewhat ghostlier implications, a meaning we have already grasped: the new Hooper is a far more "efficient clergyman" on some occasions than on others. In some situations he is consummately effective, but he utterly fails in the role of man for all seasons. The gloomy success of the morning's sermon on sin is more perfectly replayed in the afternoon's "funeral prayer"; the people tremble though they "but darkly" understand his veiled remarks about death and judgment. But his desperate failure to make human contact with each and all in the broad sunshine of the natural world is hideously repeated and exaggerated just a few hours later; the heavy pall cast by the grotesque inappropriateness of his "horrible black veil" can "portend nothing but evil to the wedding" (43) of the same evening. There might be, for every purpose under heaven, a season; a time to rejoice as well as a time to mourn, a time to love and propagate as well as a time to die; but under the aspect of the black veil it is hard to perceive any absolute significance in these naturalistic turnings. And though Hooper intends no satiric cruelty—wishing the ceremony to proceed and the wine to be drunk as before—nevertheless a quasi-sacramental occasion is jarringly disrupted. And it is impossible for us to miss the sacrilegious significance of his spilling the ceremonial wine. And thus the net result of these two services is, once again, a delicate balancing of opposite judgments.

On the one hand, at the funeral, a group of professedly religious people, not evidently accustomed to meditating on the profound significance of the "last things," have been touched, in some fairly fundamental way, with a reminder of their own mortality, and with the absolute significance of that fact for the conduct of life. It is precisely here, we must presume, that true religion as a form of "ultimate concern" might begin. And here the veil seems not only "efficient" but positively decorous, humanly appropriate as well as ritualistically apt. Indeed the service is so moving that the congregation seems aroused in some sleeping faculty: two partners in the tragic "procession of life" which leaves the church share the identical "fancy" that "the minister and the [departed] maiden's spirit were walking hand in hand" (43). Some literary critics (following Poe) might want to gloss this suggestion in a moralistic way, starting nasty rumors. Or, closer to Hawthorne's own frame of reference, some sternly theological critic (following Edwards) might protest that conversion "does not consist in any impression made upon the imagination."[29] But surely the more obvious suggestion is that the inner life of a basically pragmatic and rationalistic community has been stirred into unwonted activity. Imagination may be no satisfactory substitute for grace; but even this little gothic fancy seems, from a spiritual point of view, far more awakened than earlier speculations about madness or eye-trouble. We may fairly suppose that it includes the idea that Hooper somehow knows, in the midst of earthly life, what ordinarily is discovered only in eternity; from this dim imagining much of spiritual consequence might readily follow. And we can easily imagine a spiritual scheme according to which Hooper's funeral-success might be significant indeed.

On the other hand, however, it is almost impossible to rationalize his disastrous failure at the wedding celebration. For one thing, the disruptions seem spiritual as well as tonal. And for another, they seem to imply an unlovely sort of literalistic self-involvement mixed in with Hooper's darkly symbolic insight.

Apparently Hooper has not lost all of his "placid cheerfulness for such occasions." In spite of the gloomy distress all around, and in spite of a "deathlike paleness" on the countenance of the bride, he means—from behind his veil—to wish ordinary happiness to the newly married pair, "in a strain of mild pleasantry." So far, we may think so bad: we doubt that the gesture will, under the circumstances, produce the normal effect of "brighten[ing] the features of the guests, like a cheerful gleam from the hearth." Still, while it is only a matter of social fitness, we can always appeal to some higher good to compensate for the black veil's violation of bridal decorum. But then we immediately discover that more is at issue than a breach of social propriety on the order of placing a death's head in the wedding punch bowl, or tolling a funeral knell at a nuptial mass. What prevents us from learning (and from caring) about the social effects of Hooper's improbable pleasantry is a new fact, with graver implications: about to proffer his wedding wish, he "spill[s] the untasted wine upon the carpet, and rush[es] forth into the darkness" (43-44).

Considered simply as symbolic action, this ultimate disruption of the wedding celebration is surely ominous. As a deed of prophecy, nothing could augur less well for the newly married pair than this figure of failed communion and premature ejaculation. Applied to Hooper himself, the sign forecasts his own failure to consummate any meaningful union with Elizabeth or (apart from individual converts) with his congregation as a whole. For Hooper personally there will be only onanistic incompletion, or whatever might turn out to be its psychological equivalent; and for his congregation only the sort of separation which prevents a particular church from predicting the millennial community. Not quite an antichrist, Hooper would yet figure as a very unwelcome guest at the Marriage at Cana. And though he can scarcely be thought to embrace damnation in the manner of Ethan Brand, still one does not rush "into the darkness" outside a "Wedding Feast" without serious theological implications.

The celebration Hooper has disrupted may not be, in the explicit theology of those present, precisely sacramental; but this fact scarcely renders his spilling of the wedding wine any less sacrilegious. The typological equivalence of Christ and the Faithful with Bridegroom and Bride is the common (Pauline) property of Romanist and Puritan alike. Nowhere, according to the most elementary Christian symbolism, can one disrupt marriage without doing violence to the Church. It may be that marital union according to the flesh is *only* a shadowy type of a transcendent unity which is altogether more spiritual, and not *at all* itself a participation in and a synecdoche for the ultimate mystery of the One Body. But when is it ever valid to derange the vehicle and imagine the tenor is unaffected? Or—even if we should "puritanically" eliminate the spiritual significance of marriage altogether—can we seriously imagine that Christians ever drink wine without somehow memorializing their universal sacrament of spiritual union? The only really valid doctrinal question is whether Hooper's sacrilege here involves the desecration of two sacraments or only one. And that question begins to appear trivial in a tale which clearly implies that the two sacraments refer to only one religious mystery. It all but disappears in the context of a whole career and corpus of writing which defines as sacramental any influence which has the gracious power to save an individual from solipsism.[30]

Thus, if Hooper's spilling of the sacramental wine prefigures a whole career and a whole life of failed and disrupted communion, it also casts significant light backwards on the lapse of his Sunday dinners with Squire Saunders. A pale and secular form of communion, this; but in Hawthorne's world one does well to take whatever bread and wine may be offered. And from this same point of view we can see the misleading partiality of one critic's suggestion that in the course of the tale Hooper performs all the various functions of the ministerial office. In fact there are some very significant omissions, some absences so glaringly present that they essentially define the place where Hooper is trapped, both historically and spiritually.[31]

We (almost) hear Hooper preach; and we can easily imagine that, according to a certain evangelical model, he does very well. We see him do very badly walking among his flock. We see him marvelously succeed and grotesquely fail at funeral and wedding. And we hear of his efficacy at anxious benches and agonized deathbeds. But we never see him at the Lord's Supper. Omitted from his career, and present only by parodic implication, is that one sacramental event which endures to organize the whole of adult Christian life when all others have fallen into dispute or disuse, and which—given the actual development of the New England Mind, "from Colony to Province"—is virtually the only subject which a history of an ordinary town in New England could be significantly about. To miss either of these plain facts is secularism *tout craché*. The "essence of Christianity" is, identically, the Eucharistic Mystery. And the religious history of New England is scarcely more than the story of the early Puritan identification of the Lord's Supper as the ultimate earthly seal of Faith, through the pragmatic defense of that principle in the Half-Way Covenant and the equally pragmatic attack on it in the Stoddardean controversy about "open communion," down to the separationist revival of sacramental exclusionism in the Great Awakening. To have entirely excluded the subject from a story about the revival of authentic Puritanism in the 1730's and 1740's would be, to say the least, problematical. And to exclude it from critical discussion of the story is to run the risk of collapsing "The Minister's Black Veil" back into the paradigm of the self-indulgent, minor-Romantic sketch of the Gloomy Oddfellow.

For in fact Hawthorne does not exclude the subject; he merely elides the details. Symbolic hint and glaring absence both force us to wonder what the Lord's Supper could possibly mean to Hooper. How could he, with so many unawakened persons in his congregation, really administer that rite in good faith? Will he restrict it to his own converts, who shall have been with him behind the black veil? Might that number include Elizabeth? Will he hold spiritual communion with the woman he denies all fleshly consummation? Or is it all somehow beyond that already? As long as we are forced to imagine, are we not forced to consider an even more drastic situation? For Hooper's crucial distinction is, unlike that of Goodman Brown, *not* between the saved and all others, but rather between time and eternity, or the superficial view of man and the insight of God. By his standards, to be truly awakened is merely to know that no power on earth can ever violate the ineluctable moral secrecy of our sinful subjectivity; the "saved" man is simply the undeceived man, who knows that in this life he cannot truly know—or be known by—another. And from such knowledge, what redemption? For such knowers, the sacrament of communion might be a gloomy ritual indeed: gratuitous dreariness, if not an occasion of the sin of ironic self-pity. So perhaps Hooper will (like the young Emerson in Hawthorne's own day, though for slightly different reasons) suspend the ceremony altogether. Or perhaps he will simply go on with it, as part of his painful program of ordinariness as usual; or as he continues the marriage ceremony itself, from behind his veil, as nothing more than an earthly illusion which still manages to typify a heavenly truth to come. However we fill in the strategic vacancies of plot, the moral is always the same: Hooper spills the sacramental chalice because his insight stubbornly denies the possibility of earthly communion.

In this light it may also be significant that we never see "Father" Hooper perform a baptism. What we can think of, almost comically, as a doctrinal difference with Elizabeth denies him natural offspring. And even if she were more yielding on the point of mixed marriages, we can scarcely imagine Hooper effectively administering the sacrament which adds a new soul to the Christian community. John Cotton might, famously, delay the baptism of his son until his own admission into one of the truly reformed churches of America was secure; he would not falsify, in the "catholic" manner, the nature of the covenant promise actually being extended. But what promise would Hooper's baptism offer a child at all? The infant might or might not live to possess the true sight of his own nature, secretly sinful from the first act of consciousness (if not precisely from conception or birth); but that insight rests on no sacramental guarantee. And to us it seems less saving than merely preparatory. Hooper's salvation might indeed lie in community. A perfect "society" would indeed be for him "the redeemed form of man." But such salvation is, as he will sternly instruct Elizabeth, entirely reserved for the "hereafter" (47).

All this is much in the case against Hooper. But it is not yet all, not even all that is implied by his spilling of the wedding toast. The last word on Hooper's disruption of the marriage must concern the actual cause of spilling the communion wine and rushing out from the wedding feast. On the one hand, obviously, Hooper personally intends no sacrilege, any more than he has intended any satiric cruelty. In fact, his action seems almost as inadvertent as it is outrageous: something happens to upset his prophetic control, and he merely reacts. Nevertheless, it is precisely the sudden and unintentional quality of his most extravagant behavior which points to its obsessive quality. Somehow his own self has got itself too mixed up in his universal symbolic meaning: trying most deliberately to say something about Everyman, he suddenly remembers what kind of being is Parson Hooper, and he loses all control. And, on the other hand, just as obviously, the anti-sacramental implications of his sudden, uncontrolled revelation of deep disease are not to be thought of as his meanings alone. From the historical point of view, Hooper's most gothic eccentricities are no more than a peculiarly dramatic version of a tendency to be discovered almost everywhere in Puritan experience, though most noticeably perhaps in its more obvious phases of awakening. Hooper disrupts the marriage and nullifies the remaining Protestant sacraments only because, Puritan fashion, he seems to have uncovered something vastly more essential: himself.

This, quite literally, is why he spills the wine: "catching a glimpse of his own figure in the looking-glass, the black veil involved his own spirit in the horror with which it overwhelmed all others" (43–44). Interpreted personally, the meaning is obvious. A sudden, literal glimpse of his own outside appearance reminds him of the (still-literal) inside view he has been forced to take of himself—in what Puritan theologians, following Saint Paul, everywhere refer to as "the looking-glass of the law." The terrifying discovery, just as everywhere recorded and predicted, is that no human self will, in these terms, bear very much looking into. On this point Jonathan Edwards and Edgar Poe would be in perfect agreement: the appropriate result of a truthful look might fairly be described as "horror"; the blackness within the self would correspond much more nearly to the darkness outside the wedding into which Hooper rushes ("For the Earth, too, had on her Black Veil") than to the cheery light inside the hall.[32] Presumably Hooper already knows this very well. It is simply that, in a new moment of perfectly subjective application, it all comes home to him once again, with a disturbing power he cannot resist.

Momentarily, at least, his prophetic persona has been overwhelmed by a chance encounter with his own consciousness; literal horror sweeps away his will to figurative expression. Symbolically, and very steadily, he has wanted to "say," even at a wedding, that the true sight of sin is all on earth you know; that even conjugal knowings are grossly illusory. But the literal self has deranged the symbolic strategy—leaving Hooper himself, momentarily deranged, to rush about in his own subjective darkness.

That all of this has a powerfully Romantic or modern overtone is obvious. Less obvious, but more nearly to the point here, however, is the implication that what happens to Hooper may tend to happen to Puritanism everywhere. One thinks, most readily, of the undeniable truth of those "gloomy" cases, so dear to the liberals and the popular romancers, in which some poor soul gets lost in a dark night of humiliating preparation and never returns. But there is also, somewhat more subtly, Puritanism's abundant literature of autobiographical selves who never do quite succeed in making their literal selves quite public or representative; failing of self-transcendence, they come down to us as cases of "Conscience and Its Pathology" rather than as heroes of grace.[33]

Surely Hawthorne's historical observation is only the obvious one, well established by more "regular" historians then and now: preoccupation with the true sight of the sinful self, starkly naked of moral works and ceremonial offerings, in primary relation to God alone, inevitably renders all the various sacraments less relevant to Puritanism than to other forms of Christian experience.[34] Just so: Hooper disrupts sacraments because of his intense concern with Self. This happens publicly and in general, regardless of personal intention, because of a bias or tendency of doctrine. But it may also happen personally, wherever the Self comes to loom larger than the means instituted to save it. And this is the impression we carry away from the disrupted wedding: in the midst of a deliberate prophecy about the aboriginal importance of the Self, under the aspect of sin, Hooper glimpses again his personal self; the experience entirely destroys his prophetic detachment and suggests, already, the beginnings of self-obsession. Once this impression is firmly established, the rest of the tale reads swiftly enough.

5

Evidently Hooper has recovered his strategic composure by the time the congregational delegation visits him, to ask for hard-headed clarifications. Hooper receives them "with friendly courtesy" but waits for them to introduce their topic which, "it might be supposed, was obvious enough." But because the topic is so nominally obvious and at the same time so essentially difficult, they scarcely know how to begin. And his response to their evident discomfiture is only "the glimmering of a melancholy smile"—knowing, self-possessed, and philosophically teasing if not socially cruel: it is, as we might say, their nickel. Understandably, nothing happens. After sitting awhile, "speechless, confused, and shrinking from Mr. Hooper's eye," which—like God's—"they felt to be fixed upon them with an invisible glance," they come away "abashed," calling for a "council of the churches" if not a "general synod" (45). But since the tale is only to *imply* the sociology of revivalism and separatism, what we get instead is an interview between Hooper and his "plighted wife" Elizabeth.

Elizabeth is the only person in the village who is, as we are punningly told, "unappalled" by the black veil. She has the "calm energy" to face a difficult social situation; and she reasonably assumes a lover's "special privilege to know what the black veil concealed." Still, she does not rush off to confront and entreat Hooper. The very reverse of hysterical, she waits for his next visit; then, after a moment's realistic appraisal of the veil's appearance and effect, she launches into the problem "with a direct simplicity which made the task easier both for him and her." If she seems at first incapable of symbolic perception, still it is a mark of her sanity that she does not regard the veil with any sense of mystification. Innocent of all motives to reductivism, therefore, she begins by treating it for what it literally is, a "piece of crape," and not at all "terrible" except as "it hides a face [she is] always glad to look upon." Having made this pleasantly disarming beginning she proceeds, with equal directness and realism of expectation, to make a double request: "First lay aside your black veil; then tell me why you put it on" (45).

Now, we are entitled to feel, the contest of authorial sympathy is fairly joined. If Elizabeth has made the moment as easy as possible for Hooper, for us it still retains a certain mild electric tension. In an entirely unobjectionable and indeed a most ingratiating way, this charmingly competent young lady has asked her fiancé to reveal what is in his heart, a lover's fair request, surely. But beyond this she has, on our behalf, asked the symbolic Puritan Mind to stand up and explain itself, in language ordinarily used by men; and this, as we easily recognize, may be like asking Robert Frost's poetic star to "talk Fahrenheit, talk Centigrade." It is a very nice moment. Elizabeth's request is perfectly ingenuous, entirely without irony or any other bad faith. At the same time she has put the prophetic man of God in a very difficult situation. To drop too completely into the elementary language everybody can easily comprehend is to falsify the truth that saving insight demands that we move from our ordinary level of perception and discourse. And yet, under the present circumstances, he can scarcely repeat his own prophetic version of the star's "I burn." What *can* he say? Or, more tellingly perhaps, now that the situation is entirely personal and not at all ceremonial, what tone can he take?

He begins well enough. Faintly smiling at the naive charm of her approach, and at his own insoluble dilemma of consciousness, he speaks of the "hour to come . . . when all of us shall cast aside our veils"; against that spiritual prospect he begs her indulgence of his continuing to wear his all too literal "piece of crape." Enough said, as he might fairly hope. But the words are, to dear Elizabeth, still a mystery. Will he unveil them at least? Risky business, but he will try. The "little lower layer," then: the veil is "a type and a symbol"; and since its meaning is universally true of all mortal life, he has vowed never to remove it before any "mortal eye"; not even Elizabeth can come behind it, *ever*. Only half-comprehending, she is alarmed for her lover: what sorrow has overtaken him? Mortal sorrow enough, Hooper re-

plies, willing to take the theological effect for its cause. But what, she solici-
tously inquires, if people's minds run not to sorrow but to some secret sin?
What of the scandal? Already there are rumors . . . She is not really coming
much closer to his insight into the universal effects of Original Sin; but again
he will take whatever particular understanding she can manage: are we not
all sinners?

Now, finally, Hooper has succeeded in giving pause to the "calm energy"
of Elizabeth's self-possession. She meditates his response. The narrator supposes she is planning new methods of treating the "dark fantasy" symptomatic of his "mental disease"; but surely we have been given ample reason to
separate our point of view from his. And because her own responses now
become, for the first time, themselves ambiguous and in need of interpretation, we may as well imagine something significant.

Her meditative silence seems to indicate that the meaning of an ancestral
faith is slowly coming back; that the significance of the religious idiom in
which she has lived her whole unawakened life is beginning to dawn on her
consciousness, not "notionally" but "affectively." Subjectively. Sorrow, yes:
sorrow for sin. And for what sin? Not any grotesque or melodramatic "actual" (usually sexual) crime such as the Arminian imagination might require; only that "original" sinfulness of alienated mind and self-will which
defines our natural condition. To be human is to be sinful. To be sinful is to
be veiled. Because the "terrors" of the veil finally do fall around her, and
because Hooper recognizes her "trembling" as a sign of his own complex
feeling, we may fairly imagine that Elizabeth has taken his point—that there
are sinful meanings so totally private that they cannot be told, but only shad-
owed forth in some symbolic way, until the final judgment shall gratefully
lay bare the secrets of all hearts.

On our behalf, then, Elizabeth accepts the lesson. Unlike the narrator,
and unlike her exact counterpart in a later story of "Egotism," she does not
herself pronounce that Hooper's symbolic veil is "but a dark fantasy," or
that "what it typified was as shadowy as itself."[35] She accepts the bare fact
of sinful separation. And yet her incurably healthy mind runs to the gracious
possibility of human palliation or mitigation. Strictly speaking, the secrecy
of the inner life is invincible. But is human life entirely a matter of such ab-
solutes? And so, once more, a lover's fair request, but this time symbolically
expressed: "Lift the veil but once, and look me in the face" (47). If not
heart-to-heart, then at least face-to-face. Tell me something. If not the
worst, yet reveal some really human "trait whereby the worst may be inferred." Hooper's answer to her measured request is passionate, even shrill:
"Never! It cannot be!" And then, recovering, his equally unsettling smile
tells us that this explication has gone as far as it can; and that for him, at

least, penetrating moral insight has become dogma and obsession. For all his careful and sympathetic beginning, and for all his swift recovery, he has ended where he always ends: spiritually deranged and humanly out of control.

Hooper has educated Elizabeth's literary sensibility and brought her to a new level of spiritual awareness; but he has lost her as a lover and a wife. And for this outcome it requires a pretty stiff moral principle to convict *her*. We may forgive Hooper most of the ordinary disruptions caused by his prophetic career. We may decline to charge that his commitment to "power" in preaching is greater than to "plainness"; and that, accordingly, he has violated Pauline prescriptions for the reformed ministry. We may even agree to accept the Puritan myth of self-knowledge in place of the Catholic fiction of sacraments. But how can we forgive the tone he takes in answer to Elizabeth's not entirely simple desire for "attainable felicity"? Hysterically, he begs her not to desert him—to accept him, here, on his own astringent terms of separation *à deux*, in the promise that "hereafter" there shall be "no darkness between [their] souls" (47). But it will not do. The divine spokesman is asking a woman to espouse his career of prophecy, not to marry his manhood. Surely such a union would be as confused socially as it is inexplicable in terms of Christian symbology. Hooper may still wish to marry Elizabeth in the old way; and, however awkward and fastidious, their face-to-veil union might even be quite sexual. But it would be, from a spiritual point of view, explicitly insignificant. Elizabeth does well to refuse it.[36]

As prophet, Hooper offers his insight as a challenge to ordinary perception. But he has also decided to apply it, without any principle of mediation, to his own life. In doing so he has transformed an undeniable truth about the theological and philosophical limits of subjectivity into a working social hypothesis: rejecting the conception of any earthly "Communion of Saints," he has also denied all possibility of true sharing. Accordingly, he has erected his premise of the absolute impossibility of intersubjectivity into a perfect defense against all relative attempts at literal self-revelation. Already trapped by the personal aspect of his prophecy, he has then transformed his own self into an abstraction, with no literal history it cares to reveal. My Self is horrible; my Self is ineffable; my Self is ineffably horrible. I cannot tell you: the telling would falsify the horror. Therefore do not inquire. Trust me. I wear the Black Veil. "I burn."

In another critical idiom it would be entirely accurate to suggest that Hooper has turned himself into a sign. But not even semiological translation can save Hooper in our human sympathies: that such a metamorphosed thing can produce noticeable religious results, the remainder of Hooper's "efficient" ministry amply demonstrates; but the well-tempered critic may be excused for not wanting his daughter to marry one. And its after-career is predictable enough; even a sentimentalist narrator can be trusted with the summary.

No more attempts are made at merely human communication. The multitude cringe and children flee. The prophet's outward life continues blameless, and yet many people imagine the worst; superstitious legends grow up. Hooper grieves at all this; but he avoids mirrors and fountains, even as he continues "groping darkly within his own soul" (48) where, philosophically, he is now fairly trapped. Others similarly groping require him as their proper physician of the soul: to their New Birth he is "Father." As prophet of the true sight of sin he acquires a notable reputation. In his one most public performance he almost succeeds in reversing the otherwise inevitable process of New England's liberalization. And then he comes to die. One last time some ordinary person tries to get the whole thing explained, rationalized. As the Reverend Mr. Clark of Westbury is, in every way, a less appealing figure than Elizabeth, Hooper's sensitivity and power are once again apparent. And, as it is now too late to matter, Hooper does go fairly far toward explaining why he has felt the veil can *never* come off. And this in spite of a raging obsession with himself.

The narrator's report on Hooper's compulsive avoidance of reflecting surfaces might well suggest an advancing state of diseased spiritual self-regard. But with so many persons watching at the deathbed, there is no need to infer: amidst even his "most convulsive struggles" and in "the wildest vagaries of his intellect," Hooper maintains, by now habitually, "an awful solicitude lest the black veil should slip aside" (50–51). Such a slip would, of course, "mean" nothing, since Hooper is not in control of his intentional faculties. But the symptomatic significance is clear: the veil itself—which began as a mere symbol and then became the occasional cause of inadvertent behavior in a life of severe, ironic discipline—has now become the sort of *idée fixe* which by itself orders the entire experience of a mind otherwise out of control. Like Hooper's private self (which began as merely exemplary and altogether instrumental in regard to the art of prophecy), the veil has become an object of unique concern in itself. Thus, clinically as otherwise, Hooper's career is now complete: the obsessive object has become the sole measure of sanity; madness and common sense have perfectly changed places.

And yet, in a final lapse into lucidity, Hooper can still speak a sort of divine sense. From the depths of his all-but-otherworldly madness this Fool of Truth reasserts the coherent power of his Puritan prophecy and (once again) prevents us from declaring him too simply disturbed in his intellects. To be sure, Hooper's final "application" of his own symbolic doctrine does indeed redound to his own conviction, even as critics have suggested; and the net result of this unlooked-for irony is to leave us more or less satisfied with the narrator's unfriendly moral. But before Hooper issues his final, self-convicting challenge to friends and lovers, he has to deal with the well-intentioned but officious and finally impercipient attentions of the Reverend Mr. Clark of Westbury, "a young and zealous divine, who has ridden in haste to pray by the bedside of the expiring minister" (50). As against Clark, the burden of Hooper's spiritual seriousness and symbolic subtlety once again appears obvious and impressive, as Puritan insight always does when set beside ordinary moral intelligence. One last time—just before the last clear but damaging peroration—we are forced to see how powerful is Hooper's logic within his own world.

A paradigm of unreconstructed common sense, Clark expresses understandable concern for Hooper's earthly reputation; and, by extension, for that of the Church:

> Is it fitting . . . that a man so given to prayer, of such a blameless example, holy in deed and thought, so far as mortal judgment may pronounce; is it fitting that a Father in the Church should leave a shadow on his memory, that may seem to blacken a life so pure? I pray you venerable brother . . . Let me cast aside this black veil from your face! (51)

Now this is not entirely obtuse: unlike the rumor mongers in Hooper's world, Clark understands that it is irrelevant to search for some glaring moral fault, some singular sin of mortal gravity, hidden beneath the facade of Hooper's "blameless" exterior but obscurely revealed by his veil. There is, accordingly, no last confession to be heard; Clark feels no impulse to offer Hooper that final unburdening relief which Hooper himself has offered his own agonized converts. And since there is, by Puritan definition, no "last sacrament," the young divine proposes the only remedy his simplistic zeal can imagine: a last chance to dispel a mystery and restore a reputation. Let us clear up this whole matter once and for all, he urges, by making it plain that in the end your veil was *only* a symbol. A symbol of that generalized theologic guilt which (of course) we all share in the eyes of God. You have made your point: "we are all sinners." And it is well taken: "no man lives without faults and follies; the best have their failings; in many things we all offend." But enough is enough. Remove your veil now, at last, or everyone will suitably infer that you intend somewhat more.

Well motivated. Not entirely obtuse. And yet, by authentic Puritan standards of consciousness, entirely too easy. How utterly the meaning of the older idiom has, by now, past midway in the backsliding eighteenth century, been lost. One cringes. One almost springs to Hooper's defense at last, in spite of everything.

Unlike Elizabeth, who really did take in and apply Hooper's prophecy (but tried to look beyond it), Clark does not seem to understand at all. As with the narrator, whose detached remark about the subject to which Hooper's first new sermon "had reference," the quality of his language betrays his spiritual innocence: here it is the characterization of Hooper's life as "blameless . . . so far as mortal judgment may pronounce" which gives away his case. Technically, of course, and in the best slip-service Protestant manner, he allows for another view, namely God's. Obviously he knows and teaches, as faithfully as any Jonathan Mayhew or Charles Chauncey, any Lemuel Briant or Gad Hitchcock, that in God's revealed view we are of course all depraved.[37] But the point, surely, is that in the authentic Puritan view only that view has relevance because only that view is true. The mortal judgment is worse than irrelevant because it is inherently false and humanly pernicious. It is false because all men are sinners *really*, not just symbolically. Their so-called faults and follies and failings are, according to the only true sight of sin, horrible signs of man's willful if inevitable alienation from God. Were there only one sin, and that entirely momentary and internal, still the thing were infinite. And in fact a man's sins are infinite in number. Or if indeed there be only one depravity, it is nevertheless total: originating with the birth of consciousness, it continues to express itself at every moment of conscious life, as the reference of every fact of life to the Self rather than to Being-in-General. It is of that desperate condition, and of its painful implications for human society, that the black veil is only a symbol.

But clearly this is all beyond the Arminian range of the unctuous Mr. Clark. A minister trapped within the linguistic confines of the literature of the Puritan tradition, he automatically knows enough not to suspect or go looking for any very singular sin. But as a natural man, unawakened to the terrors of the true sight, he cannot feel the force of Hooper's prophecy at all. In fact he actually goes backwards, into that special brand of moralism to which Puritanism always must repair whenever it loses touch with its own most essential insight. His spiritual sensibilities prove so uneducable that he is forced back into precisely that area of moral melodrama which Hooper had earlier forced Elizabeth to abandon. In the face of Hooper's passionate resistance to his sensible entreaty, he changes his interpretation of the case altogether, rejecting a symbolic interpretation entirely: "With what horrible crime upon your soul are you now passing to the judgment?" (52).

Our sympathy with Hooper is never greater than at this moment. Given his premises, and given the nature of the moral inquisition to which he has been subjected, we understand how he might well go out screaming. To take off the veil now, in response to logic like that of Mr. Clark, would amount to a blasphemous infidelity to the insight he has tried to uphold throughout his entire life, in the midst of a world growing every day further out of touch with its truth and power. Hooper's meaning will simply not reduce to either of Clark's simplistic expectations. Of course the veil is a symbol. And of course Hooper is, all literally, a horrible sinner. But the veil betokens not some heinous crime as might find its way into a gothic novel or the newspapers. It symbolizes "only" the terror and the horror of being the kind of secret or subjective sinner which every man is. When most people can no longer understand that sort of symbolic utterance, it is a sign that Puritan prophecy has not done its office. And when the ministry itself shall lose its grasp of the idiom, it is the end of that world. And so, whatever is not simply clinical in Hooper's "Never!" may fairly be set down as a violent cry of (historical) prophecy against "The Danger of an Unconverted Ministry."[38]

Nevertheless, as "the true sight of sin" is not quite Hawthorne's "doctrine," the tale does not end on this note. The hysteria of the "Dark Old Man"—the Last of the Puritans, as he might almost think, with whose death a saving truth is about to die out of the world—subsides to the "faint, sad smile, so often there" (52). And as the ironies of Hooper's last speech begin to light on his own head, we are confirmed in our sense that a Converted Ministry is not without its own proper Dangers.

Smiling, Hooper means to underline the rather heavy irony that people have trembled at him alone, and at a mere "piece of crape," when in fact a far more real and terrible Black Veil is drawn over the mind and heart of every man, woman, and child in Milford and in the world. He also means to exculpate himself of the charge of undue moral secrecy. But his words suggest other meanings as well.

> When the friend shows his inmost heart to his friend; the lover to his best beloved; when man does not vainly shrink from the eye of his Creator, loathsomely treasuring up the secret of his sin; then deem me a monster. (52)

He means, of course, that in this life he could *never* be considered a moral monster. How can he be regarded as deviant when he has merely publicized what is inwardly true of everyone? And yet the troubled reader wonders why it would have been so wrong for Hooper to have made a relative human attempt at the impossible miracle of true sharing? Might he not have tried, according to some ironic model of the best-possible failed-approximate, to say to Elizabeth, or to his congregation, or to us, something of what was in his heart or soul? Of course our understanding would be false to his subjec-

348

tivity. But could we not be trusted to know this? And to understand? Or, if not, might it not be the better part of saintliness simply to bear this inevitable wrong patiently, and turn one's prophetic attention elsewhere? More outwardly?

Perhaps. But obviously Hooper's mind has never worked in this way. Despite the doubleness of his smile he is clearly moving back toward Puritan Absolutism rather than ahead to Irony. Quite obviously he has not been the sort of prophet to lead the way in showing all that might be said or done on the side of love and friendship. His marriage to Elizabeth, had it occurred, would have been a fairly transcendental affair. And though he may grieve the loss of this and all other "natural connections," his smile lets us know that he accepts his plight, even as he laments it: no one else seems able to live up to his level of insight; and his own premises prevent him from descending to meet. Trapped by an irony just short of Irony itself, Hooper must remain isolated.

The crucial clause in his last speech does not suggest that if, in some ideal but imaginable present, the friend or lover should relent from pride and privacy and show his heart, then Hooper would do the same. Hooper is no such failed-follower. What his prophecy says, much more technically, is that only when perfect sharing is shown to be possible could he be convicted of strangeness, if he then continue to wear the veil. Till then he will continue to live as a clear sign of the sinful separatism that clearly *is*, however obscurely most men may perceive it. His conscious decision has been everywhere to signify the absolute rather than to embody the relative.[39]

Further, Hooper seems to know that to remove his veil even once would deny his gesture its absolute character, and deprive it of much of its seriousness. To Clark, obviously, he would be saying something very wrong indeed: "Yes, it was *only* a symbol; I did not really mean sin literally; but only in that quaint sense we Puritans have always had in talking about ourselves in relation to God, so as not to appear presumptuous." To Elizabeth, earlier, a single removal would have conceded less, but still more than Hooper would be prepared to sacrifice. To her he would be saying: "Well, yes, I suppose there is some *thing* to tell; each of us does have a biographically trivial and a humanly embarrassing side; and on that side you will perceive that my sorrows—and yes my real sins—are not that dramatic; there are, as you may imagine, temptations as well as lonely satisfactions in my singular life as minister, and you may rest assured that they trouble me deeply, especially in those 'days of torment' we call the Lord's Supper;[40] and when I consider them in their true light, in relation to God, and as expressions of the depravity of my whole loathsome self, then you must realize that . . ." But here Arminianism as Irony turns back into Puritanism as Prophecy. And from such ironic admissions, what prophetic recovery?

Prophets, as we have been told, are not much honored in their own country: Is this not Jesus of Nazareth, whose father was a carpenter? And very probably, for many of the same good and sufficient reasons, prophets are not at all recognized by their wives; one wonders what Jonathan Edwards and Sarah Pierrepont talked about after they put out the lights. When dealing with a prophet it seems possible to know too much. To know the appropriate psychobiography—to know where the prophet is "at," or where his prophecy is coming at you "from"—is to hear human tonalities rather than the Divine Voice. The measure of Hooper's understanding of the formal nature of prophecy is his sense that, within the view of those to whom the prophecy is addressed (including Elizabeth), the mask must never be set aside. And the measure of his commitment to the absolute character of his own peculiar prophecy is that willingness to let everyone (including Clark, and all those whose mentality he represents) believe that he is horribly different from everyone else. In his world at least, the Word of God and the words of man cannot cooperate to any unified salvific result.

Forced to choose between "the absolute and the natural," his Puritanism determines all his choices one way.[41] Pressed on his choices he can only wax otherworldly and shrill: "On earth, never!" When this occurs he loses not only the moral confidence of many ordinary people in his world, and not only that "cheerful brotherhood and woman's love" which others might take as a type of eventual salvation. He also seems doomed to lose the sympathy of most readers. Ordinary moralistic and sentimental responses are both satisfactorily figured in the tale itself. An ironic response will merely recognize the inevitability of Hooper's failure to satisfy contradictory demands and (probably) blame his hysterical lapses from ironic self-possession. And even the orthodox may balk, obscurely suspecting that Hooper has somehow been stopped short of the saving insight. Very few, presumably, will hear spiritual accents in Hooper's refusals—which seem, rhetorically at least, altogether of a piece with the anathemas hurled by Digby in his cave and Brown in the forest. And fewer still will be shocked by the narrator's last "awful" thought, of Hooper's face "still" mouldering beneath the Black Veil. For it may well turn out that what is absolutely impossible in this life is impossible absolutely.

6

The thought that has kept occurring throughout our "Puritan" analysis of "The Minister's Black Veil" is that, even after the relevant theological categories have been applied, the story is yet somehow more generally psychological than specifically or historically theological. Certainly this will seem so if our standing prejudices are in favor of that "poetic" literature which is everywhere "more philosophical than history"; or if, just less generally, we have become accustomed to regarding Hawthorne as a writer who, at his most historical, "read past [Puritan] dogma and grasped . . . their essential anxiety and distress."[42] But even the historical critic seems constrained to admit that Hooper's Puritan problem of Sin everywhere threatens to lapse into a more general problem of Self; or, at very least, that the Puritan sight of sin seems to merge with Romantic Sorrow or Modern Subjectivity. And if this is so, then one may fairly ask what special claim to primacy can be made for a latter-day Puritan reading of "The Minister's Black Veil"?

Ultimately, the answer to this crucial question about misplaced historicity may lie in an understanding of the relation between Puritan and more modern forms of subjectivity. But another, simpler argument is also relevant. And so, before inquiring closely into the meaning of the notorious "ambiguity of sin or sorrow" which is said to envelop Hooper in his later career, we might do well to look again at the simpler matter of the evidence of the story's Puritan specificity. So far, we have merely evoked the context of the Great Awakening and read carefully for suggestions of meaning appropriate to that world. Closer inspection reveals that once again Hawthorne has done a surprising amount of historical source work: far too much, we ought to conclude, for one who meant for us simply to "read past" the world in which he set his fiction.

The easiest "clue" to Hawthorne's historical intention is also one of the most telling indications of the tale's contextual meaning. Surely the name of the squire who breaks off from Sunday-dinner communion with Parson Hooper is supposed to be very familiar. "Saunders" is, after all, the surname of the most famous persona created by America's most complete exemplar of liberality and enlightenment in the eighteenth century—"Poor Richard" Saunders of Franklin's best-selling *Almanac* and *Way to Wealth*. Evidently Hawthorne feels perfectly entitled to expect the association. As he says elsewhere, Franklin's widespread American fame rests not on his "philosophical discoveries . . . or even his vast political services"; rather it was "as the writer of those proverbs which Poor Richard was supposed to utter [that] Franklin became the counsellor and household friend of almost every family in America."[43] Thus it requires something short of patient archival research to recognize that "The Minister's Black Veil" means to invoke the American paradigm of secular virtue and worldly wisdom.

One does not infer, of course, that Hawthorne's Squire Saunders *is* the historical Franklin, any more than Parson Hooper *is* Edwards. The positivist in the audience, like the one present at the Showman's performance of "Main Street," will easily point out that Franklin had left New England well before any evidences of "surprising conversions" began to appear—that he broke off his relations with the Puritanism of Massachusetts well before it entered its Awakening phase. Or, less simplistically, that it is perfectly easy to imagine the cosmopolitan Franklin sitting down to a meal with a revivalist preacher—with Whitefield, for example, when that famous prophet visited Philadelphia.[44] Clearly Hawthorne's Saunders is a "fiction." And yet the conventions of his special form of fiction-as-history demand that we think about Franklin (especially in his most influential and representative Poor Richard persona) as we read the story, just as we think about Hooker or Edwards or any other such "formidable" exemplar of Puritanism's "true sight." The name "Saunders" means to suggest, with perfect intellectual economy, the precise range of religious and cultural values at issue.

The Franklin of the *Autobiography* is (for all the supposed imitation of *Pilgrim's Progress*) not much like the Edwards of the "Personal Narrative": where young Franklin builds a "wharf" in a "salt-marsh" out of a sense of public "usefulness," young Edwards joins together with some of his schoolmates to build a "booth in a swamp, in a very retired spot, for a place of prayer."[45] Both of these actions are "errata," as it turns out, but that fact does not impair their clarity as images. Franklin, who has stolen his building materials, needs to be taught that "nothing was useful which was not honest"; but he easily learns that lesson and goes on from there. Edwards lives to discover that his effort of childish piety was entirely spurious, a simplistic mistake for grace; but he also lives to assert that true salvation lies even *further* from the track of common utility as ordinarily conceived. He spends his entire adult life asserting the necessity of an intense familiarity with all the dismal swampy places of the human psyche, whereas Franklin, all the while, endeavors to fill in all such nuisances with the sane-making stuff of worldly wisdom. One almost imagines that, behind certain more proximate models, Hawthorne has Franklin in mind when, in "The Celestial Rail-road," the Slough of Despond is declared "a disgrace to all the neighborhood" and promptly filled in. Nowhere, let me repeat, is Hawthorne simply holding a brief for Puritanism. But must there not be, somewhere, "something somehow like" the sense of sin?

Even more clearly, the view of life sponsored by Richard Saunders is about as far from that to which Hooker or Edwards or (fictionally) Hooper gives witness as it is possible to imagine. If one senses the mentality of a reductive enlightenment in the verdict of the Milford physician on the condition of Hooper's "intellects," then surely it is more telling to suggest that what defines the peculiar form of spiritual impercipience in the majority of

Hooper's unawakened congregation is the Yankee secularism which first produced and then recognized itself so adequately expressed in the worldly wisdom of Richard Saunders.

His *"moral* Sentences, *prudent* Maxims, and *wise* Sayings" had been intended "to leave strong and lasting impressions on the Memory of young Persons," which they might remember "when both Almanack and Almanack-maker have been long thrown by and forgotten."[46] But even the childish listeners to Hawthorne's "Biographical Story" of Benjamin Franklin know that Poor Richard's words to the wise are insufficient. One of the more sensitive does not care for them at all: "They are all about getting money, or saving it." His story-teller Grandfather is forced to agree. Trying to do as well as he can for his historical material, without positively fostering dangerous falsehoods, and forbidden from Hawthornean irony by a "deep sense of responsibility" to the sacredness of childhood, he concedes that Poor Richard's proverbs "teach men but a very small portion of their duties."[47]

Obviously. A penny saved is not salvation earned. And if God simply helps those who help themselves, then the entire Puritan theology—from the problem of "Preparation for Salvation in Seventeenth-Century New England" right down to the famous controversy in the 1760's about "Striving to Enter at the Strait Gate"—is all monumentally irrelevant. What have early retiring and early rising to do with the "New Birth"? The worlds represented by Richard Saunders and by Awakened Puritanism are, from a strictly spiritual point of view, simply not contiguous. Edwards and Franklin, though each might be shown to be a legitimate child of the Enlightenment adequately considered, really have nothing to say to each other. Their ranges of experience and literary expression lie along different scales of reality. And a "squire" named for the affinity of his spiritual capacity to that of Richard Saunders will make no better sense of Hooper's medieval idiom and gothic masquerade than Franklin himself could make of the motivation or the religious significance of the "maiden lady of seventy" who lived in his garret in London and had "vowed to lead the life of a nun, as near as might be done in those circumstances," confessing every day to a priest because "it is impossible to avoid vain thoughts." The "true sight of sin" simply does not touch the problem of the amount of income on which "life and health may be supported."[48]

No more than any of the Franklinesque "busybodies" (44) in the congregation, so accustomed to acting as censors of ministerial mores, will a Saunders know what to say to a Hooper. They will simply leave off from meaningful relations and go their separate ways. That separation might not quite figure the distinction between "lowbrow" and "highbrow." But surely

Hawthorne did not need Van Wyck Brooks to tell him that the moral space between Franklin and Edwards amounts to a noticeable and significant division within "The New England Mind."[49]

Once we grasp the obvious point about "Saunders," we are ready for the somewhat more elegant and (to us, at least) rather more arcane one about "Clark." The two allusions work differently, but they are obviously part of the same historical pattern. "Saunders" is, in the tale itself, only a name; but the very familiar name (with the single telling detail) is quite enough. "Clark" is, perhaps, a less familiar name; but then he figures as much more than a name in the story. We see him begin well enough, in a recognizably orthodox way, only to end by lapsing into a frankly Arminian interpretation of Hooper's prophecy about secret sin, thereby making perfect nonsense of his whole spiritual commitment. With that well-intentioned but ultimately reductive performance in view, we simply ask ourselves if there is any "Clark" Hawthorne would have known who might fill the bill. How might the name "Clark" be fairly associated with the lapse of the reformed sense of sin and salvation? Once we ask this question, our only problem is the embarrassment of a whole variety of cogent answers.

Waiving the larger problem of the Enlightenment itself as a "treason of the Clarks," our first thought is likely to be of the Reverend Samuel Clarke who, though British, figures very largely in the progress of Arminianism in America, as a sort of fountainhead of liberal thought. His theories of the reasonableness of the Christian revelation and of the power of ordinary human freedom in the salvation process—expressed in his famous Boyle Lectures of 1704 and 1705, which helped to make a "thorough deist" of Franklin—inspired a whole generation of proto-Unitarians in their effort to rationalize the New England theology.[50] What better name and religious affinity might therefore be attached to a young American divine who has simply lost touch with the meaning of the older idiom of salvation? Or, if we prefer an authentic example of the new Arminianism somewhat closer to home, there is the Reverend John Clarke, the younger colleague of that redoubtable American liberal Charles Chauncey. John Clarke's pamphlet *Salvation for All Men*, signed by "One Who Wishes Well to All Mankind," helped prepare the way for Chauncey's own major contribution to the cause of Universalism; and it stirred up quite a controversy in the Boston of the 1780's. The whole affair becomes the subject of Timothy Dwight's *Triumph of Infidelity* which is, in turn, a primary source for Hawthorne's "Celestial Rail-road."[51]

Thus we should not be surprised to find the Chauncey style of liberalism implicated in a story which already accuses Franklin; and it makes fairly good sense to think of Hawthorne's "young and zealous divine" as trying to persuade himself and others that no one is ever lost utterly, not even

Hooper. Even in the end, when Hawthorne's Clark is led to infer some "horrible crime" upon the soul "now passing to the judgment," we notice that he does not at all predict Hooper's damnation. Significantly, even the tirelessly sentimental narrator comes closer to doing that.

But there is probably a still more exemplary "Clark" whom Hawthorne seems to have had still more immediately in mind. If Samuel Clarke is in the wrong country, John Clarke is in the wrong generation. We would probably have been told if Hooper had lived on into Revolutionary times, when John Clarke actually began his zealous ministry. And, less literalistically, we should be surprised if even a figurative associate of Chauncey, displaced from the Boston of the 1780's to an early decade in "Westbury," had found his way to the deathbed of a revivalist whose sermon before Belcher almost stemmed the tide of liberalism and turned New England around. Earlier in his career, before the sectarian strife of the Great Awakening, Hooper might well "have exchanged pulpits with Parson Shute" (38), despite the vaguely liberal associations of that name; but the split within the Standing Order opened very wide and deep once Boston's elite set themselves against the evangelical labors of Whitefield and Edwards.[52] Hence we can scarcely tolerate the idea of a notable recruit to the party of the future praying with a rather famous exponent of the ideology of the past. Thus, although it helps us with the moral world of the story to think about the ultimate liberalism of Chauncey (as well as about the English sources of liberal inspiration), we may still need to look elsewhere for a more essential "Clark" behind Hawthorne's allusion.

Surely the almost perfect case is that of Peter Clark, not a liberal at all, but not an Edwardsean Evangelical either; rather, an embattled "Old Light" who opposed the Awakening, and whom history remembers as an embarrassed Calvinist who gave the old game away by uncautiously admitting too many of the liberal's presuppositions into his own argument in favor of Original Sin. Chauncey himself accused Peter Clark of deserting true Calvinism in his admission of the probability of salvation for infants: did not the authentic orthodoxy teach that absolutely all human beings are, in Adam, guilty "by nature"? The problem—which dominated an extended and notorious debate on the meaning of Original Sin in the 1750's, even as Edwards' own monumental treatise on "The Great Christian Doctrine" was posthumously appearing—touched more than the matter of humane sentiments, in which Peter Clark (like virtually everyone else) was struggling to anticipate the moral tonalities of John Clarke and Charles Chauncey later; it went, in fact, to the very heart of the question of the distinction between "actual" sin as a unique and specific human intention and some "original" sinfulness of nature which is logically prior to any human act, the Adamic inheritance of which causes all of human nature to be "totally" depraved, *ab origine.*

Thus Peter Clark's problem was not principally that he felt kindly toward those children who alternately mock and are terrified of Hooper's veil. It was, rather, that he had lost the sense of the sinfulness of Original Sin. He tried to defend the intellectual cogency and moral justice of the old scheme of universal depravity, while admitting that the "principle of sinfulness" was probably not the sort of "sin" which merited hell. That is to say, the real sense of "sin" is contained in its Arminian meaning: a singular and identifiable voluntary act which an adult human being discovers his own will to have posited.[53]

And that, of course, is the precise difficulty of Hawthorne's Clark, as it is for almost everyone in the story except Hooper himself. The congregation, Elizabeth (originally, at least), and the Reverend Mr. Clark all look for the particular sin Hooper has personally committed. No one can even faintly imagine the obvious, that it is the original and alienating sinfulness of his *nature* which troubles him. Not even a fellow minister, supposed to be within his own intellectual tradition, can grasp the point of his pietistic and distinctly unmoralistic prophecy. And once we grasp the absolutely critical importance of the loss of the old sense of sin for "the Passing of the New England Theology," we easily see that "Clark" is just as strategic and telling an allusion as "Saunders."

The point is speculative, I suppose: Peter Clark's *Summer Morning's Conversation upon the Doctrine of Original Sin* (1758) is not listed among the books Hawthorne borrowed from the Salem Athenaeum; nor is Samuel Webster's *Winter Evening's Conversation*, which had provoked it; nor Charles Chauncey's *Opinion of one that has perused the Summer Morning's Conversation*, which answered Clark. But we should be slow to conclude anything from that fact. The controversy was nearly as public as it was momentous, finding its way into the very newspapers Hawthorne had before him in writing the sketches called "Old News." The first of those sketches actually refers to the same Peter Clark in question: Hawthorne pictures a desultory Boston merchant pausing at the bookstore of Kneeland and Green in order to "look over the controversy on baptism, between the Reverend Peter Clark and an unknown adversary"; and then moving on to other books, to "see whether George Whitefield be as great in print as he is famed in the pulpit." The juxtaposition of Clark with a great figure in the Awakening seems more than curious. And if Hawthorne knows about Clark in the early 1740's, why not in the late 1750's? From the same newspapers, at very least. Especially if a deft and knowing allusion just happens to make perfect sense in a story.[54]

But the Reverend Peter Clark has at least one other claim to fame—one which, indirectly at least, takes us to the heart of the historicity of "The Minister's Black Veil." On 30 May 1739 Clark delivered the official Massachusetts election sermon before Governor Belcher. The easy point, of course, is that it is *not* like the sermon we must imagine Hooper to have given. It is by no means "liberal": unlike the more famous *Throne Established by Righteousness* preached by John Barnard in 1734 (which a modern commentator has singled out as a "harbinger of the age of reason"), its *topoi* are all those of the latter-day lackluster Jeremiad. Biblical in inspiration and pedantic in manner, it enunciates all the usual clichés about New England's "apostasy": it notes a defection from the simpler mores and purer hearts of the ancestors; it predicts further judgments against further declension; and it ends with the traditional call for rulers to suppress vice in a very immoral age. Like the majority of the twelve election sermons preached before Governor Belcher, between 1730 and 1741, it is a thoroughly unmemorable piece of sociological moralism, erected on a basis of utterly tribalist filiopietism.[55] Simply considered, it is (like Hawthorne's fictional Clark himself) "Puritan" in everything but spiritual essence. It expresses complete loyalty to the moral norms of "our earliest ancestral sway" but hardly seems designed to produce a revivalistic return to piety. And in fact it had no such effect.

What gives significance to this essentially negative point concerning the latter-day indistinction of Clark's sermon, however, is the contrast between it and one or two other sermons delivered before Belcher. All the evidence indicates that Hawthorne himself had read the twelve sermons so delivered; and the story obviously suggests that the reponsible reader ought to do so as well. The result is enormously instructive: Clark's sermon is, as I have said, most unlike Barnard's appropriation of political categories from Locke and Montesquieu; and it is *just* like most of the others. Most, but not all. The crucial differences help us once again to identify the precise issues of the world we are in. Even a glance at the names of those who delivered the sermons tells us much we need to know.[56]

Thomas Prince we know as historian and annalist, Cotton Mather's most likely successor in the task of documenting the progress of New England's "Errand." Preaching in 1730, on the 100th anniversary of the arrival of Winthrop aboard the *Arabella*, he celebrates the Puritans' latter-day "Exodus." His "People of New England" gives us, in fact, a *memorable* sermon on ancestors, full of historical detail and fertile with mythic suggestion. But though he calls for a "revival of the power of piety among all about us," his memorable exercise in cultural myth-making provides no clue as to how the definitively Puritan piety might be recovered. Perhaps Wigglesworth will help. It is Samuel Wigglesworth, of course, and not his more famous ancestor, whose *Day of Doom* did much to popularize (with its relentless fourteeners) and to kill (with his merciless chop-logic) the classic Puritan view of sin and its consequences. Perhaps his is the sermon Hawthorne had in mind, as the classic instance of revivalist rhetoric as political sermon. Preached in 1733, the year of Edwards' "Divine and Supernatural Light," the year before the first "ripples" of Awakening at Northampton, "An Essay for Reviving Religion" seems to be driving at the main point. At very least it reminds us that if the revival of the 1730's and 1740's came in a surprising and unwontedly emotional form, it came nevertheless not so much by accident as in answer to an oft-repeated wish and call.[57]

According to Wigglesworth, the (perfectly Biblical) point about New England is simply this: "Thou hast a name that thou livest, and art dead." Religion survives in outward appearance but not in vital reality; the sense of sin has become a matter of habitual and notional assent rather than of personal consciousness. Declension is not ultimately a matter of "vice," as Clark and so many others would have it; far more obvious than the presence of scandalous corruption is the plain absence of conviction, compunction, humiliation. New Englanders have become "in great measure strangers to the Power and Life of Religion." With a perfect reputation for "faith, piety, chastity, justice, temperance, and sobriety," a people may yet be dying, like lukewarm Laodicea. There are plenty of "works which are materially good and laudable," plenty of ordinary moralism, plenty of what used to be called mere "civil honesty"; but where is the spirit of true piety? Is the Sabbath kept holy? Is there ever, really, any leaving off from secular affairs? Is there any genuine fear of the Lord? Is anyone really willing to "suffer convictions to ripen into conversions"? Or do people prefer to "deceive themselves with vain hopes, and impose upon the world the name that they live"? And do preachers really try to prevent this self-deception, this clumsy feint at God-deception, by frequently urging "the duty of self-examination"? Well, they had better begin to do so once again.

What New England needs to recall above all else is "God's omnisciency," the "impossibility of deceiving Him with a vain and empty show, and the vanishing hope of the hypocrite when Death and Judgment shall call them before the August Tribunal."[58] If the last clause looks backwards, very deliberately, to the "doom" prophesied by Wigglesworth's ancestor, still the thrust of the whole sermon anticipates, calls out for, and in fact predicts the world of the Awakening. When someone energetically sounds the note of alarm about "secret" sin—which foolish men "seek to hide . . . from the dread Being" (39) they daily address, but which causes men of adequate religious awareness to live their whole lives in fear and trembling—then we are getting very close to the world and the theme of Hawthorne's Hooper.

If there is any other real-life model for the fictional sermon Hooper is merely reported to have preached before Belcher, it was the one preached in 1740, the first year of New England's high Awakening, by a man named not Hooper, but Cooper—which, under the circumstances, seems close enough. The relevant circumstances involve not only the theme of his discourse, but also its quasi-official status, as well as Cooper's own familiar relation to the conduct of the Great Awakening in New England.

In our own histories of the progress of religious doctrine and sentiment in the first half of the eighteenth century, William Cooper figures as cosmopolitan Boston's most unequivocal sponsor of the revitalized Calvinism and revivalist tactics of Jonathan Edwards. Standing out very distinctly from the "free and catholic" associates of "Johnny" Barnard and Charles Chauncey, he wrote a "Preface" wholeheartedly endorsing the logic of Edwards' first published work, that quintessentially Calvinist sermon of 1731, "God Glorified in Man's Dependence." And he continued to sponsor the publication of Edwards' works in Boston, as he continued to favor and foster the revival in New England's least enthusiastic metropolis. This "official" identification with Edwards was in a sense sealed in 1741, when he provided the "Preface" for the great man's *Distinguishing Marks of a Work of the Spirit of God,* announcing that New England had entered into "the acceptable year of the Lord." He meant a spiritual season, of course, and not a literal "year"; for surely 1740 would have done as well. And indeed his election sermon of that previous year amounts to something like an official declaration, on a public and political occasion, of a year of effective revival. And if Cooper's rhetoric glows with slightly less revivalistic fervor than does Wigglesworth's earlier, nevertheless it was followed up in a way his was not, with a new set of laws concerning the "Observation and Keeping of the Lord's Day." Thus Cooper is a kind of official spokesman for the values of the revival; and the effect of that revival clearly is, according to one point of view, to bring about a return to "all the gloom and piety of our earliest ancestral sway" (49).[59]

The theme of Cooper's discourse is, like that of Wigglesworth, the need to revive a religion of "fear and trembling." And the "reason" of that theme is, quite simply, the rationale of Hooper's ministry in "The Minister's Black Veil": ours is a "God who can't be deceived and will not be mocked; who regards the intention as well as the action; who looks into the heart, and sees through all disguises."[60] However "veiled" may be the sin deep in our nature—that is, in our fixed and settled un-godliness of intention—it is perfectly apparent to the Searcher of Hearts. The first step toward salvation, accordingly, lies in the recognition of the utter deceptiveness of ordinary moral appearances.

Thus we come to see the prophecy of Hawthorne's "Hooper" as a carefully crafted reminder of a major theme of the Awakening, considered as a powerful revival of an older, less moralistic understanding of sin. Hooper is, quite simply, Hawthorne's composite figure of the preacher of the true sight of sin, in an age when that sight has come to seem more than a trifle "gothic." He stands out in sharp contrast to the figure cut by Franklin; by Mayhew, Chauncey, and Johnny Barnard; and by all the Clarks in all their various liberal postures. He is not, literally, William Cooper; for the shape of his career and the purport of his theme suggest Wigglesworth and Edwards and many other revivalists as well. He is called "Hooper," however, for the near approximation of that name to the name of the most official awakener to preach before Belcher. And for two other reasons, also related to an awakened-Puritan reading of the story.

First, if "Hooper" suggests "Cooper," it just as clearly approximates "Hooker," the name of the man whom all the American centuries have rightly identified as Puritanism's classic spokesman for the saving importance of "the true sight of sin." That phrase became Perry Miller's anthology-title for the most revealing and characteristic passage in Hooker's *Application of Redemption*; and it clearly expresses Hooker's most essential thought, the primacy of which must impress itself upon anyone who reads his writings with any care at all. Indeed, it is hardly an oversimplification to say that the entire corpus of Hooker's evangelical writing exists to convince the would-be Christian that salvation always begins with, and never *entirely* gets beyond, the recognition that "sin" is more than a conventional name for an ironic assortment of human failings or a Sunday-morning way to say that nobody's perfect. If the vaguely antinomian John Cotton is the arch-exemplar of the Puritan prophet of grace without preparation, then Hooker stands out with equal clarity as the theological counterpart: everywhere he figures as the larger-than-life exponent of the proposition that the self's utterly serious confrontation with its own disguised iniquity is the only form of preparation for grace there ever can be; and that it is the necessary (and perhaps even the sufficient) condition of grace.[61] In large measure it was Hooker's emphasis which the Awakening would need to revive.

Hooker is evoked in other ways as well. Not only does Hooper's recognized ability "to sympathize with all dark affections" recall Hooker's widespread reputation for the cure of souls shrouded in gloom and on the brink of despair, but his relation to his converts, before and after conversion, is quite like the one Hooker describes in his *Application*. And furthermore, the process which Hooper's preaching sets in motion is precisely the one Hooker recommends and defines: those parishioners first touched are seen walking "homeward alone, wrapt in silent meditation" (40). To us, of course, "meditation" is a familiar term of literary art; but whatever it may mean to poets like Donne and Herbert, in Thomas Hooker it signifies nothing else but that process of deep inwardness by which (alone) the true sight of sin is discovered and nurtured. For Hooker, God never makes the public Ministry of the Word effectual to the soul unless, privately, "He drives the sinner to sad thoughts of heart, and makes him keep an audit in his own soul by serious meditation," that carefully self-reflective process which "meets and stops all the evasions and sly pretenses the false-hearted person shall counterfeit."[62] In the context of a story of a heightened consciousness of sin, the single word identifies the mentality of Hooker with the same sort of apt precision by which the reference to "busybodies" implicates Franklin.

It even appears that echoes of Cotton Mather's famous "literary" characterization of Hooker show up in the story, as if to clarify a doubtful "theological" reference. According to the *Magnalia*, Hooker was a tireless servant of the servants of God, a lonely but faithful man whose natural relations counted for nothing: "He never took the opportunity to serve himself, but lived a sort of exile all his days." Even at Hartford, settled "among his own spiritual children . . . he was an exile. Accordingly, wherever he came, he lived like a stranger in the world." And beyond this definition of Puritan service as worldly estrangement, there is Mather's crucial description of Hooker's most proper religious gifts: in the pulpit he was always "practical" rather than "polemical"; out of the pulpit his positive genius lay in his "dealing with troubled consciences." What made him such an expert physician of the soul, so remarkably adept in treating souls that were in agony for sin, was simply his own dark experience. Lonely as well as serviceable and efficient, he once exclaimed that he could "compare with any man living for fears."[63] That claim alone would associate him with the lonely and fearful Hooper.

Thus, if it were not for Cooper, and for the explicit and meaningful setting of the story in the eighteenth century, we might almost conclude that Hooper evokes Hooker more significantly than anybody else. But plainly he evokes them both. Hooker represents original Puritanism's authentic sight of sin as pervasive and powerful though secret to all but God and the most strenuous acts of self-examination. Surely Hooper's final blast at those around his deathbed recalls Hooker's famous assertion that "they are either fools or madmen that cannot endure the presence of the physician without whose help they cannot be cured." And it is Hooker's vision which Cooper, the latter-day representative of Old-Light Puritanism, seeks to revive. Cooper may be, in the formula of one modern critic, "a strong shadow cast before the coming Jonathan Edwards"; but he is also a man very much in the long shadow of Hooker.[64] And thus we should not be unduly distressed by the ingeniousness of Hawthorne's literary formula: Hooker plus Cooper equals Hooper. It would be false wit or small verbal cleverness if the words were all we had to go on, or if the deciphering of names were the main critical act which "The Minister's Black Veil" had asked us to perform. But such is obviously not the case. For what we find to be true in the names has already abundantly appeared in the drama itself—namely, that Hooper is involved in a latter-day revival of the Puritan sense of sin. To show that

Hooper evokes both Cooper and Hooker is merely to stress the extraordinary care Hawthorne took with the historical dimension of his story.

With this stipulation, then, one last gloss on the surname of Hawthorne's haunted protagonist. According to the received wisdom of the nineteenth century, "Hooper" was the name of the very first Puritan. In fact the entire movement could be dated from that moment in 1550 when John Hooper began the first "vestarian controversy" by refusing to wear Episcopal robes. By the light of the "clothes philosophy" he had learned in Zurich, a church vestment was not at all a "thing indifferent." It was, rather, a powerful symbol of spiritual allegiance and as such had to be treated with the utmost seriousness.[65] A certain connection with our Hooper seems clear at once. Although not at all concerned with robes or surplices, he is involved in a vestarian controversy nevertheless; and one with precisely Puritan bearings. At one level his whole painful story is about nothing more (or less) significant than a single article of human vesture, employed as a religious symbol. As one woman in Hooper's congregation has tried to reassure herself, Hooper has done no more than don "a simple black veil, such as any woman might wear on her bonnet." Or, in Elizabeth's still-unawakened formulation, which Hooper will explicitly echo in his furious last speech, his veil is only a "piece of crape." A thing indifferent, surely. Except that the whole history of Puritanism exists to remind us that, under the aspect of symbol, the world contains far fewer indifferent things than carnal reason usually supposes: namely, none. And Hooper's "awful solicitude" about the black veil seems to participate in the same symbolic passion which motivated his "original" ancestor and namesake.

At some perfectly literal level, the nervous woman in the congregation seems to have forgot not only the point but even the fact of all those sumptuary laws which the Puritans passed: according to one view, a world in which any woman might all naturally wear a veil on her bonnet is a backslidden world indeed; but then the "legislative measures" inspired by Hooper's sermon before Belcher will doubtlessly remind her. And if Puritan legislators rally themselves to remind their people that all such human decorations are objectionable symbols of pride, Hooper himself lives out his whole life trying to say to those same people that his veil is nothing but a sign of his commitment to that philosophy of human existence which, brought back from places like Zurich and Geneva, had motivated the "great migration" in the first place. The historical Hooper hated vestments because he hated the whole economy of salvation they symbolized; he refused those vestments out of loyalty to another scheme. Thomas Hooker hated it equally; and the passion of his commitment to a Puritan scheme of the "application of redemption" led him to furnish a "Preface" to William Ames's *Fresh Suit Against Human Ceremonies in God's Worship*—which continued

Hooper's case against the idea that symbolic externals could be considered as things indifferent.[66] And clearly Hawthorne's Hooper shares the same mentality. He adopts rather than rejects a vestment; and the adopted vestment is one proscribed from women's bonnets; but the Puritan significance of his gesture is perfectly clear nevertheless. Formally, he means to say that a mere "piece of crape" can stand for an ultimate conviction about the nature of things. And materially, he once again asserts that in that divine order the primary fact is sinful subjectivity rather than saving ceremony or sacrament.

Hence the fully real value of Hawthorne's nominalistic formula: what John Hooper is said to have begun; what our own Thomas Hooker so clearly epitomizes for the first American century; what William Cooper sought to revive; that, Hawthorne's Parson Hooper exists to enfigure. Not really very esoteric at all. With Hooper as with Saunders and Clark, far less is required than Joyce's ideal reader with the ideal insomnia. Surely some sort of historical reading was intended to be public and available.

But not all the history of "The Minister's Black Veil" lies so near the surface. Deep down, as it turns out, there are quasi-scholarly "sources" of information about the leading events and principal personages of the Great Awakening. It comes to seem part of Hawthorne's bookish scrupulosity, his "superstitious reverence for literature of all kinds," that he will read almost any available book on a subject which interests him, even where its sectarian bias is quite foreign to his own more liberal views and more imaginative interest in moral history.[67] Of such sources Hawthorne characteristically leaves traces; and the traces almost always help with a detail in the story. So that even Hawthorne's more recondite allusions involve more than a morose literary self-delectation.

Suppose, for example, we find ourselves wondering why "the Reverend Mr. Hooper" is also referred to as "Parson" Hooper. At the end of the story, for effect, the narrator falls into the popular habit of calling him "Father" Hooper; but elsewhere he maintains the very crisp and correct Puritan style of "Mr." or "the Reverend Mr." And at the beginning of the story, this strictness calls attention to the impropriety of the congregation's use of the term "Parson." Sentimentalist that he is, the narrator is also antiquarian enough to know that "Parson" was once a distinctively Anglican usage. And surely the reader is supposed to realize that the world of Hooper's ancestors was wracked by debates about "priest" and "minister" (or "altar" and "table") as violently as by vestarian controversies. Evidently the choice between "Mr." and "Parson" is not innocent.[68]

Most simply, the congregation's loose usage might simply reinforce the image of backsliding we have seen before: just as spruce bachelors and pretty maidens can scarcely imagine that their mild flirtatiousness profanes the Sabbath, so the congregation at large little dreams that a word like "Parson" can be anything but "indifferent." Or perhaps their usage is one degree more significant: as liberalization in the eighteenth century often meant "Anglicization," perhaps the adoption of this Anglican usage signifies something more than the mere lapse of old linguistic sensitivities; perhaps Hooper's church has become, in some positive sense, more of a "parish" of nominal Christians who "worship together" because they "live together" and less of a covenanted community of visible saints.[69] Or perhaps the friendly but somewhat condescending tone of those worried about the strange new vestment of "good Parson Hooper" or about the continuing sanity or self-identity of "our Parson" is a sign of the distinctly unprophetic role he has occupied prior to his awakening. The whole world of Milford, prior to that momentous event, seems a little too cozy to be quite Puritan; more like the world of a Victorian novel than a Puritan allegory. Hooper's "amiable weakness," his "painful degree of self-distrust," has opened him up not only to the unsought advice of some Franklinesque "busybodies" but also to a sense of comfortable ownership by his whole parish. They think of him, possessively, as "our" Parson and, sentimentally, as the "good" Parson; they very distinctly do *not* regard him as a prophet of righteousness sent to expose their comfortable self-delusions and to keep their "conscience under an arrest." No one, presumably, ever thought of a searcher of hearts and a flayer of souls like Thomas Hooker as "our good Parson."

But there is also a learned explanation for the story's curiously inappropriate reference to a "parson." The theologically literate reader of Hawthorne's generation might well have been reminded of the painful but revealing career of the Reverend Jonathan Parsons, another powerful eighteenth-century exemplar and prophet of the Awakening; one who, like William Cooper, was then only a little less famous than Edwards himself. Joseph Tracy refers to Parsons as "one of the most *efficient* promoters of the revival" (my italics); and he characterizes his most famous "Account of the Revival at Lyme" as "one of the most valuable documents of the time."[70] Parsons' name appears repeatedly in Benjamin Trumbull's *History of Connecticut*, a highly plausible source of Hawthorne's knowledge of the Awakening; and his "Account" had appeared as a prominent part of *The Christian History*, to which Trumbull repeatedly refers, and which Hawthorne could easily have known.[71]

The point of a learned allusion to Parsons, however, is not just to associate Hooper with *one more* famous revivalist. Parsons is, in fact, a very early Awakener, perhaps an "original" one: his experiences at Lyme (Connecticut) are contemporaneous with those of Edwards at Northampton

Massachusetts); so that if one were to set down some absolute beginning of the Great Awakening in New England, one might almost fix on the experiences of Parsons. If William Cooper figures as an official spokesman, then Parsons is an originator. The connection between Parsons and Cooper, in relation to Hawthorne's "Parson Hooper," is strengthened by the fact that Parsons gave an election sermon in Connecticut in 1741 which was, like Cooper's, an explicit endorsement of the Awakening. Of the two sermons, Parsons' descends from Wigglesworth's famous warning—that New England "hast a name that thou livest, and art dead"—even more directly than Cooper's; and, by Parsons' own account, it surprised a crowd who had "for many years, accustomed themselves to spend [election day] in feasting, music, dancing, and gaming" into a sudden awareness of the danger of their "carnal security."[72] Once again, "secret sin" was discovered in a world which seemed happy and ordinarily good. Thus if Hawthorne's Hooper is a figure of Hooker-Cooper, he is also a sort of composite Parsons-Cooper.

But the most important fact about Parsons, perhaps, is the manner in which his own awakening to the sobering truth of the antique theology had earlier surprised all the members of his own church and touched off a long period of misunderstanding and "censoriousness." Persuaded at the outset of his career by an Anglican understanding of his "Holy Orders" by Bishop Berkeley and by his readings in that consummate Anglican Richard Hooker, he began his ministry with a thoroughly Arminian understanding of the spiritual life—based on the teachings of Archbishop Tillotson and (our now familiar) Samuel Clarke. All went perfectly smoothly, for several years, for this perfectly Anglicized Parson Parsons, who seemed well on his way to following the notorious examples of Timothy Cutler and the American Samuel Johnson into the bosom of the Arminianized Anglican Church. He even conducted (in 1731) a very popular sort of pseudo-revival, based entirely on good works and church attendance. All this changed abruptly in 1734, however, when Parsons suddenly and without noticeable preparation underwent a momentous change of heart and doctrine. Having always "abhor'd the Doctrine of God's Absolute Sovereignty," he abruptly embraced it; and with it, all the human and psychological corollaries of an awakened and "experimental" Calvinism. Painful as it must be, there was nothing to do but turn and confront his congregation with a whole range of "Hard Sayings." Their common experiences so far had all, very probably, been false and illusory. However good they all seemed, most (he feared) were still secretly lost: "An *external* Profession of the true Religion, joined with a good Degree of *doctrinal* Knowledge, *external* Devotion, *negative* Blamelessness, and the like, were not good Evidences that a Person was a *real* Christian."[73] What they had all too fatally lacked was, quite simply, the true sight of sin.

Here, then, was no itinerant intruder from the outside introducing a new standard of piety, but their own good Parson (who had expressly renounced the Calvinism of the Saybrook Platform at his ordination) telling them they had to start over with a new estimate of themselves, a new consciousness of the "secret" sinfulness of their very nature. A hard saying indeed: bad news for an unconscious world of boys and girls together. And their real surprise and dismay surely have found their way, somewhat sublimated, into Hawthorne's account of the reaction of Hooper's congregation to his sudden change. What black thought has so deranged our Parson? The historic Jonathan Parsons might yet live to see a *true* revival in his parish, in which many of his old pseudo-saints "had their countenances changed." But the original change-of-face seems the more crucial. One can only conclude that Hawthorne had indeed read *The Christian History*.[74]

There—providing the basis of Trumbull's account, and Tracy's, and all subsequent histories—he would have found all those "narratives" of all those "awakenings" which together constitute not only the richest source of information about America's religious condition in the middle of the eighteenth century but also its most essential literary history. If, as Perry Miller long ago observed, there is a sort of "Richardsonian" impulse behind Edwards' accounts of the religious experiences of Phebe Bartlet, Abigail Hutchinson, and (most intimately) Sarah Pierrepont, then surely the hundreds of "surprising" narratives of private conversions and their public results must be regarded as the true locus of biographical and social "fiction" of the period.[75] On reflection, it would seem astonishing if Hawthorne had *not* read, somewhere, something to fill in the one most significant lacuna in Hutchinson's masterful and otherwise exhaustive *History of Massachusetts Bay*. His second volume (from 1691 down to the 1750's) reads almost as if no "Great and General" event like the Awakening had ever occurred. And yet, without some sense of the inner life and outer dynamics of this transforming event, the history of latter-day New England (including the Revolution itself) is utterly unintelligible. What sense, in personal terms, could Hawthorne make of the revival at Bowdoin in the 1820's without some knowledge of its paradigm in the 1730's and 1740's? Or what would be the point, fictionally, of an extensive frame narrative centrally involving a minor and semi-comic itinerant Methodist apart from some relation to the great Whitefield? Everywhere, the Awakening provided the missing historical link.[76]

In all orthodox narratives, awakenings are staunchly defended, in spite of the personal censoriousness, the social confusion, and even the spiritual separations they produced—because, in the end, "the one desirable effect" of a conscience awakened to the true sight of sin was a good that transcended all others. It was the only adequate means to man's last end. The new consciousness, amounting to nothing less than a New Birth, might divide friends and lovers, as in fact it separated close ministerial colleagues like Charles Chauncey and William Cooper for the rest of their natural lives, without the sort of old-age reconciliation which Jefferson and Adams were to immortalize; the thing went far deeper than mere political or sectional differences. Or it might split families in half, more sharply than any Unitarian question of Hawthorne's own 1820's; more was at stake than mere doctrine. Or, to the peculiar social mind of American Puritanism, more painfully, it might divide established congregations, in a way absolutely unknown in New England before, and only threatened in the tempestuous antinomian difficulties of the 1630's; not even the settled Order of the Churches could withstand the two-edged sword of awakening consciousness.[77]

The newly conscious stood on one side; all the rest, with only their "old lights" to guide them, on the other. The duly elected minister might be on either side; and either side might depart to form a new church and perhaps a whole new town. Social reconciliation almost always seemed out of the question. Born and nurtured in an historic hatred and fear of "separation," the citizens of latter-day New England found that the newly opened gulf in their spiritual consciousness was simply too wide. And this whole infamous story—of "Revivalism and Separatism in New England"—lies directly behind the creation and just under the allusive surface of "The Minister's Black Veil."

Trumbull's long chapters on separationist scandals at first Guilford and then Milford are not quite as close to Hawthorne's emphasis as is *The Christian History*'s account of Parsons' about-face at Lyme; but they are relevant enough, in all conscience, to be labeled "sources."[78] And what orthodox historians were later forced to confess and defend, the liberal Charles Chauncey had long ago made the subject of his monumental attack on the psychology and the sociology of the Awakening; accordingly, his *Seasonable Thoughts* may also be a learned source for Hawthorne's tale of Hooper's separation. At the very least it would have provided Hawthorne with a standard of judgment based on ordinary morality and on the normal understanding of social order and personal decorum; at most it may have suggested the domestic bias that colors the narrator's presentation of Hooper's entire career. For if the orthodox can think of nothing worse than the attempt to discredit the Awakening on the grounds of its disruptive tendencies, the liberals come to identify the "unpardonable sin" as the disruption of ordinary life.[79] This liberal and ultimately sentimental norm is not identically Hawthorne's own; but he allows it to stand as preferable to that consciousness of sin which creates a paralyzing form of self-involvement and endures as the preparation for a salvation which never comes, leaving the would-be divine subjectivist in that "saddest of all prisons," the Puritan Self.

7

The narrator, of course, calls that prison by a much more general name: simply, "his own heart." By now, however, we ought to be just a trifle wary of that Story Teller's sentimental simplicities. And even if we ourselves should feel, ultimately, some critical need to "read past" all the tale's own definitive historical details and quintessentially Puritan psychology, still we may need to do this very carefully.

First of all, to notice that the surface of Hawthorne's fiction has not elaborated all the theological technicalities of the historical world of the Great Awakening—that he has, here, emphasized the psychological effects of Hooper's style of piety—is to have mastered only the obvious. The significant critical discovery is the very reverse of this: the tale itself actually does, in spite of casual appearances and in spite of its "infidel" narrator, preserve a whole sense of a latter-day Puritan world, to confer reality on Hooper's self-abstraction. What might seem to be some perfectly generalized form of "egotism" is given, with perfect precision, a local habitation and a name. Furthermore, an equally precise and usable meaning for an innocent-sounding expression like "the human heart" might not be all that easy to fix. After all, the "head-and-heart" industry has been grinding out articles on Hawthorne for several decades now without exactly revolutionizing the humane science of moral psychology; in fact, it has all but succeeded in labeling Hawthorne as anti-intellectual and simple-minded. And, finally, both our protagonist and our narrator insist that, if we are having trouble with the idea of "sin," we should try one particular alternative: "sorrow." This strategic suggestion may indeed help us to extend the range of the story's application significantly, though perhaps not quite indefinitely. For what if "sorrow" should itself turn out to be a quasi-technical term, itself infected with full historical particularity? The (indoor) sport of guessing the "essential anxiety and distress" lurking behind the Puritans' own "particular formulation of their malaise" is just not as easy as we once thought.[80]

To some readers, "sorrow" will immediately suggest a stage of that *acedia* so prominent in medieval and Renaissance literature. As linked to the theological problem of despair by Burton and other anatomists of religious melancholy, it might well apply to Hooper's inability to move out of his dark night of preparatory self-encounter and into the broad day of assured salvation. Obviously the point does not loom large in radically "preparationist" writings, but Puritanism itself did not entirely overlook the problem of getting trapped in one of the early, "sorrowful" stages of the conversion pro-

cess: conviction, compunction, and humiliation were the absolutely necessary psychological places where the spiritual journey inevitably began; but
one had to move on.[81] And, as we can easily imagine, liberal critics of Puritanism were never slow to suggest that an obsession with sin, far from being
a "true sight," was merely the ready and easy way to despair or to some
other form of "gloom." Indeed the negative psychological effects of the Puritans' heightened concern with the self as depraved became an established
topos in the "moral argument against Calvinism."

But apt as this suggestion might be in a general account of the spiritual
travails of "the New England Conscience," it is not precisely to the point
here. On the one hand, textually, it does not entirely explain Hooper's particular case: his despair is not so much of all possibility of salvation as of any
effective figure of it in this life. And on the other hand, historically, it does
not really help to extend his case to cover anything other than the theological one with which we literally began: "sorrow," as a form of acedia, is not
really different from a gloomy, paralyzing, "Puritanical" concern with secret sin.

Romantic meanings, however, do extend the comprehension of Hawthorne's terms and (hence) the story's range of philosophical references. We
think immediately of the "Sorrows" of Young Werther; and just beyond
them, to a whole range of literary personages, both real and fictional, who
obviously suffer from nothing less than "World Sorrow." Inspired by a new
philosophy of feeling and energized by the revolutionary confessional style
of Rousseau; anatomized and finally deconstructed by Goethe, only to be
universally popularized in Byron; energetically satirized and then explicitly
warned against in Carlyle; the career of the Romantic Man of Sorrows spans
and helps to unite the two literary ages most relevant to Hawthorne's own
career, that of sentiment and that of imagination as well. The "sorrow" the
new hero suffers is less from his own sins (which he is less and less willing to
call by that name) than for the sins of the world; or, more generally, for the
sin that the world is, by virtue of some lapse from righteousness that is obviously cosmic in scope and moral import. We summon up Ahab, the "man
of sorrows" with "a crucifixion in his face." And we readily recall that the
inevitable result of vicarious suffering on so universal a scale is alienation.
The man who truly sees and deeply feels the sin of the world is doomed to
suffer it uniquely: the very universality of his imagination and profundity of
his consciousness have foreclosed the possibility of human sharing. After
such knowledge, what salvation? He must bear his "sorrow" alone. What he
suffers, in the end, is his own moral isolation.[82]

Instantly we seem to recognize and re-interpret Parson Hooper as a sort
of "Byronic Puritan." That strange, ambiguous smile which "flickers" and
"glimmers" throughout his whole career, making us so uneasy, in the end is

not ambiguous at all; finally it reveals too much. The smile is painful, rueful, almost-regretful. And it is also a little too "knowing": I see something you don't see, and the color of it is Black, everywhere. Hooper knowingly feels more than he can ever communicate to any of his hearers. He does what he can, and he seems not unsuccessful in more than a few painful cases. But obviously it is all very partial. People claim to have been led, figuratively, behind the black veil; they have seen, let us suppose, the Blackness, the "Horror." But do we seriously suppose that "any man living" can compare with Hooper "for fears"? And who could ever know what is in his heart?

Hooper's problem—"finally," as we may feel ourselves tempted to say— seems more deeply that of ineluctable selfhood than necessary sin. It must seem obvious that a man who flees from mirrors and pools of water, and who is everywhere obsessively anxious about the fixed maintenance of the veil he hides behind, stands for somewhat "more" than the true sight of sin. His problems seem to have begun there; and he may well continue to make converts, within his own world, chiefly in those terms. But how many modern interpreters will he thus convert? And even in his own case, his thoughts about sin seem to have led on to thoughts about something yet more fundamental or more general: thinking about the secrecy of humanity's hidden sinfulness, he comes to dwell on the problem of secrecy *as such;* or, alternately, exploring the fears and terrors which inevitably accompany Puritan self-reflection, he discovers the Self. Puritanism, we may want to say, is merely the way in, only the vehicle. And there are, as the career of the idea of "sorrow" will amply indicate, other ways into that "saddest of all prisons."[83]

But we should proceed with caution. The discovery that a Romantic reading of "The Minister's Black Veil" has rescued Hawthorne for introductory courses in comparative literature must be announced with circumspection. The impulse to cast the pall of a World-Class Generalization over Hawthorne's provincial peculiarities is still premature.

We need to remind ourselves that the reading in terms of "sorrow" is itself an historical rather than an absolute construction of Hawthorne's meaning. For "sin" and "sorrow" are, indeed, both technical terms. Both are quite local, and neither is more "quaint" than the other. They stand to each other not as a relative to an absolute (or as vehicle to tenor) but as equals. They are both code names for "varieties" of human experience considered as particular, pluralist, and developmental. Perhaps the realities they both name may be thought always to have existed, but the "discourse" of each is known to have flourished in its own peculiar era. Puritan language cultivates the consciousness of participation in universal "sin"; Romantic idiom enables the alienating "sorrow" of heightened moral consciousness. Neither exhausts the case. Surely the substitution of a malaise that is psychological (and finally epistemological) for one that is moral (and finally theological) is more in the nature of a contingent shift of paradigmatic interest than of a necessary displacement of the apparent by the real. Without making the historicist's ultimate claim that "only particulars exist," we must still confess that some ultimate "noumenon" eludes us.

Further, and less tendentiously, we must not forget that Hawthorne's Puritan fable remains exactly what it is, even after we have discovered the Romantic clue. We may come to prefer a reading which more nearly assimilates Hawthorne to us; but the narrative itself continues to evoke the moral realities of the American 1740's—just as repeatedly, precisely, and meaningfully as the story of Goodman Brown evokes the conditions of Puritanism's third generation. The story itself, after all, is told of a Puritan and not a Romantic. "Sin" is at the center. "Sorrow" exists more hypothetically, in a sort of interpretative bracket. By choosing to elaborate the one rather than the other, Hawthorne in effect prescribes a way to tell the story of how to get trapped inside the Self (noumenal or otherwise). We are to think, primarily, of "sin" as that way. At least for the moment. Of course he *could* tell the story in another, more familiar way. And doubtless he has done so, elsewhere, more than once. But we might almost write those other, less distinctive and less distinguished stories ourselves. Nor will the search for some least common denominator ever discover anything but the least.[84] Still, if we must employ our own interpretative re-writing, then we will of course appeal from sin to sorrow. Between the first and the second hypothesis of interpretation may fall the shadow of sentimentality; but even that lapse of seriousness will not totally invalidate the point. That deleterious and thoroughly un-Puritan form of moral weakness is not nearly so bad as the "obtuse secularism" figured by the "enlightened" responses within the story. And Hawthorne will, after all, settle for "something somehow like." But we must not suppose that the theme of the shadow story is any closer to his real meaning than the moral of his "parable" itself: the dungeon of the heart is like a Puritan who ... And there we are.

Can we say, finally, just what Hawthorne's "saddest of all prisons" ultimately is? Has the story placed us in a position to define the human heart? Are we sure enough of our distinctly post-Freudian categories to feel safe in diagnosing Hooper's most "essential anxiety"? Can we confidently name that absolute reality to which we are led by *either* sin or sorrow? As I have already suggested, we might feel ready to risk something like "the Self" or "the Problem of Subjectivity." But even as we adopt these powerfully general formulae, we seem bound almost at once to make two very significant concessions, one in the direction of philosophical history and one in the direction of Puritanism.

On the one hand, very radically, it is not now evident that "the Self" is an ultimate discovery which, once made, can always be appealed to for explanation, as to some fundamental "reality." Rather, the suggestion of much recent speculation in both philosophy and psychology is that the notion of an autonomous (and hence lonely) "self-presence" is simply one more construct of an all-engendering and historical process of thought which no one as yet understands at all. Indeed it may well turn out that a whole age of philosophy based on the project of epistemology and assuming the "originary" reality of the *cogito* made not so much a great discovery as a bad mistake. The beginning of that age might be pushed back from Descartes to Plato, and it might be extended forward from Kant to some point in the Heideggerian present; but it might remain an "age" nevertheless. Deepest down, we may yet discover not "thought" or "consciousness," but "language"—or even "writing," an historical process surely.

Or perhaps it will turn out that "the Self" is indeed the true discovery and hence the necessary burden of Modernism. The concession to be made in that event is just less drastic, and not at all more helpful to the cause of the ahistorical interpretation of the writings of one Nathaniel Hawthorne. For a mounting body of evidence suggests that whether "the Self" is an ontological discovery or a philosophical construct, a psychological fact or a literary myth, the Puritans Hawthorne read and pondered will figure largely, perhaps crucially, in any true account of its evolution.

Most suggestive here, perhaps, is the recent work of Sacvan Bercovitch. His announced theme is the essential dependence of an American sense of Self on certain peculiar habits of rhetoric drawn from a unique (and outrageous) form of Biblical interpretation invented by the American Puritans. If this largest case is anything like true, then we have indeed a stunning instance of the way a "language," all quaintly historical, creates the sense of a self, which then imposes itself as an absolute. And, not incidentally, that sense of self turns out to be idolatrous in the extreme. For not only does America tend to replace the Church as the typological fulfillment of prophecy, but the sinful-saintly Self can readily exchange places with and substitute for the "holy place" itself. Thus it now seems far from absurd to claim that one powerful though altogether unlooked-for (and certainly ironic) result of Puritan hermeneutics was to advance the cause of the Self in the modern world; or, at very least, to abet the process which drew the sorrows and the triumphs of selfhood to the very center of modern problematics.[85] But even if this elegant ("linguistic") explanation should fail, even if we should utterly reject the claims of Bercovitch-as-Derrida, we are still left with that other, more old-fashioned but still essential problem of sin and self in Puritan moral experience. And even at this level, as Bercovitch implies, the relation between Puritan and modern experience appears fairly instructive.

Puritan self-analysis was undertaken, quite obviously, for the purpose of discovering the essential sinfulness of the self in question and then, somehow, moving *on*. The ultimate effect was supposed to be self-liberating and not at all self-entrapping. On the one hand, privately, no one could imagine a progress toward salvation which did not begin with a true sight of sin based on an honest self-inventory: the unexamined life was no more worth living from the spiritual point of view than from any other. But, on the other hand, a whole world beyond the self was waiting to be redeemed: the English church had to be reformed; or the American wilderness had to be made safe for Congregationalism; or the Awakening had to be preached and the Millennium prepared. Or, at the very least, one had to see and confess that the Puritan way of life was not supposed to be "individualistic" any more than it could be "selfish." Church covenants existed not to frighten people off, back into some form of spiritual isolation; still less were they supposed to send potential members into paroxysms of self-analytic self-doubt. They existed, rather, to embody and to enforce the proposition that the norm of salvation was communal. Childe Harold need not apply—no more than for a whaling voyage.

Indeed an adequate self-analysis would reveal only that the Self was the real problem: "The self was 'the great snare,' 'the false Christ,' a spider's 'webbe [spun] out of our bowels,' 'the very figure or type of Hell.' "[86] Of course one had to look at the inherent sinfulness of that self: the "secret" could not be permitted to go undetected. And obviously the sight could not be other than horrible. But one was not supposed to continue to stare, transfixed in horror. Neither should one make an entire literature out of nothing more than the "sorrows" or the "sufferings" that unavoidably accompanied the sight. In Puritan theory, psychological self-analysis was nothing but the first necessary step to spiritual self-transcendence.

And yet the evidence overwhelmingly suggests that things did not work out precisely as they were supposed to; that even at this elementary "moral" level the self got out of control. Putting the best face on the matter, Owen Watkins has suggested that the Puritan's common obligation "to speak honestly of his own experience" resulted in a significant body of personal literature which may be seen as an essential part of the growth of self-consciousness in the modern literary age. And, indeed, we are now becoming more and more aware of significant instances in which Romantic texts look backwards to a basically religious (and often explicitly Puritan) form of personal experience and expression in the previous centuries.[87] The only irony here would be the obvious one—that literary influence would be among the weaker motives of the Puritan autobiographer. More adequately stated, however, the matter is more complex and less healthy. For if the Puritans inadvertently discovered (or helped to create) a rich new subject or theme or myth for modern literature, they also seem to have opened (and then climbed inside) a Pandora's box.

Evidently the Self the Puritans invented turned out to be a particularly constricted and self-entrapping structure. The thing to be overcome is very often *not* overcome; very often the self is less transcended than it is simply heightened or featured or frozen for continuous attention. Indeed, out of all of American Puritanism's early generations, only Ann Hutchinson and her followers seemed willing to announce that such a transcendence had actually been achieved; and over her primitive form of "Transcendentalism" the victory of the "Preparationists" was utter and complete. That victory guaranteed that even the *most* assured saint could never leave off from the more or less continuous regard of his own self under the aspect of Secret Sin. And this, very likely, guaranteed obsession. Not Edward Taylor's pleasing combination of wit and dogma, not even Jonathan Edwards' stunning synthesis of idea and sensibility could quite save the Puritan conscience from the *longueurs* of secret-self-analysis.[88]

If we assent to Bercovitch's most general formulation, "we cannot help but feel that the Puritans' urge for self-denial stems from the very subjectivism of their outlook, that their humility is coextensive with their personal assertion." This relatively innocent observation will cover a fairly large number of cases—all the way from those incomparable "fears" of Thomas Hooker to the blissful narcissism of Edwards' *Personal Narrative*. At very best, Puritan self-analysis seems to guarantee self-presentation. And there is also a worst: much of the moral language of Puritan personal literature amounts to a full set of "interminable-because-unresolved incantations of the 'I' over itself" in which "every aspect of style betrays a consuming involvement with 'me' and 'mine' that resists disintegration."[89] That, I take it, is precisely the Hawthornean point, which touches far more than the recognizable morphology of "gloom." The Puritan goes looking for the root sinfulness of his deepest Self and (very often) spends a whole life in a particularly self-asserting form of self-discovery and self-denial.

For the Puritan, sin was an original fact of all human life. But though universal it nevertheless remained hidden or secret: it lay buried in the will itself; or, alternately, it somehow defined man's originary lapse into consciousness. Other theological traditions might choose to define this "sin" negatively, as the lack of some original "righteousness" which ought to be there. If those theologians were right, then one could of course never *find* the original sinfulness of the self as such. It would exist only as an absence; and to go looking for it in an analytic way would in some real sense be crazy. One could always detect an embarrassing number of "actual" sins. Of these, the most luridly fascinating might turn out to be entirely inward, without external manifestation. And some might seem to lie deep down in the life of the intention or fantasy. But how could one ever locate the presence of an absence? How could a man reasonably expect to make contact with the originally sinful *thing in itself?* And yet Puritan theory dictated a search for precisely that: in demanding that the "true sight" should capture "sin" not in its "appearance and paint" but in its original motivating "power," it set the moral consciousness on the alert for the Sinful Self Itself. The Puritan Self wanted to catch Itself not in some particular sinful act or perception but in its very own sinful noumenon. Spiritually speaking, it wanted to be Fichte rather than Hume.

That final formulation might well take us beyond the range of Hawthorne's own terms or categories. But surely that is part of the point. In directing us from a fully formed story about the "secret sin" of Puritanism toward the secret "sorrows" of Romanticism, Hawthorne has first established his own area of historical primacy and then pointed us in a certain interpretative direction, itself also historical. We may follow or not, as we wish. And we may follow it as far as we wish as long as we continue to obey the primary rule of his own narrative: not only "sorrow" but indeed all "subjectivity" may be understood to be somehow *like* the Puritan whose search for "the true sight of sin" involved him in much more (or much less) than he bargained for.

The question of "cause" or "influence" lies, similarly, just beyond the edge of valid interpretation of the meaning of "The Minister's Black Veil." We might very much like to know whether Hawthorne believed the Puritans to have invented the modern search for the Self Itself. Literally, of course, the Calvinist "I sin" was noticeably anterior to the Cartesian "I think" in the history of modern definitions of Human Being. And one can easily imagine how a nearly statistical argument might give a sort of "popular" primacy to the moral formulation: whatever we may finally discover about the relevance of ideas to history, it is unlikely to appear that Puritanism has been *less* influential than Idealist Epistemology. Nor would it be entirely irresponsible to imagine that Hawthorne may have felt a certain "Puritan" pressure behind the Romantic literature of his own day: when nineteenth-century writers looked back, it was after all to men whose writings preceded the Enlightenment, or whose thought somehow escaped Lockean sensationism, Hartleyan mechanism, and Humean skepticism. Part of what they discovered, surely, was that the Self might have a richer and more varied life than neo-classicism could admit; or that the "sorrows" of a sinful-saintly Self were among the more vital (if more melancholy) pleasures of the imagination. It might be too much to claim that when the Romantics looked back they saw "themselves" in an older intellectual dress; that they saw the Puritans' "sin" as "something somehow like" their own "sorrow." But would it not now be fair to suggest that they discovered the discovery of the Self?

Similarly intriguing (though similarly a critical "extension") would be the question of possible links between the personal literature of Puritanism and that of Romanticism. Did Hawthorne, for example, regard the Edwards of the *Treatise Concerning Religious Affections* as essentially a "Man of Feeling"? Apologists for Puritanism have continually stressed the balance or the holistic integrity of Edwards' psychology; and intellectual precision might always insist on *some* distinction between his views and those of Shaftesbury and Hutcheson. And yet there he is, weeping at Whitefield's sermons, adding his own sentimental contributions to that genre we might label "the romance of conversion," and teaching everywhere the primacy of affection in religion and life. Surely Edwards is no less America's great "pre-Romantic" than he is "the first consistent and authentic Calvinist in New England."[90] Or—as long as we are speculating—we might reverse the form of our questioning and ask about Parson Hooper's status as a "transitional" figure. Except for the fact that a certain insensitive form of public "impertinence" compels him "to give up his customary walk at sunset to the burial ground," his form of Puritanism might easily be associated with the "Graveyard School." And surely we cannot imagine him without his own brand of "Night Thoughts." Doubtlessly those would bear some relation to Hooker's famous "fears" about his own "sin"; but they might also have a share in certain later "sorrows."

Such observations are, let me repeat, speculative. Arising only when we choose to follow a "bracketed" suggestion and pursue a hypothetical line of interpretation, they lead us to questions which Hawthorne himself probably regarded as doubtful. But they do all lead, irresistibly, to the conclusion that Hawthorne tended to regard the Puritan emphasis on sin as somehow predictive of later and more famous problems of subjectivity. And, on our own premises, we must try to be as circumstantial as we can, even about Hawthorne's own speculations.

Perhaps one concrete example will suffice. And well might it come from Trumbull's *History of Connecticut,* Hawthorne's principal "secondary" source of information about the Awakening. The enormous (and crucial) eighth chapter of Trumbull's second volume—concerning the painful question of "revivalism and separatism" in New England between 1737 and 1741—ends in a very curious and (for us) suggestive way. Trumbull summarizes and then concludes his whole pro-orthodox case in an all-too-recognizable pro-orthodox way. The year is 1817, but the terms seem to have changed very little since the 1740's. And then, all suddenly, Trumbull precipitates us into his own "pre-Romantic" world.

Separations among Reformed Christians are, for Trumbull, a very bad thing and a very embarrassing topic; and (though he can think of other causes as well) he cannot fairly deny that the Awakening produced its fair share of such separations. But bad as they are, they are yet not the worst things in the world. Far more destructive to the cause of Christianity, in his view, is the anti-revivalist premise that "unregenerate men have a right to the sacramental table." Nor is all the scandal in the world, given and taken, nearly so bad as the cynical disbelief in the reality of conversion which characterized the opposition. And, scandal for scandal, nothing compares with the "contempt and abhorrence" which lead the "opposers" to speak of "the principal instruments of this work" as "the worst of men." Period and Amen. Except that beneath this literal bottom line there are appended, by way of an asterisked footnote, some twenty lines of rhymed iambic pentameter, which adumbrate this theme of Godliness maligned:

> He lov'd the world that hated him: the tear
> That dropp'd upon his bible was sincere:
> Assail'd by scandal & the tongue of strife,
> His only answer was, a blameless life.

The poem then goes on to praise the combination of Apostolic charity and zeal which characterizes its subject, and to pity his calumniated exile; the author deliberately associates the "sorrows" of his subject with those of Christ, even as his diction reduces them toward sentimentality. But the link should already be clear.[91]

Obviously we are dealing with a powerful source of Mr. Clark's view of Hooper's life as "blameless" but "blacken[ed]." But this new source is, flagrantly, "literary": it is not now a question of Hawthorne's having responded as it were "objectively" to a "regular" historian's grave attempt to set out the facts of Parsons' revival at Lyme, or of Cooper's revival at Boston, or indeed of Anybody's revival at Milford or Guilford; it is, rather, a question of Hawthorne's dramatic use of Trumbull's strategic endorsement of somebody else's sentimental portrait of some famous revivalist as a "man of sorrows." The poem's revivalist subject turns out to be not the occasionally melted Mr. Edwards but the more characteristically weepy Parson Whitefield. And the poet turns out to be a more famous "Cooper" than any discovered so far, the "incomparable Cowper": that same latter-day, self-maddened Calvinist poet to be celebrated in the famous "Man of Sorrows" passage of *Moby-Dick* as fit—along with Young, Pascal, and Rousseau—to "break the green damp mould with unfathomably wondrous Solomon."[92] Apparently Hawthorne was not alone in his ability to see Puritan connections.

377

Melville's explicit use of Cowper is not, of course, identical with Hawthorne's veiled response to Trumbull's use of Cowper's evocation of Whitefield. Melville's famous list amounts to a sort of shorthand for his own worldwide problem of the "something somehow like": Ishmael senses that *something* is sorrowing more than one poor devil of a literary sick man, of melancholy cast and introspective mood; but whether it is sin or self he "cannot," on the basis of his own experience, "precisely tell." As historian, however, Hawthorne is being a shade more precise: if a latter-day historian of the travails of New England's orthodoxy can crown his case for the Awakening by quoting the poem of an English Calvinist who yet seems to be associated with that newer class of writers who lay their stress on the deep and obscure feelings of the individual man, then evidently Puritanism does in fact have a literary history; and if the poem should amount to a frank sentimentalization of a man said to be "instrumental" in more orthodox conversions "than any man since the apostle Paul," then evidently the problem of the "true sight" is complicated indeed. Evidently what Hawthorne once called "Puritanism" was itself already "something somehow like" what we have come to call "Romanticism."[93]

The problem, however, is not to draw some direct line from New England's William Cooper in the 1740's to Old England's William Cowper in the 1780's; or from Whitefield to Trumbull; or indeed from Anybody to Anybody Else. Doubtless it will turn out that many of the ministers who carried out the Awakening in New England were as much men of sentiment (in pretty frank imitation of the available English models) as they were Calvinistic Puritans. Indeed Perry Miller has long ago suggested that such was precisely the case; and very likely one could, by poking about a bit, discover that Hawthorne himself had already foreknown the fact.[94] But that sort of positivism would not only falsify the hypothetical nature of the "Romantic" reading of "The Minister's Black Veil"; it would also reduce and simplify the nature of the connection or relation about which this hypothetical reading speculates. The point is not simply that many Puritans (back all the way to Hooker?) may have been romantically (as well as theologically) "sorrowful" before their time. Nor is it, conversely, that Romantics other than the Calvinist Cowper may have felt obscurely guilty about the "Self" which it was their lot to explore, even after Locke had found the soul a blank slate and Hume had failed to find the soul at all. The point is, rather, that Puritanism and Romanticism stand together—in spite of an apparent intervention by the empiricism of the eighteenth century—in the relentless unfolding of the obsessive modern plot of the (so far) unsuccessful search for the Self.

Solipsism has come to seem a distinctively nineteenth-century obsession, more naturally the concern of Fichte than of Descartes or Ramus, and more proper to the criticism of Byron or Poe than to that of Cotton and Hooker. But evidently Hawthorne's view of the case was less simple. Apparently he could see the outlines of the problem revealed in the absolutism and the ardor of Puritan self-search.

From Hooker's unsettling reflections on "the *true* sight of sin" to Edwards' dazzling suggestions about "the nature of *true* virtue," the Puritan refuses to be put off by the mere phenomena of selfhood. He seeks an essence, an absolute *principle* of sin or virtue. As Perry Miller very adequately suggested, the Puritan defines himself as one who will live and judge himself by only the most absolute of standards; he everywhere refuses to be put off by clichés, approximates, or palliatives.[95] Morally, he needs to find not "sins" but SIN as such. Spiritually, he seeks not "graces" but GRACE as such. And this means—"epistemologically," as we should say—he needs to locate the SELF as such. The search is arduous and lonely; one might get lost looking. Or one might even seem to find the object of search and still be lost: a man might never recover from what he saw. To some his example would be full of gloomy instruction: the Self is a black hole; stay out of caves. But apparently not to all; some would insist that "perishing" in the search is altogether preferable to the "inglorious" alternative. Not, in the end, Ishmael. But certainly Ahab. Very likely Melville. And whoever else might be on one's own private list of "Dark Romantics." Romantic "Sorrow" may indeed flatten out and sentimentalize the Puritan idea of "Sin." But evidently the search for the Noumenal Self goes on, under whatever name.

8

And yet none of these names deserves to be the last word on "The Minister's Black Veil." To re-establish the proper focus, we must return, however briefly, to Hooper's own world—and to Hawthorne's primary project of trying to make moral sense of that world. If we find we can, speculatively, treat Hooper as prolepsis of Romanticism or as epitome of Modernism, still we must recognize that the trick is accomplished by treating him in isolation. To see Hooper adequately, we must remember the community—or, rather, the failure of community—in which he is involved. Putting Hooper back in his world, and linking his experiences with those of Goodman Brown and Badman Digby, we rediscover that the real subject of which Hawthorne is our (only) adequate historian is the complicated problem of Puritanism and Community.

The history of the Puritan Mind can be regarded as a sequence of attempts to get the ideas of depravity and community into satisfactory relation. Whether the specific issue is the visibility of saints, the admissibility of hypocrites, the separability of Baptism from the Supper, or the detectability of witches, the theoretical question remains much the same: how should the reality of sin affect man's attempts to fashion a social scheme? Nor, in these terms, is there a very marked discontinuity between the seventeenth century and Hawthorne's own. The separatist aftermath of the Awakening, the Revolution as an attempt at moral and social purification, and the reformist bias of nineteenth-century evangelism are all unintelligible apart from that apparently inevitable movement of the Puritan mind from the sense of individual depravity to an idea of social perfection. In all of this there is, undeniably, an impressive concern for community as a standard of human value. Hawthorne was far from overlooking it: the community is powerfully there, and it is plausibly motivated, in all his Puritan stories. What Hawthorne questioned was not the reality of such a concern nor the good faith of those who evinced it, but the validity of the premises which everywhere gave it meaning. And his questions seem fairly cogent.

If there were no sin, the Puritan theorized, there would be no need of human government; that repressive apparatus exists only to restrain wickedness. But there would most emphatically be "society." In fact there would be, within the enduring terms of God's original covenant, perfect human solidarity; the whole human family would be nothing other than God's Body. Community would be universal because virtue unites; only sin divides. Virtue, truly considered, is nothing more than benevolence to Being in General, the self-transcending desire for the good of the whole, in loving imitation of God's own creative benevolence. In the fallen condition, however, and short of millennial reunification, there will always be divisions. How can those who are regenerate of God unite with those who are not, except to their own degradation? The "Separatist" John Robinson put the case most sharply; but the rigor of his logic epitomizes the entire "Puritan" dilemma:

> The Scriptures do expressly debar men of lewd and ungodly conversation, of all fellowship, union and communion with God. "If we say, that we have fellowship with him & walk in darkness, we lie & do not truly," saith the apostle, 1 John i, 6, "and what fellowship," saith Paul, "hath righteousness with unrighteousness? and what communion hath light with darkness? what concord Christ with Belial? or what part hath the believer with the unbeliever or infidel?" etc., 2 Cor. vi, 14–18.[96]

To be sure, many technical problems lie concealed here: definitions of "righteousness" may differ; and "conversation," "fellowship," and "communion" may take many forms. But the main point is clear and telling. Benevolence itself does not sponsor the confusion of sin and virtue, the conflation of the fallen with the redeemed. And as long as the Atonement is seen as "limited," the theological impulse to community is never quite simple; the search for a blessed unity will always be troubled by the awareness of sinful difference.

So far as we can tell from their writings, the American Puritans never faced the psychosocial implications of their vision of a world in which some are awakened to the sight of things as they truly are but where others are left to dwell amidst natural appearances. We can fairly say, I think, that they almost faced up to the question of "preparation" as the invention or at least the institutionalization of the Fearful or Sorrowful or Anxious Self: in exiling Hutchinsonian Transcendentalism to the less ruly margins of Rhode Island, they seemed consciously preferring the danger of self-analytic self-entrapment to the opposite danger of self-indulgent self-liberation. But when Roger Williams was more raggedly forced to flee to those same geographic and intellectual fringes, an equally important theoretical opportunity seems largely to have been missed. To be sure, Cotton and Williams would go on to debate, tediously, the hermeneutic implications of "the wheat and the tares." But at the crucial moment itself, no one dutifully proposed any "Sixteen Questions" about Williams' view of *all* human societies (including churches) as so many more or less "civil" outposts in a wilderness which was, theologically speaking, universal. Williams himself would come to face the prospect of discovering himself to be the only real Christian in his own invisible church; but the society at large lost this original opportunity to discuss the human meaning of "we" and "they." Indefinitely deferred, accordingly, was the chance to develop a theory of society that was Democratic as well as Christian, that might be more Christian than Separatist.[97]

What prevented full consideration, apparently, was the millennial expectation. The original moment of American Puritanism is no exception to the rule that powerful awakenings produce painful separations. But there is another rule as well: the moment of awakening is also, identically, the moment when it is possible to believe that one is at the beginning of an important (perhaps a climactic) season of salvation, and thus to imagine that (in America at least) the imminent arrival of the Kingdom will remove personal bitterness and heal social division by bringing all (or most) of town and country into some Visible Church or State of Grace. The opportunity seems unique, historic. The scandal merely temporal—and temporary.

So it was in the beginning. And so it was, in theory, whenever Awakening began the Puritan world anew. Characteristically, however, Hawthorne would not leave the Puritan problem where he found it. Critically, though only dramatically, he would lead the Puritan logic out into worldly areas or back into psychic spaces where it did not so easily apply. What happened, he wanted to know, when the world did *not* end? What became of ordinary life when the millennium did not arrive in time to effect the magical rescue of a community disrupted by awakening? Of that impious but inevitable hypothesis Parson Hooper is the crucial test case, contrived by the least apocalyptic of all American thinkers.

And why not? Why not the difficult case as well as the easier ones? When a Richard Digby shuts himself up inside his own cave of self-satisfied self-veneration, we get only the obvious and reductive case of the pseudo-Williams who discovers himself the only Saint in a supposedly Reformed World. All too inevitable: the Pope in the Parish. Much more painfully, but only a trifle more subtly, Goodman Brown is granted some magically privileged glimpse into that Heart of Human Darkness called witchcraft. Predictably, the event proves "traumatic"; equally predictably, the recovery is personally "doubtful" and theologically "partial." Practically, the case is frightful enough. But, theoretically, it is still too easy to test the Puritan theory of community as such: who has ever doubted that the Devil's half-truths are meant to divide and conquer? Some less gothic case remains untried; some poor soul remains to be lost in spite of the fact—indeed, because of the fact—that he has got the central truth of Puritanism exactly right.

That soul is Hooper's. As Puritan, Hooper may be wrong about the Self: it may be that there is *no* determinate center to human moral being. But, again as Puritan, he has come closer than most men usually get to a root fact of human life. All men are sinners. Whatever may be suggested by the bland seemings of natural appearances, casually observed amidst the comings and goings of a sunny Sabbath, the secret heart of Everyman does indeed treasure up guilt. And surely the psychological corollary is equally true: the incurable hiddenness of human depravity means that human beings never do really know each other; even the closest of intimacies are, under the aspect of eternity, illusory. And thus when the awakened Hooper shrieks that he "cannot" unveil his features, Hawthorne himself is far from denying it. The adequate ground of our sympathy with Hooper is precisely the truth of his perception that we cannot ever "show forth" our "worst"; that the secret life of human intentionality can never be satisfactorily "outered." This is also the truth which places him beyond the range of Goodman Brown, who begins by supposing that man's makeshift arrangements for Sunday morning can actually reflect God's knowledge of moral reality and ends by failing to apply any further ambiguities to himself. From the beginning Hooper is clear on both these counts. His highest view of the moral life is that it is hidden; of God's perception, that it is unavailable to men. And, significantly, all this is revealed most pertinently in his own condition; the primary application is to his own life. And yet Hooper is doomed, hardly less for Hawthorne himself than for his sentimental narrator.

Evidently Hawthorne can see, and emotionally accept, a possibility that is not available to Hooper and, without which, that sensitive minister can only suffer in sorrow. Like Hooper, Hawthorne was utterly unable to believe that salvation lay with a community of Visible Saints. Hooper may be held back from such a belief by his failure to move beyond some preparationist phase. But Hawthorne has passed beyond the entire Puritan project. And if he agrees that from one point of view there is *no* earthly salvation from moral solipsism, nevertheless he has, luckily, another view available. It is not, to be sure, quite so absolute as Hooper's. But that is only another way of saying that the author was better "adjusted" than his character, readier and abler to live in the natural, without (hypothetical) reference to God's (inaccessible) view. Far less "adamant" than Hooper, Hawthorne is entirely willing to accept universal sin as the available basis for whatever community there humanly can be.

Hooper, however, remains quintessentially Puritan in his theory of community. Or, rather, he becomes "the Puritan" once again. In the midst of a world become only outwardly religious, and at the head of a church but nominally Puritan, he revives the originary insight. Once again, divine truth is let loose in a latter-day world-without-end. Straightaway his true sight separates the pastor from the majority of his flock, and from most of his fellow shepherds. What can occur? God-like—or as a sentimentalized "man of sorrows"—he may yet "love the world which hated him." But then suppose the still more painful case: how might a newly awakened Puritan prophet come to regard his unawakened lover? The historic record revealed the unhappy separation between William Cooper and Charles Chauncey. But suppose one encountered some mismating of minds in Jonathan Edwards and Sarah Pierrepont.

What if a certain "young lady at New Haven" had been just a little less "beloved of that Great Being"? What if she had been only some plucky New England girl who insisted on her own literal sight? Or worse, perhaps, suppose she did come to catch some glimpse of her lover's vision, only to reject it as revealing too little even as it proved too much. The hypothesis is contrary not only to fact but to the "predestinarian" tendency of Puritan romance: the saint selects his own society, then shuts the door. And yet the case is thinkable; if not with Edwards, then surely with anyone less formidable. The "fact" might not make much difference to the career of Nature and Grace in the New England theology, but the hypothesis makes a pretty revealing story. The story teller might be, theologically speaking, more or less sophisticated, more or less concerned with the details of doctrine; but the tale could hardly fail to test the Puritan theory of community. If the rigorous insistence on the "true" source of fellowship and communion held good, then even the subtler and wiser sort of Puritan might end up utterly alone. He might, arguably, be alone "with himself": the fact of *con*-science probably means *something*. But his logic might well leave him without the saving community he so earnestly desired.

And so it is with Hooper, the subtlest of Hawthorne's Puritans. Or almost so. On the one hand, practically, he may be thought to share some form of self-understanding with those like-minded converts whom he has led behind the black veil; but on the other hand, theoretically, even this sharing stops well short of real community. It is all in the negative. Assurance of salvation seems unavailable. Subjective knowledge of sin is as far as man's inner researches can go. And to know oneself as a sinner is also to know that one's secrets can never be known. Sin separates. In this life sin is incurable. Separation is simply a fact. And thus, as we have seen, it scarcely matters whether Elizabeth catches Hooper's theological meaning or not. On the one hypothesis they might share the fellowship of a church or the communion of a conjugal bed; on the other, presumably, not. But in either event Hooper's absolutist view of their mutual aloneness is clear beyond cavil. And beyond violation.

Hawthorne's own hope is otherwise. It rests on a view we might venture to call "Puritan Universalism." Evidently there is not, in Hawthorne's own experience of the spiritual world, anything like a "sanctifying grace" which, by overcoming the principle of sin, heals the rents in human community and bridges the gaps in human communication. But clearly there are certain "actual graces": there is supper with an unreconstructed parishioner; and there might be an attempt at honesty with Elizabeth. These are palliatives, no doubt; second-bests, if you will. But they are partially salutary nevertheless. They might be considered "means" to a salvation which, in this life, never does fully arrive; they may even be sacramental. In any case Hawthorne is willing to accept them. They are not the highest realities conceivable. They do not flow directly from the properly "Puritan" wish to live only in the "highest imaginable excellency." But they are all that is humanly available. There simply is no visible Community of Saints. Without some Community of Sinners, therefore, no community is possible.

Surely Hawthorne knew—as sorrowfully as any seventeenth-century Puritan—that the "self" was "the very figure or type of Hell." He might even accept, more tentatively, a whole class of Puritan propositions about Sin and the Self. But in his view the last thing anybody should have to endure was a whole life looking at (or for) that self. The thing might not, in itself, even exist; and even if it did, it never *could* be adequately expressed. No one can show forth his inmost heart. But cannot one show his face? The literal face will be, of course, partially deceptive: a parson will smile and smile and be a sinner still. Deceptive too, no doubt, will be that partial revelation, that typic "trait whereby the worst may be inferred." But the alternative turns out to be worse: the symbolic veil will always be destructive of available community; it will continuously heighten and feature what cannot be overcome. Better not wear it. Better do what one can. Now. After all, there may not be the sort of "hereafter" on which Hooper bases his theory of perfect self-revelation. The "awful" thought then is that Hooper's face "still . . . moulder[s] beneath the Black Veil" (53). Or even if there should be some Last Day of Perfect Judgment, the sudden capitalization is still ominous: how should one be permitted to accomplish perfectly then what one has declined to attempt now? In either case the historic black veil of temporal separation may figure only the cosmic Black Veil of eternal alienation. In either case, Hawthorne will settle.

In the end, for Hawthorne, Hooper's arch-Puritan "sight of sin" proved too much. To be sure, spiritual maturity seemed to require it: not to know sin argued oneself unknown. Without "something somehow like" that knowledge, men and women remained merely natural; "nothing more than innocent," as Melville might say, and arguably much less. And yet such sinful self-knowledge could hardly be the whole story. One had, emphatically, to go beyond this preparatory phase. Not, indeed, into a Community of Visible Saints, however large the Judgment in Charity might make it. And certainly not "onward" to Millennium or Judgment. One simply had to go *on*. Into a world of personal and secular relationships which could never be quite "true" but which were yet not debased or dehumanized by that fact. Such an "intercourse with the world" could scarcely be regarded as beatific, but it might prove salutary nevertheless.

III

Puritanism and Revolution

℅ Seven ℞
MASQUE AND ANTI-MASQUE
A CONTEST OF HISTORIES

WHEN THE NARRATOR of the "Legends of the Province House" is "reminded of a purpose, long entertained, of visiting and rambling over the mansion of the old royal governors of Massachusetts" (239), the alert reader may hear Hawthorne announcing that he is finally going to give direct dramatic treatment to the question of the British presence in New England and the significance of its expulsion.[1] A deep interest in that "matter" had been there from the beginning of Hawthorne's career, in the "proleptic" but oblique Revolution of "My Kinsman, Major Molineux." And quite obviously it was never very far from Hawthorne's imaginings: the actions of "Endicott" and "The Gray Champion" are unintelligible without ironic reference to the critical moment of 1776; the changing political and social conditions of eighteenth-century America are the very stuff of the reflective sketches to which Hawthorne gave the oxymoronic title of "Old News"; and in the six months in which Hawthorne had recently edited the *American Magazine of Useful and Entertaining Knowledge*, he had written (or revised or condensed) the lives of no fewer than eleven Revolutionary Worthies as well as a very carefully wrought account of the Boston Tea Party.[2] He would go on to tell America's greatest story—with studied patriotism, for children—in the climactic portion of *Grandfather's Chair;* and the "signatures" of America's patriotic heroes would be carefully scrutinized in the "Book of Autographs." But, within the limits of the ironic vision, the whole story is in the "Legends." Clearly, a complicated and extended treatment of this crucial subject demands our closest attention, especially when it seems connected to so many of Hawthorne's early literary efforts.[3]

The first paragraph seems to imply it all. On what is *now* called Washington Street,[4] the Old Province House—enduring symbol of the seemingly vanished political, economic, and social presence of Britain in America—is nearly obscured by a "brick row of shops." But no very strenuous act of imagination is required to demolish those upstart democratic buildings and perceive an elemental historical reality: the House of Conservatism stands directly across the street from the Revolutionary Old South Church, bastion of Puritanism and center of organized New England resistance.[5] Small wonder that Hawthorne has his narrator notice that the gilded Indian atop the cupola of the Province House seems to be aiming his arrow "at the weathercock on the spire of the Old South." In fact, the "Legends of the Province House" are hardly less legends of the Old South Church, whose steeple clock tolls persistently and at critical moments through the tales of Britain's expulsion from America. The Old South Puritans may or may not have a century and more of democratic tradition behind them; the legend of the Puritan "founding fathers" may or may not have its grain of traditional truth. Certain it is, however, that the more general name for New England's revolutionary spirit is "Puritanism."

But before that relation can be explored in detail, it may be useful to enunciate a number of the more general strands of argument such a reading of the "Legends" will involve, and to identify the major sources of complexity in analyzing them as a unit. First of all, seeing Hawthorne succeed with four brilliantly interrelated tales about the American Revolution forces us to abandon the vestiges of the suspicion, itself anti-intellectual, that Hawthorne had merely drifted, as a dilettante or as a brooding "haunted imagination," into the gloomy but congenial moral environs of the original Puritan past. We need to keep reminding ourselves that Hawthorne's first period includes a number of historical tales that are set quite exactly and meaningfully in the *eighteenth century*. Together with "My Kinsman, Major Molineux," "Old News," "Roger Malvin's Burial," and "The Minister's Black Veil," the "Legends" supply more than adequate proof that our ingrained tendency to associate Hawthorne with the seventeenth century is uncritical and stands in the way of a proper appreciation of his most enduring achievement.

Another "external" consideration is perhaps even more crucial: the "Legends of the Province House" come to seem, upon close analysis, the most simply and unarguably historical of all Hawthorne's major tales. I do not mean that they are easy to grasp, or that their "history *as history*" is of a literal or undramatized sort; in many respects the method is still that of "My Kinsman, Major Molineux" or "The Gentle Boy." I mean, rather, that when these tales are considered as a unit, no critical response except the historical has the slightest chance of interpreting them in a significant way; or, more precisely, either they are about the meaning of the American Revolution or they are about nothing.[6]

Some critics may feel that they are, therefore, an exception to Hawthorne's rule, definitely *not* part of "the essential Hawthorne"; and some readers have no doubt found them texturally flat and thematically thin.[7] I find them a dazzling achievement and consider them a completion of the historical intentions and a validation of the historical themes found elsewhere. As is somewhat the case with "The May-Pole of Merry Mount," there is no concentration on the moral travail of any single psyche within the fictive historical world; there are, instead, a number of lesser individuals caught up in the large (*almost* mythic) historical forces. There is no Anxious Adolescent undergoing any Oedipal Initiation and no Everyman taking a Moral Fall. There is not even a Robin to stumble into the chaos of a revolutionary night of misrule and embody our own confused reactions to the ambiguities of history, not even a Goodman Brown to experience for us the moral devastation which may follow a sudden confusion in the empirics of sanctity. The "Legends" make their way solely by a relentless exposure of illusion and delusion in American history.

Other, more internal complexities also call for preliminary mention. Most obvious is the problem of interrelation: Hawthorne offers us his four legends within a single narrative frame. A rather ordinary man with, as it develops, a rather ordinary range of insight visits Boston's historic Province House; each time he visits, he hears recounted and comes away with a story of certain intriguing eighteenth-century events. Three of the tales are ascribed to a colorful tale-collector and legend-monger named Bela Tiffany, the colorful oddity of whose name seems to demand interpretation. The fourth tale owes its authorship to an Old Tory, nameless, but recognizably similar to the unreconstructed Old King's Man whose part Hawthorne takes in the last section of "Old News"—a Tory on the order of a Peter Oliver rather than a Thomas Hutchinson.[8] In every case our "outside narrator" vouches for the larger historical validity of his more-than-twice-told material, but he disavows the intention and disclaims the possibility or necessity or validity of ascertaining or preserving the authenticity of specific details. Clearly that "Fancy" mentioned in the sketch of "Governor Phips" and so ardently at work in "Alice Doane's Appeal" comes largely into play here; we are to have symbolic and (in the largest sense) moral history. And possibly irony as well. Clearly so, if the narrator turns out to know less than his tales imply.

The obvious implication is that we will be getting, by means of this paradigmatically legendary process, more of what people *say* happened than what *really* happened. This might be simply a disclaimer, one more license of Scott-inspired "history as Romantic art." Or it might mean that we are involved in a species of "intellectual history"; we may be expected to recognize that, at some level, *all* formal history is a fictive construct and that, at another, the story historians elect to tell is every bit as significant as the irreducible but irrecoverable historical "fact" itself.

And if the frame calls our attention to the problem of tellers, it is only slightly less insistent on the correlative question of hearers. The problem of "audience" (internal as well as external) must not escape our notice. All four stories are heard not only by the ordinary, democratic, outside narrator, but also by the "present occupant" of the Province House, named Thomas Waite, regularly referred to as "mine host," and begging for further critical identification. His bar-tending is a trivial and ironically reduced version of the "levees" of "vice regal pomp" held by the ancient governors, "surrounded by the military men, the councillors, the judges and the officers of the Crown" (240). Further, he owes his present situation—even more directly than most people in Hawthorne's contemporaneous Boston—to the expulsion of the British from their base in the Province House. And lest that fact and its implications be forgotten, the Old Tory (who under another historical dispensation would be a guest at a levee) is made a listener as well as a teller: he tells the last story ("Old Esther Dudley") because of what he has heard told in "Lady Eleanore's Mantle." All this is teasing enough to demand serious "literary" analysis; one would overlook its structuring significance at considerable peril.

One more preliminary. The chronological order of the tales turns out to be even more crucial to an understanding of their primary historical function than critics have yet realized.[9] After starting with a sort of "present" or primary phenomenon to be explained (a revolutionary confrontation), we "back up" twice, searching as it seems for causes. Why only twice? Because the *Democratic Review* contracted for a decidedly finite number of legends? Or for some more subtle reason? And why, in the story that marks the furthest point of our historical retreat, do things suddenly go "Spenserian," only to re-emerge into the original legendary but not allegorical texture, and into a sort of "future," one bare historical moment beyond our starting place? This too would be scanned.

The problem of the "Legends," then, is not only to discover the "history" of the individual tales, but to account for the full significance of their chronology and to explore their interrelations within a frame which calls attention to their own telling and hearing. The convolutions are not gratuitous, the constructs of an overzealous "revaluation." They are organic and necessary. They permit Hawthorne to offer a view of the irony not only of the *events* of revolutionary New England but also of the increasingly legendary *story* of those events. What fully emerges from the redoubled complexities of the "Legends of the Province House" is what was only hinted at by the prolepses of "Endicott" and the "Champion": an understanding of the relation between Puritanism and Revolution, an ironic commentary on the pattern of emerging American historiography, and an interpretation of the Legend of the Puritans as Founding Fathers, which modern historians can hardly be said to have superseded.

1

I have referred to the "outside narrator"—the person who takes us on a literal and symbolic tour of the Old Province House and whose voice actually gives us the "Legends"—as a man with decidedly ordinary perceptions. His full nature and function are not perfectly obvious from the first few paragraphs, but there are hints; and it is well to be clear about him from the outset. If not precisely "unreliable," he is yet incapable of grasping the full significance of all that is in the materials he transmits, and there are times when his comments are a bit obtuse. We may not wish to view him as totally distinct from the ultimate authorial intelligence, but it is a serious miscomprehension to take him "uncritically" as some completely unmanaged version of "Hawthorne himself." If we want to associate him with Hawthorne at all, we must see him as a version of the author's "ordinary self."[10]

Doubtlessly Hawthorne has divided himself (and his sympathies) among various characters. The simplest division is between this primary, outside narrator and Bela Tiffany; and this division seems to register the split between Hawthorne's smiling, public, worldly, comic, Jacksonian-democratic, old-house-visiting self and the deepest reaches of his legendary-historical (and ironic) imagination. Without explaining what he is doing, probably only half understanding it, the outside narrator has to pass out of the sunshine and democracy of "the busy heart of modern Boston," through a narrow archway, into the "deep shadow" of the Province House and the Past. (The action is not unlike that of the Old Manse Hawthorne moving from his garden into his study, or the Custom House Hawthorne retiring to the attic full of manuscripts.) Once passed through this "strait gate" of imagination, our narrator finds a certain class of revelation easy enough to come by. Thomas Waite—whoever that "worthy successor and representative of so many historic personages" may turn out to be—readily agrees to take him on a tour of the time-honored mansion. But that *completely* ordinary guide can help him very little. With an almost charming naiveté our narrator discovers and confesses that he was "forced to draw strenuously upon [his own] imagination, in order to find aught that was interesting in a house which, without its historic associations, would have seemed merely such a tavern as is usually favored by the custom of decent city boarders, and old-fashioned country gentlemen" (241).

The implications are fairly clear. The narrator is, much like the "external" Hawthorne in the years after 1836, himself a "decent city boarder."

He is alert enough to identify a locus of history when he sees one; he is willing to pass out of the world of obstructive present appearance to get there; but he does not, in his ordinary, worldly self, know enough; and his own imaginative powers, which he most often refers to as his "Fancy," are not powerful enough to effect any significant recovery about the past. Unless he meet with some Bela Tiffany, some more customary dweller in the house of tradition, some powerfully fictive and mythic imagination not at all inhibited by the pressures of common sense and not at all timid about the truth of legend, we will surely not get much of value.

Our narrator mentions but does not attach any significance to the "opposition" of the Old South Church and the Old Province House; he merely describes Deacon Drowne's "cunning" Indian. He conjectures that the letters *PS* which "are wrought into the iron work of the balcony" are probably "the initials of its founder's name" (240); but he does not seem to know about the princely merchant named Peter Sargent who built the mansion, in 1679, as a luxurious and extravagant private residence; and he takes no notice of the apparent contradiction when, later on, the relentlessly precise historian Thomas Hutchinson refers to the infamous Edward Randolph as "the founder of this house" (261). Clearly Hawthorne knows that the house in question has had at least two foundings, one literal and another political; and the reader is expected to notice that fact, or simply stand bewildered by some of the complexities of explicit historical reference and allusion.[11] But the narrator—who may stand for *our* ordinary, unprepared, normally unhistorical, mostly only fanciful selves, as well as Hawthorne's lesser self—merely transmits these things without much sense of their pregnancy.

And when our narrator's "imagination" rises up to its pre–Bela Tiffany heights, the results are not very impressive. Having mounted to the cupola with its once commanding view, he mentions the exaggerated prominence of the steeple of the Old South ("which seems almost within arm's length"), but his "visions" are rather the obvious ones: "I pleased myself with imagining [how] Gage may have beheld his disastrous victory on Bunker-Hill (unless one of the tri-mountains intervened), and Howe have marked the approaches of Washington's besieging army" (241). Before coming down to smack his lips over Mr. Waite's good liquor and to be gratified by Tiffany's "pleasant gossip about the Province House," the narrator goes on to imagine "huzzas" and "hats" tossed up to the dignified personage who was the King's representative and more or less to lament the fact that "now, the old aristocratic edifice hides its time-worn visage behind an upstart modern building." All this is something. But not much.

From the cupola the narrator is able to look "back" as well as "all around." This is indeed an historical vision; it is not *quite* an ordinary "sight from a steeple." But Bela Tiffany's vision takes up where the narrator's

394

ends. His spiritous "gossip," which is really the true wine of historical imagination, begins with all the old "huzzas" already silent. He will take us back,
eventually, in "Lady Eleanore's Mantle," to the days of "aristocratic splendor" in the provinces, and will offer us a parodic form of street demonstration, but his imagination does not run to the grand, the heroic, or the
patriotic. His tone is not what Emerson called "boyish hurrah," and his
focus is not on the popular but melodramatic fields of military conflict.
Other historians could be counted on not to miss that side of things; the
public and perfunctory Hawthorne had even done a certain amount of it
himself in the *American Magazine*, though usually with apologies. Bela Tiffany responds to history in another way. Like the Hawthorne who was more
interested in the youth who killed a British soldier with an axe than with the
main battle for the "rude bridge" at Concord, Bela Tiffany sees subtle confrontations and notices ironies left over after all famous battles have been
won. The opposing masques of "Howe's Masquerade" are staged even as
Boston is surrounded by Washington's besieging armies, but after the first
sentence we never hear of that. We begin with a confrontation that is symbolic rather than physical, psychological and moral rather than political and
military. And we move on, backwards and inward, from there. Not toward
historical "truth" necessarily, but into some problematic space always occupied, more or less profoundly, by the historical imagination as such.

This much ought to be obvious. The problem of distinguishing between
the ordinary outside narrator and that ironic "inside" Bela Tiffany is far less
difficult than the problem of defining the quality of Bela Tiffany's vision exactly, of comprehending what it sees in the various legends, and of discriminating between his Ironic view and the Old Tory's Loyalist view. Still—at
the risk of overexplicitness, and with a view to freeing ourselves for other
kinds of analysis as we proceed—it may be worthwhile to notice a few more
evidences of the outside narrator's inadequacies. For in the end, it is the very
deliberately drawn simplicity of the narrator's responses which alerts the
reader to the need for complexity of response to history, in relation to even
the most "patriotic" of subjects.

After giving us Tiffany's first legend, the narrator demonstrates once
again the relative weakness of his own imagination and teaches us, by negative example, how to distinguish the fancy from the imagination. Evidently
impressed by the ghostly procession in "Howe's Masquerade," he finds
himself "striving with the best energy of [his] imagination, to throw a tinge
of romance and historic grandeur over the realities of the scene" (255). But
his striving is in vain, and is more than a little comic. The rattling of spoon
and glass and the appearance of an advertisement for the Brookline stage
make the reality of the tavern too strong; he cannot hold the provincial
scene or the romantic tone in mind. Seeing a stage driver reading the *Boston*

Times reminds him how hard it is to hold "any picture of 'Times in Boston' seventy or a hundred years ago." The whole business of historical imagination is, he announces in exhaustion, "desperately hard work." And he concludes without any interpretative comment on the significance of the two masques he has seen in contention, with only a "conscious thrill of awe." The narrator is, evidently, not very different from the girls who could not respond to the true purport of the original "Alice Doane." He reacts chiefly to the aura and the tonalities of the story rather than to the substance or moral; and when present reality presses in, he finds himself powerless to preserve the illusion. The two references to stagecoach reality clearly suggest a sort of mock self-deprecation: Hawthorne knows, from rueful family experience, the difficulties involved in developing and maintaining an historical imagination in a world of stagecoaches; yet he persevered. And so must the much-distracted modern reader. The "Times in Boston" were, in their time, fully real, and their relation to the prepossessing present is both recoverable and relevant. Our problem in the "Legends" is to learn what we can of this connection from the illusion of historical fiction, even though the illusion is decidedly temporary.

The narrator's behavior is not much different in relation to "Edward Randolph's Portrait"; our instruction goes on to touch other matters, but again by negative example. The second visit to the Province House and to Bela Tiffany is the result of an interesting, probably worthy, but not *ultimately* Hawthornean motive: "I resolved to pay . . . another visit, hoping to deserve well of my country by snatching from oblivion some else unheard-of fact of history" (256). The motive is, if we may believe the language, patriotic and "antiquarian": the narrator wishes to be part of that already widespread and energetic attempt to recover and preserve everything about history's most important nation. And here again we are forced to make discriminations. The "Legends" are not, as critics have abundantly demonstrated, all that patriotic in their final significance;[12] and, in spite of the ease with which one might demonstrate the impulse to sheer factual antiquarianism in Hawthorne himself, Bela Tiffany's revelations reach a level of historical truth less positivistic than our narrator's remark suggests.

We will need to return to the problem of antiquarianism, positive research, and "moral history" later. Here it is sufficient to conclude the catalogue of our narrator's peculiarities—and to note that his own peculiar "Fancy" not only is different from Bela Tiffany's imagination, but is also in embarrassing tension with his announced antiquarian motive.

The remainder of his introduction to "Edward Randolph's Portrait" shows him busying his "Fancy" once again with a "comparison between the present aspect of the street and that which it probably wore when the British governors inhabited the mansion whither I was now going" (256). He moves from an easy lament about the present substitution of "tiresome identity" for that "picturesque irregularity" of the past to a somewhat sententious remark about the transitory quality of all human life. In this latter, he mentions the Old South Church and its clock: they seem to have something to say about continuity and change, but we have to make our own inferences about their significance in American Revolutionary History. Meeting Bela Tiffany once again, he rejoices "at the oddity of the name, because it gave his image and character a sort of individuality in [his] conception"; but it is up to us to decide that the "odd" name of this unabashedly fictive historian signifies something like "veiled revelation of the war."[13] And at the conclusion of the "miraculous" legend of the revelatory transfiguration of the portrait of Edward Randolph, he wants to know if he can still go and see the actual picture.

There is more, but this much may serve as introduction to the specific problem of the outside narrator. With mock self-condescension, Hawthorne offers, in what only the simplistic reader will take to be a portrait of "himself," a man of very small and very secondary imagination—at best a "medium" or an amanuensis. A patriotic minor antiquarian who is also, embarrassedly, a man of fancy, he fusses around the edges of the fictive historical revelations he transmits. But Bela Tiffany is also Hawthorne—unembarrassed in method and sharply ironic in attitude. And it is to his strength that the weakness of the outside narrator points.

2

"Howe's Masquerade" is, as critics have implied, the least complex of the four legends. Static and pictorial in form, and nearly "neutral" in moral judgment, it serves mainly as an introduction to the complicated problem under investigation. But it is by no means a merely "nominal" introduction: it sets the scene and identifies the combatants, but it also penetrates fairly deep into a definition of the issues, and thus is not to be lightly dismissed.[14] The historical pageants which oppose each other are more than merely colorful; and the victory of the "Puritan" masque is more than a retrospective prediction of an eventual historical outcome. Very much of what we need to know about the nature and relative force of the opposing sides is revealed by what they imaginatively project into their respective masquerades. As Bela Tiffany and his hearers sit in the "proletarian shabbiness" of the Province House bar, they are asked to think back to the "most gay and gorgeous affair that had occurred in the annals of the government," a final "ostentation of festivity" (243); and we are invited to compare the egalitarian ideas of

Jacksonian democracy with an earlier, "Puritan" idealization of the primitive simplicity of original American manners. As they sip "port sanguaree," Bela Tiffany reminds his hearers that the siege of Boston is in its last phase; and we take note that Boston has indeed become a "bloody port." But we are also to see, in contending imaginative constructs, an ideological revolution of mind and heart.

The revolution comes swiftly, as Howe's own masquerade lasts only a few paragraphs. It is abruptly disturbed and decisively abbreviated by Colonel Joliffe's anti-masque, which is the real substance of the ironically mistitled story. The contest never seems quite equal. For though there is something very properly British about the costumes worn and the roles played by Howe's guests, their whole affair seems unreal: the entire occasion is, in the light of the military situation, one of enforced gaiety; and the particular masquers assembled have no very deep relation to the American context: "The brilliantly-lighted apartments were thronged with figures that seemed to have stepped from the dark canvass of historic portraits, or to have flitted from the magic pages of romance, or at least to have flown hither from one of the London theatres without a change of garments" (243). New England knows more than a little of "historic portraits," but its own relentless idealization of the "Forefathers" is as different from the British traditionary sense as Cotton Mather is from Edmund Burke; and despite the influence of the Province House and the concerted efforts of its aristocratic retinue, the courtly cultivation of romance and comedy has yet to establish itself in the rocky soil of New England culture. Howe's steeled knights, bearded Elizabethan statesmen, and high-ruffled ladies may mingle in the British imagination—may properly mix with Merry Andrew, Falstaff, and even the appropriated Don Quixote; but none of them may withstand the stern, scornful frown and bitter smile of Colonel Joliffe. Against his "black Puritanical scowl" they possess no more force than the Comus Revellers of Merry Mount could marshall against the archetypal grimness of Endicott. A "Puritan" vision reveals their unreality at once.

But if we cannot escape the pressure of "The May-Pole" behind "Howe's Masquerade," still the relationship is a subtle one. Joliffe—a "stern old figure" standing "amid all the mirth and buffoonery"—may seem, precisely, Endicott once more, or Endicott grown older by some 140 years of history; and his name, a phonetic rendering of the historical Joyliffe, suggests "Joyless" clearly enough. But the figures he opposes are not *precisely* the equivalent of the antique Revellers. And, more crucially, the story lacks any "third" element corresponding to the Lord and the Lady (the revolutionary legend being, evidently, one of stark confrontation rather than creative encounter).

The revelry is "unreal" in both stories: here, as in "The May-Pole," critics have labeled it artificial, a mockery, a deluded attempt to mix history and myth or to arrest or resist time, a lie about history; but in "Howe's Masquerade" a slightly different temporal order is involved. "Merry Mount" is allowed to seem a bit more archetypal and mythic. The Revellers affirm, desperately and meretriciously, a return to an instinctual Eden prior to the Fall which their natures and their cultic activities so ironically reveal; Endicott's Puritanism affirms, with equal desperation, the escape into an enclave of covenant; the Lord and Lady embrace the inevitable conclusion that Miltonic time and history are, theologically speaking, real and identical everywhere. The struggle is indeed "historical," about America, but it is also somehow archetypal. In "Howe's Masquerade" the struggle is measurably less elemental. Real time and history have inevitably elapsed in the "New World," and the question is now whether that history is significant or not. At issue is "Anglicization": has experience in the *New* England made *Old* England's cultural (and political) forms more or less relevant? Granted that the absolute question is solved: we are all, under the aspect of the Fall, identically children of Adam. Still the relative question remains: what, in the cultural sense, have we to do with England?[15]

The Puritan answer is, as I have already suggested, pretty obviously given in Joliffe's assured, seemingly inevitable rout of Howe's literary, historical, and nationalistic entertainment. To the representative Joliffe, Howe's masquerade is a "stupendous impertinence." In the relative, cultural sense, British history and American history are different histories. Having "overcome" in America, Puritanism is as little involved in British high culture as it was or is in Anglo-Catholicism. Howe's last soiree, itself a provincial parody of British high culture, is as impotent in Puritan Boston as are the vice regents and tax collectors who carry on by day the charade of royal prerogative. All this may or may not be "good"; there may be here, in Joliffe's powerful scorn, the same sort of "loss and gain" critics have found in other of Hawthorne's cultural balance sheets. But it is simply a fact. The Fantastic Foolery of England can stand against Joliffe no better than against Endicott. Howe's masqueraders are by no means the same sort of "triflers of a lifetime" as the Revellers; and they may or may not be the swarm of useless, pretentious, and corrupt "Robinocrats" characterized in contemporary propaganda. Whatever may be the case in "Lady Eleanore's Mantle," their ostentation here is a function of fear and not of "pride." But they are irrelevant because they are not indigenous. The imagination of New England does not recognize them as its own, and cultural renegades like Mather Byles constitute a ludicrous minority. In the end—for good or ill—Colonel Joliffe has a powerful reality on his side: he is "the best sustained character in the masquerade" because he so completely represents "the antique spirit of his native land" (244).[16]

And thus Joliffe is the Gray Champion even more than he is Endicott. His opposition may have its ultimate roots in Puritanism's reduction of everything else to "paganism," but the present emphasis is on his representative resistance to cultural invasion as such. His scorn of Howe's buffoonery is related to Endicott's decimation of Blackstone, the one being an ironic reduction of the other; but more important is his rejection of every cultural and political form that does not spring from "the character of the people." His power to disrupt Howe's masquerade is nearly identical to the Gray Champion's power to stop the motley march of magistrates and prelates in 1689. And his "real" name, for Hawthorne, might as well be Samuel Adams.[17] Good Puritans might for a long time glory in the abstractions of English liberties, but against the advance of an "alien" social system their various champions cry "Never." And thus Howe's last desperate assertion of a viable British presence in America is really disproven well before Joliffe stages his procession of departed governors. His "black Puritanical scowl" and the eleventh-and-a-half-hour stroke from the Puritan, revolutionary Old South Church have already decided the issue. The political facts are, finally, about to catch up with the cultural realities.

One other facet of Howe's ill-fated entertainment deserves notice. The "broadest merriment was excited," we are told, not by the figures out of British history and literature, but by "a group of figures ridiculously dressed in old regimentals," portions of which "had probably been worn at the siege of Louisburg" (244). All in the "mock heroic style," the impersonations attempted include not only Gates and Lee and Schuyler, but "no less a personage than General George Washington" as well. This may look like a simple enough irony—with a victorious Washington just outside the walls; but there are subtler suggestions as well.

First of all, we recognize once again a certain appropriateness about this effort of the British imagination: mock heroic is its most proper eighteenth-century form; and it is scarcely surprising to see ruling Britannia try to deal with provincial America by casting it in this mode. Indeed the reverse would be surprising. How could London take Boston seriously? And what were Washington's origins?[18] But neither the appropriateness nor the inevitability of the response makes it any less disastrously mistaken. The Americans are serious indeed, and they may be more powerful than their tattered regimentals suggest. To be sure, Louisburg was not by British standards a victory of mythic proportions; Hawthorne himself refers to it elsewhere as a lucky raid, carried out in the spirit of a picnic or a Harvard commencement; but it was, nevertheless, a very important event in the military (and social) history of the New World. In "Old News" Hawthorne suggests that it changed the character of New England:

> After that event, the New Englanders never settled into precisely the same quiet race which all the world had imagined them to be. They had done a deed of history and were anxious to add new ones to the record. They had proved themselves powerful enough to influence the result of a war, and were thenceforth called upon, and willingly consented, to join their strength against the enemies of England.[19]

Since then, of course, their strength has grown, as their former allies against the French and Indians will discover.

But this is a minor irony. The increasing martial power and confidence of the New Englanders is an important fact for one sort of history; but for Hawthorne's proper mode a far more important one is the continuity of "Puritan" resistance or, more precisely, the re-discovery at critical moments of a basically revolutionary identity beneath the obscuring encrustations of provincial surfaces. The most significant point about the mock heroic portion of Howe's masquerade is that it misidentifies its real enemy, or chooses to imagine the less ultimate and less powerful sources of resistance. Howe's masquerade—which is contrived as an allegory of continuing British presence in Boston—is put to rout not by the physical intrusion of Washington's army but by the willful resistance of Joliffe and by his manipulation of the allegory of history which lies behind it. Massachusetts is not, as Hawthorne knows, all there is to the American resistance; and certainly General Washington is no Puritan. But Hawthorne is not the first or last historian to identify the Puritan colonies as the ultimate source of the Revolution, and his clear suggestion is that without the persistence of a Puritan spirit of dissent, resistance, and independency, the struggle between Britain and her colonies would never have entered a military phase. In the severe view of Hawthorne's moral history, Joliffe is an irreducible "cause"; Washington is an epiphenomenon.[20]

And surely Joliffe, Endicott, the Gray Champion, and Samuel Adams are less likely candidates for the mock heroic than any battlefield generals. They may not be unambiguously attractive figures, but they are not to be trivialized. Their unswerving belief in their own righteousness and their unbending rejection of compromise may not be entirely healthy, but it is deadly serious: no one has ever thought to cast Paranoia as the hero of a mock epic. And thus the English can amuse and deceive and encourage themselves only by refusing to see the resistance for what it is. The spirit that resisted Laud in the 1630's, James II in the 1680's, the encroachment of royal prerogative and of the S.P.G. in the 1760's, now in figure resists "it all"—in what Perry Miller has called, and in what Hawthorne himself will go on to identify as, an astonishingly successful "revival" of the spirit of the "Forefathers."[21]

At first glance, the presentation of Colonel Joliffe's anti-masque seems anti-climactic, even though it takes up most of the tale. Until we look closely, its details seem less interesting than the fact that he presents one at all—to supplant, after he has seriously discomfited, the mock gaiety and mock heroics of Howe's misguided and ill-fated performance. He presents a melodrama which might properly be called "the march of history"; specifically, a procession of "figures" of the Massachusetts governors from Endicott and Winthrop at the "errand" beginnings, through Bradstreet and Andros at the First-Charter crisis, through the various royal "placemen" of the eighteenth century, down to the present military governor. The procession concludes with the recently departed but "well-remembered" Hutchinson ("ill-remembered" too, as the next tale will remind us), with General Gage (Howe's immediate military, non-constitutional predecessor), and finally with a not very mysterious "figure" of Howe himself, about to join the spectral procession of "departed" governors. And we are, of course, in no danger of missing the obvious: this is a "funeral procession of royal authority in New England" (249); "the empire of Britain in this ancient province is at its last gasp tonight" (254). Howe's authority is already dead and gone. At first we may not especially regret that Howe answers Joliffe's offer of interpretation with a threat against his rebellious gray head. It turns out, however, that a little greater critical patience is necessary: the Puritan's presentation of his own history is not *entirely* transparent and self-explanatory.

Looking for subtlety in the area of "the spectral," however, is not especially rewarding. Suggestions of the magical or supernatural may serve further to associate Joliffe with the Gray Champion; and witchcraft and deviltry do become important in the second legend; but here we have no difficulty with a naturalistic explanation of what is occurring. As representative leader of the resistance, Joliffe has carefully arranged a quite human performance, complete with ghastly music; it is all as unmystifying as the carefully prepared and precisely executed parade and "review" in "My Kinsman, Major Molineux." And at this level Joliffe is simply telling Howe that he is the next to go, as all before have gone and are now ghosts. Given Howe's own manifest uneasiness, no especially magical simulation would be required to convince him that he has seen his own ghost departing, in rage and sorrow, from the governor's residence. Joliffe might well wish to believe in a supernatural guarantee for the plot he is dramatizing, but the most "spiritual" lesson to be drawn from his masquerade would concern the impermanence, generally, of the "tenure of kings and magistrates." However seriously Howe might wish to take himself, he is merely one more "moment" in that rigidly sequential march from obscurity to oblivion. The "knell of midnight from the steeple of the Old South" merely confirms, according to this view, the same "lesson of eternity" superficially taught in "A Bell's Biography."[22]

If Joliffe functions as a magician at all, it is in his role as the human artist who constructs and manages an historical presentation. Historian he unquestionably is, and critics have recognized him as such. His purpose is decidedly not, however, to offer us his pageant as a "paradigm of the 'Legends' themselves"; the structure of the "Legends" is indeed convoluted, but not in this particular way.[23] For in fact Hawthorne's four tales do not operate as a linear continuity or as a steady historical "march" to an inevitable and melodramatic terminus. Teleology there may be, but it has to be discovered by reference to still other Hawthorne tales and *in spite of* a four-part structure which violently disrupts our ordinary chronological and causal expectations. And yet Joliffe's history *is* paradigmatic—of the way in which New England customarily saw and presented its own history. What Joliffe does, as artist-historian, is to put the history of Puritan Massachusetts into virtually the only shape filiopietistic historians could imagine, from the beginnings of colonial and provincial historical consciousness down to Hawthorne's own day. In every way Joliffe's imaginative form is as properly American as Howe's is properly British; and his form is, emphatically, at least as expressive as his content. Quite simply, Joliffe's masquerade gives us history as "march," history going somewhere climactic, history "leading up to" this moment of the expulsion of "ostentation" from America.

To be sure, the individual human figures do not seem to matter very much: under the aspect of the clock on the Old South, they are all alike and all transitory; they all have their brief hour to work good or ill and then pass on, vanities all. But if the human actors are lacking in ultimate substance, History Itself is not. History is, as one may learn from Jonathan Edwards or, with certain differences of emphasis, from various of his predecessors or followers, nothing other than the record of the progress of the Kingdom of God and His Saints. To ascribe to History the same sort of vanity which orthodoxy necessarily ascribes to every other human form is to speak an ultimate blasphemy; it would be, for the orthodox historian of New England, something like the unpardonable sin. History *must* be going somewhere.[24] And where, for the New England Saints, but toward their own vindication? Where but toward the victory of the Old South Church over the Province House? And what expresses and memorializes the New England *sense* of victory so well as the displacement of a conglomerate British pageant of history by a structured and purposeful American effort? In *both* senses of the word, one "history" is replacing another. That, Hawthorne suggests, is the history of American History.

The Revolution cannot sweep through Boston without an intelligible interpretation and a memorial. It is not enough for it simply to "happen," for Washington's heroic armies to drive out Howe and his retinue of buffoons. The event must be understood according to a providential scheme, and it must be shaped and structured by the historical imagination, given its "place in a "march" which is not entirely spectral and evanescent. There cannot simply *be* a Revolution, lest cynical explanations from economics and sociology rush in to fill a vacuum of intelligibility. If Jefferson must submit "facts" to a "candid world" (a list of George III's personal "tyrannies" to an imagined congress of enlightened intelligences), the Puritan mind must do more; subsuming Jefferson's list, it must refer the revolutionary events to the march of "liberty," civil and ecclesiastical.[25] In the end, Joliffe's displacing Howe as master of the revolutionary revels figures the rejection of the British "history" of America as a provincial extension of a civilized and civilizing secular empire by the American, specifically Puritan, "history" of that same place as the "vindication" of its religious origins.

As we have seen, a good deal has changed since the beginning: Joliffe is not *quite* Endicott; and it is now a bit harder to picture British culture as simply pagan. But Joliffe *almost* sees it this way, just as the propaganda of the 1770's could scarcely keep from claiming that Britain was as corrupt an "Egypt" as the world had ever seen. Similarly, Joliffe's ideals (eliptically expressed) seem a good deal more secular than Endicott's. But then a certain secularization of content was itself part of the progressive "vindication," and it was not allowed to disrupt the form. Lockean liberties had to be read back into, or introduced as a gloss on, the original ideal of a "due form of government, civil and ecclesiastical"; it may have been quite an historical feat, but Puritan theorists were, as Perry Miller has shown, entirely up to it. The continuity of ideology may be difficult to trace, but the continuity of character or interpretation is obvious. "The Puritan" is Endicott, is the Gray Champion, is Joliffe; he is also John Wise and Jonathan Mayhew, John and Samuel Adams. His proper action—in which alone he discovers his true identity—is to "stay the march of a King"; his only comment upon that act is to tell the story of piety's own climactic and inevitable march.[26]

And thus we have no trouble inferring the main outline of the interpretation Joliffe is not permitted to offer. The "shape" of his presentation is clear, and there are hints enough. He informs us that the first group of specters pertain to "the old original *democracy* of Massachusetts," and he mentions the ultimate sacrifice of Vane (a family name about to reappear) "for the principles of liberty" (248). Governor Bellomont, the first British nobleman to hold the highest office in Massachusetts, is unlike the original rulers in more than his "very gracious and insinuating style": "unlike the early Puritan governors" he is made, in Joliffe's pageant, "to wring his hands with sorrow" (249). And Joliffe's fair granddaughter opines that the royal governors were, in general, "miserable men."

There is, from the standpoint of political accuracy, a good deal of the problematic here; but our understanding of Joliffe's view does not depend on our ability to resolve the ambiguities. We might like to know what Hawthorne himself *really* thought of Massachusetts' claim of aboriginal democracy; and a final reading of Hawthorne's politics *does* depend on a consideration of conflicting expressions elsewhere.[27] But here we need to grasp only that Joliffe formulates the standard view. Similarly, we might wonder whether Hawthorne believed the royal governors "miserable" only in the sense suggested by "My Kinsman, Major Molineux" (made miserable by the jealousy and recalcitrance of their subjects) or whether he felt them also to be mean and wretched, the dregs of a corrupt colonial bureaucracy; and the rest of the "Legends" will help us with that problem too. But, again, the point here is simply that Joliffe articulates the sanctified, "legendary" view that Puritanism and Democracy go together in Massachusetts and in God's plan. It is against this flattering self-interpretation that the other legends develop their manifold ironies.

Clearly Howe is wrong about Massachusetts: that territory, morally speaking, is not and cannot be made to appear a provincial extension of British culture; some sort of "Puritanism" is too real and too powerful for that. Its culture is still nourished by ideals Britain rejected at the Restoration. The reader accepts, readily and at face value, the superior reality and power of Joliffe's basic denial. But the real problem turns out to be more complicated than that, and we go away from "Howe's Masquerade" worried that there may be as much idealized wish in Joliffe's history as in Howe's. As the subtle contraries of Bela Tiffany continue to unfold, we grow steadily more convinced that the reciprocal attempts to put "history" into or to read it out of "legends" is "hard work" indeed, but that the effort must be made, and that a "thrill of awe" is a far from adequate response. And the subsequent legends exist to persuade us that the well-developed (in the nineteenth century, regnant) myth of the Puritans as libertarian and even democratic founders stands in need of delicate but profound alteration; that the undeniable connections between Puritanism and Revolution may imply no connection, theoretical or historic, between Puritanism and Democracy.

❦ Eight ❦

HELLISH PORTRAITS

THE LEGEND OF THOMAS HUTCHINSON

THE MOVEMENT from "Howe's Masquerade" to "Edward Randolph's Portrait" seems innocent enough: we have simply backed up a few years, to a confrontation we easily recognize as "lying behind" the one with which we began. Yet history nowhere emplots itself, and Hawthorne everywhere selects his dramatic moments with care. Significantly, therefore, the search for a "proximate cause" of the contest figured in "Howe's Masquerade" takes us not to the Intolerable Acts or to the Tea Party which precipitated them; not to the Stamp Act or the Riots it seemed to justify; not even to the Massacre which Grandfather would single out as the Rubicon of the Revolution.[1] What we get, instead, is that moment, midway between the "controlled violence" of 1765 and the military outbreak of 1775, when the British government and its American representatives—impatient with the growing disregard to their authority—decided to quarter troops in Boston. A "law-and-order" decision that backfired.

Evidently Hawthorne once again eschews the melodramatic, offering a moment of historic decision rather than of sickening bloodshed. The Massacre is forecast, as clearly as the Riots are recalled. But as all violence is amoral, so the moral historian can make no explanatory sense of blood and unreason. Less obviously, perhaps, the first movement of the "Legends" frankly proposes that the pregnant moment is the elongated one (here collapsed) in which somebody in authority felt it necessary to replace an imperial-constitutional rule with a military one. If feelings of suspicion are exacerbated to paranoia by the constitutional changes of 1774-75, even more "intolerable" than those of the 1680's, and if the Revolution is ratified by the ousting of the military governor Howe, then the proper beginning of the final phase is the introduction, for the first time since the misrule of Andros, of a "standing army" into Boston. Even if it was only a military police force. More ultimate considerations are proposed in "Lady Eleanore's Mantle," to be sure, but the point here suggested is itself far from trivial: the line from Gage's troops to Howe's expulsion seems continuous; this is the beginning of the end.

Amidst this sober logic, however, arises a prime literary suspicion —namely, that it is a "figural" rather than an "historical" Thomas Hutchinson who is asked to bear the brunt of the fateful decision. Reality and Story are at issue from the first, and that in a particularly difficult way. Joliffe and his daughter we have recognized as typic merely, even as we noticed that the famous "Mischianza Ball" had been relocated from Philadelphia to Boston.[2] Howe had been a "fact" but was easily manipulated, no match for Puritan fictions of history. Here, however, the Royalist seems so real, so responsible. Fully characterized and ambivalent enough to be convincing, Hutchinson seems at first a minor masterpiece of historical portraiture: the local authority who turned on his own. And this sense of raw historical reality is, if anything, only heightened by the knowledge that at least one of his rhetorical opponents had been solid enough to warrant a biographical sketch in *The American Magazine of Useful and Entertaining Knowledge.*[3] We sense, of course, that the *drama* here is a liberty of "Romantic history." Yet the moment seems so inevitable that we may almost forget to ask ourselves what it really *will* symbolize. And for whom.

What we need to remind ourselves, at the outset, is that the Thomas Hutchinson of history was in no way uniquely responsible for the decision to call in the troops; that the really critical decision was in fact taken in 1768, before "Lieutenant-Governor Hutchinson assumed the administration of the province, on the departure of Sir Francis Bernard" (258). The moment represented here is already late in the day. Hutchinson is changing the guard at Castle William; but as other persons and forces have conspired to bring British troops to America in the first place, the symbolism here is more convenient than exhaustive.[4] And it may have less to do with the dramatic demands of Hawthorne's fictional method than with the habit of "patriotic" historians, both popular and professional, to blame Hutchinson for everything.

Thus "Edward Randolph's Portrait" actually proposes two premises of historical explanation: the unique decision to quarter troops, on the one side; and, on the other, the steady tendency of the patriots to turn Hutchinson from a relentlessly legitimist politician into a figure of diabolic conspiracy. In this latter sense the legend focuses on Hutchinson because it *is* a legend— because Hutchinson so quickly and easily became a central portrait in the New England gallery of conspiratorial villains. His own "picture" is, like that of the blasted Randolph, one that conventional history had most blackened. And from this perspective Hawthorne's ironic purpose depends on a critical realization, from the outset, that much less may be going on here than meets the eye; that Governor Hutchinson, elaborately exonerated in

Grandfather's Chair, did not actually *do* all the things which a certain style of history had claimed; that he in no way concentrated in his own person, as he does in the legend, the whole responsibility for the decision which made bloodshed inevitable.[5]

And yet, unlike "The May-Pole of Merry Mount," the tale does not entirely deconstruct. For in another, simpler sense, the focus of the tale is proper enough: Hutchinson had considerable authority throughout the late 1760's; his letters to the home government had considerable weight in the decision that law and order required troops; and, most crucially here, he ought to have had sufficient insight to imagine the effect of the decision to quarter troops. What *is* the good of history? Or, more pointedly, who could better have predicted the response to this decision than the historian of the "Colony and Province of Massachusetts Bay"? No diabolical traitor, Hutchinson is yet "guilty" of some incredible failure of historical imagination.[6]

The decision to bring in the army is entirely "prudential," a matter of utilitarian prediction based on inference from historical experience rather than on natural or constitutional justice. Hutchinson, already New England's most authoritative historian—quoted for precedent and for doctrines of charter liberty as much by American Whigs as by American Tories—is the figure in whom historical wisdom and hence prudential judgment may most reasonably be located. He is at the head, or near the head, of Massachusetts government in the years of critical decision. He has influence and he ought to have knowledge. He is an American, as authentic in his way as are Otis and Adams, and as likely a keeper of the American "trust" as any agent of British sovereignty in America could possibly be. He *should* know. This descendant of the exiled Ann Hutchinson, this annalist of all the vicissitudes of the Puritan experiment, this man who sees himself as present occupant of the house founded by the custom of Edward Randolph, this "Essential Tory" is asked to decide whether troops can possibly help resolve the opposition between an always self-righteous, long-neglected, and now extremely suspicious Puritan state and an ungainly empire trying to preserve law and order even as it tightens up its imperial control.

Hutchinson should know what the New England response will be. How could an historian truly in touch with his subject not know? Perhaps he is not truly in touch; perhaps he never really does manage to understand, as John Adams would claim, "the true character of his native country or the temper, principles, and opinions of its people."[7] Or perhaps he does know. Perhaps some imagined "higher" consideration upsets his empirical sense at this point. At any rate, he decides for troops, for law and order; the decision may be "necessary" but it makes impossible any continuance of that essential "trust" on which political stability and social continuity are based.

Surely, then, there is some miscomprehension. And the historical miscomprehension of this most noble, most American, yet most maligned Loyalist seems to stand for the almost complete inability of a certain class of observers to understand the revolutionary point of view; or, understanding it, to appreciate the depth of historical experience from which it might draw its power to persuade conscience and motivate resistance.[8]

The movement from "Howe's Masquerade" to "Edward Randolph's Portrait" is, therefore, a double movement. In one sense it is a "backing-up" from the moment of revolutionary confrontation to the moment of decision which makes the confrontation inevitable. But in a more subtle sense it is a further elaboration of the problem of "opposing histories." If "Howe's Masquerade" gives us the opposition between two dramatized versions of the meaning of provincial America, "Edward Randolph's Portrait" shows us the contrasting operations and conclusions of two very different sorts of historians. For Alice Vane (of revolutionary name) is also an historian; and the lesson she derives from the appropriate Puritan precedent is quite different from that of her scholarly uncle. We may not be expected to agree with her patriotic "moral," any more than we agree with the larger philosophical implications of Joliffe's view; but clearly her "artist's" insights are more in touch with the crucial problems of character and psychology than is Hutchinson's flawless antiquarianism. The portrait of Edward Randolph does not mean precisely what she wants it to mean, but she does at least restore it; it does have living moral meaning for her, as it does not seem to have for Hutchinson.[9]

Ironically, Hutchinson could be saved from making his disastrous, trust-destroying decision not so much by accepting the interpretation which Alice Vane and the other proto-Revolutionaries attach to the career of Edward Randolph as by properly estimating the significance of the fact that they interpret his history as they do. Hutchinson never can and should not accept the idea that God steps in to "curse" the enemies of Puritan "liberty"—not Ann Hutchinson on the one side and not Edward Randolph on the other. But the Puritans believe He does; and believing it, they hasten to become willing instruments of the divine judgment in history. In the end, Hutchinson's study of history ought to have taught him that the Bostonians will respond to the troops of 1770 in much the same way they responded to those who followed the efforts of Randolph nearly a century earlier, or to the threat of troops in 1635; and, not less important, that they will blacken his historical portrait just as they have blackened Randolph's; or Laud's. Both cases are equally covered by the doctrine of divine vindication in the Puritan theory of history: saints *must* resist tyrants, and those who would tyrannize saints can only be diabolical, agents of the conspiracy against History's march toward Holy Liberty.

1
🎴

The first of the legend's two scenes opens with Hutchinson lost in historical reverie: instead of moving boldly to decide this issue of "deepest moment," the thoughtful and aristocratic magistrate is pondering the blackened portrait above his desk. His manner may be abstracted, but his scrutiny is careful, and something in his demeanor attracts the notice of his two kinsmen, the artistic Alice Vane and Francis Lincoln, the Provincial Captain of Castle William. The two young persons are, of course, deeply concerned in the decision about to be taken, and evidently they see a chance to use history to influence it. Their appeal may develop spontaneously, but it is not without an air of knowing complicity.

All too casually Alice Vane inquires about the subject of the portrait, and about the possibility of recovering its significance. And Captain Lincoln proceeds to relate, to the still distracted Hutchinson, "some strange fables and fantasies which, as it was impossible to refute them by ocular demonstration, had grown to be articles of belief, in reference to this old picture."

> One of the wildest, and at the same time the best accredited, accounts, stated it to be an original and authentic portrait of the Evil One, taken at a witch meeting near Salem; and that its strong and terrible resemblance had been confirmed by several of the confessing wizards and witches, at their trial, in open court. It was likewise affirmed that a familiar spirit or demon abode behind the blackness of the picture, and had shown himself, at seasons of public calamity, to more than one of the royal governors. Shirley, for instance, had beheld this ominous apparition, on the eve of General Abercrombie's shameful and bloody defeat under the walls of Ticonderoga. Many of the servants of the Province House had caught glimpses of a visage frowning down upon them, at the fire that glimmered on the hearth beneath; although, if any were bold enough to hold a torch before the picture, it would appear as black and undistinguishable as ever. (260)

All these suggestions turn out to be, in a certain ironic way, "true," but nobody there in the room believes them literally. And after having affected to tremble at these "really awful" fables, Alice Vane comes to the careful and uncasual point: "It would be almost worth while to wipe away the black surface of the canvas, since the original picture can hardly be so formidable as those which fancy paints instead" (261).

The purpose of this low-keyed little masquerade is obvious. Despite their nepotistic affection, these young people are no flatterers of "their kinsman, Governor Hutchinson." Not unlike Joliffe and his fair granddaughter in relation to Howe, they are trying to pique Hutchinson into historical realization, to make him grasp the meaning of what is, however darkly, right before his historical eyes. But the magistrate has not been fully attentive, and he may prove a trifle obtuse. He has missed the transparently conspiratorial nature of their casual artistic talk, and his pedantic response to Alice clearly indicates he has not really "heard" her own expressed reactions to the fancy and fable attached to the portrait.

Thus without realizing it, he does exactly what she has asked him to do: he correctly identifies the subject of the original picture—the not-so-formidable bureaucrat turned by legend into the Devil himself.

"I am sorry, Alice, to destroy your faith in the legends of which you are so fond," remarked he; "but my antiquarian researches have long since made me acquainted with the subject of this picture—if picture it can be called—which is no more visible, nor ever will be, than the face of the long buried man whom it once represented. It was the portrait of Edward Randolph, the founder of this house, a person famous in the history of New England." (261)

Famous indeed. A name to live in infamy, as Captain Lincoln well knows: "Of that Edward Randolph . . . who obtained the repeal of the first provincial charter, under which our forefathers had enjoyed almost democratic privileges! He that was styled the arch-enemy of New England, and whose memory is still held in detestation as the destroyer of our liberties!" *That* Edward Randolph? "The same Randolph," Hutchinson confirms, with honesty and discomfort, whose lot it was "to taste the bitterness of popular odium" (261–262).

Suddenly all distraction and pretense of casualness cease. We are very near the heart of the matter. We may want to notice that whereas the less subtle Joliffe, speaking to the less knowledgeable Howe, had referred simply to "the old original democracy," Lincoln risks only a much less impressive formula; or that while he affirms *"almost* democratic *privileges"* (my italics) in his own voice, he throws the assertion about a diabolical destruction of liberty into indirect discourse; and that this indirection continues as he goes on to repeat the story of the "curse" which "our annals" try to show working itself out in the life and death of Randolph—a people's curse which can only be, at the same time, a divine judgment, a clear case of God having given Randolph bitterness to drink. But these niceties are not the main point. What Lincoln personally believes is even less important than what side God is really on. The main point is that New England has a "history" already prepared and a "role" already waiting for Hutchinson—and that he ought to know this.

If this present occupant of the house founded by Randolph approves the transfer of Castle William (or, later, writes in favor of abridging the charter of 1691),[10] he will be the new Edward Randolph, "blasted" as the new "arch-enemy of New England." In fact it is scarcely hyperbole to say that, in the New England mind, Hutchinson will *be* Randolph. There can be many enemies, but there can be only one "arch-enemy"; and the archetypal enemy of divine-democratic purposes in history can be no other than the Devil himself. The propositions are no more true in abstract logic than they are in the concrete assertions of the New England annalists where, as we have amply seen, allegory and figure existed long before Hawthorne ever took up his allegorical pen.[11] "Arch-enemy" here signifies no more and no less than Cotton Mather's own language, which Hawthorne had quoted in "The Gray Champion." That Edward Randolph "who achieved the downfall of our ancient government" is a "blasted wretch": damned by human historians because reprobated and destroyed by God; and revealed in his absolute iniquity by his unalterable opposition to the predestined progress of the divine kingdom.

Captain Lincoln's warning, then, is most impressive, whatever may be his own commitment to supernaturalism. Do you want to incur, he implicitly asks Hutchinson, the curse of a people whose mode of cursing is to turn their enemies into Satanic figures and to resist them with all their yet-sleeping reserves of Puritanic energy?

Hutchinson tries to brush aside the real question. He knows about the "bitterness of popular odium," but of course he cannot believe in "curses"; such superstitions are as out of place in the rational historian as they are in the enlightened ruler. The traditions of Randolph's desperate end are "folly to one who has proved, as I have, how little of historic proof lies at the bottom"; they are scarcely less ludicrous than the story that the portrait is of "the Evil One, taken at a witch-meeting near Salem."

> As regards the life and character of Edward Randolph, too implicit credence has been given to Dr. Cotton Mather, who—I must say it, though some of his blood runs in my veins—has filled our early history with old women's tales, as fanciful and extravagant as those of Greece or Rome. (262)

All this is, of course, quite true—and quite beside the point. The modern historian sees, with Hutchinson, and all too easily, that Randolph is "really" only an officious, ambitious, tirelessly devoted prototype of emerging imperial bureaucracy, even though his special grudge against New England constituted a more concentrated threat to its special "privileges" than any person or agency in the 1760's or 1770's. And it is probably worth mentioning that the hysteria of the years immediately before the Revolution, the suspicion of and rage against Hutchinson, and the subsequent blackening of his reputation, are all far less "justified" than similar phenomena earlier. But in this instance the "facts" have little bearing on the "history."

Alice Vane's whispered suggestion that "such fables" may "have a moral" is far from the platitude it may seem. She makes explicit the question implied by Captain Lincoln: does Hutchinson want to risk the curse of the Puritan? The curse of such people is indeed a curse of history. The "vox populi" may or may not be a "vox Dei," but it is a powerful voice in any case. And Hutchinson ought to know.

For a moment he seems to know. Alice Vane's warning that the blackened portrait has not hung so long in the Province House without reason seems to strike upon "some feeling in his own breast, which all his policy or principles could not entirely subdue." We may well doubt that the feeling has anything to do with fear of divine retribution, for the unfailingly conscientious Hutchinson knows himself *not* to be one of those rulers who "feel themselves irresponsible"; but this tirelessly devoted annalist of his native land has every reason to hope for a better memorial in after-times than that awarded Randolph. He knows what happened to that earlier exponent of British sovereignty in America: his own history has recorded the intense and widespread popular hatred of Edward Randolph, "who, the people of New England said 'went up and down to devour them.' "[12] And he is enough of a Christian to recognize in this language a clear echo of the Biblical description of the Satanic adversary. At some level, it would seem, Hutchinson cannot *not know*. If he decides to oppose the popular will, he will invoke the same paranoic forces which "cursed" Randolph. The people will decide that he is the Devil and act accordingly.

But again Hutchinson turns aside the threat by speaking to the less real side of the problem. "Peace, silly child," he warns Alice Vane, with irony so heavy it can scarcely be lost upon himself. "The rebuke of a king is more to be dreaded than the clamor of a wild, misguided multitude" (263). This is "true," no doubt, for any traditionalist or constitutionalist or legitimist; but unless we imagine his distracted historical reverie to have been entirely empty, we cannot help feeling he knows there is more at stake. He is *not* much like Randolph, but he will become so in New England "history"; for in the history of a covenanted people, all enemies are the same Enemy.

At any rate, "it is decided." Against a last elemental plea by Captain Lincoln that he "trust yet awhile to the loyalty of the people" and not "teach them that they can ever be on other terms with British soldiers than those of brotherhood," as when they fought a common imperial enemy, "side by side through the French War" (263), Hutchinson decides to do what he feels he must. And Alice Vane does what, by some deep and mysterious historical necessity, she "must." In language that is clearly meant to recall the darkness and shadow of "The Gray Champion," this un-childish descendant of Revolutionaries, who bears the name of the most authentic Revolutionary of them all,[13] summons up the hellish forces of rebellion, even as she invokes from obscurity the meaning of Edward Randolph's portrait: "Come forth, dark and evil shape! It is thine hour!" Her cry is at once ritualistic and historical. An invocation of New England's hereditary "spirit" of revolution, it is also an historical act; it calls into play once again all the feelings and ideas, causes and meanings which shaped the Puritans' response to earlier visitations of their "arch-enemy."

Once we see the point of the first scene, the second becomes a trifle anti-climactic. Hutchinson once again resists entreaty, re-affirming loyalty to King and to order, even in the face of a *literally* unveiled portrait of Edward Randolph. Everything is a bit more explicit, but little is really changed. The lines of opposition and definition are more sharply drawn, but they are the same lines. Hutchinson feels he must proceed with the military police, and the Puritans are not about to surrender their history.

With Captain Lincoln and Alice Vane we now have a full party of "the Selectmen of Boston, plain, patriarchal fathers of the people, excellent representatives of the old puritanical fathers." Hutchinson also has his party: a small minority of the Council, "richly dressed" and "making a somewhat ostentatious display of courtier-like ceremony," and a "major of the British army, awaiting the Lieutenant-Governor's orders for the landing of the troops" (264). It is all, once again, a kind of masquerade; we have not really moved very far from Joliffe and Howe. And it is, also, all a kind of cliché. But not a cliché of Hawthorne's invention, as the very briefest look at revolutionary "propaganda" reveals. It is as if Alice Vane has summoned literary figures—rather than that Hutchinson has called together opposing political factions; as if her "come forth" has resulted in an historical revelation, or perhaps a reversion to type. The legendary fathers, the plain-patriarchal–old-Puritanical founders have appeared, or reappeared, to resist the threat to "liberty" and the encroachment of "ostentation." The truth of the scene is the truth of "legend."

But though the identity of the opponents is merely clarified to the point of mythic generality in the second scene, and though Alice Vane's final, "magical" unveiling of the portrait of New England's "blasted" enemy adds only a melodramatic note, the total effect is not one of redundancy. For the talk on both sides now becomes a good deal more direct. The crisis having arrived, the pen being now in hand, there is no further place for casual indirection. And some of the more puzzling implications of the first scene are now made quite explicit.

As the spokesman for the popular party concludes a speech rejecting in advance all responsibility for bloodshed, he appeals directly to the historian in Hutchinson: "You, sir, have written with an able pen the deeds of our forefathers. The more to be desired it is, therefore, that yourself should deserve honorable mention, as a true patriot and upright ruler, when your own doings shall be written down in history" (265). This is polite; there is still no explicit warning not to become, in deed and in memory, another Randolph; but the "historical" motive is being frankly offered for Hutchinson's consideration. And he admits feeling it, as we knew from his reverie he felt it. But he now responds with a clearer expression of his deeper concern, the "temporary spirit of mischief" abroad in the land. "Would you have me wait till the mob shall sack the Province House, as they did my private mansion?" More than the "natural desire to stand well in the annals of [his] country," Hutchinson feels the need for a stable order, under law and King.[14]

He even suggests that his listeners may yet come to share that desire above all others, that they will be grateful for the protection of the King's banner against the mob whose activities did not cease with the repeal of the Stamp Act. Echoing and answering Captain Lincoln's request earlier, he asks for *their* trust, trust in his motives and in his view of what action will produce the greatest good. Lincoln—sounding in fact a little like Burke— had pleaded for trust in the honorable intentions and the capacity for reasonable action of the people in general. But Hutchinson, as a magistrate and as a private person, has experienced the popular will as mob violence. He "trusts" the people to the extent that he believes their spirit of mischief to be only "temporary"; but he has no trust in the power of order to restore itself.[15]

The argument becomes far less polite when the British major offers his own comment on the situation, asserting the "other" conspiratorial view— that the action of the mob is not an entirely spontaneous or self-generated phenomenon: "The demagogues of this Province have raised the devil, and cannot lay him again. We will exorcise him, in God's name and the King's" (265). His "Tory" view is apt: modern historians have not failed to remark that rebellious rhetoric and revolutionary suggestions often pushed the populace further than conservative forces higher in society were really prepared to go. But this is the less important consideration. More vital is the way the transition from politeness and diplomacy to plain talk of force and violence precipitates a revelation of the primal forces at work and produces a clarification of some of the more "devilish" suggestions that have been playing through the legend.[16]

Captain Lincoln, "stirred by the taunt against his countrymen," makes reply in kind, suggesting quite frankly that force will simply be met by force: "If you meddle with the devil, take care of his claws!" But the official spokesman for the Puritan fathers—"the Venerable Selectman"—will not allow such a bare statement of real-politics or might-politics to pass as approved Puritan foreign policy; the rattlesnake's "Don't tread on me" does not tell the whole story. His answer does not abjure violent resistance, but it rationalizes it in a way we have come, only recently, to identify as absolutely definitive of the New England mind. His stipulations look simple enough, but they will bear emphasis and close analysis. "Craving your pardon, young sir," he reprimands Lincoln, "let not an evil spirit enter into your words"; remember, that is, whose side the Devil is on.

We will strive against the oppressor with prayer and fasting, as our forefathers would have done. Like them, moreover, we will submit to whatever lot a wise Providence may send us,—always after our own best exertions to amend it. (265–266)

And there it really "all" is. Condensed into two sentences is the essence of a mental operation and a political stance that can be read out of literally hundreds of Puritan sermons over at least a hundred years prior to 1775, an essence to which Perry Miller devoted several hundred pages of explanation and elaboration, growing progressively more desperate at other historians' inability to understand.

The growing British threat to American "privileges" will produce, like virtually every other threat to the Puritan state, political and otherwise, the standard "revival" procedures. There will be the prescribed days of humiliation, out of an historical habit as strong and as deep as nature itself; indeed the operations of the covenant are a kind of second nature, in every sense. In fasting and prayer, the people accuse themselves: they are being punished with the threat of loss of "liberty" for their own abuse of liberty. They are being overrun with corrupt "courtiers" (and now soldiers!) and are being devoured by bad rulers (whose aim is not "the happiness of a people") because of their own sins. This is the only logic which explains a "resistance" which begins in prayer and fasting. They will resist, but not *simply* resist. The essential point of Miller's revisionist thesis of the Revolution-as-revival provides the best gloss on the elliptical rationalization offered by Hawthorne's selectman:

What carried the ranks of militia and citizens was the universal persuasion that they, by administering to themselves a spiritual purge, acquired the energies God had always, in the manner of the Old

Testament, been ready to impart to His repentant children. Their first responsibility was not to shoot at the Redcoats but to cleanse themselves; only thereafter to take aim.[17]

They *will* resist—but not so simply as the hot and hasty words of Captain Lincoln suggest. They will cleanse themselves by "prayer and fasting"— and then take aim. Because the present crisis is no more a purely secular one than was the witchcraft or the Indian wars, they will first repent in their special, ritualistic way—and then resist *as part of* their duty, as a chosen people, to advance the cause of redemption in history. And drawing thus on deep religious-historical energies, the resistance will be fierce indeed. The God of Abraham may or may not be on their side, but it will not lessen their chances of success to think so.

Their resistance will be "enthusiastic" because it will be an act of Special Providence, of Covenant, of Holy History. In it they will recover their true revolutionary identity, always virtually present in a community of separated saints. They will *become* the fathers, the plain-patriarchal–old-Puritanical founders, the essentially revolutionary builders of 1630. In resisting the British as agents of the Devil (temporarily allowed by God to punish them for their falling away) first by self-humiliation and then by arms, the Puritan mind becomes "joyfully convinced that it had at last found its long-sought identity."[18] The selectmen facing Hutchinson *become* the founders as surely, and in the same mysterious way, as Hutchinson becomes the essential "arch-enemy."

And this too Hutchinson might be thought to understand. The hot-headed British major would exorcise a Devil raised by provincial demagogues; the heated American captain warns of the Devil's claws. But the more pious and rational selectmen talk of submission to Providence after resistance by prayer, fasting, and "exertions to amend it"; and *there,* concludes Hutchinson, "peep forth the devil's claws." From street violence and from the rhetoric which precipitated it, Hutchinson well understands "the nature of Puritan submission"—never an "unlimited" duty and, in certain cases, a sin. He may mean only that he knows violent resistance will follow as surely and as terribly from the convoluted logic of the selectmen as from the blatant threats of the major and the captain. But he ought to know more. Certainly we see more. And what we see helps us to make sense out of some of the legend's hitherto obscure suggestions.

We now see, for example, the "moral" truth of the popular legend which holds that the blackened canvas hanging in the Province House is really "an original and authentic portrait of the Evil One, taken at a witch meeting near Salem." Rebellion is hellish, the "peaceable" Hawthorne suggests in more places than "My Kinsman, Major Molineux," even when it is somehow necessary; it makes at least as much sense to talk about the Devil's being on the popular side as about God's. And certainly the rampant "distrust" of a revolutionary situation is just as devilish as that of a witch-hunt. But the Devil is present in a much more precise way as well. The really devilish thing about the Puritan resistance is the way it "be-devils" its enemies, turns all forms of opposition alike into a diabolical enemy to be overcome. Randolph (and now Hutchinson) *is* the Devil of Salem not only "logically" (because all Devils are the same "arch-enemy"), but also "historically," since they serve the same function in the Puritan drama.

The Devil-of-Salem and Randolph are, in the self-assessments of the Puritan Jeremiads, very nearly identical: both are "scourges"; both are tests; both are obstacles to godly achievement. Ultimately both are punishments for sins. Both exist by divine permission and are part of the process of trial, and error, and reformation. And hence both are dealt with in the same way: rituals of repentance and then all due resistance.[19]

What Hutchinson may almost see, what any true historian ought to see, and what we certainly see is that the Devil's claws *really* peep forth from Puritan foreign policy in its relentless be-deviling of opposing wills and forces. What a modern historian of the Boston Massacre refers to as the technique of "putting one's enemy in the wrong and keeping him there"[20] is not to be understood, Hawthorne would suggest, without some reference to the inability of a people in covenant, with the transcendent mission of a "redeemer nation," to view all enemies as the same univocal Enemy. And certainly no account of the Revolution is adequate without some reference to the complicated mental and rhetorical process which Hawthorne exposes in "Edward Randolph's Portrait." In some deep way it matters that Hutchinson is Randolph and both are the "Devil in Massachusetts." The failure to see this is indeed a serious oversight. It *must* be part of any valid historical calculation.[21]

But, finally, in some unaccountable way, Hutchinson fails "savingly" to grasp this point. His response to Alice Vane's "temporary restoration" of the portrait of the be-deviled Edward Randolph is as inadequate as many of his earlier responses. He thinks it all a cheap trick, a shallow contrivance of the "painter's art," a stage effect conceived in the "Italian spirit of intrigue." His historical failure is clearly a failure of imagination, one which the reader (and the future historian) is asked not to make. Hutchinson *knows* enough. The legalistically exhaustive pages of his *History* contain all the information necessary to make the correct prediction, to be able to imagine exactly what will happen if troops are brought in to threaten that Puritan "liberty" without which its historic mission is impossible. The event will be interpreted in just one way, and the response will be familiar. The New Englanders will not be slow to recognize the lineaments of their familiar enemy, and the techniques of arousing the holy ardor of resistance are as ready as instinct. And thus if Hutchinson compliments the New Englanders by believing their mob violence is a merely "temporary spirit of mischief," his confidence in the efficacy of British troops ultimately betrays the inadequacy of his understanding of their motives and their "spirit." The calculus of troops and mobs is profoundly altered when the human forms have cosmic significance: riot control is one sort of problem, apocalyptics quite another.[22]

2

Most a priori doubts about the "plausibility" of so modern a reading of "Edward Randolph's Portrait" can be allayed by a brief glance at the comparable sections of *Grandfather's Chair*. As always, Hawthorne is far less subtle with an audience of children, who are just learning their history; but even here it is obvious that he has thought carefully about "the problem of Hutchinson" and what beyond itself it might typify.

Grandfather introduces Hutchinson as, in his way, a superb historian: "This gentleman was more familiar with the history of New England than any other man alive. He knew all the adventures and vicissitudes through which the old chair had passed, and could have told as accurately as grandfather who were the personages that had occupied it."[23] This is high praise indeed. To know about "the old chair" is, in the symbolism of the whole work, to know about the moving center of historical significance in early Massachusetts. And hence it is not surprising that little Lawrence (Grandfather's most sensitive listener) calls Hutchinson's decision to write a formal history of Massachusetts a really "bright thought" or that he imagines Hutchinson to have been "inspired" by the spirits of former possessors of the chair, flitting around him as he writes. But this view, unfortunately, is only a childish fantasy. Although it is impossible to miss Hawthorne's profound respect for, even his feelings of historical kinship with, Hutchinson, Grandfather cannot allow this overly literary estimate to stand. Hutchinson's history is "accurate" (perhaps more ultimately reliable, it is faintly hinted, than Bancroft's),[24] but it is not very imaginative: "If Mr. Hutchinson was favored with any such extraordinary inspiration, he made but a poor use of it in his history; for a duller piece of composition never came from any man's pen" (137–138). What this means, of course, is that Hutchinson is not quite like Hawthorne, whose highly "literary" history clearly *was* the result of inspiration by the ghosts of crises past. But, as we shortly learn, it implies a bit more.

Just a few pages later Grandfather notes the "really amazing and terrible" change which came over New Englanders upon passage of the Stamp Act. The old "Puritan" characteristics had seemed to be disappearing; but "humble and loyal" subjects of the crown suddenly "showed the grim, dark features of an old king-resisting Puritan." And, the children are reminded, "the former history of our chair . . . has given you some idea of what a harsh, unyielding, stern set of men the old Puritans were" (150). What, then, would be the response of the impeccably knowledgeable Governor Hutchinson—heretofore a "wise, good, and patriotic magistrate," as well as a "devoted monarchist"—to the Stamp Act instructions? Lawrence thinks he knows immediately: "I should think . . . as Mr. Hutchinson had written the history of our Puritan forefathers, he would have known what the temper of the people was, and so have taken care not to wrong them." Indeed. He should have known. But, Grandfather answers in language similar to that put into Hutchinson's own mouth in "Edward Randolph's Portrait," "He trusted the might of the King of England . . . and thought himself safe under the shelter of the throne" (153).[25]

The moment is not *quite* the same as that of "Edward Randolph's Portrait"; and neither moment is quite adequate to Hutchinson's complex position, though the epithet of "devoted monarchist" is suggestive. But the main outline is clear enough: whereas Whig historians would have to wonder how a man like Hutchinson could be so "devilishly" disloyal to the destiny of New England's redeeming mission, Hawthorne's ironic problem is simpler and less presumptuous. How could anyone in touch with the deepest realities of New England experience and assumptions fail to see the sort of problem at hand?

The answer is simple. Only by a radical failure of historical imagination. Only by failing to take account of "fanciful and extravagant" fables which may yet have a "moral." There is, of course, ample place for enlightened and rational skepticism of a certain sort. A "too implicit credence . . . given to Dr. Cotton Mather" is certainly a pitfall for the naive or unwary, just as a too literal acceptance of the theory of history ("apocalyptic Whiggism") offered by Colonel Joliffe or Alice Vane (or Jonathan Mayhew or John Adams) is clearly risky business. But, again, the problem is to allow for the profound significance of deeply and widely held beliefs rather than to "accept" them.[26]

The Hutchinson of "Edward Randolph's Portrait" is thus a "figure" of the political failure of the "imperial" side in the American Revolution. But the political failure is based on a failure of historical re-cognition; a failure, like that figured in the irrelevant masquerade of Howe, to grasp the real nature and force of the opposition. As such it also figures a problem that historians of the Revolution have been struggling with ever since—namely, that no purely legalistic, or economic, or social explanation of the events of the 1760's and 1770's seems quite capable of explaining the precise quality and force of the "popular" opposition (fostered by the "black regiment" or the "Old South Church") to the clumsy attempts of Britain to rationalize her empire. Explanations from threats to economic or social status or to a developing theory of secular constitutionalism are, by themselves, as inadequate as the relatively "dull" legalisms of Hutchinson's own history. Something "more" seems necessary; something which can account for the hysteria and even paranoia of the popular response as more than "propaganda"; more, even, than sympathetic local response to the Jeremiad rhetoric of England's "Country Party."[27]

What is also required—and Hawthorne asserts it almost identically with Perry Miller—is some sense of the essential "features" of New England's assumptions about its own place in history. For "Edward Randolph's Portrait" makes it quite clear that more is involved than an "imaginative" theory of "the Puritan character." The essential "features" of Puritanism, which seem to be disappearing, but which are never really lost, are the belief in a transcendent historical destiny somehow tied up with a developing understanding of "liberty" and the availability of the techniques for "reviving" the spirit of the forefathers. Let matters become as confused and as seemingly secular as they may; allow, in Grandfather's words, that the old "characteristics were disappearing . . . for a good many years back" (150–151); allow the eighteenth century to be different from the seventeenth in as many ways as historical scholarship can discover. Still there are certain "features" and "characteristics" which do have a way of reappearing, ritualistically, at critical moments.

The New Englanders may have lost *most* of the doctrinal faith of their forefathers; they may even have recast those redoubtable ancestors in their own more "rationally" libertarian image. But for all that, they have a myth—or, in the terminology of Hawthorne and Wesley Craven, a "Legend"—which assures a viable continuity and a continuing logic of resistance. Their "due form of government" is the "world's best hope." Their ultimate allegiance is to a law considerably higher than martial law. Anyone who would send in troops or abridge their ancient charter liberties had better expect a devil of a time. And Hutchinson—or someone!—ought to know.[28]

3

And *we* have to know, once again, in spite of our narrator. His preliminary remarks call our attention to the Old South Church, pointing its spire into regions of darkness and storm, and becoming lost somewhere between heaven and earth; but for him this is some gratuitous gloominess. And his "moral," once again, involves transitoriness in general. Except for the Revival and Revolution we are permitted to see (and puzzle over) in "Lady Eleanore's Mantle," it is entirely up to us to imagine the activities *inside* the Old South, that representative place and mythic locus where the resistance acquires—in fasting, in prayer, and in the recollection of the character and purpose of the forefathers' resistance to "tyranny"—its intense spiritual energy.

And his concluding remarks are equally unhelpful. Or, rather, they are helpful in the same obtuse and indirect way. Our Romantic antiquarian merely fancies, in the "storm [that] had been gathering abroad," the sound of "all the old governors and great men running riot above stairs." Another thrill of Romantic awe. On the "antiquarian" side, he wonders if he could have a look at the literal—and again darkened—portrait that hung above Hutchinson's desk. The response he receives assures us we have been right in reading the significance of the narrative "around" this inadequate historian.

> Mr. Tiffany informed me that it had long since been removed, and was supposed to be hidden in some out-of-the-way corner of the New England Museum. Perchance some curious antiquary may light upon it there, and, with the assistance of Mr. Howorth, the picture cleaner, may supply a not unnecessary proof of the authenticity of the facts here set down. (269)

Of course it will not help our Romantic-antiquarian narrator to locate an actual, blackened canvas, even if one does or ever did literally exist. But here, finally, we do get a sort of paradigm of the "Legends."[29]

We can, if we are sufficiently curious, find a "portrait" of Edward Randolph in the primary documents of history, in some New England "museum" such as the *Massachusetts Historical Collections,* or the pages of Cotton Mather. We will find it doubly darkened: the true significance of a devilishly blackened reputation will be, like many other "effects" of an age and a mentality not our own, to us obscure. But a picture-cleaner may assist us. Some Hawthorne (for which Howorth seems an intentional near-anagram), some historian who does draw his inspiration from the very spirit of the past may indeed be able to illuminate the more obscure workings of historical process. He will not be a "positivist"; he may not even be, like Hutchinson, completely detailed and completely rational. He may seem, like Alice Vane, something of a magician or a trickster; certainly he will possess more of that insight founded on imaginative sympathy than our fanciful narrator. But he may also show us that the imaginative sympathy required to "unblacken" the portraits of the past does not imply total submission to the ideologies which are the source of the obscurity—and the slander.

Ideally he would see that Governor Hutchinson is, in reality, not very much like Edward Randolph, even though he lives in the house founded by that imperial agent and even though he too has a deep interest in colonial submission to royal sovereignty. He would know that Randolph himself is an "arch-enemy" only according to a very risky and self-righteous, even paranoid theory of history. But he would also know that the quartering of an "alien" army in Boston would be the crucial moment in New England resistance because that sort of threat to colonial "liberty" would serve to awaken in the popular mind all of the old cosmic equations. In prayer and fasting, a secularized progeny will become its pious ancestry, and its enemy will become the Devil himself. They will purge themselves and then resist, their "submission" being "unlimited" only to their Covenant with the God of History. At *this* level of motivation, the "liberty" of the 1770's is not very different from that of the 1630's.

❧ Nine ❧
PLAGUE, POX, PRIDE, AND CORRUPTION
THE POLITICS OF ALLEGORY

IF THE MOVEMENT from "Howe's Masquerade" to "Edward Randolph's Portrait" proves more treacherous than first appearances indicate, still it is the leap from "Edward Randolph's Portrait" to "Lady Eleanore's Mantle" that is likely to break our historical necks. Having "backed up" from 1775 to a moral territory somewhere around 1768 or 1770, we discovered a "further" elaboration of certain problems of revolutionary psychology and of historiography; now we "retreat," much more puzzlingly, to the disastrous smallpox epidemic of 1721. Although the search for ultimate revolutionary causes has led more than one historian well back into that epoch of "benign neglect" on the other side of 1763, not many interpreters have been disposed to look for explanations in the bickerings of the 1720's; and even the most imaginative theorist might wonder what line can connect a political revolution (with religious overtones) to an outbreak of infectious disease.[1] We may begin to suspect, perhaps, that the connections are not so linear as our ability to supply dates would imply. It may be that an adequate understanding of the "Legends" will force us to develop a chronology different from the apparent, literal one.

Certainly the chronology is different from the easy, sequential progress of "Old News," clearly a "forestudy" of the "Province House" material. That three-part sketch covers roughly the same historical span as the "Legends," and it is almost impossible not to use it as some sort of outside reference;[2] but in the end it apprises us chiefly of difference. Regular history properly goes one way—forward. And in "Old News," fancy's meditations on changes in social tone and habit seem to obey the same primary law: from the lethargy of the eighteenth century's early years, to the increasing military bustle of the middle decades, and on to the social upset caused by the revolutionary break. Nothing could be simpler or more natural than the "progress" of "Old News"; nothing less like the structure of the "Legends." For Bela Tiffany is evidently no minor Romantic, and we had better be prepared for a revolution in our habits of historical perception as well as in our political loyalties.

The same sort of suspicions ought to be raised by the difference in literary mode and texture we now experience. "Lady Eleanore's Mantle" is no less historical in basic intention than the first two tales, and no less legendary in its tonalities; but it is self-consciously allegorical in a way the others are not. To some critics it has seemed a separable Spenserian "apologue" on the master sin of "Pride," evidence of Hawthorne's unswerving loyalty to traditional techniques and ideas; but this view avoids the real problem.[3] Just as "Lady Eleanore's Mantle" means what it means largely as a function of its context in a complicated narrative construct, so its highly allegorical form calls attention to itself because of its very difference from the tales before and after it in the sequence. And the difference almost certainly has to do with the problem of "primacy" in the order of historical explanation. Allegory always signals *somebody's* idea of origins.

If "legend"—the popular form of "Romantic history"—is less scrupulous about particular time-past than "regular history," preferring "figures" to literal, historical singulars and conflating various concrete situations into representative instance or typic moment, then "allegory" might be thought to add the timeless dimension of the archetypal, the always and everywhere true; or, as we now say, the structural as opposed to the semantic. Thus if the allegory of "Lady Eleanore's Mantle" stood alone, it might well lead interpretation out of the realm of the historic altogether, into the world of the moral, psychic, or grammatological a priori. But in fact the "allegory" is here controlled by the "legends" which surround it; it is really an allegory within a legend. The result of this deliberate mixing of modes is curious indeed, leaving us with an allegory that is yet somehow "in history." What this suggests, in turn, is not so much ultimacy or essence as somebody's attempt to achieve it. We need to ask "whose?" And this skeptical inquiry leads to the discovery that the peculiar "Pride" of Lady Eleanore is no less significant as a fact of the Revolution than as a sign of sin.

But there is another, less Platonic difficulty. Critics of "Lady Eleanore's Mantle" have not been able to escape the impression that the frantic procession at the end of the tale seems, like the one in "Molineux," proleptic, a little revolution in itself. Certainly the climactic purgation occurs at just this point; and it would be difficult to understand why the remote cause, either in history or in the nature of things, should be the moment of highest emotional intensity unless the first cause and the prime effect were, in some special sense, the same thing; or unless, in another order of reality, the 1720's and the 1770's could be seen as somehow analogous. Thus if it is right to say that the end of "Lady Eleanore's Mantle" shows Jervase Helwyse in "full revolt," and that the procession he leads represents "the destruction of

British authority in the Revolution," then we need to develop some alternate or perhaps a multiple chronology.[4] We have not grasped the structure of the "Legends"—or penetrated to the heart of Hawthorne's view of the Revolution—until we see how the frenzy of the smallpox and the frenzy of a revolutionary revival explain each other, under the allegorical sign of "Pride."

1

The allegory of "Lady Eleanore's Mantle" looks disarmingly simple. It seems to rest on a perfectly available and inevitable formula: pride is a plague and a pox, an infection and a disease. But however strongly the equation seems to suggest (and explain) itself, we must begin by realizing that the connection between pride and pox or infection is not entirely "natural"; the connection is not one which occurred to *Hawthorne* simply because of the inherent moral suggestiveness of certain natural appearances. We can easily see how, for *someone,* pride might *be* a plague just as inevitably as, for Emerson, a brave man *is* a lion; but we miss the controlling historical bias of "Lady Eleanore's Mantle" unless we know about the "constituted" connection, in Puritan theology and in pre-revolutionary social theory, between the various manifestations of that master sin and the terrible scourge of the smallpox. Not only is "Pride" (like "Corruption") a very specialized, definitive, and technical term in the discourse of eighteenth-century moral, social, and political theorizing, but the causal connection between Pride and various plagues or scourges, including the smallpox, is as firm and settled a law in the Puritan mind as that between grace and the regenerate life.[5]

All the distressing evidences of Puritan "declension" were seen and said—in the 1720's, at the famous Reforming Synod of 1769, even back in the late 1640's—to be forms of Pride. All of the inevitable side-effects of New England's movement out of its original simplicity and into more complicated provincial relationships were greeted with dismay; and with Jeremiads which identified the problem (negatively) as an accelerating decay of the values of the founders and (positively) as a growing expression of Pride. No doubt the American Puritan Jeremiad has its beginnings in the problems which the Half-Way Covenant attempted to solve, and certainly "declension" can, at any time, refer to the specific question of the scarcity of professed "visible saints" in full communion with particular churches; but the form is never without a strong and simple social emphasis, and this emphasis tends to increase throughout the later seventeenth and eighteenth centuries. The decline of true sanctity and the growth of Pride are inseparable. Thus land disputes, business rivalries, social jealousies, status-seeking, ostentatious houses and dress, aspiration beyond one's class, the aping of the fashionable by the lower sort of people (not to mention more serious vices) were all related to that one really cardinal sin.

The social historian can explain the phenomenon rather readily: it is largely a matter of an unruly but inevitable individualism and self-interest reasserting itself against the highly corporate and communal values of Winthrop's original "Model": "This Sheba, Self." No doubt the process began almost immediately; and surely its dynamic is not specifically American or Puritan. The fact that the "Puritan" Jeremiads come to sound a bit like the "Gloom of the Tory Satirists" or the nostalgic rhetoric of the English "Country Party" suggests that the fundamental source of social disease is simply the transition from a simpler to a more complicated (more commercial, more "modern") world.[6] But these reassuring social insights do not really help us to explain the feelings of the Puritan moralist of the 1720's. For him the problem was more simply moral; its name was Pride. And he could scarcely doubt that this Pride would be punished by some scourge appropriately connected to it by God.

Increase Mather issued the warning in advance; and Perry Miller has deftly defined the moment:

The smallpox had, of course, long been considered the most deadly of scourges in the arsenal of a covenanted Jehovah; He might at any moment discharge it upon a transgressing people, yet out of respect for the terms to which He had bound Himself, He would resort to it only upon the utmost provocation. The sins of the land had been great, and He had answered them with proportional severity, but except for a slight intimation in 1678, He had held this punishment in reserve. In September 1720—reading the signs carefully—Increase Mather warned New England that smallpox was the next in order; by the end of May 1721 cases were reported, and by June 6 the disease had become epidemic.[7]

The disease came not casually or accidentally or as a result of microscopic secondary causes alone, but by an intelligible and even predictable moral law: the covenanted Jehovah scourges a backsliding people, always in proportion to their vices, and very often in kind. The smallpox epidemic was clearly *caused* by rampant Pride. And—unless one were committed to the virtually blasphemous tactic of innoculation—the *cure* was clearly a reformation of manners, a purging of Pride.

Obviously, then, Pride is a plague and a pox in "Lady Eleanore's Mantle" because the rhetoric of the 1720's makes the causal connection.[8] But this is not the entire explanation. More subtly, but with devastating implications for the analogous 1770's, Pride is a plague because of a confusing but demonstrable tendency of latter-day Jeremiads to blur cause and effect, to run sin and punishment together, to treat sin itself as a punishment or scourge—and, ultimately, to treat the vices of Pride as themselves an infection. As in the famous case of the witchcraft, an outbreak of really vicious behavior can become itself a punishment to the majority of non-witches for some other, more puzzling, less definable sense of falling away, for failing to achieve some increasingly less precise social and religious goal. Deep down, the Puritan community felt itself "plagued" or "scourged" by an "infection" of Pride long before (and long after) any ugly eruptions on the skin melodramatically appeared. The message of the Jeremiads may seem to be a clear, collective indictment: our common vices are causing our punishments. But the deeper and more troublesome implication is that social vice is *itself* a plague.[9] And with that implication comes the nagging question, answered more clearly in the 1770's than in the 1720's, about the sources of this Pride which is "plaguing us." The frenzied destruction of Lady Eleanore's mantle is a confused and ambiguous purgation of corruption in the 1720's; set in the 1770's its reforming, Pride-destroying, plague-ridding, revolutionary meaning is unmistakable. Burning the mantle and the effigy of Lady Eleanore might signify one's own repentance of flirtation with aristocratic vice; but it may also figure a more direct expulsion of "plaguing" influences.

And suggestively so. For it begins to appear that the New England colonists probably came as close to outright rebellion against British political and cultural authority in the early 1720's as at any other moment between 1689 and the 1760's. At least one critic of "Lady Eleanore's Mantle" has inferred and then implied as much; and the most authoritative historian of Boston seems certain of it. Nor can we draw any other conclusion from the alarming account of those years in Governor Hutchinson himself: "We are now arrived to the memorable year 1720 [when] the contests and dissentions in the government rose to greater height than they had done since the religious feuds of 1636 and 37."[10] Indeed the real problem for the historian may almost be to explain why a revolution did *not* occur in 1721 or 1722: most of the painful effects of England's disastrous commercial policies are "there" and, except for the hysteria related to the smallpox, no social fact stands out more clearly in the literature of the period than the virulence of the "Anglophobia raging in Boston." Or, more precisely, even as "many people in Boston looked more and more toward England for cultural inspiration and social values," the Jeremiads increasingly invoked the "values of simplicity, moderation, and sobriety" associated with the seventeenth century and with the Puritan forefathers.[11] Clearly this love-hate relation lies behind the response of Hawthorne's provincials to Lady Eleanore. It is almost clarified and simplified into rebellion as they destroy her effigy and her mantle of Pride: anything which "plagues" us will have to be purified out. At this simplest level "Lady Eleanore's Mantle" reminds us of the revolution which *almost* occurred in the 1720's. Revolution *will* occur, the story seems to suggest, when England can be identified as the source of the epidemic that is plaguing New England. (Several more decades of reading England's own Jeremiads against pride and corruption, the modern historian must conclude, will help to make that clarification.)[12]

But there is more to Hawthorne's allegory than that: "Lady Eleanore's Mantle" does more than *predict* the Revolution: it clearly suggests that the terms of the 1720's are valid terms for understanding the 1770's, that the two moments are related, allegorically, as vehicle and tenor. To read the later decade in terms of the earlier one is to be made starkly aware that the aristocratic Pride of which England is discovered to be the historical source is, apart from any outbreak of infectious disease, a plague and an infection as real and as terrible as the smallpox itself. The Jeremiad rhetoric of the two decades is surprisingly similar: in both cases one is called upon to effect the lifting of a plague or the cure of an infection by a reformation of manners. There *is*, of course, a widespread and disastrous outbreak of literal disease in the 1720's; and, medically, nothing nearly so "epidemic" in the 1770's. But that fact scarcely seems to matter. To the Puritan mind in distress, Pride *itself* is a plague and a pox, even when no one's face oozes corruption.[13]

In the 1720's the Jeremiad formula means, primarily, that the repentant elimination of Pride in all of its various social manifestations and a return to the simpler ways of the founders will induce the covenanted Jehovah to withdraw the scourge of the smallpox; but the confused feeling that Pride itself is a scourge is also present, and (apparently) there is even some desire to purge English social influence as the source of corruption. In the 1770's the formula is simpler, reduced as it is to a purely moral or symbolic essence: we are plagued with the ugly outward marks of Pride—gifts, perquisites, places, pensions, avarice, luxury—and our government is corrupted because "the infection of vice [has] become universal."[14] To secure release from infection should be quite easy because the infection is, as it were, "only" allegorical. Quite simply, *all* one should have to do to secure release from the plague of English social and political corruption is to repent of that Pride which made the plague inevitable, to repent of one's flirtation with the values of Lady Eleanore.

The problem is not, as we might think, that the smallpox seems more like a literal "act of God" than a plague of proud, luxurious, corrupt ministers and courtiers. The logic of the covenant makes no such distinction. And according to *some* logic, the problem of the 1770's ought to be easier than that of the 1720's since the later problem is, considered *as disease*, "only" moral or allegorical. Would that it were so: that one did not, at some point, have to "take aim" at Redcoats and "persecute" Tories (those latter-day worshipers of Lady Eleanore); that Reformation alone could baffle Hutchinson and his patronage machine, foil the deep-laid plots of the Bute ministry, decimate the forces of Howe and Gage.

And yet this irony is not quite final in the order of Hawthorne's conflation of the 1770's with the 1720's. For, as he seems to have recognized, the perilous moment of the 1720's involved action which, from the standpoint of the Jeremiad rhetoric of moral reformation, seems almost as direct, human, and physical as that of the 1770's. Led by the frenzied Jervase Helwyse, a mob does exorcise the image and burn the prideful "effects" of Lady Eleanore. In the sense in which this activity comes "after" the selectman's vow to Hutchinson that the resistance will begin in fasting and in prayer, and to the extent that the procession itself seems religious (if only parodically), we are justified in feeling that the provincials' response to Lady Eleanore is not "merely" physical: burning the clothing of infected persons is ordinary enough medical practice, but burning effigies is another matter altogether. Still, religious or "magical" as the causality of Helwyse's wild procession seems dominantly to be, there is something threateningly physical about mob action in front of the Province House.[15]

That mobs roamed the streets of Boston during the exacerbated moments of the medically and politically disturbed days of 1721 we may well imagine: Governor Shute did not press the legislature for riot-control measures without reason; and one may well doubt that the smallpox was the only reason for removing the legislature to Cambridge.[16] In one sense we have no problem: to the *moral* historian, all revolutionary mobs are the same; any one is fair enough type of any other. But there may be more to the case than this. The whole story seems fraught with some deeper, unstated significance. And more may be involved than Hawthorne's famous "groping" for allegorical significance.

Considered from the vantage of the 1720's, the most peculiar feature of "Lady Eleanore's Mantle" is what it leaves out. In Hawthorne's 1830's, no less than now, the celebrated story connected with the smallpox epidemic of 1721 is the question of inoculation, that vaunted triumph of science over superstition, that one time when the Mathers were right and the Franklins were wrong. Hawthorne himself tells the story that way in *Grandfather's Chair,* complete with the bombing of Cotton Mather's study. He has obviously read in "the war of words . . . against Cotton Mather and Doctor Boylston"; and he is able, in one dependent clause, to identify something close to the essential issue—"that, if Providence had ordained them to die of the small-pox, it was sinful to aim at preventing it." He evokes the specter of mob violence by suggesting that "the people," furious, "threatened vengeance against any person who should dare to practise inoculation."[17] But his children's account is, in the end, completely apolitical. "Lady Eleanore's Mantle," on the other hand, is totally political (once we learn the lexicon of the Jeremiad), and the names of Mather, Boylston, and Douglass do not even appear. The only "physician" who does inhabit the story is a certain Doctor Clarke, and he seems important primarily as a "famous champion of the popular party" (275). In short, "Lady Eleanore's Mantle" outrageously omits that one consideration which a nineteenth-century reader would instinctively expect in a story about the smallpox epidemic of 1721.[18]

Surely some crucial displacement has occurred; and with it, once again, some radical reordering of the significance of seemingly well-known events. Of central importance in the analysis of "Lady Eleanore's Mantle," then, must be the question of direct, human action and its "political" motivation. What do American provincials *do*, in this story of the 1720's, that is in any manner so "revolutionary" as Cotton Mather's decision that it is "safe" actively to prevent a covenanted punishment by the merely human or secondary means of inoculation?

2

In the first of the four scenes, we *seem* to see Pride arriving in the New England colonies, but minor ironies abound. The "rich and high-born Lady Eleanore Rochcliffe" has been sent from London to the provinces "in the hope that a beautiful young woman would be exposed to infinitely less peril from the primitive society of New England than amid the artifices and corruptions of a court" (273). That seems sensible. To be sure, not all Englishmen were prepared to believe that a purified Christianity had been translated to an apocalyptically defined "New" England; but long ago the un-Puritan poet George Herbert had feared something not unlike that might happen, and the Enlightenment evocation of America as "primitive" in a favorable sense found a continuing echo in England's eighteenth-century Opposition, or "Country Party."[19] And who could deny that Boston was a less "tempting" environment than London, that the society which produced Franklin's satires in the *New England Courant* was less "artificial" than the one which produced *The Rape of the Lock*, that "corruption" (in either its generalized social or its technical political sense) was far less advanced in the provinces than at court? On *one* scale, to be sure, Boston might seem very much like Babylon: its own Jeremiahs could keenly sense the desperate state of its declension from the ideals of Winthrop's original City. However reluctantly, they could testify to the truth of the latter part of Herbert's poem as well as the former: that "as the Church shall thither Westward fly / So Sinne shall trace and dog her instantly." But they knew, at the same time and just as clearly, that "Hell is a city very much like London"—much *more* like London than Boston. Doubtlessly the number of spiritual deaths from Pride and the number of physical deaths from plague and pox were, between the wholesome atmosphere of the New World and the crowded cities of the Old, roughly proportional.[20]

Into this *relatively* safe atmosphere, enter Lady Eleanore, "remarkable for a harsh, unyielding pride, a haughty consciousness of her hereditary and personal advantages, which made her almost incapable of control" and which amounted almost to "monomania." And so, woe to her, our impressionable narrator-as-Jeremiah thinks to reflect: "it seems due from Providence that pride so sinful should be followed by as severe a retribution" (274).

But though Lady Eleanore has brought with her Imperial Self enough Pride to doom herself and plague a purer people, and though she proceeds, melodramatically, to wrap herself ever more fatally in the mantle of her Pride, still the world she enters is already somewhat contaminated. Or, if that is too strong, a world far from immune. Her relative, Governor Shute, has preceded her by several years, and Shute is not the first "needy nobleman" to have been granted the prerogative of setting up a miniature court society in the New England provinces. Phips may have been crude in spite of his fortune and his knighthood, but Coote (the Earl of Bellomont) and the aristocratic Dudley had been as anxious to affect the princely manner as Shute; all had been greeted with the same sort of provincial attempt at ceremonious pomp which attends the passage of Lady Eleanore from Newport to Boston. And it is obviously not a completely uncorrupted populace which gives its "simultaneous acclamation of applause" to Lady Eleanore's "emblematic" action of placing "her foot on the cowering form" (276) of Jervase Helwyse, even as she shakes hands with the governor.[21]

The image is, of course, a telling one, and Lady Eleanore suggests far more than she realizes in declaring that "when men seek only to be trampled upon, it were a pity to deny them a favor so easily granted—and so well deserved" (276). The people's applause, which they will bitterly repent and actively reverse, signifies their acceptance not only of the "essential" rightness of Lady Eleanore's prideful scorn of a self-abasing lover, but also their own "Anglicized" flirtation with the pride-inspired vices of aristocracy and luxury. The people who applaud the prideful arrival of Lady Eleanore are the same people who in the Jeremiads are charged with, and in their own rituals confess, that all their troubles are solely the result of their failure to remain true to the pristine social values of their very un-Cavalier forefathers; who are daily corrupting themselves with gorgeous mantles and other imports from the transatlantic world of Lady Eleanore. And though Lady

Eleanore is not herself a political figure, she is a kind of courtly hanger-on who will have to be supported in style; and hence it is not really far-fetched to see in her clasping of the royal governor's hand—across the prostrate body of Jervase Helwyse—an emblem of the (temporary) ascendency of the "Court" Party; and in the people's applause, a temporary and half-conscious acceptance of this ominous development.

The political and social emphasis is strengthened by Hawthorne's inclusion of the otherwise trivial information that Helwyse had met Lady Eleanore when he was "secretary to our colonial agent in London." Of course he has had to fall in love with her (and, symbolically, become familiar with and enslaved by English court values) *somehow;* and probably one reason he is named Hell-wise is just *because* "Hell is a city very much like London."[22] But unless Hawthorne's writing is more casual than we have so far found it, we are also expected to recognize that "historically," the fictional Jervase Helwyse could have been secretary *only* to the famous Jeremiah Dummer, the man Thomas Hutchinson says fared well in New England politics precisely *because* he knew England well, and whose famous *Defence of the New England Charters* (1721) is well recognized as a document of enormous revolutionary potential. At very least, the association with Dummer concentrates our attention on the possibility that Helwyse may be conceived as an important "figure" of political knowledge and activity.[23]

But the first scene does more than define a moment of provincial flirtation with "Pride," "Luxury," and "Corruption"; and it provides more than a fleeting image of knowledge to be repented and slavish loyalties to be withdrawn. It also bristles with revolutionary hostility. We are expected, I think, to feel Endicott turning in his grave when we hear that Lady Eleanore's coach is escorted by "the prancing steeds of half a dozen cavaliers" (274), and we are forced to feel more than the obvious moral meaning when the instant of her arrival is greeted by the bell of the Old South "tolling a funeral." Doctor Clarke invokes the allegory of "King Death" easily enough; but the reader, who has *already* heard the "midnight knell from Old South" marking "the funeral procession of royal authority in New England," knows that Lady Eleanore's welcoming parade leads just as surely in that political direction as Pride leads to a Fall. And as events develop, there is reason to believe that Doctor Clarke's "populism" is founded on premises more specific than those shared with John Donne.

His emphasis continues to be moralistic, to be sure; as moralistic as that of any Jeremiad preacher striving to subdue stubborn new political and social problems with the time-honored rhetoric and the magical causality of the covenant. And perhaps the tolling from the Old South *is* only an "awkward coincidence." Still this physician and "famous champion of the popular party" may, like Colonel Joliffe, know more than he lets on. Certainly there

433

is a curiously threatening note in his confident prediction that "nature" will surely claim Lady Eleanore "in some mode that shall bring her level with the lowest!" (276). Historically, Clarke's "levelism" is not known to have been especially metaphysical. Increase Mather might threaten a whole backsliding, prideful people with a pox without any imputation of revolutionary activism; but we may well wonder if this noteworthy opponent of Governor Shute, royal prerogative, and the whole Court Party should enjoy the same privileged status. Perhaps we are to see something of the "devil's claws" peeping forth—here, and again in his mysterious behavior at the end of the second scene.

Many of the implications of the setting and action of that scene—the gorgeous provincial ball—are extraordinarily plain. First of all, the very existence of such an affair in the Boston of this period is a significant commentary on the desperate progress of aristocratic Pride: "Look," Cotton Mather had cried out in 1718, "on our Cloathing, our Furniture; our Tables, our Children; and if it were not for shame I had said our Balls."[24] Other things are just as clear: the representative, aristocratic significance of Lady Eleanore's four most ardent admirers; her holding aloof from the "mob" of guests; the moral implications of Helwyse's plea that she renounce her Pride by taking one sip of the holy wine of universal human communion. We may pause momentarily to wonder whether the "silver cup . . . appertaining to the communion plate of the Old South Church" can symbolize any notion quite so "catholic"; but only momentarily. The real ambiguities of the scene surround Doctor Clarke—his knowledge, his motives, and his relation to other persons present and to the dramatic events of the evening.[25]

We hear of him only at the end of the scene, only after the no-longer-prostrate Helwyse has confronted the aloof and scornful Lady Eleanore. And then we learn that he, too, had "stood apart," and that he was "separated from Lady Eleanore by the width of the room" (281). At one level, his "opposition" to Lady Eleanore is easy enough to appreciate: from the first the democratic moralist and the aristocratic lady have been poles apart. But we should know, as Hawthorne knows (from Hutchinson, if from no more original source), that he and she are also "parties" apart. Clarke is, at this precise historical moment, the Speaker of the *very* insubordinate lower house of the Massachusetts General Court; he may be merely the Popular Party's second choice (after Elisha Cooke, Jr., who never *could* get himself approved by Shute as Speaker), but he is opponent enough to have got himself "negatived" several times before 1720, when the representatives simply stopped *asking* for Shute's approval. We cannot, I think, read "Lady Eleanore's Mantle" clearly unless we realize that Doctor Clarke literally embodies the most deliberate insult yet offered to Governor Shute and his party, and the most rebellious challenge offered to British authority in America since 1689. A serious ambiguity, then, is implied by Clarke's very presence at Governor Shute's symbolic celebration of the arrival of the symbolic Lady Eleanore. Later, in the midst of the smallpox epidemic, when Clarke is at the Province House in his role as physician, we are teasingly told that "he was an infrequent guest in more prosperous times" (285). And he seems as flagrantly out of place as Joliffe does at Howe's masquerade.[26]

The aristocratic Captain Langford, who has been aggressive in subduing Helwyse, notices that the confident, reserved Clarke has been eyeing Lady Eleanore "with such sagacity that [he] involuntarily gave him credit for the discovery of some deep secret" (281). To draw Clarke out, he facetiously suggests that the doctor has been "smitten" with Lady Eleanore's charms. Clarke rejects the suggestion as preposterous ("God forbid!") and then waxes prophetic: "If you be wise you will put up the same prayer for yourself. Woe to those who shall be smitten by this Lady Eleanore!" (281–282).

Again, this might be no more than Jeremiad rhetoric: the standard prescription of moral cure for an essentially moral disease. Clarke is perhaps entitled to such language since, in the anti-prerogative politics of the 1720's, the Puritan clergy and the champions of charter liberties find themselves on the same side (an unstable coalition, to be sure, but the only one potent enough to produce eventual rebellion). On our alternate time scale, however, Clarke's speech is as clearly recognizable as a threat against "damned Tories" as the speech of the selectman in "Edward Randolph's Portrait" is a prediction of more-than-passive resistance. And perhaps one is not being overly sensitive to the possibility of "conspiracy" to suspect that Doctor Clarke may be something more than a prophet. He has come to Shute's ball, we must imagine, directly from a meeting of the Boston Caucus—which observers as diverse as Peter Oliver and William Gordon seemed to know has just then come into existence.[27] Obviously he is no more a casual spectator of the weird performance turned in by Jervase Helwyse than Joliffe is of the spectral march shown to Howe.

And what if Helwyse's activities are literally a performance? Certainly there is something highly theatrical about them; and he seems to have adopted a very different attitude toward Lady Eleanore since their first meeting in America. In their confrontation we seem to see the figure of British, courtly, aristocratic Pride seal her own moral doom and invite direct divine punishment by disdaining the proffered Cup of Human Communion and then refusing to throw off her fatally infectious Mantle of Pride. But there are serious ambiguities, even apart from the oppressive moralism of the blatant allegory. Just as the first scene undercuts the self-flattering, patriotic response by implicating the "applauding" populace in the Pride of the foreign visitor, so this scene also provides its own very drastic counterreading: Jervase Helwyse does, after all, spill something on Lady Eleanore's mantle, something which someone in the story thinks is poison. And this possibility clearly reinforces the (allegorical) suggestion that the cause of the coming scourge is not really foreign at all.

It is, of course, possible that Lady Eleanore already *has* the smallpox, and that Doctor Clarke's "keen sagacity" simply notices the symptoms in the "fervent flush and alternate paleness of her countenance" (278). The narrator, later, seems to give his own patriotic endorsement to the universal belief of an infected and crazed populace that, all along, "the contagion had lurked in that gorgeous mantle" (284). And, on this hypothesis, we can speculate that the festival comes to its "premature close" when the exceedingly sagacious Doctor Clarke reports his medical observations to the private ear of Governor Shute, the very instant after he has prophesied "woe" to the "smitten." Somehow, though, the Providential and Patriotic reading seems not quite satisfactory. For one thing, Clarke's communication to the governor is too casual and calm: "But yonder stands the Governor—and I have a word for his private ear. Good night!" (282). One doubts that the "unforeseen circumstances" which cause the "sudden change in his Excellency's hitherto cheerful visage" have anything to do with ordinary preventive medicine, since no measures are taken and since it is the ball itself and not any threatened epidemic which "supplied the topic of conversation for the colonial metropolis for some days after its occurrence" (282).

More credibly, Clarke's communication is of some embarrassing or threatening political news: the Speaker of the lower house, the governor's powerful political enemy, has decided to pass it on "casually," at a vice-regal entertainment, to discomfit the royal representative as Joliffe unnerves Howe. Perhaps the representatives have just contrived some new challenge or insult—disbanded *themselves,* or declared their *own* fast day to atone for their own sins of Pride and as direct "antidote" to Shute's ball. Or perhaps Clarke has to report rumors that a mob will try to disrupt the governor's gorgeous but heaven-tempting festivities. Perhaps there is to be an early appearance of Helwyse's revolutionary mob.

And perhaps, finally, Clarke himself is somehow behind it all.[28] Though no longer in England, Helwyse may very well be Clarke's "agent" still, still working on behalf of the so-called Popular Party, against the Royalists. We may wish to resist the really dire possibility—that Doctor Clarke has conspired either to "poison" Lady Eleanore or to infect her with smallpox, even though the story's own ambiguities do not prevent such a *literal* reading; even though it would seem to be precisely true at the *allegorical* level; even though the *historical* Clarke was thought to have been responsible for (accidentally) infecting a fellow member of the House; even though other physicians were, in the frenzied days of 1721, accused of deliberately dispatching people through the horrendous practice of inoculation; even though Cotton Mather was "bombed" for recommending that "unsafe" procedure; and even though Hawthorne appeared to believe the "dire" opinion that Shute himself was eventually "driven from the province by the whizzing of a musket ball."[29] Still, it is just possible that Helwyse believes he is poisoning or infecting Lady Eleanore, that he changes his mind in the midst of his performance, and that this accounts for his second petition, that Lady Eleanore cast off and burn her accursed mantle. He has spilled something deadly on it, but "it may not yet be too late!" She will not, of course, and so Helwyse can only conclude that when next they meet, her "face must wear another aspect—and that shall be the image that must abide within me" (281).

Though neither the story itself nor an application to the historical sources behind it will solve these ambiguities, it is absolutely necessary to take account of them. They exist to remind us of the inherent treacherousness of the attempt to discover the source and describe the transmission of the infection of Pride in the religious and social history of New England. This historically created ambiguity—and not any moral dogma concerning the magnetic chain of moral democracy—is the real subject of "Lady Eleanore's Mantle." Is the problem Lady Eleanore's presence in America, or Helwyse's original aspiration and the people's applause? Does the smallpox lurk in her mantle or in Helwyse's chalice? Does the Province House itself become the central symbol of New England's problem of Pride only when it is appropriated to the use of royal officials who descend from "founder" Edward Randolph? Or was the problem "founded" there when the local merchant Peter Sargent built this palatial residence in 1679, the very year when the Reforming Synod (in Hawthorne's words) "gave its opinion that the iniquity of the times had drawn down judgments from heaven, and proposed methods to assuage the divine wrath by a renewal of former sanctity."[30]

Furthermore, the political ambiguities which surround the figure of Doctor Clarke seem entirely of the same order as those one encounters in trying to find out about the secret activities of the Anti-Prerogative Party in the troubled years following 1719. A baffled Thomas Hutchinson was forced to admit that he did not know how to account for the actions of the Popular Party in 1720 and 1721. And the understated conclusion of the most recent historian of that difficult subject is that the Cooke-Clarke party made certain decisions for resistance in 1719, but that "there is so much mystery involved in the early years of the Caucus that care must be exercised."[31] It may well be that the unresolvable ambiguities of "Lady Eleanore's Mantle" are intended as Hawthorne's necessarily inconclusive version of "the problem of conspiracy" in early American history. One simply cannot find out who is causing what, with whatever degree of intention.

The conclusion about which there is no ambiguity, however, is that Hawthorne somehow connected the moral climate of the smallpox epidemic with that of revolution. Both were the very opposite of clean, safe, and antiseptic. And we will surely not do justice to the complexity of Hawthorne's response to the principal glory of American history unless we appreciate the seriousness of the allegory which he *himself* invented: considered as scourge and plague and pox, Revolution is far more terrible than Pride ever was.

The "ambiguity and weariness," the "pity and terror," and the "frenzied merriment" of "My Kinsman, Major Molineux" only partly prepare us for the literally terrific climax of the "Legends." "Old News" takes us just a bit further: not only are all revolutions "pernicious to general morality" (despite any rhetoric of "Reformation") but, with specific regard to 1776, "almost all our impressions . . . are unpleasant, whether referring to the state of civil society, or to the character of the contest, which, especially, where native Americans were opposed to each other, was waged with the deadly hatred of fraternal enemies. It is the beauty of war, for men to commit mutual havoc with undisturbed good-humor."[32] Very likely Hawthorne would have agreed with the view of a modern historian that the American Revolution was, in reality, "more of a Civil War than the better-known conflict of 1861–1865."[33] Even as an inevitable "coming of age," it is an affair of relatives: Major Molineux and Governor Hutchinson are alike uncles to Revolutionaries. And here, in the final two sections of "Lady Eleanore's Mantle," the Revolution is seen as a total breakdown of brotherhood, of "civil friendship," of that mutual trust without which human relations become literally barbarous.

It is obvious that Hawthorne intends to offer us more than a melodramatic "journal of the plague year," more than an evocative account of the social upheaval that inevitably accompanies pestilence in superstitious and medically primitive times. The story is too firmly based on the "constituted," covenant connection between the social diseases of Pride and Pox for that. The scene itself continues to supply abundant political hints. And in fact, when the matter under investigation is the multiple relation between social sins somewhat grossly labeled Pride, an outbreak of infectious disease, and certain obscure revolutionary activities, the only problems to which an historian *not* bound by the logic of the covenant could validly address himself were political.

Granted—of course!—that Pride is metaphorically a Pox. And granted that *some* sort of God might order secondary natural causes in precise accordance with the moral behavior of a chosen group. Granted, that is, that Lady Eleanore's damnable Pride merits the leveling punishment of the smallpox and may itself either cause or constitute a sort of plaguing influence. The significant (and fearsome) question remains: what does a Covenanted People *do* when an ever more treacherous moral proposition turns into a medical fact? In this story they first go mad and then ritualistically expel a scapegoat.

Significantly, the frenzy of the smallpox epidemic which follows Shute's disrupted festival, and which culminates in Helwyse's mob action in front of the Province House, is like nothing so much as that "Universal Madness" which ran "riot in the Main Street" in 1692. In the witchcraft frenzy there had been, "among the multitude . . . horror, fear, and distrust; and friend [had looked] askance at friend, and the husband at his wife and the wife at him, and even the mother at the little child; as if, in every creature God has made, they suspected a witch, or dreaded an accuser."[34] Here, at the height of yet another predicted and avowedly providential scourge, there is that "fear so horrible and unhumanizing . . . which makes man dread to breathe heaven's vital air lest it be poison." To be sure, the scourge temporarily enforces a frenzied version of the moral democracy which Helwyse and Clarke had earlier espoused, compelling "rich and poor to feel themselves brethren." But the dominant result is hideously amoral: everyone fears "to grasp the hand of a brother or a friend lest the gripe of pestilence should clutch him" (283). Thus, finally, and with brutal efficacy, does the tale defeat any wish we might have to dwell on Hawthorne's "moral" or "allegorical" acceptance of Puritan logic.[35] Whoever caused the scourge, and whatever it "signifies," the prophetic Helwyse and Clarke have got more than they bargained for. Elemental "Trust" is the virtue which Captain Lincoln had warned (or *will yet warn*) Hutchinson not to compromise. And here we glimpse the frenzied result of its total disappearance.

In this desperate situation, the first moment is one of universal paralysis. As happened in Boston in 1721 (just after Doctor Clarke was thought to have introduced the infection into the meetings of the General Court),[36] "the public councils were suspended." And the people temporarily disregard all problems concerning political enemies, obsessed as they are with the "bloody red flag" of that "direful conqueror," the smallpox. For one fearful historical moment the people are without resource—except for that "rage and despair" which sometimes take "the semblance of grinning mirth" (284). Raving against the "pride and scorn" of the "luxurious" Lady Eleanore whose "gorgeous" mantle of Pride they universally and paranoically believe to be the only source of the scourge, they fantastically hail each of her new infectious triumphs. In bitter self-mockery and in obvious parody of their earlier actions and attitudes, they now applaud every new "red flag of pestilence" hoisted over "yet another door."

Their earlier applause for the triumph of the courtly Eleanore over her Provincial Worshiper had signified, we must assume, their own growing acceptance of aristocratic values, including their own lust for the gorgeous mantles (and other such foreign finery) which Cotton Mather had allegorized as "Flags of Pride."[37] Now they madly applaud those Flags of Pestilence which the inexorable logic of the covenant has decreed are *also* Flags of Pride. Their frenzied, mirthful rage against Lady Eleanore is far from a rational repentance of an earlier flirtation; perhaps they will never be quite capable of that. But in their paralysis and hysteria, the psychology of revolution has already begun.

The hysterical phase continues unabated through Helwyse's final confrontation with Lady Eleanore. However we interpret the ambiguities of his earlier behavior and, whatever we decide about his relation to Clarke, his madness is now evident. The confrontation begins with his delusion (in contradiction of his earlier prediction) that Lady Eleanore sits "in state, unharmed herself by the pestilential influence." Along the way it may embody the moral of Lazarus and Dives, but it ends with the cry of "insane" merriment which identifies Helwyse with the frenzied, applauding populace in hailing "another triumph for Lady Eleanore" (287). And the reader begins to wonder whether madness is an infected people's only resource.

Historically, however, there were two others: Reformation, hitherto "the Only Sure Way to Prevent Calamity,"[38] and (lately) that secular alternative almost more fearsome to many than the calamity itself, Inoculation. Once again, therefore, we are reminded of Hawthorne's fantastic omission: Doctor Clarke may possess the sort of "calm, stern eye" which can occasionally quell a frenzy, but no one in the story seems to possess the new medical secret. The fictional result is that all of the historical frenzy directed against the blasphemous inoculators has been absorbed into the equally historical frenzy against Anglophiles. And the reason pretty clearly has to do with the political intentions of Hawthorne, the tale's ultimate teller: he is forcing us to look at Pride and Politics, not at Pride in its moral essence, and certainly not at Pride and the Confusions of Colonial Medicine; and he is presenting an allegory in which the 1720's are vehicle and the 1770's are tenor. In this light it is perfectly clear why "Lady Eleanore's Mantle" concludes not with an active medical defense against the literal infection which the people have "traced back" to "that gorgeous mantle" but with an equally active, equally revolutionary (and still more than a little hysterical) scapegoat ritual in which repentance and political threat are dangerously mixed.

The political implications of the feud over inoculation in the 1720's are

440

not entirely clear: the literature of the period does contain some suggestions that this new practice is yet another dangerous foreign innovation, but there seems to be no direct correlation between medical and political opinion. What is perfectly clear, however, is that the hysterical fear and distrust bred by the Pride-scourging outbreak of the smallpox was exacerbated by the moral objections against inoculation and by the widespread suspicion of the motives of its practitioners; and that this paranoid social condition greatly increased the revolutionary potential of an already volatile political situation.

If Hawthorne's historical picture seems garish and melodramatic, it may be reassuring to hear a very "regular" modern historian evoke the same moment:

> Boston seemed ripe for revolt. In the people's name [their leaders] directly confronted royal authority over issues inherently involved with constitutional dependence on England. Disease and financial chaos placed unbearable pressure on the people's nerves. Violence lurked just beneath the surface of every issue. Most of the traditional institutions of reason and restraint were divided, confused, or discredited. Hatred for things English had reached new heights. The town and the province were on the brink of rebellion and everyone knew it.[39]

Cover this impossible situation with the Jeremiad's allegorical confusion of Pride and Pox as plague and scourge, and the result is the state of social psychosis which the accelerating frenzy of "Lady Eleanore's Mantle" seeks to approximate. The melodrama is no gothic invention.

3

In the final "act" of the story, Helwyse snatches the "fatal mantle" and rushes out of the Province House—to assume religious and political leadership of a confused, distrustful, and rebellious people. The account is worth quoting:

> That night, a procession passed, by torchlight, through the streets, bearing in the midst, the figure of a woman, enveloped with a richly embroidered mantle; while in advance stalked Jervase Helwyse, waving the red flag of the pestilence. Arriving opposite the Province House, the mob burned the effigy, and a strong wind came and swept away the ashes.

Evidently this ritualistic activity proves extraordinarily efficacious; it was reported, at any rate, that "from that very hour, the pestilence abated" (288). But the precise nature of the activity being performed is very mysterious indeed.[40]

Perhaps it is partly medical, though the part played by the wind and the report of instant, magical efficacy ruin any emphasis on that aspect. More pronounced is the moral and social symbolism: in this third phase of their response to Lady Eleanore, the people have recovered not only from their semi-voluntary flirtation with Lady Pride, but also from the paralysis of their bitter self-mockery and self-parody; they are actively destroying the symbols of their own idolatrous disloyalty to their Fathers. Perhaps they are burning up the very gods after which they have been whoring. But the symbolic or ritualistic quality of their repentance and reformation points to its ultimately religious nature. And here is where the dangerous ambiguities begin. The quality of their religious activity is "magical," just as causality within the covenant is always "constituted."[41]

It would be one thing for the "infected" populace to burn *all* their *own* mantles, literally to destroy and make unusable all the luxurious imports which have corrupted their common moral life as surely as they have blighted the "tender plant" of their provincial economy. But it is quite another thing to deal entirely in symbols. An apologist might argue that for children of the Puritans—who are relatively sophisticated in the use of allegory, and who know that the doctrine of "weaned affections" does not imply literal poverty—ritual destruction is enough; that actual destruction would be entirely too crude and literalistic. Perhaps so. But the danger of self-deception remains, especially when the symbols destroyed are considered "alien" rather than "proper."

And the social historian would have to observe that the literalistic sort of repentance of British "Pride" and "Luxury" is precisely the sort which the children of New England almost never seriously attempted, despite the increasingly detailed catalogues and increasingly energetic exhortations of the Jeremiads, and despite the growing importance of sumptuary laws. This is precisely the point of Perry Miller's history of the Jeremiad mentality in New England: the descendants of the (idealized) founding Puritans persisted obsessively in ritualistic, fast-day "repentances" of social "vices" which they seemed either powerless or simply unwilling *really* to leave off.[42] They continued for a very long time to try to cure social disease by rhetoric and by magic ritual alone. For a very long time, but not forever. One is tempted to say, simply, that "just as" the practice of Inoculation eventually displaced the rhetoric and ritual of Reformation as the first line of defense against the scourge of the smallpox, "so" Revolution eventually ended the scourge of Pride. But the two cases are not precisely analogous, and the precipitate comparison obscures part of what is happening in Helwyse's ritual. Considered as symbolic action, what happens "opposite the Province House"—*in front,* that is, of the Revolutionary Old South Church—is in one sense what always happens in the troubled mind of latter-day New England Puritanism. The people *symbolically* repent, and certain biased observers validate the magical causality of the covenant by reporting a marvelous success: *"It was said,* that, from that very hour, the pestilence abated, *as if* its sway had some mysterious connection, from the first plague-stroke to the last, with Lady Eleanore's Mantle" (288). Obviously, as my italics mean to suggest, Hawthorne commits himself to this "legendary" version of historical cause and effect only very indirectly. The process is magical whether one is talking about literal or symbolic infections: the people's belief in the power of ritual *alone* to secure release from the metaphorical infection of Pride and Luxury is as superstitious as their belief in the medical potency of Lady Eleanore's "Flag of Pride"; and roughly the same sort of self-flattering self-deception is involved in the idea that all corruption comes from without (as "a curse to our shores") as in the basic conception of a National Covenant. The history here is the history of what, in Hawthorne's ironic view, always happens in a Puritan "history."[43]

In another sense, however, something "new" happens; or, if not "new" precisely, something that happens only occasionally, in moments of extreme crisis; something at once recalled and predicted and begun in "Edward Randolph's Portrait." For clearly what happens "opposite the Province House" is not *entirely* ritualistic and religious. The most active part of the action of Helwyse and his mob is still symbolic, no doubt, but its intimations of political activism are as potent as its medical implications are mad. The point to stress is not the obvious one—that the effigy-burning in front of Lady Eleanore's (and Governor Shute's) residence is either a threat or a symbolic pre-enactment of violence; that Helwyse's "red flag of the pestilence" is really a red flag of revolution. The important consideration is, rather, the precise nature of the psychological change which takes the populace from the frenzy of ironic applause to the frenzy of image-burning.

The people have turned, quite evidently, from the profitless "rage and despair" of their own self-punishing but ineffectual repentance to a more concentrated and satisfying attack on an object (unhappily a person) outside themselves. One essential element in the mentality of the Covenant and the Jeremiad has come loose from all the rest. The people are still being scourged for Pride. And Pride is still as real a plague as the smallpox. But now, with wonderful psychic release and terrible revolutionary energy, the disease is discovered to have a source *outside* the body of the people, as that body enthusiastically and revivalistically experiences itself. Corporate self-accusation and convenantal repentance have turned into an attack on an alien source of corruption. What is plaguing us? Pride! And what is Pride? Not, now, our very own unruly aspirations, collectively considered; but Lady Eleanore and her deadly Mantle, all her party and all her friends, all her pomps and all her works. And what is to be done? The body must rid itself of alien corruption. Lady Eleanore must be destroyed, or expelled, or at least "leveled."

The final "action" of "Lady Eleanore's Mantle" is, as I have suggested, easier to associate with 1776 than with 1721. But the essential point is that Hawthorne locates a crucial break in New England's corporate identity at the earlier date, in the midst of the smallpox frenzy. The action (as well as the frenzy) is like that of looking for witches in 1692, but in 1692 there is no visible source of corruption at all comparable to the Court Party of Lady Eleanore. It would be a strange sight indeed if Peter Sargent were to burn an effigy of Peter Sargent in front of the Old South Church, "opposite" his own palatial town house. It would be a heartening sight to see an infected populace burn all its own infecting luxuries "opposite the Province House" in 1721 (as if, today, we should destroy all our own devices of pollution instead of cheering for Ralph Nader). Or it *might* be enough if, in burning the mantle and the effigy of Lady Eleanore, the infected populace really felt they were repenting and rejecting their very own Pride. But it is not reported that any one of the people put on Lady Eleanore's mantle before it was burned.

4

Even in explicating fiction, one must be quite fair to the "Puritan" mentality as it persisted, "anachronistically," into the more complicated world of the provincial eighteenth century. Of course it could not prevent or secure release from smallpox epidemics. And probably it never could have become completely at home with questions of paper currency versus specie. It might welcome Lockean political immunities into its own theories of Covenant and Destiny easily enough but, holding that God's higher law alone is truly sovereign, what could it authentically teach on the question of "dividing" human sovereignty between the British Parliament and the provincial legislatures? On some issues both the mystical Jehovah and the mystified Charter were silent. Still, as Hawthorne clearly knew, its categories were not entirely irrelevant.

Followed literally and with perfect faith, the Puritan prescription for social health and stability would have worked: if the people, *all* of the people, all organically related in the National Covenant (if not all members of the Body of Christ), had truly repented of their flirtation with Lady Eleanore and left off the conspicuous pursuit of Mantles and Balls, the political crisis and moral catastrophe figured in "Lady Eleanore's Mantle" would almost certainly never have occurred. In all human probability, the same people would have contracted the smallpox in 1721; but there would have been no pre-existing allegorical disease for it to embody. And the political disease of the 1770's would have had to be conceptualized in a far less dangerous way. If *all* the people *truly* reform, the worst social pestilences do indeed abate at once. But, as always, the Puritan prescription demanded too much in practice—just as, in theory, it always managed to prove too much. And, always, the result of the Puritan theory and practice of piety was to leave dangerous moral vacuums which ordinary human beings filled up with their own needs and fears.

Apparently Puritan theory was worse than nothing against a literal outbreak of smallpox: a whole people seemed to go almost literally insane in 1721 over Cotton Mather's suggestion that it was "safe" to try, by means of the secondary causation of inoculation, to prevent a scourging pestilence whose prime cause could only be a people's decline into Pride and whose truly efficient agent could only be a justly wrathful Jehovah. The Puritan had to take the highest view: he had to see the world in the mind of God. Did not Inoculation threaten to tear the world out of His Mind?[44]

Perry Miller has audaciously suggested that the most "revolutionary" fact of 1721 is not Jeremiah Dummer's *Defense* of the New England charter (which was once again under attack in England) on certain frankly secular grounds; not the increasing boldness of the Popular Party which controlled New England's lower house; and not the increasing tendency of Puritan sermons to stress Whig philosophy as well as Reformation. Above all these he places the drastically revolutionary implications of the smallpox controversy: to defend inoculation was to admit that men might validly anticipate and try to ward off Judgments passed according to the Covenant. The immediate result was, in the words of one pamphleteer, "a state of War, Sin and Contention in our very prayers."[45] One "party" was "confessing" sins of Pride in the approved traditional way. The inoculationists were confessing the very same sins but *also* thanking God for showing them a way to avoid the perfectly just and (according to the old way of thinking) perfectly "natural"consequences of those sins; they were, quite simply, ruining the allegory by divorcing the moral tenor from its divinely constituted vehicle.

The traditional party wondered what sense could any longer be made of their whole history as a covenanted, backsliding, and therefore scourged people. What was being risked (and what, according to Miller, never was

quite regained) was "the conception of the covenant itself": "Spokesmen for
that national philosophy could never again authoritatively contend that what
the people suffered was caused by their sins and that repentance alone, as
directed by hierophants, could relieve them." Part of this is overstated, as
Miller himself would have later implicitly to admit. The National Covenant
endured at least until the Revolution, and sins continued to be blamed for
sufferings of all sorts.[46] But part is exactly right: never again could repentance *alone* be counted on to relieve an afflicted people. And there, of
course, lies the "easy" revolutionary implication. A people who had learned
to inoculate against the literal infection of smallpox could more easily purge
themselves of the allegorical one of Pride and Luxury and Corruption. This
argument could be worked out perfectly, even when constitutional and legal
questions remained hopelessly tangled. As the Hutchinson of "Edward
Randolph's Portrait" too dimly realizes, "Puritans" thus liberated could
quite comfortably confess and take aim. They might even grow careless
about the order of operations.

Hawthorne's explanations, it seems to me, are of the same order as
Miller's. In general, his commitment to the primacy of what John Adams
called "the minds of the people" is no less monolithic than Miller's, although he would include more of the frenzied and irrational within the area
of "mind"; and in particular, his view of the Revolution is even more auda-
cious. Yet it seems true in its own terms. And beyond all doubt it is a positively stunning view to have advanced in 1838, a virtually treasonable view
to have published in the pages of the *Democratic Review.* Read opposite the
"boyish hurrah" and Transcendental Whiggism of Bancroft (whose ideas
the "Legends" come more and more to implicate and challenge), its pene-
tration is almost unbelievable.

In connecting the Revolution of 1776 with the smallpox epidemic of
1721 (but in outrageously omitting all mention of the famous inoculation
controversy), Hawthorne has directed our attention to the more difficult
revolutionary implications of the single most chaotic year in New England's
period of "benign neglect." The basic terms of his highly "unoriginal" allegory consciously preserve the Puritan connection between the scourge of
Pride and the scourge of the smallpox; but they deliberately stultify all attempts to take the story as a moral allegory simply. Instead it forces us to
see that the 1770's and the 1720's are related as vehicle and tenor. Or, more
precisely, that given the Puritan symbology, the story of the 1720's is a
perfect, and that of the 1770's an imperfect, allegory: the two decades are
alike in frenzied distrust, alike in moralistic concern about Pride, Luxury,
and Corruption; still the earlier decade has a literal infection and the later
decade has none. And finally—brilliantly—"Lady Eleanore's Mantle"

forces us to see that in the 1720's the trust and the allegory broke down together.

For Hawthorne, the really revolutionary fact about the 1720's is not the release from Reformation as the *only* sure defense against plaguing influences; rather it is the breakdown of the corporate identity and the accompanying rise of the party spirit. We have seen that Hawthorne thought Revolution more of a plague than Pride ever was. No doubt he also agreed with the clergyman of 1721 who suggested that "the spirit of party is worse than any disease." Quite simply, "Lady Eleanore's Mantle" is about the sort of "party" strife and suspicion which amounts to "a state of War, Sin and Contention in our very Prayers." It is one thing for Clarke to cultivate a different personal and political style from Governor Shute, but it is quite another to call down (in effect) a curse on the head of Lady Eleanore. It is one thing for a *whole* people truly to repent the social vices which cause a disease in the body politic, but quite another for a leader and a people (themselves quite wise in the ways of hell) to fasten their attention on a single, "alien" plaguing influence.[47]

Once again, perhaps, the Puritan mind failed disastrously by demanding too much. *All* it required, as we have said, is that *all* the people truly repent. In times of affliction, at any rate, there should be no Boston versus Country, Court versus People, Governor versus Legislature. For if there is, the breakdown of Trust will be frenzied indeed: the party of wholesome virtue will fiercely oppose the party of infectious vice; those who will (to their own mind, at least) repent and who will (metaphorically, at least) take the cup of communion with the Old South Church will rage against those who will not. "Opposite the Province House," they will constitute themselves into an "opposition" formidable indeed, the kind of "opposition" neither Howe nor even Hutchinson will quite be able to define.

Insofar as Helwyse's mob action takes place in front of the Province House, it both constitutes and symbolizes the threat of direct revolutionary action. But insofar as it exists "opposite" the Province House—in front of or perhaps even inside the Old South Church—it stands for the religious validation of a "Popular" (or at least anti-Royal) party. No doubt the simple political differences were not invented in 1721: Governor Dudley and Elisha Cooke, Sr., were real enough political enemies. And no doubt the language of political opposition is not absolutely unique to New England: English Country Party Jeremiads about Pride, Luxury, and Corruption have almost as venerable a history as their American Puritan counterparts; and they had, it now seems clear, a far more avid and receptive readership in the provinces than at home.[48] But the course of events and emotions in the Boston of 1721 seem to define, momentarily, proleptically, the potent force of a political ideology raised to a religious level and adopted as the only acceptable definition of native health and virtue. Here (and hereafter) the infecting influence will be treated as alien to the body of the people who are backslidden but still fundamentally virtuous.

In a very real sense, what happens "opposite the Province House" is all the things which the selectman in "Edward Randolph's Portrait" predicted. And, conversely, something very like Doctor Clarke's definition of Lady Eleanore and his curse upon all who are "smitten" by her is clearly required before Governor Hutchinson can be made into an alien and plaguing influence. In "Lady Eleanore's Mantle," the treatment of cultural disease begins, as always, in "prayer and fasting"; but it proceeds directly to the task of "waving the red flag of pestilence," in rhetoric and then in revolutionary fact, in the face of the party of infectious vice.

❦ Ten ❧

THE DEATH OF THE PAST
HISTORY, STORY, AND THE USE OF TRADITION

I F THE LAST MOMENT of "Lady Eleanore's Mantle" provides the emotional climax of Hawthorne's cunningly constructed "Legends," and if indeed it does present a double vision in which root psychological cause and eventual revolutionary purgation are intentionally conflated, then we are bound to see "Old Esther Dudley" as a sort of strategic anticlimax. The reversal of view implied in an Old Tory's prejudicial version of British expulsion can hardly be as unsettling as the complexity to which we have already been exposed. For one thing, the sentiments of the unreconstructed "old loyalist" do not come to us directly but must be passed through the "medium of a confirmed democrat." Beyond that, moreover, it has been the function of Hawthorne's irony to divide our loyalties in ways which no calculated "casebook" assemblage of conflicting explanations can ever approximate.

Superficially, of course, there is just such a "balance"—as the Old Tory is moved to strike back and try to have the last word.[1] Evidently he has not grasped any more of the irony implicit in the tale of Pride and its cure than have any of the other listeners; he seems as obsessed with his old personal loyalties as the narrator and his host are complacent in the patriotic abstractions offered by Joliffe, the selectman, and Clarke. In response to these, the Old Tory invokes the powers of Providence and Magic on the Royalist side; he opposes the figure of Lady Eleanore, the Prideful Destroyer, with the figure of Esther Dudley, the Faithful Preserver.[2] And yet in many ways the ironic mode of "Old Esther Dudley" is indistinguishable from that of the other "Legends": our feckless narrator still does not fully understand the ironic implications of his material or indeed of his own position; and everywhere those implications involve incompleteness, contradictory explanations, and missed opportunities. And there is thus a sense in which the effect of "Old Esther Dudley" simply "follows" from all that has gone before. Its tone of fatality and even of calm is not only relative (in comparison with the "frenzy" of "Lady Eleanore's Mantle") but absolute and necessary, the inevitable result of a logic of events and of a single ironic design.

In terms of the explicit chronology, we have returned to the original point of departure; having "backed up" twice, we now find ourselves only one significant historical moment beyond that of "Howe's Masquerade." The expulsion predicted earlier is here accomplished: Howe retreats in ignominy, surrendering to an inevitability though not really defeated by any army. What has fallen between the last shadow of Joliffe's typic masquerade and the act itself may be read simply as an excursion into the past in search of causes: close to hand, the colonial response to the simplistic decision to treat Boston as a disciplinary problem; and further back (in time and in psychological reality) the beginnings of party spirit and of the revolutionary definition of royalism as an alien plague. What has intervened, in retrospect, is simply the significant history of the "Puritan" mind in the eighteenth century.

But there is also a sense in which the movement of the "Legends" has been perfectly sequential, their ironic, emotional order as "regular" and straightforward as the linear chronology of "Old News." We begin, in "Howe's Masquerade," with a picture of the parties and a definition of the conflict and proceed from there. As "Champion" and as "almost-Endicott," Joliffe gives us the essential note of Puritan loyalty to its own vision of history and destiny as somehow involved with Holy Liberty. In "Edward Randolph's Portrait" we see that by the latter half of the eighteenth century this vision has become atavistic, or at least "historical"; that the identity it creates—though somehow always "there"—must yet be reactivated by a fairly conscious renewal of antique historical perception. Before taking any revolutionary action, the descendants of the Puritans must redefine themselves in terms of the purposes of their forefathers, and they must be taught to see the truly diabolical visage of their historic enemy. What then "follows" in "Lady Eleanore's Mantle" is the creation of an ideology based on that vision as well as a definition of its less mysterious "party" basis.

Given this completely demystified view of Puritanism and Revolution, it is hardly necessary for "Old Esther Dudley" to offer an alternate or contending explanation. More appropriately, it suggests the straitened limits a culture imposes upon itself if it chooses to explain events precisely as Joliffe, the selectman, and Doctor Clarke would explain them. What "Old Esther Dudley" asks us to understand, finally, is not only that revolutionary events do not *have* to be seen exactly as the neo-Puritan ideology of Apocalyptic Whiggism sees them; indeed, Hawthorne's final emphasis is less on the inherent truth or falsity of that view than on the cultural cost of persisting so relentlessly in seeing things just this way. Obviously past events never *were* quite what an enlisted history says they were; still, the point of "Old

Esther Dudley" is slightly more subtle. Let the "true" history of the American Revolution be just what the Puritan preachers of the period (or Bancroft) would have it be. Admit that "vision" is an ultimate in one order of explanation: that in one absolute sense human beings do exactly what they truly believe they are doing; that intention is to action as soul is to body. And then concede that very many provincials really did experience the Revolution as an act of political purgation, cultural purification, moral reformation—guided by Providence and vitalizing the teleology of Salvation. Grant, that is, the crucial distinction between "ideology" as widely shared definition or motive and "propaganda" as managed rationalization.[3] And still the problem of cultural gain and loss remains: are we better or are we worse for demanding, in 1776 or in 1838, so grand a meaning for the war which ended our colonial status? For the price of certain visions can be very high indeed.

Among American writers who begin their careers in the first half of the nineteenth century, Hawthorne was not of course unique in worrying that the cost of "the American Vision" might be exorbitant. Most obviously, Irving and Longfellow seemed to regret the purchase of a moral future at the expense of a cultural past. And Cooper, at moments, seems to have approximated to Hawthorne's sense that America was perhaps taking rather higher ground than it might be comfortable permanently to occupy. But Hawthorne, whose vision was the most genuinely historical of the group, faced the problem most directly and steadily. And more pointedly, other writers who entertained such doubts did not contribute their literary embodiment to the pages of the *Democratic Review,* whose editorial policy affirmed that America's futuristic destiny was not only guaranteed by Providence but was in fact indistinguishable from "the cause of humanity" or "the cause of Christianity"; and whose ordinary contributors never dreamed that America might yet be only "a word's shape."[4]

Only in the context of the *Democratic Review*—in the midst, that is, of Bancroftian History, Jacksonian Democracy, and Manifest Destiny—can we understand the anticlimactic concluding function of "Old Esther Dudley," or account for the involuted complexity of Hawthorne's narrative point of view. The story of America's "loss" in the Revolution is only partly suggested by Howe's embittered retreat and Esther Dudley's pathetic death. The more significant loss is implied by America's official refusal to give Tory views and values a fair hearing.

1

It is between "Lady Eleanore's Mantle" and "Old Esther Dudley" that our ordinary narrator most directly calls attention to his own twice-tellings. At the conclusion of "Lady Eleanore's Mantle" he displays what he evidently regards as his growing sophistication; whereas earlier he had shown an embarrassingly naive interest in the *actual* portrait restored by Alice Vane, he now waxes ironical about all such literalistic expectations:

> The reader can scarcely conceive how unspeakably the effect of such a tale is heightened, when, as in the present case, we may repose perfect confidence in the veracity of him who tells it. For my own part, knowing how scrupulous is Mr. Tiffany to settle the foundation of his facts, I could not have believed him one whit the more faithfully, had he professed himself an eye-witness of the doings and sufferings of poor Lady Eleanore. Some sceptics, it is true, might demand documentary evidence, or even require him to produce the embroidered mantle, forgetting that—Heaven be praised—it was consumed to ashes. (288)

In itself, no doubt, this little development is trivial enough; the Story Teller having lapsed, Hawthorne is not yet creating a Coverdale. Still the passage does function as a narrative signal, an important (if momentary) dropping of the ironic mask. We are once more alerted to questions of "reliability."

Then, at the beginning of "Old Esther Dudley" the narrator finally reveals the true nature of his own bias, from which we infer the precise import of the duplicity in Hawthorne's overall literary strategy. The "excitable" Old Tory, we are told, seemed not quite in possession of his faculties when he told his story. Alternately melting into tears and clenching his fists, he was evidently betrayed by wine, ardor, and imagination.[5]

> Under these disadvantages, the old loyalist's story required more revision to render it fit for the public eye, than those of the series which have preceded it; nor should it be concealed, that the sentiment and tone of the affair may have undergone some slight, or perchance more than slight, metamorphosis, in its transmission to the reader through the medium of a thorough-going democrat. (291)

Most simply, the ordinary narrator is justifying his use of greater editorial liberty in one story than in the others. The motive would seem to be decorum. But somewhat more is also at stake: the nervous admission that the "metamorphosis" is "perchance more than slight" because the "medium" is "democratic" calls our attention to Hawthorne's relation to O'Sullivan's *Democratic Review* as pointedly as to his ineffectual narrator.[6]

Read with this relation in mind, the apology reminds us that somebody who has just been taken up by a magazine dedicated to the proposition that "all history has to be rewritten" in the light of the nineteenth century's retrospective and evolutionary sense of America's manifest democratic destiny does not begin by risking a perfectly full and sympathetic rendition of the views of Loyalists like Joseph Galloway or Jonathan Boucher or Samuel Seabury or Daniel Leonard or Peter Oliver. Not, at least, if that somebody is trying to *stop* being "the obscurest man of letters in America." And certainly not if one sort of "intercourse with the world" looks as though it may be opened up by the political patronage of George Bancroft, whose *History* has already made more than a modest beginning of the re-write called for in O'Sullivan's democratic "medium."[7]

As we have seen, "The Gray Champion" looks very much like some sort of response to Bancroft's first volume, appearing not only to reinforce Bancroft's "typological" view of the events of 1689 but in fact to adopt the "vindication" theme announced at the end of the first volume.[8] Of course it does not; many of Bancroft's emphases are deliberately stood on their head. And similarly here. The "Legends" imply an awareness of Bancroft's culturally dominant ("Whig") interpretation of American history as clearly as they remind us of O'Sullivan's editorial bias. Only now the problem is more delicate. By the time "Howe's Masquerade" is published (May 1838), Hawthorne is not quite so independent as he was in 1834 and 1835: he has already published several stories in the *Democratic Review;* and his negotiations with George Bancroft are already well under way.[9]

We need not accuse Hawthorne of bad faith in accepting an invitation to contribute to the *Democratic Review* or of crass opportunism in accepting patronage at the hands of Bancroft. He was, in some fairly complicated way, a "democrat"; he was, on balance, satisfied as to the essential rightness of America's political separation from England; and he would eventually accept the age's dominant ("spiral") theory of Progress. Yet neither his politics nor his view of American history is in tone (or in "mode") very close to that of O'Sullivan or Bancroft. And it seems perfectly obvious that if either man had been able to recognize the ironies built into the "Legends" (or into "The Gray Champion" or "Endicott"), Hawthorne's career after 1837 would not have developed as it did.[10]

We know, of course, that several of Hawthorne's friends were recommending him to Bancroft (who was in the process of assuming control of the Democratic machine in Massachusetts) as early as the first week in April

1837, just several weeks after the appearance of the *Twice-told Tales*. And we also know that, later in April 1837, Hawthorne was invited by J. L. O'Sullivan to contribute to the soon-to-be-launched *Democratic Review*.[11] It seems highly likely that the two events are related, that Bancroft's first (and most logical) action on Hawthorne's behalf was to suggest that O'Sullivan and the *Democratic Review* might do something for Hawthorne at once, in a purely literary way. For, as it turns out, the letter inviting Hawthorne's contribution to the *Democratic Review* did not come to him from O'Sullivan directly. It went, rather, to Elizabeth Peabody, who in turn delivered it to Hawthorne in a personal visit. The only modern biographer to notice this little peculiarity can make no sense whatever of the round-about procedure. The explanation, however, is pretty easy to imagine. Elizabeth Peabody was, after all, one of those who were appealing to Bancroft on Hawthorne's behalf. And since at this point (April 1837) neither Bancroft nor O'Sullivan knew Hawthorne directly, it would seem obvious that Bancroft passed Elizabeth Peabody's request on to O'Sullivan, who then contacted Hawthorne by way of Elizabeth, his original well-wisher.[12] And this makes Bancroft doubly Hawthorne's patron: by the time the first legend appears in O'Sullivan's relentlessly democratic "medium," Hawthorne knows that his entry to that magazine depends on Bancroft as directly as his forthcoming political appointment.

Under such circumstances, what sort of literary behavior might be appropriate? How was one to be faithful to a certain historical vision without alienating powerful political friends who viewed American history and destiny through other lenses? The "purest" alternative, doubtlessly, would have been to decline all forms of patronage at the hands of George Bancroft: to refuse all association with the unflaggingly simplistic ideology of the *Democratic Review* and to decline all appointments to all customs houses. But having decided, so recently, to take up a fully active part in the contemporary world, such a decision would have implied retreat from the outset. Must complexity of vision mean political disaffiliation, alienation, paralysis? Why not at least attempt to introduce some element of "criticism" into the very sphere of public myth-making? The risk would be great. At very least one would have to gamble more on the unbiased intelligence (including the openness to irony) of the average magazine reader than on the acumen of editors and politicians; the conditions of literary success were that the ones should see what the others should miss. But no doubt Hawthorne felt that the idea of democracy itself was premised on some such risk.[13]

Irony, no doubt, would have been enough: O'Sullivan and Bancroft would miss the subtle countercurrent of the "Legends" in just the same way (and for exactly the same single-minded reasons) they had missed it in "The Gray Champion" and in "Endicott." But Hawthorne does not let it go at that. For reasons that may cause us to see political shrewdness where we have preferred to see only moral ingenuousness, he placed his four "Legends" in a frame which deliberately calls attention to the precarious condition of their publication.[14]

The sly reference to the *Democratic Review* as "medium" is fairly obvious. More subtle, it now comes to appear, is the precise function of the outside narrator: that public and banal version of Hawthorne discovers that relieving the boredom of ordinary life amidst surfaces with a little Romantic antiquarianism is not so harmless or trivial an action as it once seemed; to be writing history in New England in the 1830's may be an *intensely* political act. The contemporary historian William Hickling Prescott worried about George Bancroft's unembarrassed and unimpeded ability to "woo the fair muse of history and the ugly strumpet of faction with one and the same breath." He referred, of course, to Bancroft's equal facility at marshalling historical evidence and managing a political machine. And indeed Bancroft was surprisingly able at both. But once we grant that Hawthorne never would become a "machine" or even a "party" politician, and that his ironic self-awareness was unrelenting, we can hardly be more precise than to apply Prescott's *mot* to the literary strategy of Hawthorne's "Legends."[15]

Basically, the narrator has wanted to cultivate certain Romantic "thrills" of heroism, or grandeur, or "awe." And he has further rationalized that his little self-indulgences will be neither solipsistic nor open to partisan interpretation: he will simply "deserve well of [his] country by snatching from oblivion some else unheard-of fact of history." Just so, no doubt, many "Romantic" historians have assumed. But evidently neither history nor patriotism is quite that simple. For now our unwitting narrator finds himself caught between the "Whig" affirmations on the surface of Bela Tiffany's three narratives and the "Tory" lament on the surface of the Old Loyalist's excited reply. And in editing the Loyalist's story on other than the literary grounds of "history as Romantic art," he becomes guilty, however ineffectually, of "trimming."

Obviously, however, the narrator's political prudence is not to be identified with Hawthorne's, since his own hints have alerted us to the historical and political naiveté of the narrator from the beginning, and since Hawthorne's revisions are the result of literary strategy and not personal bias. Behind all other tellings and hearings stands Hawthorne's own ironic intelligence, performing what we may safely take to be the historian's true duty—to criticize that "story" called "the past" which power elites always enlist as "sanction" for an existing order, particularly for one of comparatively recent ascendancy.[16]

And thus the logic behind the narrative convolutions of "The Legends of the Province House": to publish in the official organ of the National Democratic Party, at the express invitation of the party's official propagandist and with the concurrence of the party's all-but-official ideologist and patron, a fictional "criticism" of the particular "past" which that party needed most desperately to enlist as "handmaid of authority"; and to contain that complex, legendary fiction within a narrative frame which should point out the implications of the act of writing history in such a context. The "Legends" themselves effectively put asunder the providential links by which an "enlisted" American historiography had been trying to join Puritanism, Liberty, Revolution, and Democracy all together: Puritanism and Revolution might indeed be related, but that was all; and the result of that, as we are yet to see, might not be entirely happy. Beyond or "outside of" this, the frame of the "Legends" shows us a naive, Romantic, antiquarian narrator nervously discovering what the extraordinarily perceptive author already knows: writing about the past may be the most political of actions, with implications for the present and future as well as for the past.

The figure of Thomas Waite may give us further reason to think about the implications for Hawthorne of Prescott's pithy sentence. Paradoxically, however, the personal hints *within* the work itself are far less available—far more nearly a rueful private joke—than the flagrant external fact of the very appearance of Hawthorne's "Legends" alongside the political rhetoric and under the political aegis of O'Sullivan and Bancroft. In the end, perhaps, Hawthorne was just a bit too careful, though it is easy to understand why.

The basic consideration connecting Waite with Bancroft is his identity as "present occupant" of the Province House. Literally, of course, that structure was indeed being used as a tavern in 1838; and we have no reason to doubt that Hawthorne, the "decent city border," did take an occasional beverage there. But as the strategic confusion about "founders" Peter Sargent and/or Edward Randolph makes clear, we are everywhere to pay attention to the political continuities the Province House may embody; and surely somebody besides a local bartender is being implicated as the "worthy successor and representative of so many historic personages" (241). In fact Bancroft comes as close as anybody to occupying the position once held by the antique political inhabitants of the Province House. He is not, to be sure, the governor of the Commonwealth of Massachusetts, any more than Randolph ever was. But as collector of customs of the Port of Boston, he inherits the function which Randolph so officiously brought into being.[17] Further, his position as collector makes him the chief dispenser of patronage for the party which (reputedly) ousted those degenerate British office-and-influence mongers in 1776. This consideration implicates Hawthorne himself in a modern repetition of the political "vices" which an earlier generation identified as a "plot" to "enslave" Massachusetts, making him one of those minor "placemen" so obnoxious in revolutionary propaganda. But Hawthorne is at least *aware* of his situation. And irony covers a multitude of sins.

The Province House is also, clearly enough, New England's House of History—which Bancroft has come, by 1838, to occupy pretty comfortably.[18] Thus when Waite takes our narrator on one historic tour of that house, we can almost see Hawthorne himself begin to cringe: the minor romancer must play "guest" to the approved historical "host," patronized in the field of history as surely as in the house of customs. More painful, perhaps, would be the irony behind the observation that the "fortunate conjunction" of the narrator and Bela Tiffany has produced a markedly "increased custom" for Mr. Waite's establishment. More readers for the *Democratic Review,* obviously enough; but probably Hawthorne's wicked little fictions of Revolution were inadvertently to increase the popularity of Bancroft's already more popular volumes on Liberty. Popular audiences being what they are, the canny deconstructions only advertised the construct. Then as now, quite likely, readers found their way "back" from the romancer Hawthorne to the historian Bancroft with no proper sense of the political, modal, or narratological gulf that lies between.

There may be other, more private clues, but it is hardly necessary to follow them out.[19] The frame of the "Legends" does not have to be *entirely* allegorical. Nor could the allegory be made *too* clear; for seeming to endorse the views of Bancroft and O'Sullivan was the condition of publishing in the *Democratic Review* at all. And whatever the extent of private self-delectation, the instructions to the critical reader are perfectly clear: "Old Esther Dudley" will present the basis of that view of the Revolution which confirmed Democrats have declared heretical—but which the sheer force of their bias had made them unable to detect and edit out. (Ironists can understand and even perhaps accept some idea of Providence; but a single-minded commitment to the re-writing of history under the sign of Progress tends to deaden the sense of irony.) And beyond this elementary concern for the "other" view, "Old Esther Dudley" forces consideration of the cultural loss America suffered because first Puritan and then Democratic ideologists persisted in defining the Revolution as they did.

As it turns out, progressive ideology is inimical not only to the idea of true history, forcing interpreters to select only those events and ideas which received some later "vindication," but it is inimical also to the possibility of cultural richness and diversity. Progressive history reduces multiplicity to unity, not only in "explanation" but in "reality." What is edited out from the past will not be available soon again.

2

The superficial "loyalism" which political prudence has *not* needed to edit out of "Old Esther Dudley" is as easy to accept as it is obvious. The explicit attention paid to the Tory point of view is entirely of a piece with the obtuse and more than slightly arrogant deference which "the Republican Governor" Hancock pays to "the stately and gorgeous prejudices" of the "tottering" Esther Dudley at the end of the story. It is permitted to look at such things as long as one does not take them seriously. Accordingly, the ordinary narrator has preserved loyalism as an object of "fancy" merely—a colorful antiquarian curiosity rather than a challenging political or cultural commitment. Necessarily so. He is not Sir Edmund Burke, nor was meant to be. He can imagine a vital conservatism as little as he could seriously countenance tearing down the vulgar row of shops which obscure the entrance to the Province House.

Surely he courts no imminent political danger by ascribing a certain courage and discipline to General Howe, who would prefer heroic death to ignominious withdrawal. With the military conflict now at more than sufficient distance, the winners can afford to be generous; especially as they occupy the house and sip the wine of those they have displaced. Besides, romance fairly thrives on indestructible devotion to irrecoverably lost causes. And how is it possible not to be a *little* sympathetic to that ancient aristocrat whose stubborn pleasure it is "to be the last in this mansion of the King"? Esther Dudley is, after all, "Old," like England herself. Colorful and picturesque, no doubt, but powerless and irrelevant. Even her Patriot neighbors in revolutionary Boston had found her tolerable. A "rude mob" might revile other Loyalists who remained behind after Howe's desperate masquerade and bitter departure; the full story of what precisely happened to those Tories who continued to visit her at the Province House "during those days of wrath and tribulation" and who "quaffed healths to the King, and babbled treason to the Republic" (296) might very well bear painful elaboration. That story, of course, would have to come to us through some other medium.[20] But there is no evidence that the narrator feels he has anything to suppress where his title character is concerned. She was well treated by Revolutionaries then, he seems to think, and it would now be ungenerous for even staunch Republicans to refuse a certain tribute to her departed shade.

And so Esther Dudley is allowed as full a measure of integrity as Howe.

She clearly believes that "Heaven's cause and the King's are one," and her confidence that Heaven will "bring back a Royal Governor in triumph" (292) certainly does not suffer by superficial comparison with the beliefs of Joliffe, the selectman, or Clarke. In *this* view of the Tories, at least, no one's *sincerity* is at issue.

There is, to be sure, "much haughtiness in her demeanor": she regards everyone acting under the new authority as an intruder, and her self-assurance is such that "it was really an affair of no small nerve to look her in the face." But even this does not earn the hostility of "stern republicans." At one, easy level of moralistic response they are content that she should stay on to "haunt the palace of ruined pride and overthrown power, the symbol of a departed system embodying a history in her own person" (295–296). At this level she is simply appropriated into a Puritan-Republican allegory of social and political virtue—an aged Lady Eleanore whose pride is no longer a real threat. Everyone seems to know she is invincibly persuaded that the colonies either were or soon would be "prostrate at the footstool of the King," but no one wishes to make this "enemy" the footstool of their feet, not even when she audaciously celebrates the King's birthday. The people do not throw mud at her illuminated windows. They only laugh—pitying "the poor old dame, who was so dismally triumphant amid the wreck and ruin of the system to which she appertained" (299).

Beyond the reductions of their allegory, then, there is in the people's response to the zeal of Old Esther Dudley chiefly the condescensions of pity. She is so unswervingly loyal, so unbendingly committed, so unquestioningly faithful. But so pitifully mistaken.[21] As she lives on alone in the Province House, the armies of Britain are *not* proving "victorious on every field"; nor, setting such empiricism aside, are they "destined to be ultimately triumphant" (298). Not even Howe could believe that Massachusetts would ever receive another royal governor. And Esther Dudley's tolerant neighbors know as well as readers of the *Democratic Review* and of Bancroft what outcome is "destined." A person must be "partially crazed" to think otherwise. And what response is so appropriate to invincible delusion as pity?

Thus the attitudes implied by Hancock's final speech about the values of Esther Dudley are, within the story, not at all remarkable. His flat rejection of the history she symbolizes is perfectly predictable; and even his willingness to "reverence, for the last time, the stately and gorgeous prejudices of the tottering Past" (301) requires no very impressive breadth of cultural generosity. What he calls for is anything but a renewal of her loyalties. And the idea that her values might somehow be subsumed within others which only *seem* dialectically opposite could never enter into a mind capable of a cold-prose declaration of independence from "the Past." For Hawthorne's

Hancock-figure, the past is not precisely useless. Rather, it has just one more use before it dies. Like the pitiful Esther Dudley, it is "tottering"; but before it lapses into non-existence, we can look once more at what we have been, before actively becoming that totally "other" thing which we are destined in the future to be.

Obviously such an attitude is far from Hawthorne's own. But the first point to be grasped about "Old Esther Dudley" is not simply that Hancock is no spokesman for Hawthorne himself, that he may be portrayed less sympathetically than Howe, that he is in fact "satirized." Of primary importance, rather, is the recognition that Hancock merely gives final and sententious expression to a collective attitude toward the past which is really worse than open hostility would be: one last, complacent "reverence" to "the principles, feelings, manners, modes of being and acting" which "time has rendered worthless," and then "onward" as a "new race of men—living no longer in the past, scarcely in the present—but projecting our lives forward into the future." What "Hancock" asserts, in language far more appropriate to an editorial in the *Democratic Review* than to his own historical voice, is nothing short of *total* victory for the forces of revolutionary futurism as such.[22] Unthreatened by the past as competing value, presuming to understand its limited (negative) moral use, and asserting the autonomous freedom of the present to "project" the future *ex nihilo*, the representative figure of Hancock is given the truly rare opportunity not only to declare a radically new beginning but even to bury a figure of the now defunct and irrelevant past. The past "hath done [its] office." The past is dead. Now, "onward"! "We are no longer children of the Past!" (302).

If all this is indeed too easy, then it follows that criticism which stresses the "tenderness" of the portrait of Old Esther Dudley is even less to the point than that which discusses the relative sympathy invested in Howe and Hancock.[23] The ordinary narrator can be kind to Esther Dudley—kinder, certainly, than most Revolutionaries and most Patriotic Historians were to most Tories—simply because he does not regard her any more seriously than do her neighbors or Hancock. Neither her neighbors nor the narrator feels the need to burn Esther Dudley in effigy. But in the end the explicit (condescending) sympathy toward the figure of Esther Dudley is no more significant than the explicit (superficial) function of the whole story as a "balance" to what has gone before. Once again, the operative literary effects exist at the level of latent irony and inhere in certain undeveloped suggestions which run counter to the import of the most obviously "interpretative" rhetoric which the tale supplies. At this level the discerning reader sees that Esther Dudley has performed certain "offices" that Hancock cannot even conceive and which the editorial mentality of the *Democratic Review* would utterly reject if it could recognize.

* * *

Of these, her office as historian of a particular (aristocratic) past and embodiment of a whole style of approach to the past in general is only the most obvious. We do not need to care much about the reality of her legendary power to cause "all the pageantry of gone days" (295) magically to appear in her mirror. As "Romantic art," history might well be able to summon "the shadows of the Olivers, the Hutchinsons, the Dudleys, all the grandeurs of a bygone generation" to the spiritual view of the inward eye as "really" as an antique and eccentric old gentlewoman can assemble "a few of the staunch, though crestfallen, old tories, who had lingered in the rebel town" (296). As always, Hawthorne is aware of the more problematic aspects of his own artistic tradition.[24] Yet he no more ultimately depends on the "spectral" powers of the imagination here than in "Howe's Masquerade." The populace may "fear" such a power as much as they "pity" the "partially crazed" mind of its reputed possessor; and the fear may be as potent as the pity in assuring that "neither wrong nor insult ever fell on her unprotected head" (295). But clearly their attitude is merely superstitious. Confident that "destiny" is on their side and not hers, assured that they and not she will ultimately be "vindicated," it is not the retaliation of "history" which they fear. They will overcome, and no amount of re-interpretation or re-valuation will ever entirely discredit their achievements with generations yet unborn.[25]

The stories she is allowed to tell the children of the rebels, however, involve other and more serious considerations. Here is where her real power as historian lies, and it appears that in this domain her power is greater than her tolerant neighbors quite realize. It is not, in any obvious sense, a "political" power. No amount of faith or imagination on her part can ever effect the return of a royal governor. In the last analysis her "Hope" *is* only "Memory in disguise," and she herself seems half-aware of that fact. Furthermore, unlike the Tory historians Hawthorne could have known, she does not even seem to have a moral or a constitutional case to prove. Still, as she works her fictional spell on her childish visitors at the Province House, a generation of Americans even "newer" than Hancock's seems to be slipping back into the past again. Washington will defeat Howe—as decisively as Joliffe defeated him earlier and as surely as the selectman and Doctor Clarke defeated Hutchinson and Lady Eleanore. But the same Hawthorne who accepts all that without the slightest trace of Tory bitterness is also plotting for Esther Dudley to defeat Hancock. In writing his "Legends" for (that is, "against") the *Democratic Review,* he is himself carrying on the same contest.

At first glance Esther Dudley's influence might seem to be "only" literary. As the children leave her legendary sphere within the Province House, they have become "bewildered, full of old feelings that graver people had long ago forgotten, rubbing their eyes at the world around them as if they had gone astray into ancient times, and become children of the past" (297). At home they talk, with familiarity and without self-consciousness, about "all the departed worthies of the Province, as far back as Governor Belcher and the haughty dame of Sir William Phips." It is as though they had been "sitting on the knees of these famous personages." And to their puzzled but indulgent parents they protest that they most certainly did "really see." No mere notional understanding this. As "Romantic historian" Esther Dudley has been as successful as any Walter Scott, or as Hawthorne's "Phips" had announced his own wish to be.

Such a literary success is not without worldly consequences. Not precisely political, still they touch a person's (even a child's) deepest sense of his own manner of being in the world. The point is not exactly that the conservative or Tory imagination has methods interdicted to the professors of futuristic American patriotism. There is probably *some* significance to the fact that Irving, Longfellow, and Hawthorne are at once more imaginative *and* more conservative than, say, Bancroft, Prescott, and Motley; but in some sense they are *all* disciples of Scott. More simply, it is here a question of what aspects of the past a person is willing to allow within the range of sympathetic apprehension. Whig historians are interested in progress and in the future. They thrive on teleological generalization. They can "vivify" only part of the relevant past, often that Puritan or bourgeois-democratic part which was itself least sympathetic to the concerns of art and culture. Like those prophets of an American literature to be enlisted on the side of the "new," they can receive inspiration only from such moments of the "old" as seemed pregnant with typological significance.[26] But clearly the children of Esther Dudley will suffer none of these crippling immunities.

What the children receive from Esther Dudley is, all simply, a lively and personal sense of the way the most "British" segment of the American past really was, quite without regard to the question of whether that past will, in any form, "return in triumph." In her own "desolate heart" she may hope for eventual vindication, but what she allows "childhood's fancy" to discern are the "ghosts that haunted there" (297). That is to say, the children know the past *as past* and not as destiny; they develop a remarkable feeling for an older order without ever being the least confused about "the progress and true state of the Revolutionary War."[27] If we choose to believe that she herself does *not at all* recognize her own "hopes" for what they are (loving and nostalgic memory), and if we decide she remains unalterably convinced that Providence has indeed arranged the triumphant return of Governor Howe, still the ironic point is abundantly clear. Esther's history is no less valid and true and ultimately "usable" simply because it does not validate any future. Indeed it may be more valid. The naive narrator, the canny author, and the prudent editors of "Old Esther Dudley" all share, we may presume, a certain predilection for the relatively idealistic premises that underlie Esther Dudley's legendary art. But what Hawthorne alone understands—and emphasizes, over the shoulder of his fictive narrator and under the nose of his quite real editors—is that providential assumptions and typological methods constitute an overbelief which is incompatible with valid history. Hawthorne may well have a quarrel with "regular" modern historians about the proper limits of the imagination and figural representation in the writing of history, but he is clearly at one with them in realizing that history *as history* attempts no more than to recover the sense of what was; *as such,* it does not validate what is or predict what will be. And thus the multiple irony latent in the position of Esther Dudley as historian: whereas her revolutionary neighbors (including Hancock) treat her as the literal embodiment of a past that is about to die and depart once and for all from American historical memory, and whereas virtually all the Puritan characters in the first three "Legends" see their own present as validating a certain limited portion of the past, according to a providential guarantee, she herself simply keeps alive and lovingly transmits a sense of a reality that "was."

If we think of Esther Dudley as someone whose attachment to the past is merely a conventional "given," as someone whose one automatic statement is simply "How I love everything old," then it will not be difficult to account for the narrator's sympathy. Practically committed to the "new," he is nevertheless attracted to the past as color and to antiquity as a tone. Though Hawthorne is satirizing this minor-Romantic-antiquarian side of himself, and though he hopes to stand for a more profound relation to the past, he sees that even this sort of attachment is not without value. For its very premise is the *pastness* of the past. But it is not necessary to see Esther in just this way. Not political, and half-aware that her Hope is indeed only Memory, she seems nevertheless a True Tory Believer—as our narrator manifestly is not. It is probably most useful to think of him as personally sympathetic with Esther Dudley because of his antiquarian predilections, as consciously (prudently) suppressing any overt discussion of the way the Revolutionaries customarily treated the Loyalists, and as unaware of the irony in his formulation about the confusion of Hope and Memory.

Irony there undoubtedly is, however, since such confusions exist far more radically in the orderly assumptions of a mind like Bancroft's than in the disorderly mind of this ancient Tory. It is that renowned historical guide who most noticeably expects the unknown future to vindicate the well-remembered past. Or, if we regard the future less as unknown and more as "projected," then it is a question of disguising Millennial Hope as Historical Memory: earnestly desiring and anticipating a progressive and libertarian future, one is strongly tempted to invent a history which embodies the progress of liberty. Such historical difficulties, everywhere beyond our narrator's grasp, are raised in connection with the activities of Old Esther Dudley as clearly as with those of Alice Vane. And only in Esther Dudley's legend is Hawthorne's attitude perfectly unarguable: by deliberately forcing the *reader* to dissociate Esther Dudley's loving memory and zealous commitment from any conceivable political hope, he has stressed the inviolable pastness of her past; and in doing so he has effectively separated the difficult and often discouraging idea of true history from the easier and more ideologically useful one of typological vindication.[28]

Even further from the narrator's notice lie the story's conservative suggestions about revolution and temporality or the historical process as such. For once we have learned to distrust the adequacy of Hancock's final declaration of independence from "the Past," and to view the narrator and his entire story in a critical and ironic spirit, it becomes evident that the revolutionary changes which are swirling around the uncomprehending head of Esther Dudley are not nearly so radical as the new governor's rhetoric would have us believe. To be sure, the last Loyalist tenant of the Province House dies, and death is as clear a break as we can imagine; Governor Howe does *not* return, and the permanent expulsion of an hitherto legitimate government is no small matter; the governor who *does* return is a governor once more elected by the people, and Hawthorne never thinks of discrediting the normal workings of ordinary political democracy. And yet none of this even approaches the story's more subtle implications. Quite apart from the question of the children reclaimed for the past by Esther Dudley's historical tales, there are clear suggestions that even under the most favorable circumstances it is not possible to accomplish the sort of revolution Hancock sententiously proclaims. Probably such a total end and aboriginal beginning would not be good if it *were* possible; and certainly this princely merchant is not the man to accomplish or embody or even preside over the abrupt historical change of phase from aristocracy to democracy. But above all, the stress is on the relatively incomplete nature of *any* revolution, however radically motivated.

The "New" John Hancock is destined to outlive—and to read a moral into the life and death of—the "Old" Esther Dudley; not the other way around. It is as certain as Endicott's victory over the Lord and Lady of the May. But it is no more ultimate. At a level that can only be called "metaphysical," Esther Dudley's simply living through the Revolution, in the

Province House, is even more important than her telling children about its pre-revolutionary occupants. In the last analysis what Esther Dudley *is* looms larger than anything she does.

What then *is* Old Esther Dudley? She is, first of all, a "Dudley." The name reminds us once more of the partly "internal" character of the Revolution; for if her immediate ancestor is the royal governor who was so bitterly opposed by Cotton Mather, her lineage nevertheless runs back to the founding of New England: to Thomas Dudley, father of Anne Bradstreet, guardian and eventual governor of the Puritan Israel.[29] Latterly her family name may connote "Tory," but its nuance was not always so; and even as Tory, it is (like Hutchinson) as venerable a name as the colony has to show. If the pitiable helplessness of Esther Dudley's antique gentility seems somehow to capture the strange, lady-like impotence of the Tories generally, still the name reminds us that, prior to the last stage of crisis, the people who came to be called Tories were far from insignificant in the "democratic" but still "deferential" politics of Massachusetts Bay.[30]

As Esther Dudley refuses to leave the Province House (and Boston, and New England) with Howe (and the other departing Loyalists), her motivation appears to be fairly complex. Already fallen into "poverty and decay," she has long had "no resource save the bounty of the King, nor any shelter except within the walls of the Province House" (292). Long since a royal pensioner, she has had only "nominal duties"; and she can, if she chooses, simply continue to be a royal pensioner elsewhere, in Halifax or back in England. But clearly her commitment to the old order will reduce to an economic explanation no more easily than that of, say, Thomas Hutchinson or Peter Oliver. Her loyalty to the Province House may have something to do with the "punctilious courtesy which it was her foible to demand" there. But as with the famous (and, of course, literal) Tories, her loyalism has a strong if tenuous and hard-to-define moral, almost religious quality.[31]

In one sense she functions as a sort of "spirit of place": gliding mysteriously through the passages and public chambers of the Province House, fabled to have entered "in the train of the first Royal Governor," and fated "to dwell there till the last should have departed" (293) she is the essence of whatever the British presence in America has been or meant. Her Republican neighbors, including Hancock, easily reduce her to a type of outworn and rejected aristocracy: once the spirit of an operable system; now anachronistically urging her claims upon a progressively "neglectful world." Even Howe, whose own reluctance to leave ought to produce a sympathetic response, is inclined to write her off, in a moment of irritation, as foolish and obstinate: "the very moral of old-fashioned prejudice" (294). But the sympathetic reader cannot quite let it go at this, even though Howe and the Rebels seem to agree. Everywhere Esther Dudley seems more important than any of the explicit statements made about her: somehow an essential and irreducible fact of the situation, she is necessary according to a higher law of historical reality. She simply cannot be *talked* out of existence; not by Howe, not by her neighbors, not by Hancock.

Royal influence will never come again to the Province of Massachusetts Bay, but it *has been*. And having been, it will partly determine whatever follows—all revolutionary rhetoric to the contrary notwithstanding. The past will never come again, but neither will it quite go away. Massachusetts remains the same "place." The Province House still stands. And expressly loyal to her own "Forefathers," Esther Dudley lingers: in fact and in body, as long as she can; longer presumably in "spirit."

But the dogged determination which provokes the departing Howe is not to be explained in metaphysical or superstitious terms alone. Esther Dudley has (in our narrator's version, at least) no constitutional argument to make, but she does have her commitment, her "immutable resolve." Her "pertinacious" refusal to accept Howe's version of reality and necessity and her seemingly obsessive determination that "King George shall still have one true subject in his disloyal province" (294) are not so much "crazed" as they are suggestive of dominant Tory attitudes. Everywhere those attitudes seem remarkable for their tenacity, not to say their inflexibility. If the American Rebels seem volatile and not a little "Puritan" in their hot desire for radical transformation, the American Loyalists seem invincibly (if sometimes nervously) committed to the status quo. Tory language is different but it is also strong: without ready appeals to apocalyptic expectation, or simplistic contractualism, or even common sense, it has its own "mystic" resources. The inability to believe in the possibility of British defeat calls for no comment. But the quasi-religious "Tory" commitment to the King and to the existing order will bear some analysis.[32]

3

It is noteworthy that although Esther Dudley is absolutely steadfast in her refusal to leave with Howe, she is far from hysterical at his departure or the general Tory exodus. She seems to accept political and military necessity at this level: the governor cannot remain, and there is no real point in his hallowing the Province House with a "blood-stain on the floor." Howe regrets his inability to leave some lasting, public "testimony that the last British ruler was faithful to his trust"; but this consideration seems not at all to trouble the voice with which she replies: " 'Heaven's cause and the King's are one,' it said. 'Go forth, Sir William Howe, and trust in heaven to bring back a Royal Governor in triumph' " (292). Esther Dudley is by no means complacent at the turn things have taken, but she does not regard Howe's forced departure as crucial to the ultimate cause which they both serve. He may leave—though she may not. They both talk of "trust," but they do not mean quite the same thing. And it is on the ambiguities of "trust" that the story's latent conservatism makes its way.

Evidently certain higher "trusts" may remain unbroken even as the political order which seems to embody them is visibly shattered. In "Edward Randolph's Portrait" both sides accused the other of breaking the fundamental trust on which the legitimacy of British rule in America had long depended. In "Lady Eleanore's Mantle" we were forced to look at a positively virulent, revolutionary distrust, which resembled nothing so much as a witch-hunt in its "frenzy." In the present story Howe sadly confesses that despite his moral faithfulness, he has in fact lost "the Province which the King entrusted to [his] charge" (293). And Hancock, though he does not use the word, is really declaring, at the end, that all the old trusts are dead and that a totally new order of allegiances has taken their place. All of this is real enough: revolutions introduce discontinuities and break old allegiances, personal and political. And yet the symbolic career of Old Esther Dudley suggests that this is not an ultimate reality. What she stands for, finally, is the continuity which endures even the most radical of revolutions, a trust which at its deepest level is not political but is the equivalent of historical process itself.[33]

The politics of her "trust in Heaven" are, as we have seen, not the essential point: both sides trust Providence; only one side wins; and "history" must resist the conclusion that right made might.[34] Of crucial importance, rather, is the fact that her prayerful exhortation to Howe is quickly replaced by a different language (and ritual) of trust. Howe's moment of irritation with Esther Dudley comes, we should notice, between two vastly more significant and characteristic ones in which he explicitly invests in the "old-fashioned prejudice" she embodies.

First of all he offers her money—coin of the British realm, impressed with the graven image of King George. His motives, to be sure, are largely personal (he will not leave "this wretched old creature to starve and beg"), and his original thought is that the money will "buy a better shelter than the Province House can now afford"; but his speech also affirms the values of subordination and continuity, whose defense in Massachusetts he feels he is being forced to abandon: "King George's head on these golden guineas is sterling yet, and will continue so, I warrant you, even should the rebels crown John Hancock their king" (293). The principal irony connected with

467

"King Hancock" will become clear later: an upstart rebel can continue to ape royal ways even at the head of a republican government. And the rueful reality of the provincial monetary situation need only be mentioned: the long-standing dependence on British specie will endure beyond and in spite of drastic constitutional alterations.[35] But Howe's affirmation seems at least to raise the question of larger, "moral" dependencies, and cryptically to suggest a whole set of attitudes at least as important to Hawthorne as Hancock's: certain realities of the corporate life lie deeper than all talk about them; certain continuities of trust and value defy all "declarations" to the contrary.

All sorts of British values, Hawthorne seems to imply, will "pass current" for some time to come. Revolution is a dangerously speculative enterprise, and some pledges take longer to redeem than others. The *Democratic Review* could call into existence and define an autonomous American literary experience no more successfully than the newly independent colonies could create a fully trustworthy and stable currency.[36]

But more important than the coin given Esther Dudley is the key. Again, a "harmless" interpretation is possible: irrationally disturbed at the idea that Esther Dudley is somehow more loyal than himself, but persuaded that this shrewish "old fool" does indeed intend to remain in the very Province House whose "charge" was "entrusted" to him, Howe makes the best of things by giving "the Province House in charge to" a vicarious representative. It is absurd, of course. He cannot help "smiling bitterly at himself and her." The ritual is empty because she is so patently ineffectual. Given the practical accomplishment of Joliffe's earlier prediction, how can it possibly matter that "King George shall have one true subject in his disloyal Province"? It is all so reductive and materialistic: one person, one key, one house. Still, the victims may as well play out their parts in the bad romance which history has written for them: "Take this key, and keep it safe until myself, or some other Royal Governor, shall demand it of you" (294). And yet the ritual comes to seem less absurd when, several revolutionary years later, Esther Dudley believes she is surrendering the key to a royal governor once more.

As pathos, her mistake about Hancock—to whom she triumphantly offers the carefully guarded key to the Province House—is no more interesting than her other "partially crazed" beliefs about the "true state of the Revolutionary War." It is somewhat more interesting as irony, as not a mistake at all. Her inability to doubt that Hancock is the "long-looked-for" royal governor "to whom she was to surrender up her charge" depends on more than her own fixed idea. Expecting a return of the "pomp and splendor of bygone times," Esther witnesses the following scene:

Advancing up the court-yard, appeared a person of most dignified mien, with tokens, as Esther interpreted them, of gentle blood, high rank, and long-accustomed authority, even in his walk and every gesture. He was richly dressed, but wore a gouty shoe, which, however, did not lessen the stateliness of his gait. Around and behind him were people in plain civic dresses, and two or three war-worn veterans, evidently officers of rank, arrayed in a uniform of blue and buff. But Esther Dudley, firm in the belief that had fastened its roots about her heart, beheld only the principal personage. (300)

If one looks only at Hancock, the mistake is entirely understandable. Though chosen in a relatively democratic manner, and though accompanied by plain-dressing citizens, he is still the same hereditary aristocrat he has always been, the man Hawthorne elsewhere described as having the appearance of a "skillful courtier" at the "footstool of King George's throne," and as concerned "quite as much [with] his own popularity" as with "the rights of the people."[37]

Indeed, if Esther is mistaken about the "royal" quality of Hancock, she is far from alone in the error. To be sure, it had long passed as a "byword" in Boston that she might "look for a Royal Governor again" only when "the golden Indian on the Province House shall shoot his arrow" or when "the cock on the Old South spire shall crow." But this is not the whole story. For when "at last . . . Esther Dudley knew, or perchance she only dreamed, that a Royal Governor was on the eve of returning to the Province House, to receive the heavy key," it was also a fact that "intelligence bearing some faint analogy to Esther's version of it was current among the townspeople" (299). Evidently our narrator can make no better sense of this rumor than he can of the double founding of the Province House. But Hawthorne expects the import of the rumor to be fairly clear: many of the ordinary people in Massachusetts openly referred to the pompous new governor (who had been "born to the inheritance of the largest fortune in New England") as "King Hancock"; and still more must have doubted that the much-heralded change in political constitution could make very much practical (that is, economic or social) difference to them.[38]

To us it is obvious that not all "revolutionary" changes in the personnel or even in the constitutional mechanics of government issue in a radical or "democratic" redistribution of wealth and power. And it is very nearly as obvious that American historians have not yet spoken the last word on the question of "the American Revolution considered as a Social Movement." Hawthorne himself appeared to believe that the long-range results of the American Revolution were more liberal and democratic than otherwise. But he did not hold the opinion with anything like the simplicity and fervor of O'Sullivan and Bancroft. And whatever his own beliefs, this was the appropriate place to consider the other side of the argument—although again, of necessity, only by ironic implication.

And thus the almost-central irony of "Old Esther Dudley": the continuity of political "trust" in Massachusetts based on the personal indistinguishability of Governor Hancock from the various royal placemen who preceded him. For all appearances, for most practical purposes, and to many people's minds, he might as well be a royal governor come again.[39] He might represent a *different* aristocratic oligarchy than that headed by the Hutchinsons and the Olivers, but it is not clear on the face of it that one is better off being ruled by tax-evading, mob-inciting merchants who (in private life) cultivated the aristocratic style than by certain appointed and professed courtiers who were to the manner born. And if a "democratic" election of governor is still so "deferential" as to choose a Hancock—merely to substitute a Whig Oligarch for a Tory Oligarch—then what ultimate use the Revolution? Despite the "people in plain civic dresses," are we not indeed witnessing the return of the old "pomp and splendor" to the Province House? How different is Hancock from Governor Bernard (who proposed the official creation of an American aristocracy) or from Governor Shute (who first established the Province House as an exemplar of the British courtly style) or from one Peter Sargent (who built the palatial residence for all these later inhabitants)? Or, to press the argument bitterly in another direction, how really different would a fastidiously aristocratic historian of the march of transcendental liberty seem to an obscure writer in plain civic dress, a decent city boarder forced to accept the patronage of the "new" order?

It is no wonder that the popular "intelligence bearing some faint analogy" to Esther's "mistake" is not explained or even emphasized. For a frank and honest estimate of the degree of truth concealed in Esther Dudley's reaction to "what she construed as the Royal Governor's arrival" makes Hancock's final speech about "newness" (in the manner of the *Democratic Review*) seem patently absurd and even a little asinine. British social values are still alive and at least as healthy as British currency. If Hancock would "reverence, for the last time, the stately and gorgeous prejudices of the tottering Past," then he ought to conduct his own burial procession: his own resemblance to the style of Lady Eleanore is far more striking than is that of Old Esther Dudley. Unfortunately for the cause of social democracy, however, Hancock cannot be seen to "totter," despite his "gouty shoe." And unfortunately for our aged Loyalist, she is incapable of seeing the element of truth in the mistake of her aged eyes and traditionalist vision.

No ironist, Esther Dudley does *not* hand the key over to Hancock. Rather she clutches it back, horrified that she has come so close to bestowing that precious symbol of legitimacy on an upstart rebel, "the monarch's most dreaded and hated foe." And this is as it should be, for it is not the ironic continuity of social appearances that the story means in the end to emphasize. The truth and reality of Old Esther Dudley are partly independent of what happens to the key. It is, to be sure, a suggestive symbol of the legitimacy conferred by continuity; and Esther's holy devotion to the task of conferring it is meant to contrast sharply and definitively with Hancock's utter disinterest in receiving it. But in the last analysis the key is no more a symbol of Hawthorne's own ultimate meaning than was the mantle.

The last scene—describing the fate of the key—is carefully managed as strategic anticlimax. It begins on a very high note indeed: as Hancock advances toward the Province House, we find that Howe's personally embarrassed and politically modest "Take this key" has turned into Esther Dudley's triumphant and potent "Receive my trust." But then her dismal error becomes swiftly apparent; and after it has called forth Hancock's "reverence," she pulls herself free of his terrifying support and sinks down "beside one of the pillars of the portal." And so her ordeal ends, not in triumph, but in bewildered non-performance of the holy duty she hoped would be her last act. Of course the narrator knows just how to emphasize the final pathos: "The key of the Province House fell from her grasp, and clanked against the stone" (302). Old Esther Dudley has indeed remained "faithful unto death," but her touching personal loyalty seems without reward and without public consequence. No one bothers to pick up the key she has dropped or to take up the trust she has finally had to lay down.

If the Old Tory were telling his own story, we can easily imagine how critical this moment would be: a radical break in political continuity has indeed occurred; the heavenly gift of authority, transmitted down the generations as if from parent to offspring, has been willfully (that is, rebelliously) rejected, perhaps totally lost.[40] From such a fall, what redemption? Our narrator, of course, will give us none of this: antiquarianism and sentiment are one thing, but Robert Filmer is quite another. And obviously Hancock would be the last man in the world to pick up Esther Dudley's key: armed with the rhetoric of newness, and trusting the future to validate his legitimacy, he can see no need to align himself with *anything* that has gone before; or if he were to notice continuity, he would not be able to speak as he does.

And thus it seems to end: the past simply dies, unable to transmit anything to a present so revolutionary as to be interested only in the future. The party of the past has been *so* mindlessly "faithful" to its own terms that it has rendered itself obsolescent. The party of the future is projecting itself so vigorously that it scarcely believes in any moment "present" long enough to be touched by the past. Just so the American experience seemed to many in the 1830's. A clean break and a new beginning, without political embarrassment and without cultural regret. And just so, obviously, would Hawthorne's patrons be pleased to have his "Legends" conclude—with Esther Dudley's useless, dying "God save the King" followed by Hancock's vigorous and ringing "We are no longer children of the Past."

But because Hawthorne knew that neither the American Revolution nor historical process itself could be adequately described that way, "Old Esther Dudley" forces the reader's final response to be somewhat different. Not only has the historical power of Esther Dudley begun to reclaim the newest generation of "children" away from an ideologue completely unaware of his own totally familiar political appearance; but some of her power has worked on Hancock, in spite of himself. It is rather like the victory which the Lord and the Lady win over Endicott. Like Endicott, Hancock has the last word; but before he has it, he—like Endicott—is forced to pay tribute to values he is not supposed to recognize. We have said that his final "reverence" is condescending rather than profound. And so it is. But this is not its only significant aspect. Without the force of some Burkean "prejudice" in favor of chivalry, it would not occur at all: Hancock supports Old Esther Dudley "with all the reverence a courtier would have shown to a queen" (301). At another level the reverence seems drawn out of him, by the power of a reality he simply cannot disregard; conservative beliefs are too deeply held to be ignored. Thus he may quibble with Esther Dudley about the limits of royal sovereignty, but he cannot refuse to echo her "God save King George." And though he ends with a radical declaration, his projection of the future is delayed by a last pilgrimage "to the tomb of her ancestors" (302). It is, indeed, far too little, but it is something. In the end, all unwittingly, the tottering Esther Dudley forces the future to take account of (in fact even to touch) the past.

This moment of enforced contact between the past and future suggests a number of significant considerations. Most obviously it defines the nature of the fully historical present: conscious plan for the future, unable to evade awareness of the past. Beyond that, it not only figures the reality of the American Revolution far better than it is described by Hancock's rhetoric of projected newness, but it also serves to remind us once again that the most radical implications of that rhetoric are more proper to the *Democratic Review* of 1838 than to the majority of American Patriots of the 1770's.

On the one hand, the actual Revolution *was* more conservative than Hancock's rhetoric allows; and the picture of the princely merchant chivalrously supporting an ancient Royalist counts for more than all his words. On the other hand, his words themselves do not sound much like the dominant ideology of 1776, which recognizes (and even glories in) a certain conservative intention. The Revolution may have been an awakening *to* the millennial reality of the Apocalyptic "New," but it was also a *re*vival of older virtues, political and social as well as moral. "Old Esther Dudley" does not offer an appropriate occasion for a full rehearsal of the complicated argument about conservatism versus liberalism in the American Revolution; but Hancock's final, enforced, inadequate "reverence" for the past does call our attention to the fact that as the ideology of America as "revolutionary" became more and more secularized, it also became more and more simply futuristic. Bancroft's "typological" interest in the Puritan past is far less genuinely historical than that of the revolutionary Patriots who searched the pages of Hutchinson's history for constitutional and moral precedent; it is also, obviously, far less valid than Hawthorne's almost religious regard for the ontological integrity of past reality. But it is, at the same time, far more faithful to historical reality than that of the frankest spokesman for a manifest destiny of newness.[41]

Taken together, Hancock's actions and his speeches seem to figure the reality of a partly conservative revolution being smoothly covered over with an almost totally futuristic rhetoric. Hancock himself is *very much* part of an aristocratic tradition, in and out of a basically "deferential" colonial politics and social structure; according to one view, he helped to engineer a "popular" uprising in the protection of private interests, the very reverse of liberal democracy. In any event he bids an entirely premature farewell to the "stately and gorgeous prejudices" of the past—even as he himself seems to embody and profit by many of them. And finally he offers a mere lip service to the "Forefathers." As Esther Dudley's commitment "to the tomb of my forefathers" is not very different from the sort that fired Puritan "ancestor worship" even down to the Revolution, so her Forefathers and Hancock's own are not that different. Hancock is as truly a child of the aristocratic Governor Dudley as is Esther. And in the Revolution itself the idea of "ancestry" mattered far more than Hancock's momentary pause indicates.

The aroused present of the American Revolution really *was* a touching of the present and the future: as implied in the other three ("Puritan") "Legends," a generation intensely aware of a heritage or "trust" it passionately thought of as libertarian took a step it considered crucial to the divine scheme of human destiny. But in the factitious divisions produced by the narrative conditions of "Old Esther Dudley," all of this is obscured. In a modern antiquarian's prudent, minor-Romantic version of Tory prejudice, concern for the past (embodied in Esther Dudley's devotion to the Province House and its key) threatens to seem less a rational concern for vital and operative continuity of belief than an obsessive preoccupation with legitimacy as consecutiveness and with the mechanics of transmission; and concern for the future turns into the mindless, secularized "onward" of

473

latter-day political "projectors." Joliffe, or the selectman, or Doctor Clarke would accept Esther Dudley's literal key no more readily we may presume, than would Hancock; and certainly the tradition they embody is not now, by reflex, given uncritical endorsement. Still, the clear implication is that the terms of the first three "Legends" have made a far different sense of the problem of past and future. On behalf of the *Democratic Review*, Hancock adopts a rhetoric of pure futurism, but he is of the past as much as "Old" Esther Dudley; and though even his obtuseness is forced to take *some* account of the past, he does not understand why and how his remarks turn into lip service. As everywhere, the secularized version of the apocalyptically "New" cannot really come to terms with the "Old."[42] Ultimately Hancock's chivalry and the narrator's interest in the past as tone amount to pretty much the same thing.

But the miscomprehensions and inflations of Hancock's final behavior and rhetoric are only one element in the "anticlimax" of the conclusion of "Old Esther Dudley." If Esther Dudley is more real than Hancock has the perception or language to grant, and if she is more real to the literal children than to the children of Hancock's rhetorical future, she has become still more real to the reader. We cannot escape the fact that she fills up an otherwise vacant interregnum between Howe and Hancock: she really does connect the two regimes, despite the dropped key and the apparently missed communication.

To demand an actual, physical transfer of key, charge, and trust would be as reductive and simplistic in its way as Hancock's attitudes are in theirs. Disciples of Filmer might require such a literal and explicit continuity, and some of the more rigid of the American Tories might be thought to demand some such transfer; but clearly Hawthorne's sympathy with such Tories was never complete or fundamental. Whenever he wrote of them most specifically, his main purpose was the "noble" (and for his generation remarkable) one of proving, against universal American prejudice, that they were not evil or mean-spirited people. Beyond this, he has a remarkable feeling for the position and problems of Thomas Hutchinson. If Hawthorne were to prove Hutchinson's disciple, we could well understand: anyone trying to touch the solidities of the past itself might feel like declaring such an allegiance. And one *can* find more in most of the notable American Tories than a sort of desperate and legalistic concern for the constitutional "legitimacy" of every new belief, action, or institution. Nevertheless, when Hawthorne wrote his sketch of "The Old Tory," he was very careful to distinguish: for him to get the character right, it was necessary to transform himself from a "modern Tory" into such a "sturdy King-man as once wore that pliable nickname." And just so here, as we pursue the "Hawthorne" who stands behind all his various narrators.[43]

What values can we ascribe to this "modern Tory"? First of all, he appears to "comprehend" (that is, contain but also understand and judge) the limited imaginative commitment of his narrator, to pastness as color and tone, to nostalgia. He also comprehends the political counterpart of such "minor-Romantic" values: the reverential feeling which aristocratic and cultural classes have for inherited forms of political and social organization— the conservative prejudice in favor of monarchy, established religion, and chivalry, all on the ground of their antiquity and "esthetic" appeal, rather than on that of mere self-interest. Both these prejudices appear to serve the writer, who quickly observes that the purely progressive imagination lacks external resource and can "project" itself only so far. Thus a "modern Tory" might be a "literary" (as opposed to a political) follower of Edmund Burke. Disregarding questions concerning the validity of some and the invalidity of other revolutions, he would be less concerned with where things stayed right or went wrong than with the value of the past as such. And probably he would care less about prescribing the manner in which institutions ought to develop than with the fact of development as such. Perhaps we should call him a "philosophical" follower of Burke, even if this tends to mean merely a disciple of Scott and Irving.[44]

Yet possibly there is a political influence as well. The facts of Hawthorne's "borrowing" are by no means clear, but it seems difficult to appreciate the function of Esther Dudley as bearer of a sacred trust apart from some of Burke's more memorable formulations. If we look for a motto for the narrower, more nearly political aspects of her behavior, we can find nothing in Hutchinson, or Oliver, or Galloway, or Boucher as appropriate as this: "The very idea of the fabrication of a new government is enough to fill us with disgust and horror. We . . . wish to derive all we possess as *an inheritance from our forefathers.*" And are we not asked to regard Hancock precisely as one of Burke's "temporary possessors and life-renters" in the state who are "unmindful of what they have received from their ancestors"? If Esther Dudley anticipates Hepzibah Pyncheon as prisoner of traditional prejudice, then surely Hancock is a forestudy of Holgrave in what Burke called the "unprincipled facility of changing," the upshot of which is that "no one generation would link with the other" and that "men would become little better than flies of a summer." And most fundamentally, what is Esther Dudley herself but a living embodiment of that trust which Burke described as the vital and organic partnership "between those who are living, those who are dead, and those who are yet to be born"?[45]

Again, the point is not that Hawthorne judged the American Revolution as right or wrong as it did or did not base itself on Burke's premises. The story does not force us to decide whether someone *should* or *should not* have picked up the key; for us, Esther Dudley's personal faithfulness and trust, surviving years of fraternal hatred and bloodshed, are the only real consideration. And Hawthorne's own concern is not so much with government or even society as with the nature of historical change. At this level his suggestion is clearly that Burke is right and Hancock (or the *Democratic Review*) is wrong: continuity is true and radical innovation is false. Hancock is not exactly like Howe; but linked by the analogy of the "aristocratic" and "deferential" Esther Dudley, their regimes are far from discontinuous. For Hawthorne it was an inviolable law that what followed owed its existence in some measure to what went before; it was, therefore, in some frame of reference "like" what went before. The historian's prime task, in consequence, was to define historical causation by discovering analogies—to find the Esther Dudley between the Howe and the Hancock.

Most critics would agree with R. W. B. Lewis that Hawthorne's best writing is characterized by a "passion for sources and beginnings, for traditions and continuities." History, we might well conclude, was his privileged way of understanding the world. His motto might even come from Henry Osborne Taylor: "Discontinuity in history is an illusion. More real is the overlapping of thought and feeling through the succession of forms."[46] Though Hawthorne worked with figure and in irony, he nevertheless remained committed to the historian's main ends: to understand the past as it was and to define historical continuity or "overlap" by such discriminating analogies as allowed for significant (relative) similarities amidst irreducible (simple) differences. And of this complex concern, "Old Esther Dudley" stands as an epitome.

4

The conclusion of "Old Esther Dudley" is anticlimactic, then, because the clanking of Esther Dudley's key against the stone does not matter; and because our experience of the reality she represents makes Hancock's final speech ring hollow and irrelevant. Even had the American colonists intended the totally new beginning suggested by later rhetoric, they could not have achieved it. America was to remain the same place and, as the Howe-Dudley-Hancock analogy suggests, its people remained largely the same people. Absolute discontinuity or complete change of phase is against the law of history. And more particularly, as Hawthorne would later suggest, "our relations with England remain[ed] far more numerous than our disconnections." It is even to be hoped that the spirit of Esther Dudley, the preserver, the protectress of continuity, will come *consciously* to prevail in the hearts of future American generations over the spirit of Hancock. For like her stories to the children, "Old Esther Dudley" means to inspire not one final reverence for a "departed system," but rather a sacred regard for "the bonds of history, of literature, and all that makes up memories"—a Burkean reverence for "the institutions that have grown out of the heart of mankind."[47]

Such values Hawthorne evidently wished to associate with the American Tories; or, rather, he preferred to attend to this deepest strain of conservatism in them more than any other; more, certainly, than to such political conservatism as effectively makes revolution impossible. The approach is partial, of course: England, not America, produced Burke; and his profoundest views were called forth on the occasion of the French, not the American, Revolution. And yet there seems a kind of fairness in it, not only to right a balance of historical judgment in which the Tories seemed not to weigh at all, but also because some American Loyalists at least do approach a Burkean conception of human development. "The High Tories," as their most able modern historian has aptly remarked, "regarded society almost as an organism, a living, breathing thing, its mysteries beyond the wit of man."[48] Reading them today, one finds the "caution and reverence" they embody at least as attractive as the apocalyptic zeal of the Puritans, the revolutionary restlessness of Jefferson, or the simplistic contractualism of Paine.

But it would be quite wrong, let us repeat, to say that "Old Esther Dudley" presents, in reply to the previous "Legends," the Tory view of the American Revolution. In a complicated, indirect, and ironic way it affirms the highest values with which the Tories may be fairly associated; it does so in self-conscious and almost direct contradiction of the *Democratic* "medium" in which it appears; but it does not follow the logic of the American Tory historians in explaining "the Origin and Progress of America's Rebellion." To understand why this is so is to comprehend, finally, the anticlimactic function of "Old Esther Dudley" itself in Hawthorne's overall design.

The principal reason is that the Tory view is already embedded, as irony, in the first three "Legends": not only do those tales give us plenty of opportunity to imagine concrete "conspiratorial" activities for the various Puritan "demagogues" who feel themselves opposing a Diabolic Enemy engaged in an Historic Conspiracy; but the basic thrust of Revolutionary Opposition is as clearly identifiable as Puritan in those tales as it is in the writings of Oliver, Galloway, Boucher, or Chandler. Clearly it was no novelty in the 1830's to claim that Puritanism caused the American Revolution. The Tories almost unanimously believed in the predominance of a Boston clique, and with only a few exceptions they ascribed Independence to a "settled plan" of the New England Puritans. One of the most notable exceptions was Hutchinson; but as "Edward Randolph's Portrait" shows, Hawthorne did not consider this immunity to suspicion of Puritanism as a sign of superior perception. Again it is worth quoting a modern historian of the Tories:

> If the element of moral praise or reproach is removed, there is, after all, no great difference between the Tory belief that New England Puritanism was in permanent and wicked conspiracy against the British government, and John Adams' belief that the settlement of New England by the Puritans was part of a divine plan for the liberation of man from the tyranny of Church and State.[49]

And even Bancroft's views, as modern historians of historians have dutifully noted, are not that different from those of the Tories, including those of George Chalmers, against whom Bancroft seems most directly to have reacted.[50]

There is considerable disagreement, of course, about exactly when a conscious design to achieve Independence became fully articulated; but up to the 1830's almost everyone agreed that there was in Puritanism what Edwards might have called a "steady tendency" toward independence. Beyond this, disagreement was partly a question of value. What was one to think of such a tendency? But there were also the subtler questions: how was independence related to a developing Puritan conception of "liberty"? and to what extent might "democracy" be implicated in or be likely to develop out of such a tendency?

The burden of Hawthorne's first three "Legends," as we have clearly seen, is to stress the Puritan impetus in various moments of American revolutionary consciousness, but at the same time to question the liberal implications of the liberty sought at those moments; and, more reflexively, to examine the validity of "typology" and "vindication" as a general explanation of the Independent tendency in American history. That the Puritans were, at more than one moment, significantly rebellious seemed to Hawthorne undeniable; that the whole thing should be seen as a providential progress toward a predestined state of millennial human freedom seemed highly questionable. Not that he would think the world going steadily to hell if, under the aegis of Puritanism, it *were* steadily going to what Bancroft called "the people"; if things really appeared so, he might even add his own "hurrah." But since they seemed more than a little ambiguous, his first three "Legends" present America's revolutionary Puritans in a more complicated way: talking always about Providence and the Progress of Liberty, they nevertheless reveal themselves in attitudes which suggest the partial justice of their nasty and demagogic reputation among the Tories.

Essentially modern in his approach to this complicated question, Hawthorne sees that Puritanism contains (perhaps *is*) a powerful dynamism for political change: judging all "merely" human arrangements by its own higher law and convinced of its own mission to accomplish divine ends within human history, it is always ready to stay the march of a king or to send a royal governor packing. Indeed it may be truly at peace with itself only when it is at war with what most other men take to be the inevitable product of *human* history so far. If from one point of view the Puritan's dialectical opposite is the Pagan Reveller, from another it is the High Tory: the latter is the ultimate conservative, the former the ultimate revolutionary. But because Hawthorne is not convinced that all revolutionary change is for the better, and because his cardinal doctrine is the anti-apocalyptic belief that Mankind is never to be permitted one final and direct stroke against diabolic oppression and for the libertarian millennium, he is left with such doubts and ambiguities as make up his first three "Legends"—with the less holy elements of Puritan motivation and action, and with the seamy side of Providence.[51]

And then the problem of Puritanism seems to vanish from "Old Esther Dudley" entirely, the figure of the Revolutionary as Puritan being replaced by Hancock, the proleptic spokesman for a somewhat more secularized, open-ended futurism. The one story which is ascribed to an ultimate Tory source seems—after the sound and fury of "Lady Eleanore's Mantle"—calmly to take up other issues. The effect is curious, but intelligible. And probably it is more telling than any more obvious, argumentative strategy could be.

Having given us in "Lady Eleanore's Mantle" not only a literary but also an historical climax, and having imbued that story with all the Tory criticism one could ask for, why should Hawthorne attempt yet another crescendo? To have hinted that there may indeed be poison in the communion cup of the Old South Church was to have presented, in an obvious metaphor, the substance of the Tories' most desperate charge against the "Black Regiment." And to have stressed the element of "frenzy" was to have given the Tory response to the violent upheaval of the 1760's and 1770's more than its due. "Frenzy" is their own melodramatic word for the sociology of the Revolution. They use it almost unanimously and always in the same context: the frenzy of the rebellion is like the frenzy of the witchcraft. Enough said. Grant that all rebellion is hellish, even when carried out by the Boston Saints. Accept for the sake of argument even Peter Oliver's strained identification of revolution as a species of witchcraft.[52] Still, the war was now over: it could not by act of moral will be undone; and its validity could not be judged by the degree of violence that went into it, since (*ex hypoth-eosi*) *all* revolution has its hellish side.

And so, what final note to stress? Surely not the providential; the usefulness of that handsome a priori had already been severely impugned. And surely not, in a "Legend," the legalistic or constitutional. The Hawthorne who expressly enunciated as few political "beliefs" as religious ones held fast to the justifiability of the American Revolution; but he has no wish to argue about Esther Dudley's key. What remained, quite simply, and what his peculiar form of fiction was perfectly equipped to approach, was the question of gain and loss.

This pragmatic question continued vital, for although the War of Independence was over, the American Revolution was still going on, especially in contemporary rhetoric. If the locus of the essential battle was indeed, as John Adams suggested, "in the minds and hearts of the people," then the affair had no more ended in the early 1780's than it had begun in the mid-1760's. And so as the first three "Legends" (whatever their operative chronology) look back to the proto-Revolutionary attitudes of Puritans which caused or perhaps *were* independence, the last story points to the continuing problem of the values the American Revolution could or should be made to justify. The first three "Legends" worry the view of American history ultimately sanctified by Bancroft—that the entire Puritan past was pregnant, at least typologically, with that glorious liberty which was the predestined End of Man. The final one then turns directly against the purely futuristic philosophy of the *Democratic Review,* which seemed to Hawthorne even more destructive of a valid regard for the integrity of the past.

To tell the story of "Old Esther Dudley" was, quite simply, to take up a significant part of her opposition to Hancock once again. To affirm her values was to affirm what O'Sullivan had tried to slander as "that specious sophistry . . . by which old evils struggle to perpetuate themselves." To construct a story so as to win a more profound sympathy for Esther Dudley than for Hancock was to deny that the "gigantic boldness" of the American Revolution set mankind free, once and for all, for the "onward march" of improvement; it was to deny that "the eye of man looks [so] naturally forward" that he is almost certain "to stumble and stray if he turn his face backward"; and it was to deny that Americans have interest "in the scenes of antiquity, only as lessons of avoidance of nearly all their examples." It was to try to ensure that, in the minds and hearts of a people with a genuinely revolutionary heritage, a "contagion of liberty" might not spell the death of the past.[53]

As one assessed the problem in the 1830's, the "loss" of the Revolution seemed precisely the loss of the conservative point of view. The intellectual defeat of the Tories had been utter and abject. And now the fatuous and jejeune sound of a rhetoric of projective futurism suggested that the "philosophical" (including the literary) loss might yet overbalance the perfectly undeniable political and social gains. In point of philosophical fact, "the Tories' organic conservatism . . . failed to reappear in America after the Revolution."[54] And to Hawthorne this fact seemed serious indeed.

Hawthorne was perfectly aware that a mindless perpetuation of a mythic past may have crippling political and social consequences. He thoroughly understood what O'Sullivan meant by warning that the evils of the past tend to perpetuate themselves by means of a sophistical appeal to the "wisdom of the forefathers"; and he did not need the recent historian and critic J. H. Plumb to tell him that the first duty of history *as history* is to criticize the popular or political use of the storied or legendary past as "sanction" or as "destiny." Hawthorne's credentials as critic are established beyond cavil not only by his perfectly lucid revelation in "The Gray Champion," "Endicott," and the first three "Legends" that the tendency of American Puritanism is less clearly liberal-democratic than it is simply revolutionary, and that even this tendency is more intelligible as the result of a potentially paranoic overbelief than (as Bancroft concluded) of Divine Decree; they are also established by the subtle implications of "Old Esther Dudley" itself—where the figural identity of Hancock and the *Democratic Review* suggests that even America's *pure* futurists need to capture *one* past event (the Revolution) as sanction. But the main impulse of "Old Esther Dudley" is not critical; rather it is frankly mythic. Indeed the strength of its tendency toward mystification reveals Hawthorne's belief that the loss of the sense of the past might be a more serious danger than any uncritical misuse.[55]

If we wish, we can say that the history of Hawthorne's "Legends" is three parts critical and one part mythic. But such a literary calculus does not allow for the strong effect produced by the anticlimactic suggestion of "Old Esther Dudley"; that, psychologically considered, America's Revolution might yet become entirely too successful; that in the minds and hearts of the American people a significant portion of their historic experience might entirely die. And so "Old Esther Dudley" seems, above all else, to affirm the conservative habits of reverence for the past and respect for continuity, simply and as such.

At the same time we should resist the temptation to conclude that the affirmative implications of Hawthorne's position as "modern Tory" are as full of "mystery" as those of his more political predecessors. To be sure, "Old Esther Dudley" has evoked an attitude of receptivity toward the past without at the same time supplying an unambiguous political doctrine or a "theory of history"; it has raised some important questions which it does not solve. And hearing our narrator conclude his performance by allegorizing the "dying gleam" of a lamp as the vanishing of the "glory of the ancient system . . . from the Province House" (302), we may find ourselves wondering if Hawthorne is not perhaps escaping too easily. Sensing the ease with which the "knell of the Past" from the clock of the Old South transports this Hawthornean persona into a region where, undisturbed at last by stagecoaches, or paperboys, or rattling spoons, he and his tavern-haunting companions can babble "about the dreams of the past," we may find ourselves dissatisfied with just one more image of this too-easy response. Has Hawthorne adequately distinguished, we may find ourselves demanding, between the values of his narrator and those we are supposed to abstract from the commitment and career of "Old Esther Dudley"?

Perhaps not. But before we decide that Hawthorne is merely one of those whom Emerson identified as "imaginative persons in this country" to whom a certain "fantastic" loyalty to old things "may be pardoned," we should recall what we have learned about that same Old South Church—thanks to Hawthorne's shrewd political and historical intelligence, and *in spite of* our narrator. And we should recall that Hawthorne's Hancock-figure brilliantly anticipates Emerson's own rebuke of the pure Revolutionary: "The past has baked your loaf, and in the strength of its bread you would break up the oven."[56] Nor should we forget that the "unanswered" questions are something like ultimate ones: what *is* the truly human use of historical understanding? Or, just less absolutely, what are the true claims of the conservative impulse as against the revolutionary? An appeal to relevant moments in "Old News," or "A Bell's Biography," or even *Grandfather's Chair* might help us give greater clarity to the moral Toryism suggested by "Old Esther Dudley." Here, however, it is enough to suggest one theme for the conclusions of this volume: that Hawthorne, Jacksonian Democrat that he undeniably was, nevertheless remained at least as committed as Irving and Longfellow to the proposition that those "historical associations" which render "more valuable the things that have been long established" are nothing less than a kind of "grace."[57]

✂ PROBLEMATIC CONCLUSIONS ✄
"ON THE COUCH" AND IN THE WORLD

IN ONE FAIRLY IMPORTANT SENSE, a study of the present sort—
lengthy, detailed, empirical—really permits no "conclusions" beyond
those particular interpretative hypotheses already proposed and tested. Each
of the tales we have examined adumbrates its own thematic considerations,
even as it discovers the clues and disposes the evidences proper to its own
invention: as history is plural, so Hawthorne's fictions are various. Thus any
moral or psychological ideal general enough to organize all of Hawthorne's
assembled particulars threatens to become entirely nominal in the formulation and positively embarrassing in the argumentative insistence. And any
"theory of history" that would seek to impose a cosmic teleology on the
provincial details of his local investigations tends not only to misidentify at
last the nature of his own literary project but also to repeat, at some ultimate, "literary" level of abstraction, the very "theology" he tried so hard to
evade and even to neutralize.[1]

Evidently Hawthorne "believed in" the power of the past; arguably, he
even felt "trapped" by it. That, in all its locality, was the really real, against
which all possible futures (including the fantasy of some perfect, millennial
one) figured as merely ideal.[2] And even his own present, when he should get
around to considering the nature of its own transitory validity, would seem
most potent as an incipient past: the individual might constitute himself by
recalling an experience whose *present* form he never had been quite competent to grasp; and a people might look back on a formative influence.
Thoreau (and behind him Emerson) might seek to valorize the active and
original present of "consciousness"; but for Hawthorne—at once more
conservative and more modern—"reflection" was the distinctively human
operation, and history was the most vital and humanizing of its "aids." And
that was why it was too important to be left to antiquarians or ideologues.[3]

But as some such propositions seem everywhere implied by the various
"readings" already proposed, it were surrogation (as well as idealism) to

press them here; especially as all summations tend to rationalize. Perhaps it will be more useful, and even somehow more frank, to consider some of the leading reasons why a writer whose major project is so obviously oriented toward the past has yet fallen so largely out of the domain of historical criticism; to reason away these reasons if we can; and thus to make the premise of "moral history" stand for somewhat more than the aggregate of its own interpretive details. Not for everything, to be sure, for Hawthorne's early experiments were indeed various; but for more than is usually credited. For more, certainly, than a congenial displacement of psychological themes into some convenient past.

1

Obviously our survey of Hawthorne's "early tales" has been as partial and selective in matter as it has been overcommitted in method. Not only have historical readings been everywhere treated with privilege, but a very great deal of competing (and possibly contradictory) evidence has been left out. That is to say, roughly two-thirds of the seventy-odd tales and sketches Hawthorne succeeded in publishing between 1830 and 1838 have not been taken into significant interpretative account; and obviously these would have to count for much in any *fully* empirical account of the methods and themes which variously occupied Hawthorne, and possibly even competed for primacy, in that fascinating but still murky "Salem" period of his career.[4] What if it should turn out that for every Goodman Brown there were two Old Maids in a Winding Sheet?

Actually, of course, and fortunately for Hawthorne's overall reputation, the situation is far more complicated than any such two-to-one formula can possibly suggest. On the one hand, defensively, there probably are a fair number of other tales which will yield to the same sorts of historical-allusive investigation demonstrated here. The two tales of the Shakers would be only the most obvious examples: though both are located in the near-present, both lie along one of the most prominent lines of "moral history" we have been tracing; in Hawthorne's career, and just possibly in literal fact, the Shakers provide a link between the life-denying idealism of Puritan (and Quaker) theology and the weird assortment of apocalyptic expectations he would anatomize in the 1840's.[5] Similarly, though a little less drastically, certain "local" tales like "The Ambitious Guest" and "The Great Carbuncle" seem to turn on attitudes and even on specific references that are distinctively New Englandish.[6] Further back in time, and more conventionally therefore, "The Duston Family," "A Bell's Biography," and "The Prophetic Pictures" all reveal clear evidences of Hawthorne's persistent dialogue with the sources of American moral culture, and with its rejected alternatives as well.[7] And most generally—as we begin to realize that, for Hawthorne, "the historical" (as a critical motive) and "the gothic" (as an available style) were never truly opposing categories—even tales like "The Wedding-Knell," "Peter Goldthwaite's Treasure," and "John Inglefield's Thanksgiving" may also make themselves most intelligible within some framework of historical reference.[8]

The esthetic yield of all this might well be mixed, as the best of the historical tales have (very probably) already been so identified. And the raw count would (in all likelihood) still be against their total in the early canon. But when we begin to realize that what balances them, on the other, more open hand, is not some formal or thematic monolith, but in fact a wide variety of genres, tones, and styles, the historical series epitomized in this study may well begin to bulk as large as it has always loomed significant. For though it has been possible to fold "Wakefield," "Fancy's Show Box," and "Dr. Heidegger's Experiment" into a pseudo-historical recipe for "the Hawthornesque," no one (I think) should want to whip up a counterformula out of ingredients mixed equally from "Sir William Pepperell," "Little Annie's Ramble," "A Rill from the Town Pump," "The Toll-Gatherer's Day," "Mrs. Bullfrog," and "The Lily's Quest."[9]

In the end, however, the problem is not really statistical: neither popular images nor professional structures can be thought to arise in quite that way. Nor could any mere counting undo the conclusion that "Young Goodman Brown" really is all about the implications of the Puritanic problem of "specter evidence"; and no weight of comparative-canonic (or other "extrinsic") probability can nullify the discovery that "The Minister's Black Veil" quite evidently means to evoke an entirely historical understanding of "sin and self." It may be difficult to imagine how these massively objective and ruthlessly critical tales *could* have been written by the man who indulged himself in "Sights from a Steeple" or projected himself as "Monsieur de Miroir." But as the problem is one of fact and not of possibility, we must evidently learn to deal with it the best way we can, even if this threatens to involve us (once again) in the weary premise of the "two Hawthornes."[10]

Clearly *some* problem really does remain. For psychological critics (and now, more radically, structuralist critics as well) seem always able to absorb the latest report from the historical provinces with perfect equanimity, adjusting a detail here and there, but leaving the generalized and ever-familiar portrait of Hawthorne as "psychological romancer" pretty much untouched. What we need to consider, then—unless we wish to accuse the majority of our professional colleagues of bad faith—is what really happens when we alter the focus, enlarging both the biographical and the critical field. Generalizations are always attractive, and apparently certain comparisons *demand* to be made. What *then* happens to our own bright image of Hawthorne as "moral historian"?

Suppose we concede that, after all, Goodman Brown's is indeed a noticeably "Haunted Mind"; or that it is scarcely an irresponsible flight of fancy to regard him as a sort of Puritanic "Wakefield," existential "outcast" in spite of his perfectly fixed local habitation. Or, less metaphorically, suppose we grant that the account of Hooper's unfortunate alienation is not to be separated from a whole cycle of "moralized fictions" which, characteristically but without entire conviction, "celebrate the common highway of life and deplore all attempts to step aside from it"; that despite an apparent separation by historic generations, he really is a close fictional relative of David Swan, Sylph Etherege, and Edward Fane. Or again, most generally, suppose we pause to observe that both of our most redundantly historical tales (and others besides) are *also* prime examples of "Hawthorne's Dreams."[11] How, finally, can we think to divorce them from the uneasy Romantic sensibility which preferred to spend its own "Sunday at Home"; or which, somewhat more daringly, enjoyed making "Night Sketches Beneath an Umbrella"; or which, at its own self-inhibiting limit, always found its own "Devil in Manuscript"?

All of which is really to raise the enduring objection of a tradition in Hawthorne criticism which is at once both venerable and *au courant:* on what ground of theory or observation can one responsibly oppose the Jamesean dictum that, whatever may seem to be Hawthorne's specific literary "given," the "really fine thing" about him is his care for "the deeper psychology"? If even the crudest of our available psychologies *can* always subsume the very most elaborate of our historicisms, why not simply *let* it? Why resist the conclusion that, in the end, it is simply the timeless "haunting" in Hawthorne which truly matters?

A complete answer to this complex but really single question would almost certainly involve an extended (and itself historical) analysis of our own "reader expectations," as these are now so fully "psychologistic" (or at least Jamesean) in kind: why *do* we regularly prefer, as handmaiden to literary interpretation, those disciplines which structure and generalize as opposed to the ones which elaborate and specify? And surely it would involve a fuller grasp of the exact workings of Hawthorne's "non-historical" tales than can be provided here, in conclusion, by an interpreter with the wrong biases. But the outline of a partial answer, already anticipated in the previous analyses, deserves to be stated very simply: Hawthorne's best tales keep turning out to be those which do involve us in history; a fair number of these, like "The May-Pole" or the various "Legends of the Province House," do not

lend themselves to psychological analysis at all; and even those which obviously do are not evidently improved by the full and perfect translation into
that idiom.

Though simple, the point is worth emphasizing. In plain defiance of our
prevailing assumptions, and in formal affront to our most available categories, Hawthorne's characters are most credible and interesting when they
have been conceived in organic relation to their appropriate historical world;
his themes are most vital—least susceptible to nominal reduction, least productive of post-structuralist ennui—when they are won by historical dialectic rather than propounded as psychic truism. Nor, unless one insists on
confounding Roy Harvey Pearce with Fredric Jameson, does one need to
be a "Marxist" to notice this. It is simply that the psychic experiences of
Goodman Brown and Parson Hooper, not to mention Tobias Pearson,
Reuben Bourne, and Robin Molineux, are more plausibly motivated and indeed more completely intelligible when understood as representatives of
"the mind" haunted by assumptions or grappling with events that are recognizably historical. This, I take it, is what Pearce has meant by suggesting
that we take Hawthorne's characters off our couch and restore them each to
his own world. And this restoration is scarcely the aim of any form of psychostructural conflation.[12]

To be sure, some least common denominator is always there, identifying
characters from various centuries under a single analytic term, identifying
them too with characters who seem to float outside time altogether. But
whether the term is from Freud or Dugald Stewart, it always manages to
leave us with the least. We can call that least "the lowest," insisting that it is
therefore "the deepest"; but we always end up with less than what Hawthorne at his best has studied and plotted to give us. Indeed the essence we
abstract often seems hostile to the existence we first observed. Pearson,
Brown, Bourne, Molineux, and Hooper come to us each from a different
phase of our own *quite* peculiar past; specific allusions insist in fact that we
place each one in his own provincial decade.[13] We murder to conflate. And
never more so than when we choose, in anything more than a passing structuralist aside, to merge all or any one with the flitting image of minor-Romantic sensibility—now idly, now earnestly—dramatizing the pleasures of
cultivated imagination, or confronting the fear of encroaching solipsism.
That too is Hawthorne, in one of his several moods. But it is not the
Hawthorne who worked close-in to the problem of available pre-conception
versus actual experience; and, in his early phase at least, more or less continuously with the historic record of American moral assumptions.

"The Haunted Mind" thus remains a perfect epitome only so long as our
own categorical choices insist that it is. Perhaps it may be fairly thought to

give us the primal dream of a writer whose works do involve us everywhere in the language, imagery, and machinery of dreaming. But even if so, it self-consciously declines to give us precisely those things we find of interest in the majority of tales we most value. Better they should transcend it than it reduce them. For if it is an essence, it yet forbids most real existence. And this of its own generic nature.

Certainly it gives us a mind we readily recognize—one which, though it has just fallen *out* of sleep, evokes our "hypnagogic" expectations nevertheless.[14] Yet its discoveries are not at all transcendental or "Poe-esque." It may feel itself somehow suspended between what it can term "yesterday" and "tomorrow"; and it may wish for an extension of its atemporal fantasy into some territory neutral enough to defy time and free the imagination from its customary, too dismally lawful train of associations. But, as if to suggest that Coleridge and Plato are of no avail against the Scots and the Stagyrite, the tomb of fancy releases only the decaying images of personal memory. And these so generalized (as Sorrow, Hope, and Fatality) that we must agree to understand without really recognizing. Even the specter of "Remorse" offers us nothing specific enough to really grasp, requiring another, kindred but more "theological" sketch for its own show-box elaboration. And that, as it turns out, from the casuistical speculations of Jeremy Taylor and John Cotton.[15]

What "The Haunted Mind" offers, then, in almost literal terms, is the quite special problem of Hawthorne (or some narrative surrogate) "on the couch." And the revelations are hardly surprising: freed of all opposing objectivity (except perhaps a "spire" and a "firmament" on the other side of a frosted pane of glass), the "mind" in question merely enacts an altogether predictable sequence of abstract possibilities. Yesterday these might have been elaborated and arranged according to the known laws of plot, or placed in some relation to the moral or political expectations of an audience; and tomorrow—well, tomorrow is only another potential yesterday. For "now" all the mind can do, to stay its fearful flight from mortality, is to fantasize an ideal female "other" and pray that something called "the soul" may yet find a home elsewhere. If this dream vision manages to remind us at all of Robin Molineux's famous moment of moonlit suspense, or of Goodman Brown's starless suspension, it can only be for a brief, pre-interpretative moment. For the train of figures which erupts into Robin's dream really does violate it from the outside, and Brown must return to the faithful wife and community his vision has so weirdly transformed. Leaving us to suspect that *all* attempts to essentialize "Hawthorne's psychological themes" are likelier to produce parody than epitome.[16]

Or perhaps it will yet appear that Hawthorne's own intentions are themselves parodic, throughout "The Haunted Mind." Possibly his *evident* reliance on the embattled Scottish model of association is merely his way of suggesting that one's fictions are always dealing with *some* mind, never *the* mind.[17] Such a discovery would move this sketch a good deal closer to something we might call "history," but still a significant distinction would seem required. For a tale which deconstructs some modish mentalism is quite different from one in which a character is baffled by the relation between his assumptions and his experience. Leaving Hawthorne still to dream the dreams of the antinomian on the scaffold, the antique lady in the cent shop, and the mad poet at the pig farm.

Nor do any of Hawthorne's other most *purely* psychological fictions manage to alter this figure—of a specialized, and quite probably parodic, attempt to create the portrait of a mind too fine to suffer more than a momentary violation by any reality beyond itself. The "Night Sketches" may be, as delicately read by Hyatt Waggoner, the personally considered and generically controlled affirmation of a man who, though sufficiently "acquainted with the night," was yet determined to stay within the small circle of illumination available.[18] Or it may be, more nearly, a sensitive and fairly forgiving parody of some not-quite-dark Romantic, some Irving before Irving. But for the purposes of the present argument it scarcely matters, for the narrator is safe in a way Hawthorne's historical characters never are.

Whatever "fearful urgencies" may seem to dissuade Hawthorne's decidedly domestic adventurer from taking his midnight plunge into elements less clement than those surrounding the "fireside" of his study, he seems to know, from repeated experiment, that he will positively enjoy the wind and the rain without; they may not be his most *natural* element, but what else to do when the fancy has gone dry or stale? And if he does encounter any "dim terrors" more metaphysical than the mud-puddle he calls a "Slough of Despond," his pious sentiments, which he keeps closer about him than his shaggy overcoat, seem perfectly proof against them. "Luckless lovers" may slip on a remnant of ice and find themselves (more in literary melodrama than in personal bathos) "precipitated into a confluence of swollen floods," but we know our strolling artist is far too self-possessed ever to lose his own balance. Nor, like the Coverdale he altogether predicts, will he lift a finger to help: "Were it in my nature to be other than a looker-on in life, I would attempt your rescue. Since that may not be, I vow, should you be drowned, to weave such a pathetic story as shall call forth tears enough to drown you both anew"(430).[19] On he goes, therefore, catching a gleam or absorbing a shadow from all he observes. On him, too, the dark patches fall. Or so he would convince us.

Not that his is an "altogether chameleon spirit, with no hue of its own": he *will* assert his own self, plunging "onward, still onward into the night." But he chooses not to follow some ultimate stranger out of the light and into the "unknown gloom." Nor does he speak to him, any more than some unspoken vow or convention could permit converse with the "drowning" lovers. As the scene is really somehow all "mental," so it would be quite literally insane to address a figment of one's own fantasy.

In fact no one really "speaks" in this extraordinarily self-enclosed exercise of the vagrant fancy. The narrator has seemed to move from the faraway of his travel books to the near-at-hand of his own New England town, but he might as well be dreaming still. An ancient mariner has seemed to ask "How fare ye, brother?" (429)—as if in hearty recognition of the condition which is as common as it is elemental. But even this single brief quote, rippling the surface of a fiction so placid not even a typhoon could really disturb it, is but the projection of an all-disposing narrator determined to have everything his own psychic (and not *too* gloomy) way. He passes, observes, moralizes the darkness of "Death and Sorrow" into his own golden meaning, and returns "to that same fireside" he whimsically left; mildly dubious about the shape of affairs under the (hidden) moon, but content on the whole to "bear the lamp of Faith" alone. Goodman Brown should be so blessed. Even the Wives of the Dead had to face each other.

The problem, of course, is that there is an obvious *generic* difference between this and those other, less predictable, more fully appointed "night sketches." It would be grotesque, therefore, to flog this one for failing to deliver what it cannot on premise have. But then that is also somehow the main point: fictions in which an authorial intelligence ventures forth to deploy itself are widely different from—and provide a very poor norm for—ones in which a full-fledged character has to mix it up with other full-fledged characters who dare to talk back. The present sketch will appear better or worse, I think, as we ascribe more or less irony to the invention and disposition of its narrative persona: better Charles Lamb should bear this lamp than Hawthorne, wherever his own nightly excursions happen to have taken him. But no construction of our own can make it shed more than the wannest of lights on explorations which, though metaphorical, happen also to have been historical.[20]

Not even the solipsistic fascination of "Wakefield" can provide us with the existential metaphor we essentially seek; though it clearly presents us with a more complex and in a sense "worldly" case, it also belongs essentially to the genre or syndrome of dissociated mentality.[21] Subject though he is to the common-sense criticism of the narrator (rather than propounding his fantasies in his own nameless voice), and liable as he remains to objectification in the eyes of the wife he might at any moment chance to meet, Wakefield yet floats free of all relationality; and as his one real assertion of "individuality" seems more like whimsy than moral choice, he strikes us as a mind entirely without assumptions. Like a Bartleby without courage or conviction, or a Rip Van Winkle without plausible motive to drift away, he precipitates the story of a character as devoid of "character" as he is bereft of social function.[22]

Appearing to have no thoughts except those touching the systematic maintenance of an elongated "whim-wham," he asks no questions of his existence and answers none about ours—except, perhaps, what it would be like if trivial subjectivity were infinite. A "morbid vanity," surely. He can move about and observe all of "busy and selfish London" (God's plenty of selfish business, surely), but no one can recognize his own precise way of being. The narrator asserts that he falls into an entirely "new system," but we see nothing of this. He neither eats ginger nuts nor yet deals apples. And as Hawthorne will elsewhere suggest that "nothing wearies the soul more than an attempt to comprehend" a character who seems to be "on the outside of everything,"[23] perhaps we are dealing with a less impressive moral than the narrator's climactic capitalization would imply. Possibly Wakefield is more silly than tragically inevitable. We can easily imagine Goodman Brown greeting him not as a Brother Outcast but only as a very small man gone unaccountably wrong: once there were *reasons* to explore the limits of human relation.

We probably make some advance in our understanding of the career of Wakefield if we think to "modernize" him—either philosophically, as some minimum example of subjective alienation, or sociologically, as a slender figure of urban anomie.[24] But as it is scarcely plausible to consider Hawthorne's other, more famous exempla in precisely these ways, we merely emphasize his own specific difference to do so. Someone might yet think to connect him with the historic Wakefield who, from the chilly bosom of the Church of British Unitarianism in the eighteenth century, declared against the efficacy of all "social praying"; perhaps this is why our own Wakefield's one mid-course encounter with his wife occurs outside a church, and why she carries "a prayer book in her hand."[25] But, again, this premise leads us not downward into psychic essence, or outward into categorical generalization, but only somehow backwards, into the lost (and repented) world of Roger Williams, whose story has already been more appropriately told elsewhere.

It seems best, therefore, to leave Wakefield exactly where he seems to be: nowhere. And to define his tale precisely as our instincts first suggest, as the most intriguing of those "haunted" sketches which worry the proposition that alienation may somehow be its own excuse for being. Agreeing perhaps, that in Hawthorne's view all men are potentially Wakefields, and that some of his historical characters, however they begin, actually end up in pretty much Wakefield's own condition, we must also notice that elsewhere the starting point has seemed more intensely to matter. And that even if "nothing" may be thought, hauntingly, to motivate this condition as power-fully as any stated reason of history, still the more "reasoned" tales are everywhere more credible in conception and more powerful in effect. For alienation is evidently best studied as a function of the reality of the world *from which*. And that distance is as hard to measure in the sketchy world of "Wakefield" as it is in the purely neutral one of "The Haunted Mind" and "Night Sketches."

At one level, therefore, the historicist argument plainly suggests that ob-vious generic differences resist and threaten to impoverish all but the most carefully formulated (and avowedly anti-semantic) attempts to bracket the world and collapse "the Hawthornesque" into a psychological essence. Far from essentializing the peculiar psychologies of the historical tales, freeing them up for categorical abstraction, the "haunted" sketches actually high-light their own problematic status by calling into question the notion of art as an exploration of the psychic-as-such. As their subject seems to vanish the moment it comes into view, they actually throw us back on "the historical" as the only suitable model of mental completion. Far from providing the terms that everywhere apply, they more nearly expose the emptiness of their own.

Nor do these sketches provide any but the most treacherous of metaphors for the problem of Hawthorne's own "self" in relation to his most serious project of fiction, "Alice Doane's Appeal" remaining the best early example we have of that. The "Oberon" pieces appear to be thoroughly ironic about the "Romantic" possibility of art as self-expression, even as Hawthorne's later prefatorial remarks suggest they ought to be. And the playful conceit of "Monsieur du Miroir" becomes serious only when we observe that it de-liberately discredits itself as a model of full or present self-possession.[26] Epistemologically as well as morally, it turns out, Hawthorne has made self-seeking appear everywhere an enterprise of diminishing returns.

In spite of our psychobiographical earnestness, "The Devil in Manu-script" actually reads off best as comedy, funnier in its way than the disaster of the Story Teller in "Mr. Higginbotham's Catastrophe." Whatever mo-tives of personal desperation may have once led Hawthorne to burn some of his early tales, it requires an extreme commitment to the literal not to recog-nize the artistic distance Hawthorne achieves in this remarkable little exer-cise in self-exorcism.[27] Oberon's tone is everywhere melodramatic to the point of mania; his critical language is as mawkish as his literary self-conceit is extreme. And the narrator—who sounds a lot like Horatio Bridge, but who also figures as the artist's only really sane self—actually gets much the best of the literary debate he patiently transcribes: surely there is some ordi-nary value in those fiendish tales; and certainly the writing was not all a hellish suffering. But the haunted writer, more firmly established in his romantic clichés than even the disillusioned poet of "The Canterbury Pilgrims," *will* not be denied his mad transfiguration.

So he burns his tales, starting a real-life conflagration no mere rill from the town pump can extinguish, and concludes with a frenzy of exultation that utterly unmasks the strategy of determined self-irony: "Huzza! Huzza! My brain has set the town on fire. Huzza!" No doubt Bridge could only be encouraged: his fame-seeking friend may have suffered serious personal disappointments, but he could still make fun of the problem; he may have betrayed a marked tendency to self-involvement, but he could still write fiction. And probably it were risky for our own criticism to press much closer in. The personal plot is too thick, the literary evidences too carefully managed.[28]

Even an extraordinarily suggestive sketch like "Sunday at Home" proves far more oblique than first appears, resisting where it seems to encourage psychobiographical epitome. Surely, we tend to imagine, here is "the real Hawthorne," spending his introspective Sundays (as all his other days) "behind the curtain" of a window which, though now open to the light of common day, can yet admit only those evidences which the mind of the artist is well prepared by reverie to manipulate. And this in spite of the *moral* knowledge, here duly inscribed, and everywhere else thematically implied, that it were well to take the risk of going out to mix with the multitude, even with one so relatively unmixed as may appear at a Congregational church on a New England Sabbath. The action were the prayer, whatever partial or misguided words should fall from the lips of the reverent but unlovely local preacher. The hymn, the organ, and the bell would comprehend all personal differences in common spiritual aspiration, even as the sunshine will bless all honest purposes under heaven. "Oh [he] ought to have gone."[29] To hang back were, essentially, "Digby-ism."

But alas—we think to interpret—he *cannot* go forth. Though his "inner man goes constantly to church," he cannot bear congregation, any more than could, essentially, the Reverend Mr. Hooper. Still less can he bear dismissal, though "the Sabbath eve is the eve of love." Knowing too well his unchangeable place, the psychological artist is doomed to the mere reading of "printed sermons"; and to these only as they start some "train of thought" as can be allegorized as "those colleague pastors," his own "Mind and Heart." How well he knew himself—how puritanically well—in spite of the coyness of his continental image in the *miroir*. In broad daylight he must whistle in the dark: at midnight he "shall glance aside and shudder."[30] Now, surely, we know the man who wrote "The Minister's Black Veil."

Unless perhaps we should chance to notice a poem which "Hawthorne as Editor" thought to include in the *American Magazine of Useful and Enter-*

taining Knowledge for May 1836. Just there, we can observe, appears to have originated this "Hawthornesque" conceit of cheerful Sabbath bells falling oddly on the ear

> Of the contemplant, solitary man
> Whom thoughts abstruse or high have chanced to lure
> Forth from the walks of men, revolving oft,
> And oft again, hard matter, which eludes
> And baffles his pursuit[.]

Suddenly we realize that, whatever may be the complex truth of the obscure biographical case, we are *also* dealing with an already standard Romantic literary situation; that whatever else may be true of "Sunday at Home" it too is clearly a twice-told tale. The diction is the diction of prose, as the setting is that of the American sketcher; but the argument is the invention of Charles Lamb. And suddenly our confident psychologism is balked at its very "source."[31]

Suddenly we remember not only the inherent arrogance of the psychoanalytic project, but even Hawthorne's own most patient "explanation" of himself to Sophia: some "involuntary reserve" has given such an "objectivity" to his writings that people surely mistake to imagine he pours himself out in those writings; he tells what is "common to human nature, not what is peculiar" to himself. Thus where we suppose we have recognized his psyche as such, the fact may be that he has well succeeded in pre-viewing our own assumptions.[32] In this case the problem would be that "we" understand the Romantic alienation of Charles Lamb, as a sort of half-way Byronism, altogether too well. Ourselves, too, "thought-sick and tired / Of controversy, where no end appears," we too easily grasp the situation and too readily forgive the attitudes of "the lonely man" who (in Lamb's perfectly predictive formula) *"Half* wished for society again" (my italics). Somebody evidently feels satisfied to learn that the "relenting soul" of this artist-scholar still "Yearns after all the joys of social life, / And softens with the love of human kind"; but perhaps we are not supposed to be. Possibly Hawthorne's prosy translation—which elaborates without really explaining anything—exists to suggest that Lamb's half-hearty conclusion only half covers the case. Why not *go?*

Yet to propose that "Sunday at Home" was conceived in irony and dedicated to the proposition that all Romantics are more equal is not to deny its biographical relevance altogether. It is merely to recommend a certain critical caution. As the sketch reveals attitudes which are widely shared rather than intimately personal, it may actually serve us best as a reminder of all that it is not telling; of all that we, perhaps, should yet like to know, in spite of Hawthorne's own systematic reticence.

Would the psychobiographer be *so* badly advised, for example, to consider precisely what church it was, propositionally speaking, that Hawthorne declined to attend after his return from Bowdoin to Salem? Or exactly what "printed sermons" he seems most likely to have read, in lieu of presenting himself to the influence of the spoken word? Sooner or later we really will have to consider just how, in his particular case, the dispute between the "Heart" of Puritan Piety and the "Mind" of Enlightenment Criticism may be imagined to have arranged itself. For the assembled evidence of life and works does not suggest a temperament so modern or so secular as to render religion as such entirely beside the point; some standard seems everywhere implied, though its embodiment seems nowhere to be observed. Or if Hawthorne himself merely disbelieves in "social praying," then more than one minor sketch is trickier than anyone has yet imagined; for then "bad faith" would replace "irony" as the key to an entire career. He *ought* to have gone.

All the available evidence suggests that the passing of "the New England Theology" was indeed a complicated and painful process, that Old-Light Puritanism could evolve slowly (and not quite satisfactorily) into various sorts of "Liberal Christianity," but that the whole thing could scarcely lapse, all at once, into Modernism, Symbolism, Psychologism, or any sort of more or less strenuous Romantic religion of the Self. The passage of so complex an historic ideology into Hawthorne's art may have been, as James suggested, "exquisite"; but only the dogmatism of categorical transcendence will assert that such transactions are ever perfect. Psychology will reduce religion only if we insist that it must. And art can scarcely subsume it without leaving a single doctrinal trace. Yet unless we rest satisfied with the Melvillean supposition of some temperamental Calvinist residuum, the entire transaction remains exactly as mysterious as James once indicated— subtle, efficacious, and "best known to [Hawthorne] himself."[33]

Nor can mere *literary* history quite force the issue: twice-told tales invite the inconclusions of irony, but irony never tells us more than what cannot possibly be the case. Trivial affirmations occur, to be sure, especially in tales we seldom read and have little reason to value. But the power is in the denials, in a series of tales founded in history and connected by propositions we recognize but did not ourselves invent. Clearly this state of affairs will bear the closest biographical scrutiny. Meanwhile, however, it remains a little naive to assume that a single psychic intention will adequately represent the entire Hawthorne premise or project.

2

The best evidence of Hawthorne's own perception of his (precarious) status as artist-in-the-world may yet be derived, cautiously and indirectly, from the design of his "Story Teller" project, so far as we are indeed able (imperfectly) to reconstruct it. More importantly, perhaps, that third of Hawthorne's early attempts to assemble a fully organic collection of tales may also provide our most credible metaphor of significant literary intention in Hawthorne's early phase. It may even afford us our one most legitimate opportunity to consider how Hawthorne might have presented himself to posterity if certain merely bibliographical conditions of his career had been otherwise.

Of course the argument is beset with difficulties, not the least of which is that in one sense it runs contrary to fact. For in the end it was the *Twice-told Tales* which Hawthorne *did* succeed in publishing as a literary unit; and that according to some design which probably seemed significant enough at the time, and which some critics can even now find ways to praise.[34] Thus, as "The Story Teller" has an only slightly more secure bibliographical foundation than our own "collection" of "Tales of the Puritans," the Melvillean caveat remains cogent: "The might-have-been is but boggy ground to build on." And even if we could perfectly succeed in reconstructing this most complex of Hawthorne's early projects, it would remain, for our present purposes, a mere metaphor of unified literary design. As such it could scarcely comprehend everything of value, any more than the collection itself can be imagined as an *omnium gatherum* somehow transfigured to literary perfection. The part never will quite stand for the whole.[35]

Yet the thought remains worth thinking, despite these significant objections. For if Hawthorne did eventually settle for a collection which represents his widest spectrum of literary effects—even as it noticeably omits some of his most intense colorations—it is also true that he had earlier tried his best to offer something quite different: something geometrically more complex in structure; something which in fact sought to define the terms of his most pervasive literary problem even as it embodied a fair sampling of the available solution. And it remains significant that he was deeply disappointed by his failure to represent himself in this sufficiently subtle way,[36] with the result that there is something half-hearted (if not positively dimwitted) about much that gets written into the *Twice-told Tales.*

An author who seems to know, intuitively, that he will surely perish by failing to publish will undoubtedly seek ways to accommodate the audience he actually addresses, or the publishers he has in fact to satisfy. No doubt the case of *Fanshawe* versus the "Seven Tales" had already provided the necessary if gloomy "professional" lesson. Thus it is scarcely surprising to discover that, after the dismantling of "The Story Teller," a somewhat dispirited Hawthorne found the means to keep the pot boiling; or that the tales so produced often read like parodies of the earlier work, the firmly achieved historical problematics degenerating into thematic doggerel.[37] Nor should it be very startling that he did, in the end, agree to prepare a miscellany like the *Twice-told Tales,* even as he went to work on a masterpiece of dramatic narrative like "The Legends of the Province House." The really remarkable fact is that, given the failure of first the "Seven" and then the "Provincial Tales," he should have attempted something so elaborate and risky as "The Story Teller" at all. For it evidently meant to dramatize his peculiar problem of telling tales both "New Englandly" and "slant," even as it actually told a number of just such tales. And thus it remains, despite the tantalizing uncertainty of its exact table of contents, a unique index of authorial strategy.

Accordingly, the altogether ironic spectacle of the provincial writer's splendidly determined but disastrously misdefined literary self-launching—and the cautious consideration of what might follow from that—remains full of sober if oblique instruction. An aspiring author goes forth to meet the world: to experience it; to subdue it, in some manner, by imaginative transformation; but above all, perhaps, to address it, in terms of its own recognition and value. And yet something is painfully wrong from the outset. An emergent persona is trapped in a self-definition which his creator understands as hopelessly reductive. Whether we consider his situation as defined by "The Seven Vagabonds" or (somewhat later) by the various segments of the "Passages from a Relinquished Work," the problem is pretty much the same: despite his references to the noble ancestry of authorship, our "outsetting bard" has clearly introjected, from the provincial world he would address, an entirely debased notion of the social (and even the religious) significance of story-telling.[38] How can he make contact without trivializing? Pandering, even?

In his first incarnation our author is merely a "strolling gentleman," eager to convince a motley tribe of "Vagabonds"—showmen, gypsies, and confidence artists—that he is up to their own level of vocation; that a carefree lad of eighteen, aspiring to become an "itinerant novelist," has as much right as anyone to help divert an anxious populace about to be dismissed from a Methodist camp meeting. And though he wins this first, local battle, for acceptance as the seventh vagabond, he does so more by quoting the invocation to Mirth in "L'Allegro" than by appealing to his chosen "Oriental" precedent. And he still must endure the "sly wink" of the vagrant fortune teller in the group, whom he half-humorously identifies as the Devil, freshly arrived in New England from his jaded career of "wandering up and down upon the earth" (362).[39] The moment is less fraught than a similar one, later, in "Ethan Brand"; and it produces none of the ironic self-apology which Hawthorne lets loose in the exasperated "Custom House." But the attentive critic scarcely needs to read backwards: *somebody* is having "theological" scruples about the literary career.

Quite probably, as one recent commentary has marvelously observed, our proto–story teller well remembers how his entire life and character are predicted and judged by the story of "Youth" in the *New England Primer*, a recent edition of which he has thought to notice in the "circulating library" of the traveling bookseller among the group. Parodying the tale's own Miltonic pre-text, and more than anticipating later works on the subject of "Christian Sobriety" in New England, that "antique" but still "venerable" *Primer* not only prophesies spiritual doom for the lad or maid who opts for the un-Puritanic pursuit of "Sports and Plays," "Joy and Mirth," it even has the Devil promise the appropriate earthly reward for this spiritual sell-out:

> If thou wilt but be rul'd by me,
> An Artist thou shalt quickly be.[40]

No wonder the old fortune teller repeats his "peculiar wink" at our fledgling Story Teller, or that he takes leave of the general company "chuckling within himself as he took the Stamford road" (369). Much work remains, apparently, among the Methodists released from their meeting; but the pact with this particular youth can be considered well concluded. Idleness has been redefined as the literary workshop, and the Devil has a new disciple.

Just less drastic—and potentially more sobering, therefore—is the moment just before this general breakup and leave-taking, itself so abrupt as to have confused the Story Teller's original (and otherwise very able) bibliographer.[41] What disperses the whole traveling tribe, by obvious and structural design, is not any external change of literary plans but the single devastating sentence delivered by the itinerant Methodist preacher, heading "westward" *from* the Stamford revival: "Good people, . . . the camp meeting is broke up" (369). Deprived of the available audience, now, as well as of any purpose plausibly held in common, these more mirthful itinerants are themselves quite "broke up"; and each must take his separate way as before. Nor is that fact without obvious interpretative significance: story-telling may or may not be the Devil's own confidence game, but without a more or less earnest world to address, it utterly loses its reason for being.

But what stings the narrator most, apparently, and what may leave the most lasting impression on our critical memory, is the image reflected back on himself from the solitary Methodist on horseback. As that worthy looks down on this "singular" collection of drifters, the narrator may easily feel a certain condescension in the formal charity of his "good people." Though the preacher smiles, the would-be Story Teller cannot fail to notice the reproving force of "the iron gravity" about the mouth of this intensely committed man; so that we almost expect the entire retinue to vanish in an instant, like so much "fantastic foolery" before the gaze of Endicott. And it is not without sad self-insight that our aspiring author feels himself absorbed—equally with the rest, though only in the projection of his own imagination—"under the general head of Vagabond" (368). Neither he nor the minister may be quite mindful of the classic place in Genesis (where Cain is doomed to be a "fugitive and a vagabond upon the earth"),[42] but clearly *someone* here is feeling that this altogether improbable yet somehow heroic *eighth* itinerant has chosen the only true way of wandering; that this doubtlessly untutored and evidently ungrammatical circuit-rider personally embodies and theologically exhausts the one legitimate possibility of living off the Word. You may tell us, Uncle Robert, what's a writer to do?

A tight spot, surely, but also a nice moment—in an underinterpreted story that makes its own way and deserves to be more widely read than it is. Evidently the secular artist is going to have real problems in a world where a single, sacred text has ousted all others; and where the only appropriate commentary on or extension of that text is taken to be "evangelical." The prospect is almost enough to throw one back on the abstract terrors of "The Haunted Mind," as if for relief. For how *can* the mere Story Teller open intercourse with such a world?[43] And if the tale succeeds in raising more questions than it quite answers, still this seems only proper for a highly dramatized introduction to the problem of literary origins.

Perhaps we are invited to suspect that the seventh vagabond is really the Methodist Itinerant, and not our Story Teller at all; that in the end it is literature and not evangelical preaching which escapes reduction to mere showmanship. The structure, after all, calls for six clear cases of amusing vagrancy, plus one ambiguous seventh; perhaps Revivalism fills up that list better than Imagination. As both the text and our own independent sources of sociological insight permit us to regard a camp meeting as a "great frolic and festival" (358),[44] perhaps we are expected to strike back at once, cutting off a Puritanic problem root and branch: people need diversion in this weary world, and sliding into home for Jesus has seemed to work for some. Wherefore hold your tongue and let the writer notice the general "nonsense of *all* human affairs" (352, my italics). We all wander without aim; we all put on motley and play the fool. The writer merely sets it all down as "God's plenty."

Or perhaps, somewhat more soberly, the titular irony is that there are really *eight* "Vagabonds" here, as there are clearly eight "Itinerants." As the narrator begins "to think that all the vagrants in New England were converging to the camp meeting" (361), so we reflect that, once upon a time, in the age before Whitefield, no one moved: the local congregation and its settled minister defined Reality. But then the Gospel itself went strangely on the road, to outrageous assemblages such as "camp meetings," at outlandish places like "Stamford," dear God. With Truth itself wandering up and down upon the earth, why *not* take a walking tour of Canada or a canal-boat trip to Detroit? Then, since the center will *not* hold, buy your own ticket on the Celestial Rail-road. As Melville's Redburn would find out to his sorrow, it is indeed a moving world. Possibly it is, therefore, a playful one as well.

And as there may be rather more vagabonds than we initially suspect, so there may be fewer categories than first appear—not three, but only two; or even one. Instead of the faithful populace spiritually assembled, the peripatetic Evangelical earnestly making his appointed rounds, and some biblically namable but otherwise insignificant *tertium quid,* perhaps there are only the settled and the mobile, the fast fish and the loose. With even the fast coming loose. Perhaps the typology of "vagabondage" is not quite so simple as it seems. For under the aspect of modern life, who ain't a vagrant?

And doubtless the literary problem is itself a little more complex than any *Primer* may cause it to appear. "Merry Andrew" may still count as an alien in this latter-day world of Puritanic zeal. And none of our putative Vagabonds is thinking to set up a maypole. But perhaps the institution of literature may yet establish itself in this newer New England. To be sure, no Renaissance is yet in sight: Irving and Cooper both work out of New York; and our modest Story Teller is scarcely the prophet come to unsettle all things. But as things themselves are looking already a little unsettled, perhaps even this world is ready to permit a little recreation of fiction. Especially if that fiction were addressed to such persons who still knew the difference between a revival and a circus, a Whitefield and a Barnum. It might be some time yet before the local readership could take seriously the final command of the old showman: "Come, fellow labourers, . . . we must be doing our duty by these poor souls at Stamford" (367). But perhaps "moral history" at least could be counted a *pardonable* sin.

Obviously some such hope is embedded in the strategic literary misdefinition of "The Seven Vagabonds." How, otherwise, could Hawthorne have continued the project of story-telling at all? And as his own progress is into neither silence nor Byronism, we must assume that the blighting specters of Satan, Cain, and the Wandering Jew have been laid to rest at the outset; or that the Grim Reaper of Irony has finally cut them down to puny human size. It is pretty hard, after all, to ascribe a tale which implies a whole tradition of satire, and which actually notices the literary examples of Cervantes, Shakespeare, Swift, Fielding, and Scott, as coming from the pen of a man troubled above all else by his own perception of the Sin of Art.[45] Under the aspect of *the world*, the literary career is *evidently* valid. It is merely a little harder to pursue within the province of Puritanic Piety than elsewhere.

And so the same ironies continue—in those curious "Passages" from the larger work which was "Relinquished," it turns out, only after its worldly situation and historical ambition had become abundantly clear.[46] The same intolerable dichotomy appears: literary art, forced to define itself as defiantly trivial, is once again set over against the preaching of the Word, and that again in the evangelical (or "Methodist") manner. Once again the teller of tales is forced into the position of personal idler and social parasite by a culture that has totalized the One Story worth telling. But the point is, once again, the intense local absurdity of this Puritanic collapse of all literary *parole* into the common *langue* of Scripture. It may succeed in temporarily invalidating fiction, but it can scarcely enhance any valid Gospel thereby. It merely forces the writer into rebellion.

Nothing is easier, apparently, than slipping out from under the moralistic supervision of old Parson Thumpcushion: merely deny that your God-given "nature" or "peculiar character" fits you for physics, law, Gospel, store, or farming (not to mention the stagecoach business), gather up your modest inheritance, and hit the road—quoting Childe Harold and Don Quixote all the way. A hasty "Flight in the Fog," a hundred-mile ramble, a "fictitious name," and *voilà:* the Story Teller proper: escaped from the "dismal chamber," foot-loose and fancy-free. Anyone puzzled by the prospect may consult the earlier "encounter with several merry vagabonds in a showman's wagon" (407).[47]

What can occur? A number of stories, no doubt: merely manufacture a "great variety of plots and skeletons of tales," keep them "ready for use" in memory (or in *Notebooks*), and trust always that "the inspiration of the moment" will fill them up with a "unity" or "wholeness" which defies mechanism (416–417). A plausible project for a Minor Romantic, surely. What if one's tales seem but "air-drawn pictures"? Will they not be set in "frames"—"perhaps more valuable than the pictures themselves, since they will be embossed with groups of characteristic figures, amid the lake and mountain scenery, the villages and fertile fields, of our native land" (408–409)? What more could be wanted? If Irving be thought a wonder for appropriating "the storied" places of the Old World—and for smuggling in, here and there, a German tale or two in order to confer tradition upon unsuspecting New Amsterdam—what might not be done with a series of entirely *American* sketches?[48]

All that is required, apparently, is the *sense* of history or of place. Nothing really germane: nothing about Salem Village or Lovewell's Rock, for example. Something about "Niagara," of course, since American nature is nothing if not sublime. And balance that, perhaps, with a little color from a "Canal Boat" and a "Steamboat." For antiquity, a rumination on "Old Ticonderoga." And how omit the rural and rugged contours of New England's own "White Mountains"? Such richness. Just *walk*, and the thing will write itself. Call the Story Teller "Oberon," if only at the moralistic conclusion. But remember to claim the substantive result as a truly American Literature.[49]

Unless, of course, some other story is unfolding on its own. Suppose, for example, the Story Teller happens to meet up, at the outset, with an Endicott-Thumpcushion-Methodist by the name of Eliakim Abbott, fresh out of Andover or the Valley of the Shadow, and himself afoot with his vision. What then? Suddenly the stories will have context beyond the limits of mere geography: every time the Story Teller shall call upon his unfolding resources of observation and wisdom for some spontaneous effort of "pathos and levity" (416), that outlandish Evangelical will be addressing an audience of "sinners on the welfare of their immortal souls" (418). He will even take his own turn at trying to convince our vagrant-vagabond-scapegrace of the "guilt and madness of [his own] life" (421). A turn for the Hawthornesque, surely. Evidently it is not going to be so easy as it has seemed.

Once you come down "from the steeple," or out from "behind the curtain" or midnight glass, once you start sketching things in daylight and on the broad highway, certain real problems immediately assert themselves. On the one hand, all too drastically, you have to fight for your own definitional existence: if you are not, evidently, a preacher (or a lawyer or a politician), what is your right to come before the public at all, in your own name or under any conceivable mask or persona? But on the other hand, a question altogether more valid and productive: how will your themes hold up in a world still naive enough to believe that the play of literature is never quite "free," still earnest enough to demand that the word associate itself always with some needful thing of truth or value? How will your variously managed efforts *compare* with "the one desirable effect" of the "efficient clergyman"?[50] It is one thing to notice that the religious and the literary have been set in drastic opposition. But it is quite another to demonstrate the error of this dichotomy.

For help in this crucial situation, few critics would think to appeal to the evident absurdities of "Mr. Higginbotham's Catastrophe"—which, coming "next" in the career of "The Story Teller," is really the only tale in the project for which we have the precise context. While Eliakim Abbott seeks to evangelize his first audience, smallish and mostly female, the newly emancipated but still hounded Story Teller takes the stage of "The Village Theatre" to rehearse the life and literary experiences of one Dominicus Pike, himself a story teller, whose fortune it is to hear, repeat, and elaborate certain very circumstantial (yet false) rumors about the hanging-murder of one Higginbotham. Pike is forced to endure the embarrassment of a "sad resurrection" by that worthy gentleman; but he is also permitted to enjoy a marriage to his lovely daughter, happily ever after. No one much understands, then or now; but the original audience laughs, uproariously and ever louder, at every mention of the preposterous and mildly obscene name of "Higginbotham"; and also, a bit more bawdily, at the "stiff queue of horse-hair" (420) which a mischief-loving little epicene has suggestively attached to the Story Teller's collar. They laugh till they break their benches, falling on their "bothams," if not quite rolling in the aisles.

Q.E.D., we might readily assume. Thumpcushion and Abbot rest their case: the Artist as Buffoon, filling in the space between the turgid rhetoric of "The Tragedy of Douglas" (418) and some afterpiece hardly more significant than an absurd erection of horse-hair. And this while sober persons adhere to these anxious benches of evangelical sorrow. Somebody close down the theaters. And send this evident vagabond back to his spiritual guardian.

Except that, as we may now realize, the Story Teller's tale has a serious turn in *somebody's* mind; and we must notice this even if we cannot chart its ultimate tendency. However this local entertainer may define his project, and whatever his original audience may derive from his premier performance, his Higginbotham text actually reads off as a knowing and wicked parody of the argument between Mr. David Hume and the host of Christian apologists who sought to confute his skeptical view of human testimony and the credibility of miracles. If somebody is having trouble with the theological status of mere literature, somebody *else* is noticing the entirely "literary" status of the regnant theology. And just as evidently.[51]

The basic premise of "Mr. Higginbotham's Catastrophe" merely inverts the ordinary skeptical suspicion regarding the Christian events. Instead of a real death and a merely rumored return to life, we have a hanging so faithfully reported and so circumstantially corroborated as to seem proven; so much so that Higginbotham's ability to survive this onslaught of rumor comes to seem itself miraculous, and is in fact referred to as a "resurrection" (110).[52] He is never said to have been "crucified," of course; but being hanged on a tree has always seemed close enough for typological purposes. And when the tree is needlessly overspecified as a "St. Michael's Pear," the grounds of our own skepticism are altogether lost: anyone who has ever sung "The Twelve Days of Christmas" is supposed to know where he is. Especially when the rest of the apologetical fit is too perfect to be either accident or idleness.

The spread and the elaboration of the false intelligence concerning Higginbotham proceed exactly as Hume had predicted—with love of novelty and public attention on the one side, and eager credulity on the other. Moreover, the language of witnesses, evidence, and testimony is as legalistically complete as it had been in the "textbook" defense of the Christian case which Hawthorne had been asked to internalize at Bowdoin; or as it currently appeared in the religious magazines. The apologetic paradigm embraces even the story's own most particular details: the first reporter of the supposed hanging is called a "prophet" (111); when Dominicus Pike begins to spread the alarming report, his auditors immediately take it "for gospel" (109); indeed, Pike soon finds himself in a position Eliakim Abbott might envy, broadcasting "a new edition of [his] narrative, with a voice like a field preacher" (113). And when it comes time to explain how, in someone's complex plot, the rumor of Higginbotham's death had got weirdly out in front of supposed fact, the narrative takes ironic refuge in the definitive formula of Christian typology: somehow a " 'coming event' was made to 'cast its shadow before' " (119).[53]

But as truth is everywhere simpler than fiction, the one-sentence clarification comes only after Dominicus Pike, tobacco-peddler turned Seeker, has been forced to endure a faithful parody of true conversion in his own quite secular person. The moment his story is most effectively challenged, he takes up the classic role of the "Doubting Thomas": "May I be hanged myself," he anxiously exclaims, "if I believe old Higginbotham unhanged till I see him with my own eyes, and hear it from his own mouth." But then, as it *is* rather late in the historical day for this original sort of spiritual encounter, he thinks to add the following "confidential" proviso: "And as he's a real shaver, I'll have the minister or some other responsible man for an indorser" (117).

Yet even this (Melvillean) impurity drops away, as the evangelical paradigm rushes to its own absurd completion. As all revelation can be of God's "hinder parts" merely, so Pike comes to recognize "the rear" of Mr. Higginbotham, "dim and unsubstantial" before him, a "figure" merely. There—as the local laughter increases, no doubt—he finds that "for [his] soul" he cannot quite pass through some strait "gate." Yet he must see for himself. And so, with "old Nick" behind and the object of his "mysterious" quest uncertainly ahead, he rushes on to his own personal, experimental encounter: "Have you been hanged or not?" (119). In some outrageous penultimate irony he manages to save Higginbotham, rather than the other way round. Yet he manages, in the end, to reap his appropriate reward: Higginbotham's attractive daughter and "a large tobacco manufactory" in the Story Teller's native village. Many mansions, indeed. But heed the Call, apparently, and the worldly calling takes perfect care of itself.

And that, very probably, is as far as it is safe to go in the present state of scholarship. Certainly it is as far as we need to press our own argument, concerning Hawthorne's picture of the *origins* of the artist-in-the-world. Taken together, "Passages" and "Higginbotham" define both the point of departure and the enduring problematic: a story teller, in flight from the established (bourgeois-Calvinist) orthodoxy, and tending to accept that orthodoxy's own definition of the literary career, begins his own self-dramatized career by telling a story which *just happens* to parody the single story which that orthodoxy regards as adequate and therefore privileged; and this while some late-come and marginally official spokesman of that story tries to rehearse its simple outline and complex application, in a situation which, though undoubtedly reduced by the circumstances of latter-day New England history, merely flirts with the borders of the Province of Irony. A rather strikingly contrived situation, surely. Perhaps we might try the experiment of imagining Hawthorne as just "there," for the next twenty or thirty years, rather than hiding behind a curtain or dreaming behind a frosted glass.

Of course there are problems. Does the Story Teller himself, for example, understand the import of his text?—any more than the audience which laughs itself senseless throughout? It seems unlikely, given the rest of his characterization; yet where the game is so rare, one hesitates to dogmatize. And what, in any case, would be the precise reach of Hawthorne's own "theologic" intention? To identify the witty blasphemy of his persona?—consigning him to the tender mercies of the Shorter Catechism. Or merely to satirize the witless inspiration of the would-be Artist, unaware of his own implication and echo? Or would it be, on the other hand, to savor the explicit (if covert) demolition of the absurd epistemological pretensions of an embattled and repressive orthodoxy?—making it clear, from the outset, that the creed which has won the day has already lost its own originary argument. Or yet again, more modestly, merely to insist that whatever is true of story-telling is true *as such,* that there are *no* exceptions to the general rules of faith in fiction?—thus to win but a little space for some miscellaneous tales to compare and compete with the One Story.

The questions are fair, no doubt. And fascinating, if the critical wind is right. Yet as our own moral is perfectly plain, there seems no reason to argue or decide: any of these possibilities introduces us to a Hawthorne both more worldly and more capable of complex fictions than we are accustomed to assume. If we see that clearly enough, we may yet get the rest.[54]

Indeed the literary project which climaxes Hawthorne's more or less continuous early efforts to anthologize himself presents us with a thematic problem so intensely historical (and, not incidentally, with a narrative problem so subtly indirect) that interpretation itself does best merely to pause and consider the case. What moralism of "the head and the heart" could possibly cover the matter at issue between the Story Teller and Eliakim Abbott? Or, for that matter, between the Story Teller and his own audience? And what insight of psychology or magic of structural collapse can possibly render adequate account of a narrative and social situation so deliberately worldly? Evidently even a dismal chamber may assimilate and then "imitate" more of reality than can appear to many critical philosophies. And if we can *just* bear the reduction of the "haunted" mind to the historic model of Dugald Stewart, what will we say when a Story Teller, in flight from a Calvinist guardian, but in the company of an itinerant evangelist, plunges over his head into the world of Hume and Paley? Perhaps we may yet think of something. But it might take a while.

3

A similar caution may endure to guide any future efforts to reconstruct the "remainder" of the "Story Teller" project, including our own brief, heuristic re-vision. What we seem to know best about the problem is how much we never *can* know. Yet somehow the notion of two whole volumes of interconnected "frame-stories" seems to justify the curiosity it generates. What *could* it have been like?

We can be fairly sure that certain particular tales (some of them manifestly historical) were supposed to have appeared "there." But, except as they were all somehow to *follow* from the treacherous narrative beginnings of "Passages," we hardly know where "there" might be. After "Higginbotham" we know next to nothing about the order of the tales. Nor can we know with what "site" the various tales (historical or otherwise) might have been associated. And, most unhappily, we have lost all the "connecting" materials which were to situate the various tales, as "Passages" necessarily prepares the ground for "Higginbotham." Thus we can never be certain just how any given tale might have proceeded from the Story Teller's development or his unfolding relation with his unlikely road-fellow.[55] All we can know is that, although this had seemed to be a very important aspect of his project, Hawthorne nevertheless did agree, finally, to publish the rest of the tales *separately:* devoid, that is, of all preparations and surroundings. And that he bitterly regretted this radical paring away of literary and social context.[56]

Perhaps this latter (psychological) fact best expresses the needful caution. As these tales once had a fully dramatized (and obviously "faulty") narrator, better learn to trust the "rhetoric" less than we have often tended to do. And as they were once told on the road that leads from one real place to another, *cherchez le monde.* Perhaps Hawthorne may yet teach us the art of literary inference.

Of all that we can merely infer about the complex design of "The Story Teller," perhaps our most intriguing suspicion concerns Hawthorne's plans for Eliakim Abbott. Evidently he had been quite serious about the Story Teller's fellow "pilgrim"; for when, in his own latter and *personally* more worldly days, he found himself the subject of a spiritual visitation from the madly prophetic Jones Very, he could think of no characterization more apt than to declare that Very "more than realized the conception of entire subjectiveness he had tried to describe in the preacher of 'The Story Teller.' "[57] Indeed the whole episode must have seemed like *déjà vu,* or like life imitating art, as some utterly implausible latter-day gospelizer earnestly sought to deliver our now-accomplished literary professional of his Bosom Idol of Imagination. The psychological "conception," of "entire subjectiveness," is scarcely lost, working itself out well enough in "Egotism; or, the Bosom Serpent."[58] But we should like to know how Abbott's own quality of subjectiveness might have been deployed; or, more cogently, what light it might throw on the more subjective tales of our most worldly Teller. For evidently this one "other" constant character, though he may strike his un-covenanted companion as a "stray patient" from a "lunatic asylum" (415), was meant to be more than a mere foil.

How, for example, might the entire subjectiveness of Abbott have either provoked or responded to the performance of "The Minister's Black Veil"?—which we really must, on the available evidence, assign to the "Story Teller" project.[59] If this tale predicts the concerns of "Egotism" (in which Jones Very fulfills Eliakim Abbott), it just as obviously points back to Abbott's own spiritual ancestry; and it clearly passes the lips of some scapegrace narrator. Would not the Story Teller, here at least, have some sense of his irony? And would not his present-day subjectivist be forced to take the point? Could he respond?—countering the argument from "gloom" with a word on behalf of Hooper's "one desirable effect." Might his responses (here or elsewhere) have affected the Story Teller's own sense of life and career? Could the effect be reversed? Or would the two of them simply continue to walk?—agreeing, though "without any formal compact" (415), to divide the world between them?[60]

The questions are speculative, of course. Yet they seem also somehow inevitable. And surely part of their legitimacy resides in the fact that they are more important to *ask at all* than to *answer correctly.* For to consider "The Story Teller" at all is simply to imagine how, in the terms of Hawthorne's early career, the literary circuit sought to complete itself. Just so, in this instance, it is sufficient merely to imagine "The Minister's Black Veil" as a theological and a literary issue between the Story Teller and the Lonely Evangelist, whether their actual comments are lost or not. A larger story completes itself in *any* event. Perhaps the example may yet teach us to be more genuinely "dialectical" about all of Hawthorne's themes, including that of the mind and the world.

But our speculations can also take a more biographical form: what had Hawthorne meant his literary odd couple to reveal about his own career definition? Clearly his two partialists could simply have gone *on*, embodying the competing misdefinitions of the available literary career, and leaving the reader to wonder just how Hawthorne himself might understand secular literature as, at once, both diverting and salutary. To teach by pleasing, we might always think to say. Except that the thematic burden of some of the tales—the bitter patriotism of "The Gray Champion" and "Young Goodman Brown," for example—seems a bit too heavy to "please" in the ordinary sense. Perhaps their only *pleasure* would consist in such altogether ironic satisfaction as an honest reader may, sometimes, without too much self-congratulation, take on the occasion of discovering something he did not exactly wish to learn. Somewhat after the manner of evangelical "conviction" itself. A complex fate.

The best example, quite probably, would have been "The May-Pole of Merry Mount," the conception and terminology of which derive from the false dichotomies of "The Seven Vagabonds" as plainly as from the texts of the "annalists" themselves. If the local motives of the Story Teller are past finding out, still the Hawthornesque motive is perfectly apparent: the playful life is perfectly typified in the demeanor of the Revellers, even as the Christian Sobriety of Eliakim Abbott is classically embodied in the arch-Puritanic aspect of Endicott. The past of Merry Mount merely repeats the present of the "Vagabonds," as allegories proliferate themselves with a spontaneity that might baffle playfulness and sobriety alike.[61] Meanwhile, evidently, someone is supposed to be learning something about the origins and subsequent shape of moral history in New England. But how could Eliakim and the Story Teller learn the lesson without disestablishing themselves?

Once again, perhaps, the actual conversation of our two protagonists matters less than their historic opposition. No doubt it were Ideology to claim that Dialectic matters more than any particular dialogue. But how can we imagine the antagonists in question ever agreeing to cooperate upon the invention of the project of "historic deconstruction"? Perhaps we have not, indeed, lost everything, despite a critical ignorance which seems, for the most part, genuinely invincible.

* * *

And yet there may be one significant gap, so to speak, in our otherwise provocative ignorance. The two tales *set* in the White Mountains appear to have been *told* just there; and the sketch which introduces them is thematic as well as geographical. Those facts may actually help.

We do not know precisely where the tales of Endicott, Brown, and Hooper got themselves told. Though they have clear enough geo-thematic implications—as, for example, "The Old Maid in the Winding Sheet," "The Vision of the Fountain," and "The Three-Fold Destiny" do not—we cannot assume that the Story Teller's "Flight" led him conveniently through Mount Wollaston (or is the tale about Naumkeag?), Salem Village, and one or another available Milford. Nor can we quite imagine what tales (extant or destroyed) may have attached themselves to the fully developed sketches of "Niagara" or "Rochester," or "Old Ticonderoga" or the "Ontario Steamboat." But the Story Teller's "Pedestrian" recollections of "The Notch of the White Mountains" and of his "Evening Party Among the Mountains" prepare the way for "The Ambitious Guest" and "The Great Carbuncle" with more than a little plausibility.[62] And the fully assembled figure may actually give us some idea of the extent to which Hawthorne's moral history is "local."

Most obviously, the sketches in question assemble a cast of characters into the enforced domesticity of Crawford's Inn, to share a little security and warmth amidst the "mysterious brilliancy," and the "slides" (422) of the relatively awesome region in question. And there is also, of course, an adequate opportunity to test the lure of the legend of "the 'Great Carbuncle' of the White Mountains" (428). Most significantly, however, the introductory matter also propounds a sort of theme, in explicit (religious) language as well as in images. The awesome character of this most sublime of New England settings has no trouble leading the mind "to the sentiment, though not to the conception, of Omnipotence" (423).[63] Thus the theological bearing of the stories which follow can come as no surprise.

The tireless contextual labors of Kenneth Cameron have long since suggested that a whole *world* of literary and theological culture lies behind the overtly topical story of "The Ambitious Guest"; that for a "proper appreciation of what this story sought to accomplish and what it meant to [Hawthorne's] contemporaries," it may be necessary to consult not only the "typical press reports" which widely publicized the disaster of the Willey family of New Hampshire but also a significant body of sermonic literature on the "themes of necessity, free will, sin, judgment . . . and especially what theologians call 'the problem of evil.' " And if this seems a labor of more love than most critics can quite bestow on a relatively simple (and apparently sentimental) tale, then perhaps a more recent suggestion will sufficiently cover the case. Namely, that the tale's basic conception and even its diction owe more than a little to the terrific vision of Sovereignty expressed in Edwards' "Sinners in the Hands of an Angry God."[64] Evidently the naturally ambitious visitor and the naturally pious family are equally instructed, suitably if too late, that "their foot shall slide in due time." The "sentiment of Omnipotence" indeed.

Of course we can scarcely imagine the Story Teller *preaching* on this theme, even late in his career, on his way back home; some somber enough moral is rigged up, to be sure, in his fragmentary "Journal of a Solitary Man," but it is scarcely High Calvinist.[65] Nor is there any reason to suppose that Eliakim Abbott ever *told a story*. But no doubt it all worked somehow, ironically, as do the Humean implications of "Higginbotham." For the mountainous matter of sovereignty surely constitutes a large measure of what is culturally at issue between the Narrator and the Preacher. And where better to have *this* matter out in the open?

The same mountainous problematic is continued, even more elaborately, in "The Great Carbuncle" which, if it presents a less compressed and dramatic instance, nevertheless contains an even more complex sample of New England's theological culture, strengthening our sense that the worldly bearing of "The Story Teller" was to have been more or less continuous. Most obviously, the tale is redundantly peopled with seventeenth-century satiric "characters," whom we easily recognize as nineteenth-century religious "types." And though the satire is fairly broad, still the spray of Biblical allusions suggests another level of seriousness, somewhere. In the end a provincial quest for the sacred object of some scarcely credited Indian legend turns out to look quite like the necessary search for "the pearl of great price," as variously misconceived by a whole gallery of religious misfits.[66]

The most empirical doctor of natural philosophy—rejoicing in the absurdly significant name of "Cacaphodel," and wishing merely to reduce the sought-for treasure to its essential elements—may surely pass as one of the Story Teller's less startling improvisations. So perhaps may his theological counterpart, a cynical disbeliever in *all* reports concerning transcendent objects: him we know without benefit of Hume. Nor is there anything unprecedented in his fate: for "willful blindness" to all mysterious light, he is literally blinded and turned loose to become an Unpardonable Wanderer, up and down upon the earth. A bit more teasing, however, is the case of Ichabod Pigsnort, the "weighty merchant and selectman of Boston" who is also an "elder in the famous Mr. Norton's church"; and who, before taking an unlicensed sabbatical to search for this new form of wealth, was rumored to enjoy "wallowing naked among an immense quantity of pinetree shillings" (151).[67] Humorous, at least, is the providence according to which he is captured by Indians and transported to Canada; there to be held for (allegorical) ransom, till he should pay all that was due. Evidently the Story Teller *himself* knows an odd fact or two. And perhaps his personal hostility to the supposedly august Way of New England is coming out in the open just a bit, though the audience is probably still laughing at the names.

Most intriguing of all, perhaps—though satiric still, clearly—is the oddly familiar figure of the Seeker. In love with *the search as such*, he collapses and dies at what appears to be the sudden and unlooked-for satisfaction of his ingrained spiritual lust. All he had ever hoped (against hope, as he himself concedes) was to bear the precious jewel "to a certain cave" he knows of, and there, "grasping it in his arms," to "lie down and die, and keep it buried with [him] forever" (154). Title his story: "The Man of Adamant Meets the Great Carbuncle; and Dies of His Own Realized Presumption."[68] And try not to be too surprised if his drastic example makes some more modest aspiration appear altogether preferable.

Yet as there is something parodic about all these (and several other, less memorable) instances of not-quite-spiritual searching, so there is something too pat and reassuring about the moralistic alternative. The Matthew and Hannah of our tale, themselves scarcely distinguishable from some of Hawthorne's other domestic "Pilgrims,"[69] have sought the Great Carbuncle only for "its light in the long winter evenings" (156) of their unfolding marital relation; and they appear to abandon the object of their search at the very moment of discovery. Settling for but a single drink from the "lake of mystery" which marks "the long sought shrine of the Great Carbuncle" (161), they seem entirely content to return to their "humble cottage." And, as if they knew that *mere* homeliness were not by itself enough to resolve so elaborate a case of questing, they offer a sort of "political" rationale for their decision: "never again will [they] desire more light than all the world may share" (163). Not a *bad* idea, surely: sinew the sentiment of "the domestic" with the more resilient ideology of "democracy," and it can resist the lure of "the adventurous" every time.[70] And yet there may be certain more-than-literary reasons to resist the conclusion that our model couple has entirely earned the right to live happily *ever* after.

As they must continue to dwell amidst the awful surroundings of the White Mountains, perhaps their assurance of safety is less than absolute. From the moment we see Hannah "tottering" on "one of the rocky steps of the acclivity" (160), we are forced to wonder whether *her* foot too will also slide, in due time. For all her leaning on Matthew, and their common leaning on one another, perhaps they are, in historic figure, merely the same domestic couple who *cannot* avoid the Slide in "The Ambitious Guest." Though it may be pretty to think otherwise, perhaps no mere natural combinations are proof against the icy implications of Edwardsean theology. "Omnipotence" may yet know to "keep the feet of [the] saints," but it may require more than a humble cottage in democratic America to prove that saving case.[71] The most we can say, apparently, is that the point is still at issue in the world of Eliakim Abbott and the Story Teller.

Even more sobering, perhaps, is the gradual recognition that, above or behind all this local theology, conceived in parody and resolved in sentiment, the tale is actually pressing to evoke the American Master-Theme: somehow the Carbuncle, bunk or not, represents the Idea of America itself. As we may surmise from its strategic absence at the center of the story (and as source-study will duly confirm), there never *was* any mysterious jewel or stone; nothing but the lake itself, the "mysterious" one from which Matthew and Hannah take their one (familiar) communion-sip. A poetically brilliant body of water, to be sure, catching and reflecting a marvelous refulgence all around; and a "prophetic" one, no doubt, in the White Man's own spiritualizing mythology. But an actual "gem" only by an awkward literalization of the original Indian legend. Significant, therefore, is the Story Teller's preliminary confession that he is "shut out" from Indian lore as "the most peculiar field of American fiction" and that he "does abhor an Indian story" (429).[72] For his entire tale, whatever its simplistic moral, rests entirely on some fundamental historic misprision.

More significant still becomes our realization that the mysterious object in question (whatever it turns out to be), and even the story which reveals its concealment, must still be wrested away from its situation amidst Indian idolatry. A lake become a carbuncle must also become, through the typological intermediation of the Gospel according to Matthew, a light unto the nations, or America itself remains undiscovered in Scripture. A British nobleman, otherwise utterly out of place in the story, wishes to bear the transcendent American grace or virtue back to his own ancestral halls, as if Columbia's "gem," which is also a "beacon light" set upon a hill, could be stolen before it were quite realized.[73] As if all truly American claimants, enlightened beyond the *simpliste* politics of Matthew and Hannah, did not know that their light *is* one which "all the world may share" (163).

Again, clearly, all of this is *well* beyond the Story Teller himself. Beyond Eliakim Abbott too, we must suppose, unless that ragged Prophet of the Spiritual Kingdom has been especially attentive to the cardinal object of American idolatry, America itself. But it is scarcely too much for Hawthorne himself to have plotted, even as he permits his vagabond spokesman to drag to the valley of the Amonoosuck elements of a legend that belongs near the Connecticut. And if it may take yet a while for our own criticism to unravel it all, perhaps the instance may stand to remind us how complex the plot of "The Story Teller" could easily become. And as a symbol of what we lose when stories are forced out of historic relation and into literary autonomy—where "The Great Carbuncle" can seem only an inept rehearsal of psychological themes better developed elsewhere.[74] Things might have been otherwise. And they could have been quite splendid.

At very least the White Mountains would have their own story, or pair of stories, even as (Irving-fashion) the Catskills have theirs. One of them, though borrowed (again, Irving-fashion), would have had its own ("inglorious") Ichabod; and even the terms of its borrowing might have mattered. All of this can seem rather trivial, of course; as if reality were insufficient without our (regionalist) stories about it. Or, pressed a little too earnestly, it can become the basis of some local arrogance or national idolatry; anybody who thinks the United States themselves are the greatest poem probably knows too little about either the states or poetry. And yet there is a reason to believe that Hawthorne was not *entirely* ironic about the geographical "frames" of his air-drawn pictures, that he would have regarded an Irving-esque reading of his "Story Teller" as meaningful in its own terms, however limited.

Years later, in a mood of particular seriousness, he offered his own moral and deeply conservative theory of "the storied":

the more historical associations we can link with our localities, the richer will be the daily life that feeds on the past, and the more valuable the things that have been long established: so that our children will be less prodigal than their fathers in sacrificing good institutions to passionate impulses and impracticable theories.[75]

As the subject here is his country's own most destructive Civil War, we scarcely flatter Hawthorne's intelligence to imply that the bloody footprints of that war were sufficiently redeemed by such memorial or fictional "herbs of grace" as might grow from them; the price and the benefit are clearly incommensurate. Yet if it is not quite immoral to hope for *some* good out of *every* evil, perhaps America itself might yet become a storied land, despite its first Puritan and then revolutionary penchant for newness. What else could you do with some battlefield in Pennsylvania, after all, except add it to a Hill in Salem Village and a Rock near Lovewell's Pond? Surely not make a speech on American Destiny.

How much simpler, therefore, the case of the Story Teller and the Ordinary Reader. How is it other than innocent to appropriate—"domesticate"—the White Mountains for literature? We *do*, after all, live in cottages and (except for Californians, perhaps) out of the way of the Slide. Or, if literature *must* recognize "the abyss," then let the stories subtly imply the Absolute which threatens to annihilate all our relatives. No one is ever damned, we must assume, for believing that God is Love, or that democracy is by and large a good idea. And as Calvinist orthodoxy itself must admit that where these insights fail, we are all in beyond our intelligence anyway, why worry about how the argument comes out? Or even whose argument it ultimately is, in the literary sense? Mountains force cottages, in America no less than elsewhere. And the shadow of the Theological Sublime, God knows, must capture an image wherever it can. So why *not* tell just those stories in their most available New England setting? One small jaunt for a Story Teller, but a giant stride for American literary culture.

Yet there was supposed to be more. Not more regionalism, to be sure. For Hawthorne, at least, all of New England was a single moral region. And not more of that complex "world" in any descriptive or naturalistic sense. For we can scarcely imagine Hawthorne *ever* becoming that kind of writer.[76] Only more of such historical intelligibility as may reveal itself to an observer who, though suspicious of "origins," has yet read the available records of the local past and has set out to notice what passes for novelty on all sides. Perhaps certain problematic connections could be observed, above and around the limitations of the strolling observers. Perhaps others might be led to notice them as well—to *see*, where the dramatized protagonists merely struggle—how a local legend might epitomize the whole national story. Nothing recapitulates anything else; but everything has a history, and the world is full of echoes if we can hear them. So the writer is forced to go out and listen, even in the figure of a tone-deaf story teller. It were metaphysics to assert that what is "behind the curtain" is, after all, only what one has been reading. But clearly language is a prison house until somebody gets out on parole and talks to somebody else. So open the intercourse.

Or is the writer himself very shy?—will he *not* serve up his own heart "delicately fried, with brain sauce"? Then he'll *have* to let his narrator do the talking. Call him the Story Teller—a silly fellow, as everyone seems to know. But then the literary voice will *always* sound like a parody of the Self. Or is the writer also very earnest, like the old-time Puritans? Then he'll have to let their conscience be his guide. Call that peculiar phenomenon Eliakim Abbott. And let them have at it. Let them wander wherever the road leads. The Soul will not necessarily accomplish herself by the way, but something of interest may turn up; in symbolical New England it usually does. Let them say whatever *they* may, each according to his own painfully mimetic conception. Trust the world to reject whatever local misdefinition may occur. Or, if that too is metaphysics, remember at least that, since literature is itself inherently ironical, one's own opinions must shift for themselves in any event.

So let the introspective silences end. And let the dialogue begin, in and about the world the Puritans have left behind. In a world so clearly in process, who shall demand dogma, who forbid debate? Perhaps the gesture will indeed matter more than the propositional aggregate. Or, if the old conventions yet endure, perhaps there will arise, somewhere between the preaching and the performance, the outlines of a moral history of the province spread around the writer's haunted chamber. The thinnest of worlds is thick enough. Someone may notice.

4

One is tempted to end by calling Hawthorne's entire career—with his publishers, with his contemporaries, and with a fair sampling of his commentators—a "tragedy," as poignant in its way as that of Miller's Edwards: he began his literary life in a garret, but *they* forced him out of relation. The villain of the piece, as the conception itself verges toward melodrama, is no one but the nefarious Park Benjamin, who broke up "The Story Teller" and published its "tales" separately; robbing them of their connective tissue of drama, dialectic, development, and world; preparing the way for a mere miscellany of twice-tellings and forecasting a whole academy of literary isolationists, including such inspired precursors as Melville and James. A bit extreme, perhaps, and yet Rufus Griswold himself could scarcely do more, in the case of Edgar Poe, to bias the beginnings of criticism.[77] For if there *had* been a "Story Teller," then Hawthorne's various metaphors of literary solipsism (including the famous upper rooms of both Manse and Custom House) could scarcely enjoy their peculiar power to define, as if inevitably, the precise point of Hawthorne's literary departure.

Perhaps those later metaphors would not even exist. But, as this is a little like suggesting that "The Story Teller" might have opened intercourse with someone other than Sophia Peabody, no doubt we should resist the speculation. Especially as *everyone* would regret the loss of such quasi-personal introductions as the *Mosses* and *The Scarlet Letter* actually came to enjoy. Yet as someone's accident is always someone else's providence, perhaps we should pursue the thought in some less drastic form.

No one, it is to be hoped, would have thought to identify Hawthorne as, himself, his own identical Story Teller, even if he should adopt the familiar name of "Oberon" at the end. And the lesson in distance would have helped. For one thing, all those "morals" which, absent at the outset, begin to be provided as the "Provincial Tales" give way to "The Story Teller" would have to be situated in their own fictionalized world and referred to the intelligence of some dramatized persona. The head and the heart would still be *there*, of course; but they might look more like an available literary appeal than a personal *summa theologiae*. And the later "Prefaces" might themselves have come to be taken in obliquity—protests against the appeal to "personality" quite as much as invitations to "sympathy"; for they are everywhere more ironic than our passion for intimacy and/or literary guidance has ever quite allowed.[78] Long before Hawthorne ever spoke, it might have appeared, he dramatized, in a way that even James might have appreciated. And in a way that we, despite the desperate literalness of our approach to Hawthorne's moralistic "talk," might have learned to construe. Children of the Puritans are earnest enough, in all conscience; but literature is *play*. And the Hawthorne text teaches the second lesson no less clearly than the first.

Call me Oberon, perhaps. Bridge does; he thinks of me as his "literary friend," and neither of us plays tennis. But do not suppose this proffered familiarity permits any shortcuts to interpretation: a text is a text. And do not imagine that "I" am any more the infatuating figure "behind the curtain" than the fatuous narrator of "Higginbotham." And why indeed should you care about the "I" at all? For that you have Rousseau and Byron—and soon will have Henry Thoreau himself, all sincere in his own personal disclaimers. I wrote these stories: what can I tell you?[79]

Perhaps Melville might have taken instruction, whatever his (highly ironic) "Virginian" might profess. If he found the earlier work, even as disarranged into the *Twice-told Tales,* more solid and substantial than the rarified matter of the *Mosses,* what might he have concluded from the frank secularity of "The Story Teller"? Surely the man who set Dominicus Pike on the road from Morristown to Parker's Falls remembered to patronize the butcher as well as the tobacco merchant. "Plump sphericity" there might never have been, in this blue-eyed wonder who learned to lisp the world in Spenserian stanzas. But with the elaborated image of Eliakim Abbott at large in his own historic world, perhaps Melville would have been less eager to propose a psychograph of Hawthorne on the basis of a tale which anatomizes the "Egotism" of Jones Very.[80] And even the generalized form of the lesson—Hawthorne dramatizes, he does not confess—might have suggested the essential fact about the entirety of the *Mosses:* its world is the world of Transcendental illusion; its body is not "the world's body" but only the "phenomena" of those rare philosophers who whisper, to the cow they milk, "you are not true."[81]

James is not so easy to forgive, or to blame on Benjamin. Writing a whole book, and speaking as a professional critic rather than as a passionate partisan, he might be expected to have informed himself about not only the Eliakim connection but the entire matter of the plan and fate of "The Story Teller." Yet Lathrop himself, whose book on Hawthorne's neo-Puritan solemnity James was in effect answering, seemed ignorant of that material in 1876; and Conway would not publish the relevant recollections of Elizabeth Peabody until 1890. So James went elsewhere to build his own anti-Puri-

tanic case, to the undeniable basis of a psychology somehow "deeper" than
that of John Calvin. Or perhaps James *did* catch some sense of the peculiar
"world" of the Story Teller: possibly there, along with the *Notebooks,* is
where he formed his own idea of that impoverishment of society and manners that forced the American decision for psychological romance. For with
his standards of social texture, how could the New Englandish arena of
Eliakim and the Story Teller seem anything but a provincial half-world of
satiric tonalities and intellectual loose ends? How could he know that, beyond the local problem of rescuing Hawthorne from the orthodoxies of familiar piety, the enduring task would be to save this admirable literary
precursor from a psychological inquiry that would deepen into solipsism?[82]

Doubtless James solved his own anti-Lathrop problem fairly enough:
"Young Goodman Brown" was anything but a personal cry of "metaphysical despair." Indeed it was "the very condition of production" of this and
the other "unamiable tales" of the Puritans "that they should be superficial,
and, as it were, insincere." Or, as if that quaint formulation were somehow
too Jamesean, the telling dictum: the tale of Goodman Brown is "not a parable, but a picture, which is a different thing."[83] James cannot think to call it
a specimen of "moral history," but his "picture" comes close enough to our
own sense of Hawthorne's studied objectivity to relieve him of ultimate
blame. Perhaps we should have been able to go on from there, to recognize
the precise world Hawthorne had sought to *picture.* Not James's own great
world, to be sure, but somewhat more than the world of "the mind," in one
or another state of gloomy self-haunting.

And even Melville was not entirely unaware of the ground Hawthorne
most authoritatively occupied. Or so we can surmise if we are willing to seek
intelligence in the suggestive detail. Whatever Melville's curious "Virginian" may propound by way of theology (as if to answer Edgar Poe's too
"artful" view of Hawthorne's claim), and however he may puff his "American Shiloh" to the status of a Shakespearean "Master Genius," his very first
ploy may be his most significant. He has been spending his "mornings in the
haymow" reading "Dwight's Travels in New England," we learn; now he is
offered a different sort of literary fare. Not the ironic pilgrimage of the
Story Teller, to be sure, but only Hawthorne's decidedly latter-day *Mosses,*
containing (along with "Roger Malvin's Burial" and "Young Goodman
Brown") chiefly such "travels" as Hawthorne had more recently made,
chiefly in Transcendental Concord. And yet the pairing seems significant,
the displacement apt: off to the barn with the *Mosses,* "and good-by to
'Dwight.' "[84]

Ironic Nathaniel Hawthorne rather than orthodox Timothy Dwight is
the true and revealing traveler. And his domain is truly New England.
Melville is not able to say that the older histories lead straight on to the

newer ones, that the death-by-idealism theme elaborated in "The Gentle Boy" and bitterly compressed into "The Shaker Bridal" entirely forecasts the thematic preoccupations of the tales of the 1840's and actually inspires (or "sanctions") his own skeptical and "naturalist" investigations. Others would have to notice the transit from the Conscience of the Puritans to Consciousness in Concord.[85] But nowhere does Melville suggest that Hawthorne's world is the world of dreams. For him the "deeper psychology" is always emphatically moral or theological; but even less than James could he imagine such concerns abstracted from all space and time. That were to work backwards from the Transcendental reverie of Emerson to the Platonic hypnagogy of Edgar Poe. Hawthorne, on the contrary, shared and battled for the neo-orthodox world of Dwight. Better than that, he won it. Evidently it would require a whole fleet of Yale Colleges and of Harvards to discover otherwise.

So that the tragedy, if tragedy it is, is scarcely perfect or inevitable. We have had "our Hawthorne" pretty much the way we have wanted him. And it were vain, at this remove, to resurrect Park Benjamin merely to cuff him some about the face and neck. The irony and the distance are still there, in the tales "themselves," even without the carefully constructed framework of dramatic control. And a whole world of historical allusion remains, in the major tales, regardless of our anthology, there for us to trust or not, at the pleasure of our theories.

There is just no telling, at this distance, what sort of a writer Park Benjamin thought he had on his hands—or what sort of a deed he thought he was doing, on behalf of what audience, when he decided that two volumes of tales existed more agreeably in isolation than *in situ*. Possibly he preferred a Hawthorne more simply and neatly (domestically) moral than the dramatic ironies of the assembled "Story Teller" quite implied. More likely, he merely preferred the safe alternative of many (unsigned) tales in a magazine to some riskier form of publication.[86] Who reads an American *book?* And all that the subsequent critical case will ever prove is that, like Benjamin, we can still have whatever Hawthorne we seem to want. We no longer want the domestic moralist, evidently; but the choice of Hawthorne in or out of his historical situation remains open. Even as we grow weary of his psyche "on the couch," preferring instead some newer paradigm of the professional writer "in the study," we can still find ways to avoid the problem of the tales in their own thematic world.[87]

What conclusion, then? What possible way to bias, at the last, a critical freedom of which Park Benjamin is scarcely the prophet? Many morals press, and only an Eliakim Abbott would insist that any One will cover the case. We might well consider taking that risk, if only to remind ourself that Historicism is no *less* well provided, from the variegated Hawthorne text, than other forms of readerly address. Yet what final form can we think to give Hawthorne's peculiar worldly urgency?

There is scarcely any need to review all the patent instructions we have been given in the preface-like beginning of "Governor Phips," the coda-like conclusion of "The Man of Adamant," or the entirety of the tightly framed revision of "Alice Doane"—all of which *tell* us, clearly enough, to read for history; they even show us how this might be done. All that is required, apparently, is the decision to be instructed by this sort of authorial directive. Likewise, the hermeneutic significance of certain "provincial" headnotes (and of one "colonialist" footnote) is already part of the record: an "editor" has told us where to look for aids to interpretation and objects of ironic reference. All we have to do is *believe:* that Hawthorne knows his subject, and that he might help us with the history of our peculiarly political religion.

If we do believe, the case for "intention" is already sound enough. And if not, it will scarcely help to struggle, here, with the elaborate ironies of mocking self-definition propounded in "Main Street," even though the summary-idea of a fanciful history of the principal route through original New England accords with and even grounds, retroactively, the controlling metaphor of "The Story Teller." A fortiori, therefore, a full historicist account of the imaginative transfiguration of all this into the spectral confrontations of "The Custom House" and the fleshly encounters of *The Scarlet Letter* must wait some further monograph; or *volume,* if the course of this self-declared argument from history were to be appropriately continued— through the *Seven Gables, Blithedale,* and the fragmentary "Ancestral Footstep." Call that project "The *Progress* of Piety," from the odd provinces of sketch and tale to the sovereign domain of romance.[88] Settle here for a single intuition.

More than "the power of the past," Hawthorne believed in the reality of time. Well before he met Emerson, or read that sage's glowing remarks on the largely Platonic significance of "History," or sought to answer them (in "The Old Manse") with his own modest reflections on "Genius" and "the times," he had been bold enough to set down this: "All philosophy that would abstract mankind from the present is no more than words."[89] An historicist maxim, surely. For as the "present" in question is really an intensely local past, revealing itself in an antique volume of what were once *news*papers (and this under the oxymoronic conceit of "Old News"), the emphasis is less "presentist" than *temporal as such.* Man and his given World: it takes no more, but also no less, to make the circuit of reality.

The world in question, the Boston of the 1730's, once enjoyed as full an existence, absolutely speaking, as the mind is able to conceive. The "life" of those times was, we learn, obviously and even comically provincial: nothing so intense as had been lived a century earlier, in the first flush of the Puritan's apocalyptic zeal; and only a trifle as varied and interesting as it was yet to become, or as it might even then be enjoyed back in London. But there it was, full of its own worldly preoccupations, some of which touched on matters appropriately regarded as "spiritual"; and reflective enough to set the more engrossing ones down as "news." None of it *absolutely* new, perhaps, as there may be, under the sun, nothing truly such. And all oddly old now, like our own New Cricism; or, to change the frame, like the Newness of Transcendental Concord. All of it "vain," therefore, if we wish to regard it with wisdom. Yet all of it real enough to be set down in language which earnestly sought, according to the laws of its own genre, to cover the existing case. And real enough *still*, within the competence of syntax and the comprehension of reference, to be known by anyone willing to take up and read.

Indeed, Hawthorne here suggests and everywhere else implies, what could ever be more fully known than what someone had once set down as adequate to the present concern? Or what more, in any genre, could anyone even imagine or contrive to set down? And since all literature reduces itself to that status in the end—the record of a moment altogether "mutable" and the measure, therefore, of the difference between one moment and the next—why not convert this "Irvingesque" limitation into an enabling premise? Why not seek to understand, as such, precisely such moments as have been real enough to inscribe themselves?

True enough, all this so-called reality merely was. And about the final reason of such entities William Faulkner may well debate Waldo Emerson forever. But surely the more anxious metaphysical objections fall away the moment we realize that all our words lapse from themselves in the moment of their conception. As "the past" is but the lengthening shadow of *difference,* so its news is no further off from the truth than anything else we might happen to hear. So why *not* embrace the career of literature as historical? Especially if there were powerful political and religious reasons for doing so.

For where had one encountered a more flagrant abstraction from time than in America itself? Where, between a spiritualized ancestor worship and a naturalized apocalyptics, had a Party of Irony more plainly cried out for existence? And how could its irony have been other than historical? What it needed to insist on, beyond such local ironies as amateur research may always set before an historical laity, was precisely the full reality of all times and places.[90] Or at least of all those we ever know as such. And where is this lesson better taught than in Hawthorne's early tales? In both the "Provincial Tales" and "The Story Teller," they constitute as intractably historical a body of literature as it has been possible for anyone in America to produce. In precisely this sense: without suggesting that their own mimesis ever approaches that of "naturalism," and without ever lapsing into what we recognize as "regionalism," they steadfastly insist on the significant temporality of their own local settings; and this in direct opposition, very often, to certain recognizably meta-historical uses which others were inclined to make of the same materials.

The local past was not particularly edifying. And it usually embarrassed attempts to redeem it by typology. It was merely real: its personages had had to work out their own destinies in the terms available. Probably they could not be recovered in all their particularity; but as long as the dialectical process could be intelligibly represented, it was scarcely necessary to re-invent all the precise details. They played the hand they were dealt. Nor could one satisfactorily isolate any generalization more substantive or salutary. People lived out their premises, and then their stories simply stopped. Someone might *yet* learn from the unhappy endings of Tobias Pearson, Reuben Bourne, Robin Molineux, Goodman Brown, Parson Hooper; but no post facto arrangement of their experiences rendered any general law. Even the Story Teller, it appears, was required to endure rather than enabled to transcend the situation which made his project seem so problematic. And when Hawthorne finally got around to questioning himself on the larger significance of "history," the best he could do was to satirize the presumption of the question itself.

Thus it appears in *Grandfather's Chair,* which attempts to summarize his own New England "story," in child-like good faith. Addressing the very "chair" which, passed down from moment to moment, might be thought to have witnessed it all, Hawthorne's least wickedly ironical narrator puts his own earnest version of Ahab's inquest of the decapitated head of a whale: "You certainly have had time enough to guess the riddle of life. Tell us poor mortals, then, how we may be happy."[91] A less naive questioner would have demanded, here, some proposition more to the meta-historical taste of Cotton Mather or Henry Adams. But we know where we are: what law do we *learn* from this elongated history lesson?

Embarrassed, and with all the reticence of a symbol, the chair is loathe to speak at all; finally it ventures only a pre-critical truism: "Justice, Truth, and Love are the chief ingredients of every happy life." This may be, depending on one's philosophical style, a bit better than learning that "Life is a rubber ball," but Grandfather is understandably distressed: we needed two centuries to learn *that?*—of which "every human being is born with the instinctive knowledge." History, we should imagine, justifies itself by revealing something we *do not already know.* Then this, from the chair, "drawing back in surprise":

Ah! . . . From what I have observed of the dealings of man with man, and nation with nation, I never should have suspected that they knew this all-important secret. And, with this eternal lesson written in your soul, do you expect me to sift new wisdom for you, out of my petty existence of two or three centuries?

"But, my dear chair," says Grandfather. But me no buts, saith the chair. This is quite enough for you to "tell" your audience. And what matter if you merely repeat the lessons of Bronson Alcott or Horace Mann? The children have ample time to learn that Life is not Conclusion. And they also have, after all, the text itself; to which they can always return.

And so have we—the texts themselves, outrunning all conclusions, as history defies while yet informing all our own theoretic observations. Perhaps we can yet find a way to be interested in their particular way of playing with "old news." Not merely because Hawthorne wanted us to, for our own psychic and political health, as if we were all neo-Puritanic still. But principally, I imagine, because we can yet find the link between authorial intention and literary satisfaction: Hawthorne may yet turn out to be more fun when we learn to play the game his way.

Spite of all the moralism on the hither side of his Puritanic soul, Hawthorne himself seems perfectly to have realized that literary value resides always in the controlled play and never in the achieved status of meaning. What he played with, again and again, was precisely the phenomenon of historical *difference:* the implausible sufficiency of every world that was. And in the midst of this world, where the war of words will always lapse into the play of meaning, Hawthorne criticism has yet to prove itself more richly, skeptically, and intellectually playful than his own historical tales. *His* conclusions return us, always, to *their* semantic textures. These are woven, most of them, from the pieties once at large in the historic world of provincial New England. And these are offered as but a token of what truly is. We may accept them as such. For so too is everything else.

NOTES

INDEX

❦ NOTES ❦

PROLOGUE

1. At different levels of abstraction, David Levin and Hayden White both emphasize the "literariness" of all historical writing; see "The Literary Criticism of History," in *In Defense of Historical Literature* (New York: Hill and Wang, 1967), pp. 1–33; and *Metahistory* (Baltimore: Johns Hopkins University Press, 1973), pp. 1–42.

2. Richard Harter Fogle has warned that future source studies need to pay careful (philosophical) attention to "the relation between 'source' and 'end,' of the work we are primarily discussing"; and, further, that "renewed care must be taken to distinguish positive external evidence from inference"; see his review of John Caldwell Stubbs, *The Pursuit of Form*, in *American Literature*, 42 (1971), 570. Though I am not writing a source study primarily, I have tried to take his warning seriously. Yet I have concluded his two rules are probably self-contradictory: the more we essay to "prove," positivistically, an undeniable "source," the less interesting become our *essentially speculative* efforts to grasp its vital relation to the literary "end."

3. The works of Doubleday and Bell are amply cited in my own text. The reviewers of Bell's book are, respectively, Blake Nevius, *Nineteenth-Century Fiction*, 27 (1972), 241–243; and Lewis Leary, *New England Quarterly*, 44 (1971), 664–665.

4. Far from claiming future territory, I wish instead merely to concede certain failures of self-consistency. Written over many years, different chapters respond to different critical pressures. And some of the older analyses—"Young Goodman Brown" and "The Legends of the Province House"—remain a bit intuitive, underdocumented. But as art is longer than life, perhaps the reader will take the wish for the fact.

POLEMICAL INTRODUCTION

1. Melville's review originally appeared in *The Literary World* (17, 24 August, 1850). I quote from the (normalized) reprinting in the Critical Edition of *Moby-Dick* (New York: W. W. Norton, 1967), pp. 540–541.

2. The second installment of Melville's "Mosses" begins with the Virginian's

(clearly fictional) assertion that he had "not at all read" "Young Goodman Brown" when he wrote his first remarks. To gauge the extent of Melville's own self-involvement here, one would compare the "Mosses" with certain crucial passages of *Moby-Dick* (especially chap. 96, "The Try-Works") and also with Melville's excited letters to Hawthorne; see Merrell R. Davis and William H. Gilman, ed., *The Letters of Herman Melville* (New Haven, Conn.: Yale University Press, 1960), esp. pp. 123–133, 141–143.

3. James's *Hawthorne*—originally published in the English Men of Letters series in 1879—is explicitly directed against the familial pieties of George Parsons Lathrop's *Study of Hawthorne* (Boston: Houghton Mifflin, 1876). Given the state of Melville's reputation in the 1870's, it would not be surprising if James had not seen Melville's review.

4. *Hawthorne* (rpt. Ithaca, N.Y.: Cornell University Press, 1956), p. 46.

5. "Hawthorne and His Mosses," quoted from the Norton *Moby-Dick,* p. 549. The argument for Melville's internalization of "Young Goodman Brown" would depend on the similarities between Brown's rebellion and the cosmic protest of Ahab and Pierre.

6. *Hawthorne,* p. 81. James is opposing Lathrop's Melvillean view of "Young Goodman Brown" as a "terrible and lurid parable."

7. I use "interpretation" and "commentary" in their original scriptural-hermeneutical senses, to signify the critical activities performed by persons who accept the thematic import of a given text and want to deepen their understanding of its truth or extend its range of application. "Analysis" suggests a less believing, more "deconstructive" frame of mind: the analyst wishes to know how a text was put together or how it produces its esthetic or moral effects.

8. See William Crary Brownell, *American Prose Masters* (rpt. Cambridge: Harvard University Press, 1963), pp. 52–53; Van Wyck Brooks, *America's Coming of Age* (rpt. Garden City, N.J.: Doubleday, 1958), pp. 35–36; and Vernon L. Parrington, *Main Currents in American Thought* (New York: Harcourt, Brace, 1927), II, 450.

9. "Maule's Curse, or Hawthorne and the Problem of Allegory," *In Defense of Reason* (New York: W. Morrow, 1947), pp. 157, 174–175.

10. Doubtlessly the "Jamesean" view originates in Hawthorne's own later self-evaluations. The humorous ("Aubépine") headnote to "Rappaccini's Daughter" and the self-renouncing conclusion to "The Old Manse"; the self-satire of "Main Street" and the self-criticism of "The Custom House"; the anxious "Preface" to *The House of the Seven Gables* and the more resigned ones to the 1851 *Twice-told Tales* and to *The Snow-Image*—all beg to be denied by a sympathetic critic who will see more in Hawthorne's art than its often quaint allegorical form. But James and many others—including not a few modern commentators on the "theory of art" contained in Hawthorne's "Prefaces"—have prided themselves on simply believing Hawthorne: either they have been taken in by his ironic self-deprecation, or else they have agreed that Hawthorne's own *worst* view of the case is indeed the true one.

11. See Marius Bewley, *The Eccentric Design* (rpt. New York: Columbia Univer-

sity Press, 1963), pp. 113-146; Martin Green, "The Hawthorne Myth: A Protest," in *Re-Appraisals* (New York: W. W. Norton, 1963), pp. 61-86; and Lionel Trilling, "Our Hawthorne," in Roy Harvey Pearce, ed., *Hawthorne Centenary Essays* (Columbus: Ohio State University Press, 1964), pp. 429-458.

12. See Paul Elmer More, "Hawthorne: Looking Before and After," in *Shelburne Essays in American Literature* (rpt. New York: Harcourt, Brace and World, 1963), p. 129; and D. H. Lawrence, "Nathaniel Hawthorne and *The Scarlet Letter*," in *Studies in Classic American Literature* (rpt. Garden City, N.J.: Doubleday, 1951), pp. 92-110.

13. "Introduction" to *Hawthorne* (New York: American Book Co., 1934), pp. xix-xl. The only statement of Hawthorne's Puritanism *at all* approaching the literalness of Warren is Barris Mills, "Hawthorne and Puritanism," *New England Quarterly*, 21 (1948), 78-102.

14. See Herbert Schneider, *The Puritan Mind* (New York: Henry Holt, 1930), pp. 262-263; F. O. Matthiessen, *The American Renaissance* (New York: Oxford, 1941), p. 192; and Harry Levin, *The Power of Blackness* (New York: Vintage, 1960), p. 55. For other more or less revealing attempts to wrestle with or to adjust the notion of Hawthorne's "Puritanism," see Mark Van Doren, *Hawthorne* (New York: Sloane, 1949), pp. 70-79; Joseph Schwartz, "Three Aspects of Puritanism," *New England Quarterly*, 36 (1963), 192-208; Larzer Ziff, "The Artist and Puritanism," in Pearce, ed., *Centenary Essays*, pp. 245-270; and J. Golden Taylor, *Hawthorne's Ambivalence Toward Puritanism* (Logan: Utah State University Press, 1965).

15. I employ the words "re-enact" and "re-cognize" to make public my reliance on the parallel analyses of R. G. Collingwood and E. D. Hirsch, who both defend the imaginative "reproducibility" of humanistic experience; see "History as Re-enactment of Past Experience," in *The Idea of History* (rpt. New York: Oxford, 1956), pp. 282-302; and *Validity in Interpretation* (New Haven, Conn.: Yale University Press, 1967), esp. pp.1-67, 127-163, 209-264.

16. See "Hawthorne and his Mosses," in the Norton *Moby-Dick*, p. 537.

17. Among the "new" biographies, Randall Stewart's *Nathaniel Hawthorne* (New Haven, Conn.: Yale University Press, 1948) long remained "standard" and is actually rather convincing on the purposive character of Hawthorne's study in the 1820's and 1830's (pp. 27-44). For a review of the entire "normalizing" tendency in Hawthorne scholarship, see Seymour L. Gross and Randall Stewart, "The Hawthorne Revival," in Pearce, ed., *Centenary Essays*, pp.335-366. The recent discovery of the hitherto "lost" portions of Hawthorne's earliest notebook threatens to re-open this old controversy.

18. See Hyatt Waggoner, *Hawthorne* (Cambridge: Harvard University Press, 1955), pp. 12-25; "Art and Belief," in Pearce, ed., *Centenary Essays*, pp. 167-195; Leonard J. Fick, *The Light Beyond* (Westminster, Md.: Newman Press, 1955), esp. pp. 35-70, 171-175; and Henry G. Fairbanks, *The Lasting Loneliness of Nathaniel Hawthorne* (Albany: Magi Books, 1965), esp. pp. 185-202. Waggoner expressed serious reservations about the schematic quality of Fick's conclusions (in "Art and Belief"); but essentially all three of

these critics agree that Hawthorne's sense of sin and salvation is more Arminian-Protestant—and in a sense more "catholic"—than it is Calvinist-Puritan.

19. See Lathrop, *Study*, p. 296; Edward Wagenknecht, *Nathaniel Hawthorne: Man and Writer* (New York: Oxford, 1961), pp. 172-201; W. Stacy Johnson, "Sin and Salvation in Hawthorne," *Hibbert Journal*, 50 (1951-52), 39-47; Allen Flint, "The Saving Grace of Marriage in Hawthorne's Fiction," *ESQ*, 19 (1973), 112-116; Hyatt Waggoner, "'Grace' in the Thought of Emerson, Thoreau, and Hawthorne," *Emerson Society Quarterly*, 54 (1969), 68-72; and Chester E. Eisinger, "Hawthorne as Champion of the Middle Way," *New England Quarterly*, 27 (1954), 27-52. In my view Crews's chapter on "Psychological Romance" really *does* destroy, on behalf of D. H. Lawrence, all *simplistic* versions of Hawthorne's religion—but only those. Waggoner himself had already objected to the placidity of the Hawthorne offered by Wagenknecht; see "Hawthorne," *American Literary Studies: An Annual / 1963* (Durham, N.C.: Duke University Press, 1963), pp. 21-23. But Crews tended to conflate the two critics into a single neo-orthodox image; see *The Sins of the Fathers* (New York: Oxford, 1966), pp. 3-26.

20. For the beginnings of an analysis of the "Lawrentian" assumptions of Crews and other critics of psychoanalytic tendency, see my own essay "The Symbolic and the Symptomatic: D. H. Lawrence in Recent American Criticism," *American Quarterly*, 27 (1975), 486-501. And for Crews's own strategic redefinitions, see "Reductionism and its Discontents," in *Out of My System* (New York: Oxford, 1975), pp. 165-185.

21. Romanticism parts company with Enlightenment at precisely this point: where the single-term analyses of the eighteenth century explicitly intended to reduce all of the supernatural to the natural, the various "spiritualistic" monisms of the nineteenth century mean to elevate all phenomena to a virtually supernatural dignity or miraculous complexity; see Thomas Carlyle, "Natural Supernaturalism," in *Sartor Resartus* (rpt. New York: Odyssey, 1937), pp. 254-267. This "elevationist" tendency was ably criticized by Orestes Brownson only a few years after the fact; see "Transcendentalism" (1845), in *Works* (Detroit: T. Nourse, 1882-1902), VI, 1-113. And the whole episode in intellectual history has been brilliantly analyzed by M. H. Abrams; see *Natural Supernaturalism* (New York: W. W. Norton, 1971).

22. The best example of the criticism that takes all of these contextual considerations seriously and yet holds back from defining either Hawthorne's explicit intention or his major achievement as primarily historical is the work of Neal Frank Doubleday; see *Hawthorne's Early Tales: A Critical Study* (Durham, N.C.: Duke University Press, 1972).

23. See "Hawthorne's 'My Kinsman, Major Molineux': History as Moral Adventure," *Nineteenth-Century Fiction*, 12 (1957), 97-109; "Hawthorne's Revision of 'The Gentle Boy,'" *American Literature*, 26 (1954), 196-208. Curiously, Gross's other essay of this period expresses an unreconstructed historicism quite like the one his "Molineux" article rejects; see "Hawthorne's

'Lady Eleanore's Mantle' as History," *Journal of English and Germanic Philology*, 54 (1955), 549-554.

24. Wagenknecht, *Hawthorne*, pp. 33-34; Crews, *Sins*, pp. 3-9, 27-43. For a sample of responses to Crews's psychological ahistoricism, see the reviews by Philip Rahv, *New York Review of Books*, 7 (1966), 21-23; E. M. Holmes, *New England Quarterly*, 39 (1966), 537-539; W. B. Stein, *American Literature*, 38 (1967), 564-565; and H. A. Murray, *American Scholar*, 36 (1967), 308-312. Nearest to an historicist protest is A. N. Kaul's defense of the Leavis approach in *Yale Review*, 56 (1956), 148-152.

25. "Hawthorne as Poet," *Sewanee Review*, 59 (1951), 179-205, 426-458; *Form and Fable in American Fiction* (New York: Oxford, 1961), pp. 99-168; *The American Vision* (New Haven, Conn.: Yale University Press, 1963), pp. 139-173.

26. See Walter Blair, "Nathaniel Hawthorne," in James Woodress, ed., *Eight American Authors* (New York: W. W. Norton, 1971), p. 100 and (more generally) pp. 93-114. Besides appealing to the anti-historical authority of Gross, Crews could also cite the psychoanalytic example of R. P. Adams, "Hawthorne's Provincial Tales," *New England Quarterly*, 30 (1957), 39-57; and Melvin R. Askew, "Hawthorne, the Fall, and the Psychology of Maturity," *American Literature*, 34 (1962), 335-343. There was really no reason to assume things were headed in the direction of an impoverished historicism.

27. "Shadows of Doubt: Specter Evidence in 'Young Goodman Brown,'" *American Literature*, 34 (1962), 344-352; and "Romance and the Study of History," in *Centenary Essays*, pp. 221-244. See also Pearce's earlier essay, "Hawthorne and the Sense of the Past," *ELH*, 21 (1954), 327-349.

28. "Romance and the Study of History," pp. 223-224.

29. See Milton Stern, *The Fine Hammered Steel of Herman Melville* (Urbana: University of Illinois Press, 1957), pp. 1-25. Robert Lowell's historicist "reading" of Hawthorne is clearest in his adaptation of "My Kinsman, Major Molineux"; see *The Old Glory* (New York: Farrar, Straus and Giroux, 1964), pp. 65-114.

30. The latest critic to defend Hawthorne against reduction to the "fixities and definites" of history *as history* is Nina Baym. Her book is anxious to make Hawthorne's historical interest loom as small as possible, and she has elsewhere made answer to my own earlier historicist suggestions; see *The Shape of Hawthorne's Career* (Ithaca, N.Y.: Cornell University Press, 1975), pp. 15-52; and "Hawthorne," in *American Literary Studies: An Annual / 1974* (Durham, N.C.: Duke University Press, 1976), p. 25.

31. See "Fathers, Sons, and the Ambiguities of Revolution in 'My Kinsman, Major Molineux,'" *New England Quarterly*, 44 (1976), 559-576; and "Hawthorne's Ritual Typology of the American Revolution," *Prospects*, 3 (1977), 483-498.

32. Pearce has brought his own position into dialectic relation with that of the "psychoanalysts" in "Robin Molineux on the Analyst's Couch: A Note on the Limits of Psychoanalytic Criticism," *Criticism*, 1 (1959), 83-90.

33. Hawthorne's review of Simmes appeared in the *Salem Advertiser* (2 May 1846); of Whittier in the *Literary World* (17 April 1847). Both have been reprinted by H. Bruce Franklin in *The Scarlet Letter and Related Writings* (New York: Lippincott, 1967), pp. 285–287, 289–291.

34. See Michael Bell, *Hawthorne and the Historical Romance of New England* (Princeton, N.J.: Princeton University Press, 1971), esp. pp. 3–14, 193–211.

35. Doubleday wishes to include "Dr. Heidegger's Experiment" among "The Masterpieces in the *Twice-told Tales*"; and many critics would hold out for "Wakefield" or for some of the sketches in what I shall end by calling "the Haunted Mind Group." But the existing anthologies still confirm the verdict of Gross and Stewart in favor of the tales with a discernable New England setting, as against "such prefabricated tales as 'The Lily's Quest' or 'The Three-Fold Destiny.' "

36. The first of these critical-discriminatory tasks has already been well begun by the historicist analyses of Leavis, Pearce, Levin, Bell, and (to a lesser extent) Doubleday. To this basic list might be added R. W. B. Lewis' cogent essay "The Return into Time: Hawthorne," in *The American Adam* (Chicago: University of Chicago Press, 1955), pp. 110–126. Other critics involved in the post–New-Critical "return to history" have been more interested in Hawthorne's *theory* of history and hence have been concerned to deduce and elaborate his own theoretical premises: see G. G. Jordan, "Hawthorne's 'Bell': Historicial Evolution Through Symbol," *Nineteenth-Century Fiction*, 19 (1964), 106–124; Johannes Kjorven, "Hawthorne and the Significance of History," in Skard and Wasser, ed., *Americana Norvegica* (Philadelphia: University of Pennsylvania Press, 1966), I, 110–160; Ursula Brumm, "Nathaniel Hawthorne," in *American Thought and Religious Typology*, John Hoagland, trans. (New Brunswick, N.J.: Rutgers University Press, 1970), pp. 111–161; John E. Becker, "Allegory and History," in *Hawthorne's Historical Allegory* (Port Washington, N.Y.: Kennikat Press, 1971), pp. 155–179; Leo B. Levy, " 'Time's Portraiture': Hawthorne's Theory of History," *Nathaniel Hawthorne Journal*, 1 (1971), 192–200; R. H. Fossum, *Hawthorne's Inviolable Circle: The Problem of Time* (Deland, Fla.: Everett/Edwards, 1972); and Harry B. Henderson, "Hawthorne: The Limits of the Holist Imagination," in *Versions of the Past* (New York: Oxford, 1974), pp. 91–126. To my mind, this more ontological approach is *two* levels of abstraction above what is at present most needed: Hawthorne's "philosophy of history" seems even less important than his "theological doctrines."

If I am right about this, then it will follow that a modest historical essay like J. H. Plumb's *The Death of the Past* (Boston: Houghton Mifflin, 1971) will provide a more useful term of current reference than an enormously more pretentious theoretical treatise like Hayden White's *Metahistory* (Baltimore: Johns Hopkins University Press, 1973). Except in the special case of *The Marble Faun*, Hawthorne's proper historical task involved the deconstructive criticism of local political "mythologies" rather than the creative emplotment of some universal or totalizing "Myth." Hawthorne was (so to speak) a follower of Roland Barthes rather than of Northrop Frye. More responsibly: his point of departure is from an essentially Bancroftian historiography. On the one hand, he seems to accept much of the "Romantic" epistemology implied by the idea of the freedom of the historical artist to create representative figures or to contrive representative dramatic moments; see David Levin, *History as Romantic Art* (rpt. New York: Harcourt, Brace and World, 1963), pp. 1-23. On the other hand, however, he utterly rejects and bitterly denounces the "progressive" historiography which understands American Democracy as a necessary outcome of Nature, or as a providential outgrowth of True-Whig Ideology, or as the ultimate antitype of the Puritan Israel; see Levin, *Romantic Art*, pp. 24-45; Pearce, "Romance," pp. 221-231; and compare Herbert Butterfield, *The Whig Interpretation of History* (rpt. New York: W. W. Norton, 1965); Bernard Bailyn, *The Ideological Origins of the American Revolution* (Cambridge: Harvard University Press, 1967); E. L. Tuveson, *Redeemer Nation* (Chicago: University of Chicago Press, 1968), esp. pp. 1-136; Sacvan Bercovitch, *The Puritan Origins of the American Self* (New Haven, Conn.: Yale University Press, 1975), esp. pp. 136-186; and N. O. Hatch, *The Sacred Cause of Liberty* (New Haven, Conn.: Yale University Press, 1977).

If "theory" has any other relevant task, it might be the monumental one of establishing the abstract possibility of historical criticism itself. That is to say, we not only should have to defend the historical legitimacy of Hawthorne's literary procedures, but we should also validate *our* own ability to recover, historically, *his* own historical intentions. My own sense is that the effort might begin with the work of Collingwood and Hirsch (see note 15). It might draw practical aid and comfort from Roy Harvey Pearce's "Historicism Once More" and (a little less directly) from David Levin's "Literary Criticism of History"; see *Historicism Once More* (Princeton, N.J.: Princeton University Press, 1969), pp. 3-45; and *In Defense of Historical Literature* (New York: Hill and Wang, 1967), pp. 1-33. But given the present hermeneutical disarray, probably nothing short of a philosophical revolution will suffice; before we get a criticism willing to base itself on some "realistic"ontology, the present "linguistic idealism" will have to run its course, as did its "psychologistic" predecessor. Everyone has his favorite example of the regnant confusion. My own is a book on some putative "New Historicism," which (wildly) treats the work of Murray Krieger as a likely source of some new historicist methodology and then (more sensibly) concludes that no concluding statement is possible; see Wesley Morris, *Toward a New Historicism* (Princeton, N.J.: Princeton University Press, 1972), esp. pp. 187-216.

37. Melville, "Hawthorne and His Mosses," in the Norton *Moby-Dick*, p. 540; James, *Hawthorne*, p. 45.

38. See Lloyd Morris, *The Rebellious Puritan* (New York: Harcourt, Brace, 1927); Schneider, *Puritan Mind*, pp. 256-264; Kaul, *American Vision*, pp. 139 ff. Gross and Stewart rightly identify Newton Arvin's *Hawthorne* (Boston: Little, Brown, 1929) as the biography which "gave final form to the 'dismal chamber' view of the subject" ("Revival," *Centenary Essays*, p. 339). But in the related and perhaps more fundamental matter of "ancestral footsteps," Arvin must share responsibility with Morris, pp. 5-43; with Frank

Preston Stearns, *The Life and Genius of Nathaniel Hawthorne* (Philadelphia: Lippincott, 1906), pp. 11-34; and with Edward Mather [Jackson], *Nathaniel Hawthorne: A Modest Man* (New York: Crowell, 1940), pp. 7-30. That this "ancestral" bias was invented rather than inevitable is proven by such older biographies as George E. Woodberry's *Nathaniel Hawthorne* (Boston: Houghton Mifflin, 1902) and Herbert Gorman's *Hawthorne* (New York: G. H. Doran, 1927). The "new" biographies returned to a consideration of Hawthorne's actual nineteenth-century beginnings; besides Stewart and Wagenknecht, see Robert Cantwell, *Nathaniel Hawthorne: The American Years* (New York: Holt, 1948); and Hubert Hoeltje, *Inward Sky: The Mind and Heart of Nathaniel Hawthorne* (Durham, N.C.: Duke University Press, 1962). Most recently, Arlin Turner has emphasized Hawthorne's *conscious* identification with region and heritage; see *Nathaniel Hawthorne* (New York: Oxford, 1980), pp. 3-44.

39. Vernon Loggins, *The Hawthornes* (New York: Columbia University Press, 1951), p. 199.

40. Bentley's first mention of the fact that Elizabeth Manning had married Captain Nathaniel Hawthorne is on the occasion of the latter's death, four years later; see *The Diary of William Bentley* (rpt. Gloucester, Mass.: Peter Smith, 1962), III, 353. Lathrop, defending Hawthorne's *inner* religion, admits that although "he had a right to a pew in the First Church, which his family had held since 1640 . . . he seldom went to service after coming from college" (*Study of Hawthorne*, p. 156). The assumption that Mrs. Hawthorne went back to the church of the Mannings after her husband's death lies behind Wagenknecht's remark that "the East Salem Church, which Nathaniel attended as a boy, was . . . then on the verge of Unitarianism" (*Hawthorne*, p. 177).

41. For a full discussion of the theological positions of the churches and ministers in Salem (and in New England generally) in the crucial years around 1800, see Conrad Wright, *The Beginnings of Unitarianism in America* (Boston: Starr King, 1955), pp. 252-291. Wright stresses the importance of Arminian doctrines rather than the question of Trinitarianism, but his conclusions about the doctrinal agreement are supported by the older, more official histories of Unitarianism; see G. W. Cooke, *Unitarianism in America* (Boston: American Unitarian Association, 1902), pp. 69-90; and E. M. Wilbur, *A History of Unitarianism* (Boston: Beacon Press, 1965), II, 379-434. For supplementary accounts of the unstable theological conditions of this period, see F. H. Foster, *A Genetic History of the New England Theology* (rpt. New York: Russell and Russell, 1963), pp. 273-315; Joseph Haroutunian, *Piety Versus Moralism* (New York: Henry Holt, 1932), esp. pp. 177-219; and H. Shelton Smith, *Changing Conceptions of Original Sin* (New York: Scribners, 1955), pp. 37-85. When Loggins asserts that Hawthorne's "First Church . . . was to remain rigidly conservative for another thirty years" (*Hawthorne*, p. 191), he can be referring only to its explicit stand on the "secondary" question of Unity versus Trinity.

42. Fick, *Light Beyond*, p. 172.

43. See William Ellery Channing, *Works* (Boston: American Unitarian Association, 1899), pp. 459–468.

44. In Waggoner's view, Hawthorne occupies a "classic" position at the "center of Christian orthodoxy"; see *Hawthorne* (1955 ed.), pp. 12–25. Although my own theological biases are atavistically Thomist, I hold no brief for Hawthorne's proto-Catholicism, except as Waggoner's definition of Hawthorne's Christianity resembles C. S. Lewis' conception of Milton's: "Catholic in the sense of basing [itself] on conceptions . . . held 'always and everywhere and by all' "; see *A Preface to Paradise Lost* (New York: Oxford, 1961), p. 61.

45. As my hypothetical title suggests, the view to be answered is that of Haroutunian's *Piety Versus Moralism*. The answer would propose that the New England theology never *did* develop a rational structure competent to support the weight of its aboriginal piety—without which the piety lapsed. The beginnings of such a more-than-liberal answer might draw support from Conrad Wright's essay "The Rediscovery of Channing"; see *The Liberal Christians* (Boston: Beacon Press, 1970), pp. 22–39.

46. "Main Street," in the Centenary *Snow-Image* (Columbus: Ohio State University Press, 1974), p. 67. The telling phrase reveals Hawthorne's continuing concern with "The Moral Argument Against Calvinism."

47. Thus Cantwell quotes, for contrast, Horace Mann's account of his own education; see *American Years*, p. 89.

48. Stewart, Cantwell, and Hoeltje all infer that Hawthorne's early home discipline was benign, and all characterize his Maine experiences as Wordsworthian and "idyllic"; see *Hawthorne*, pp. 1–12; *American Years*, pp. 38–44; and *Inward Sky*, pp. 29–42. The "Sybaritic" characterization of Clifford Pyncheon seems strategically autobiographical: thus "Phoebe" saves Hawthorne from the self-indulgences of fantasy as effectively as she saves his Holgrave-self from artistic objectification.

49. As Cantwell observes, Hawthorne was involved in a "struggle, lasting almost twenty years," with this most conscientious uncle, who was (perhaps not incidentally) the only member of the Manning-Hathorne household to go "back" to Calvinism when the public split within Congregationalism occurred. The struggle certainly involved the regularity of Hawthorne's education; and very probably it concerned "his hopes and plans for his own career" as a writer (*American Years*, pp. 46–62). And yet the "Story Teller" version of this is surprisingly free of angst: the figure of Oedipal Calvinism, named "Thumpcushion," is humorously characterized; and the Story Teller is himself made a fairly trivial fellow. One doubts that the struggle was violent.

50. The choice of Bowdoin College seemed to depend on its proximity to the Manning residence in Maine and on its relatively low tuition (Stewart, *Hawthorne*, p. 13). For the career and the (missed) influence of Appleton, see Cantwell, *American Years*, pp. 94–95.

51. The career of Emily Dickinson provides at least as instructive a contrast as that of Horace Mann: once more we are permitted to observe what a really powerful "Puritan" influence would look like in the nineteenth century. James was surely right to observe that people responded to the heritage of

Calvinism in different ways. But he almost certainly overstated the extent to which Hawthorne's aboriginal mind was held by that tradition; see *Hawthorne,* pp. 45–8.

52. For discussion of "the mental scale" of Bowdoin, see Stewart, *Hawthorne,* pp. 14–20; Cantwell, *American Years,* pp. 60–97; and Hoeltje, *Inward Sky,* pp. 50–58. For the most "direct" account of the Bowdoin curriculum, see L. C. Hatch, *Bowdoin College 1794–1927* (Portland: Loring, Short and Harmon, 1927), pp. 36–60, 269–280.

53. "The College Years of Nathaniel Hawthorne" (Ph.D. diss., Yale University, 1932).

54. Stewart's observation remains true: "Hawthorne had got a good education . . . in Christian philosophy" (*Hawthorne,* p. 25). Even more important, however, are Waggoner's suggestions about Hawthorne's tactics for "The Discovery of Meaning." Adumbrating Julian Hawthorne's authoritative observation that, as contrasted with Emerson, Hawthorne more and more questioned "the expediency of stating truth in its disembodied form," Waggoner observes that "Hawthorne's thinking outside his tales is much less impressive than his thinking in his tales." Thus his *Notebooks* are everywhere less impressive and revealing than the *Journals* of Emerson and Thoreau. Apparently Hawthorne felt that his fiction "could apprehend 'more of the various modes of truth' than he could grasp by 'direct effort.'" See *Hawthorne* (1955 ed.), pp. 60–64; and compare *Hawthorne and His Circle* (New York: Harper, 1903), p. 68.

55. Elizabeth Peabody's account of the great Congregational schism makes it clear that Hawthorne could not have missed it: "The religious controversies that ended by changing all the old Puritan churches of Boston and Salem from Calvinism to Liberal and Unitarian Christianity, were raging in 1818, and divided all families; our own family, and especially our mother, who was very devout, remained Liberal"; see Julian Hawthorne, *Hawthorne and His Wife* (Boston: Houghton Mifflin, 1884), I, 60–61.

56. The Bowdoin curriculum had been expressly patterned after that of Harvard, where theological opinion ranged from the majority liberalism to a minority of moderate, and not wholly consistent, Old-Light or "federal" Calvinism. At Bowdoin the majority and minority were probably reversed. The really powerful stronghold of Old-Light Calvinism was, of course, Andover. Only if Hawthorne had somehow found his way to Yale would he have encountered the vigorous and "consistent" New-Light Calvinism of Edwards, Bellamy, and Hopkins. See Stewart, *Hawthorne,* pp. 15–17; Hoeltje, *Inward Sky,* pp. 52–55; Hatch, *Bowdoin,* pp. 23–84; and Wright, *Beginnings of Unitarianism,* pp. 252–280. The letter concerning Hawthorne's nonparticipation in the Mead incident is to his sister Maria (4 May 1823); see Hoeltje, pp. 55–56, 69. The letter relating to the progress of Revival at Bowdoin is to his Aunt Mary Manning (26 November 1824); see Hoeltje, p. 75.

57. For Hawthorne's collegiate peccadilloes and pranks, see Cantwell, *American Years,* pp. 73–74, 81–89; and Hoeltje, *Inward Sky,* pp. 61–74. The first ref-

erence to the "Sunday sickness" is in a letter to Maria (14 April 1822); and see Cantwell, pp. 88–89.

58. For the likelihood of parody in Hawthorne's first published work, see Roy Harvey Pearce's "Introduction" to the Centenary *Fanshawe* (Columbus: Ohio State University Press, 1964), pp. 301–316. In the "Story Teller" project, it seems clear that Hawthorne is implicitly rejecting the available dichotomy between preaching as serious and writing as foolish and irresponsible. Still, if one had to choose, Hawthorne "would not that cowléd churchman be."

59. For the convention-ridden source of "Sunday at Home," see Lamb's "The Sabbath Bells," which Hawthorne reprinted in the *American Magazine of Useful and Entertaining Knowledge*, 2 (May 1836), 399.

60. The view of Hawthorne as possessing, in his maturity, a firm but largely unarticulated religious faith is, of course, the "official" family view—first articulated by Lathrop (see note 19) and then repeated by Julian Hawthorne: "He had a deep and reverent religious faith, though of what purport I am unable to say"; see *Hawthorne Centenary at the Wayside* (Boston: Houghton Mifflin, 1905), p. 114. Such would surely have been the impression created by Hawthorne's habit of leading family prayer and of his "dumb" readings of Spenser, Bunyan, and Milton. And it accords well enough with the rest of the available evidences: the love letters repeatedly suggest that matters of faith lie too deep for discourse; and even the famous comment on Melville's "morbid state of mind," his inability either to "believe" or yet to "be comfortable in his unbelief," suggests a "fideistic" temperament as strongly as a skeptical conclusion; see *The English Notebooks of Nathaniel Hawthorne*, Randall Stewart, ed. (New Haven, Conn.: Yale University Press, 1941), pp. 432–433.

61. A continuation of this present study would have to deal not only with Nina Baym's account of Hawthorne's artistic development but also with the most "modern" accounts of Hawthorne's "poetics"; see Baym, *Hawthorne's Career*; Edgar Dryden, *Nathaniel Hawthorne: The Poetics of Enchantment* (Ithaca, N.Y.: Cornell University Press, 1977); and Kenneth Dauber, *Rediscovering Hawthorne* (Princeton, N.J.: Princeton University Press, 1977). For the moment it is enough to suggest that even "structuralist" attempts to account for Hawthorne may have to begin with the problem of his involvement in history.

62. See Richard Harter Fogle, *Hawthorne's Fiction* (Norman: University of Oklahoma Press, 1952, 1964), pp. 3–131; Roy R. Male, *Hawthorne's Tragic Vision* (Austin: University of Texas Press, 1957), pp. 3–89; Waggoner, *Hawthorne* (1955, 1963); and Crews, *Sins*, pp. 3–135.

63. See R. P. Adams, "Hawthorne: The Old Manse Period," *Tulane Studies in English*, 8 (1958), 115–151; John J. McDonald, "The Old Manse Period Canon," *Nathaniel Hawthorne Journal*, 2 (1972), 13–40; "'The Old Manse' and Its Mosses," *Texas Studies in Language and Literature*, 16 (1974), 77–108; Baym, *Hawthorne's Career*, pp. 84–117. The unpublished scholar-

ship on Hawthorne's literary involvement in the intellectual problems of the 1840's is even more instructive: see the Cornell dissertations of Bruce Jorgensen (" 'The True Madmen of This Nineteenth Century': Cases of Consciousness in Concord," 1977) and David Van Leer ("The Apocalypse of the Mind: Idealism and Annihilation in the American Renaissance," 1977).

64. Of the twenty-three tales published between May 1842 ("The Virtuoso's Collection") and April 1845 ("P's Correspondence"), only four are not appropriately introduced by the range of experience and ideas evoked in "The Old Manse"; two of these are children's stories ("Little Daffydowndilly" and "A Good Man's Miracle"), and two take us back to Hawthorne's "colonialist" concerns ("Drowne's Wooden Image" and "A Book of Autographs").

65. "The Custom House," which refers back to "The Old Manse" in many significant ways, invokes Alcott as the climax of a series of remarkable "experiences" that includes Brook Farm, Emerson, Ellery Channing, Thoreau, Hilliard, and Longfellow (Centenary Edition of *The Scarlet Letter*, p. 25). Hawthorne's comparison of Very with his own Eliakim Abbott is reported in a letter of Elizabeth Peabody quoted in Edwin Gittleman, *Jones Very: The Effective Years, 1833–1840* (New York: Columbia University Press, 1967), p. 283. The phrase about "the madmen" is from Ellery Channing's "Youth of the Poet and the Painter," but the sentiment is close to the one Hawthorne expressed in "The Old Manse."

66. I see no need to divide Hawthorne's Salem years into two literary periods, as Nina Baym has done (*Hawthorne's Career*, pp. 15–83): the historical—and even the specifically "Puritan" interest—is continuous through 1838.

67. See *The Blithedale Romance*, "Rappaccini's Daughter," and "The Old Manse"—in the Centenary Edition, III, 52; X, 91, 18–32.

68. The philosophy of "newspapers" and of the present moment propounded in "The Old Manse" (Centenary Edition, X, 20–21) is already a redaction and an echo of the moral of "Old News" (Centenary Edition, XI, 133).

69. In addition to the works cited in note 63, see H. P. Miller, "Hawthorne Surveys His Contemporaries," *American Literature*, 12 (1940), 228–235; N. F. Doubleday, "Hawthorne's Satirical Allegory," *College English*, 3 (1942), 325–337; Frank Davidson, "Thoreau's Contribution to Hawthorne's *Mosses*," *New England Quarterly*, 20 (1947), 535–542; A. H. Marks, "Two Rodericks and Two Worms," *PMLA*, 74 (1959), 607–612; M. J. Colacurcio, "A Better Mode of Evidence," *Emerson Society Quarterly*, 54 (1969), 12–22; and David Van Leer, "Aylmer's Library," *ESQ*, 22 (1976), 211–220.

70. Such an argument would of course deny that Hawthorne was in any significant sense a "Platonist." It would thus oppose itself, in various ways, to the positions of Rudolph Von Abele, *The Death of the Artist* (The Hague: Martinus Nijhoff, 1955); B. R. McElderry, "The Transcendental Hawthorne," *Midwest Quarterly*, 2 (1961), 307–323; Marjorie Elder, *Nathaniel Hawthorne: Transcendental Symbolist* (Athens: Ohio University Press, 1969); and M. S. Schreiber, "Emerson, Hawthorne, and 'The Artist of the Beautiful,' " *Studies in Short Fiction*, 8 (1971), 607–616. It would try to build on the work

of Millicent Bell, *Hawthorne's View of the Artist* (New York: State University of New York Press, 1962); J. K. Folsom, *Man's Accidents and God's Purposes* (New Haven, Conn.: College and University Press, 1963); and D. A. Berthold, "Hawthorne's Esthetics of the Imperfect," *Dissertation Abstracts International*, 33 (1972), 2885-A; but it would take Hawthorne's anti-Platonism in a theological as well as an esthetic direction.

71. The Hawthorne-Melville relationship remains underinvestigated and mysterious on the Hawthorne side; see Harrison Hayford, "Melville and Hawthorne," (Ph.D. diss., Yale University, 1945); Sidney Moss, "Hawthorne and Melville," *Literary Monographs*, 7 (1974), 45–84; and E. H. Miller, *Melville* (New York: Braziller, 1975), esp. pp. 15–44, 178–255. The question of Hawthorne and novel versus romance still supports an industry; for its theoretical basis, see Lionel Trilling, "Manners, Morals, and the Novel," in *The Liberal Imagination* (rpt. New York: Doubleday, 1957), pp. 199–215; Northrop Frye, *Anatomy of Criticism* (Princeton, N.J.: Princeton University Press, 1957), pp. 303–315; Richard Chase, *The American Novel and Its Tradition* (New York: Doubleday, 1957), pp. 1–28; and Perry Miller, "The Romance and the Novel," in *Nature's Nation* (Cambridge: Harvard University Press, 1967), pp. 241–278. For a brief but perceptive "review" of certain recent embarrassments of this popular critical gambit, see Cushing Strout, "From Trilling to Anderson," *American Quarterly*, 23 (1971), 601–606. For a useful introduction to the problem of Hawthorne and Europe, see Terrence Martin, "Hawthorne's Public Decade and the Values of Home," *American Literature*, 46 (1974), 142–152.

72. For Hawthorne's romances as triumphs of Romantic form—rather than evidences of decline—see John Caldwell Stubbs, *The Pursuit of Form* (Urbana: University of Illinois Press, 1970), pp. 81–137. For the identification of a "Major Phase," see Baym, *Hawthorne's Career*, pp. 123–215.

73. The "negative-Romantic" context of "Ethan Brand" has long been clear; see (for example) G. K. Anderson, *The Legend of the Wandering Jew* (Providence: Brown University Press, 1965), pp. 174–227. Equally important, however, is the precise way in which the tale sets the Byronic (and Shelleyan) note against the softer tonalities of the early Wordsworth (and Coleridge), and the way that linguistic drama is placed within the theological tradition of Puritan attempts to prevent the "unpardonable sin" of despair. If the tale is, as some critics have held, *strategically* "abortive," that fact only heightens Hawthorne's short-circuited rejection of negative Romanticism: the fate of the Puritan "reprobate" had already exhausted the possibilities of the Romantic "man of sorrows."

74. We have no adequate "reading" of "Main Street." Michael Bell understands the "modernity" of its historical views of the Puritans (*Historical Romance*, pp. 62–64), and Nina Baym is alert to the uneasiness of its formal dialectic (*Hawthorne's Career*, pp. 119–122). But we have yet to grasp its full significance as an "Introduction" to *The Scarlet Letter* almost as essential as "The Custom House" itself.

75. I make only the tentative beginnings of an adequately historical reading of

The Scarlet Letter in "The Footsteps of Ann Hutchinson," *ELH*, 39 (1972), 459-494. I am at present working on a monograph titled " 'The Woman's Own Choice': Theology and Sexual Metaphor in *The Scarlet Letter*," which ought to be able to make the full case. It will have to recognize the enormous moral authority of John Winthrop. And it will have to take primary account of the views of Charles Feidelson, *"The Scarlet Letter," Centenary Essays*, pp. 31-78; Austin Warren, *"The Scarlet Letter:* A Literary Exercise in Moral Theology," *Southern Review*, 1 (1965), 22-45; E. W. Baughman, "Public Confession and *The Scarlet Letter*," *New England Quarterly*, 40 (1967), 532-550; Bell, *Historical Romance*, pp. 149-190; Becker, *Historical Allegory*, pp. 88-154; M. A. Isani, "Hawthorne and the Branding of William Prynne," *New England Quarterly*, 45 (1972), 182-195; and Frederick Newberry, "Tradition and Disinheritance in *The Scarlet Letter*," *ESQ*, 23 (1977), 1-26.

76. Although "Main Street" ends the Showman's historical past with the "great snow" of 1717, the less histrionic narrator of *Grandfather's Chair* marks the beginning of a new era with the accession of Phips, the first New-Charter governor of Massachusetts (*Centenary Edition*, VI, 55-67).

77. The contemporaneous social inspiration of *Seven Gables* is well established: see Matthiessen, *Renaissance*, pp. 322-334; Hall, *Critic of Society*, pp. 160-167; Male, *Tragic Vision*, 119-138; Bewley, *Eccentric Design*, pp. 175-183; Alfred Marks, "Hawthorne's Daguerrotypist: Scientist, Artist, Reformer," *Ball State Teachers College Forum*, 3 (1962), 61-74; and (much more recently) Jonathan Arac, "The House and the Railroad," *New England Quarterly*, 51 (1978), 3-22. The beginnings of an analysis of Hawthorne's philosophy (or "theology") of history in the book have been made by Waggoner, *Hawthorne* (1963 ed.), pp. 160-187; R. A. Yoder, "Transcendental Conservatism and *The House of the Seven Gables*," *Georgia Review*, 28 (1974), 33-52; and John Gatta, "Progress and Providence in *The House of the Seven Gables*," *American Literature*, 50 (1978), 37-48. The most convincing account of the book as a "sustained attempt to establish connections between Puritan past and nineteenth-century present" is Michael Bell, *Historical Romance*, pp. 214-226.

78. James ingratiatingly confesses that, as a critic, he "hardly know[s] what to say" about this "lightest and brightest and liveliest" of Hawthorne's longer works; about the "lightly indicated identity" of Coverdale he remarks only that "it has a great deal in common with that of his creator" (*Hawthorne*, pp. 104-105). Evidently James recovered himself in fiction: *The Bostonians* is an evident redaction of the "matter" of Blithedale; and more importantly, James would spend much of his later career experimenting with problematic narrators like Coverdale. Among modern critics, James's critical blindness is shared most noticeably by Robert C. Elliott, whose essay on *The Blithedale Romance* found its way into the *Centenary Essays* (pp. 103-118). For more percipient commentary on the function of Coverdale, see Frederick Crews, "A New Reading of *The Blithedale Romance*," *American Literature*, 29 (1957), 147-170; W. L. Hedges, "Hawthorne's *Blithedale:* The Function of the Narrator," *Nineteenth-Century Fiction*, 14 (1960), 303-316; John

Schroeder, "Miles Coverdale as Actaeon, as Faunus, and as October," *Papers on Language and Literature*, 2 (1966), 126-139; and Louis Auchincloss, "*The Blithedale Romance:* A Study of Form and Point of View," *Nathaniel Hawthorne Journal*, 2 (1972), 53-58.

79. The best treatments of the reformist "matter" of *Blithedale* are Irving Howe, "Hawthorne: Politics and Pastoral," in *Politics and the Novel* (New York: Horizon, 1957), pp. 163-175; Male, *Tragic Vision*, pp. 139-156; and Kaul, *American Vision*, 196-213.

80. See E. H. Davidson, "The Unfinished Romances," in *Centenary Essays*, pp. 141-163; and compare the "Historical Commentary" of Davidson and C. M. Simpson in the Centenary Edition of *The American Claimant Manuscripts* (Columbus: Ohio State University Press, 1977), pp. 491-521.

81. For the continuity of Hawthorne's investigation of "Past and Present" from *Seven Gables* to *Ancestral Footstep*, see Bell, *Historical Romance*, pp. 226-242. For *The Marble Faun* as "international" precursor of Howells and James, see Cushing Strout, "Hawthorne's International Novel," *Nineteenth-Century Fiction*, 24 (1969), 169-181. And for the temporal exhaustiveness of Hawthorne's threefold conception of "eternal" Rome, see M. E. Brown, "The Structure of *The Marble Faun*," *American Literature*, 28 (1956), 302-313; C. R. Smith, "The Structural Principle of *The Marble Faun*," *Thoth*, 3 (1962), 32-38; and Sidney Moss, "The Symbolism of the Italian Background in *The Marble Faun*," *Nineteenth-Century Fiction*, 23 (1968), 332-336.

82. *Hawthorne (*1963 ed.), pp. 209-211.

83. For other "solutions" to the problem of Hawthorne's final failure, see E. H. Davidson, *Hawthorne's Last Phase* (New Haven, Conn.: Yale University Press, 1949), pp. 142-157; Waggoner, *Hawthorne* (1963 ed.), pp. 226-246; Crews, *Sins*, pp. 240-257; and Baym, *Hawthorne's Career*, pp. 251-278.

84. Though I would agree with Neal Doubleday (as against Nina Baym) that "the 1825-1838 time span is as clearly defined a period as we are likely to find in the study of any writer" (*Early Tales*, p. 3), I am aware of the need (eventually) to take account of the difference between Hawthorne's major (historical) tales and the other (lesser) productions of his Salem years.

85. Melville's point (concerning the "higher criticism") is somewhat more complicated than David Levin's (concerning "Young Goodman Brown"), but the example will serve; see Marvin Fisher, "Melville's 'Jimmy Rose,' " *Studies in Short Fiction*, 4 (1966), 1-11.

86. See Hawthorne's "Prefaces" in the Centenary *Snow-Image*, p. 4, and *Seven Gables*, p. 1.

1. NATIVE LAND

1. See Randall Stewart, *Nathaniel Hawthorne* (New Haven, Conn.: Yale University Press, 1949), pp. 19-20.

2. For the "conventional" conditions of Hawthorne's literary apprenticeship, see

Neal Frank Doubleday *Hawthorne's Early Tales, A Critical Study* (Durham, N.C.: Duke University Press, 1972), pp. 3-71.

3. The question of Hawthorne's early development is fraught with difficulties. There are, first of all, some remaining "canonic" problems. Most scholars accept the authenticity of "An Old Woman's Tale" (*Salem Gazette*, 21 December 1830), although the Centenary Edition refers to it, as to "The Battle Omen" (*Salem Gazette*, 2 November 1830) and "The Haunted Quack" (*The Token*, 1831), as "attributed"; and Gerald R. Griffin has argued for the authenticity of "The New England Village"; see *Essex Institute Historical Collections*, 107 (1971), 268-279. And, just possibly, there could be still other (unsigned and uncollected) tales and sketches in the *Salem Gazette*, *The Token*, or the *New England Magazine;* Hawthorne seems to have implied this in a letter to William Ticknor (7 June 1854), responding to a request for material to fill up the enlarged (1854) edition of the *Mosses.* Furthermore, there is reason to believe Hawthorne may have destroyed a fair number of early tales: scholars can account, even conjecturally, for less than half of his projected "Seven Tales of My Native Land"; and if the (highly fictionalized) evidence of "The Devil in Manuscript" can be trusted at all, Hawthorne may at some point have despaired of more than three or four of his earliest fictional lucubrations. And most crucially, perhaps, the precise chronology of *composition* of the surviving tales is far from certain. The Centenary Edition prints an authoritative list of these tales in order of *publication;* see *The Snow-Image and Uncollected Tales* (Columbus: Ohio State University Press, 1974), pp. 483-488. But the certainty of this list may be falsely reassuring: we cannot be absolutely certain where *Fanshawe* (1828) fits in; and no argument moving "from" one "to" another early tale or sketch can quite take refuge in secure chronology. Accordingly, my own strategy in this chapter remains tentative and "unscientific": I treat the accepted tales in their (approximate) order of publication (with some organizational grouping for convenience) and look for larger indications of literary orientation or direction. The most useful scholarly aid in this undertaking remains Nelson F. Adkins' seminal study of "The Early Projected Works of Nathaniel Hawthorne," *Papers of the Bibliographical Society of America*, 39 (1945), 119-155.

4. "Main Street," in *Snow-Image*, pp. 67, 68, 78, 57.

5. The principal irony of "Main Street" involves the audience's inability to recognize moral-metaphorical dependences: insisting that "Anna Gower, the first wife of Governor Endicott . . . left no children," Hawthorne's listeners fail to recognize their own "energetic" application of Manifest Destiny as descendent from Endicott's Puritan Errand.

6. For the critical prescription (by Rufus Choate and others) of the "matters" of a native American literature, see Doubleday, *Early Tales*, pp. 18-26.

7. The letter from Goodrich (dated 19 January 1830, and answering Hawthorne's of 20 December 1829) mentions "The Gentle Boy" and "My Uncle Molineux" [*sic*]; but "Roger Malvin's Burial" would also appear in Goodrich's *Token* for 1831 and was almost certainly part of the group. See Adkins, "Projected Works," 127-129.

8. Ultimately, of course, Hawthorne rejected the simply patriotic prescriptions of the nativists. Evidently he learned to see what Rufus Choate could not—the "useful truth" in the "persecutions of the Quakers" and the "controversies with Roger Williams and Ann Hutchinson"; see Doubleday, *Early Tales,* pp. 24-25.

9. Adkins refers to "Alice Doane's Appeal" as "the only extant story we may be quite certain belonged to the "Seven Tales" ("Projected Works," p. 125); he means, of course, that "Alice Doane" referred to by Elizabeth Hawthorne and later revised as "Alice Doane's Appeal." Thus "The Hollow of the Three Hills" (HTH), published in the *Salem Gazette* for 12 November 1830 but very probably intended for the "Seven Tales" of 1827, seems a fair enough place to begin.

10. All citations of HTH, given in parentheses, refer to *Twice-told Tales* (Columbus: Ohio State University Press, 1974). The invocation of "strange old times" provides the basis for Terrance Martin's discussion of the "method" of Hawthorne's tales; see *Nathaniel Hawthorne* (New Haven, Conn.: Twayne Publishers, 1965), pp. 49-51; and compare "The Method of Hawthorne's Tales," in Roy Harvey Pearce, ed., *Hawthorne Centenary Essays* (Columbus: Ohio State University Press, 1964), pp. 7-30.

11. In Hyatt Waggoner's original view, witchcraft offered itself as a subject "ideally suited to the young writer of 'sensibility' in the age of the romantic quest for the *outré"*; see *Hawthorne: A Critical Study* (Cambridge: Harvard University Press, 1955), p. 36.

12. Poe refers to the "subject" of HTH as "commonplace," but praises its artistry nevertheless: "Every word *tells,* and there is not a word which does *not* tell"; see "Twice-Told Tales" in M. Alterton and H. Craig, ed., *Poe* (New York: American Book Co., 1935), pp. 362-363. F. O. Matthiessen cites this view with approval; see *The American Renaissance* (New York: Oxford, 1941), p. 206.

13. The most elaborate treatments of HTH are both "technical" (or "structural"), and neither can do much with the question of theme; see C. S. Burhans, "Hawthorne's Mind and Art in HTH," *JEGP,* 40 (1961), 286-295; and Kenneth W. Staggs, "The Structure of Hawthorne's HTH," *Linguistics in Literature,* 2 (1977), 1-18. For explicit discussion of the tale's *struggle* toward significance, see David Downing, "Beyond Convention: The Dynamics of Imagery and Response in Hawthorne's Early Sense of Evil," *American Literature,* 51 (1980), 463-476.

14. Clearly "the sentimental" (or perhaps "the domestic") is as important to HTH as "the gothic." In fact, the lady of the tale, who refers to herself as a "stranger in this land" (200), may remind us more of the seduced and abandoned heroine of *Charlotte Temple* than of the standard European villain in "the earliest examples of American gothic"; see Nina Baym, *The Shape of Hawthorne's Career* (Ithaca, N.Y.: Cornell University Press, 1976), pp. 26-27.

15. Ely Stock seems correct in suggesting that the conception of witchcraft in HTH is in some sense "Biblical," but this insight has scarcely furnished a de-

finitive interpretation; see "Witchcraft in HTH," *American Transcendental Quarterly*, 14 (1972), 31-33.

16. Unlike "Young Goodman Brown" (YGB), HTH does not insist that we refer its witchcraft "vehicle" to the "tenor" of thought of 1692. The "elegant" interpretation proposed would be similar to H. J. Lang's psychological reading of "The Wives of the Dead" (rather than David Levin's historical interpretation of YGB); see "How Ambiguous is Hawthorne?" in A. N. Kaul, ed., *Hawthorne* (Englewood Cliffs, N.J.: Prentice-Hall, 1966), pp. 86-98.

17. My "positive" proposals about HTH are frankly based on the dangerous (negative) assumption that arguments about theological despair are probably *not* relevant. Accordingly, I should not be entirely displeased if someone could furnish an apposite text from Cotton Mather's *Brand Plucked* or Thomas Hooker's *Firebrand*—which clearly *do* apply to a story such as "Ethan Brand."

18. At issue here would be something like the logic or law of "compulsion" which Frederick Crews has proposed as an explanation for the self-destructive behavior of Reuben Bourne; see *Sins of the Fathers* (New York: Oxford, 1966), pp. 80-95.

19. My argument *against* the New England historicity of HTH extends that of Arlin Turner; see *Nathaniel Hawthorne: An Introduction and Interpretation* (New York: Holt, Rinehart and Winston, 1961), pp. 18-21. My larger case *for* a genuine historicity as an essential element in the "Hawthornesque" takes issue with the generic definitions of Doubleday; see *Early Tales*, pp. 42-71.

20. Hawthorne refers to his own investment in the supernaturalism of New England in the letter to Goodrich of 20 December 1829; see Adkins, "Projected Works," p. 127. Of all the literature now called "pre-Romantic," Hawthorne's intense familiarity with the gothic is the most obvious; but a writer who began with sentimental effusions of poetry, and who announced in 1820 (in a letter to his sister) that he had read "all most [*sic*] all the books which have been published for the last hundred years," may easily be supposed to have read Thompson, Young, Gray, Collins, and the Whartons.

21. All that has been written against Hawthorne's interest in "history *as history*" seems perfectly true of Hawthorne's boyhood and college days. His sister Elizabeth confirms some such disinterest; and no doubt his concern never became quite professional or academic. But the tales themselves eventually demonstrate an amazing historical awareness. Nor are we without significant evidence touching Hawthorne's eventual feelings of competence and power: the man who scolded his sister's "naughty notions" about Hamilton and arbitrary government, who seriously entertained Duyckinck's suggestion of (someday) writing a proper history of witchcraft, and who suggested (in "The Custom House") that he might indeed write a "regular history" of Salem is clearly a man who had come to feel himself (at least) the equal of his antiquarian or Romantic-historical contemporaries.

22. For the view of *Fanshawe* as forecast, see Carl Bode, "Hawthorne's *Fanshawe*: The Promising of Greatness," *New England Quarterly*, 23 (1950), 235-242; and Robert E. Gross, "Hawthorne's First Novel: The Future of a

Style," *PMLA*, 78 (1963), 63–68. Oddly, "An Old Woman's Tale" (OWT) has never been fully treated in this "proleptic" way: neither of the recent books on Hawthorne's "poetics" (Dryden and Dauber) even mentions the tale; and Nina Baym *merely* mentions it as one of the "three earliest surviving stories [which] share a preoccupation with visions" (*Shape*, pp. 26–27). Much more critical interest has been invested in the paradigmatic quality of "The Haunted Mind."

23. See Vernon Loggins, *The Hawthornes* (New York: Columbia University Press, 1951), pp. 3–11.

24. All citations of OWT refer to the Centenary *Snow-Image*. The tale first appeared in the *Salem Gazette* for 21 December 1830.

25. In the end, of course, we do not *know* what besides the original "Alice Doane" was supposed to go into the "Seven Tales"; but critics as widely divergent as Turner and Baym have accepted the plausible inclusion of OWT (see *Hawthorne*, p. 20; and *Shape*, p. 24). For Hawthorne's own "critical" language about the "fireside legend," see his "Review" of Whittier's *The Supernaturalism of New England*, re-published (from *The Literary World*, 17 April 1847) in H. Bruce Franklin, ed., *The Scarlet Letter and Related Writings* (Philadelphia: J. B. Lippincott, 1967), pp. 289–291.

26. According to Baym, "The lovers in OWT fall asleep and dream something that really happens" (*Shape*, p. 27).

27. For a definitive review of the problems of dating the inception and identifying the intention of *Fanshawe*, see Roy Harvey Pearce's "Introduction to *Fanshawe*," in *The Blithedale Romance and Fanshawe* (Columbus: Ohio State University Press, 1964), pp. 301–316.

28. All citations of *Fanshawe* refer to the Centenary Edition (above). The work first appeared in October 1828. Pearce concludes that "Hawthorne must have had *Fanshawe* in hand by . . . the end of 1826," but that it was probably written *after* such stories as were intended for the "Seven Tales," and possibly for a different audience ("Introduction," p. 301–303).

29. For the contested geography of *Fanshawe*, see P. E. Burnham, "Hawthorne's *Fanshawe* and Bowdoin College," *Essex Institute Historical Collections*, 80 (1944), 131–138; and Robert Cantwell, *Nathaniel Hawthorne: The American Years* (New York: Holt, Rinehart and Winston, 1948), pp. 119–120. For the somewhat more profitable argument about its *literary* location, see G. H. Orians, "Scott and Hawthorne's *Fanshawe*," *New England Quarterly*, 11 (1938), 388–394; and J. S. Goldstein, "The Literary Source of Hawthorne's *Fanshawe*," *Modern Language Notes*, 60 (1945), 1–8. More recently, Nina Baym has argued for the adapted or "Americanized " gothic of *Fanshawe*, in "Hawthorne's Gothic Discards," *Nathaniel Hawthorne Journal*, 4 (1974), 105–115; and Robert Sattlemeyer has suggested the relevance of Scottish Common Sense philosophy, in "The Aesthetic Background in Hawthorne's *Fanshawe*," *Nathanial Hawthorne Journal*, 5 (1975), 200–209.

30. Rejecting Bowdoin for Dartmouth, Cantwell nevertheless insists that Edward Walcott "seems plainly modeled on Franklin Pierce" and that Fanshawe was "obviously inspired by Gorham Deane," the hard scholar whose life and ulti-

mately death "made a profound impression on Hawthorne" (*American Years*, pp. 122–123). Leo B. Levy seems blissfully unaware that Bowdoin was not in existence "about eighty years since," relative to the date of *Fanshawe;* but this is only a minor flaw in his generally unconvincing argument for the significance of time and place in *Fanshawe;* see "Hawthorne's World of Images," *Studies in the Novel*, 2 (1970), 440–448.

31. For the "solemn wager" with Cilley, see Horatio Bridge, *Personal Recollections of Nathaniel Hawthorne* (New York: Harper, 1893), pp. 47–48.

32. Marion Kesselring's famous "list" shows Hawthorne borrowing Brown's *Wieland* in 1838; see *Hawthorne's Reading* (New York: New York Public Library, 1949), p. 45. But in the light of his avowed interest in gothic fiction, it seems highly likely that Hawthorne first read *Wieland* much earlier.

33. I agree with Nina Baym that the incest motif in "Alice Doane" is largely conventional; see "Gothic Discards," pp. 112, 115; and cf. Henri Petter, *The Early American Novel* (Columbus: Ohio State University Press, 1971), pp. 242–256. But I am persuaded with Crews that "Walcott and Fanshawe are complementary sides of Hawthorne" (*Sins*, pp. 161–162). Cantwell's suggestion about Pierce and Deane supports this reading: Hawthorne would clearly be viewing his own identity choice in terms of the visible and available alternatives—wherever the novel is "set."

34. The evidence clearly suggests that Hawthorne really did repent his early tendencies to "solipsism." The famous language about trying to "open an intercourse with the world" is, of course, retrospective (from the "Preface" to the 1851 *Twice-told Tales*) and so could be colored by the wisdom of much later experience; similarly, the repeated tributes to the saving power of Sophia (in the love letters) might be largely a convention of courtship. But the 1837 letter to Longfellow is absolutely persuasive. It protests that the young Hawthorne never "meant" to be "carried apart from the main current of life" but that he had in fact "secluded [him]self from society": "I have made a captive of myself, and put me in a dungeon, and now I cannot find the key to let myself out"; quoted from George Parsons Lathrop, *A Study of Hawthorne* (Boston: Houghton Mifflin, 1893), pp. 175–176.

35. Pearce is almost certainly correct in arguing that Hawthorne's efforts were directed toward concealing his authorship of *Fanshawe* rather than trying to "suppress" or to "recall" it (see "Introduction," pp. 307–312).

36. There is, to be sure, a certain amount of "gloomy" material in the newly discovered manuscript of *Hawthorne's Lost Notebook 1835–1841* (University Park: Pennsylvania State University Press, 1978), and criticism has not been slow to notice this fact; see Hyatt Waggoner's "Introduction," which (in part) expands his suggestions in "A Hawthorne Discovery: The Lost Notebook, 1835–1841," *New England Quarterly*, 49 (1976), 618–626. Yet none of this "gloom" bespeaks "Calvinism." And it remains true that *Fanshawe* is in some ways "comic"; see E. Cifelli, "Hawthorne as Humorist," *CEA Critic*, 38 (1976), 11–17; and James G. Janssen, *"Fanshawe* and Hawthorne's Developing Comic Sense," *ESQ*, 22 (1976), 24–27.

37. No doubt Hawthorne was, from the first, a prolific and omnivorous reader; and clearly his writings allude to all sorts of readings. But the evidence also suggests that he began a conscious program of readings in New England history just after his Aunt Mary Manning acquired a share of the Salem Athenaeum. We cannot locate any very specific knowledge of Puritanism earlier; and the records show that relevant works by Ames, Barclay, (Alden) Bradford, Hubbard, (Thomas) Hutchinson, Increase and Cotton Mather, (Nathaniel) Morton, Neal, Sewell, Trumbull, Ward, and Winthrop (as well as some significant collections of sermons and state papers) were all first borrowed between December 1826 and November 1828 (see Kesselring, *Reading,* pp. 43–64).

38. Neither "Sir William Phips" nor Hawthorne's two other early historical sketches have yet appeared in the Centenary Edition; accordingly, all citations of "Phips" refer to vol. XII of the Riverside Edition: *Tales, Sketches, And Other Papers* (Boston: Houghton Mifflin, 1883), pp. 227–234.

39. See David Levin, *History as Romantic Art* (New York: Harcourt, Brace and World, 1959), pp. 3–23.

40. The principal "sources" of "Phips"—considered simply as such—would clearly be Mather's *Magnalia* and Hutchinson's *History,* which Hawthorne borrowed in late 1826 and early 1827; see Kesselring, *Reading,* pp. 53, 56. For modern consultation, see *Magnalia Christi Americana* (Hartford, Conn.: S. Andrus and Son, 1855), I, 164–230; and *The History of Massachusetts* (Cambridge: Harvard University Press, 1936), I, 336–341, 460–466, and II, 51–60, 63–68.

41. Hawthorne's own gallery of Yankee "positivists," who know what they know all too well, is fairly impressive. Among others: the bespectacled "Cynic" of "The Great Carbuncle"; Peter Hovenden of "The Artist of the Beautiful"; the biographically exact critic in the audience of "Main Street"; and (especially) Judge Pyncheon of *The House of the Seven Gables.* In all these instances Hawthorne clearly gives the Devil his due, even while attacking him *as* the Devil.

42. So powerfully entrenched is this ideal-affective theory of saving knowledge that Emerson and Ripley can both appeal to it (with only a minimum sense of their own "natural-supernaturalism") in the 1830's: Norton's religion is a *mere* "historical Christianity"; Unitarianism generally is "key-cold." The classic American text would be Jonathan Edwards' *Treatise Concerning Religious Affections,* especially the Fifth and Sixth Signs of Part III; see John E. Smith, ed. (New Haven, Conn.: Yale University Press, 1969), pp. 291–340.

43. For the Coleridgean argument in America (beyond the limits of Emerson's *Nature*), see John J. Duffy, ed., *Coleridge's American Disciples* (Amherst: University of Massachusetts Press, 1973).

44. Quoted from Perry Miller, ed., *The Puritans* (New York: Harper and Row, 1963), p. 292. Hawthorne would, of course, have had to encounter the original version of Hooker's *Application of Redemption* (London, 1659); but that was less difficult then than now. Hawthorne mentions Hooker (along with

Cotton) in *Fanshawe* (Centenary, p. 402) and again in *Grandfather's Chair* (Centenary, *True Stories*, p. 29); more significantly, Hooker seems to loom up behind the figure of Parson Hooper in "The Minister's Black Veil."

45. For Edwards' classic *reductio*, see *The Freedom of the Will* (New Haven, Conn.: Yale University Press, 1957), pp. 169–194. For a tentative but telling comparison of Hawthorne and Edwards on the special problem of sin and history, see Roy Harvey Pearce, "Hawthorne and the Sense of the Past," *ELH*, 21 (1954), 333–334.

46. It would be totally misleading, of course, to suggest that Hawthorne was, in any acceptable sense, an Edwardsean Calvinist. Waggoner's impressionistic conclusion remains valid: "No one who knows Hawthorne's works can suppose he believed in the doctrine of total depravity in the sense in which Jonathan Edwards did" (*Hawthorne*, 1955, p. 43).

47. The one serious reading "Phips" has received rightly emphasizes its dramatic-ironic or "literary" character; see Edward J. Gallagher, "Hawthorne's 'Sir William Phips,'" *ESQ*, 19 (1973), 213–218.

48. See Perry Miller, *The New England Mind: From Colony to Province* (Cambridge: Harvard University Press, 1953), pp. 130–190.

49. Endicott is Hawthorne's primary exemplar of the "holy warrior" in American Puritanism, although the sword-and-Bible *picture* appears in *The House of the Seven Gables*. For the prominence of this paradox in contemporary fiction, see Michael Bell, *Hawthorne and the Historical Romance of New England* (Princeton, N.J.: Princeton University Press, 1971), pp. 17–81. For Cotton Mather's contribution to the sacramentalizing of American *realpolitik*, see Sacvan Bercovitch, *The Puritan Origins of the American Self* (New Haven, Conn.: Yale University Press, 1975), esp. pp. 140–186.

50. Aside from his part in "The Judgment of the Witches," Phips distinguished himself in the theopolitics of the anti-Catholic wars against the French in Canada. In fact, Mather makes this involvement flow directly from his baptism into the Covenant; see *Magnalia*, I, 182–217.

51. Gallagher cites Bercovitch on Mather's creation of the "Franklinesque" theme of "rags to riches" ("Hawthorne's 'Phips,'" p. 213); but more is at issue than "the New World success story." Actually, Hawthorne is out for Bercovitch's larger theme: the power of Puritanism's rhetorical ability to sanctify all sorts of American works; see *Puritan Origins*, pp. 35–71.

52. Mather's "Life Of His Excellency Sir William Phips, Knt." is in fact dedicated "To his Excellency the Earl of Bellomont, Baron of Coloony in Ireland, General Governour of the Province of Massachusetts in New England, and the Provinces annexed" (*Magnalia*, I, 164); and it was clearly offered to this minor nobleman, hopefully, as a pious *exemplum*.

53. All citations of "Mrs. Hutchinson" refer to vol. XII of the Riverside Edition (pp. 217–226). The sketch first appeared in the *Salem Gazette* for 7 December 1830. For Hawthorne's later feminist-theological speculations, see my own "Footsteps of Ann Hutchinson," *ELH*, 39 (1972), 459–494.

54. For the excised reference to the Puritans' "original bond of union," see *Twice-told Tales*, p. 614.

55. The most likely source of Hawthorne's knowledge of Mrs. Hutchinson's famous self-incrimination is an appendix to the second volume of Thomas Hutchinson's *History of Massachusetts:* "Number II, November 1637, The Examination of Mrs. Ann Hutchinson at the court at Newtown." For modern reference, see Hutchinson, *History,* II, 366–391. Beyond this, Hawthorne had also read the relevant accounts in Winthrop's *Journal* and Mather's *Magnalia,* and he may well have consulted Winthrop's *Short Story of the Rise, Reign, and Ruine of the Antinomians, Familists, and Libertines* (see "Footsteps," pp. 461–478).

56. For a similar verdict on Cotton, see Miller, *Colony to Province,* pp. 59–65.

57. For Winthrop's account of the monstrous birth, see his *Journal,* J. K. Hosmer, ed. (New York: Charles Scribner's Sons, 1908), I, 266–269.

58. On this question Winthrop gave Puritanism's authentic answer in his famous "little speech" on liberty; see *Journal,* II, 237–239. His "doctrine" is entirely consistent with that originally proposed by John Cotton in his "Letter to Lord Say and Seal"—which was published as "Appendix Number III" in the first volume of Hutchinson's *History* (pp. 414–418).

59. Hawthorne's Puritans are, despite what *The Scarlet Letter* calls the "Utopian" character of some of their expectations, decidedly conservative, not unlike the men whose "Mind" Perry Miller so splendidly evoked; see *The New England Mind: The Seventeenth Century* (Cambridge: Harvard University Press, 1939), esp. pp. 365–462. It is Hawthorne's Quakers who embody the emphasis on "Spirit," which may also be thought of as characteristic of the Puritan impulse; compare Geoffrey Nuttall, *The Holy Spirit in Puritan Faith and Experience* (London: Oxford, 1946), esp. pp. 90–133.

60. Writing of John Cotton's more elegant objections to the doctrines of John Wilson, Winthrop offers the following: "It was strange to see, how the common people were led, by example, to condemn him in that, which (it was very probable) divers of them did not understand, nor the rule which it was supposed to have broken"; see *Journal,* I, 205.

61. Mrs. Hutchinson urged that "there lyes a clear rule in Titus [2:3–5] that the elder women should instruct the younger"; but Winthrop replied that, in the light of 1 Corinthians 14:34–35, the rule could mean only that "elder women must instruct the younger about their business, and to love their husbands" (see Hutchinson, *History,* II, 368). Elsewhere Winthrop took an even harder line: according to 1 Timothy 2:12, "I permit not a woman to teach"; compare his *Short Story,* reprinted in David D. Hall, ed., *The Antinomian Controversy* (Middletown, Conn.: Wesleyan University Press, 1968), p. 267.

62. The Quaker connection is clear: when Mrs. Hutchinson was commanded to withdraw herself "as a leper . . . out of this Congregation," she left holding hands with Mary Dyer. And it was as an avowed Quaker that Mary Dyer returned to Boston in 1656, walking (as it were) in "the footsteps of the sainted Ann Hutchinson"; see Rufus Jones, *The Quakers in the American Colonies* (rpt. New York: W. W. Norton, 1966), pp. 20–21.

63. George Bancroft was shortly (in 1834) to argue that "the principles of Ann Hutchinson were a natural consequence of the progress of the reformation,"

and he would compare her to Descartes as "a prophetic harbinger of the spirit of the coming age [which] established philosophic liberty on the method of free reflection"; see *History of the Colonization of the United States* (Boston: Little, Brown, 1856), I, 388–394. For the continuation of this emphasis, see Brooks Adams, *The Emancipation of Massachusetts* (rpt. Boston: Houghton Mifflin, 1962), pp. 214–248; Charles Francis Adams, *Three Episodes of Massachusetts History* (Boston: Riverside, 1892), I, 363–532; James Truslow Adams, *The Founding of New England* (rpt. Boston: Little, Brown, 1949), pp. 165–174; and Marion L. Starkey, *The Congregational Way* (New York: Doubleday, 1966), pp. 21–80.

64. For a review of the process by which Ann Hutchinson was turned from a heretic into a seducer, see my own "Footsteps," pp. 466–478.

65. All citations of "Dr. Bullivant" refer to vol. XII of the Riverside Edition (pp. 78–87). The sketch first appeared in the *Salem Gazette* for 11 January 1831.

66. Critics of *The Scarlet Letter* often fail to read the lesson of chaps. 7 and 8, at Bellingham's mansion, and especially of chap. 21, "The New England Holiday," back against the book's opening image. In that latter chapter, as in "Bullivant" and "Main Street," Hawthorne is careful to warn that one can easily overemphasize "the gray or sable tinge" of the original Puritans, and to suggest that it was "the generation next to the early emigrants [who] wore the blackest shade of Puritanism."

67. The precise sources of Hawthorne's knowledge of "the declension" of Puritanism might prove hard to fix. Certainly they include Mather's *Magnalia,* with its treatment (in Book V) of "The Reforming Synod of New England" (pp. 316–338); but very likely they number, as well, many of the same Jeremiad sermons from which Perry Miller has told the story of New England's movement "from colony to province."

68. The Riverside Edition is in error at this point. It refers to "a work of Increase Mather, the 'Remarkable Providences of the Earlier Days of American Colonization' " (84). The text of the *Salem Gazette,* however, mentions "a work by Cotton Mather, the 'Remarkables' of his Father"; and the "nearly forty years" chronology makes it clear that the "source" in question must be Cotton's *Parentator, or the Remarkables of Increase Mather* (Boston, 1724) rather than Increase's *Essay for the Recording of Illustrious Providences* (Boston, 1684), informally titled "Remarkable Providences."

69. The premise of "The Story Teller" is that, in New England, evangelical preaching has come to seem the only legitimate use of "the word," that the "play" of secular literature is usually debased and is at best irrelevant. Some such view seems to haunt the narrator of "The Custom House," who finds himself accused by his ancestors of being a "degenerate fellow." And thus the final word of the "sociology" of chap. 21 of *The Scarlet Letter,* itself reminiscent of the rhetoric of "The May-Pole of Merry Mount": in the end Puritanism (as it became) "so darkened the national visage ... that all the subsequent years have not sufficed to clear it up. We have yet to learn again the forgotten art of gayety." All this might be taken as a cogent specification of what Q. D. Leavis meant by the "poetic" loss, as balancing the "spiritual"

gain, of American Puritanism; see "Hawthorne as Poet," rpt. in A. N. Kaul, ed., *Hawthorne* (Englewood Cliffs, N.J.: Prentice-Hall, 1966), pp. 29–35.

70. See Matthiessen, *Renaissance*, p. 215. And for rough approximations to my three categories of historicist doubt, see Lewis Leary's review of Bell's *Historical Romance*, *New England Quarterly*, 44 (1971), 664–665; Nina Baym's review essay on "Hawthorne," in James Woodress, ed., *American Literary Scholarship: An Annual/1974* (Durham, N.C.: Duke University Press, 1976), p. 25; and Barton Levi St. Armand's article on "Hawthorne's 'Haunted Mind': A Subterranean Drama of the Self," *Criticism*, 13 (1971), 1–25.

71. For the "centrality" of American colonial history to the early (1826–1838) period of Hawthorne's borrowings, see Kesselring, *Reading*, pp. 6–13. Kesselring's view that such reading "filled in the background of local color" (p. 13) represents the *minimum* view which needs to be challenged.

72. If Parson Hooper were said to have been reading Dante or Shakespeare or Milton, very many literary critics would take up the clue at once; but most (apparently) have trouble believing in the interpretative relevance of a New England Election Sermon.

73. Quoted from Lathrop, *Hawthorne*, p. 176.

74. Even as Hawthorne honestly laments the unintentional solipsism of his years in the "dismal chamber," he begins to undervalue the best work he did there. This sense of the "moral" (or at least the personal-psychological) triumphing over the "literary"—which also affected his judgment about the relative merits of *The Scarlet Letter* and *The House of the Seven Gables*—must always be counted into the argument about "Hawthorne's Estimate of His Early Work"; see Neal Frank Doubleday, *American Literature*, 37 (1966), 403–409; and compare *Early Tales*, pp. 182–238.

75. Following D. H. Lawrence, much Hawthorne criticism has espoused his "imagery" as against his explicit "rhetoric"; see (especially) Crews, *Sins*, passim. But, as I have suggested in connection with the "rose-bush" of *The Scarlet Letter*, historical allusion must be treated as (at least) the theoretical equal of natural imagery in construing the meaning of any literary text ("Footsteps," pp. 459–460).

76. See Bell, *Historical Romance*, pp. 3–14.

77. See Kesselring, *Reading*, pp. 45, 53, 48, 56.

78. Ibid., pp. 56, 57, 53, 64, 50, 56, 45, 60. Hawthorne's borrowing of various "collections" disguises, with a mere name, a wide assortment of very particular readings; and Kesselring explicitly suggests that such readings were to have "counteracted any wrong impressions" created by the general histories (p. 10).

79. Ibid., pp. 50, 61, 55, 48, 62, 56, 64, 47, 53, 48, 42, 51, 54.

80. Ibid., pp. 47, 46, 62, 52, 58, 53, 57, 58, 61, 60, 45, 58, 43.

81. Ibid., pp. 58, 55, 50, 51, 61, 44, 53, 62.

82. Stewart and Cantwell agree on the extremely purposive character of Hawthorne's "reading period"; see *Hawthorne*, p. 44, and *American Years*, pp. 98–99.

83. The work of Sacvan Bercovitch suggests that *most* Puritan literature amounts to a concerted attempt to raise American reality to the status of Biblical myth; see *Puritan Origins,* pp. 109–135.

84. With regard to the nineteenth century, Bercovitch's argument has been anticipated by Fred Somkin, *The Unquiet Eagle* (Ithaca, N.Y.: Cornell University Press, 1967); and Ernest L. Tuveson, *Redeemer Nation* (Chicago: University of Chicago Press, 1968). J. H. Plumb suggests that the historian's most *essential* task is to criticize both popular and political re-visions of the past as mythic; see "The Role of History," in *The Death of the Past* (Boston: Houghton Mifflin, 1971), pp. 102–145.

85. The gothic provenance of "Alice Doane's Appeal" (ADA) is well treated by Waggoner, *Hawthorne* (1955), pp. 37–45; and by Baym, "Gothic Discards," pp. 111–114. For the question of editorial response, made on behalf of an American ladies-magazine audience, consult Seymour Gross, "Hawthorne's ADA," *Nineteenth-Century Fiction,* 10 (1955), 232–236. The classic psychoanalytic reading is, of course, that of Crews (*Sins,* pp. 44–60); and the original historicist emphasis is that of Pearce ("Sense of the Past," pp. 337–339).

86. All citations of ADA refer to *Snow-Image.* The tale first appeared in *The Token* for 1835, though some form of "Alice Doane" was demonstrably in existence by the end of 1829 and may well date back to the inception of the "Seven Tales"; see Adkins, "Projected Works," pp. 121–128.

87. Compare *Wieland* (rpt. New York: Hafner, 1926), chap. 6, pp. 56–69.

88. In one sense Hawthorne's literary development involved the progressively more strenuous attempt to control his own imaginative excesses and to heighten the moral impact of his own work. This moral concern (rather than any supposed anti-historicism) is the real basis of his rejection of the novels of William Gilmore Simms and, eventually, even the example of Scott: "the world, nowadays, requires a more earnest purpose, a deeper moral, and a closer and homelier truth than he was qualified to supply it with" ("P's Correspondence," *Mosses,* p. 369).

89. In *Grandfather's Chair* Hawthorne's scrupulously careful narrator is at great pains not to slander the reputation of Cotton Mather: pressed on the point, he concedes that Mather was "the chief agent in the [witchcraft] mischief," but that one should "not suppose he acted other than conscientiously"; and he concludes, quarreling with the recent "biography, written by Mr. Peabody, of Springfield," that "his life should have been written by one, who, knowing all his faults, would nevertheless love him"; see *True Stories from History and Biography* (Columbus: Ohio State University Press, 1972), pp. 94, 105.

90. The "historian" in question is almost certainly Charles W. Upham; see Baym, *Shape,* pp. 38–39.

91. The one critic closest to an adequately "technical" reading of "Alice Doane's Appeal" is Michael Bell (*Historical Romance,* pp. 68–76). For other historical analyses more or less compatible with my own, see Robert H. Fossum, "The Summons of the Past," *Nineteenth-Century Fiction,* 23 (1968), 294–303; *Hawthorne's Inviolable Circle* (Deland, Fla.: Everett/Edwards,

1972), pp. 13–22; Stanley Brodwin, "Hawthorne and the Function of History," *Nathaniel Hawthorne Journal*, 4 (1974), 116–128; and, most subtly, Charles Swann, "ADA: or, How to Tell a Story," *Literature and History*, 5 (1977), 4–25.

92. The classic charge against the "contradiction" of "Alice Doane's Appeal" is Waggoner's; see *Hawthorne* (1955), pp. 43–44. The epistemological problem at issue, however, is quite like that quintessentially Puritan problem of faith and evidence, which David Levin discovered at the heart of "Young Goodman Brown"; see "Shadows of Doubt," *American Literature*, 34 (1962), 344–352. Bell presses toward a defense of the historicity of ADA but ends by noting a "confusion" that is cleared up only in YGB; see *Historical Romance*, pp. 71–76.

93. Those characters in *Wieland* who unquestioningly accept the sexual guilt of Clara Wieland seem clearly caught up in some version of the problem of "specter evidence." Thus that gothic work may well function as an important "mediation" between Hawthorne and the historical materials of the Salem Witchcraft.

94. I point to the connection between Spenser and ADA, by the way, in "Visible Sanctity and Specter Evidence," *Essex Institute Historical Collections*, 110 (1974), 259–299. For a more extended assertion (with rather different implications), see John Schroeder, "Alice Doane's Story," pp. 129–134.

95. For an "absolution" of the wizard, see Helen L. Elias, "Alice Doane's Innocence: The Wizard Absolved," *Emerson Society Quarterly*, 62 (1971), 28–32. The point is (parenthetically) "answered" by Dennis Coffey; see "Artist Absolved," pp. 230–240.

96. Ultimately, of course, one must follow Frederick Crews in looking for the nature of the psychic transaction in question. One looks for that law, however, in the materials (that is, the language) of Puritanism itself, according to the suggestion of David Levin; and cf. Swann, "How to Tell," pp. 14–23.

97. Michael Bell and Nina Baym both look for some analogy or link between Leonard Doane and Cotton Mather (*Historical Romance*, p. 72, and *Shape*, pp. 37–39). Somewhat less convincing is the suggestion, of Dennis Coffey, that "the narrator, the wizard, and Cotton Mather are [all] transformations of the same character" ("Artist Absolved," p. 238).

98. For Sewall's confession of guilt in the witchcraft, see *The Diary of Samuel Sewall*, M. Halsey Thomas, ed. (New York: Farrar, Straus and Giroux, 1973), I, 366–367.

99. Calef, *More Wonders of the Invisible World* (London, 1700); quoted from George Lincoln Burr, ed., *Narratives of the Witchcraft Cases* (New York: Charles Scribner's Sons, 1914), pp. 300–301. Besides the original edition, Hawthorne could have known the work from three later reprintings— Salem, 1796, 1823, and Boston, 1828.

100. To Cotton Mather, Calef seemed merely "a very wicked sort of a Sadducee . . . raking together a crue of Libels," but his book clearly made a more subtle and powerful impression on Hawthorne. He seems to have agreed that Mather had "let loose the Devils of Envy, Hatred, Pride, Cruelty, and

Malice"; and his emphasis on the breakdown of faith everywhere (cf. *Grandfather's Chair* and "Main Street") echoes Calef's charge that the witchcraft proceedings had caused "Brother to Accuse and Prosecute Brother, Children their Parents, Pastors their immediate Flock unto death"; see Burr, *Proceedings*, pp. 293, 299.

101. *Grandfather's Chair* reads off, almost everywhere, as a considerate and even "charitable" revision of the historical tales. What it ordinarily reveals is less change or development than the simple omission of ironies that are too "wicked" (that is, "adult") for childish simplicity.

102. Although not all modern scholarship has been kind to Robert Calef, it remains true that Upham's *Lectures on Witchcraft* (Boston, 1831) is "chiefly responsible" for the view that Cotton Mather "instigated witchcraft trials to satisfy his own lust for fame and power"; see Chadwick Hansen, *Witchcraft at Salem* (New York: George Braziller, 1969), p. 220. Thus Hawthorne has had a word to say against Upham long before he pilloried that "smiling, unctuous man of God" as Judge Pyncheon in *The House of the Seven Gables*. Undoubtedly we are to read the praise of his "better wisdom, which draws the moral as it tells the tale" (267) as ironic: Upham's simplistic moralism had succeeded—famously!—precisely where Hawthorne's imaginative complexity had failed to win him an audience.

103. For Miller's famous, embattled re-statement of the not-at-all "popular" case against Mather, see *Colony to Province*, p. 204. And even Chadwick Hansen concedes that the *Wonders* represents a "hasty, ill-considered, overwrought, partisan defense of [Mather's] friends"; see *Witchcraft*, p. 221. For the conservative or "charitable" use of Biblical warnings, see *The Return of Several Ministers Consulted* (1692), in David Levin, ed., *What Happened in Salem?* (New York: Harcourt, Brace and World, 1960), pp. 110–112.

104. Clearly it is possible for historical criticism to be just a little too simple about the tale's second attempt to move its audience, and a little too solemn about the final "monumental" moral; see, for example, Fossum, *Inviolable Circle*, pp. 20–22; and Brodwin, "Function of History," pp. 121–125. For a radical reading of the final episode as the height of a dramatized narrator's "inhumane exploitation," see Mark M. Hennelly, Jr., "ADA: Hawthorne's Case Against the Artist," *Studies in American Fiction*, 6 (1978), 125–140. The more conventional, semi-autobiographical view of the narrator is reasserted by James L. Williamson, "Vision and Revision in ADA," *American Transcendental Quarterly*, 40 (1978), 345–354.

105. Upham's work has controlled very much of modern critical response to the events of 1691–92—not so much through the 1831 *Lectures* as through the two-volume *Salem Witchcraft* (Boston, 1867), which "made him the standard authority in the field" (Hansen, *Witchcraft*, p. 220). George Lyman Kittredge and Marion L. Starkey both cite Upham's authority without critical comment; see *Witchcraft in Old and New England* (rpt. New York: Atheneum, 1972), pp. 588, 594, and *The Devil in Massachusetts* (rpt. Garden City, N.J.: Doubleday, 1961), pp. 271–291, passim. Paul Boyer and Ste-

phen Nissenbaum (in turn) refer to Starkey's work as "the best researched and certainly the most dramatic account of the events of 1692"; and they criticize Upham chiefly for "idealiz[ing] the sturdy yeomen who figured in his narrative"; see *Salem Possessed: The Social Origins of Witchcraft* (Cambridge: Harvard University Press, 1974), pp. xi, x. All this makes Hawthorne's (implicit) criticism of Upham seem telling indeed.

106. If *Wieland* "mediates" Hawthorne's relation with the witchcraft materials, *The Faerie Queene* had long since prepared his moral understanding. For the pervasiveness of Spenser's influence, see (especially) Randall Stewart, "Hawthorne and *The Faerie Queene*," *Philological Quarterly*, 12 (1933), 200–212; Arlin Turner, "Hawthorne's Literary Borrowings," *PMLA*, 51 (1936), 534–562; and Buford Jones, "The *Faery Land* of Hawthorne's Romances," *Emerson Society Quarterly*, 48 (1967), 106–124. More tendentiously, John Schroeder has repeatedly argued Hawthorne's concealment of his enormous debt to Spenser; see "Hawthorne's 'Egotism' and Its Source," *American Literature*, 31 (1959), 150–162, and, more recently, "Alice Doane's Story" (see note 94).

107. The crucial Spenserian locus is, of course, *The Faerie Queene* (I:i 29–I:ii 11).

108. William Stacey testified that he was tempted by the specter of Bridget Bishop in his chamber at night; apparently she also "hovered over the beds of Samuel Gray and Richard Colman and Jack Louder." Or so, at least, had "honest men, unable to keep her scarlets and laces out of their minds, interpreted their night thoughts"; see Starkey, *The Devil*, pp. 153–154. For the original testimony, compare Cotton Mather, *Wonders of the Invisible World*, in Burr, ed., *Narratives*, pp. 223–229.

109. For the virtually paranoid climate or context of "The Judgment of the Witches," see Miller, *Colony to Province*, pp. 149–208.

110. Beneath the level of Miller's intellectualized "sociology," the small-town dynamics of Salem Village have been studied by Boyer and Nissenbaum (*Salem Possessed*). And for the argument that there actually were more than a few practicing witches in New England in 1692 (including Bridget Bishop), see Hansen, *Witchcraft*, esp. pp. 93–120.

111. In the "Preface" to *The Snow-Image* Hawthorne described himself as a man who had long been "burrowing, to his utmost ability, into the depths of our common nature, for the purposes of psychological romance." Though the self-definition proves somewhat less than anti-historical critics often imply (see Crews, *Sins*, pp. 3–26), it certainly helps to clarify the difference between his approach and that of Upham, who is everywhere interested in singular personalities.

112. The texts in question are (of course) *The House of the Seven Gables*, which explicitly links mesmerism to witchcraft and the "evil eye," and "Egotism; or, The Bosom Serpent," which tries to make moral sense out of the popular and borderline-scientific belief in the swallowed snake. For the critical significance of mesmerism, see Taylor Stoehr, *Hawthorne's Mad Scientists* (Ham-

den, Conn.: Archon Books, 1978), pp. 32-63, 83-102. At present, herpe-
tology threatens to displace cetology as American criticism's preferred mode
of indoor naturalism.

113. "Main Street," in *The Snow-Image*, p. 68.

114. "Malvin," "Molineux," and "The Gentle Boy" all appeared (along with
"The Wives of the Dead") in *The Token* for 1832; but they (like the *ur*
"Alice Doane") were also in existence by late 1829; see Adkins, "Projected
Works," p. 128. As we shall see, Hawthorne's borrowings from these
"sources" point toward 1827-1829 as the most likely period of composition.
"Young Goodman Brown" first appeared in the *New England Magazine* for
April 1835; its most likely period of composition is 1833-34.

115. No one would want to claim that the representations of "Young Goodman
Brown" are essentially "realistic" or that its thematic import is primarily
"sociological"; see Taylor Stoehr, "YGB and Hawthorne's Theory of Mimesis," *Nineteenth-Century Fiction*, 23 (1969), 393-412. And yet it both
invokes and comments upon a world that is quite recognizably latter-day
American Puritan.

116. One can plausibly argue that the existing "Alice Doane's Appeal" is actually
anti-gothic in its effect, but it would be very difficult to make that case for
the interest of the original "Alice Doane"; see Manfred Markus, "Hawthorne's ADA: An Anti-Gothic Tale," *Germanisch-romanische Monatschrift*,
Neue Folge, 25 (1975), 338-349.

117. The vital point to grasp—as against the generic analyses of Neal Doubleday—is that there is no such thing as "the Hawthornesque before Hawthorne." One discovers his powerful originality only by counting in the
seriousness and the aptness of his New England historical themes; the rest
he may well share with "Scott and William Austin" (*Early Tales*, pp.
42-52).

2. PROVINCIAL TALES

1. The disheartening fact about our knowledge of Hawthorne's early attempts
to publish a "framed" collection is that the critic still learns almost as much
from a 1940's article as from a 1970's book: see Nelson F. Adkins, "The
Early Projected Works of Nathaniel Hawthorne," *Papers of the Bibliographical Society of America*, 34 (1945), esp. pp. 127-131; and cf. Alfred Weber,
Die Entwicklung der Rahmenerzählungen Nathaniel Hawthornes (Berlin:
Erich Schmidt, 1973), esp. pp. 61-99. The American critic who has studied
the bibliographical problem most closely, in recent years, is Nina Baym; see
The Shape of Hawthorne's Career (Ithaca, N.Y.: Cornell University Press,
1976), esp. pp. 30-34. And for the most elaborate "literary" guess about
Hawthorne's plot in the "Provincial Tales," see R. P. Adams, "Haw-
thorne's *Provincial Tales*," *New England Quarterly*, 30 (1957), 39-57.

2. Though the historicist premises of Weber's "reconstruction" of the "Provincial Tales" seem more credible to me than the purely esthetic ones of

Adams, I am extremely wary of the attempt to discover such "inner criteria" as would permit us to move from comparative thematics to descriptive bibliography; see *Die Entwicklung*, pp. 74–83. In one sense "The Story Teller" is a *less* treacherous case: there we have a clear beginning, laying out a frame as well as proposing a theme.

3. For the psychological ground of similarity between "My Kinsman, Major Molineux" (MKMM) and YGB, see Richard C. Carpenter, "Hawthorne's Polar Explorations," *Nineteenth-Century Fiction*, 24 (1969), 45–56. And for the more strenuous versions of a psychostructuralism which tend to conflate all the major tales, see Frederick Crews, *The Sins of the Fathers* (New York: Oxford, 1966), pp. 44–116

4. Unlike "Roger Malvin's Burial" (RMB) and MKMM, "The Wives of the Dead" (WD) has never been "discovered" by modern critical ideology, and "readings" of the tale have been brief and "analytic" (rather than "interpretative"): see Mark Van Doren, *Nathaniel Hawthorne* (New York: Viking, 1949), pp. 82–84; Hans-Joachim Lang, "How Ambiguous Is Hawthorne?" in A. N. Kaul, ed. *Hawthorne* (Englewood Cliffs, N.J.: Prentice-Hall, 1966), pp. 87–89; Neal Frank Doubleday, *Hawthorne's Early Tales* (Durham, N.C.: Duke University Press, 1972), pp. 215–218; Patricia A. Carlson, *Hawthorne's Functional Settings* (Amsterdam: Rodopi, 1977), pp. 115–118; and John Selzer, "Psychological Romance in Hawthorne's WD," *Studies in Short Fiction*, 16 (1979), 311–315.

5. Adkins, "Projected Works," pp. 121–122.

6. For an account of "the domestic" as the countertheme of a basically "exploratory" national literature, see William C. Spengemann, *The Adventurous Muse* (New Haven, Conn.: Yale University Press, 1977).

7. See Baym, *Shape*, pp. 30–34. Weber, who believes that "The 'Provincial Tales' are undoubtedly historical stories" (p. 74), has nothing to say about the themes of WD; see *Die Entwicklung*, pp. 74–83.

8. All citations of WD refer to *The Snow-Image* (Columbus: Ohio State University Press, 1974).

9. See Louise Dauner, "The 'Case' of Tobias Pearson," *American Literature*, 21 (1950), 464–472.

10. Critical concern with the household lantern threatens to obscure the more potent image of the (federated) household itself; see Carlson, *Settings*, pp. 115–118.

11. Carlson has elaborated Lang's grammatical suspicion (about the "she" who "suddenly awoke" in the last line) into a structural chart; but the original "insight" remains unconvincing. The problem is not only that this reading requires an "entirely dishonest narrator" (Doubleday, *Early Tales*, p. 217), but even more drastically that it bungles the story's management of point of view: there simply is no plausible point of transition from one dreaming consciousness to the other.

12. In Hawthorne's ironic typology, Margaret and Mary are—both of them—both wise and foolish "virgins" at the same time. For the Biblical account (famous in America since Thomas Shepard's mammoth sermon), see Matthew

25: 1–13; and for the story of Martha and Mary, see Luke 10: 38–42. No doubt Hawthorne also has in mind John 11, where Martha and Mary are asked to believe that Jesus can raise their brother Lazarus from the dead. "Margaret" may well find her way into the story by way of the "domestic" influence of Wordsworth's "Ruined Cottage"; and such an influence would strengthen the possibility that WD was originally one of "Seven Tales," which had Wordsworth's "We Are Seven" for a motto.

13. Doubleday considers the ending most unusual "for a story written in the 1820's," yet it proves possible to construct "a completion of the domestic incidents and relationships of the tale" (*Early Tales*, p. 216).

14. What Hawthorne stops just short of imitating is that whole world of "Romantic" false delicacy which Howells would eventually satirize, particularly in *The Rise of Silas Lapham*. In that world the serious characters soberly worry that *all* happiness is at someone else's expense; and the others rejoice that people are always "making the most wildly satisfactory and unnecessary sacrifices for each other."

15. So I interpret James's famous remark about Hawthorne's caring for the "deeper psychology": his quasi-scientific concern for psychic law was often stronger than his literary concern for full or "round" characterization; and this turn of mind underlies his entire "allegorical" habit. See *Hawthorne* (rpt. Ithaca, N.Y.: Cornell University Press, 1956), p. 59.

16. Thus I name the dominant tendency in "modern" Hawthorne criticism, as it has not yet given way to the "post-modern" interest in the linguistic conditions or the meta-thematic possibilities of literariness as such. A "psychologism" rather than a "linguisticism," the merely "modern" way still affects to discover semantic meaning as a function of literary form; but it blissfully assumes that "deep" psychological meanings—whether conscious or unconscious in the order of authorial intention—are always ultimate in the order of critical explanation.

17. Aside from the classic "source studies," few substantial readings of RMB have paid much attention to the story's one-paragraph historical "headnote"; and ironically even these original source critics have created the impression that Hawthorne's "imagination" quickly left the real past behind; see G. H. Orians, "The Source of Hawthorne's RMB," *American Literature*, 10 (1938), 313–318; and David S. Lovejoy, "Lovewell's Fight and Hawthorne's RMB," *New England Quarterly*, 27 (1954), 527–530. The significant (historicist) exceptions would be Ely Stock, "History and Bible in Hawthorne's RMB," *Essex Institute Historical Collections*, 100 (1964), 279–296; and Robert Daly, "History and Chivalric Myth in RMB," *Essex Institute Historical Collections*, 109 (1978), 99–115. David Levin has warned against a simplistic reading of Hawthorne's opening tone, yet it still seems to me ironic; see "Modern Misjudgements of Racial Imperialism in Hawthorne and Parkman," *Yearbook of English Studies*, 13 (1983), 145–158.

18. All citations of the text of RMB refer to *Mosses from an Old Manse* (Columbus: Ohio State University Press, 1974).

19. The most fitting comments on the tale's inherent moral complexity are (still)

those of Hyatt H. Waggoner, who essentially "discovered" RMB for modern criticism; see *Hawthorne* (Cambridge: Harvard University Press, 1955), pp. 78–86.

20. Given Waggoner's inspired suggestions, Frederick Crews's more systematic "discoveries" about RMB seem a bit too gleeful, even as they have subsequently come to appear a little tendentious and one-sided. See "The Logic of Compulsion in RMB," *PMLA*, 79 (1964), 457–465; and compare *Sins of the Fathers* (New York: Oxford, 1966), pp. 80–95.

21. The influence of Jeremy Taylor was first proposed by Neal F. Doubleday, who connected Taylor's *Ductor Dubitantium* (which Hawthorne borrowed in 1834) with "Fancy's Show Box"; see "The Theme of Hawthorne's FSB," *American Literature*, 10 (1938), 431–433. In his later work, Doubleday also noticed that Hawthorne "had withdrawn all three volumes of Taylor's *Discourses on Various Subjects*," in 1826, 1829, and 1831—dates more appropriate to the conception, writing, and possible revision of RMB. Austin Warren seems to have intended this connection in treating the author of RMB "as an artist, writing about conscience [who] 'worked up' his subject through reading . . . the books of Increase and Cotton Mather, Bishop Jeremy Taylor on cases of conscience, The Newgate Calendar, The State Trials of England"; see *The New England Conscience* (Ann Arbor: University of Michigan Press, 1966), p. 135.

22. According to G. D. Josipovici, Hawthorne's modernism reveals itself as the concern "not with moral truths but with psychological truths"; see "Hawthorne's Modernity," *Critical Quarterly*, 8 (1966), 351–360. A stronger case could be built on the notion that RMB exaggerates the "particularist" (psychological) emphasis of classic casuistry to the precise point where its "universalist" (ethical) ambition fails.

23. For Malvin as unwitting Satan, see Daly, "History and Chivalric Myth," pp. 103–104.

24. The Biblical context of Reuben's "temporizing" and evident moral "instability" was first identified—in the story of Joseph and his brothers (Genesis 37)—by W. R. Thompson, "The Biblical Context of Hawthorne's RMB," *PMLA*, 77 (1962), 92–96.

25. Simulating the "right reason" of effective conscience at this point is precisely the "heroic" standard of "wildly satisfactory and unnecessary sacrifice" identified by Howells. It may also be thought of as "chivalric"; see Daly, "History and Chivalric Myth," pp. 110–115.

26. It is not precisely accurate to say that "the author relieves Reuben Bourne of any guilt for abandoning Malvin" and that "his guilt first comes when he allows Malvin's daughter . . . to believe . . . that he stayed with her father . . . and after that when he breaks his vow"; see Arlin Turner, *Nathaniel Hawthorne* (New York: Holt, Rinehart and Winston, 1962), p. 31. And it is seriously misleading to suggest that "the second section of [RMB] introduces a set of moral and spiritual problems rather different from those of the first"; see Doubleday, *Early Tales*, p. 194. *Of course* the narrator absolves Reuben from any "censure" for simply "leaving Roger Malvin" (349), but the struc-

ture of the tale insists on the identity of his mixed and problematic intention throughout.

27. See Daly, "History and Chivalric Myth," p. 111.

28. See Crews, "Logic of Compulsion," p. 458. For criticism of this semi-ethical position, see Daly, "History and Chivalric Myth," pp. 101–103.

29. Jeremy Taylor, *The Rule and Exercise of Holy Living*, in vol. IV of *The Whole Works of the Right Rev. Jeremy Taylor*, Reginald Heber, ed. (London: Ogle, Duncan, 1822), p. 24. Books I and II of the *Ductor Dubitantium*— which provide a rich context for RMB—are little more than a philosophical elaboration of Taylor's originary rule of intention.

30. Taylor, *Holy Living*, p. 24.

31. Puritan casuists, from Ames and Baxter in England to the Mathers and Samuel Willard in America, are in the same (Thomistic) philosophical tradition as the Anglican Taylor. That is to say, the Calvinist doctrine of the *total* depravity of *every* human intention does not everywhere matter as much as it might. With Edwards, however, the Calvinist difference makes *all* the difference. *The Nature of True Virtue* insists that the only *really* virtuous intentions comprehend the gracious notion of Being-in-General. And the *Freedom of the Will*—in its relentless attempt to avoid the infinite regress of a will before the willing—virtually excludes the notion of intention, excluding all conscious motions prior to execution from the domain of the voluntary, and identifying the moral quality of human actions entirely with their "nature" rather than their "origins or cause."

32. RMB has undoubtedly profited from the intense psychoanalytic study it has received; anticipating Crews in this mode, there were (besides Waggoner) Adams, *"Provincial Tales,"* pp. 39–57; Louis B. Salomon, "Hawthorne and His Father: A Conjecture," *Literature and Psychology*, 13 (1963), 12–17; and Agnes McNeill Donohue, "From Whose Bourne No Traveler Returns," *Nineteenth-Century Fiction*, 18 (1963), 1–19. The most noteworthy followers of Crews in the "case-study" of RMB are Gloria Chasson Erlich, "Guilt and Expiation in RMB," *Nineteenth-Century Fiction*, 26 (1972), 377–389; and Dieter Schulz, "Imagination and Self-Imprisonment: The Ending of RMB," *Studies in Short Fiction*, 10 (1973), 183–186.

33. Critical followers of D. H. Lawrence have been most aware of the "territorial" aspect of American literary consciousness. For example: Leslie A. Fiedler, *The Return of the Vanishing American* (New York: Stein and Day, 1968); Richard Slotkin, *Regeneration Through Violence* (Middletown, Conn.: Wesleyan University Press, 1973); and John Seelye, *Prophetic Waters* (New York: Oxford, 1977).

34. Orians, Lovejoy, Stock, and Daly (see note 17) all call attention to the currency of the Lovewell myth, though only the latter two attempt to make that fact thematically significant. For further information on the "matter of Lovewell" as of 1825, see Fanny Hardy Eckstorm, "Pigwacket and Parson Symmes," *New England Quarterly*, 9 (1936), 378–402; and Gail H. Bickford, "Lovewell's Fight, 1725–1958," *American Quarterly*, 10 (1958), 358–366.

35. Arlin Turner's comment seems representative: "The action begins at Lovell's Fight, a historical event of 1725, but the setting serves only to place two wounded men in the wilderness" (*Nathaniel Hawthorne,* p. 31). And this too literal view of the significance of Lovewell's Fight is in fact sponsored by source-critic Lovejoy, who concludes that the tale quickly breaks free of its sources to become simply "a psychological study of a young man burdened by the torment of his secret guilt" ("Lovewell's Fight," p. 530).

36. For the "vital significance" of the Lovewell legend, see Bickford, "Lovewell's Fight," pp. 358–362. For the discrepancies between history and legend, see Eckstorm, "Pigwacket and Parson Symmes." And for the ironies of Hawthorne's first paragraph, see Stock, "History and Bible," pp. 279–286; and Daly, "History and Chivalric Myth," pp. 112–114.

37. Eckstorm's principal villain is Parson Symmes; but she also makes it clear that "everybody in official circles must have known," and that "no one hindered him" in his instant revision of history ("Pigwacket and Parson Symmes," pp. 400–401).

38. The *physical* monument to Lovewell was constructed only in 1904, but Bickford indicates that "it had always been the custom to conduct visitors . . . to the battleground at Lovewell's Pond" ("Lovewell's Fight," pp. 363–364).

39. Daly, "History and Chivalric Myth," p. 112.

40. Stock, "History and Bible," pp. 280–282.

41. The brief suggestion of Diane C. Naples is essentially apt: "RMB . . . may be Hawthorne's parable for the nineteenth-century historian"; see "RMB—A Parable for Historians?" *American Transcendental Quarterly,* 13 (1972), 45–48.

42. Daly's (historical) explanation of Reuben's last name seems more complete and telling than Donohue's earlier (linguistic) proposal; see "History and Chivalric Myth," pp. 104–105; and compare "From Whose Bourne," pp. 9–10.

43. See Perry Miller, *The New England Mind: From Colony to Province* (Cambridge: Harvard University Press, 1953), p. 204.

44. For the "geopolitics," consult Seelye's *Prophetic Waters;* for the "hermeneutics," see Sacvan Bercovitch, *The American Jeremiad* (Madison: University of Wisconsin Press, 1978).

45. Edwin Fussel offers only two pages on RMB, but he clearly recognizes the "daydream" passage as "parodic to the point of cruelty"; see *Frontier* (Princeton N.J.: Princeton University Press, 1965), p. 76. Slotkin treats RMB only briefly, and Seelye has not yet extended his analysis this far; but as they review much of the literature that *evidently* lies behind RMB, their terms marvelously illuminate the significance of Reuben's "westering" experience. Led on by Seelye's "esthetic" of the frontier, Reuben's only regeneration is the deadly one achieved through Slotkin's "violence."

46. Thus I read Seelye's essential thesis: only the walled-in "Citty" of Puri-

tanism—and that only imperfectly and temporarily—could at all restrain the American territorial "esthetic."

47. Such is the initial, as yet unmythic conclusion of William Bradford, as Hawthorne would have read it in the faithful transcription of Nathaniel Morton; see the John Davis edition of *New England's Memorial* (Boston: Crocker and Brewster, 1826), p. 35. And for the appropriate reminder of French and Indian guilt, see Levin, "Modern Misjudgements," pp. 151–154.

48. Slotkin points out that Daniel Boone was himself "a neglectful husbandman, hostile to society and plagued by lawsuits" (*Regeneration*, p. 478). But Hawthorne may well intend to invoke the more widespread phenomena: everywhere a mania for "Land!" and everywhere lawsuits over the "boundaries" of what had once been Indian territory; see Miller, *Colony to Province*, pp. 33–52; and more specifically, Richard L. Bushman, *From Puritan to Yankee* (New York: W. W. Norton, 1970), pp. 41–103.

49. For a "covenantal" reading of RMB, see Stock, "History and Bible," pp. 286–296. If this sort of reading is correct, then William J. Scheick may have overemphasized the *natural* ambiguity of this symbolically insistent rock; see "The Hieroglyphic Rock in RMB," *ESQ*, 24 (1978), 72–76.

50. Again Hawthorne had quite enough of the Pilgrim story available in Morton, not only the departure from Holland but also (by way of an editor's "Appendix") the very moving breakup of the Plymouth Church, as many original members sought more land; see *New England's Memorial*, pp. 406–407.

51. For the filiopietistic vicissitudes of Plymouth Rock, together with a largely unironic version of the "Apotheosis" of the Pilgrim "Forefathers," see George F. Willison, *Saints and Strangers* (New York: Reynal and Hitchcock, 1945), pp. 408–435.

52. Since the Biblical discoveries of Thompson (1962) and Stock (1964), and despite the criticism of their significance by Crews (1966), still other Biblical places have been firmly located. John R. Byers, Jr., convincingly argues for "the well known Laban-Jacob-Rachel story (Gen. 23–31); see "The Geography and Framework of Hawthorne's RMB," *Tennessee Studies in Literature*, 21 (1976), 11–20. And Burton J. Fishman proposes, with equal cogency, the paradigmatic rock-experience of Moses (Isaiah 48:21 and Numbers 20:7–12); see *Studies in American Fiction*, 5 (1977), 257–262. Indeed it seems scarcely an overstatement to suggest that Hawthorne seems to have had the *whole* of the Old Testament in mind—at least insofar as that complex work can be read as a unified epic of religious tribalism; and, significantly, as it had been willfully applied to the ragged matter of Land, the Indians, and the Generations in the pseudo-typic externalities of provincial New England.

53. One might almost wish Cooper's *Deerslayer* had been written in the 1820's; but *The Last of the Mohicans* (1826) had already accomplished the magic revitalization of Bumppo as Hawkeye. And, less tendentiously, Hawthorne probably has the Boone legend itself directly in mind: "In the fire hunt Boone mistakes Rebecca for a deer and nearly shoots her"; see Slotkin, *Regeneration*, p. 478. Here, however, there is *no* magical rescue: no ram appears in the

brush to atone by substitution; and nobody goes on to inherit any pastoral promises.

54. The story's explicit eighteen-year chronology takes us from 1725 down to 1743, the year before the Battle of Louisburg, which—according to Hawthorne's "Old News"—seems to have aroused *explicitly* imperialist feelings in the "quiet race" of New Englanders; see *The Snow-Image* (Columbus: Ohio State University Press, 1974), p. 144.

55. John Samson, "Hawthorne's Oak Tree," *American Literature*, 52 (1980), 457-461. Hawthorne's use of the Farmer and Moore *Collections* is well documented in Orians and Lovejoy, and is rightly assumed by Stock, Daly, and others.

56. Virginia O. Birdsall's original (impressionistic) account of Hawthorne's oak tree seems innocent enough, but Patricia Ann Carlson's recent (diagrammatic) manipulation of both the tree and the rock seems retrograde. See "Hawthorne's Oak Tree Image," *Nineteenth-Century Fiction*, 15 (1960), 181-185; and compare "Image and Structure in Hawthorne's RMB," *South Atlantic Bulletin*, 41 (1976), 3-9.

57. J. Farmer and J. B. Moore, ed., *Collections, Historical and Miscellaneous* (Concord, N.H.: J. B. Moore, 1823) II, 33-42.

58. Thus "the matter of the Indians" figures far more powerfully in Hawthorne's fictional thought than we have recognized. Though "few incidents of Indian warfare [seemed] naturally susceptible of the moonlight of romance," RMB effectively does its job. Moreover, the matter lurks everywhere on the periphery of Hawthorne's historical fiction; and surely the neglected "Duston Family" (1836) could be read back against its source in Mather's *Magnalia*, in precisely this context.

59. Crews, I take it, has satisfactorily accounted for the geographical coincidence of Reuben's fateful return, on internal ("compulsive") grounds (*Sins*, pp. 82-92). Within these ("literal") terms, the falling branch is indeed a "pathetic fallacy," but its true explanation is contextual and historical: Reuben is, *per figuram*, the reason why the Charter Oak "appears to have lost its upper trunk." And for an apparently competing (but really supplementary) account of Hawthorne's concern for the calendar, see J. T. McCullen, "Ancient Rites for the Dead and Hawthorne's RMB," *Southern Folklore Quarterly*, 30 (1966), 313-322.

60. The *Salem Gazette* (15 April 1825), p. 30. George F. Willison points to a similar problem about the official veneration of Plymouth Rock: "When the calendar change from Old Style to New Style had been made in 1752, the difference between them amounted to eleven days, and the Old Colony Club had set Forefathers' Day accordingly. But this was an error, for at the time of the landing in 1620 the difference . . . was only ten days" (*Saints and Strangers*, p. 425).

61. Placing the "Fight" itself on Saturday (May 8, Old Style) rather than Sunday (May 9, Old Style), and congratulating itself on the Protestantism, Science, Commerce, and Civilization of its decision to add eleven rather than ten days

to the modern calendar, the *Salem Gazette* argues for a New-Style celebration date of May 19. Reuben's own "anniversary" is, of course, given by Hawthorne in the Old Style; and it commemorates not the "Fight" (May 9) but his abandonment of the dying Malvin (May 12). According to J. T. McCullen, "the twelfth of May" is significant because it "falls within the period of the *Lemuria,*" a sacred Roman festival which, unlike the more comfortable and benign *Parentalia*, shows a "gloomy, fearful atmosphere," as if a people were not at ease with their dead ("Ancient Rites," pp. 314–322). This seems relevant as far as it goes; but the real point would touch far more than Hawthorne's debt to "folk consciousness." Along with certain tribalist (and even Oedipal) paradigms from the Old Testament, Hawthorne is bringing Roman rite to bear on the peculiar quality of New England's own intense and uneasy "ancestor worship"—long since characterized by Perry Miller as "such a veneration of progenitors as is hardly to be matched outside China" (*Colony to Province,* p. 135). Thus Hawthorne's logic, in McCullen's own terms: Reuben's own anniversary seems indeed a superstitious, barbarous, and tragic *Lemuria;* but the public events of 1825 read off as a bitterly ironic *Parentalia,* for according to the spirit of that festival the people have nothing to fear from ancestors "so long as the living members performed their duties towards them under the supervision of the State and its Pontifices" ("Ancient Rites," p. 314).

62. Unlike RMB, MKMM was "discovered" by the historicists: Q. D. Leavis stressed its evident (if "proleptic") connection with the Revolution; and Roy Harvey Pearce elaborated its implicit "theology" of history. See "Hawthorne as Poet," *Sewanee Review,* 59 (1951), 198–205; and "Hawthorne and the Sense of the Past," *ELH,* 21 (1954), 327–334. Accordingly, a great deal of the "classic" criticism of MKMM has involved the attempt to deny that these historical considerations can fully (or even *adequately*) account for the greatness of this tale. See, for example, Waggoner, *Hawthorne* (1955), pp. 46–53; Seymour Gross, "Hawthorne's MKMM: History as Moral Adventure," *Nineteenth-Century Fiction,* 12 (1957), 97–109; Richard Harter Fogle, *Hawthorne's Fiction* (Norman: University of Oklahoma Press, 1964), pp. 104–116; and Crews, *Sins,* pp. 72–79. Still, the impulse to historical investigation has remained strong—stronger, perhaps, than in any of Hawthorne's other early tales. For further examples of this "school," see Robert H. Fossum, "The Shadow of the Past," *Claremont Quarterly,* 11 (1963), 43–56, and *Hawthorne's Inviolable Circle* (Deland, Fla.: Everett/Edwards, 1972), pp. 26–31; Julian Smith, "Coming of Age in America," *American Quarterly,* 18 (1965), 550–558, and "Historical Ambiguity in MKMM," *English Language Notes,* 8 (1970), 115–120; John Russell, "Allegory and MKMM," *New England Quarterly,* 40 (1967), 432–440; Doubleday, *Early Tales,* pp. 227–238; A. B. England, "Robin Molineux and Young Ben Franklin," *Journal of American Studies,* 6 (1972), 181–188; P. L. Abernathy, "The Identity of Hawthorne's Major Molineux," *American Transcendental Quarterly,* 31 (1976), 5–8; Peter Shaw, "Fathers, Sons, and the Ambiguities of Revolution in MKMM," *New England Quarterly,* 49

(1976), 559–576, and "Their Kinsman, Thomas Hutchinson," *Early American Literature*, 11 (1976), 183–190; Dennis M. Murphy, "Poor Robin and Shrewd Ben," *Studies in Short Fiction*, 15 (1978), 187–190; and Robert G. Grayson, "The New England Sources of MKMM," *American Literature*, 54 (1982), 545–559.

63. The best non-clinical account of the tale's psychological plot is that of Gross ("Moral Adventure," pp. 54–58).

64. Again, the famous psychoanalytic reading is that of Crews; and (again) his analysis implies a "systematic" simplification of the eclecticism of Waggoner. For the more clinical anticipations of Crews, see Franklin B. Newman, "MKMM: An Interpretation," *University of Kansas City Review*, 21 (1955), 203–212; Simon O. Lesser, *Fiction and the Unconscious* (Boston: Beacon Press, 1957), pp. 212–224; and Louis Paul, "A Psychoanalytic Reading of Hawthorne's MK," *American Imago*, 18 (1961), 279–288. Lesser's article called forth a significant critique and caveat by Pearce: "Robin Molineux on the Analyst's Couch," *Criticism*, 1 (1959), 83–90. For a more recent example of psychoanalytic interpretation, see Robert M. Strozier, "Dynamic Patterns: A Psycho-Analytic Theory of Plot," *Southern Review: Australia*, 7 (1974), 254–263.

65. "Sense of the Past," pp. 329–330. All citations of the text of MKMM refer to *Snow-Image*.

66. Pearce, "Sense of the Past," pp. 327–328.

67. Many early psychological readings of the tale tended to compromise with rather than to contradict the historical interpretation. And, following Leavis, the historicists themselves have generally accepted as inevitable the relation between Robin's "Coming of Age" and the American Revolution. Fossum explicitly suggests that "America's break with England, Robin's break with his home and father, and every young man's break with the parental bond, are in the story interchangeable and mutually supporting" (*Inviolable Circle*, p. 27); and Shaw suggests that "by making ritual connections between coming of age and revolution [Hawthorne] provides a clear insight into the nature of both" ("Fathers, Sons, and the Ambiguities," p. 576).

68. *True Stories from History and Biography* (Columbus: Ohio State University, 1972), p. 171. Leavis originally proposed "Old News" as the ideal gloss on MKMM, but (as we shall see) that work is far more nearly related to the "Legends of the Province House"; and the relevance of *Grandfather's Chair* is by now well established. See Doubleday, *Early Tales*, p. 230; Shaw, "Fathers, Sons, and the Ambiguities," p. 562; and also—relevant to the "Hutchinson connection"—"Their Kinsman, Thomas Hutchinson," pp. 183–190.

69. An adequate description of the strategic counterpoint of child-like piety and adult irony in *The Whole History of Grandfather's Chair* remains to be written. The fullest account so far is that of Nina Baym, *Shape*, pp. 85–96; and see also John W. Crowley, "Hawthorne's New England Epochs," *ESQ*, 25 (1979), 59–70.

70. Kesselring's list reveals that Hawthorne borrowed vol. I of Hutchinson's *History* in 1826 and again in 1829 (the year he first submitted the tale for publi-

cation); see *Hawthorne's Reading*, p. 53. Critics justifiably infer that he had read the entire work, however, for it is vols. II and III which contain the events alluded to in his headnote; see Doubleday, *Early Tales*, p. 230; and Shaw, "Fathers, Sons, and the Ambiguities," pp. 562–563. Vol. III (containing Hutchinson's own "ordeal" with the Boston mob) remained unpublished until 1828, and so we may fairly ascribe the "composition" of MKMM to that year; but its experiential roots almost surely go back to the celebrations of 1826.

71. "Though standing at the opposite pole from Sam Adams on the issues of the day, Hutchinson, in his *History of Massachusetts*, provided the patriot party with a wealth of material—enough, indeed, to lend credence to Ezra Stiles's observation that the publication of the history in 1764 had 'contributed more than anything else to reviving the ancestral Spirit of Liberty in New England' "; see Wesley Frank Craven, *The Legend of the Founding Fathers* (rpt. Ithaca, N.Y.: Cornell University Press, 1965), pp. 39–40. Catherine Albanese has more recently noticed the same irony: "a Royalist was . . . providing grist for the patriot mill"; see *Sons of the Fathers* (Philadelphia: Temple University Press, 1976), p. 20. For the true (unideological and even skeptical) temper of Hutchinson's historiography, see Bernard Bailyn, *The Ordeal of Thomas Hutchinson* (Cambridge: Harvard University Press, 1974), esp. pp. 16–20.

72. Russel B. Nye suggests that Bancroft's "determination to write the definitive history of the American people" may have been provoked by his reading of the work of George Chalmers, which he had characterized as acute but "written in a Tory spirit, full of spleen against our ancestors"; see *George Bancroft* (New York: Knopf, 1945), p. 94. But surely Bancroft was also attempting to supplant Hutchinson; for although Hutchinson's third volume (1828) had not enjoyed great popularity, his whole work was surely recognizable as "by far the best of the loyalist histories" (Bailyn, *Ordeal*, p. 384). The most "usable" history of the Revolution remained David Ramsay's influential two-volume work of 1789; but Ramsay could not tell the story from a New England ("apocalyptic") point of view; see Lawrence J. Friedman, *Inventors of the Promised Land* (New York: Knopf, 1975), pp. 18–30.

73. For the apocalyptic mood of 1826, see Robert P. Hay, "The Glorious Departure of the American Patriarchs: Contemporary Reactions to the Deaths of Jefferson and Adams," *Journal of Southern History*, 35 (1969), 543–565. As Hay makes clear, the celebrations of Independence Day in 1826 had been the most flamboyant in American history so far, even *before* anyone learned of the providential "departures" of Jefferson and Adams on the same Fourth of July. And, just as clearly, much more was at issue in the overwhelming tide of rhetoric that followed this news than the cooperative (or competitive) contributions of these two Patriarchs: the seal was being set on the civil-religious meaning of the American Revolution. See also L. H. Butterfield, "The Jubilee of Independence," *The Virginia Magazine of History and Biography*, 61 (1953), 119–140. For the local tone of the celebrations in Hawthorne's New England, see George Bancroft's "Fourth of July Oration, 1826," at North-

ampton, in H. A. Hawken, ed., *Trumpets of Glory* (Granby, Conn.: Salmon Brook Historical Society, 1976), pp. 81–93; and Daniel Webster's encomium to "Adams and Jefferson," (2 August 1826), in *The Writings and Speeches of Daniel Webster* (Boston: Little, Brown, 1903), I, 285–324. And cf., in the same volume, Webster's orations on "The First Settlement of New England" (Plymouth, 1820) and "The Bunker Hill Monument" (Charlestown, 1825).

74. The constant ("psychologistic") premises of Hawthorne criticism infect even the most informed interpreters: according to Shaw, "Hawthorne modified history and folklore to explore individual psychology" ("Fathers, Sons, and the Ambiguities," p. 566).

75. Shaw, "Fathers, Sons, and the Ambiguities," p. 564. For a fuller analysis of Hawthorne's typological mode—which stops just short of uncovering its deconstructive irony—see Shaw's more general article: "Hawthorne's Ritual Typology of the American Revolution," *Prospects*, 3 (1977), 483–498.

76. According to Hawthorne's headnote, Robin's adventures "chanced upon a summer night, not far from a hundred years ago" (209). Not far indeed, if we count from 1832; for the (economic) pre-history of the Revolution might well begin with the "Molasses Act" of 1733. Renewed and made "perpetual" in 1764, on the eve of the Stamp Act itself, the law was "designed to compel the rum distillers and dealers of New England . . . to buy molasses . . . of British, instead of foreign, colonies in the West Indies"; see Arthur M. Schlesinger, *The Colonial Merchants and the American Revolution* (New York: Atheneum, 1968), p. 19. The Molasses Act was met by "popular" protests "proleptic" of the Stamp Act violence, and it accelerated the depreciation of paper money (so lamented by Governor Hutchinson). Thus the (learned) connection between the "sexangular piece of parchment" (209) Robin receives as change from the ferryman and the tavern cheer he cannot afford to purchase, a bowl of rum punch "which the West India trade had long since made a familiar drink in the colony" (212). Grayson sets the tale in 1730; see "New England Sources," pp. 546–550.

77. For a summary of the Tory view of the "Rebellion" which allies its "theology" with that of Lord Clarendon, see William H. Nelson, *The American Tory* (Boston: Beacon Press, 1964), pp. 170–183. Hawthorne, of course, had known Clarendon's *History of the Rebellion and Civil Wars in England* since 1826 (Kesselring, *Reading*, p. 47). Of the Tories mentioned in Nelson, Hawthorne had probably read works by Daniel Leonard, Jonathan Boucher, William Galloway, and George Chalmers. And though Hawthorne could not have read Peter Oliver's *Origin and Progress of the American Rebellion* (which remained in manuscript until 1961), the chapter on him in *Grandfather's Chair* makes it clear that Hawthorne knew his theology of rebellion very well (see *True Stories*, pp. 191–197).

78. Peter Shaw has suggested that "the critical problem with MKMM has become that of establishing Hawthorne's attitude toward the American Revolution in the light of his disapproval of its crowd excesses" ("Ritual Typology," p. 491). A couple of extreme cases seem exemplary: to avoid asking the reader to identify with Robin, Russell has made him a composite of Hutchin-

son's six royal governors ("Allegory," p. 439); and admitting that he is "confused" about the story's disposition of our sympathies, Smith can conclude only that "Hawthorne is morally ambivalent toward the Revolution," fully aware of "the guilt we inherited with our independence" ("Historical Ambiguity," p. 120). From another perspective, Alexander W. Allison rejects historical readings altogether since they tend to "impute ... High-Tory opinions to Hawthorne"; see "The Literary Contexts of MKMM," *Nineteenth-Century Fiction*, 23 (1968), 305. And thus it should be noted that "moral" (and "myth") critics do not have this problem at all: for them Robin enters not Boston in 1733 (or the 1760's) but simply "hell" (or the "city of night"); see also Arthur T. Broes, "Journey into Moral Darkness," *Nineteenth-Century Fiction*, 19 (1964), 171–184; Carl Dennis, "How to Live in Hell," *The University Review*, 37 (1971), 250–258; Sheldon W. Liebman, "Robin's Conversion," *Studies in Short Fiction*, 8 (1971), 443–457; and Mario L. D'Avanzo, "The Literary Sources of MKMM," *Studies in Short Fiction*, 10 (1973), 121–136.

79. Nelson, *American Tory*, p. 182.
80. Pearce, "Sense of the Past," pp. 327–328.
81. Hutchinson, *History*, I, 271–273.
82. Thus Hawthorne's original title, for the Irish Molineux was in fact the uncle of the trader. Abernathy has identified this Irish Molineux and shown that he was available to Hawthorne through the *Drapier's Letters* of Jonathan Swift, where he appears in significant conjunction with the effigy-ritual of his kinsman, William Wood. But he seems unaware of Pearce's original identification of the American Molineux, and (following Doubleday) he has failed to notice that Hutchinson refers to the Irish Molineux as well as the American; see "Hawthorne's Major Molineux," pp. 5–8. Too late to influence the present argument, John Franzosa has suggested that this same Irish Molineux's *philosophic* relation to Locke bears on the problem of Robin's sensory disorientation; see "Locke's Kinsman, William Molyneux: The Philosophical Context of Hawthorne's Early Tales," *ESQ*, 29 (1983), 1–15. And from a rather different perspective, Nathan A. Cervo has associated Hawthorne's Molineux with Miguel de Molinos, the father of "quietism"; see "The Gargouille Anti-Hero," *Renascence*, 22 (1969), 69–77.
83. The modern reader will most likely know about "Robinocracy" from Bernard Bailyn's brilliant study *The Ideological Origins of the American Revolution* (Cambridge: Harvard University Press, 1967)—or from the historians of British politics (Robbins, Plumb, Pocock) on whom Bailyn depends. But as Bailyn makes clear, the "definitive" works on Robinocracy were reprinted many times in America during the eighteenth century and were in fact enormously influential (*Ideological Origins*, pp. 39–40). And though Kesselring is silent on the matter, the internal evidence of MKMM strongly suggests that Hawthorne had read in the pages of Bolingbroke's *Craftsman* as well as in the *Cato's Letters* of Trenchard and Gordon.
84. Quoted from Bailyn, *Ideological Origins*, p. 50.
85. Among the many similarities between Robin Molineux and the young Ben

Franklin, none is more arresting than their relation to political patrons, with Robin's Uncle Molineux here playing the role of Franklin's Governor Keith; see Smith, "Coming of Age," p. 554. Drawing on this same historical comparison, Dennis M. Murphy has suggested that "Robin" invokes the "Poor Robin" who gave his name to the title of the almanac of Franklin's brother James ("Poor Robin and Shrewd Ben," p. 189).

86. Again Bolingbroke, quoted from Bailyn, *Ideological Origins*, p. 50.

87. For the real limits of Hutchinson's own success as Walpolean Robinarch, see Bailyn, *Ordeal*, pp. 176-184.

88. Historians have usually dated the beginning of America's political parties—in the fully modern (neutral) as opposed to the "Puritan" (pejorative) sense—from the period immediately following the outbreak of the Revolution; see Jackson Turner Main, *Political Parties Before the Constitution* (New York: W. W. Norton, 1974). But it is now clear that some form of "opposition" had begun to organize in Boston as early as 1719-20, under the leadership of Elisha Cooke, Jr., and in concerted response to the more "courtly" interests of the Dudleys and Governor Shute. Indeed a recent commentator credits Cooke with "creating a distinctly modern organization . . . to organize and politicize [the electorate]"; and he notes that Cooke was to be accused of controlling elections with "bribes and election-time liquid treats"; see Gary B. Nash, *The Urban Crucible* (Cambridge: Harvard University Press, 1979), p. 87; and cf. G. B. Warden, *Boston 1689-1776* (Boston: Little, Brown, 1970), pp. 92-101. For Hutchinson's account of these phenomena, see *History*, II, 163-218; Hawthorne's "whizzing musket ball" is discussed on p. 217.

89. The fullest treatment of the beginnings of Court versus Country in New England is T. H. Breen, *The Character of the Good Ruler* (New Haven, Conn.: Yale University Press, 1970), pp. 203-269. For Hawthorne's fully ironic understanding of the provincial response to the invasion of "courtiers," see his 1838 tale of "Lady Eleanore's Mantle."

90. As Richard L. Bushman has made clear, American fear of "corruption" began with the understandable suspicion that the impoverished (and "alien") noblemen being appointed as royal governors would simply enrich themselves out of the public treasuries of a country whose "true interest" they neither shared nor always fully understood; and that it expressed itself not only in the long and wearing battles over governors' salaries but also in a jealous guarding of the "constitutional right . . . to control public funds." Only later did "corruption" take on its full British meaning of "subversion by ministerial appointment." See "Corruption and Power in Provincial America," in *The Development of a Revolutionary Mentality* (Washington, D.C.: Library of Congress, 1972), pp. 63-91. All of this economic strife is fully (if tediously) treated by Hutchinson; see *History*, II, passim.

91. Julian Smith proposes that the "country representative" is "either the governor himself or a royal official" ("Historical Ambiguity," p. 118). But this incoherent political suggestion misses Hawthorne's irony and leads to intolerable critical confusion.

92. Modern study of the particular quality of mob violence may well begin with

Arthur M. Schlesinger's Hawthornean reminder that "the patriot element comprised diverse elements and motives, and that a posterity, grateful for the end result, has preferred to remember only the more genteel aspects"; see "Political Mobs and the American Revolution," Massachusetts Historical Society *Proceedings*, 99 (1955), 244-250. For the clearest view of the organized and unspontaneous character of *much* eighteenth-century mob activity, see Edmund S. and Helen M. Morgan, *The Stamp Act Crisis* (Chapel Hill: University of North Carolina, 1953), esp. pp. 159-168, 231-240. Hutchinson's *History* clearly expresses his own belief that the mobs which intimidated Peter Oliver and then sacked his own house were no spontaneous overflow of political emotion (III, 86-92). And elsewhere he is even more direct in his characterization of "the present model of government among us": "When anything of more importance is to be determined, as opening the custom house or any matters of trade, these are under the direction of a committee of merchants, Mr. Rowe at their head, then Molyneux, Solomon, Davis, etc.; but all affairs of a general nature [begin with] a general meeting of the inhabitants of Boston where Otis with his mobbish eloquence prevails with every motion"; quoted from Morgan, *Stamp Act*, p. 235. Hawthorne seems to have understood—as clearly as the horrified Tories, or as the ambivalent John Adams—that "mobs were a necessary ingredient" of the Whig program.

93. The source of Julian Smith's (frankly admitted) confusion about the "political ambiguity" of the politics in MKMM surely lies in his all-too-certain identification of the spot where Robin is standing—on the steps of the "Old South Church," across from "the Province House, the royal governor's mansion from 1717 until the Revolution" ("Historical Ambiguity," p. 116). Grayson agrees about the story's prime locus, though he makes the politics considerably less ambiguous; see "New England Sources," pp. 550-559. Yet another corner seems equally consistent with Hawthorne's meager architectural details; see Hugh Morrison, *Early American Architecture* (New York: Oxford, 1952), pp. 426-442.

94. For the classic instance of credulity about the "kindly stranger," see Gross, "Moral Adventure," pp. 104-105; and cf. Daniel Hoffman, *Form and Fable in American Fiction* (New York: Oxford, 1961), pp. 69-70.

95. It is scarcely to be denied that there is "something dream-like" about MKMM, or that Robin falls into something like a "hypnagogic state" while alone at the church; or, even more cogently, that the tale abounds in references to "A Midsummer Night's Dream." And yet the thing can clearly be overdone—as, in the old style, by Newman, "MKMM: An Interpretation"; or, in the new, by Rita K. Gollin, *Nathaniel Hawthorne and the Truth of Dreams* (Baton Rouge: Louisiana State University, 1979), pp. 116-123.

96. Robin's final identification of his church-step companion with all his "other friends" unmasks that personage utterly: Robin's "shrewdness" (that is, naiveté) has been marked by its absolutely single-minded inability to see *anything* two ways at once; precisely here, however, he commands moral (and literary) authority by learning, finally, the adult use of irony. Behind Hawthorne's literary characterization of Robin may well lie Cotton Mather's polit-

ical protest against the flatteries of Governor Dudley's courtiers—"enough to Dazzle an Honest Countryman, who Thinks every Body Means what he Speaks"; quoted from Breen, *Good Ruler*, p. 233.

97. Though Lowell changes the moral character of Robin's "friend"—making him a somewhat pathetic (modern) political weathervane and timeserver (who would "see a sign")—he correctly identified him as a "Clergyman," the pastor of the church in question. See *The Old Glory* (New York: Farrar, Straus and Giroux, 1964), pp. 121–134.

98. The political role of the clergy in the course of American resistance and then Revolution has always been well recognized, if not precisely defined; John Adams, on the one side, and Tories like Hutchinson and Oliver, on the other, clearly saw the power of clerical rhetoric—whether "propaganda" or "ideology." Hawthorne may here be suggesting that at least some clergymen may have had a more direct role. At very least he is evoking our memory of Jonathan Mayhew's provocative sermon on the text "I would that they were even cut off which trouble you," which Hutchinson believed to have inspired the attack on his own house; see *History*, III, 89. Mayhew, who died in 1766, was pastor of the West Church, which cannot possibly figure in the geography of the Molineux parade. But the pastor of the First Church, from 1727 to 1787, was also well known as a leader of the Black Regiment; indeed the rhetoric of Charles Chauncey was often more volatile than Mayhew's own, and Peter Oliver characterized him as "the Head Master of the School of Prophets." Of course Chauncey was an economic and social conservative as well as an ideologue of resistance, but even this fact fits Hawthorne's pattern; for the cool detachment with which Hawthorne's minister admits to knowing the mob leader but "not intimately" (225) characterizes the aristocratic Chauncey better than any other Boston clergyman.

99. As Morgan observes, the politically purposive mob activities of Boston in the 1760's took their rise in the Puritanic "Pope's Day" clashes between the South End and the North End mobs, vying in blood for the right to burn an effigy of the Pope; see *Stamp Act*, pp. 159–160. Nash makes it clear that, though merchant leaders (like Molineux) might simply take over and manage these "ritualistic" pageants of "misrule," they could come to have a political life of their own; see *Urban Crucible*, pp. 260–261, 292–300, 309–311, 339–362. But that of course is also part of Hawthorne's point: ritual activity is born in violence and may not subsume it permanently; an effigy may turn into somebody's uncle.

100. By my geographical (and political) lights, the Molineux procession advances down King Street, from the Long Wharf, turns the corner where the First Church and the Town House face each other, and sweeps on down Cornhill Street to a meeting at the Old South: I refer to the famous "Bonner Map" of 1722, which is printed as the frontispiece in Warden's *Boston*. For the political plausibility of such a route, see Hiller B. Zobel, *The Boston Massacre* (New York: W. W. Norton, 1971), pp. 78–79; and cf. Warden, *Boston*, pp. 280–283, 311–313.

101. Gross, "Moral Adventure," p. 106. We are now in a position to reverse the old critical orthodoxy: Robin's quest, without reference to the politics of conspiracy, substitutes "dreamy" analytic abstractions for the real world.

102. For the more virulent evocations of the connection between British plots and "the Scarlet Whore," see Philip Davidson, *Propaganda and the American Revolution* (Chapel Hill: University of North Carolina, 1941), pp. 122-128. For a more sober view of "the Anglican Connection," see Carl Bridenbaugh, *Mitre and Sceptre* (New York: Oxford, 1962); and of the Biblical theory in question, James West Davidson, *The Logic of Millennial Thought* (New Haven, Conn.: Yale University Press, 1977), esp. pp. 213-254.

103. Again Hawthorne reveals his flawless mastery of the Revolutionary lexicon: "contagion" begins as a word expressing the paranoic Whiggish suspicion of the epidemic spread of "corruption" and ends as a shorthand for the hysterical Tory fear of the riotous end of respect for all duly constituted authority; see Bailyn, *Ideological Origins*, esp. pp. 230-319 ("The Contagion of Liberty").

104. For the most sophisticated treatment of MKMM under the aspect of myth and ritual, see Peter Shaw, "Fathers, Sons, and the Ambiguities," and "Hawthorne's Ritual Typology." Shaw's work is anticipated by that of Daniel Hoffman; see "Yankee Bumpkin and Scapegoat King" (in *Form and Fable*); ultimately it derives from the seminal "historicist" essay of Q. D. Leavis ("Hawthorne as Poet"). For the professional historian's awareness of the ritual origins of American resistance, see Nash, *Urban Crucible*, pp. 260-263.

105. Thus the "compromising" tendency of most "historicist" criticism (see note 67). The tendency permanently to associate the political with the familial is only strengthened, of course, by the readiness of both Loyalists and Revolutionaries to think of Great Britain as "in the same relation to the colonies as a parent to children" (Bailyn, *Ideological Origins*, p. 313).

106. For a keenly critical view of the Revolutionary afterlife of the original Puritan ideology, see Bercovitch, *Jeremiad*, pp. 93-175. And for the definitive study of the literary and intellectual history of the Revolution as *rite de passage*, see Michael Kammen, *A Season of Youth* (New York: Knopf, 1978), esp. pp. 186-220.

107. Cf. Russell: "The easiest way to see why Robin cannot represent young America is to observe that his *antagonists* perform this representation. Singly or in groups as they appear . . . they are a rough-and-ready lot, reeking of self-sufficiency and . . . obviously are not to be trifled with where their independence is concerned" ("Allegory," p. 434).

108. According to Kammen, one unhappy result of Americans' easy acceptance of their Revolution as national rite of passage has been the tendency "to minimize the most revolutionary aspects of the Revolution"; another has been "the reductive inclination to simplify our past by flattening out the diversities and uncomfortable complexities" (*Season of Youth*, pp. 213, 221).

109. Absent from MKMM is any explicit reminder of the attempted destruction

of Hutchinson's historical manuscripts, "containing secrets of our country's history" (*True Stories*, p. 158)—the accidental (or providential) survival of which made Hawthorne's own story possible. But perhaps the entire tale stands for this problem, for it simultaneously enacts and forbids the literary transcendence of historical secrets.

110. We misjudge Hawthorne's historical competence *utterly* if we try to infer it from the literal informations of *Grandfather's Chair*. For everywhere a kindly old narrator—who ends his performance with an account of his confrontation with his own ironic muse (parodying the experience of Milton's Adam with the Angel)—knows much more than he is telling. Most obviously, he censures Charley's chauvinistic wish that "the people had tarred and feathered every man" of Hutchinson's Junto (*True Stories*, p. 177); and, on the other hand, he patiently corrects Lawrence's more sensitive but still hasty (child-like) inference that the mobbish New Englanders were "not worthy of even so much liberty as the King was willing to allow them" (pp. 159, 171). Even more knowingly he denies Lawrence's suggestion that Hutchinson wrote history with a degree of romantic inspiration (pp. 137–138). But mostly he knows how to keep silent: when Clara observes it "odd . . . that the liberties of America should have had anything to do with a cup of tea," we tremble on the verge of a truly Hawthornean ("provincial") irony; but Grandfather merely "smile[s] and proceed[s] with his narrative" (p. 179). His auditors, after all, are children; he can afford to wait.

111. The quotation—and the "vision," pure and simple—comes from D. H. Lawrence's (poetic) remarks on Whitman in *Studies in Classic American Literature* (rpt. New York: Doubleday, 1951), p. 186. For Lewis' more academic (dialectical) account, see *The American Adam* (Chicago: University of Chicago Press, 1955), esp. pp. 1–13.

112. An adequate account of the beginnings and early flourishings of the historical romance in America remains to be written. For the present, see G. H. Orians, "The Romance Ferment After *Waverly*," *American Literature*, 3 (1932), 408–431; Ernest E. Leisy, *The American Historical Novel* (Norman: University of Oklahoma Press, 1950), pp. 3–113; John C. Stubbs, *The Pursuit of Form* (Urbana: University of Illinois Press, 1970), pp. 3–48; Michael D. Bell, *Hawthorne and the Historical Romance of New England* (Princeton, N.J.: Princeton University Press, 1971), pp. vii–xii, 3–14, and passim; and Doubleday, *Early Tales*, pp. 3–71.

113. For the anxious underside of American optimism in the early nineteenth century, see Somkin, *Unquiet Eagle*, pp. 1–90; and cf. Bercovitch, *Jeremiad*, pp. 142–143.

114. The Massachusetts Historical Society dates from 1791 and the American Antiquarian from 1812; but, as Kammen rightly observes, "the first distinctive movement to establish state and local societies occurred between 1820 and 1828" (*Season of Youth*, p. 26). See also David D. Van Tassel, *Recording America's Past* (Chicago: University of Chicago Press, 1960), esp. pp. 31–40; and cf. Walter Muir Whitehill, *Independent Historical Societies* (Boston: Boston Athenaeum, 1962), esp. pp. 3–12.

115. See Russel B. Nye, *The Cultural Life of the New Nation* (New York: Harper and Row, 1960), pp. 235–267. For a generous selection of texts calling for a literature that would "use American materials," see Richard Ruland, ed., *The Native Muse: Theories of American Literature* (New York: Dutton, 1972), I, 85–260. Unfortunately Ruland omits Rufus Choate from his collection; for his discussion of the principal "matters" of America, see "The Importance of Illustrating New-England History by a Series of Romances like the Waverley Novels," in *The Life and Writings of Rufus Choate* (Boston: Little, Brown, 1862), I, 319–346.

116. Solomon Stoddard, *An Appeal to the Learned* (1709); quoted from Perry Miller, ed., *The American Puritans* (New York: Doubleday, 1956), p. 222.

117. Stoddard, *Appeal;* in Miller, *American Puritans*, p. 223. Hawthorne's version of this remark appears as the famous "moral" of *The House of the Seven Gables:* "the wrong-doing of one generation lives into the successive ones, and, divesting itself of every temporary advantage, becomes a pure and uncontrollable mischief."

118. See "Main Street," in *Snow-Image*, pp. 67–68, 55–60; "Liberty Tree," in *True Stories*, p. 171.

119. Pearce, "Sense of the Past," p. 348; Lewis, *American Adam*, pp. 7–8.

120. Instead of Choate's proposed "series of romances" dramatizing the crucial significance of New England's typic instances, Hawthorne gives us only an assortment of tales conceived as gloomy memorials or anti-mythic deconstructions.

121. For the latter-day Puritan attempt to reduce the inhibiting power of "ancestors" without fully empowering "the self," see Emory Elliott, *Power and the Pulpit in Puritan New England* (Princeton, N.J.: Princeton University Press, 1975), esp. pp. 136–200.

122. The most learned of recent attempts to deal with Hawthorne "historically" holds that, "like his contemporaries Hawthorne sought the meaning of American history in its origins"; and that, like Bancroft, he "answers the question of how America will turn out by exploring the origins of New England" (Shaw, "Ritual Typology," pp. 483–484). One should beware of this proposition, especially as it associates Hawthorne with the frankly neo-typological epistemology of Bancroft. Without quite offering Hawthorne as an exemplar of the modernism which holds that "origins are lost," one must always allow for his ironic play with existing literary oversimplifications about the past.

3. THE PURITAN BIAS

1. Most criticism of "The Gentle Boy" (GB) is based on Seymour Gross's contention that Hawthorne's revisions made the tale less historical, more archetypal; see "Hawthorne's Revisions of GB," *American Literature*, 26 (1954), 196–208. The most significant exception of Gross's view is that of Michael Bell: while GB "can be read as a 'timeless' tale of human suffering, . . . it is far more profoundly set at a particular time, a particular mo-

ment in American history"; see *Hawthorne and the Historical Romance of New England* (Princeton, N.J.: Princeton University Press, 1971), p. 112.

2. Thus Neal Doubleday invokes a parenthetical remark by Hyatt Waggoner; see *Hawthorne's Early Tales: A Critical Study* (Durham, N.C.: Duke University Press, 1972), pp. 169–170.

3. For Hawthorne's ambivalent estimate of this early tale, see his "Preface" to *GB: A Thrice Told Tale* (Boston: Jordan, 1839). This is the edition for which Sophia Peabody drew a "portrait" of gentle Ilbrahim. But the tale may already have had a personal significance for Hawthorne, since it had aroused the interest of the Peabody sisters more than any of his other early (anonymous) publications; more than any other, this tale had served "to open [his] intercourse with the world."

4. For a view which tries to balance Hawthorne's motives of guilty "atonement" with other, more publicly historical motives, see Doubleday, *Early Tales*, pp. 159–163.

5. The quotation is from Manzoni, but the sentiment would hold true for the serious work of Scott as well; see Leslie Fiedler, *Love and Death in the American Novel* (New York: World, 1966), p. 164. For the epistemology of America's romantic historians, inspired by Scott, see David Levin, *History as Romantic Art* (New York: Harcourt, Brace and World, 1963), esp. pp. 3–23. A careful application of these ideas to Hawthorne is made by Roy Harvey Pearce, who distinguishes Hawthorne's *critical* from his contemporaries' *metaphysical* theory of history. The point is well taken: obviously Hawthorne does not share the prevailing attitudes concerning "nature" and "progress." Still, the simpler note seems worth stressing: Hawthorne shares with these contemporaries many assumptions about the importance of history as dramatic-affective rather than documentary-positivist; see "Romance and the Study of History," *Hawthorne Centenary Essays* (Columbus: Ohio State University Press, 1964), esp. pp. 221–231.

6. The basic "source study" of GB long ago identified Hawthorne's explicit allusion to "the historian of the [Quaker] sect" (69) as William Sewell, whose *History of the Rise, Increase, and Progress of the Christian People Called Quakers* (Burlington, N.J., 1774) Hawthorne borrowed from the Salem Athenaeum in January 1828 and October 1829. Besides this massive Quaker fundament, Hawthorne also drew facts and attitudes from William Hubbard's *General History of New England* (1677), Cotton Mather's *Magnalia Christi Americana* (1702), John Neal's *History of New England* (1720), Thomas Hutchinson's *History of Massachusetts* (1764), and Isaac Backus' *History of the Baptists in New England* (1777). See G. Harrison Orians, "The Sources and Themes of GB," *New England Quarterly*, 14 (1941), 664–678. It also seems likely to Orians that Hawthorne knew George Bishop's anti-Puritan *New England Judged* (in the London edition of 1703) and John Norton's anti-Quaker *Heart of New-England Rent* (Cambridge, 1659), both of which lie behind Sewell; to me Bishop and Norton seem certain. Thus I take Orians' work for granted and heartily agree with Doubleday that "the representative quality of the tale . . . has its foundation in the history of Puritan-Quaker relationships" (*Early Tales*, p. 163). All

citations of the text of GB refer to *Twice-told Tales* (Columbus: Ohio State University Press, 1974).

7. Contrary to Gross's argument ("Revisions," pp. 196–198), Hawthorne's substantial deletions from his preliminary sketch change neither its historical import nor its essential ethical balance. The canceled passage does go well out of its way to make allowances for the Puritans' behavior, but it returns to their "polemic fierceness" after all. Further, Hawthorne's literal and brutal attack on Endicott ("the person then at the head of the government") is allowed to stand, so that the guilt is "balanced" with or without the deletions. And since the movement of the canceled passage perfectly imitates the movement of the sketch as a whole, its deletion can be accounted for in terms of literary economy: Hawthorne would tell it less and rely more on his showing. For all of Hawthorne's deletions, see *Twice-told Tales*, pp. 613–619.

8. Gross's suggestion that the tale is really a sort of Manichaean parable about the "Evil Principle" has been elaborated by Agnes McNeill Donohue in "The Fruit of that Forbidden Tree," *The Hawthorne Question* (New York: Crowell, 1963), pp. 158–170. The psychoanalytic reduction is, of course, one of Crews's *Sins*.

9. See Roy R. Male, *Hawthorne's Tragic Vision* (New York: W. W. Norton, 1964), p. 45. Michael Bell gives the story a similar reading in terms of the "tragedy" of New World home and identity; see *Historical Romance*, pp. 110–117. And for a subtler formula concerning Evil and History in Hawthorne, see Roy Harvey Pearce, "Hawthorne and the Sense of the Past," *ELH*, 21 (1954), 333–334.

10. W. R. Thompson's reading of GB in terms of an opposition between Old and New Testament may be a little too pat, but he successfully demonstrates the tale's effective range of Biblical references; see "Patterns of Biblical Allusion in Hawthorne's GB," *South Central Bulletin*, 22 (1963), 3–10. To his long list I should like to propose the parable of the Good Samaritan (Luke 10: 30–37), the various versions of the Sermon on the Mount, and Matthew's account of the standards of the Last Judgment (25: 31–46).

11. Lines 5–6 from Williams' poem "Boast not, proud English . . . ," originally published in his *Key into the Languages of America* (1643). That work may have been originally familiar to Hawthorne from its partial reprinting in vol. III of the *Collections of the Massachusetts Historical Society* (Cambridge, 1794), 203–238—which Hawthorne borrowed on 8 November 1827; see Marion L. Kesselring, *Hawthorne's Reading* (New York: New York Public Library, 1949), p. 56. Not surprisingly, however, that filiopietistic reprinting omits all of Williams' pungent poetic criticisms of Massachusetts Puritanism's special pretensions to grace. That distortion was promptly corrected by the publication of the entire work as vol. I of the *Collections of the Rhode Island Historical Society* (Providence, 1827); and on the basis of internal evidence I conclude that Hawthorne had seen this edition (p. 61).

12. Matthiessen's judgment accords pretty well with the impression generally conveyed by Perry Miller's *The New England Mind: The Seventeenth Century* (Cambridge: Harvard University Press, 1939). Among the more noteworthy

modern attempts to answer this view are J. F. Maclear, " 'The Heart of New-England Rent,' " *Mississippi Valley Historical Review*, 42 (1956), 621–652; and Robert Middlekauff, "Piety and Intellect in Puritanism," *William and Mary Quarterly*, 3rd series, 22 (1965), 457–470. Much of this aspect of the reaction against "the Harvard School" seems to be beside the point, based on an uncareful reading of Miller's book or (at very least) on a failure to appreciate the qualifications Miller provided in "From Edwards to Emerson"; see *Errand into the Wilderness* (New York: Harper, 1964), pp. 184–203.

13. The Williams poem is again from the Rhode Island Edition of the *Key* (p. 32). It has been cogently suggested that Melville's idea of redemption coming through the pagan savage Ishmael owes something to Hawthorne's use of Ilbrahim; see Matthiessen, *Renaissance*, pp. 215–216; and cf. Gerhard Friedrich, "A Note on Quakerism and *Moby Dick*," *Quaker History*, 54 (1965), 94–102. It seems equally likely that Hawthorne's own sense of comparative religion and culture came to him more powerfully from Roger Williams than from any of the Enlightenment writers with whom he was familiar. For this aspect of Williams' thought, see Perry Miller, *Roger Williams: His Contribution to the American Tradition* (New York: Atheneum, 1965), esp. pp. 49–54.

14. The "relevant" (but redundant) passage reads as follows: "The inhabitants of New England were a people, whose original bond of union was their peculiar religious principles. For the peaceful exercise of their own mode of worship, an object, the very reverse of universal liberty of conscience, they had hewn themselves a home in the wilderness." My own sense of Puritan "tribalism" derives from Edmund Morgan, *The Puritan Family* (New York: Harper, 1966), pp. 161–186; and *Visible Saints* (Ithaca, N.Y.: Cornell University Press, 1965), pp. 64–112.

15. How much Hawthorne knew, in the later 1820's, about the Islamic world one can only infer. But it seems certain that he knew Ilbrahim (or Ibrahim) was the Moorish equivalent of Abraham; that it was the name of several prominent leaders in the eighth-century origins of Islam; and that the Islamites ultimately traced their origins to Ishmael (the son of Abraham by the slave girl Hagar), through whom the Israelites' covenant did *not* descend and who in Pauline typology became the figure of the whole lost world of the flesh outside of Christianity. Thus where Melville has a pagan savage redeem his bastard-outcast of an Ishmael, Hawthorne sends salvation to his covenanted Puritans in the name of that religion organized in most explicit opposition to the Christian scheme of salvation history.

16. The explicit reference to Ward's *Simple Cobbler* occurs further on in the original text, at the beginning of the scene in the meeting-house. At that point a canceled passage notices "a few high headdresses, on which the 'Cobbler of Agawam' would have lavished his empty wit of words," but even this reference calls the reader's attention to a classic Puritan argument against "toleration." The deletion of the passage neither exonerates Ward nor dismisses history; it merely prompts us to look for other models of Hawthorne's Puritan minister as well.

17. For an instructive comparison, see Perry Miller's extended discussion of "the hidden rationalism" of Puritanism in *The Seventeenth Century*, pp. 111-206. Geoffrey Nuttall accepts Miller's conclusion as valid for the *conservative* wing of Puritanism; see *The Holy Spirit in Puritan Faith and Experience* (London: Oxford, 1946), pp. 35-36.

18. For Hawthorne's doctrine of Providence, see Leonard J. Fick, *The Light Beyond* (Westminster, Md.: Newman Press, 1955), pp. 16-20, 173-174. And for Hawthorne's sense of democracy as a function of a common guilty (though not "totally depraved") identity, see Hyatt H. Waggoner, *Hawthorne* (Cambridge: Harvard University Press, 1955), pp. 12-16.

19. The classic document for the study of this problem in Hawthorne is "The May-Pole of Merry Mount"; but what is given there with schematic clarity is powerfully suggested by GB (as also by his two Shaker tales, "The Canterbury Pilgrims" and "The Shaker Bridal"). A modest beginning of analysis of the idea of grace in Hawthorne has been made by Hyatt Waggoner—in his *Hawthorne*, but more directly in two later essays; see "Art and Belief," *Centenary Essays;* and " 'Grace' in the Thought of Emerson, Thoreau, and Hawthorne," *Emerson Society Quarterly*, 54 (1969), 68-72. As always, Waggoner is perceptive and careful. He sees that grace in Hawthorne takes the form of saving contact with a human Other. But even he holds back, noticing in conclusion that Hawthorne is "far more successful in portraying guilt, isolation, and darkness than he is with their contraries" (" 'Grace,' " p. 72).

20. If Hawthorne had indeed been, as criticism used to imply, a truer citizen of the seventeenth than of the nineteenth century, then clearly his spiritual home would have been closer to the wilderness outpost of Providence than to the meta-Zion of Boston or Salem. My own discussion of Hawthorne and Williams owes much, obviously, to the modern account of Perry Miller (*Williams*, pp. 74-192); but *The Bloody Tenet of Persecution* (1644) is a book Hawthorne is likely to have known. And, failing first-hand familiarity, he would have found a surprisingly informative account of Williams' views in Isaac Backus, *A History of New England with Particular Reference to the Denomination of Christians Called Baptists*, 2 vols. (Boston: Draper, 1777); see especially chap. 2, "Mr. Roger Williams's Sentiments, and his Banishment, with Other Affairs, from 1634 to 1644."

21. Williams was, if anything, ultra-Puritan about his doctrine of grace. As Perry Miller has pointed out, his separatism existed for the sake of the true church, not the democratic state. He does find that all men are equal in the wilderness of nature; and he does attach a certain importance to that natural life. Nevertheless, the regenerate life remained his ultimate goal and good. His major argument—contra Cotton—was that by connecting the state to the idea of grace, one was bound to commit political mystification and theological idolatry: the Kingdom of God and His grace were by definition interior.

22. For the relation between preparationism and antinomianism, see Miller, *Colony to Province*, pp. 53-67. And for the unresolved debate which engulfed New England after Edwards, see Joseph Haroutunian, *Piety Versus Moralism*

(New York: Holt, 1932), pp. 43-96; and Conrad Wright, *The Beginnings of Unitarianism in New England* (Boston: Starr King Press, 1955), pp. 9-134. I argue for Hawthorne's ability to deal with the theology of such matters in "The Footsteps of Ann Hutchinson," *ELH*, 39 (1972), 459-494.

23. As with Williams, the evidence for Hawthorne's familiarity with Edwards is largely inferential. So far as I can determine, Hawthorne mentions Edwards only once in his writings: in "A Book of Autographs" (1844) Hawthorne exclaims that Aaron Burr was certainly a "wild off-shoot to have sprung from the united stock of those two singular Christians, President Burr of Princeton College, and Jonathan Edwards!" There are some knowing ironies here—the anti-tribalist unpredictabilities of grace and the edge on the idea of "singular"—but they are not much to go on. Yet it would be naive to imagine that a Bowdoin education made no mention of orthodoxy's arch-spokesman or that Hawthorne was otherwise illiterate in his works.

24. See *The Nature of True Virtue* (Ann Arbor: University of Michigan Press, 1960), pp. 75-97. As Perry Miller makes clear, Edwards is a "benevolist" and, in a sense, a "sentimentalist" where virtue is concerned, but his object of attack is precisely that easy sentimentality of the ordinary "good-hearted man"; see *Jonathan Edwards* (New York: Sloane, 1949), pp. 285-297.

25. The Edwardsean opposition between natural and true virtue finds its modern analogue in Anders Nygren's distinction between love which does and love which does not take account of personal good to be derived from the "object"; see *Agape and Eros*, trans. P. S. Watson (New York: Harper, 1969).

26. James's formula concerns the matter of *The Bostonians.* For Hawthorne's anticipation of Henry Adams, see H. G. Fairbanks, *The Lasting Loneliness of Nathaniel Hawthorne* (Albany: Magi Books, 1965), pp. 121-144.

27. Source studies of GB have ignored Nathaniel Ward, even though he is mentioned by name in the 1832 text, and though Hawthorne is known to have borrowed *The Simple Cobbler of Aggawam* (London, 1647) from the Salem Athenaeum on 27 June 1827. Writing well before the Quaker "invasion," Ward's emphasis is on the dangers of toleration in general; but he does seem to be aware of a proto-Quaker party in England, and of course he knows about Ann Hutchinson. Thus he issues a special warning against "a new-sprung Sect of phrantastics" who "cry up and downe in corners such bold ignotions of a new Gospel, new Christ, new Faith, and new gay-nothings, as trouble unsettled heads, querlous hearts, and not a little grieve the Spirit of God"; quoted from the modern edition by Paul Zall (Lincoln: University of Nebraska Press, 1969), p. 20. John Norton has received only brief mention in the criticism. Orians suggests (in a footnote) that "the prototype of the preacher to whom [Catherine] listened was either John Wilson, the high-priest of Boston ... or Reverend John Norton, author of *The Heart of England* [sic] *Rent"* ("Sources," p. 673). More recently Doubleday proposed "that Hawthorne may have been thinking of the Salem minister Edward Norris" (*Early Tales,* p. 163). But apart from this (lesser) question of a personal model for a particular (minor) character, Norton clearly has a crucial importance. Only his extended and libelous attack on the Quakers as dealing

in new revelations and as sponsoring moral enormity could justify Hawthorne's reference to "a history of that sect, and a description of their tenets, in which error predominated, and prejudice distorted the aspect of what was true" (80); see *New-England Rent*, pp. 34–40.

28. For the personal models of Quaker Catherine (Elizabeth Horton, Joan Broksup, Mary Wright, Mary Taylor, Ann Austin, Mary Fisher, and especially Mary Dyer) and the sources of these personal details (Hutchinson, Hubbard, Mather, and Neal on the one side; Sewell and probably Bishop on the other), see Orians, "Sources," pp. 671–674. As Orians notes (p. 672), Catherine is "a representative Quaker figure," created from a mixing of details from many accounts. Her "martyr complex" (p. 675) cannot be said to represent *all* of Quakerism, or the *best* of Quakerism, but it is there in all the sources, friendly as well as hostile; Hawthorne has very little to do in the way of slanderous invention. And the presence of widespread aberration in the sources marks Hawthorne's treatment as more the analysis than the indulgence of "psychological excess" (see Crews, *Sins*, p. 62). For latter-day Quaker admissions of the excessive tendencies of "militant" seventeenth-century Quakerism, see Rufus M. Jones, *The Quakers in the American Colonies* (rpt. New York: W. W. Norton, 1966), pp. 51–89.

29. Hawthorne's language in this scene is both precise and suggestive. Most obviously, "rational piety" is, historically considered, an oxymoron and not a cliché: rationalism and pietism are commonly supposed to be opposite tendencies in seventeenth- and eighteenth-century religious psychology; by blending these opposites in the character of Dorothy Pearson, Hawthorne suggests a balance that is imaginable, at least, in a person whose "nature" is adequately developed. Less obvious, and more tendentious, is Hawthorne's deliberate expression of his own perfectly conscious Arminian Protestantism. On the one hand he is very careful: Dorothy is blameless *only* "so far as mortal could be so"; but on the other, contra Edwards, he makes the (resistible!) grace to Catherine come in the form of a *merely* "natural love." Hawthorne may be claiming more than he can quite show, but he knows very well what he is claiming.

30. The temptation, of course, is to beg the Edwardsean question and say that Dorothy "truly" loves Ilbrahim. No doubt she does, but that is not Hawthorne's emphasis. His purpose is to counter the pervasive Puritan tendency to separate natural loves from godly loves. His unified image suggests a love which is both natural and salutary.

31. Dorothy's use of the word "conscience" rather than "light" and Catherine's reference to her "voice" further adumbrate the idea of "rational piety." Dorothy's "conscience" is clearly prior to the categories of formal theology, but it is still an aspect of her reason as formed by the Word of God. Catherine's "voice," on the other hand, would signify some sort of special and direct intuitive revelation from God—prior to reason, higher than the dictates of natural law, and possibly beyond the range of Scripture. For the Quaker doctrine of "light" as different from the traditional powers of reason and conscience, see Nuttall, *Holy Spirit*, pp. 34–61.

32. Obviously Hawthorne does not "sentimentalize childhood." But critics who stress the depravity of the Puritan children simply invert the problem of sentimentality and end up sounding like the embattled Calvinists of Hawthorne's day—reduced to defending orthodoxy on the liberals' own ground of the moral characteristics of infants and children; see Leonard Woods, *Reply to Dr. Ware* (Andover, 1822), pp. 152–163, 181–202.

33. Tobias' "talent . . . for failure" has been overstated by Crews (*Sins*, pp. 66–67). His "unprosperous fortunes" in England (76) signify only his worldly ("civil, honest") motives for coming to New England. And though his religious dis-ease does plainly lead him, wearily, into all sorts of worldly failures, he is, when we first meet him, "a man of some consideration, being a representative to the General Court, and an approved lieutenant in the trainbands" (77).

34. See Louise Dauner, "The 'Case' of Tobias Pearson," *American Literature*, 21 (1950), 464–472; and cf. Crews, who would throw the blame on the "one final parent" (*Sins*, p. 71).

35. *English Literature in the Sixteenth Century* (New York: Oxford, 1944), pp. 453–454.

36. As J. William Frost has written, both Puritans and Quakers "agreed upon an absolute separation between man and the divine. God was and man was, and since man had sinned there was no contact. If anything, the Quakers had a lower view of man's abilities than the Puritans"; see "The Dry Bones of Quaker Theology," in *The Quaker Family in the American Colonies* (New York: St. Martin's Press, 1973), p. 12. Frost's extended comparison of Puritan and Quaker is based in part on Hugh Barbour's authoritative treatment of *The Quakers in Puritan England* (New Haven, Conn.: Yale University Press, 1964), esp. pp. 127–159. And for the general "context" of Puritan-Quaker similarity, see Nuttall, *Holy Spirit*.

37. The straitened condition of "analogy" in Puritanism is nowhere better evidenced than in Edwards' *True Virtue*. Images or shadows are, of course, everywhere in Edwards, for "it pleases God to observe analogy in his works." Accordingly there is a "secondary beauty" in the universe, distinct from, but not entirely unlike the primary beauty of true virtue. It may consist of either "natural" or "cordial" consents; and in either case it is a fit image of universal benevolence *for the saint*. Yet Edwards' main point is not to affirm the existence of the analogy between either esthetic or ordinary ethical beauties and True Virtue, but rather to deny that the lesser can ever lead on to the greater, the partial to the true. Perceiving the analogy is "the consequence of the existence of [true] benevolence, and not the ground of it." In short, we can recognize in the partial consents of this world a shadow of True Virtue only *after* the gracious experience of True Virtue itself. In a very real sense, Edwardsean analogy works *down from* but not *up to* God; as in Edgar Poe and other Puritanical Platonists, the way up and the way down are only *theoretically* the same; see *True Virtue*, pp. 27–41.

38. As Robert Penn Warren has written, "the two abstractions, Puritanism and Quakerism, though seeming to be contrasted, one on the side of rigor and ar-

579

rogance, the other on the side of love and humility, in reality conspire to destroy the Gentle Boy with his fund of 'unappropriated love'—love that such a world does not know how to appropriate"; see "Hawthorne Revisited: Some Remarks on Hellfiredness," *Sewanee Review*, 81 (1973), 83.

39. Nuttall's view of the continuity of Puritan and Quaker has been widely accepted in modern scholarship: besides Frost and Barbour (note 36), see W. S. Hudson, "Mystical Religion in the Puritan Commonwealth," *Journal of Religion*, 28 (1948), 51-56; G. A. Johnson, "From Seeker to Finder," *Church History*, 17 (1948), 299-315; and Maclear, "Heart." For a more recent account of the continuity of radically Spiritist ideas throughout the Puritan world,' see Christopher Hill, *The World Turned Upside Down* (New York: Viking, 1972). Finally, however, we must notice that Nuttall is as convincing in distinguishing the "spiritual" doctrines of Puritan and Quaker as he is in making their original association; see *Holy Spirit*, pp. 151-168.

40. Besides the polemical works of Quakers Bishop and Sewell and Puritans Norton and Mather, I think we may be fairly certain that Hawthorne had read one of the many English and American reprintings of George Fox's *Journal or Historical Account* (London, 1694). Significantly, however, Hawthorne was not without more "systematic" sources. On the Quaker side there was Robert Barclay's definitive *Apology for the True Christian Divinity* (London, 1678), the 1775 edition of which Hawthorne borrowed from the Salem Athenaeum on 7 February 1828; see Kesselring, *Reading*, p. 44. On the other side there was, principally, Richard Baxter: Hawthorne borrowed Edmund Calamy's *Abridgment of Mr. Baxter's History of his Life and Times* (London, 1713) on 30 April 1828; and later, but well before the publication of GB, he borrowed Mathew Sylvester's famous compilation of the work, titled *Reliquiae Baxterianae* (London, 1696); see Kesselring, pp. 44, 46.

41. One often has trouble persuading students of Hawthorne's "balanced" view; they can easily understand how Elizabeth Peabody imagined GB was written by a former Quaker. And eventually, of course, Hawthorne expressed an estimate of George Fox that was only a little less enthusiastic than Emerson's own: "The Virtuoso's Collection" (1842) refers to Fox as "perhaps the truest apostle that has appeared on earth for these eighteen hundred years."

42. The critical "parameters" of the following speculations would include Waggoner's various defenses of Hawthorne's "classically Christian" orthodoxy and Fick's extended discussion of his view of Christ (*Light Beyond*, pp. 24-31). My most explicit point of departure would be Austin Warren's inferential conclusion that Hawthorne held "quite literally to belief . . . in some sort of Christology (of the conservative Unitarian variety, it would appear)"; see *Hawthorne*, p. xxv.

43. Although Crews wrongly identifies "the Father above—the arch-sadist of a lunatic universe" as the immediate cause of Quaker Catherine's "spiritual" masochism, we recognize the portrait nevertheless (*Sins*, p. 71). William Ellery Channing came close to saying as much about the Puritans' "Father" in "Unitarian Christianity" and "The Moral Argument Against Calvinism," whose angry rhetoric may well have provided a clue to the creation of Mel-

ville's Ahab; see *Works* (Boston: American Unitarian Society, 1899), pp. 376–380, 462–466.

44. Emerson's well-known respect for Quakerism is most easily studied in his lecture on "George Fox"; see *The Early Lectures of Ralph Waldo Emerson*, S. E. Whicher and R. E. Spiller, ed. (Cambridge: Harvard University Press, 1966), pp. 164–182. The classic expression of Transcendental "Spiritism" occurs not in Emerson but in George Ripley's ongoing attacks on the rationalistic historicism of the Unitarians, beginning in the early 1830's; Perry Miller has anthologized some of the crucial documents in *The Transcendentalists* (Cambridge: Harvard University Press, 1960), pp. 95–97, 132–140, 214–220, 251–257, 284–293.

45. In charging that Channing's "Unitarian Christianity" essentially misstated the orthodox teaching of the Trinity, Moses Stuart of Andover nevertheless conceded that *some* of its Patristic formulations were clearly neo-Platonic rather than Biblical; see *Letters to the Rev. William Ellery Channing* (Andover, Mass., 1819). Here Andrews Norton pounced: the doctrine was *all* Greek in origin; "Statement of Reasons," *Christian Disciple*, 7 (1819), 316–333, 370–431. It remained for Samuel Miller of Princeton to argue, against fellow Calvinist Stuart, that the *eternal* Sonship was indeed both Biblical and vital; see Stuart, *Letters on the Eternal Generation of the Son* (Andover, Mass., 1822), and Miller, *Letters on the Eternal Sonship of Christ* (Princeton, 1823). All this is only a small part of a much larger pamphlet debate, of which Hawthorne could scarcely have been unaware; see E. M. Wilbur, *A History of Unitarianism: In Transylvania, England, and America* (Boston: Beacon Press, 1945), pp. 416–434.

46. As Miller so well demonstrated, the Puritans never lacked a keen appreciation of the marvelous rationality of God's various dispensations; given the "voluntarism" of their predestinarian theology, however, the human propriety of God's ways could only seem a "gratuitous" condescension; see "The Marrow of Puritan Divinity," in *Errand*, esp. pp. 63–68.

47. According to Hugh Barbour, Nayler was "confused": his triumphal entry was "intended to symbolize the coming of the inward Christ into every heart; but the women sang 'Holy, holy, holy,' and Nayler would not condemn them" (*Quakers in England*, pp. 62–65).

48. Surely Hawthorne's famous exclamation in "Main Street"—"How like an iron cage was that which they called liberty!"—expresses a direct judgment on Winthrop's famous "little speech" of 1645. That passage virtually organizes the *Journal*, as it records the gradual unfolding of Winthrop's neonomian theopolitics, and (as such) lies directly behind *The Scarlet Letter*. And indeed the main (historical) point of *The Scarlet Letter* is the discovery that the spiritual-passional element in Puritanism was not to be the distinguishing mark of its existence in America: having had their Ann Hutchinson, the Puritan Establishment would be as ready to fear and persecute the Quakers as certain underground pietists were prepared to welcome them; see Maclear, "New-England Rent," pp. 630–645; and compare my own "Footsteps" (note 22).

49. *The Seventeenth Century*, p. 45.

50. Although Hawthorne could have grasped the "Fatherly" tendency of Puritan theology elsewhere, it would be surprising if he were not keenly aware of John Norton's classic defense of the New England orthodoxy. As Mather's prominent treatment makes clear, Norton had been a crucially important first-generation figure: having famously arrived with Shepard, he went on to provide a definitive *Answer* to English questions about the apparent exclusiveness of the New England Way; he was a leading architect of the Cambridge *Platform of Church-Discipline;* and he lived long enough to become the hand-picked (and dream-revealed) successor (and official biographer) of John Cotton. Well before he confronted, refuted, and (as Mather ruefully admits) persecuted Quakers, he had been appointed by the General Court to answer an attack on the Puritans' peculiar version of the atonement; and in *this* effort Mather positively glories. His defense of Christ's having "exactly fulfilled the first covenant"—in substitution for Adam and Every Christian—was endorsed by "Cotton, Wilson, [Richard] Mather, Symmes, and Thompson"; and even though such legalistic propositions struck Richard Baxter as "fictions, falsehoods, forgeries, ignorant confusions, and gross errors," Norton offered them as "the 'Faith once delivered unto the saints,' " and Mather defends them as "the sense of all the churches in the country" (*Magnalia*, I, 291–294). Out of this representative but deeply problematical tract ("A Discussion of . . . the Sufferings of Christ") grew his more scholastic treatise *The Orthodox Evangelist* (London, 1654), which Cotton's "Preface" declared might be "fitly communicated to all churches."

51. See James J. Jones, *The Shattered Synthesis* (New Haven, Conn.: Yale University Press, 1973), pp. 26–27. Jones quotes the most relevant passages from *The Orthodox Evangelist;* but he also cites, not incidentally, *The Heart of New-England Rent.*

52. Jones makes it clear that Norton's only "distinction" lies in the consistency with which he weds the predestinarian (Calvinist) emphasis on divine will and decree to the substitutionary (Anselmian) theory of atonement (*Synthesis*, pp. 3–31). The "tendency" may be traced back at least as far as the scholastic distinctions of William Ames: "Christ is not the meritorious or compelling cause of election . . . In the work of redemption, Christ himself is said to be an effect of the first act of redemption. He is the means given for the salvation of man, as this salvation is the election of God"; see *The Marrow of Theology* (Boston: Pilgrim Press, 1968), p. 155.

53. "The Experience," lines 11–12, in *The Poems of Edward Taylor* (New Haven, Conn.: Yale University Press, 1960), p. 9. For a fuller sense of Taylor's "difference," see his *Christographia*, Norman S. Grabo, ed. (New Haven, Conn.: Yale University Press, 1962), esp. pp. 5–105.

54. *American Poets* (Boston: Houghton Mifflin, 1968), p. 15.

55. According to Perry Miller, "We need to remind ourselves that the Quakers who, in those first intoxicating days, followed George Fox and Edward Burrough were not the sober citizenry of today but a mob of crassly assertive,

ignorant, and reckless fanatics" (*Williams*, p. 241). This probably sounds harsh to most students of Fox's *Journal* and most apologists for the genius of the Quaker Meeting. But just as we may overrefine seventeenth-century Quakerism by judging it retrospectively as Fox's movement solely, so we tend to forget that the *Journal* itself is a retrospective document which rather tones things down; see Hill, *World Turned,* pp. 186–207, 302–306. Thus Baxter and Mather are not entirely wrong in regarding the Quakers as "proper fanatics" and "Energumens." And Williams and Mather are within their rights in fastening on Fox's astonishingly radical *Great Mystery of the Whore Unfolded* (London, 1659): the *Journal* was as yet unpublished, and the *Great Mystery* might fairly be taken as Quakerism's official answer to Baxter's *Quaker Catechism* (London, 1655).

56. The primacy of embattled "proclamation" in early Quaker experience (and literature) has been firmly established by Barbour and Roberts (*Early Quaker Writings,* pp. 27–29, 49–55). The psychology and tone of such a proclamation is extremely revealing: assuming that men "naturally believe that God has reason to love them," the early Quakers have "almost nothing to say about love"; the message is one of judgment and of wrath (52). And even the sympathetic pages of Quaker apologies make it clear that the early tactic of enthusiastic testimony did not actually *work;* or, if it did, only in an indirect and unpleasant way. Again and again the Quakers proclaim their Spirit to some embodiment of Officialdom that is known to be grossly unsympathetic. Almost universally that Officialdom responds in a highly predictable way— with violence more or less controlled. As often as not there is a "backlash" effect: sober people are turned off from the Quaker cause. If converts are actually made, the reasons rarely concern stated Quaker positions; mostly they have to do with sympathy for Quaker sufferings. This dynamic is ultimately what one would understand as the "masochism" of the early Quakers—their calculated willingness to shed their own blood in what they called "the Lamb's War." That war abated somewhat in England after the trial of Nayler (Barbour, *Quakers in England,* pp. 62–71); but it continued in New England until after the Restoration (Jones, *Quakers in the Colonies,* 90–110), and its stalemated battles dominate vol. I of Sewell's *History.*

57. Baxter, *One Sheet Against the Quakers* (London, 1657), quoted from Nuttall, *Holy Spirit,* p. 162; Williams, *George Fox Digg'd out of his Burrowes* (Boston, 1676), quoted from Miller, *Williams,* p. 248. Cotton Mather's (derivative) version of the same charge is that "the Quakers made themselves to be Christs as truly as ever was Jesus the Son of Mary" (*Magnalia,* I I, 523).

58. *Magnalia,* I I, 524.

59. See Barbour, *Quakers in England,* pp. 140–141.

60. The emphasis on "subjective faith" is, of course, everywhere in Quakerism, but James Nayler's famous formula became a sort of watchword: "If I cannot witness Christ nearer than Jerusalem, I shall have no benefit by him"; see Hugh Barbour and Arthur Roberts, *Early Quaker Writings* (Grand Rapids: Eerdmans, 1973), p. 245. The classic Quaker "exposition" of the point

would be Barclay's "proposition" concerning "Inward and Unmediated Revelation"; see Barclay's *Apology in Modern English* (Elberton, N.J.: Dean Freiday, 1967), pp. 16–45.

61. Nuttall, *Holy Spirit*, p. 146.

62. In one sense Hawthorne's "Christology" seems orthodox in the extreme: "adoption" is Saint Paul's seemingly inevitable figure for the "gratuitous" character of man's acceptance by God as son and heir with Christ (Galatians 4; Romans 8). As such it becomes an important "stage"—after "Calling" and "Justification," but before "Sanctification" and "Glorification"—in the Puritans' own account of "the Application of Christ" (Ames, *Marrow*, pp. 149–174). The massively technical problems (and the possibility of heresy) enter only when one is tempted to think of Christ Himself as God's "adopted" rather than "begotten" or "generated" Son; that is, either as a "mere man"or yet as a created demi-god who was, on the basis of proven loyalty, selected for the task of reconciliation and then exalted to divine honors. The structure of Mark's gospel suggests such a view, beginning as it does with the "adoptive" birth of a baptism rather than with the events at Bethlehem; Paul himself may have regarded the resurrection as proving some such adoption; and the view could be defended on the basis of Jesus' own repeated statements of subjection to the Father. But amidst the doctrinal controversies of the early Christian centuries, the Council of Nicea (325) defined all such views as heretical, insisting that Jesus of Nazareth was (somehow) the incarnation of the pre-existent Logos, who was Himself of the same substance (*homoousios*) with the Father; see Adolph Harnack, *The History of Dogma*, trans. Neil Buchanan (Boston: Roberts Brothers, 1895), I, 183–203; III, 1–118, 288–315; IV, 1–59; A. C. McGiffert, *A History of Christian Thought* (New York: Scribners, 1932), I, 232–290; and Jaroslav Pelikan, *The Emergence of the Catholic Tradition* (Chicago: University of Chicago Press, 1971), pp. 172–277. Of these later technicalities Hawthorne may well have been innocent; or he may have rejected them as a form of that "stupendous impertinence" in which theological distinctions do not "touch upon their ostensible object."

63. For Ilbrahim as doubly victimized Christ-figure, see R. H. Fossum, *Hawthorne's Inviolable Circle* (Deland, Fla.: Everett/Edwards, 1972), pp. 45–46.

64. Nuttall, *Holy Spirit*, pp. 145 (quoting Ernst Troeltsch), 159.

65. Richard Baxter found the Quakers "mostly the same with the Ranters," both setting aside everything except "the light which every man hath within him"; see J. M. L. Thomas, ed., *The Autobiography of Richard Baxter* (London: J. M. Dent, 1925), pp. 73–74. But by the time of the *Journal*, at least, Fox clearly insisted on "the reality of Jesus' historical life" (Barbour, *Quakers in England*, p. 146)—as in his confrontation with Rice Jones, who held that "there was never any such thing" as the Christ who suffered at Jerusalem; see J. L. Nichals, ed., *The Journal of George Fox* (Cambridge: Cambridge University Press, 1952), p. 63.

66. Modern apologists are anxious to convince us—against the standard Puritan charge—that the Quaker Christ-within did not *entirely* nullify the objective,

historical Christ, that Quaker theology continually stresses "the unity of the subjective and the objective in Christian experience" (Nuttall, *Holy Spirit,* pp. 44–45). The point is well taken. And yet the distinctive note of Quaker theology is surely its *extreme* emphasis on the Spirit. One evidence of this is the stress on possession of "the Spirit Proper" rather than "the Gifts of the Spirit" (Nuttall, pp. 48–61). Even more crucial would be the whole tendency to merge "the Seed of God, or the Spirit of God within man, with Christ" (Barbour, *Quakers in England,* p. 145).

67. Part of the change that takes place within Quakerism—after the period of Hawthorne's tale—involves a movement toward genuine pluralism; Mather noticed it as the difference between Fox and Penn (*Magnalia,* 11, 523). As the apocalyptic expectation fades, one senses a movement from that guarded spiritual "tolerance" which is a function of some highly normative "liberty of the Spirit" to a more recognizable ethical and political stance of "toleration." But as Nuttall put's the case, any description of tolerance among the original Spiritists must recognize "this attitude as purely personal, or as confined to the fellowship of the Church" (*Holy Spirit,* p. 118). Thus, although much has been written about the "group consciousness" of the Quakers, it seems more proper to stress the essentially individualist (and revolutionary) nature of their "original" experience: the "Friends' distinctive experience has always been simultaneously of radically inward worship and ethics and of apocalyptic change" (Barbour and Roberts, *Early Quaker Writings,* p. 14). That formula would seem to account very well for the Quakers of Hawthorne's story and for the real persons on whom they are based.

68. See Frost, "Dry Bones," p. 14; and Barbour, *Quakers in England,* pp. 144–149.

69. The phrase is that of Mark Van Doren, *Nathaniel Hawthorne* (New York: Sloane, 1949), p. 72; compare Male, *Tragic Vision,* pp. 45–48. And for Hawthorne's transcendence of "pathos," see Doubleday, *Early Tales,* p. 170; and Warren, "Hawthorne Revisited," pp. 81–85.

70. Morgan, *Puritan Family,* p. 1. The quotation within Morgan's summary is from Thomas Hooker's *The Christian's Two Chief Lessons.*

71. Only doctrinaire liberals will ever believe that Hawthorne could have been, even at the beginning, a "Channing Unitarian," in spite of the religious leanings of his immediate family. And yet certain similarities to Channing are worth noticing. The most important of these would be in the "negative": both men seemed interested in the deleterious moral effects that Calvinistic Puritanism "tended" to produce; or which seemed somehow "proper" for it to produce, even if the looked-for effect did not *always* follow. Channing's own (troubled) efforts to define this problem occur, successively, within "Unitarian Christianity" (1819), "The Moral Argument Against Calvinism" (1820), and "Unitarian Christianity Most Favorable to Piety" (1826); see *Works,* pp. 377–378, 467–468, 385–387.

72. The argument about moral "striving" came to its parodic climax in the 1760's: Jonathan Mayhew could see only an Arminian meaning in the Gospel command to "strive to enter at the strait gate"; the Edwardsean answer,

given by Samuel Hopkins, could only be that anyone who can "truly" strive is of course already regenerate (see Haroutunian, *Piety,* pp. 43–71). At issue, obviously, is the failure of a whole culture to give imaginative credibility to the spiritual "case" we might call "The Once-born Sick Soul." The absence of any such category in James's *Varieties of Religious Experience* speaks volumes not only about the Calvinistic incapacity of the New England "Mind" but also about the significance of Hawthorne's achievement in Tobias Pearson. Ultimately Hawthorne himself—along with Melville and Emily Dickinson—belongs in this crucial category.

73. Behind the final speech of the old Quaker zealot, Orians has identified Marmaduke Stevenson's call to leave his own "dear and loving wife and tender children" ("Sources," p. 669). Doubleday concludes that he "exists primarily for his historical representativeness" (*Early Tales,* p. 163).

74. The phrase is adapted from the title of a proto-Unitarian pamphlet by Lemuel Briant: *The Absurdity and Blasphemy of Deprecating Moral Virtue* (Boston, 1749)—which observes that it is possible to succeed entirely too well in the orthodox case against the "filthy rag" of "merely human" virtue.

75. Rebutting Briant—and other liberals who charged that the "tendency" of Calvinist doctrine was to weaken the affective basis of natural virtue—the Edwardseans merely repeat Edwards' own distinction: whereas virtue is "true" only according to a consideration of Being-in-General, sin is sin not only against this "spiritual and divine sense of virtue, but . . . also against the dictates of that moral sense which is in natural conscience" (*True Virtue,* p. 92). Compare Samuel Hopkins, *The True Character of the Unregenerate* (New Haven, 1769), pp. 144–146, 169–171.

76. Seymour Gross has interpreted Hawthorne's criticism of Simmes's superficial play with "lights and shades" as evidence of Hawthorne's own movement away from history; to me it seems more fairly a criticism of the failure of significant history *as history.* See "Hawthorne's 'My Kinsman, Major Molineux': History as Moral Adventure," *Nineteenth-Century Fiction,* 12 (1957), 97–109. My own view of Hawthorne as critic of the historical "tendency" of Puritanism would associate him with the "pragmatic" logic of Henry Bamford Parkes, which assumes that "all ideas have practical consequences and that the best method of evaluating ideas is to explore those consequences," a logic that is as much Channingesque as Jamesean; see *The Pragmatic Test* (New York: H. Wolff, 1941), p. 4.

77. Fox, *Journal,* p. 12.

78. For Miller's classic definition of "the Augustinian Strain of Piety" within Puritanism, see *The Seventeenth Century,* pp. 3–34.

79. Fox's experience of conversion reaches its crucial turning-point at the moment a "Voice" instructs him that "there is one, even Jesus Christ, that can speak to thy condition" (*Journal,* p. 11). The joy of this spiritual opening effectively saves him from mournful night-walking as a "man of sorrows," and it releases him from the authority of "priests" and "separate preachers"; but at the very next moment it leads him into his unresolved ambiguities about Christ and the Father. In the end Fox seems to have "merged Christ and the

Spirit and [then] asserted that Christ was not distinct from the Father" (Barbour, *Quakers in England,* p. 145). What gets lost in all of this is not so much the unique redemptive importance of the historical Jesus of Nazareth as the Christic significance of the human Other.

80. In discussing the Quakers as an instance of violent "enthusiasm," Chauncey defines (and recommends) *"Gentleness"* as "a disposition to treat one another with Candour and Mildness," one which is never "fierce and destructive, calling for Fire from Heaven to devour all who don't think as we do"; *Seasonable Thoughts on the State of Religion in New England* (Boston, 1743), p. 30. For the identification of this source of Ilbrahim's "gentle" spirit (as well as one in Spenser), see James Duban, "Hawthorne's Debt to Spenser and Chauncey in GB," *Nathaniel Hawthorne Journal,* 6 (1976), 189–195.

81. After 1820, "the two wings of congregationalism were . . . spiritually divided, and the division ran through many congregations and even through families" (Wilbur, *Unitarianism,* p. 431). The debate about the precise relation between the historic Christ and the metaphysical Logos remained more or less "academic" (see note 45); and even the presumably central question of the divinity of Christ remained a reflex rather than a direct issue. The Unitarians could not discover that such a thing was *clearly* taught in Scripture; nor could they discover why human salvation demanded any such thing. The Calvinists, for their part, continued to require it almost exclusively for reasons of "Anselmian" coherence: if man was totally depraved, and if God continued to require infinite satisfaction for sin, then obviously Christ *had* to be God and man at once. After Channing's initial brush with these questions in "Unitarian Christianity," they continued to absorb popular attention in the notorious "Wood'n Ware Controversy." See, principally, Leonard Woods, *Letters to Unitarians* (Andover, Mass., 1820), and Henry Ware, *Letters Addressed to Trinitarians and Calvinists* (Cambridge, 1820); for a full bibliography of the controversy, see Wilbur, *Unitarianism,* p. 430.

82. On the problematic substitution of the Grotian ("governmental") theory of the atonement for the traditional Anselmian ("vindictive") theory, see F. H. Foster, *A Genetic History of the New England Theology* (Chicago: University of Chicago Press, 1907), pp. 113–115, 177–182; Haroutunian, *Piety,* pp. 160–176; and Wright, *Beginnings of Unitarianism,* pp. 217–222.

83. What one requires, perhaps, is that a book like that of Conrad Wright contain a separate chapter on "The Atonement" or, more generally, on "Christology in New England"—as well as the more obvious chapters on "Original Sin," "The Freedom of the Will," and "Justification by Faith" (*Beginnings of Unitarianism,* pp. 59–134).

84. The most convincing account of Channing's intellectual position is Robert Leet Patterson, *The Philosophy of William Ellery Channing* (New York: Bookman Associates, 1952); see esp. pp. 97–148 ("Man") and pp. 149–182 ("Christ"). On the one hand Channing's (very literal) Christ is quite explicitly an Arian demi-god rather than a "begotten" and then "incarnate" Son; on the other hand, however, his "essential sameness" with God reveals man's own perfectionist possibilities. And just here Hawthorne's crucial difference ap-

pears most plainly: whatever his cold-prose belief about the literal Christ, his strategic use of the figure of adoption expresses his more orthodox sense of the gratuitousness of salvation of the whole human race. And as to the third "person" of the Trinity, even Emerson at least came to realize that the Spirit signifies somewhat more than the personal self: the concluding "Prospects" of *Nature,* the Transcendental proclamations of "The Divinity School Address," and even the embattled affirmations of "Self-Reliance" all point to some doctrine beyond perfect moral self-culture.

4. PIOUS IMAGE AND POLITICAL MYTH

1. For an account which sets out to minimize the significance of the matter of the Puritans in Hawthorne's early tales, see Nina Baym, *The Shape of Hawthorne's Career* (Ithaca, N.Y.: Cornell University Press, 1975), esp. pp. 53–83. And for a critical justification of the miscellaneous nature of the *Twice-told Tales,* see J. Donald Crowley, "The Unity of Hawthorne's *Twice-told Tales,"* *Studies in American Fiction,* 1 (1973), 35–61.

2. The title proposed here is that of Harry Levin's widely used anthology (Boston: Houghton Mifflin, 1960). For Hawthorne's own plan for a volume of "Old-Time Legends," see Arlin Turner, *Nathaniel Hawthorne* (New York: Oxford, 1980), pp. 192–193.

3. There is no need to review the critical history of Hawthorne's attitude toward Puritanism—though it may be pointed out that crucial works of re-vision are Hyatt H. Waggoner, *Hawthorne* (Cambridge: Harvard University Press, 1955), esp. pp. 12–25, and Leonard J. Fick, *The Light Beyond* (Westminster, Md.: Newman Press, 1955); and that the fullest elaboration of Hawthorne's (apparent) division of feeling about Puritanism is J. Golden Taylor, *Hawthorne's Ambivalence Toward Puritanism* (Logan: Utah State University Press, 1965).

4. For Melville's peculiar mix of orthodox and liberal sympathies, see T. Walter Herbert, *Moby-Dick and Calvinism* (New Brunswick, N.J.: Rutgers University Press, 1972), esp. pp. 21–92.

5. Still carrying some slender brief for Waggoner's view of Hawthorne's "classic" Christianity, I can scarcely agree with his assertion that "Hawthorne had a typical nineteenth-century view of his ancestors"; see *Hawthorne* (1963), p. 14.

6. According to J. Franklin Jameson, Bancroft "caught, and with sincere conviction repeated to the American people, the things they were saying and thinking concerning themselves"; see *The History of Historical Writing in America* (Boston: Houghton Mifflin, 1891), p. 103. The insight is elaborated by Fred Somkin; see *Unquiet Eagle* (Ithaca, N.Y.: Cornell University Press, 1967), esp. pp. 175–206.

7. George Bancroft, *History of the United States* (Boston: Little, Brown, 1856), I, 469.

8. The possible connection between Bancroft and "The Gray Champion" has

been (briefly) explored by Michael Davitt Bell, who opposes the ironic reading of the tale and concludes that, "like Bancroft," Hawthorne "expressed the conventional typological view of the Revolution of 1689"; see *Hawthorne and the Historical Romance of New England* (Princeton, N.J.: Princeton University Press, 1971), p. 50. Though Hawthorne himself "took great care" in placing all the items in the *Twice-told Tales*, the idea of calling the collection "The Gray Champion, and Other Tales" may originally have been that of the publisher; see J. Donald Crowley, "Historical Commentary," *Twice-told Tales* (Columbus: Ohio State University Press, 1974), pp. 502–503.

9. The fullest "ironic" reading of the tale is that of Frederick Newberry; see " 'The Gray Champion': Hawthorne's Ironic Criticism of Puritanic Rebellion," *Studies in Short Fiction*, 13 (1976), 363–370. Newberry builds on the insights of Fossum and Crews and opposes the more "patriotic" readings of Bell, Doubleday, Hoffman, Pearce, Schwartz, and Fisher (p. 363). Other "ironists," it seems to me, are John E. Becker and Kenneth Dauber, though both of these critics have wider concerns; see *Hawthorne's Historical Allegory* (Port Washington, N.Y.: Kennikat Press, 1971), pp. 30–39; and *Rediscovering Hawthorne* (Princeton, N.J.: Princeton University Press, 1977), pp. 53–56. The most learned and subtle of the "patriotic" readings is Ursula Brumm, "A Regicide Judge as 'Champion' of American Independence," *Amerikastudien*, 21 (1976), 177–186.

10. For the "other" side of the Andros affair, see Viola F. Barnes, *The Dominion of New England* (New Haven, Conn.: Yale University Press, 1923). The modern, "balanced" account is David S. Lovejoy, *The Glorious Revolution in America* (New York: Harper and Row, 1972).

11. All citations of the text of "The Gray Champion" (GC) are from *Twice-told Tales* (Columbus: Ohio State University Press, 1974). The tale first appeared in the *New England Magazine* (January, 1835).

12. For a close, "constitutional" review of the issues leading up to the uprising in 1689, Hawthorne had before him (obviously) Thomas Hutchinson's own painstaking account. Though critical of the Andros regime, Hutchinson is far more level-headed than the various Puritan historians Hawthorne had read; see *The History of the Colony and Province of Massachusetts Bay* (Cambridge: Harvard University Press, 1936), I, 297–351.

13. According to his most recent biographer, "it was through his writing that Cotton Mather participated in the Glorious Revolution"; see David Levin, *Cotton Mather* (Cambridge: Harvard University Press, 1978), p. 162. Levin refers primarily to a document called *Declaration of the Gentlemen, Merchants, and Inhabitants of Boston, and the County Adjacent* (Boston, 1689), which Hawthorne may well have read. Certainly he had read Mather's summary account of the affair in his life of Governor Phips; see *Magnalia Christi Americana* (Hartford, Conn.: Silas Andrus, 1855), I, 174–180. For the classic definition of the "paranoia" that characterized the latter days of the Puritan (and the beginnings of the American) covenant, see Perry Miller, *The New England Mind: From Colony to Province* (Cambridge: Harvard University Press, 1953), pp. 149–172. As the conception is political rather than clinical,

it may be safely associated with the chiliastic theology of Cotton Mather, however we should assess his own level of sanity.

14. According to the powerful thesis of Miller's New England Masterplot, Puritanic accounts of King Philip's War, the Andros administration, and the outbreak of the witchcraft all obey the same "Jeremiad" logic: a people in covenant are, by God's permission, being "scourged" for their sins by agents of the Devil's own latter-day conspiracy; see *Colony to Province*, pp. 130–208. For David Levin's more temperate view of much of the same material, see *Mather*, pp. 66–222.

15. For the "ritualistic" character of these proto-revolutionary events—which Miller recognizes as simply the "rejection, in the venerable English spirit, of Popery" (*Colony to Province*, p. 158)—see Peter Shaw, "Hawthorne's Ritual Typology of the American Revolution," *Prospects*, 3 (1977), 483–498; and, more generally, *American Patriots and the Rituals of Revolution* (Cambridge: Harvard University Press, 1981).

16. Compare "Endicott and the Red Cross," *Twice-told Tales*, p. 439.

17. According to Perry Miller, "Randolph was a fussy, devoted, unimaginative and exasperating man, one of those who want to tidy up the universe and who therefore expend a lifetime of energy on the first detail they find amiss. He tried to make good Englishmen out of New Englanders, for which most of them hated him—'blasted wretch,' Cotton Mather cried—as cordially as he did them" (*Colony to Province*, p. 137). This conception has been elaborated in M. G. Hall's *Edward Randolph and the American Colonies 1676–1703* (Chapel Hill: University of North Carolina Press, 1960).

18. As Thomas Hutchinson recounts the affair of 18 April 1689, the people of Boston—smarting under the Andros regime, and in possession of rumors of the accession of William of Orange—were too "impatient" to wait for the new order of things; instead they rose in arms and rashly "seized and confined" Andros and the principal members of his royal party. Though Randolph would accuse Increase and Cotton Mather of conspiracy in the affair, Hutchinson tends to believe the published claim of the Puritan leadership, that they were "surprised with the people's sudden taking of arms." Thus Hutchinson's own account, though critical, supports the idea of a spontaneous expression of the popular "spirit"; see *History*, I, 315–323. For a less credulous interpretation of the same episode, stressing the wish of the leadership to make it seem "a widely supported undertaking," see Lovejoy, *Glorious Revolution*, pp. 239–245. Levin also allows the possibility of *some* prior collaboration; see *Mather*, pp. 162–168.

19. The standard account of Hawthorne's various sources for the idea of a New England "Champion" is G. Harrison Orians, "The Angel of Hadley in Fiction," *American Literature*, 4 (1932–33), 257–269.

20. Ursula Brumm is correct to insist, against Orians, that Scott's *Peveril of the Peak* (1822) is a very important part of the process going on "behind" Hawthorne's text. For it was Scott who first indicated how the problem of real versus miraculous politics could be transcended at the level of "myth"; see "Regicide Judge," pp. 180–181.

21. Neal Frank Doubleday also stresses the importance of Scott; but, like Orians, he can see only an "extension of the legend," in both Scott and Hawthorne; see *Hawthorne's Early Tales* (Durham, N.C.: Duke University Press, 1972), pp. 85–92. What *nobody* has seen is that Hawthorne notices the *political* implications of "Natural Supernaturalism" in New England. For Hawthorne's criticism of the *simpliste* Romantic approach, see his 1847 review of John Greenleaf Whittier's *The Supernaturalism of New England*, conveniently reprinted in H. Bruce Franklin, ed., *The Scarlet Letter and Related Writings by Nathaniel Hawthorne* (Philadelphia: J. B. Lippincott, 1967), pp. 289–291.

22. Orians, "Angel of Hadley," pp. 257–259; Doubleday, *Early Tales,* pp. 86–87.

23. At issue, finally, is Hawthorne's exact relation to the quasi-typological patriotism of the nineteenth century, of which Bancroft is the prime exemplar. According to Peter Shaw, Hawthorne is "like his contemporaries" in finding "a primitive democratic spirit among the Puritans that is proleptic both of the Revolution and the future of America" ("Ritual Typology," pp. 483–484). Sacvan Bercovitch, it appears, may wish to espouse a subtler version of the same view; see *The Puritan Origins of the American Self* (New Haven, Conn.: Yale University Press, 1975), pp. 178–180; and cf. *The American Jeremiad* (Madison: University of Wisconsin Press, 1978), pp. 205–208. My own view (shared with Frederick Newberry) is that the irony of GC is too radical to support this interpretation.

24. Orians, "Angel of Hadley," p. 264. Orians has no doubt that Hawthorne had read both McHenry and Barker; but he sees, again, only "the idea of transferring the sphere of [the champion's] movements and of spanning the life of the regicide until the Salem Delusion in 1692."

25. Cotton Mather, *Wonders of the Invisible World,* in Samuel G. Drake, ed., *The Witchcraft Delusion in New England* (Roxbury, Mass.: W. Elliot Woodward, 1866), I, 15–16. For a completely unparanoid account of the continuity between revolution, witchcraft, and millennium in the mind of Cotton Mather, see Levin, *Mather,* pp. 143–173; and cf. Sacvan Bercovitch, "Cotton Mather," in Everett Emerson, ed., *Major Writers of Early American Literature* (Madison: University of Wisconsin Press, 1972), esp. pp. 106–118.

26. According to Bercovitch, the American end-time is always about-to-be; see *Jeremiad,* p. 79.

27. Miller, *Colony to Province,* p. 204.

28. Hawthorne could not have known Sewall's *Diary,* of course, but the story of his public confession was famous—appearing (among other places) in Calef's *More Wonders of the Invisible World,* which had itself been reprinted in 1823.

29. If Mather's logic of 1688–1692 had held good, the witchcraft episode would have appeared in "The Seventh Book" of his *Magnalia* rather than in the "Sixth." It remained for Mather a matter of "science" (and not of "superstition"), but it utterly lost its link with the millennium in America. And so it lapsed as a literary subject, except for those writers who were explicitly *critical* of Puritanism. Thus, oddly, when Hawthorne took it up directly, as a subject in itself, he would have to see *more* in it, not less, than his

contemporaries—which is to say, "Young Goodman Brown" is *not* a deconstruction but an original psychotheological research.

30. Shaw, "Ritual Typology," p. 491.

31. Certainly we must suppose Bancroft interpreted Hawthorne in the patriotic/ typological sense. For an account of how thick the personal-political plot could become, the reader is referred to Part Three of this study.

32. Lovejoy, *Glorious Revolution*, p. 184. By 1837 Bancroft will have the story of Wise's resistance to Andros, in vol. II of his *History;* one of his primary sources will be Joseph B. Felt's *History of Ipswich* (Cambridge: Charles Folsom, 1834). Given the date of GC (January 1835), Hawthorne could also have relied on Felt.

33. Lovejoy finds it curious that "no single leader emerged" in the revolution against Andros—as if the leaders of the uprising wished it to seem "a unanimous outburst of the 'people' " (*Glorious Revolution*, p. 244). This is indeed what Mather's *Declaration* would have us believe—that the revolution of Andros was an expression of "New England's hereditary spirit." Yet Hawthorne's critical view suggests that we look for local, conspiratorial activity merely covered over with some typological myth, and that we contrast this with the altogether more ingenuous style—both political and literary—of John Wise.

34. The text of Wise's *Vindication* had been reprinted several times in 1772 and remained readily available. For Perry Miller's cautious evocation of Wise's "championship," see *Colony to Province,* pp. 288-302.

35. As his one full-scale biographer notices, the question of Wise's exact influence on the leaders of the American Revolution remains problematic; see George Allen Cook, *John Wise: Early American Democrat* (New York: Octagon Books, 1966), pp. 150-156. Clearly it *could not* have influenced the neo-Puritanic typologists among them. And my assumption is that Hawthorne alludes to it for that very reason—its politics are as rational as its historiography is ordinary.

36. For criticism which stresses the link between GC and "Endicott and the Red Cross" (ERC), see Frederick Crews, *Sins of the Fathers* (New York: Oxford, 1966), pp. 30-43; Robert H. Fossum, *Hawthorne's Inviolable Circle* (Deland, Fla.: Everett/Edwards, 1972), pp. 31-36; Bell, *Historical Romance,* pp. 44-60. Doubleday connects the tale with both "The Gray Champion" and "The May-Pole of Merry Mount" (*Early Tales,* pp. 85-108). Robert Lowell has compressed "Endicott" and "The May-Pole" into a single drama; see "Endicott and the Red Cross," in *The Old Glory* (New York: Farrar, Straus and Giroux, 1970), pp. 3-79.

37. All citations of the text of ERC are from *Twice-told Tales.* The tale first appeared in *The Token* for 1838.

38. As the original passengers aboard the *Arabella* had to be carefully instructed (by Winthrop himself) that they had indeed entered into a covenant, so it appears likely that some must have been surprised by its terms, as these gradually unfolded themselves. Hutchinson notes the dismay of certain Anglicans

and calls the decision to admit only (reformed) church members to full citizenship "a most extraordinary order or law" (*History*, I, 18-25).

39. For the regnant Puritan theory of Church/State "cooperation," see John Cotton's "Letter to Lord Say and Sele," in Hutchinson, *History*, I, 414-417.

40. Doubleday cites Felt's *Annals of Salem* as the undoubted source for Hawthorne's "specimens of seventeenth-century punishments" (*Early Tales*, p. 102). Yet the more important issue concerns the Puritans' use of their historic opportunity; and on this issue Hawthorne clearly follows the lead of the Tory historians. For example, the account which appears to have inspired the patriotic reaction of Bancroft asserts that the Puritan establishment was conceived in a spirit of "retaliation" and that Puritan behavior proves "how apt men are . . . to inflict what they will not patiently endure"; see George Chalmers, *Political Annals of the Present United States* (London, 1780), pp. 153-154.

41. In Bradford's formula, there was not more "wickedness" in New England than elsewhere but much less. It was merely that sins were there "more discovered and seen and made public by due search, inquisition and due punishment"; see *Of Plymouth Plantation* (New York: Random House, 1952), p. 317. The irony of Hawthorne's own disclaimer is nicely observed by Frederick Newberry, the ablest reader of ERC as of GC; see "The Demonic in ERC," *Papers on Language and Literature*, 13 (1977), 251-259.

42. The parallel moment in *The Scarlet Letter* is chap. 3, "The Market-Place," which yokes together the crimes of a "heterodox religionist" and of a "vagrant Indian." One larger irony informing the scene is that "Governor" Bellingham had himself, *in reality,* just been voted out of office for sexual misconduct. For a modern study of the public and the private in the Puritan world, see David H. Flaherty, *Privacy in Colonial New England* (Charlottesville: University of Virginia Press, 1972).

43. Hawthorne's outright condemnation of Endicott is from the unrevised portion of the headnote to "The Gentle Boy" (*Twice-told Tales*, p. 69).

44. Hawthorne's debt to Swift has been noticed but not fully explored; see Alice Lovelace Cooke, "Some Evidences of Hawthorne's Indebtedness to Swift," *University of Texas Studies in English*, 18 (1938), 140-162. The exact quality of his interest in *A Complete Selection of State-Trials*, 6 vols. (London, 1742), also remains to be considered; see Marion L. Kesselring, *Hawthorne's Reading, 1828-1850* (New York: New York Public Library, 1949), p. 48.

45. For Endicott as Bunyan's Diabolus, see Sacvan Bercovitch, "Diabolus in Salem," *English Language Notes*, 6 (1969), 280-285. And for his identity as a Spenserian antichrist, see Newberry, "The Demonic," pp. 257-258.

46. As certain ironies lie much nearer the surface of ERC than of GC, so Endicott has been harder to praise as a "spirit" or "representative" of "Puritanism" than the Gray Champion. Early critics of ERC thought it voted for the *politics* of Puritanism, however, in spite its *religious* intolerance; see Barriss Mills, "Hawthorne and Puritanism," *New England Quarterly*, 21 (1948), 78-102; Joseph Schwartz, "Three Aspects of Puritanism," *New England*

Quarterly, 36 (1963), 192–208; and Taylor, *Hawthorne's Ambivalence*, pp. 21–23. Then Crews insisted that the irony touches politics itself: Puritan "liberty" is no such thing, and not all revolutions are democratic in tendency (cf. *Sins*, pp. 30–43). Since Crews, most critics have emphasized Hawthorne's ambivalence toward the Revolution itself, accepting Endicott as a "type" of its morally mixed character; see Edward J. Gallagher, "History in ERC," *Emerson Society Quarterly*, 50 (1968), 62–65; Sacvan Bercovitch, "Endicott's Breastplate," *Studies in Short Fiction*, 4 (1967), 289–299; Bell, *Historical Allegory*, pp. 53–61, 109–110; Fossum, *Inviolable Circle*, pp. 33–36; Doubleday, *Early Tales*, pp. 101–109. The only critics who really insist on Hawthorne's outright hatred of Endicott are John Halligan, "Hawthorne and Democracy," *Studies in Short Fiction*, 8 (1971), and Newberry, "The Demonic."

47. The "Swiftean" strategy of ERC may actually *dare* Bancroft to notice for, despite the absence of the red-cross incident from his laudatory account of Endicott in the pages of his first volume (see pp. 354–382), this is *his* ideology.

48. Behind the emphasis of critics like Bell and Doubleday lie the original insights of Q. D. Leavis and Roy Harvey Pearce; see "Hawthorne as Poet," *Sewanee Review*, 59 (1951), 179–205, 426–458, and "Hawthorne and the Sense of the Past," *ELH*, 21 (1954), 487–506; and cf. Sacvan Bercovitch, "How the Puritans Won the American Revolution," *Massachusetts Review*, 17 (1976), 597–630.

49. For these "representative" Puritan distinctions concerning the right use of liberty, see Cotton's famous "Answer" to Williams, published as part of Williams' *Bloody Tenet of Persecution*, reprinted in Miller, *The Puritans*, I, 217–218; Ward's satire on the notion of toleration in his *Simple Cobbler of Aggawam*, Paul Zall, ed. (Lincoln: University of Nebraska Press, 1969), esp. pp. 5–25; and, most famously, Winthrop's "little speech" of 1645, in *Winthrop's Journal*, J. Franklin Jameson, ed. (New York: Barnes and Noble, 1908), II, 237–239.

50. Compare "Main Street," in *The Snow-Image and Uncollected Tales* (Columbus: Ohio State University Press, 1974), p. 58. The image of the iron cage is, in all probability, from Bunyan; see Leavis, "Hawthorne as Poet," p. 19. But one suspects that the definition on trial—here and in *The Scarlet Letter*—is from Winthrop. For a critical analysis of Winthrop's political theory and behavior, see G. L. Mosse, *The Holy Pretense* (New York: Howard Fertig, 1968), pp. 86–106.

51. See *The Whole History of Grandfather's Chair*, in *True Stories from History and Biography* (Columbus: Ohio State University Press, 1972), pp. 22–25. For an account of Hawthorne's politics which takes *Grandfather's Chair* as Hawthorne's normative political statement, see Nelson F. Adkins, "Hawthorne's Democratic New England Puritans," *Emerson Society Quarterly*, 44 (1966), 66–72.

52. Like Orians before him, Doubleday has discovered and assembled together many things that are undoubtedly *true* about Hawthorne's use of his sources.

But when something problematic occurs, he merely suggests that Hawthorne is ever willing to adapt his materials "to his narrative purpose"; thus he merely observes that the confrontation between Endicott and Williams "has no historical justification" (*Early Tales*, p. 102). The habit is catching: sooner or later everybody is saying that history, for Hawthorne, "was completely at the beck of his creative imagination"; see Gallagher "History in ERC," p. 64. Yet as Michael Bell more soberly notices, Hawthorne's "use of Williams is one of the more curious features of ERC"; and, as he implies, we do not get the story till we get that right (*Historical Romance*, p. 57).

53. *Grandfather's Chair*, pp. 22–23.

54. The "source critic" loses the game the moment he decides that the bare details of Felt's *Annals* were more important to Hawthorne that the whole troubled narrative of Winthrop's *Journal*—or the retrospective evaluations of Mather's *Magnalia* (II, 495–505) and Hutchinson's *History* (I, 34–37); see Doubleday, *Early Tales*, p. 102. If one may not "argue with" (as well as "borrow from") a "source," then "influence" is everywhere without "anxiety" and the "sins of the fathers" are just no problem at all.

55. Winthrop, *Journal*, I, 61–135, passim; and cf. Hutchinson, *History*, I, 18–40. For instructive modern accounts of the situation and the issues, see Perry Miller, *Orthodoxy in Massachusetts* (Cambridge: Harvard University Press, 1933), esp. pp. 102–262; and Edmund S. Morgan, *The Puritan Dilemma* (Boston: Little, Brown, 1958), pp. 34–133.

56. Winthrop, *Journal*, I, 62, 117, 119.

57. Ibid., 127–145.

58. For an account which stresses the extent to which some decisive break had *already* occurred, consciously or not, see Morgan, *Puritan Dilemma*, pp. 44–53.

59. Winthrop, *Journal*, I, 149–150.

60. Ibid., 149, 162–163, 137.

61. The primacy of Winthrop becomes evident as soon as we move from the "sources" of Hawthorne's words and images to the shapers of his understanding and "ambivalence." At this level the example of Bancroft may also matter, very intensely: Bancroft omits Endicott from his account of 1634 and advances the "championship" of Williams—as if "*his*" spirit" were the guiding genius of revolution in America; see *History*, I, 348–382.

62. *Grandfather's Chair*, p. 24.

63. Winthrop, *Journal*, I, 137; and cf. Mather, *Magnalia*, II, 495–502.

64. For the American proto-revolutionary notion of the indivisible unity of political and religious "liberty" in America—and the contrary union of tyranny in England—see Carl Bridenbaugh, *Mitre and Sceptre* (New York: Oxford, 1962), esp. pp. 207–287.

65. See Miller, *Orthodoxy in Massachusetts*, pp. 102–211. And for Miller's full elaboration of this intensely "Hawthornean" view of Williams, see *Roger Williams* (New York: Atheneum, 1965), esp. pp. 22–48.

66. As Sacvan Bercovitch clarifies a matter left blurred by Perry Miller, Williams' use of typology precluded the idea of any religious state after the lapse

of the Biblical Israel; see "Typology in Puritan New England," *American Quarterly*, 19 (1967), 166–191. For an account of the dominant culture which followed from the defeat, at the outset, of Williams, see Bercovitch, *American Jeremiad*, pp. 31–131. And for a discussion of the explicitly "imperialist" implications of Puritan theological attitudes—barely restrained by an esthetics of enclosure—see John Seelye, *Prophetic Waters* (New York: Oxford, 1977), esp. pp. 131–216.

67. Winthrop, *Journal*, I, 62.

68. Ibid., 116–117. The careful reader of Winthrop can make out that Williams means explicitly to preclude the idea of an "elect nation"; and this fact will make him an odd hero for Bancroft indeed.

69. Chalmers, *Political Annals*, p. 269.

70. Winthrop, *Journal*, I, 162–163. For Williams as "harbinger of Milton," see Bancroft, *History*, I, 375–376.

71. For a sampling of the rhetoric Endicott "echoes," see Philip Davidson, *Propaganda and the American Revolution* (Chapel Hill: University of North Carolina Press, 1941), esp. pp. 139–245. The same rhetoric is less cynically treated in Perry Miller, "From the Covenant to the Revival," *Nature's Nation* (Cambridge: Harvard University Press, 1967), pp. 90–120, and is elaborately studied in Bridenbaugh, *Mitre and Sceptre*, pp. 207–287. The classic (if problematic) account of the religious springs of the American Revolution is Alan Heimert, *Religion and the American Mind* (Cambridge: Harvard University Press, 1966).

72. See Bancroft, *History*, I, esp. pp. 366–382.

73. For the wicked suggestion that Endicott, standing for "Anglo-Saxon energy—as the phrase now goes," is the father of America's territorial destiny, see "Main Street," *Snow-Image*, pp. 56–60.

74. Endicott does not seem to have been an explicit hero of the Revolutionaries, any more than of Bancroft. Yet he was, very clearly, the villain of the Tories. See, for example, Peter Oliver, *Origin and Progress of the American Rebellion* (Stanford, Calif.: Stanford University Press, 1961), p. 20. Or, for a text Hawthorne (like Bancroft) had almost certainly read, see Chalmers, *Political Annals*, pp. 157–158.

75. Winthrop, *Journal*, I, 149–150.

76. For Hawthorne's tenderness regarding Winthrop—both here and in *The Scarlet Letter*—see Bell, *Historical Romance*, pp. 47, 135–137. For his "hiding" of sources, see John W. Schroeder, "Hawthorne's 'Egotism; or the Bosom Serpent' and Its Source," *American Literature*, 31 (1959), 150–162.

77. Ann Hutchinson and Roger Williams are often paired, as they are in Bancroft (*History*, I, 372–395), as heretical co-champions of Puritanic liberty. And yet there are some very important differences. Clearly Winthrop can denounce (and exile) Hutchinson without violating the English understanding of New England's constitutional relation to the "mother country." Indeed he can count on large-scale English support for his own "neonomian" principles. But he cannot openly denounce the "separatism" of Williams without exposing

(or lying about) his own heterodox view of New England's independence from the Church of England.

78. For the crucial text and blank space, see Winthrop's *Journal*, I, 135. The interpretation, which Hawthorne clearly anticipates, is that of the (1908) editor, J. Franklin Jameson. His footnote reads, in full: "How far the colony had abandoned the temper shown in the *Farewell to the Church of England*, of three years before, Winthrop's entry makes plain, though the 'conclusion' is not stated. It would have gone hard with Puritanism in New England, had not King and bishops now begun to feel the heat of a back-fire at home" (135).

79. For Winthrop's crucial role in the invention and disposition of the proto-American "world" of Puritanic Massachusetts, see Samuel Eliot Morison, *Builders of the Bay Colony* (Boston: Houghton Mifflin, 1930), pp. 51-104; Morgan, *Puritan Dilemma*, esp. pp. 45-173; Darrett B. Rutman, *Winthrop's Boston* (Chapel Hill: University of North Carolina Press, 1965); and Seelye, *Prophetic Waters*, 131-158.

80. See Bell, *Historical Romance*, pp. 53-61.

81. Winthrop's now familiar "Model of Christian Charity" was not readily available before 1838, when it appeared in vol. VII of the third series of the *Collections of the Massachusetts Historical Society* (Boston: Charles C. Little and James Brown, 1838), pp. 33-48. But as its editor notes (*Collections*, p. 32), its spirit is diffused throughout the *Journal* itself; and its essence is summarized in a single entry for 22 September 1642 (II, 83-84), which itself "echoes" much of Endicott's own rhetoric.

82. See *Patriotic Gore* (New York: Oxford, 1962), pp. ix-xxxii, 99-130.

83. A deletion from the original headnote to "The Gentle Boy"; see *Twice-told Tales*, p. 614.

84. *The Marble Faun*, as I read it, tries hard but fails to vote for the America of Hilda and Kenyon. For a brief review of Hawthorne's initial willingness to abandon the American Union as "unnatural" and to settle for New England as a *mere place*, see Turner, *Hawthorne*, pp. 362-364.

85. For Hawthorne's retrospective (10 September 1841) verdict on "The Man of Adamant" (MA), delivered in response to some criticism offered by Sophia Peabody, see *Love Letters of Nathaniel Hawthorne* (Washington, D.C.: NCR/Microcard Editions, 1972), p. 41.

86. The "archaeological" interest in MA has discovered literary sources in Spenser, in Scott's *Old Mortality*, and (most recently) in William Austin's "The Man with the Cloaks"; see John W. Schroeder, "Hawthorne's MA," *Philological Quarterly*, 41 (1962), 744-756; Buford Jones, "MA and the Moral Picturesque," *American Transcendental Quarterly*, 14 (1972), 33-41; Henry W. Gautreau, "A Note on Hawthorne's MA," *Philological Quarterly*, 52 (1973); and R. L. Bland, "William Austin's 'The Man with the Cloaks: A Vermont Legend': An American Influence on Hawthorne's MA," *Nathaniel Hawthorne Journal*, 7 (1977), 139-145.

87. The psychosexual reading is, of course, that of Crews (*Sins*, pp. 114-166). Bell, Fossum, and Doubleday all offer basically historical readings: Bell stresses the tale's reduction of the theme of "The Minister's Black Veil" (*His-*

torical Romance, pp. 64–68); Fossum, the complete escape from temporality (*Inviolable Circle*, pp. 66–68); and Doubleday, the reduction of Puritanism itself, with Digby "coming out of American Puritanism" and conceived as "an absurd extreme of a Puritan direction" (*Early Tales*, pp. 218–222). The most vigorous, unembarrassed (theological) reading remains that of Hyatt Waggoner; see *Hawthorne* (1955), pp. 95–100.

88. On the origin of the Puritan movement as a preaching brotherhood, see William Haller, *The Rise of Puritanism* (New York: Columbia University Press, 1938), esp. pp. 3–82. On the American experiment as a repudiation of this identity, see Edmund S. Morgan, *Visible Saints* (Ithaca, N.Y.: Cornell University Press, 1965), esp. pp. 1–112. Hawthorne's knowledge of the "brotherly" character of the original Puritan movement in England seems to have depended principally on John Neal's *History of the Puritans, or Protestant Nonconformists*, 5 vols. (Portsmouth, N.H., 1816–17); see Kesselring, *Reading*, p. 58.

89. All citations of the text of MA are from *The Snow-Image and Uncollected Tales* (Columbus: Ohio State University Press, 1974). The tale first appeared in *The Token* for 1837.

90. For a sober dialogue on the precise role of "separation" in the actual beginnings of America, see Miller, *Orthodoxy*, pp. 73–147; and cf. Larzer Ziff, *The Career of John Cotton* (Princeton, N.J.: Princeton University Press, 1962), pp. 47–78.

91. Edward J. Gallagher has proposed Sir Kenelm Digby's account of a petrified city as a likely explanation for the name of Hawthorne's arch-separatist turned to stone; see "Sir Kenelm Digby in Hawthorne's MA," *Notes and Queries*, 19 (1970), 15–16. To me it seems likely that Hawthorne also implies the trenchant maxim of George Digby, though I have been unable to locate Hawthorne's exact source. According to a modern authority, "Digby expressed what was in many minds" when he remarked, in opposition to certain church reforms proposed in 1640, that "instead of every Bishop we put down in a Diocese, we shall set up a Pope in every Parish"; see William Haller, *Liberty and Reformation in the Puritan Revolution* (New York: Columbia University Press, 1955), pp. 21–22. Hawthorne would have found much information on this Digby, and on the sentiment here represented, in Clarendon's *History of the Rebellion and Civil Wars in England*, 6 vols. (Oxford, 1705); see Kesselring, *Reading*, p. 47. For the "separatist" use of the Pauline text separating light from darkness—a favorite of John Robinson, the "Pilgrim" pastor in Holland—see George D. Langdon, *Pilgrim Colony* (New Haven, Conn.: Yale University Press, 1966), pp. 100–105. Neal's *History* contains a very full (and critical) account of Robinson and other non-tarrying "Brownists"; see (in an available edition) *The History of the Puritans* (New York: Harper and Brothers, 1843), I, 149–151, 242–44, 269–70.

92. As of 1820, Channing was "persuaded" that Calvinism had "passed its meridian" and was in fact "giving place to better views"; see "The Moral Argument Against Calvinism," *Works* (Boston: American Unitarian Association, 1899), p. 468. Jefferson was even more optimistic, assuring Benjamin Wa-

terhouse in 1822 of his "trust" that "there is not a *young man* now alive in the United States who will not die an Unitarian"; see *The Writings of Thomas Jefferson* (New York: G. P. Putnam's Sons, 1899), X, 220. Yet the career of Holmes (and others) clearly goes to show that certain New Englanders, however fleshly their hearts, never could "get the iron of Calvinism out of their souls"; see William H. Shurr, "The Persistence of Calvinism," in *Rappaccini's Children* (Lexington: University of Kentucky Press, 1981), pp. 19-33.

93. According to the exilic prophet Ezekiel, the Lord will convert the nation he has gathered by taking "the stony heart out of their flesh and giv[ing] them a heart of flesh" (11:19); and, as he repeats the formula (36:26), this shall be His way to "vindicate the holiness of my great name" (36:23). Thus are Puritan stoniness and national idolatry parodied together.

94. In the memorable formula of Schroeder, "the allegory of MA explores the case of a bigoted Red Cross Knight who enters the Wandering Wood already separated from Una and ensnared by Duessa masking as Fidessa, discovers Error's Den and makes his home there, refuses Una's saving truth, rejects the Water of the Well of Life and the balm of the Tree of Life; and consequently, on the evening of the crucial third day, is vanquished by the old dragon of Sin and Death, his defeat being symbolized by the completion of his Spenserian metamorphosis from adamant-hearted man to Man of Adamant" ("Hawthorne's MA," p. 755). Thus Endicott is not, apparently, Hawthorne's only Puritanic Red Cross Knight errant.

95. The Abraham reference is Genesis 25: 1-18; the Elijah, I Kings 19: 4-18. Significant also, in the light of Digby's total abstinence, may be the Lord's miraculous feeding of Elijah (I Kings 17:5 and 19:5); and finally, of course, his failure to be carried up to heaven, Elijah-like, in a chariot of fire (II Kings 2:11).

96. See Miller, *Williams*, pp. 22-32; and "The Theory of the State and of Society," *The Puritans*, I, 186-187.

97. Winthrop, *Journal*, I, 149, 154.

98. Ibid., 309. Winthrop's parodic account is, it should be noted, our only real source for this moment in Williams' career.

99. Winthrop's scorn is perfectly evident in the phrase "all comers." Mather's extended satire on Williams' "quixotism" culminates in an account of Thomas Hooker's extended *reductio* of his separatism to the teaching that it would be "unlawful for a [Christian] father to call upon his child to eat his meat"; see *Magnalia*, II, 497-498. Yet the entire burden of Mather's masterwork is to defend the latter-day constitution of New England Congregationalism as a society of "Visible Saints."

100. Miller's implication is Morgan's explicit theme: the separating zeal of the Puritans' "non-separatist congregationalism" had led their pure churches an indefensible distance away from the real world; see *Visible Saints*, pp. 113-152. Thus one rejects the argument of Neal Frank Doubleday—that since "Puritanism did not breed anchorites," Hawthorne's Digby "cannot seem representative enough to be important" (*Early Tales*, p. 221).

101. Winthrop, *Journal*, I, 309.

102. Doubleday recognizes that Digby is offered "a sort of sacrament" (*Early Tales*, p. 218), but does not explore the complexities. Schroeder is closer to the real problem: "The cup which Mary proffers is a most richly condensed sacramental symbol, figuring both the water of baptism and the wine of the eucharist" ("Hawthorne's MA," pp. 750–751). The heart of the matter, as Hawthorne seems to have realized, is that any radical "conversionist" Christianity is forced to interpret *both* sacraments as mere "seals" of holy status, and that sooner or later it will become very hard to tell them apart. For extended analysis of this Puritanic dilemma, see Norman Pettit, *The Heart Prepared* (New Haven, Conn.: Yale University Press, 1966), and E. Brooks Holifield, *The Covenant Sealed* (New Haven, Conn.: Yale University Press, 1974).

103. As we noticed in connection with GB, the key text for Williams' proto-naturalism is his treatise on the language (and the courteous hospitality) of the Indians: *A Key Into the Language of America* (London: Gregory Dexter, 1643), which Hawthorne probably knew in its 1827 edition by the Rhode-Island Historical Society (Providence: John Miller, 1827).

104. In my view, the sexual suggestions of MA, emphasized by Crews (*Sins*, pp. 114–116), must be thought of as fully conscious on Hawthorne's part and must be related to problems of demography—of biology, really—which ultimately embarrassed the Puritan ecclesiology (see Morgan, *Visible Saints*, 125–129). My assumption, further, is that Hawthorne himself was in fact very widely read in the sacramental controversies of the seventeenth century: Kesselring's list itself shows Cotton Mather's *Companion for Communicants* and, among a miscellany of "Sermons, Pamphlets, Tracts," a fifteen-volume collection of "Controversial Pamphlets (including Ecclesiastical Councils)"; see *Reading*, pp. 56, 60–61. Further, Hawthorne confidently alludes, in "Old News," to "the controversy on baptism, between the Reverend Peter Clarke and an unknown adversary" (*Snow-Image*, p. 140). But in any event, the *Magnalia* itself contains more than enough: Book V ("Acts and Monuments") is identically a reprinting of and commentary upon the decisions arrived at by all the various synods called to address the problem of faith and sacramental discipline (II, 177–338); and Mather's "Life of Mr. Jonathan Mitchel," the second longest in his entire work, is precisely an explication and defense of the "Half-Way Covenant" (of which Mitchel was the principal architect) as the best way to resolve the problem of biology and purity (II, 66–113).

105. For the "laboratory" metaphor, see Miller, *Colony to Province*, p. x. It remained for Morgan to publish the scientific results: "The Puritans had in fact moved the church so far from the world that it no longer fit the biological facts of life" (*Visible Saints*, p. 128).

106. *Magnalia*, I, 324–325. Significantly, Mather titles his life of Davenport "Puritanismus Nov-Anglicanus"—as if in recognition of an epitome. Significant also is the fact that Doubleday does not mention Davenport as one of the Puritans Digby might seem to evoke. Though he might imply him

among the "scores of less well known persons" who became dissenters the moment "the Puritans established their Holy Common Wealth," he cites only Roger Williams, Ann Hutchinson, and Thomas Hooker; see *Early Tales*, p. 221. Williams is indeed relevant, as we have seen. But not the other two: Hutchinson was not, after all, self-exiled; and Hooker—unlike those founders who contemplated or executed a "further withdrawal to an isolated area from which [the] 'mixed multitude' should be excluded" (Morgan, *Visible Saints*, p. 120)—was actually seeking a more *inclusive* church. The point is small, perhaps; but it is worth noticing that Hawthorne got it right.

107. Mather, *Magnalia*, I, 325.

108. According to the summary conclusion of Norman Pettit, "it was Davenport's point of view, not Bulkeley's, Hooker's, or even Shepard's, which came to stand for the New England Way" (*Heart Prepared*, p. 221). For similar modern judgments, see David D. Hall, *The Faithful Shepherd* (Chapel Hill: University of North Carolina Press, 1960), pp. 75-88, 98-107, 201-203; and Robert G. Pope, *The Half-Way Covenant* (Princeton, N.J.: Princeton University Press, 1969), pp. 15-18.

109. Mather, *Magnalia*, I, 328.

110. Ibid., 325. The reader who agrees that Mather's "Life of Davenport" is indeed a principal source for MA will find a rich reward of irony in the Scriptural accounts of Zebulon and Issachar. First of all, both of these "tribal" sons of Jacob are conceived in the midst of a positively covenantal lust for offspring; furthermore (as Mather's typological scheme well understood) both are—according to the pattern of Abraham, Sarah, and Hagar—"legitimate," being sons of Leah rather than of some mere hand-maiden (see Genesis 30:1-24). And yet, as the plot unfolds itself, in fact it is the (trans-Jordanian) "haven" of Zebulon (Genesis 49:13) which the Lord will "make glorious"; and so "the people who walked in darkness [will] have seen a great light" (Isaiah 9:1-2). Thus does Mather himself, despite his own political compromises, hold out for the chiliastic spirit of New Haven as the truly American way.

111. Holifield, *Covenant Sealed*, p. 174. Though Mather declines to name Davenport (anymore than he will name his own father) as an obdurate opposer of the Half-Way Covenant, his role as "obstructionist" (Pope, *Half-Way Covenant*, p. 18) is clear in at least two other histories Hawthorne most certainly had read: see Benjamin Trumbull, *A Complete History of Connecticut* (Hartford, 1797), I, 298-313; and Hutchinson, *History*, I, 192. Hutchinson also makes it clear that when the *Result* of the Synod of 1662 was published, Davenport "opposed it in print." And indeed Hawthorne may well have read this document, published (with a "Preface" by Increase Mather) as *Another Essay for the Investigation of the Truth* (Cambridge, 1663).

112. Miller, *Colony to Province*, p. 107; and cf. Pope. *Half-Way Covenant*, p. 152. Hutchinson takes the split precipitated by Davenport as an occasion to meditate at length on "the perverseness of human nature," according to which "separations, and divisions, in churches and religious societies, are

liable to subdivisions ad infinitum" (*History*, I, 229-234)—Q.E.D., George Digby.

113. Mather, *Magnalia*, I, 331. Though Mather must be critical of Davenport's lack of policy, and though he even hints that Davenport may have been deficient in "rational charity," yet his final estimate is resoundingly positive: his true glory is that, like Mather himself, he was granted, "by the special favor of Heaven unto him," the power to discern the coming of the Kingdom in America.

114. Miller, *Orthodoxy*, pp. 113-114. I do not know where Hawthorne learned of this (Steven) Goffe; he is mentioned in Hutchinson (*History*, I, 75), but not in this regard. Of course Davenport is also known as "one of the key links in the underground train of correspondence between the regicides William Goffe and Edward Whalley"; see Larzer Ziff, *Puritanism in America* (New York: Viking Press, 1973), p. 185. Yet unlike GC, MA does not seem to press this (or indeed any other) political connection.

115. Mather, *Magnalia*, I, 265. Mather mentions the birth of Cotton's "Seaborn" son, but only as a "mercy" God had long denied. But Winthrop had long since recorded the logic according to which Cotton delayed the child's baptism until he himself had duly professed his faith to a properly covenanted congregation; see *Journal*, I, 107.

116. Doubleday is correct to observe that "Puritanism did not breed anchorites"; and that, literally at least, Digby may be thought to represent "a spiritual peril more characteristic of [Hawthorne's] own time than of Puritanism" (*Early Tales*, p. 221). Yet Morgan's verdict is also apt: if the Puritans *had* been willing (Shaker-fashion) to form "monasteries instead of churches, they might have concentrated on their own purity and left to others the task of supplying the church with new members" (*Visible Saints*, p. 128). In the end, however, Hawthorne's own point is both simpler and more telling: separatism is very hard to do by halves; thus many a John Cotton and Cotton Mather may be Davenport under the skin.

117. "Alice Doane's Appeal," *Snow-Image*, pp. 266-267.

118. All citations of the text of "The May-Pole of Merry Mount" (MM) are from *Twice-told Tales*. The tale first appeared in *The Token* for 1836.

119. Richard P. Adams and Melvin R. Askew try hard with the (psychological) theme of "the fall" in MM; see "Hawthorne's Provincial Tales," *American Literature*, 30 (1957), 39-57; and "Hawthorne, the Fall, and the Psychology of Maturity," *American Literature*, 34 (1962), 335-343. But Crews rightly sees that "the didactic example of Edith and Edgar" is "banal"; more largely at issue, he argues, are "the emotional qualities of Puritanism and hedonism" (*Sins*, p. 18). Even Richard Harter Fogle recognizes that, as "allegory," the conflict in MM is a little too pat; see *Hawthorne's Fiction* (Norman: University of Oklahoma Press, 1952), pp. 59-69. For criticism which identifies the mythic elements in Hawthorne's tale, see Norris Yates, "Ritual and Reality," *Philological Quarterly*, 34 (1955), 56-70; John B. Vickery, "The Golden Bough at Merry Mount," *Nineteenth-Century Fiction*, 12 (1957), 203-214; Daniel G. Hoffman, *Form and Fable in American*

Fiction (New York: Oxford, 1961), pp. 126–148; Robert Deming, "The Use of the Past," *Journal of Popular Culture,* 2 (1968), 278–291; and Shaw, "Ritual Typology," 484–487.

120. Source criticism of MM is both field day and nightmare. G. Harrison Orians rightly points out that Hawthorne could not have known Bradford directly; but he fails to notice how much of Bradford is literally repeated by his nephew, Nathaniel Morton, in *New England's Memorial.* Further, he is unwarrantably dogmatic about Hawthorne's ignorance of Thomas Morton's *New English Canaan.* Worst of all, he uniformly imagines that Hawthorne was merely "looking for material" in the pages of all the various accounts that were available; see "Hawthorne and MM," *Modern Language Notes,* 53 (1938), 159–167. Doubleday rightly emphasizes the local fame of Endicott in the 1820's; and he notices that writers like Nathaniel Morton and Thomas Prince are (in the main) but redactors of Bradford. But he missummarizes the historical events themselves, imagines the entire tale as a *tour de force* in the amalgamation of historical materials, and concludes that this *"Paradise Lost* in provincial miniature" has been arranged to tell us that "neither a whipping post nor a maypole can stand for the best in life" (*Early Tales,* pp. 92–101). J. Gary Williams does much better, supposing that a sort of creative historicism may actually account for Hawthorne's manipulation of Blackstone and of Strutt's *Book of Sports;* see "History in Hawthorne's MM," *Essex Institute Historical Collections,* 108 (1972), 173–189. And a competent historian has recently observed that an extraordinarily large number of inexcusably biased reports, from both historians and more literary tale tellers, had badly blurred the events at Wollaston–Merry Mount–Dagon before Hawthorne ever lifted his pen; see John P. McWilliams, "Fictions of Merry Mount," *American Quarterly,* 29 (1977), 3–30.

121. The problem of "origins" which are themselves somehow "historical" might constitute the true paradox of "Hawthorne's Historical Allegory"; see Becker, *Historical Allegory,* pp. 21–30.

122. Peter Shaw, as we have seen, finds Hawthorne like Bancroft in seeking "the meaning of America in its origins" (*Ritual Typology,* 483–484). And the "historical critics" of MM have been, similarly, a little too credulous and moralistic in their accounts—as if Hawthorne had, after all, found the incident which, in itself, explained or forecast everything else. See John C. Stubbs, *The Pursuit of Form* (Urbana: University of Illinois Press, 1970), pp. 75–78; Bell, *Historical Romance,* pp. 119–126, 130–134; and Fossum, *Inviolable Circle,* pp. 59–64.

123. For the moralistic point of departure in MM (and for a reading which probably will not survive the criticism of Frederick Crews), see Chester E. Eisinger, "Hawthorne as Champion of the Middle Way," *New England Quarterly,* 27 (1954), 27–52.

124. Somewhere at the back of MM we hear echoes of almost everything significantly said in the truly historic debate between Puritan and Cavalier; see Deming, "Use of the Past," 279–287; and Doubleday, *Early Tales,* 97–100.

125. For a full-scale account of the prediction that all species would "degenerate"

in America (whether anyone, following Thomas Morton, "went native" or not), see Antonello Gerbi, *The Dispute of the New World* (Pittsburgh: University of Pittsburgh Press, 1973). If from nowhere else, Hawthorne would certainly have been familiar with this (non-Miltonic) argument from Jefferson's *Notes on the State of Virginia.*

126. The classic study of the "American" fear of moral degeneration in the New World is Roy Harvey Pearce, *Savagism and Civilization* (Baltimore: Johns Hopkins Press, 1953), esp. pp. 3-49. For the appropriate countertheme— of the redemptive quality of "savage" life—see Richard Slotkin, *Regeneration Through Violence* (Middletown, Conn.: Wesleyan University Press, 1973). Michael Zuckerman draws on the analysis of Slotkin in his study of the clash of values at Merry Mount; see "Pilgrims in the Wilderness," *New England Quarterly,* 50 (1977), 255-277.

127. For evidence that MM was to have been part of "The Story Teller" (even if left over from "Provincial Tales"), see Seymour L. Gross, "Four Possible Additions to Hawthorne's 'Story Teller,' " *Papers of the Bibliographical Society of America,* 51 (1957), 90-95. See also the proposals in my own final chapter.

128. For the best that moral commentary can do—the reader must choose between Christianity and paganism—see Sheldon W. Liebman, "Moral Choice in MM," *Studies in Short Fiction,* 11 (1974), 173-180.

129. Since Fogle first proposed that Hawthorne *sympathized* with the Revellers but recognized that "the Puritans are closer to reality" (*Hawthorne's Fiction,* p. 64), few critics have been able to avoid the premise of "ambivalence"; some have even made this "the point." Taylor has made MM occupy the dead center of Hawthorne's spectrum ("Hawthorne's Ambivalence," pp. 22-29). And Joseph J. Feeney proposes that "the plot manifestly favors the Puritans" while "imagery" as well as "sound and rhythm . . . favor the people of Merry Mount"; see "The Structure of Ambiguity in Hawthorne's MM," *Studies in American Fiction,* 3 (1975), 211-216. Eisinger proposes an "Hegelian" solution, with Edith and Edgar as the magical synthesis of an opposition otherwise supposed to be unresolvable; see "Middle Way," pp. 34-35.

130. *Hawthorne* (Ithaca, N.Y.: Cornell University Press, 1956), pp. 45-46. Hawthorne's specific language for the probable shadow-effects of Puritanism may well contain an ironic echo of Cotton Mather's "halcyon" prediction: despite unprecedented opposition by the Devil, the Puritan Way has planted its root deep, sent its boughs and branches both east and west, till all "the Hills were covered with the Shadow thereof" (*Wonders,* pp. 15-16).

131. Rightly sensing that Hawthorne has seized on the fact that a "decisive minority set themselves in absolute hostility to the immemorial culture of the English folk with its Catholic and ultimately pagan roots," Q. D. Leavis immediately notices that some deep game is being played with the man Endicott "identifies" as Blackstone; see "Hawthorne as Poet," pp. 187-189.

132. The nice parallelism of Endicott's outrageous accusation clearly re-recalls that of Mather's classic formula, itself echoed by Hutchinson, Alden Brad-

ford, and Thomas Davis. Blackstone "would never join himself to any of our churches, giving this reason for it: 'I came from England, because I did not like the *lord-bishops;* but I can't join you, because I would not be under the *lord-brethren'* " (*Magnalia,* I, 243).

133. It has been perfectly clear since 1938 that Hawthorne's use of Blackstone is, in the most basic sense, "unhistorical"; but few critics have known what to make of this odd but self-emphasized fact. Orians himself observes that "Hawthorne had to have an English priest for the exigencies of his plot," but wishes he had chosen somebody like John Lyford, "a name more sullied in the pages of history" (that is, of Bradford); see "Hawthorne and MM," pp. 163–164. Doubleday agrees that Blackstone makes no *ordinary* historical sense in this tale; yet he wonders why Hawthorne did not follow the advice of William Howard Gardiner (in the pages of the *North American Review*) and give Blackstone his own sketch or tale (*Early Tales,* p. 97). Terrence Martin proposes that Hawthorne had originally *meant* the name which appeared in the *Token* version of MM—namely, the Ranter-Anabaptist Lawrence Claxton; and both he and Bell speculate learnedly on Hawthorne's reason for changing Claxton to Blaxton (or Blackstone) in the *Twice-told Tales;* see *Nathaniel Hawthorne,* (New York: Twayne Publishers, 1965), p. 87; and *Historical Romance,* p. 123. Taylor "concludes" his essay on the paradigmatic "ambivalence" of MM with a fascinating and largely accurate account of the "real" Blackstone; but, unable to make any decent sense of Hawthorne's historical intentions, he merely nominates the undercutting of Endicott's identification as "the strangest footnote in fiction" (*Hawthorne's Ambivalence,* pp. 29–35). Only Leavis and (more precisely) Williams seem to sense that Hawthorne's motives are in fact deeply historical; see "Hawthorne as Poet," pp. 188–189; and "History in MM," pp. 182–185.

134. The critical history of MM may truly be said to begin with the observation of G. H. Orians: "To the student, Hawthorne's MM would seem so patently historical as to make a study of its sources unnecessary." What ensues then is a "source study" which indeed causes the question of history to disappear: "Hawthorne's fancy falsified the true conflict" but realized the higher objective of a "fancy delicately spiritualized"; see "Hawthorne and MM," pp. 166–167. Yet it remains true that without *some* sense of the matter of Hawthorne's "annalists," MM is the next thing to unintelligible; and so it seems permissible to be as careful as possible.

135. See McWilliams, "Fictions of Merry Mount," pp. 4–15. And cf. Minor W. Major, "William Bradford versus Thomas Morton," *Early American Literature,* 5 (1970), 1–13.

136. The recoverable chronology would seem to be this: the Wollaston community was established in 1625, with Morton taking it over in 1626 and observing his first official May Day in 1627; he was arrested, by Standish, for violation of a "royal edict" against providing Indians with firearms, in June 1628, even as Endicott was preparing to sail for New England; Endicott's ship probably "crossed" that of the deported Morton on his way back to

England; Endicott arrived in New England in September 1628 and seems to have proceeded to the "discipline" of the leaderless (and hapless) Merry Mount almost at once. For the fullest review of these facts, see Charles Francis Adams, ed., *The New English Canaan of Thomas Morton* (Boston: Prince Society, 1883), pp. 15–32. A clear enough summary is also provided by McWilliams (above).

137. See "Governour Bradford's Letter Book," *Collections of the Massachusetts Historical Society*, 3 (1794), 60–65. Orians refers to this document but does not propose it as a "source" ("Hawthorne and MM," p. 164).

138. See Nathaniel Morton, *New England's Memorial*, John Davis, ed. (Boston: Crocker and Brewster, 1826), pp. 135–141. Both Orians and Doubleday agree that this is one of Hawthorne's prime sources.

139. Morton, *Memorial*, pp. 135–137. And cf. Bradford, *Plymouth*, pp. 204–205. Though D. H. Lawrence did not think to make a culture-hero of Thomas Morton in his 1923 *Studies in Classic American Literature*, William Carlos Williams quickly corrected the oversight in his 1925 study, *In the American Grain;* and scholars such as Slotkin, Seelye, and Zuckerman (all cited above) have more than rescued this early prophet of "natural liberty" and/or non-Puritanic community.

140. Morton, *Memorial*, p. 137. And cf. Bradford, *Plymouth*, pp. 205–206.

141. Bradford, *Plymouth*, p. 206.

142. As Taylor observes, Bradford does indeed "bewaile" at length the socio-political wickedness of Morton's (alleged) arms policy ("Hawthorne's Ambivalence," pp. 30–31). But as the example of his redactors clearly indicates, it is not so much too little as too late: the chronology has already been blurred, and one allegorical image may outweigh any number of historical words.

143. Having omitted Bradford's crucial indication of the true chronology, Nathaniel Morton proceeds drastically to foreshorten his diatribe against the guns—"lest [he] should hold the reader too long in the relation of the particulars" (*Memorial*, pp. 137–139). A formula for allegorical misprision, surely.

144. As Orians points out, Neal's *History of New England* treats only Morton's (alleged) "trading in arms and ammunition," and Morse and Parish's *Compendious History of New England* (which Hawthorne may also have known) mentions only his (later) "arrest for the theft of a canoe" ("Hawthorne and MM," p. 160).

145. *Memorial*, p. 141. The editor is John Davis (see note 138).

146. Ibid. Orians suggests that Hawthorne could have learned the correct chronology only in Felt's *Annals of Salem* ("Hawthorne and MM," p. 164). Yet the point is there, most explicitly, in Davis' footnote to Nathaniel Morton; and this footnote is clearly more crucial than anything in Felt.

147. Hawthorne borrowed the volume containing Bradford's letter (see note 137) in November 1827 (Kesselring, *Reading*, p. 56). That he knew what he was reading is the burden of the present (not altogether positivist) argument.

148. To claim that the allegory here is ultimately Endicott's own is merely to no-

tice that Hawthorne's "annalists" were able to "recognize" in his actions far more meaning than most historians have been able to detect in those annalists themselves. Endicott's authoritative biographer points out that, by the time Endicott arrived in New England, the entire Merry Mount affair had become "what might be called 'ancient history.' " And, furthermore, "there is no reason to suppose that he believed Merrymount to be within his jurisdiction, though it later turned out so to be"; hence his entire venture had sprung "from a sense of curiosity or from a sense of duty, or both"; see Lawrence Shaw Mayo, *John Endicott* (Cambridge: Harvard University Press, 1936), p. 17. In McWilliams' equally innocent formulation, Endicott's most notorious deed "was historically little more than a dramatic gesture of moral disapproval" ("Fictions of Merry Mount," p. 8). It would seem to depend on what you mean by "history."

149. Bradford makes much of the "recognition" his small company received from the Puritans who, along with Endicott, began to arrive in the Bay; and Nathaniel Morton dutifully repeats his words; see *Plymouth*, pp. 223–225, 234–236; and cf. *Memorial*, pp. 142–161. Yet for Hawthorne's brand of history, the more significant fact had been the "prior" recognition of Endicott's originary allegorical deed.

150. Clearly (contra Orians and Martin) Blackstone was inevitable. Lyford was long since exposed as a *mere* scoundrel, belonging to ordinary history as ineluctably as Thomas Granger, the turkey-bugger. And Claxton was surely an editor's misprision or a typesetter's bungle: Ranters may fall to licentious behavior, predictably enough, but they seldom think to cloak their lusts in "the surplice."

151. For Blackstone as Europa-figure, see Harry Levin, ed., *The Scarlet Letter and Other Tales of the Puritans* (Boston: Houghton Mifflin, 1960), p. 106. For his embodiment of "European" arts and graces, see Leavis, "Hawthorne as Poet," p. 189; and Bell, *Historical Romance*, p. 130.

152. Much of the relevant information on Blackstone is conveniently summarized in Williams, "History in MM," pp. 180–183.

153. *The House of the Seven Gables* (Columbus: Ohio State University Press, 1965), p. 6. It seems obvious that the "Original Sin" in that romance has as much to do with the dispossession of Blackstone as with the more famous matter of witchcraft.

154. *Magnalia*, I, 243.

155. See Edward Johnson, *Wonder-Working Providence of Sion's Savior*, in *Collections of the Massachusetts Historical Society*, 2nd series, II (1814), 70; and William Hubbard, *General History of New England*, in *Collections of the Massachusetts Historical Society*, 2nd series, V (1815), 113. Hawthorne is known to have borrowed both these reprints of seventeenth-century histories (see Kesselring, *Reading*, p. 56); and Orians cites them both as "sources" ("Hawthorne and MM," p. 163).

156. One of Hawthorne's most authoritative sources of information about Blackstone, clearly, had been a certain "Memoir of Mr. William Blackstone, An Early Planter of Boston," in *Collections of the Massachusetts Historical Society*,

2nd series, X (1823), 170–173. The phrase about "living waters" occurs (all innocent of typology) in the very next article, by the same hand, titled "On the Question—What Is the Meaning of the Aboriginal Phrase *Shawmut?*" (pp. 173–174).

157. Caleb Snow, *History of Boston* (Boston: Abel Bowen, 1825), p. 52.

158. Hubbard refers to Salem (despite its Old Testament provenance) as "the Christian name" of Naumkeag (*General History*, p. 112). Just so (*pace*, Williams), *Shawmut*—already "civilized" to *Blackstone's Neck*—had to be "christened" as *Boston*. Being repeated, of course, is the most complex instance of all: *Passonagessit, Wollaston, Merry Mount, Dagon, Quincy;* the mind boggles. The crucial *difference* between the dispossession of Thomas Morton and that of William Blackstone is that, as no plausible charge could ever be brought against Blackstone, he never could be deported; so he simply had to be left out of the record—till Hawthorne reattached him to the myth he helps define.

159. Johnson's point, barely intelligible through his turgid prose, is that as "Mr. John Indicat" is the "fit instrument to begin [the] Wilderness-work" of temple-building, Blackstone is inappropriate in the extreme (*Wonder-Working Providence*, p. 69); and Hubbard as much as labels Blackstone a mere "pretender" to true priesthood (*General History*, p. 113).

160. "Eccentric" is the word of Caleb Snow (*Boston*, p. 51). Truly so, for the Puritan secret sat in the center and *knew*.

161. As Williams notes, Hawthorne was well acquainted with the theological essence of the "vestarian controversy" from Neal's *History of the Puritans;* see "History in MM," pp. 182–183. And he would also seem to have read William Ames's *Fresh Suit against Human Ceremonies in God's Worship* (Rotterdam, 1633), complete with Thomas Hooker's own "Preface"; see Kesselring, *Reading*, p. 43.

162. See Williams, "History in MM," pp. 183–185.

163. Quoted from Joseph Strutt, *The Sports and Pastimes of the People of England* (London: Chatto and Windus, 1876), p. 44. Hawthorne had borrowed the 1810 edition of this (1801) work in March 1827; see Kesselring, *Reading*, p. 62.

164. Bradford, *Plymouth*, pp. 97, 86–87. Nathaniel Morton omits many of Bradford's "Puritanical" details, but he faithfully repeats the symbolic fact which concludes Book I: the Pilgrims celebrated their very first Christmas in the New World (referred to merely as the twenty-fifth day of December) by erecting "their first house for common use" (*Plymouth*, p. 72).

165. Quoted from the Adams edition of *New English Canaan* (see note 136), pp. 278–283. For Hawthorne's probable acquaintance with this work (contra Orians), see Williams, "History in MM," pp. 177–180.

166. Criticism which stresses the "Puritan" sympathy of MM is likely to be assuming Bradford's own theologistic evaluation of Morton's revels (for example, Orians, Doubleday); that which finds a bit of the Reveller in Hawthorne the Artist is usually assuming a more mythic perspective (for example, Vickery, Deming). Hawthorne's own view is less ultimate, more

historical than either: Puritanism defines itself as the supplantation of the Myth of Nature by its Ramean opposite, the Myth of Grace. The odd result of this cultural totalization will be that the "liberal" Jonathan Mayhew will come to write the book—*Christian Sobriety* (Boston, 1763)—which turns Hawthorne's Story Teller into a wandering reprobate (see the final chapter in this book).

167. If I am correct to infer that Hawthorne's interest in Strutt is more theo-political than mytho-sociological, then it is probably irrelevant to decide whether William Hone's *Every-Day Book* (London: William Tegg, 1826) was also a "source" for the "masques, mummeries, and festive customs, described in the text" (54) of MM. The proposal was first made by Hoffman (*Form and Fable*, pp. 134-140), but it is disputed (on chronological grounds) by Doubleday: Hawthorne first borrowed Hone in September 1835, too late to influence a tale bound for the 1836 *Token* (*Early Tales*, p. 94).

168. *Sports and Pastimes*, p. 513.

169. For the "element of pleasure in legal violence" as the essence of the Puritan mentality here portrayed, see Crews, *Sins*, pp. 18-19. And cf. the formula of Leavis: "And what did the Puritans worship? We are left in no doubt as to Hawthorne's answer: Force" ("Hawthorne as Poet," p. 191). While this verdict seems indeed more adequate than all talk of "balancing the claims of the heart and the head," the true analysis may be deeper still: the Puritan's application of power is often accompanied by some subtler sleight of symbols, whether or not naming is always itself an act of force.

170. For a modest defense of the traditional interests of theme and form in Hawthorne, see my own critical review of much recent Hawthorne scholarship: "The Sense of an Author," *ESQ*, 27 (1981), 108-133.

171. To my knowledge, the nearest approach to the "theme" of self-reference in Hawthorne criticism so far is Kenneth Dauber's suggestion that what interests us in Hawthorne is his self-dramatized act of communication and not any of his various moral or historical messages; see *Rediscovering Hawthorne*, pp. 3-46. For the moment at least, the more pressing problem may be the tendency of literary historians themselves to reject as unconscionably "provincial" any criticism which refers the meaning of a Hawthorne text to the world and the words of his (undisputed) colonial sources; see William R. Spengemann, "Review Essay," *Early American Literature*, 16 (1981), 173-186, and also his "Reply to Professor Elliott," *Early American Literature*, 17 (1982), 98-99.

172. The case for Milton's *Comus* seems obvious and has in fact been well argued; see Sheldon W. Liebman, "Hawthorne's *Comus*: A Miltonic Source for MM," *Nineteenth-Century Fiction*, 27 (1972), 345-351. Yet any Lawrentian critic of MM will surely feel that the son of Dionysius survives, even in Hawthorne, the worst that Milton could do.

173. Bell finds MM to end on "a hope underlined by the insistent echoes, as Edith and Edgar are led from Merry Mount, of the ending of *Paradise Lost*" (*Historical Romance*, p. 124); and Doubleday complacently agrees that "in its closing paragraphs, MM becomes, in Harry Levin's fortunate phrase,

'a *Paradise Lost* in provincial miniature' " (*Early Tales,* p. 100); yet the reader will want to watch the ironies of all this very closely. Something is indeed being narrowed down rather drastically, but the miniaturization is less Hawthorne's provincial reduction of Milton's grand scope than his observation that the high Miltonic argument is itself parodied by the peculiar eschatology of American Puritanism—as if some narrow-minded Endicott had appeared to "arrest" Milton's Adam and Eve at the precise moment the necessary Angel had cast them out into history. Once again, a fact in Hawthorne's subtext underlines the nature of his irony quite precisely: the narrator of MM makes bold to declare Edith and Edgar well married by the Anglican Priest of Nature; but in fact (as Taylor is baffled to observe) "Endicott actually performed Blackstone's marriage" (*Hawthorne's Ambivalence,* p. 35). That is to say: the bourgeois (anti-sacramental) sociology of Puritanism, aligning itself with an essentially idolatrous theory of history, has managed to control the "springs" of everything.

174. I do not mean to set R. W. B. Lewis in opposition to Sacvan Bercovitch (and others who have told the story of the "rhetoric" of America as "Redeemer Nation"); indeed *The American Adam* (Chicago: University of Chicago Press, 1955) endures as a truly "seminal" book. Yet it remains true that the story of our transition from history's only remaining grace to "Nature's Nation" is still to be written. In the meantime, Hawthorne.

5. VISIBLE SANCTITY AND SPECTER EVIDENCE

1. I do not mean to suggest that "Young Goodman Brown" (YGB) and "The Minister's Black Veil" (MBV) treat some reality entirely unmediated by texts; only that here Hawthorne treated his "sources" as indicators of psychological dis-ease rather than as overdetermined political argumentations.
2. I accept the common view that the excitable narrator of Melville's essay on Hawthorne's "Mosses" responds a little too *personally* in flattering Hawthorne's *own* ability "to penetrate, in every bosom, the mystery of sin"; see "Hawthorne and his Mosses," in Harrison Hayford and Herschel Parker, ed., *Moby-Dick* (New York: W. W. Norton, 1967), p. 549.
3. Levin's widely reprinted article originally appeared as "Shadows of Doubt: Specter Evidence in Hawthorne's YGB," *American Literature,* 34 (1962), 344–352. Levin approves the following precursors: D. M. McKeithan, "Hawthorne's YGB," *Modern Language Notes,* 67 (1952), 93–96; Thomas F. Walsh, Jr., "The Bedeviling of Young Goodman Brown," *Modern Language Quarterly,* 19 (1958), 331–336; and Paul W. Miller, "Hawthorne's YGB: Cynicism or Meliorism," *Nineteenth-Century Fiction,* 14 (1959), 255–264. He might also have cited Thomas E. Connolly, "Hawthorne's YGB: An Attack on Puritanic Calvinism," *American Literature,* 28 (1956), 370–375. The most direct "answer" to Levin is Paul J. Hurley, "Young Goodman Brown's 'Heart of Darkness,' " *New England Quarterly,* 37

(1966), 410-419—which argues, wrongly I think, that Levin trivializes the story by blaming everything on supernatural agency. Other, even less cogent answers include Gordon V. Boudreau, "The Summons of YGB," *Greyfriar*, 13 (1972), 15-24; and John B. Humma, "YGB and the Failure of Hawthorne's Ambiguity," *Colby Library Quarterly*, 9 (1971), 425-431. Critics who accept and try to build on Levin's historicist insight include the following: Darrel Abel, "Black Glove and Pink Ribbon," *New England Quarterly*, 42 (1969), 163-180; Michael Davitt Bell, *Hawthorne and the Romance of New England* (Princeton, N.J.: Princeton University Press, 1971), pp. 76-81; Neal Frank Doubleday, *Hawthorne's Early Tales* (Durham, N.C.: Duke University Press, 1972), pp. 200-212; and B. Bernard Cohen, "Deodat Lawson's *Christ's Fidelity* and Hawthorne's YGB," *Essex Institute Historical Collections*, 104 (1968), 349-370.

4. See Thomas E. Connolly, ed., *Nathaniel Hawthorne: YGB* (Columbus, Ohio: Charles E. Merrill, 1968), pp. 6-8; James W. Clark, Jr., "Hawthorne's Use of Evidence in YGB," *Essex Institute Historical Collections*, 111 (1975), 12-34; Cohen, "*Christ's Fidelity*," p. 370; and Levin, "Shadows," p. 352.

5. For the "classic" psychoanalytic reading of YGB, see Frederick Crews, *Sins of the Fathers* (New York: Oxford, 1966), pp. 98-106. For other more or less "scientific" models, see Reginald Cook, "The Forest of Goodman Brown's Night," *New England Quarterly*, 43 (1970), 473-481; Dennis Brown, "Literature and Existential Psychoanalysis," *Canadian Review of American Studies*, 4 (1973), 65-73; and Edward Jayne, "Pray Tarry with me Young Goodman Brown," *Literature and Psychology*, 29 (1979), 100-113.

6. For the beginnings of a "structuralist" account of the famous "ambiguities" of YGB, see Harold F. Mosher, Jr., "The Source of Ambiguity in Hawthorne's YGB," *ESQ*, 26 (1980), 16-25.

7. For a translation of Hawthorne's psychological themes into the language not of Freud but of Scottish Common Sense, see Rita K. Gollin, *Nathaniel Hawthorne and the Truth of Dreams* (Baton Rouge: Louisiana State University Press, 1979), esp. pp. 123-128, 134-138.

8. Doubleday, *Early Tales*, p. 202.

9. For the sense of Hawthorne's personal revulsion from the affair of 1692, see "Main Street," in *The Snow-Image* (Columbus: Ohio State University Press, 1974), pp. 73-78. And for the clear, "spectral" connection between YGB and ADA, see Bell, *Historical Romance*, pp. 76-78.

10. All citations of the text of YGB refer to *Mosses from an Old Manse* (Columbus: Ohio State University Press, 1974). The tale first appeared in the *New England Magazine* (April 1835).

11. "Fancy's Show Box," in *Twice-told Tales* (Columbus: Ohio State University Press, 1974), p. 220.

12. The conjecture as to the exact "night of all nights" is that of Daniel Hoffman; see *Form and Fable in American Fiction* (New York: Oxford, 1966), p. 150.

13. See Richard S. Carpenter, "Hawthorne's Polar Explorations," *Nineteenth-Century Fiction*, 24 (1969), 45-56; Donald A. Ringe, "Hawthorne's Night Journeys," *American Transcendental Quarterly*, 10 (1971); and Brown, "Ex-

istential Psychoanalysis." The tradition carried out here is that of Crews (and of his predecessors, Adams and Askew).

14. For the appropriate Christian lore, see Joseph T. McCullen, "YGB: Presumption and Despair," *Discourse*, 2 (1959), 145–157.

15. See his "Introduction" to *Young Goodman Brown*, p. 8. This "Introduction" is the third of Connolly's contributions to the ongoing debate: the first is cited in note 3; the second—"How Young Goodman Brown Became Old Badman Brown," *College English*, 24 (1962), 153–154—is conceived as an answer to Robert W. Cochran, "Hawthorne's Choice: the Veil or the Jaundiced Eye," *College English*, 23 (1962), 342–346.

16. In ways it might be impossible to "document," YGB appears to depend on Cotton Mather's *Magnalia Christi Americana* (esp. Books IV and V) as crucially as on his *Wonders of the Invisible World*. We have long known that Hawthorne read the *Magnalia* as early as 1827; see Marion L. Kesselring, *Hawthorne's Reading, 1828–1850* (New York: New York Public Library, 1949), p. 56. Furthermore, *Grandfather's Chair* invites us to suppose that it was a book he kept re-reading; see *True Stories from History and Biography* (Columbus: Ohio State University Press, 1972), pp. 92–95. But beyond that, we are forced to imagine that the *Magnalia*—along with Daniel Neal's *History of New England* and Benjamin Trumbull's *History of Connecticut* —provided Hawthorne with "sociological" information he could use in a fairly speculative way; that if Hawthorne could worry the matter of "declension" in "Bullivant," he could also epitomize it in YGB. For clearly all the "Jeremiad" themes are collected (if not quite compressed) into that one book.

17. "Revisionist" interpretation of the Half-Way Covenant begins with Edmund S. Morgan, *Visible Saints* (Ithaca, N.Y.: Cornell University Press, 1965), esp. pp. 113–138. For its continuation, see Norman Pettit, *The Heart Prepared* (New Haven, Conn.: Yale University Press, 1966), pp. 158–216; Robert G. Pope, *The Half-Way Covenant* (Princeton, N.J.: Princeton University Press, 1969); and E. Brooks Holifield, *The Covenant Sealed* (New Haven, Conn.: Yale University Press, 1974), pp. 169–186.

18. See, for example, Emil Oberholzer, *Delinquent Saints* (New York: Columbia University Press, 1956), pp. 7–12.

19. This, as I have argued elsewhere, is precisely the problem faced by Edward Taylor: once there was *some* approved place for the doubtful, the final step became even *harder* to take; see *"God's Determinations* Touching Half-Way Membership," *American Literature*, 39 (1967), 298–314.

20. Besides "Bullivant," "Main Street" also ponders the problem of Puritanic "inheritance"; see Bell, *Historical Romance*, pp. 62–64. E. H. Davidson has also noticed Hawthorne's fascination with "that era when the Puritan conscience was [most] troubled by its inner disharmonies"; see "The Question of History in *The Scarlet Letter*," *Emerson Society Quarterly*, 25 (1961), 2–3.

21. For the "antinomianism" of Brown's premises, see James W. Matthews, "Antinomianism in YGB," *Studies in Short Fiction*, 3 (1965), 73–75; and,

somewhat more testingly, Claudia G. Johnson, "YGB and Puritan Justification," *Studies in Short Fiction,* 11 (1974), 200–203.

22. Roy Harvey Pearce, "Romance and the Study of History," in *Hawthorne Centenary Essays* (Columbus: Ohio State University Press, 1964), p. 233.

23. *The New England Mind: From Colony to Province* (Cambridge: Harvard University Press, 1953), p. 135.

24. *Memorable Providences, Relating to Witchcrafts and Possessions,* quoted from David Levin, ed., *What Happened in Salem?* (New York: Harcourt, Brace and World, 1960), p. 102. Mather makes it clear that although witchcraft is indeed the "furthest Effort of our *Original Sin*" (99), still all are "tempted hereunto" (102). In itself it is a kind of despair, since "All the *sure Mercies* of the *New Covenant* . . . are utterly abdicated" (98). But the *way into* witchcraft often involves presumption: *"Let him that stands, take heed lest he fall"* (102).

25. Levin, "Shadows," p. 352.

26. Hurley, "Brown's 'Heart of Darkness,' " p. 411.

27. The best way to "prepare" to read YGB is to make one's way through G. L. Burr's *Narratives of the Witchcraft Cases* (New York: Charles Scribner's Sons, 1914) and Levin's *What Happened in Salem?* It also helps to have read the standard modern commentators: see Miller, *Colony to Province,* pp. 149–208; Marion L. Starkey, *The Devil in Massachusetts* (New York: Doubleday, 1949); and, for the revisionist emphasis, Chadwick Hansen, *Witchcraft at Salem* (New York: New American Library, 1969).

28. *An Essay For the Recording of Illustrious Providences* (Boston, 1684), p. 200. The relevance of Mather's remark is not intended as an argument against other sources. See—in addition to Cohen (note 3) and Clark (note 4)—G. H. Orians, "New England Witchcraft in Fiction," *American Literature,* 2 (1930), 54–71; Fannye N. Cherry, "The Sources of Hawthorne's YGB," *American Literature,* 5 (1934), 342–348; Arlin Turner, "Hawthorne's Literary Borrowings," *PMLA,* 51 (1936), 543–562; and E. Arthur Robinson, "The Vision of YGB," *American Literature,* 35 (1963), 218–225.

29. As I indicated in my original version of this chapter, the psychological dynamics of ADA and YGB are so essentially Spenserian that the Red Cross/Archimago episode in Book I of *The Faery Queene* must be regarded as the common "mythos" of both tales; see "Visible Sanctity and Specter Evidence," *Essex Institute Historical Collections,* 110 (1974), 277–278. This insight, which takes us well beyond earlier speculations about Spenser's "influence," is elaborated (relative to ADA) by John Schroeder; see "Alice Doane's Story: An Essay on Hawthorne and Spenser," *Nathaniel Hawthorne Journal,* 4 (1974), 129–134.

30. Again the explicit warning of Increase Mather seems cogent: "we may not in the least build on the devil's word"; if we do, "the matter is ultimately resolved into a diabolical faith" (*Providences,* p. 200).

31. For the reality of practicing witches in Salem Village, see Hansen, *Witchcraft,* esp. pp. 93–120.

32. "Shadows," p. 351. *Contra* the charge of Hurley, Levin does not argue that

all discussion of the nature and extent of "depravity" is beyond the proper limits of fiction; only that *this story* is designed to suggest that Goodman Brown's particular evidences do not touch the "heart" of that question.

33. "Fancy's Show Box" (*Token*, 1837) provides a useful gloss on the implied theology of YGB not only because it stresses the "spectral" quality of Mr. Smith's solid-seeming outer life, but also because it emphasizes the variability of the inner life as well: wicked intentions may indeed produce "a stain upon the soul," yet this is only half the traditional formulation; a reversal of intention blots out the stain and leaves "the canvas white as snow" (*Twice-told Tales*, p. 225). Indeed the dominant idea of the sketch seems to be the virtual impossibility, given the *extreme* variability of intention, of fixing oneself, once and for all, in a settled moral state. For the most part, Hawthorne hypothetically argues, we really do not know a firm purpose from a flitting fantasy: "There is no such thing in man's nature, as a settled and full resolve . . . except at the very moment of execution" (p. 226). Before an "act," all intention is hypothetical; and afterwards, it can always be repented. It is this thought, quite likely, which drives the self-reprobated Ethan Brand to blasphemous suicide; certainly it controls Hawthorne's attitude toward witchcraft. Not believing in predestination, he cannot construe it as the reprobate's *real* embracing of the inevitable. To be sure, the will-to-evil exists; and it may well wish, at moments, to totalize itself. But as the thing is impossible, Brown does indeed pull back. His problem, apparently, in his inability to believe that most others (who do not commit blasphemous suicide) probably do the same.

34. As is clear from a book like Morgan's *Visible Saints* (or Mather's *Magnalia*), the defining essence of American Puritanism is the ambition to identify the Visible with the Invisible Church. The most powerful protest from *within* the premises of Calvinism came, as we have observed in earlier chapters, from Roger Williams. For a full account of his criticism of the Puritan "Way," see Edmund S. Morgan, *Roger Williams: The Church and the State* (New York: Harcourt, Brace and World, 1967); and cf. Perry Miller, *Roger Williams* (New York: Atheneum, 1953).

35. Crews's famous formula for Hawthorne's guilty relation to his hated ancestors (*Sins*, p. 38) actually applies most appropriately to the witches themselves. For the case in Winthrop, see his *Journal* (New York: Charles Scribner's Sons, 1908), I, 230. For other accounts of the psychosocial meaning of the Salem Witchcraft, see Hansen, *Witchcraft*, pp. 121–155; and Kai T. Erikson, *Wayward Puritans* (New York: Wiley, 1966), pp. 137–159.

36. See Erikson, *Wayward Puritans*, pp. 185–205. The Emersonian formula occurs in defense of "Self-Reliance," where it seems to answer an orthodox objection from his Aunt Mary Moody.

37. For Goodman Brown's refusal of baptism as part of a pattern of contrary motivation, see Walter J. Paulits, "Ambivalence in YGB," *American Literature*, 41 (1970), 577–584.

38. Ever since Richard Harter Fogle suggested that in YGB "Hawthorne wishes to propose, not flatly that man is primarily evil, but instead the growing doubt lest this should be the case"—see "Ambiguity and Clarity in YGB," *New*

England Quarterly, 18 (1945), 448—most critics have been sensitive to a whole range of "ambiguities" which cloud the premise of Total Depravity. One effort, of which mine is a part, has been "historical": what are Brown's premises and what is the nature of his evidence? Another has been "narratological": what does the story actually "say"? The prime example would be that of Mosher (see note 6), but his work builds on that of Taylor Stoehr, Sheldon W. Liebman, Leo B. Levy; see "YGB and Hawthorne's Theory of Mimesis," *Nineteenth-Century Fiction,* 23 (1969), 393–412; "The Reader and YGB," *Nathaniel Hawthorne Journal,* 5 (1975), 156–169; and "The Problem of Faith in YGB," *JEGP,* 74 (1975), 375–387. Without benefit of Levin, the entire project seems to me a bit "operose," yet Mosher effectively disputes, on narrative grounds alone, Levy's certainty that Brown's literal wife indeed attended a literal witch-meeting, so that the problem of YGB remains that of the nature of faith rather than the character of Faith.

39. For the latter-day Puritan subtlety, see *The Return of the Several Ministers Consulted,* reprinted in Levin, *What Happened,* pp. 110–111. For the "classic" text on the identification of hypocrites, see the selections Perry Miller has made from John Cotton's *The New Covenant,* in *The Puritans* (New York: Harper and Row, 1938), I, 314–318.

40. Williams' solution, as outlined by Miller and Morgan (see note 34), was finally to declare the *true* Church an altogether invisible affair and thus to consign all "visible" churches to the realm of politics and the flesh. Stoddard, remaining a staunch Calvinist *and* a formidable theocrat, settled for the proposition that the Lord's Supper was merely a *means* to (rather than a seal of) converted sainthood; see Miller, *Colony to Province,* pp. 227–302. The Arminians' answer was the simplest: disbelieving in "final perseverance," they merely observed that the game of salvation is "not over till it's over."

41. I have argued the "Rappaccini" case elsewhere: see "A Better Mode of Evidence," *Emerson Society Quarterly,* 54 (1969), 12–22.

42. The speaker is Sister Soulsby, the female evangelist in Harold Frederic's *Damnation of Theron Ware.* The context is the more crassly revivalistic Methodism in the long since "burned-over" district of upstate New York; but the problem of election to visible sainthood remains the same.

43. For efforts to discover *political* relevance in the case of Goodman Brown, see Robert E. Morsberger, "The Woe That Is Madness," *Nathaniel Hawthorne Journal,* 3 (1973), 117–182; and, somewhat more substantially, Barton Levi St. Armand, "YGB as Historical Allegory," *Nathaniel Hawthorne Journal,* 3 (1973), 183–197. Most cogent, perhaps is the argument of Frank Shuffleton, who relates the scene of the witch-meeting in YGB to Mrs. Trollope's account of Methodist camp meetings in her *Domestic Manners of the Americans;* see "Nathaniel Hawthorne and the Revival Movement," *American Transcendental Quarterly,* 44 (1979), 16–25. Yet this "social" question may be better left for the context of "The Minister's Black Veil"—and its placement in the clearly contemporaneous project of "The Story Teller."

44. For evidence of the "enthusiastic" fervor behind the original Puritan decison to admit only tested saints to church membership, see David D. Hall, *The An-*

tinomian Controversy (Middletown, Conn.: Wesleyan University Press, 1968), pp. 3–20. For a selected analysis of intimidating Puritan autobiographies, see Daniel B. Shea, Jr., *Spiritual Autobiography in Early America* (Princeton, N.J.: Princeton University Press, 1968). The solemn charge quoted here is from Thomas Shepard to his son; see Michael McGiffert, ed., *God's Plot* (Amherst: University of Massachusetts Press, 1972), p. 36.

45. See Bell, *Historical Romance*, pp. 99–100. As suggested earlier, the explicit moralizing of ADA parodies Upham.

46. For the classic view that there was "nothing Puritan" about the Salem Witchcraft, see George Lyman Kittredge, *Witchcraft in Old and New England* (Cambridge: Harvard University Press, 1929). Miller's classic answer runs as follows: "We shall avoid confusing ourselves by an irrelevant intrusion of modern categories only when we realize that what struck Salem Village was intelligible to everybody concerned . . . within the logic of the Covenant" (*Colony to Province*, p. 192).

47. *Wonders of the Invisible World* (Boston, 1693), p. 7. For the full context of Mather's end-time thoughts on witchcraft, see David Levin, *Cotton Mather* (Cambridge: Harvard University Press, 1978), pp. 174–222.

48. "Several Ministers," quoted from Levin, *What Happened*, p. 111.

49. *Wonders*, p. 8. As the court of Oyer and Terminer followed the practical advice rather than the theoretical warning of the "Several Ministers," and as the *Wonders* did defend the results of those determinations, so Miller charged Mather with having "prostituted a magnificent conception of New England's destiny to saving the face of a bigoted court" (*Colony to Province*, p. 204). For Hawthorne the issue was just a shade less personal: a whole world rested upon the ability to tell saints from witches.

50. For Cotton versus Williams on the parable of wheat and tares, see Miller, *Williams*, pp. 101–128. Since Williams came to hold that the only *real* church was invisible, the problem of human distinction disappeared: *obviously* saints and sinners were mixed in the world, and *ex hypothesi* the invisible church was pure. Cotton went on with the old problem, bequeathing it to numberless literal and cultural descendants: he might come to accept (and even *defend*) the presence of weedy hypocrites in the Garden of the Church, but he never for a moment abandoned the regulative ideal of congregational separation.

51. See *Snow-Image*, pp. 77–78.

52. Modern historians often seem to echo Hawthorne: according to Starkey, the witchcraft "had brought a division and a sore sickness of spirit on the people. Husband had 'broken charity' with wife and wife with husband, mother with child and child with mother"—and all on the very strangest sort of "evidence" (*The Devil*, p. 248).

53. As noted in connection with ADA, II Corinthians 11:14 became a crucial text during the witchcraft episode; yet its application proved ambiguous. What precisely followed from the fact that "Satan himself is transformed into an angel of light"? For Increase Mather the fact implied warning to prosecutors: be careful, for the Devil *can* assume the specter of an innocent person; see *Cases of Conscience Concerning Evil Spirits Personating Men*, in Levin, *What*

Happened, pp. 117–129. Yet Robert Calef charged Cotton Mather with using the text in the opposite way, to "compass" the execution of George Burroughs: the Devil assisted this witch in his saintly simulation; see *More Wonders of the Invisible World,* in Burr, *Narratives,* pp. 360–361. Levin disbelieves Calef's account (see Mather, pp. 215–216); I believe it and suspect Hawthorne did also. Still the point is simply that Calef unerringly locates the fatal flaw in Puritan epistemology: invisible matters are seldom what they seem.

54. *Wonders,* p. 152. Clark proposes James Brown of Swansea as the prototype of Hawthorne's bedeviled protagonist; see "Use of Evidence," pp. 13–17. More likely, Hawthorne remembered a name from the *Wonders* itself—one William Brown, who "testified to the bewitchment of his most pious and prudent wife" (75), a member of the Curwen family.

55. *Wonders,* p. 80. One ventures to suggest that, politics aside, Goodman Brown is what Cotton Mather would have become without the Peculiar Faith provided by his own Special Angel: "I and my Faith" with a vengeance.

56. See *True Stories,* p. 55.

57. Starkey retains a hint of the older, wishful version: the people suddenly realized "their leaders had suffered the devil to guide them. They were turning from such leaders" (*The Devil,* p. 249). In Miller's chastened formulation, "The onus of error lay heavy on the land; realization of it slowly but irresistibly ate into the New England conscience" (*Colony to Province,* p. 208).

58. For the spread of Stoddardism *up to* 1692, see Pope, *Half-Way Covenant,* esp. pp. 239–260. For the relation of Stoddardism to the Brattle Street Church, see Morgan, *Visible Saints,* pp. 139–152. Thomas Brattle's letter of 1692 is included in its entirety (along with most of Calef's *More Wonders*) in Burr's *Narratives.* And for Judge Sewall's change of heart, see his *Diary* for 19 August 1962 and 15 January 1696/7. And (finally) for a slightly different view of Salem Witchcraft and the end of the authentic Puritan world, see Erikson, *Wayward Puritans,* pp. 155–159.

6. THE TRUE SIGHT OF SIN

1. In treating Hooper as a "case of conscience," I invoke the example of Austin Warren; see *The New England Conscience* (Ann Arbor: University of Michigan Press, 1966), pp. 132–142.

2. For the classic view of unresolvable ambiguity in "The Minister's Black Veil" (MBV), see Richard Harter Fogle, *Hawthorne's Fiction* (Norman: University of Oklahoma Press, 1952), pp. 33–40.

3. The most meaningful comment on the sermon before Belcher is the brief reference by Glenn C. Altschuler in "The Puritan Dilemma in MBV," *American Transcendental Quarterly,* 24 (1974), 25–27. The "fact" is also mentioned by Michael Davitt Bell, *Hawthorne and the Historical Romance of New England* (Princeton, N.J.: Princeton University Press, 1971), p. 68; and Neal Frank Doubleday, *Hawthorne's Early Tales* (Durham, N.C.: Duke Uni-

versity Press, 1972), p. 171. For other generally "historical" interpretations, see Robert H. Fossum, *Hawthorne's Inviolable Circle* (Deland, Fla.: Everett/Edwards, 1972), pp. 56–59; Harry B. Henderson, *Versions of the Past* (New York: Oxford, 1974), pp. 101, 109; and Robert E. Morsberger, "MBV: Shrouded in Blackness, Ten Times Black," *New England Quarterly*, 46 (1973), 454–462. For explicit rejections of significant "historicity," see Raymond Benoit, "Hawthorne's Psychology of Death," *Studies in Short Fiction*, 8 (1971), 553–560; and Nina Baym, *The Shape of Hawthorne's Career* (Ithaca, N.Y.: Cornell University Press, 1976), p. 58.

4. For the psychoanalytic reading of MBV, see Frederick Crews, *Sins of the Fathers* (New York: Oxford, 1966), pp. 106–111; for the outlines of a semiological approach, see W. B. Carnochan, "MBV: Symbol, Meaning, and the Context of Hawthorne's Art," *Nineteenth-Century Fiction*, 24 (1969), 182–192.

5. The "knowing" view of Hooper as guilty of some explicit (probably) sexual crime drives from Poe's (widely reprinted) review of *Twice-told Tales*. For a carefully guarded comparison with Dimmesdale, see Doubleday, *Early Tales*, pp. 177–178. And for the classic case *for* Hooper (as against Brown), see Robert W. Cochran, "Hawthorne's Choice: The Veil or the Jaundiced Eye," *College English*, 23 (1962), 342–346.

6. The similarity between Digby and Hooper is well established in the criticism. For their relative status as images of "the Puritan," see Michael Bell, *Historical Romance*, pp. 64–68. For their similarity as Romantic "egoists," see Millicent Bell, *Hawthorne's View of the Artist* (New York: New York University Press, 1962), pp. 23–24. And for Digby as the "grotesque" version of Hawthorne's sexual "escapists," see Crews, *Sins*, pp. 114–116. MBV was first published in *The Token* for 1836 and was almost certainly part of "The Story Teller" as it existed in 1834; "The Man of Adamant" appeared in *The Token* for 1837.

7. Baym, *Shape*, p. 55.

8. Hooker, *The Application of Redemption;* quoted from Perry Miller and Thomas H. Johnson, ed., *The Puritans* (New York: Harper and Row, 1963), p. 292.

9. Cf. C. C. Goen, *Revivalism and Separatism in New England, 1740–1800* (New Haven, Conn.: Yale University Press, 1962), esp. pp. 1–114; and, a bit less specifically, Edwin Scott Gaustad, *The Great Awakening in New England* (New York: Harper and Row, 1957), pp. 102–125.

10. Fogle's premise of radical ambiguity has found relatively few supporters; it has seemed necessary to decide. Against Hooper, see W. B. Stein, "The Parable of Antichrist in MBV," *American Literature*, 27 (1955), 386–392; E. E. Stibitz, "Ironic Unity in Hawthorne's MBV," *American Literature*, 34 (1962), 182–190; and Nicholas Canaday, Jr., "Hawthorne's Minister and the Veiling Deceptions of Self," *Studies in Short Fiction*, 4 (1967), 135–142. In favor, see Benoit, "Psychology of Death"; Cochran, "Hawthorne's Choice"; G. P. Voight, "The Meaning of MBV," *College English*, 13 (1952), 337–338; Victor Strandberg, "The Artist's Black Veil," *New*

England Quarterly, 41 (1968), 567-574; and G. A. Santangelo, "The Absurdity of MBV," *Pacific Coast Philology*, 5 (1970), 61-66.

11. All citations from the text of MBV refer to *Twice-told Tales* (Columbus: Ohio State University Press, 1974).

12. See *Faithful Narrative*, in C. C. Goen, ed., *The Great Awakening* (New Haven, Conn.: Yale University Press, 1972), pp. 144-149. And for the more general relevance of Edwards (as well as of Bunyan and Shepard), see Morsberger, "Shrouded in Blackness."

13. Evidently something like a "Puritan" problem lies behind our own critical tendency to disregard the literal in Hawthorne; see David Levin, "Shadows of Doubt," *American Literature*, 34 (1962), 344-352.

14. The creator of the flamboyant Awakening "style" was Whitefield rather than Edwards. Even the famous "imagistic" "Sinners in the Hands of an Angry God" was delivered by Edwards in monotone, with "his eyes fixed on the bell-rope;" the upset came from the auditors. See Perry Miller, *Jonathan Edwards* (New York: William Sloane, 1949), pp. 145-146.

15. The narrator may be confusing "secret sin" with the related but secondary problem of other "sad mysteries"; but the theologically literate reader should not do so. The primary sense of "secret sin" should clearly be Calvin's sense of sinfulness rooted in our nature which we (while unregenerate) are unaware of. For Puritans, this should all be an "open secret"; and confusion on this point marks the narrator's (or the critic's) loss of touch with the Calvinist idiom.

16. Cf. "Passages from a Relinquished Work," published in the *New England Magazine* (December 1834). The bibliographical argument for the inclusion of MBV within the projected "Story Teller" was first advanced by Seymour Gross, "Four Possible Additions to Hawthorne's 'Story Teller,' " *Papers of the Bibliographical Society of America*, 51 (1957), 90-95. The argument has been rejected by Doubleday (*Early Tales*, p. 170) and Baym (*Shape*, p. 40); but the tale's narrative peculiarities would seem to support inclusion. For the most complete discussions of "The Story Teller," see Nelson F. Adkins, "The Early Projected Works of Nathaniel Hawthorne," *Papers of the Bibliographical Society of America*, 39 (1945), 119-155; and Alfred Weber, *Die Entwicklung der Rahmenerzählungen Nathaniel Hawthornes* (Berlin: Erich Schmidt, 1973), pp. 142-307.

17. Thomas Hooker, *Application of Redemption;* quoted from Miller and Johnson, *Puritans*, p. 305.

18. Quoted from Miller and Johnson, *Puritans*, p. 312.

19. For the innocent response to "efficient," see Stibitz, "Ironic Unity," p. 189. The official status of the word may be inferred from Joseph Tracy's favorable characterization of Edwards as "perhaps the most efficient preacher in New England"; see *A History of the Revival of Religion* (Boston: Tappan and Dennet, 1842), p. 214. For Hawthorne's interest in revivalist phenomena, see Frank Shuffleton, "Nathaniel Hawthorne and the Revival Movement," *American Transcendental Quarterly*, 44 (1979), 311-323.

20. See *Distinguishing Marks*, in Goen, *Great Awakening*, pp. 266-267.

21. The critics *most* hostile to Hooper are Stein and Stibitz (see note 10).
22. Accepting the Melvillean hint, we may yet stop short of the argument which would make Hawthorne himself a latter-day Puritan whose system emphasizes sin but omits grace; see Austin Warren, "Introduction," *Nathaniel Hawthorne* (Cincinnati: American Book Co., 1934), pp. xix-xxi.
23. Lying in wait for those who overvalue the commonplace in Hawthorne is (still) Frederick Crews. His arguments answer not only a simplistic theology like that of Edward Wagenknecht in *Nathaniel Hawthorne* (New York: Oxford, 1961), pp. 172–201, but also the sort of truistic moralism associated with Chester E. Eisenger's "Hawthorne as Champion of the Middle Way," *New England Quarterly*, 27 (1954), 27–52.
24. Hooper might conceivably pass the test of the *Religious Affections*: his consciousness is arguably "spiritual," and his outwardly irreproachable life agrees well enough with Edwards' "neonomian" Twelfth Sign, which insists on "Christian practice." But the relevant standard might be in the earlier *Faithful Narrative*: Hooper would not seem to possess that "holy repose of soul" which marks the last stage in Edwards' simplified morphology; and the unrelieved blackness (or monochromatic grayness) of his veiled vision might associate him with those unregenerate men who would discuss the precise hue of salvation knowing only the "names of colors" (see Goen, *Awakening*, pp. 173–174).
25. It is as if Hooper had experienced Thomas Shepard's preparatory phases of "conviction," "compunction," and "humiliation," without going on to "faith," with its "privileges" of "justification," "reconciliation," and "adoption"; see *The Sound Believer*, in J. A. Albro, ed., *The Works of Thomas Shepard* (Boston: Doctrinal Tract and Book Society, 1853), I, 115–284.
26. Perry Miller himself seems always flirting with the temptation to regard Edwards as primarily "literary": see not only his *Edwards* (1949) but also "The Rhetoric of Sensation," in *Errand into the Wilderness* (Cambridge: Harvard University Press, 1956); and "Introduction," *Images or Shadows of Divine Things* (New Haven, Conn.: Yale University Press, 1948).
27. Cf. Sacvan Bercovitch, *The Puritan Origins of the American Self* (New Haven, Conn.: Yale University Press, 1975), esp. pp. 1–34.
28. Though some critics have, undeniably, worked too simply with the positive or affirmative values in Hawthorne, the problem itself remains valid and important; and a book like Leonard J. Fick's *The Light Beyond* (Westminster, Md.: Newman Press, 1955) does not *entirely* collapse under the attack of Frederick Crews.
29. Edwards, "The Divine and Supernatural Light"; quoted from Faust and Johnson, ed., *Jonathan Edwards* (New York: Hill and Wang, 1962), p. 104.
30. The Christian typology of marriage and the Church derives most explicitly from Paul's Epistle to the Ephesians, though it draws much of its richness from the "mystical" interpretation of the Song of Solomon. For the general Puritan acceptance of this system of privileged metaphors, see Gordon S. Wakefield, *Puritan Devotion* (London: Epworth, 1957), pp. 32–37.
31. Doubleday notes that we see Hooper at Sunday service, wedding, and funeral;

he concludes (too simply) that these exhaust "the rituals for what is really important in human experience" (*Early Tales,* pp. 171–172).

32. The full case for the "Puritan" character of Poe's "horror" remains to be made; I make only the beginnings of such an argument, incidentally, in "The Example of Edwards," in Emory Elliott, ed., *Puritanism and American Literature* (Urbana: University of Illinois Press, 1978).

33. For example, Bercovitch persuades us of Cotton Mather's success in making John Winthrop figure as an American-Puritan Everyman; but many of the more *auto*biographical cases clearly fail in their representative attempts; and Mather himself surely fits more readily into the "pathological" schema of Austin Warren. See *Puritan Origins,* pp. 12–25; and cf. *New England Conscience,* pp. 1–28, 76–87.

34. For the Puritan "ambivalence" toward the remaining Protestant sacraments, see Geoffrey Nuttall, *The Holy Spirit in Puritan Faith and Experience* (London: Oxford, 1946), pp. 90–101; John F. H. New, *Anglican and Puritan* (Stanford, Calif.: Stanford University Press, 1964), pp. 59–76; and Norman Pettit, *The Heart Prepared* (New Haven, Conn.: Yale University Press, 1966), pp. 74–93, 134–136. A partially revisionist argument holds that Puritanism gradually outlived its "experimental" bias and, in the years *before* the Great Awakening, enjoyed a sort of "Sacramental Renaissance"; see E. Brooks Holifield, *The Covenant Sealed* (New Haven, Conn.: Yale University Press, 1974), pp. 139–224.

35. Such is the "Transcendental" verdict of Rosina, at the end of the "Puritan" career of Roderick Ellison, in "Egotism; or, The Bosom Serpent." But as Roderick goes on to show, in "The Christmas Banquet" (1844), the idealist cure may be worse than the moralist disease: self for self, the nineteenth century beats the seventeenth all hollow; or, paraphrasing Crews, a "snaky" identity may be better than none.

36. For a sexual interpretation of Hooper's self-veiling, see Crews, *Sins,* pp. 106–111; and, less drastically, R. D. Crie, "MBV: Mr. Hooper's Symbolic Fig Leaf," *Literature and Psychology,* 17 (1967), 211–217. Certain details of Crews's reading are criticized by James Quinn and Ross Baldessarini in "Literary Technique and Psychological Effect in MBV," *Literature and Psychology,* 24 (1974), 115–123. Any very stern case against Hooper must come to terms with Elizabeth. For Stein she signifies, "by common biblical association," a person "consecrated to God" ("Antichrist," p. 389); but a more strenuous argument might point explicitly to that Elizabeth who was the cousin of the Virgin Mary and the miraculous mother of John the Baptist. The effect would be ironic, of course, but the ironies would redound on Hooper primarily; no miraculous birth occurring, Hooper remains—literally, at least—outside the line of salvation; as partial a "Father in Faith" as is Digby in the role of Abraham. For a common-sense justification of Elizabeth as "the norm of human wholeness and love in the story," see Canaday, "Veiling Deceptions," p. 141.

37. For the tendency of liberals to retain a strict nominal loyalty to the orthodox language of sin, see Joseph Haroutunian, *Piety Versus Moralism* (New York:

Henry Holt, 1932), pp. 3–71; and Conrad Wright, *The Beginnings of Unitarianism in American* (Boston: Starr King Press, 1955), pp. 59–90, 115–134.

38. The famous sermon on "The Danger of an Unconverted Ministry" (1740) is by Gilbert Tennent; see Alan Heimert and Perry Miller, ed., *The Great Awakening* (Indianapolis: Bobbs-Merrill, 1967), pp. 71–99. As Heimert and Miller show, the theme is a dominant one among defenders of the Revival.

39. My treatment of Hooper as "absolutist" follows Stibitz, who charges him with "harmfully exalting one idea" ("Ironic Unity," p. 182). But critical discussion of the typical Hawthorne protagonist as an overly rigid idealist has had a long and distinguished history, going all the way back to Randall Stewart's identification of "the scholar idealist" as "perhaps the most important single type of character in Hawthorne's works"; see the "Introduction" to *The American Notebooks* (New Haven, Conn.: Yale University Press, 1932), p. xliv.

40. The reference is to Solomon Stoddard's *Doctrine of the Instituted Churches* (London: Ralph Smith, 1700), p. 22. My point is simply that Hooper can treat the Supper neither (traditionally) as a sign nor (revolutionarily) as a means; his isolationism has rendered any sacrament of unity meaningless.

41. The phrase is that of Milton Stern; see *The Fine Hammered Steel of Herman Melville* (Urbana: University of Illinois Press, 1957), p. 1. Stern treats Melville as a unique anti-Transcendentalist founder of American naturalism; but if such terminology is indeed applicable, it would clearly apply to Hawthorne first, from whom much of Melville's "Christian naturalism" clearly derives.

42. Nina Baym, "Hawthorne," in James Woodress, ed., *American Literary Studies: An Annual/1974* (Durham, N.C.: Duke University Press, 1976), p. 25.

43. *True Stories from History and Biography* (Columbus: Ohio State University Press, 1972), pp. 273–274.

44. Franklin is anxious that we understand "the terms" of his friendship with Whitefield: he invites the great revivalist to lodge at his own house "not for Christ's sake" but for Whitefield's; and his way of listening to the Evangelist's message is to compute the distance at which his clear, loud, and articulate voice may be heard. It is, all too plainly, a matter of communications theory; and it is a little like his being interested in *The Pilgrim's Progress* mainly for its mixture of narrative and dialogue. See *The Autobiography of Benjamin Franklin* (New Haven, Conn.: Yale University Press, 1964), pp. 175–180.

45. Franklin, *Autobiography*, pp. 53–54; and Edwards, "Personal Narrative," in Faust and Johnson, p. 57.

46. "Preface to Poor Richard, 1747," in F. L. Mott and C. E. Jorgensen, ed., *Benjamin Franklin* (New York: Hill and Wang, 1962), p. 193.

47. *True Stories*, p. 274.

48. *Autobiography*, pp. 102–103.

49. See *America's Coming of Age* (New York: E. P. Dutton, 1915), pp. 3–35.

50. For the influence of Samuel Clarke on the American clergy, see Wright, *Beginnings of Unitarianism*, passim; and Henry F. May, *The Enlightenment in America* (New York: Oxford, 1976), pp. 11–21. Mott and Jorgensen specu-

late that either Bentley or Derham may be the villain of the Franklin piece (*Franklin*, p. cxvii); but the editors of the Yale *Autobiography* more plausibly suggest Clarke. Not only did his *Demonstration of the Being and Attributes of God* (1704) affect Hume and Holbach just as Franklin says he was affected, but even more significantly, when Franklin describes his return to virtue, he sounds very much like the Clarke of the *Discourse Concerning the Unchangeable Obligations of Natural Virtue* (1705), arguing that virtue is part of the "Reason of Things."

51. For the Universalist controversy provoked by John Clarke and Charles Chauncey, see Wright, *Beginnings of Unitarianism*, pp. 187–193. And it is obviously Dwight's response to this controversy which mediates between Bunyan and Hawthorne—controlling the emphasis on hell and also providing the model for Smooth-it-away in the "smooth Divine, unus'd to wound/The Sinner's heart, with hell's alarming sound"; see *The Triumph of Infidelity*, in W. J. McTaggart and W. K. Bottorff, ed., *The Major Poems of Timothy Dwight* (Gainsville, Fla.: Scholars' Facsimiles, 1969), esp. pp. 356–358.

52. For the likely associations of Shute, see the biographical note of "Daniel Shute, D. D.," in William B. Sprague, *Annals of the American Pulpit* (New York: Robert Carter, 1865), I, 18–22.

53. For Peter Clark's dangerous concession to the liberals, see *The Scripture-Doctrine of Original Sin, stated and defended. In a Summer Morning's Conversation* . . . (Boston: Kneeland, 1758), esp. pp. 2–25, 42. For Chauncey's ruthless response, see *The Opinion of one that has perused the Summer Morning's Conversation* . . . (Boston: Green and Russell, 1758); Clark only makes things worse in *Remarks on a late Pamphlet* . . . (Boston: Edes and Gill, 1758). The whole controversy is reviewed by Haroutunian, *Piety*, pp. 15–42; Wright, *Beginnings*, pp. 37–90; and H. Shelton Smith, *Changing Conceptions of Original Sin* (New York: Scribners, 1955), pp. 37–39.

54. The mention of "Peter Clarke" occurs in "Old News, I"; see *The Snow-Image and Uncollected Tales* (Columbus: Ohio State University Press, 1974), pp. 140–141. The treatise at issue would be Clark's *Scripture-Grounds of Baptism* (Boston: Kneeland and Green, 1735). For Hawthorne's reading of the various newspapers in question, see Marion Kesselring, *Hawthorne's Reading* (New York: New York Public Library, 1949), p. 45. My own suspicion is that Hawthorne knew the works of Peter Clark directly. He was by no means an obscure figure: his ministry at Danvers (formerly "Salem Village," the site of the witchcraft episode) lasted from 1716 to 1768; and over that period he published at least sixteen separate titles; see C. K. Shipton and J. E. Mooney, *National Index of American Imprints Through 1800, The Short-Title Evans* (Worcester, Mass.: American Antiquarian Society, 1969), p. 153.

55. *The Ruler's Highest Duty and the People's Only Glory* (Boston: Kneeland, 1739; Evans, 4350). For Barnard, see A. W. Plumstead, ed., *The Wall and the Garden* (Minneapolis: University of Minnesota Press, 1968), pp. 223–280.

56. For identification of all of the twelve sermons delivered before Belcher, see R. W. G. Vail, *A Check List of New England Election Sermons* (Worcester,

Mass.: American Antiquarian Society, 1936). The first hundred years of New England election sermons have been studied by T. H. Breen in *The Character of the Good Ruler* (New Haven, Conn.: Yale University Press, 1970); and the election sermons of the 1760's and 1770's have become a staple in studies of "Puritanism and the American Revolution"; but there is no adequate discussion of the import of these sermons in the middle of the century. For Hawthorne's reading of such sermons, see Kesselring, *Reading*, p. 61.

57. *An Essay for Reviving Religion* (Boston: Kneeland and Henchman, 1733; Evans, 3735). For Prince's sermon, see Plumstead, *Wall*, pp. 179–220.

58. Wigglesworth, *Essay*, pp. 1, 4, 5, 7, 18, 23, and esp. p. 31.

59. At his ordination in 1716, William Cooper distinguished himself by "publicly drawing up a confession of faith in the articles of Calvinism" (Miller, *Edwards*, p. 21). Many of his (numerous) early publications stress the need for a revival; and after sponsoring the Calvinism of "God glorified" in "free and catholic" Boston, he went on to co-author a "Preface" to Edwards' *Faithful Narrative*—plainly declaring the "wonderful work at Northampton" an authentic "effusion" of the Spirit (in Goen, *Awakening*, pp. 136–141). Aside from his election sermon, his major publications of 1740 and 1741 stress the connection between the Revival and a strict orthodoxy of sin and grace (see Gaustad, *Awakening*, pp. 56–61). His very aggressive "Preface" to the *Distinguishing Marks* not only repeats Edwards' charge that opposition to the Awakening stems from Arminianism and may amount to the "unpardonable sin"; it also proposes the creation of a journal (like *The Christian History*) which would "transmit accounts" of all local revivals (in Goen, *Awakening*, pp. 223–224). A final sign of Cooper's absolute loyalty to the ideals of the Revival would be his suggestion (in 1743) that perhaps Edwards had gone too far in exposing the faults of certain revivalists (Goen, p. 80). Once again, the argument is *not* that Hooper *is* Cooper. But certain bits of evidence are scary indeed: Cooper's "Preface" to the *Distinguishing Marks* opens with a citation of the precise chapter and verse in Corinthians in which Paul discusses the self-veiling of Moses, which W. B. Stein ("Antichrist") long ago proposed as the Biblical source of MBV; see Goen, *Awakening*, pp. 215–217.

60. *The Honours of Christ* (Boston: Draper, 1740; Evans, 4498), p. 18.

61. Miller long ago identified Hooker as the founder of an American tradition of preparationism stressing conviction, humiliation, and contrition; and he also noticed that, although Hooker's views became normative, they did not escape criticism for making preparation theologically too all-inclusive; see " 'Preparation for Salvation' in Seventeenth-Century New England," *Nature's Nation* (Cambridge: Harvard University Press, 1967), pp. 50–77. Elaborating and emending Miller, Norman Pettit admitted that "the preparatory phase was by far the most important single activity in Hooker's conception of conversion" (*Heart Prepared*, p. 100). Hooker's recent biographer is careful to explain that Hooker really does have some sense of a light beyond; but clearly his own emphases and his later (very considerable) influence have to do with the idea of an elongated and painful preparation; see Frank Shuffleton, *Thomas Hooker, 1586–1647* (Princeton, N.J.: Princeton University Press, 1977), pp.

78–97, 247–261, 282–307. Furthermore, Pettit has recently made it quite clear that it was Hooker who effectively turned the Puritan Mind inward, by emphasizing a "preparatory anxiety [that] put off assurance"; see "Hooker's Doctrine of Assurance: A Critical Phase in New England Spiritual Thought," *New England Quarterly*, 47 (1974), 518–534. Thus Hawthorne's evocation of Hooker comes to seem not only fair but in a sense inevitably right: of all the "original" American Puritans he came the closest, intellectually at least, to getting "stuck" in preparation. He might cure sick souls by distinguishing their needful anxiety from gratuitous despair; but he could also be accused of separating "a good faith" from any "relish and sweetness" (Pettit, "Assurance," p. 521).

62. Quoted from Miller and Johnson, *The Puritans*, p. 305. Miller also reproduces a brief portion of Hooker's remarks on "Repentant Sinners and their Ministers" (pp. 309–314). Hooker's point is that the converted eventually realize that their induced terrors were necessary, and that (ironically, in Hooper's case) the minister himself eventually "feasts [with] them as guest."

63. *Magnalia Christi Americana* (Hartford, Conn.: Andrus, 1853–1855), I, 343, 346.

64. Cooper sounds most like Hooker when advising his hearers to love and advance their preparatory motions: "If your Convictions are but superficial, beg God to make them deep. If they are but transient, beg God to fasten them as a Nail in a safe place"; see *One Shall be Taken and Another Left* (Boston: Fleet, 1741), p. 14.

65. For the career of Hooper as first Puritan, see Daniel Neal, *The History of the Puritans* (New York: Harper, 1843), I, 51–52. Hawthorne borrowed the 1816–17 edition of Neal in April 1827; see Kesselring, *Reading*, p. 58.

66. Hawthorne borrowed Ames's *Fresh Suit* in May 1827; see Kesselring, *Reading*, p. 43.

67. Such, it seems to me, is the just reading of Hawthorne's much quoted remarks in "The Old Manse": Hawthorne reads *everything*, with "reverence," and always in search of some "Truth." If "books of Religion" usually frustrate his search, it is because they "so seldom touch their ostensible subject"—and not, as is often assumed, because the subject itself was outside his concern. It is always with "sadness" that he turns away from such books. Nor is the rejection of "theological libraries" quite absolute: it is only "for the most part" that they amount to a "stupendous impertinence"; and even when they do not advance Hawthorne's own quest, they always reveal (as in a sort of "newspaper") the history of the general search. See *Mosses from an Old Manse* (Columbus: Ohio State University Press, 1974), pp. 19–21.

68. The O.E.D. makes it clear that "parson" is, etymologically, the same word as "person" but that, historically, it refers to the legal person in whom ownership of the local (English) parish church is invested. Thus it was both properly Anglican and inherently objectionable to Congregationalists.

69. For Solomon Stoddard's famous re-invention of the parish, see *Instituted Churches*, pp. 7–8. And for the full purport of "Anglicization," see T. H. Breen, *The Character of the Good Ruler* (New Haven, Conn.: Yale University

Press, 1970), pp. 203–239; and Joseph Ellis, *The New England Mind in Transition* (New Haven, Conn.: Yale University Press, 1973), pp. 34–81.

70. Tracy, *Revival*, p. 133.

71. Kesselring's evidence makes it impossible to decide whether it was Samuel Peters' *General History of Connecticut* (London, 1781) or Benjamin Trumbull's *Complete History of Connecticut, Civil and Ecclesiastical* (New Haven, 1818) which Hawthorne borrowed on 31 October 1827; but the evidence of MBV makes Trumbull appear more likely. And, working in the next decade, Joseph Tracy found the volumes of *The Christian History* "not very uncommon" in New England at the time (*Revival*, p. v.).

72. Parsons' sermon was a local and not an official performance, and so it was not immediately published. But Parsons gives a full account of its text, doctrine, and impact in his "Account"; see *The Christian History . . . for the Year 1744* (Boston: Kneeland and Green, 1745), pp. 133–143.

73. "Account," pp. 120–125.

74. Now a fairly rare book, to be read by most people in microtext (*American Periodical Series*, film 639a, no. 18, reel 10), *The Christian History* is an extremely important work in the intellectual and literary history of America. Suggested by Edwards and supervised by Thomas Prince, Jr., it began (on 5 March 1743) as an eight-page weekly periodical to which revivalist ministers, seized by a sense of an approaching millennium, submitted their own accounts of the revivalistic progress of salvation in their own congregations. Then, after the Awakening had run its Great and General course, it was separately reprinted as *The Christian History, Containing Accounts of the Revival and Propagation of Religion in Great-Britain and America For the Years 1743 and 1744*, 2 vols. (Boston: Kneeland and Green, 1744, 1745). Parson's "Account" appears as pp. 118–162 of vol. II.

75. *Edwards*, pp. 137–138.

76. In many ways Trumbull's *Connecticut* is the perfect complement to Hutchinson's *Massachusetts*, providing not only an overview of New England's "other" colony but also a perspective which took the religious affairs of revival and separation as seriously as secular matters such as warfare and constitutional problems. Supplemented by *The Christian History*, it would have been sufficient.

77. As Goen makes clear, men touched by the New Light saw "no middle ground" with ordinary men, as these "separatical times" saw the formation of "nearly a hundred [new] churches" (*Revivalism and Separatism*, pp. 66, 68).

78. The separations at Guilford and Milford both involve the withdrawal of an awakened congregation from an unawakened minister, but they seem necessary to complete the whole "world" which inspired MBV; especially suggestive is the former, in which a minister sows the seeds of separation by "hiding his real sentiments." See Trumbull, *Complete History*, II, 114–134, 177–179, 335–339.

79. Chauncey's attack on the Awakening—frightening women and children, confusing many a "little flock," and upsetting the ordinary arrangements of

society—clearly has elements of domestic as well as of social, political, and theological conservatism. And it is his attack, made on the basis of his own survey, that later historians (like Trumbull and Tracy) were still answering. See *Seasonable Thoughts on the State of Religion in New England* (Boston: Rogers and Fowle, 1743; Evans, 5151); esp. pp. 103-119 of Part I.

80. Baym, *American Literary Scholarship, 1974*, p. 25. Baym's article on "The Head, the Heart, and the Unpardonable Sin" (*New England Quarterly*, 40, 1967, 31-47) arranges these traditional counters as well as anybody else's, without rescuing Hawthorne's moral psychology from the charge of banal simplicity; see Martin Green, *Revaluations* (New York: Oxford, 1965), pp. 61-85.

81. For the intimate relation between sorrow (*tristitia*) and sloth (*acedia*), see Siegfried Wenzel, *The Sin of Sloth* (Chapel Hill: University of North Carolina Press, 1960), pp. 23-28, 51-55, 155-162, 171-174. Sorrow also figures crucially in Burton's climactic chapter on "Religious Melancholy"; see *The Anatomy of Melancholy* (London: William Tegg, 1854), esp. pp. 713-716. The standard Puritan text is Richard Baxter's *Preservations Against Melancholy and Over-much Sorrow* (London, 1716); but we should not forget the ironic fact that Hooker's early reputation rested on his cure of souls driven by sorrow to the brink of despair (see Mather, *Magnalia*, I, 334).

82. The "anatomy" of Romantic "sorrow" remains to be written. Morse Peckham's theory of a "negative Romanticism" might provide a primitive conceptual beginning; see "Towards a Theory of Romanticism," *PMLA*, 66 (1951), 5-23. The "conclusion" might sound like Geoffrey Hartman's formulations concerning "Romanticism and 'Anti-Self-Consciousness,'"; in Harold Bloom, ed., *Romanticism and Consciousness* (New York: W. W. Norton, 1970), pp. 46-56. A preliminary table of contents would be offered by the later chapters of G. K. Anderson's *The Legend of the Wandering Jew* (Providence: Brown University Press, 1965). By themselves, however, Anderson's anti-Christ-ian instances provide a morphology too Byronic and unsubtle. One needs to throw in a certain amount of Coleridgean "dejection" and Wordsworthean "despondency" to strike the uneven balance.

83. For hints of Hooper's Byronism, see Bell, *Artist*, pp. 23-24, 68. For the implication of later, more advanced forms of subjectivity, see Santangelo, "Absurdity"; and Benoit, "Psychology of Death."

84. The search for minimum psychological essence is epitomized by Baym's discussion of Hawthorne's *"Twice-told Tales* Period" in terms of a troubled minor Romanticism; see *Shape*, pp. 53-83.

85. Bercovitch, *Puritan Origins*, pp. 1-34.

86. Quoted from Bercovitch, *Puritan Origins*, p. 18.

87. See Owen Watkins, *The Puritan Experience: Studies in Spiritual Autobiography* (New York: Schocken, 1972), pp. 164, 238. Romantic re-interpretation of earlier varieties of spiritualism is a major theme of M. H. Abrams' *Natural Supernaturalism* (New York: W. W. Norton, 1971). For the specific case of Wordsworth and earlier religious autobiography, see F. D. McConnell, *The*

Confessional Imagination (Baltimore: Johns Hopkins University Press, 1974); and R. E. Brantley, *Wordsworth's "Natural Methodism"* (New Haven, Conn.: Yale University Press, 1975).

88. For Taylor's poetic attempt to laugh Every Puritan out of his Melancholy Humor, see John Gatta, Jr., "The Comic Design of *Gods Determinations,*" *Early American Literature,* 10 (1975), 121–143.

89. Bercovitch, *Puritan Origins,* pp. 17–19.

90. The "transitional" quality of Edwards was regularly recognized in the nineteenth century. Miller skillfully maintains some of this "pre-Romantic" emphasis, even as he carefully distinguishes Edwards from Shaftesbury and Hutcheson; see *Edwards,* pp. 238–244. For a relatively stiff rejection of this approach, see Conrad Cherry, *The Theology of Jonathan Edwards* (New York: Anchor, 1966), pp. 176–181.

91. Trumbull, *Connecticut,* II, 260–264.

92. Ibid., p. 264. And cf. chap. 96 ("The Try-Works") in *Moby-Dick.*

93. The realization that concepts like "Romantic" and "pre-Romantic" are largely the invention of criticism should not obscure the facts of literary history itself, where the plot is fairly thick. For example, Melville's famous opposition of his literary men of sorrows to Rabelais recalls Hawthorne's use of Cowper and Rabelais at the end of "The Virtuoso's Collection" (*Mosses,* p. 493); and Hawthorne's Virtuoso is himself a version of the Wandering Jew, considered as a sort of ultimate Romantic (but anti-Christian) man of sorrows. Moreover, Melville's prior reference to "Virginia's Dismal Swamp" seems to embody his recognition of Hawthorne's allusion, in "Ethan Brand," to the Bartram who named that landscape (and influenced Wordsworth, also alluded to in "Ethan Brand").

94. Miller, *Edwards,* pp. 17–23.

95. *The New England Mind: The Seventeenth Century* (Cambridge: Harvard University Press, 1939), pp. 35–63.

96. Quoted from G. D. Langdon, Jr., *Pilgrim Colony* (New Haven, Conn.: Yale University Press, 1966), pp. 101–102.

97. For the ambiguous question between Cotton and Williams, see Perry Miller, *Roger Williams* (New York: Atheneum, 1953), esp. pp. 74–205; and Sacvan Bercovitch, "Typology in New England," *American Quarterly,* 19 (1967), 166–191. For the debate between Cotton and the preparationists, see David D. Hall, ed., *The Antinomian Controversy, 1636–1638* (Middletown, Conn.: Wesleyan University Press, 1968).

7. MASQUE AND ANTI-MASQUE

1. All citations of the text of "Legends of the Province House" (LPH) refer to *Twice-told Tales* (Columbus: Ohio State University Press, 1974). All four tales appear to have been written after the publication of the first edition of *Twice-told Tales* (March 1837) and probably in response to the direct solicita-

tion of John L. O'Sullivan; see Neal Frank Doubleday, *Hawthorne's Early Tales* (Durham, N.C.: Duke University Press, 1972), pp. 117-121. All first appeared in his newly created *United States Magazine and Democratic Review*: "Howe's Masquerade" (HM), May 1838; "Edward Randolph's Portrait" (ERP), July 1838; "Lady Eleanore's Mantle" (LEM), December 1838; and "Old Esther Dudley" (OED), January 1839. All were collected, back-to-back, into the 1842 *Twice-told Tales*.

2. The account of the Boston Tea Party appears in the *American Magazine* for April 1836, pp. 317-319. The most substantial biographies are those of Washington (March, pp. 265-266), Major General Lincoln (March, pp. 267-268), Hamilton (May, pp. 354-355), and John Adams (August, pp. 481-484). Briefer notices are of figures as various as Schuyler, Clinton, Jay, Barry, Dale, Cooper, and Marion.

3. LPH remains the most "underinvestigated" of Hawthorne's major literary projects. The most satisfactory account is John P. McWilliams, " 'Thorough-Going Democrat' and 'Modern Tory,' " *Studies in Romanticism*, 15 (1976), 549-571. The other full-scale modern reading treats the artistic uneasiness at the basis of Hawthorne's historical imagination; see Evan Carton, "Hawthorne and the Province of Romance," *ELH*, 47 (1980), 331-354.

4. As Boston's principal thoroughfare had turned from King Street into State Street, so the street in question had formerly been called, variously, High, Main, and Cornhill-Marlborough-Newberry-Orange.

5. The revolutionary primacy of the Old South was perhaps as much geographical as ideological: it was a capacious meeting-house to which "the Body of the People" could march—from Faneuil Hall, past the Town House—to hear the inflammatory rhetoric of Otis or Samuel Adams, just "opposite" the Province House. See Thomas Hutchinson, *History of the Colony and Province of Massachusetts Bay* (Cambridge: Harvard University Press, 1936), III, 137-143; and cf. Hiller Zobel, *The Boston Massacre* (New York: W. W. Norton, 1970), pp. 78-97.

6. Crews omits LPH altogether. Kenneth Dauber provides a perfunctory psychoanalytic reduction, but his real (modernist) point is that they are indeed "without a content—that is, pure form, 'about' nothing"; see *Rediscovering Hawthorne* (Princeton, N.J.: Princeton University Press, 1977), pp. 65-81.

7. The case "against" LPH is largely one of silence. The significant exception is Doubleday, who finds Hawthorne embarrassed by his own gothic ("Hawthornesque") devices; see *Early Tales*, pp. 122-137.

8. The "framed" structure of LPH—first noted by Nelson F. Adkins, "The Early Projected Works of Nathaniel Hawthorne," *Papers of the Bibliographical Society of America*, 39 (1945), 144—has been stressed by the "historicist" readings of R. H. Fossum and Julian Smith; see "Time and the Artist in LPH," *Nineteenth-Century Fiction*, 21 (1967), 337-348; and "Hawthorne's LPH," *Nineteenth-Century Fiction*, 24 (1969), 31-44. More "artful" speculations are offered by Margaret V. Allen, "Imagination and History in LPH," *American Literature*, 43 (1971), 432-437; Jane Donohue Eberwein, "Tem-

poral Perspective in LPH," *American Transcendental Quarterly*, 14 (1972), 41–45; and P. L. Reed, "The Telling Frame of LPH," *Studies in American Fiction*, 4 (1976), 105–111.

9. Most critics are careful to "date" each tale, and Eberwein finds the perspective "elongated" so as to make the near past seem more distant and legendary ("Temporal Perspective," p. 41); but no one identifies the chronology as particularly "revolutionary."

10. Much of Hawthorne's artistic anxiety seems relieved by the clear evidences of ironic narrative manipulation; see Carton, "Province of Romance," pp. 332–334.

11. The building in question was not used as the governor's official residence until the (gorgeously celebrated) arrival of Samuel Shute (in 1716), the fourth governor under the new, "Royal" Charter. Randolph, who first came to America in 1676, never lived in Sargent's elegant house; what Hutchinson means, of course, is that Randolph founded the British customs service in Massachusetts (which the royal governors tried to carry on), and that his various reports on local avoidance of trade regulations ultimately produced the charter under which Massachusetts had to suffer royal governors. The standard modern account of Randolph is M. G. Hall, *Edward Randolph and the American Colonies* (New York: W. W. Norton, 1960). And for the vicissitudes of Peter Sargent's house, see Walter Muir Whitehill, *Boston: A Topographical History* (Cambridge: Harvard University Press, 1959), pp. 17–18.

12. Now taken for granted, the existence of the "subtle counterstatement" undercutting the obvious patriotism had to be *discovered*; see Seymour Gross, "LEM as History," *JEGP*, 54 (1955), 549–554; and Thomas F. Walsh, "Hawthorne's Satire in OED," *Emerson Society Quarterly*, 22 (1966), 31–33.

13. "Bela," I take it, suggests *bellum*; and "Tiffany," a word for a not entirely opaque veil, appears to be related to the word "epiphany."

14. There are no separate articles on HM. Fossum and Smith both treat it briefly, as "paradigmatic" or "introductory." The only sustained analysis is John E. Becker, *Hawthorne's Historical Allegory* (New York: Kennikat Press, 1971), pp. 43–49.

15. Critics (e.g., Fossum and Smith) regularly recognize the forced and irrelevant character of Howe's entertainment; but only Becker sees it as a sort of cultural "allegory," to be opposed by a counterallegory of explicit Puritan construction; see *Historical Allegory*, pp. 45–46.

16. Despite his famous advocacy of obedience to a single tyrant three thousand miles away rather than to three thousand tyrants less than one mile away, Hawthorne offers Mather Byles less as a "representative Tory" in the sober "constitutional" sense than as a convert to British "style."

17. As McWilliams notices, a certain John Joyliffe is prominently mentioned by Thomas Hutchinson in connection with the 1689 opposition to Andros; see "Thorough-Going Democrat," pp. 562–563. For Hawthorne's portrait of Samuel Adams as neo-Puritan "Champion," see *Grandfather's Chair* in *True*

Stories from History and Biography (Columbus: Ohio State University Press, 1972), p. 173; and "A Book of Autographs," in *The Snow-Image and Uncollected Tales* (Columbus: Ohio State University Press, 1974), p. 366.

18. As Fumio Ano points out, General Howe was part of the audience amused by a farce called *The Blockade of Boston* (performed in January 1776), in which Washington is similarly caricatured; see "The Mischianza Ball and Hawthorne's HM," *Nathaniel Hawthorne Journal*, 4 (1974), pp. 231–234.

19. "Old News, II," in *Snow-Image*, p. 144. Everywhere Hawthorne emphasizes both the casual, almost accidental quality of the victory at Louisburg *and also* its very serious consequences; cf. "Sir William Pepperell," in *The Works of Nathaniel Hawthorne* (Boston: Houghton Mifflin, 1883), XII, 234–235; and *Grandfather's Chair*, in *True Stories*, 113–120.

20. Such, of course, is the "Tory" view—Hawthorne's own relation to which remains ambiguous until OED.

21. See "From the Covenant to the Revival," in *Nature's Nation* (Cambridge: Harvard University Press, 1967), esp. pp. 90–108.

22. "Alas for the departing traveler, if thy voice—the voice of fleeting time—have taught him no lessons for Eternity"; see *Snow-Image*, p. 110. Close analysis of "A Bell's Biography" will reveal, however, a much less moralistic concern with the ugly details of *realpolitik* in the eighteenth century.

23. See Fossum, "Time and the Artist," p. 340.

24. Of course there are major differences among American historians—from the final disillusion of Bradford, to the revived expectations of Mather and Edwards (whether pre- or post-millennial), to the sacralization of secular liberty in Bancroft; and yet it is striking how easily they all unite under the banner of "the Kingdom of God in America," and that as the redemption of human history itself, which were otherwise all but meaningless. For the continuity of Bradford, Mather, and Edwards, see Peter Gay, *A Loss of Mastery* (Berkeley: University of California Press, 1966); for a studied comparison of Edwards and Bancroft, Fred Somkin, *Unquiet Eagle* (Ithaca, N.Y.: Cornell University Press, 1967); and for the largest sense of historical continuity, E. L. Tuveson, *Redeemer Nation* (Chicago: University of Chicago Press, 1968), and Sacvan Bercovitch, *The American Jeremiad* (Madison: University of Wisconsin Press, 1978).

25. The concern of virtually all prominent American Revolutionaries with "the lessons of history" has been amply documented by H. Trevor Colbourn in *The Lamp of Experience* (Chapel Hill: University of North Carolina Press, 1965); and it would be false to claim that New Englanders worried less about "the rights of Englishmen" than other American colonials. Yet a "Puritan" emphasis seems distinguishable: whereas Jefferson and other secular minds take refuge in natural rights, the Puritan's last resort is to Salvation History; for the Puritan, English tyranny is most of all a sin against New England's proper past and apocalyptic destiny. The development of Puritan history as a revolutionary weapon is deftly summarized by Carl Bridenbaugh, *Mitre and Sceptre* (New York: Oxford, 1962), pp. 172–178. Cf. also Wesley Frank

Craven, *The Legend of the Founding Fathers* (rpt. Ithaca, N.Y.: Cornell University Press, (1965); and Sacvan Bercovitch, "How the Puritans Won the American Revolution," *Massachusetts Review,* 17 (1976), 597-663.

26. What Hawthorne helps us see is that the mythic identity of "Puritan" can be embraced—meta-politically—by both liberals and conservatives: the essential note is the inflexible determination to stand firm against all threats to the meta-historical plan of divine liberation in New England, however the terms of that plan are variously conceived. Thus the political writings of John Adams are as "Puritan" as the character of Samuel Adams; see *American Magazine,* pp. 481-482; and cf. Craven, *Legend,* pp. 27-32; Tuveson, *Redeemer Nation,* pp. 20-24; and Edmund S. Morgan, "John Adams and the Puritan Tradition," *New England Quarterly,* 34 (1961), 518-529. This logic seems clear enough in Bridenbaugh (see *Mitre and Sceptre,* pp. 224-229) and also, on a larger scale, in Michael Walzer's *Revolution of the Saints* (Cambridge: Harvard University Press, 1965). Confusions occur only when the problem of Puritanism and Revolution slides over into a consideration of the entirely more subtle one of Puritanism and Democracy; see Alice Baldwin, *The New England Clergy and the American Revolution* (Durham, N.C.: Duke University Press, 1928); and Alan Heimert, *Religion and the American Mind* (Cambridge: Harvard University Press, 1966).

27. For various shadings of Hawthorne's belief in a fundament of democracy within Puritanism, see Herbert W. Schneider, "The Democracy of Hawthorne," *Emory University Quarterly,* 22 (1966), 123-132; Nelson F. Adkins, "Hawthorne's Democratic New England Puritans," *Emerson Society Quarterly,* 44 (1966), 66-72; Peter Shaw, "Hawthorne's Ritual Typology of the American Revolution," *Prospects,* 3 (1977), 483-498; and McWilliams, "Thorough-Going Democrat."

8. HELLISH PORTRAITS

1. According to *Grandfather's Chair,* "the angry feelings between England and America might have been pacified" at any moment before "the king's soldiers [should] shed one drop of American blood"; see *True Stories from History and Biography* (Columbus: Ohio State University Press, 1972), p. 169. The less "child-like" logic of ERP accords better with the judgment of modern historians; cf. G. B. Warden, *Boston, 1689-1776* (Boston: Little, Brown, 1970), pp. 189-190; and Hiller Zobel, *The Boston Massacre* (New York: W. W. Norton, 1971), pp. 180-181.

2. See Fumio Ano, "The Mischianza Ball and Hawthorne's HM," *Nathaniel Hawthorne Journal,* 4 (1974), 231-235.

3. For Hawthorne's sketch of "Major General Lincoln," see the *American Magazine* for April 1836, pp. 267-268. Though Hawthorne's Lincoln is, here, scarcely literal, yet some historical irony attaches to the fact that he was afterwards "elected Lieutenant-Governor" and "appointed collector of Boston."

4. Bernard departed for England on 1 August 1769—whereupon "the administration devolved upon Mr. Hutchinson, the lieutenant-governor," though his commission did not arrive until "the beginning of March, 1771"; see Thomas Hutchinson, *The History of the Colony and Province of Massachusetts Bay* (Cambridge: Harvard University Press, 1936), III, 184, 239. British troops (which never *had* been formally requested) had begun to arrive in the fall of 1768.

5. For the "patriotic" blackening of Hutchinson, see Peter Shaw, *American Patriots and the Rituals of Revolution* (Cambridge: Harvard University Press, 1981), pp. 26–47.

6. The literal basis for this legend is Hutchinson's account of his scrupulously carrying out, in 1770, "an order of the king in council, demanding that a garrison of troops should be placed in Castle William, and the provincial garrison dismissed" (*History*, III, 221). This decision came after the "Massacre" but seems to have established Hutchinson's reputation as a "traitor"—well before Franklin's publication of his letters to the home government in 1773. Ultimately, of course, it was those letters (and those of Bernard) which persuaded British authority that Boston had become ungovernable. Warden has called these letters "hysterical" (*Boston*, p. 190), but other authorities disagree; see Zobel, *Massacre*, pp. 61–105; and especially Bernard Bailyn, *The Ordeal of Thomas Hutchinson* (Cambridge: Harvard University Press, 1974), pp. 70–155.

7. *The Works of John Adams* (Boston: Little, Brown, 1850–1856), IV, 67–68.

8. See Bailyn, *Ordeal*, pp. 109–138.

9. In one critical formula, "Hutchinson . . . is too much the man of fact, too little the man of fancy"; see R. H. Fossum, "Time and the Artist in LPH," *Nineteenth-Century Fiction*, 21 (1967), 341.

10. Letters recommending "some abridgment of what is called English liberty" were indeed made public, along with those giving the impression that troops were needed; but Hutchinson was far less responsible for the Intolerable Acts than was Randolph for the infamous revisions of 1684 and 1691.

11. As Warden has noted, even the customs commissioners became "agents of antichrist" (*Boston*, p. 185).

12. Hutchinson, *History*, III, 270.

13. Joliffe has referred to Henry Vane as "the wisest head in England" and suggested that he laid it on the block "for the principles of liberty" (248). *Grandfather's Chair* is willing to allow Vane a "martyrdom," but in "Mrs. Hutchinson" he seems a dark enthusiast, pleased by the prospect of "change and tumult, the elements of his power and delight"; see *The Works of Nathaniel Hawthorne* (Boston: Houghton Mifflin, 1884), XII, 220.

14. The complexity of Hutchinson's motivation (beautifully stressed by Bailyn's *Ordeal*) is evident on nearly every page of his climactic third volume. He remarks that he and Peter Oliver "were to be *blackened,* and rendered odious to the people" (p. 295, my italics); but he also records his sickening worry over outbursts of lawless violence; and above all raises his concern for legitimacy, as in the matter of Castle William (pp. 221–224).

15. How seriously Hawthorne took the violence directed at Hutchinson may be inferred from his sketch, in *Grandfather's Chair*, of "The Hutchinson Mob"; see *True Stories*, pp. 154–160.

16. Virtually all the Tory historians (including Hutchinson) believe in a "conspiracy" of demagogues; and (unlike Hutchinson) Peter Oliver refers this work to the Devil. Yet the belief in conspiracy is not *quite* equal on both sides, as the Tory's Devil is not part of a cosmic arrangement; lack of such a distinction weakens Bernard Bailyn's "Note on Conspiracy" in *The Ideological Origins of the American Revolution* (Cambridge: Harvard University Press, 1967), pp. 144–159.

17. "From the Covenant to the Revival," in *Nature's Nation* (Cambridge: Harvard University Press, 1967), p. 97.

18. "Covenant to Revival," p. 99. What Miller "revises" is the view that cynical leaders provoked popular violence through the skillful manipulation of "propaganda." His argument also prepares the way, it seems to me, for the yet more recent sense of "ritual violence": such violence is usually preceded by the ritualistic confirmation or rediscovery of a long-lost but essentially revolutionary "Puritan" identity; see Shaw, *Rituals of Revolution*, pp. 5–26.

19. For the historical basis of Puritan Jeremiad-logic, see Perry Miller, *The New England Mind: From Colony to Province* (Cambridge: Harvard University Press, 1953). For further political elaboration, see Sacvan Bercovitch, *The American Jeremiad* (Madison: University of Wisconsin Press, 1978), esp. pp. 93–175.

20. Zobel, *Massacre*, p. 32. James Truslow Adams makes the same (representative) point about Samuel Adams, regarded as "a Puritan of the Puritans"; see *Revolutionary New England 1691–1776* (Boston: Atlantic Monthly Press, 1923), p. 302.

21. It is also fair to note, of course, that the animus against Hutchinson was (if anything) greater than that against Randolph because Hutchinson was a native New Englander.

22. Ultimately Hawthorne's Hutchinson betrays a strain of what Miller would call "obtuse secularism"; see "Covenant to Revival," p. 99. For a modern study of the "apocalyptics" of the Revolution, see Nathan O. Hatch, *The Sacred Cause of Liberty* (New Haven, Conn.: Yale University Press, 1977).

23. *True Stories*, p. 137. Further references are cited in the text.

24. The context implies an uncomfortable choice: Hutchinson for "accuracy," Bancroft for "brilliancy or philosophy"; see *True Stories*, p. 138.

25. Grandfather goes on to suggest that if Hutchinson had learned from his own history, "he need not, in after years, have been an exile from his native land" (*True Stories*, p. 157).

26. A recent historian of the Salem Witchcraft judges that although "Hutchinson's account is more balanced than those of most of his successors," still he is a "typical eighteenth-century rationalist"—concluding, against fair evidence to the contrary, that "all witchcraft [is] a matter of fraud"; see Chadwick Hansen, *Witchcraft at Salem* (New York: Braziller, 1969), pp. xi, 50.

27. I have no wish to quarrel with the illuminating work of Bernard Bailyn, who

(following the lead of Caroline Robbins) has established beyond cavil that the rhetoric of England's own Jeremiahs evoked a deep and powerful "Country" opposition in New England; see *Ideological Origins*, pp. 22–143. Yet Miller's "Hawthornean" thesis also endures, sinewing the logic of Hatch (*Sacred Cause*) and Shaw (*Rituals of Violence*). For an attempt to reconcile Miller and Bailyn, see Gordon S. Wood, *The Creation of the American Republic* (Chapel Hill: University of North Carolina Press, 1969), pp. 3–124.

28. It is hard to see that anyone since Hawthorne has faced the problem of Puritanism and the history of the 1760's and 1770's more directly. And what he says is what Wesley Frank Craven and others (such as Miller, Hatch, Shaw, Bridenbaugh, Heimert, and Tuveson) *almost* say—that the crucial fact about the revolutionary decade is the transformation of a diffuse filiopietism into a concentrated revolutionary ideology, complete with symbolic antecedents and ritual occasions; that, as the magical invocations of Alice Vane suggest, the descendants *become* the ancestors, even as these are recreated in a presentist image; see *The Legend of the Founding Fathers* (rpt. Ithaca, N.Y.: Cornell University Press, 1965), pp. 33–45.

29. Contra Fossum, who sees the spectral march of "Howe's Masquerade" as paradigm; see "Time and the Artist," pp. 341–342.

9. PLAGUE, POX, PRIDE AND CORRUPTION

1. In the standard view, events before 1763 figured as long-range background; see John C. Miller, *Origins of the American Revolution* (Boston: Little, Brown, 1943); and Lawrence Henry Gibson, *The Coming of the Revolution* (New York: Harper and Row, 1954). A minor variant would be Bernhard Knollenberg, *Origin of the American Revolution 1759–1766* (New York: Free Press, 1960). Of eighteenth-century observers, David Ramsay covers the period 1492–1763 in one chapter (of twenty-seven). Tory writers seek a longer-term explanation, in reference to some original "conspiracy" of Puritanism; but after invoking that Master-Explanation, they skip quickly enough to the 1760's.

2. Q. D. Leavis uses "Old News" to gloss "Molineux"; see "Hawthorne as Poet," in A. N. Kaul, *Hawthorne* (Englewood Cliffs, N.J.: Prentice-Hall, 1966), p. 38. But John P. McWilliams presses it close in to LPH; see " 'Thorough-Going Democrat' and 'Modern Tory,' " *Studies in Romanticism*, 15 (1976), esp. pp. 558–561.

3. For allegorical interpretation of LEM, see Hyatt H. Waggoner, *Hawthorne* (Cambridge: Harvard University Press, 1955), pp. 87, 101–102; and (in spite of his facts) Neal Frank Doubleday, *Hawthorne's Early Tales* (Durham, N.C.: Duke University Press, 1972), pp. 128–130. For the partial restoration of history, see Seymour Gross, "LEM as History," *JEGP*, 34 (1955), 549–554; R. H. Fossum, "Time and the Artist in LPH," *Nineteenth-Century Fiction*, 21 (1967), esp. pp. 343–345; Julian Smith, "Hawthorne's LPH," *Nineteenth-Century Fiction*, 24 (1969), esp. pp. 36–40; Sheldon W. Liebman,

"Ambiguity in LEM," *Emerson Society Quarterly,* 58 (1970), 97–101; and McWilliams, " 'Thorough-Going Democrat.' " And for some sense of Hawthorne's historical distance from his allegory, see John E. Becker, *Hawthorne's Historical Allegory* (Port Washington, N.Y.: Kennikat Press, 1971), pp. 49–60.

4. Smith, "Hawthorne's LPH," pp. 38–39.

5. Even Becker is confusing at this point: "Hawthorne's problem . . . was to build and maintain a causal nexus between Lady Eleanore's pride and the ravages of the plague" (*Historical Allegory,* p. 53). And yet it seems more accurate to say that Hawthorne had to observe and deconstruct that nexus.

6. For the economics of the eighteenth-century Jeremiad, see John E. Crowley, *This Sheba, Self* (Baltimore: Johns Hopkins University Press, 1974). For the earlier, less secular attack on "selfishness," see Sacvan Bercovitch, *Puritan Origins of the American Self* (New Haven, Conn.: Yale University Press, 1975), pp. 1–35. The classic study of the Jeremiad and its issues is, of course, Perry Miller, *The New England Mind: From Colony to Province* (Cambridge: Harvard University Press, 1953). Darrett B. Rutman has argued that the rhetoric of declension—from corporation to individuality—was there from the first; see *Winthrop's Boston* (Chapel Hill: University of North Carolina Press, 1967), esp. pp. 2–23, 135–163.

7. *Colony to Province,* p. 346. See also Robert Middlekauff, *The Mathers* (New York: Oxford, 1971), p. 357. Whether Hawthorne has seen Increase Mather's actual sermon is unclear; but evidently he had read an account of its import in Cotton Mather's *Parentator*—from which he quotes in "Dr. Bullivant." See also Cotton Mather, *The Angel of Bethesda* (Boston, 1722).

8. Epitomized here is the cardinal principle of Roy Harvey Pearce: Hawthorne derives his symbols mainly "from the facts of history itself—the factuality of American historical experience as he studied and understood it"; see "Romance and the Study of History," in *Hawthorne Centenary Essays* (Columbus: Ohio State University Press, 1964), p. 222.

9. According to Miller, "corruption itself" swiftly began to appear "not as a cause but as a visitation of wrath"; and sinfulness itself became the chief "curse upon the body politic" (*Colony to Province,* p. 28).

10. *History,* II, 174. What Hutchinson "take[s] no pleasure in relating . . . in this and the next two years" (182) is obviously a constitutional crisis of the first magnitude—involving Royal Prerogative versus Charter Privilege; and, as he makes clear, popular opinion was highly aroused by "pamphlets, courants, and other newspapers" claiming that "civil liberties were struck at" (174). The Hawthorne critic in question is Gross: "the tenure of Governor Shute [was] a period marked by severe conflict, which in 1722 reached almost rebellious proportions" ("LEM as History," p. 549). The modern historian is G. B. Warden: "After 1715 almost every problem and conflict which had complicated life in Boston in earlier years erupted violently, nearly . . . bringing Boston and the province to the edge of revolution. It is something of a miracle that a revolution did not occur in the 1720's"; see *Boston 1689–1776* (Boston: Little, Brown, 1970), pp. 80–81.

11. Warden, *Boston,* pp. 90–91.

12. In Warden's cogent analysis, "the Bostonians of the 1720's were unable or unwilling to appreciate in explicit terms just how deleterious their enforced economic dependence on England was"—stressing, instead, their own prideful lust for English imports (*Boston,* pp. 84–85).

13. The 1770's were not entirely free of the smallpox nor of inoculation controversy—as in Marblehead and Salem in 1773–74. The episode is "frenzied" enough, but the controversy is fairly local; and it distracts from (rather than typifies) the main political issues of the moment. See G. A. Billias, "Pox and Politics in Marblehead, 1773–1794," *Essex Institute Historical Collections,* 92 (1956), 43–58; and G. H. Garfield, "Salem's Great Inoculation Controversy, 1773–1774," *Essex Institute Historical Collections,* 106 (1970), 277–296.

14. The formula is that of Samuel Langdon's "Government Corrupted by Vice," a famous and widely reprinted sermon preached "before the Honorable Congress of the Colony of Massachusetts, on the 31st of May, 1775"; see Frank Moore, ed., *Preachers of the American Revolution* (New York: For Subscribers, 1860). The representative character of Langdon's rhetoric may be studied in the other sermons in this volume, and in those by J. W. Thornton, *The Pulpit of the American Revolution* (Boston: Gould and Lincoln, 1860). Miller makes important use of these sermons in "Covenant to Revival." The persuasive generality of such medical/political language in the eighteenth century in established by Caroline Robbins, *The Eighteenth-Century Commonwealth* (Cambridge: Harvard University Press, 1959); and Bernard Bailyn, *The Ideological Origins of the American Revolution* (Cambridge: Harvard University Press, 1967); and Gordon S. Wood, *The Creation of the American Republic* (Chapel Hill: University of North Carolina Press, 1969). What emerges is that the eighteenth-century "Opposition" is everywhere obsessed with the "health" of the body politic; that social disorder everywhere figured itself as infectious disease; and that the "Puritan" contribution was the sense that such political disease could be as much a "scourge" as an outbreak of the pox.

15. If much of the causality here is "magical" (see Becker, *Historical Allegory,* p. 54), and if the psychology is evidently "ritualistic" (see Peter Shaw, *American Patriots and the Rituals of Revolution* [Cambridge: Harvard University Press, 1981]), still the upshot *is* violence.

16. Hutchinson records that the May 1721 session of the General Court "resolved that considering the small pox in Boston . . . they were very desirous the court should be removed to Cambridge" (*History,* II, 189). This seems innocent enough, and yet his (early) comparison to the constitutional disorder of 1637–38 is very suggestive; for then the Court was moved to Cambridge for self-consciously political reasons. And the modern historian of Boston is more frank: "supposedly Shute"—who was then deeply embattled against the "popular" leaders of the lower house—"wanted to avoid the small pox in Boston, but he wrote a letter condemning the levelling tendencies" there. And when his letter became public, it caused "such a turn in Boston that he

wanted a riot act to prevent any uprising in the capital"; see Warden, *Boston*, p. 98. This larger climate of violence appears also in almost all accounts of the "bombing" of Cotton Mather; see O. T. Beall and R. H. Shyrock, *Cotton Mather* (Baltimore: Johns Hopkins University Press, 1954), pp. 93–122; and Daniel J. Boorstin, *The Americans: The Colonial Experience* (New York: Random House, 1954), pp. 223–227.

17. See *True Stories from History and Biography* (Columbus: Ohio State University Press, 1972), pp. 102–103.

18. Lawrence Clayton treats inoculation as the "key" to LEM, but handles this principle reductively; see "A Metaphorical Key to Hawthorne's LPH," *English Language Notes*, 9 (1971), 49–51.

19. According to Herbert's "Church Militant," "Religion" had stood in England "on tip-toe" and was "Readie to pass to the American strand." And much of Britain's "Opposition" rhetoric risked the same suggestion concerning "Virtue"; see Bailyn, *Ideological Origins*, pp. 38–85.

20. Unlike Hawthorne, New Englanders of the 1720's lacked Shelley's famous association of Hell and London; but as Warden observes, "Those few Bostonians who visited England would have agreed" on the similitude (*Boston*, p. 19). If New Englanders increasingly lamented their own luxuriating depravity, still they never admitted an equality of corruption. Wigglesworth had refused to do so in "God's Controversy with New England" (1662), which codified the Jeremiad form in America. And if Increase Mather had been willing, in the 1690's, to repeat "the Judgment of very Learned Men, that in the Glorious Times promised to the Church on Earth, New England will be hell," it was only to arouse the moral energies necessary to prevent the prospect. Just so in the 1720's and 1770's: the attack on corruption was designed to stay the tendency. It can even be called "optimistic"; see Sacvan Bercovitch, *The American Jeremiad* (Madison: University of Wisconsin Press, 1978), esp. pp. 3–30.

21. The significance of the American applause was first noticed by Gross, "LEM as History," pp. 550–551. Hawthorne elsewhere assigns various dates for the appearance of Pride-Luxury-Corruption in America: "Old News" points to the 1750's as the best image of imitative, provincial "splendor" in contrast to an earlier simplicity; *Grandfather's Chair* invokes "the example . . . set by the royal governors" in a chapter dealing with the 1730's and 1740's; *The Scarlet Letter* provides a striking imagery of an aristocratic magistracy in the first generation; and *The House of the Seven Gables* pictures a community celebrating the vicious aristocracy of the House of Pynchon. Yet LEM seems exactly right in identifying the 1720's as an early crisis of anglophilia and anglophobia; see Warden, *Boston*, pp. 80–101.

22. "Jervase" is, for Hawthorne, an ancestral name; but "Helwyse" points only to a more generalized background.

23. John Adams found Dummer's *Defence* "one of our most classical American productions," containing "the feelings, the manners, and the principles which produced the Revolution"; see *The Works of John Adams* (Boston: Little, Brown, 1850–1856), X, 343.

NOTES TO PAGES 434-439

24. Quoted from Miller, *Colony to Province,* p. 307.
25. For the subtle counterallegorical ambiguities surrounding Clarke, see Smith, "Hawthorne's LPH," pp. 39-40; and especially Liebman, "Ambiguity in LEM," pp. 99-100.
26. Of the struggles of 1720-1722, the most bitter involved the presumed right of the House to choose its own Speaker, not subject to the Governor's veto; and Hutchinson "take[s] no pleasure in relating" the dispute over the choice of John Clarke, in which the popular party strove to establish their "revolutionary" constitutional point; see *History,* II, 188. Thus Clarke is almost as potent a name for "popular liberties" as Cooke. And its "figural" significance is further enhanced by the fact that a *William* Clarke was also involved in lower-house opposition to royal prerogative—and by the fact that both these Clarkes were also physicians, as Elisha Cooke was not. Thus the medical "vehicle" of LEM demands Clarke as surely as its political tenor required the exclusion of Mather, Douglass, and Boylston. For a modern reworking of the political matter of the 1720's, see Warden, *Boston,* pp. 80-101; and for the British "background," see Jack P. Greene, "Introduction" to *Great Britain and the American Colonies* (New York: Harper and Row, 1970), esp. pp. xiii-xxxi.
27. See Warden, *Boston,* pp. 92-95; also his "Caucus and Democracy in Colonial Boston," *New England Quarterly,* 43 (1970), 19-45. And compare William Pencak, *War, Politics and Revolution in Colonial Massachusetts* (Boston: Northeastern University Press, 1981), pp. 62-76.
28. Liebman proposes that Clarke has Helwyse offer Lady Eleanore an "antidote" he (Clarke) knows is poison; see "Ambiguity in LPH," p. 100.
29. Hawthorne repeats Hutchinson's view of Shute's departure (in 1722) in his headnote to MKMM. For the charge that Clarke accidentally introduced (literal) infection into the legislative chambers, see Hutchinson, *History,* II, 204; one irony here was that the literal victim was William Hutchinson, a distant relative of the man popular ideology would ultimately "poison."
30. See "Dr. Bullivant," *Works of Nathaniel Hawthorne* (Boston: Houghton Mifflin, 1883), XII, 83.
31. Warden, *Boston,* p. 95.
32. See "Old News," in *The Snow-Image and Uncollected Tales* (Columbus: Ohio State University Press, 1974), p. 160.
33. Wallace Brown, *The Good Americans* (New York: William Morrow, 1969), p. 2.
34. See "Main Street," in *Snow-Image,* pp. 77-78.
35. At issue is less Hawthorne's theological view of pride than his literary (and political) use of allegory. Taking the allegory "straight" entitles us to a salutary moral about democracy and brotherhood; see (for example) A. N. Kaul, *The American Vision* (New Haven, Conn.: Yale University Press, 1963), pp. 170-171. But it also leaves us with a Hawthorne who rejoices in the Puritanic premise of divine punishment by magical providence. And this conclusion may come to seem as barbarous as that produced by a "pious" reading of RMB; see Frederick Crews, *Sins of the Fathers* (New York: Oxford, 1966),

pp. 90–95. The issue is partially clarified by Peter Berek's sense that Hawthorne (as contrasted with Spenser) writes an "allegory of doubt"; see *The Transformation of Allegory* (Amherst, Mass.: Amherst College Press, 1962). Even more to the point would be Edwin Honig's suggestion that a most fertile form of allegory arises when "some venerated or proverbial (old) story has become the pattern for another (the new) story"; see *Dark Conceit* (New York: Oxford, 1966), p. 12. Yet the crucial consideration here is the "deconstruction": acting as critic, Hawthorne elaborates only to undo a (political) allegory all too well made. Thus the fatal error of taking Clarke, uncritically, as "the tale's raisonneur" (Gross, "LEM as History," p. 554) or as our "allegorical guide" (Becker, *Historical Allegory*, p. 52). Clarke is so far from political disinterest as to be, in all probability, the very subject and center of the tale's problematic: it is one thing for Increase Mather, acting as spokesman for a covenanted people, and including himself in the list of sinners, to warn of approaching wrath; it is quite another for the leader of a newly self-conscious political party to threaten "woe" to royalism and aristocracy. And the difference expresses the history of American politics in the "provincial" period.

36. Hutchinson, *History*, II, 204.

37. See Miller, *Colony to Province*, p. 308.

38. The formula is that of Samuel Willard's election-day Jeremiad of 1682, but it epitomizes the covenant premise.

39. Warden, *Boston*, pp. 98–99.

40. One regrets that Peter Shaw has treated LPH so briefly: a few words on ERP in *Rituals of Revolution* (pp. 37–38), and a few on HM in "Hawthorne's Ritual Typology of the American Revolution," *Prospects*, 3 (1977), 494–495. But surely LEM is the drastic case, for which the logic of Miller must also be invoked.

41. In Becker's formula, "the Puritan notion of a providence which redresses the balance of wrongs on earth was a primitive belief, without the excuse of primitive times" (*Historical Allegory*, p. 54).

42. In Miller's famous formulation, the Puritans were trapped in their own covenantal version of the "Protestant Ethic": to do "right" was to prosper in the worldly calling, but this seemed always to produce the "wrong" of a costly mantle of pride; see *Colony to Province*, pp. 40–52. The first result was moral confusion, but the last might well be political hysteria.

43. At one level, as Miller has argued, the logic of the covenant precluded both perfect success and utter failure: the one ended History, the other American Election. Nevertheless, as Bercovitch has shown, every Jeremiad does hold out the perfect hope. And indeed there had been notable successes: Increase Mather's *Brief History of the Wars with the Indians* could trace the end of "King Philip" to the remarkable repentance ritual of 9 May 1676; and Cotton's *Magnalia* is full of stunning success stories. Here and elsewhere "it is said" that ritual repentance and relief from the scourges of reality are the vital principles of history.

44. For a bibliography of the "war of words" over inoculation—in which (oddly,

to our sense) the laity seem more radically Puritan than the ministers—see John Duffy, *Epidemics in Colonial America* (Baton Rouge: Louisiana State University Press, 1953), pp. 252–254.

45. Quoted from *A Letter from One in the Country,* in Miller, *Colony to Province,* p. 364.

46. For the overstatement, see *Colony to Province,* p. 363; the balance is redressed by "Covenant to Revival."

47. Some "biographical" distinction may be useful at this point. On the one hand, Hawthorne was scarcely a "party man" in the Jacksonian sense. But neither, obviously, did he subscribe to the "primitive" Puritan myth of a "whole people" united under a "Christian magistrate"; see T. H. Breen, *The Character of the Good Ruler* (New Haven, Conn.: Yale University Press, 1970). Nor did he quite share the eighteenth-century prejudice against all political parties as "factional"; see Richard Hofstadter, *The Idea of a Party System* (Berkeley: University of California Press, 1969), esp. pp. 1–39. Accepting the inevitability of political-interest combinations, he warns everywhere of groups which mystify a single standard of purity or patriotism.

48. See Pencak, *War, Politics, and Revolution,* pp. 9–59; Robbins, *Commonwealthmen,* pp. 378–386; and Bailyn, *Ideological Origins,* pp. 94–143.

10. THE DEATH OF THE PAST

1. See Julian Smith, "Hawthorne's LPH," *Nineteenth-Century Fiction,* 24 (1969), 40–44.

2. In the psychoanalytic terms of Kenneth Dauber, the "bad mother" is deposed, the "good mother" remains; see *Rediscovering Hawthorne* (Princeton, N.J.: Princeton University Press, 1977), p. 78.

3. For Miller's version of this distinction, see "From the Covenant to the Revival," in *Nature's Nation* (Cambridge: Harvard University Press, 1967), pp. 91–92; and cf. Gordon S. Wood, "Rhetoric and Reality in the American Revolution," *William and Mary Quarterly,* series 3, 23 (1966), 3–32.

4. The phrase is from Archibald MacLeish's poem "American Letter." For Hawthorne as balancer of cultural accounts, see Q. D. Leavis, "Hawthorne as Poet," in A. N. Kaul, ed., *Hawthorne* (Englewood Cliffs, N.J.: Prentice-Hall, 1966), pp. 25–63. For a version of Cooper in similar terms, see A. N. Kaul, *The American Vision* (New Haven, Conn.: Yale University Press, 1963), pp. 84–138.

5. The portraits of the Old Tory offered in "Old News" and *Grandfather's Chair* are tinged with sentiment, but their presentation is ultimately less dismissive than that of the narrator here. In "Old News" the purpose is less to arouse sympathy for "the Americans who clung to the losing side" than to stress the credibility of their claim: "The state of the country . . . was of dismal augury for the tendency of democratic rule"; see *The Snow-Image and Uncollected Works* (Columbus: Ohio State University Press, 1974), p. 159. And similarly, the sketch of Peter Oliver's "Farewell" in *Grandfather's Chair*

contains no hint that "deep love and fierce resentment" disqualify him as an historical observer; see *True Stories from History and Biography* (Columbus: Ohio State University Press, 1974), pp. 195–196. For a brief account of the "disqualification" of the Tory historians, see Douglas Adair and John Schutz, "Introduction" to *Peter Oliver's Origin and Progress of the American Revolution* (Stanford, Calif.: Stanford University Press, 1961), pp. vii–xxi.

6. Seymour Gross first called attention to the problem of publishing LPH in the *Democratic Review;* see "LEM as History," *JEGP,* 54 (1955), 550. The point is further stressed by Neal Frank Doubleday and John P. McWilliams: see *Hawthorne's Early Tales* (Durham, N.C.: Duke University Press, 1972), pp. 132–133; and " 'Thorough-Going Democrat' and 'Modern Tory,' " *Studies in Romanticism,* 15 (1976), 561.

7. O'Sullivan's "Introduction" to vol. 1, no. 1 of the *United States Magazine and Democratic Review* (October 1837) is partly a plea for a national literature, but much of it also reads like a ground-plan for Bancroft: "All history has to be rewritten; political science and the whole scope of moral truth have to be considered in the light of the democratic principle" (p. 14).

8. Cf. Michael Davitt Bell, *Hawthorne and the Historical Romance of New England* (Princeton, N.J.: Princeton University Press, 1971), pp. 34–35, 41, 49–50.

9. Prior to HM, Hawthorne's contribution to the *Democratic Review* included only "Footprints on the Sea-Shore" and "Snow-Flakes," both for February 1838 and both apolitical. Yet by the time the final arguments were made to Bancroft (late in 1838), Hawthorne could be represented as a worthy exponent of the "national" literature and also as the author of the sketch of the democrat Jonathan Cilley, in the *Democratic Review* for September 1838. Thus by the publication of OED (January 1839) Hawthorne was in the thick of Massachusetts politics.

10. McWilliams forgives the publication strategy of LPH because he feels Hawthorne has in fact "justified" the rebellion; see "Thorough-Going Democrat," pp. 560–561. On the other hand, James R. Mellow has recently stressed the "talent for rationalization" Hawthorne developed in regard to his curious political career; see *Nathaniel Hawthorne in His Times* (Boston: Houghton Mifflin, 1980), esp. pp. 255–257. My own sense is that Hawthorne is testing the limits of his own subversive power.

11. *Twice-told Tales* was published 8 March 1837. By March 26 Bridge informed Hawthorne that he had sent a copy to Cilley, whose assistance (in Washington) "would be needed." Bridge's next letter (April 7) informs Hawthorne of a note sent to Bancroft the previous day. O'Sullivan's letter of invitation is dated (at Washington) April 19. See Julian Hawthorne, *Hawthorne and His Wife* (Boston: Houghton Mifflin, 1884), I, 152, 156, 159.

12. Robert Cantwell finds it "extraordinary" that Elizabeth Peabody delivered the O'Sullivan letter, as the two seemed not yet acquainted; see *Nathaniel Hawthorne: The American Years* (New York: Holt, Rinehart and Winston, 1948), p. 232. But this seems a false problem: Elizabeth Peabody knows Bancroft—well enough to sponsor Hawthorne to him on her own; and Ban-

croft knows O'Sullivan—well enough to contribute to the early issues of his magazine. Thus the probable sequence: Elizabeth Peabody contacted Bancroft; Bancroft wrote to O'Sullivan (as well as to other, less literary persons in Washington), mentioning Elizabeth's sponsorship; O'Sullivan contacted Hawthorne by way of Elizabeth. The hypothesis is further supported by the fact that "Hawthorne never answered O'Sullivan's letter" (Cantwell, *Hawthorne*, p. 232); by the end of April he evidently knew the real chain of events. Nor is the Bancroft-O'Sullivan link surprising; for though the *Democratic Review* had its own financial integrity, Bancroft owned its ideology.

13. For the element of overbelief in Hawthorne's politics, see "The Hall of Fantasy," where democracy is set down as one form of Faith in the Ideal; see *Mosses from an Old Manse* (Columbus: Ohio State University Press, 1974), p. 179. For the Christian bases of Hawthorne's democratic values, see Hyatt H. Waggoner, *Hawthorne* (Cambridge: Harvard University Press, 1955), pp. 15-16; and cf. Gabriel Vahanian's Hawthornesque argument that since all of us are so bad, none has the right to "pull spiritual rank"; *Wait Without Idols* (New York: George Braziller, 1964), pp. 49-71.

14. Here is how the political sub-plot might look: GC (*New England Magazine*, January 1835) is indeed a reaction to Bancroft's first volume (1834), an ironic response turning on the ambiguities of "vindication." This tale leads off the 1837 *Twice-told Tales* (almost titled "The Gray Champion and Other Tales"); and it, at least, was seen and misread by both Bancroft and O'Sullivan, as both prospered Hawthorne's career. Yet as GC is early, it is also relatively innocent; it invites misreading, but not by specific (political) persons. The same cannot be said with certainty of ERC (*Token*, 1838). This cunning little sketch may have been written *after* political negotiations were under way, as further proof of ideological "loyalty," yet specifically designed to deceive the ideologues. Finally, of course, the LPH themselves are written and published even as Hawthorne's friends sponsor his name in the highest Democratic circles, not noted for historical irony.

15. Prescott is quoted from R. B. Nye's "Introduction" to an abridged version of Bancroft's *History of the United States* (Chicago: University of Chicago Press, 1966), p. x. See also Nye's "The Historian and the Politicians," in *George Bancroft* (New York: Knopf, 1945), pp. 85-136.

16. For the "critical" responsibility of the historian, see J. H. Plumb, *The Death of the Past* (Boston: Houghton Mifflin, 1971), pp. 19-101.

17. For Randolph's role in establishing effective trade regulation in New England, see Thomas Hutchinson, *History of the Colony and Province of Massachusetts Bay* (Cambridge: Harvard University Press, 1936), I, 278-320; and cf. Michael G. Hall, *Edward Randolph and the American Colonies* (New York: W. W. Norton, 1960), pp. 21-153. On the explicit function of the royal governors, see L. W. Labaree, *Royal Government in America* (New Haven, Conn.: Yale University Press, 1930); and Jack P. Greene, *The Quest for Power* (Chapel Hill: University of North Carolina Press, 1963). And for a detailed account of the customs service, see Thomas C. Barrow, *Trade and Empire* (Cambridge: Harvard University Press, 1967), esp. pp. 39-83.

18. By 1835 Bancroft's first volume—inscribed with the motto "Westward the star of empire takes its way," and informed with the thesis of a "steady march from tyranny to liberty"—had already "found its way into nearly a third of the homes of New England"; and Bancroft's name "was well on the way to becoming a household word"; see Nye, *Bancroft*, p. 102. The second volume (covering the years 1660–1668) was published in 1837, was equally clear about where American history was going, and was equally popular.

19. Bancroft was Hawthorne's literal "host" at various times during 1838—while political negotiations were proceeding and the "Legends" were appearing. Thus there is probably some private referent of the otherwise gratuitous "orality" (see Dauber, *Rediscovering Hawthorne*, pp. 75–77) of the oyster supper which precedes LEM.

20. Presumably Hawthorne's own sense of "wrath and tribulation" came from Hutchinson's third volume, first published in 1828. Though Hutchinson takes the story only as far as June 1774 (the date of his departure), he makes much of the sufferings of his own family, the Olivers, and other faithful Loyalists; see *History*, III, 85–92. Also available to Hawthorne were the Tory histories of Boucher, Chalmers, and Galloway.

21. Into Esther Dudley Hawthorne has compressed a number of "typical" Tory attitudes. With Peter Oliver she believes that "the God of Heaven hath repeatedly checked rebellion"; see Adair and Schutz, ed., *Origin and Progress*, p. 168. But she also embodies the initial Tory trust in British military might; see Wallace Brown, *The Good Americans* (New York: William Morrow, 1969), p. 58. More particularly, Esther Dudley evokes those rather famous "female Loyalists who were not claimants or even exiles," those quintessential Tories, Catherine and Mary Byles. Of those two descendants of Cottons and Mathers, Wallace Brown offers the following portrait: "Among their souvenirs and royal portraits, the sisters, sipping 'loyal tea,' relived the festivities of the Boston siege when Earl Pearcy and Lord Howe visited them . . . (Catherine even wrote to George IV on his accession, assuring him of her loyalty.)" See *The King's Friends* (Providence: Brown University Press, 1965), pp. 41–42.

22. In "A Book of Autographs" Hawthorne would treat Hancock not as the "actual man" characterized by one of his associates as "without a head or heart," but simply as a "majestic figure, useful and necessary in its own way"; see *Snow-Image*, p. 367. T. F. Walsh detects the "satire," but neglects to mention that it is the ideology of the *Democratic Review* which is satirized; see "Hawthorne's Satire in OED," *Emerson Society Quarterly*, 22 (1961), 31–33.

23. Like Walsh, Julian Smith also makes a bit too much of the narrator's sympathy; see "Hawthorne's LPH," p. 42.

24. For the view which makes the problems inherent in an art loyal to history the self-reflexive *subject* of LPH, see Evan Carton, "Hawthorne and the Province of Romance," *ELH*, 47 (1980), 331–354; and cf. Kenneth Dauber, *Rediscovering Hawthorne* (Princeton, N.J.: Princeton University Press, 1977), pp. 65–81.

25. Clearer than almost anything else about "the New England Mind" is that its constant revisionism is never recognized as such: later "vindications" permit a clearer distinction between the "transient" and the "permanent" in their destiny, as "typology" turns inevitably into "natural supernaturalism"; but the mind is never changed. Besides Miller's various analyses ("Errand into the Wilderness," *Colony to Province,* and "Covenant to Revival"), see Carl Bridenbaugh, *Mitre and Sceptre* (New York: Oxford, 1962), pp. 171–340; Wesley Frank Craven, *The Legend of the Founding Fathers* (rpt. Ithaca, N.Y.: Cornell University Press, 1965), pp. 1–101; and A. W. Plumstead, *The Wall and the Garden* (Minneapolis: University of Minnesota Press, 1968), pp. 3–38.

26. The ultimate defect of Bancroft's *History* is not that it presents "an *ex parte* case for the American cause, a patriotic celebration of the Revolution as a milestone of human progress"; see Jack P. Greene, *The Ambiguity of the American Revolution* (New York: Harper and Row, 1968), pp. 48–49. Neither is it quite that "his deep faith in Jacksonian democracy encouraged him to see liberty and equality everywhere in the American past, including places and times where it did not exist"; see Nye, ed., *History,* p. xxiv. The problem, much more simply, is that the observer who knows where History is going will be interested less in the past *as past* than in its shadowy prefigurations of the more perfect future; he will be dead to the ironies of history in which good does *not* come out of evil; and he may become totally incapable of "re-enacting" (in R. G. Collingwood's famous phrase) the moments of the past which do *not* prefigure the preferred future. That is to say, "typology" may not be the only "meta-history," but it is certainly the most disabling one we know.

27. Consider the probable intent of *Grandfather's Chair:* to inculcate a positive appreciation of democratic values without erecting the "Americanism" of the 1830's and 1840's into an exhaustive standard of value.

28. Never utterly skeptical, Hawthorne never abandons his premise of "moral history": his imaginative recreations ultimately serve the notion that "history is 'for' human self-knowledge"; see R. G. Collingwood, *The Idea of History* (rpt. New York: Oxford, 1956), p. 10. Yet OED also suggests that "mere antiquarianism" may be more valuable than a "history" unconsciously overcommitted to some specific entelechy.

29. In the terms set up by HM, there are Dudleys on "both sides": Thomas Dudley (first chosen governor in 1634) appears with Endicott, Winthrop, and others in a line Colonel Joliffe refers to as "rulers of the original Democracy"; his descendant Joseph Dudley (appointed in 1702 under the Royal Charter of 1691) was a notorious Anglophile, appearing in the group labeled "miserable men."

30. For a sample of the widespread twentieth-century argument about democracy versus deference, see Michael Kammen, ed., *Politics and Society in Colonial America* (New York: Holt, Rinehart and Winston, 1967); and George A. Billias, ed., *The American Revolution: How Revolutionary Was It?* (New York: Holt, Rinehart and Winston, 1965).

31. Disputed here is the reductive claim that Loyalists were so for financial or so-

cial advantage; for their "welter of conflicting motives," see Brown, *Good Americans*, pp. 44–81.

32. As little given to mysticism as any historian one can name, Thomas Hutchinson's concern for "legitimacy" has nevertheless an almost religious character—suggesting that "the past" can inspire as holy a devotion as "the future."

33. Fossum invokes "the organic nature of both time and humanity" ("Time and the Artist," p. 346), but seems hesitant to embody that belief in Esther herself.

34. Without questioning the relevance of Bancroft's Enlightenment and Romantic precursors (see Nye, *Bancroft*, pp. 95–97), one should remember that he also belongs to a tradition of Holy Historians that stretches back to Eusebius, whom William Bradford preferred to Augustine. Along with his American contemporaries and Puritan predecessors, who also had to explain the triumph of Anglo-Saxon Puritanism in America, he is also always on the verge of discovering the unique conclusion of Special Providence: so far, so God.

35. No reader of Hutchinson's *History* can miss the importance he attaches to English (*specie*) currency throughout the entire colonial period: a hard-headed hard-money man, he makes coinage a virtual symbol of legitimacy. Nor did the problem cease with the Revolution: after a brief period in which "Continental currency held its value . . . without any security," it swiftly suffered a disastrous collapse; see E. James Ferguson, *The Power of the Purse* (Chapel Hill: University of North Carolina Press, 1961), pp. 18–19. For Hawthorne's contemporaries, the expression "not worth a Continental" was not yet a dead metaphor; and the principal irony here is that, behind the Patriot's vaunted trust in God, the revolution against King George only increased the already pre-eminent value of coins stamped with his image.

36. As Hawthorne plays with money as a metaphor for trust, he may well be recalling the view expressed in David Ramsay's *History of the American Revolution:* the *temporary* stability of colonial currency "was in some degree owing to a previous confidence, which had been begotten by honesty and fidelity, in discharging the engagements of government"; quoted from Ferguson, *Power of the Purse*, pp. 18–19. As Ferguson goes on to point out, "the Revolution destroyed that confidence."

37. See *Grandfather's Chair*, in *True Stories*, p. 174. Though Hawthorne later records that Hancock was "the first [governor] whom the people had elected, since the days of old Simon Bradstreet" (p. 201), he spends a whole paragraph here on Hancock's regal appearance and manner.

38. William H. Nelson records the skeptical view of one John Ross: "Let who would be king, he well knew that he should be a subject"; see *The American Tory* (rpt. Boston: Beacon Press, 1964), pp. 91–92.

39. Here Julian Smith joins hands with Frederick Crews: one more pseudo-revolution or "inessential reversal"; see "Hawthorne's LPH," p. 43; and cf. *Sins of the Fathers* (New York: Oxford, 1966), pp. 38–43. Yet the ease of an Oedipal generalization should not obscure the tough political point: virtually alone among his contemporaries, Hawthorne was willing to consider the Rev-

olution as in part a struggle between two opposing power elites within the colonies. On this issue, see Jack P. Greene, *The Reinterpretation of the American Revolution* (New York: Harper and Row, 1968), pp. 19–31.

40. Behind this scene in OED lies Hutchinson's studied account of his own surrender of the keys of Castle William, conveying at a stroke his scrupulous concern for the constitutionally legitimate transfer of power: "he [that is, Hutchinson himself] went to the castle, and, calling for the keys, in the presence of the commissioners of the customs and many other persons, he delivered them to lieutenant-colonel Dalrymple, and, by virtue of the authority he derived from his commission to govern the province according to the royal charter, committed to him the custody of the Fort. The formality of delivering the keys had been the usual way of signifying the change of command" (*History*, III, 222).

41. Perhaps Hawthorne could indeed distinguish between O'Sullivan and Bancroft. Though he came to like the one and scorn the other (as a sort of "blatant beast"), he may well have recognized that Bancroft, the historian, could look back long enough to discover a type.

42. As Walsh has suggested, the concluding moment of OED is significantly glossed in "Earth's Holocaust": Hancock's "onward" turns into the "onward" with which a whole generation casts into an apocalyptic fire all the accumulations of the past; see "Hawthorne's Satire," p. 33.

43. See "Old News," in *Snow-Image*, p. 153. McWilliams argues for full authorial sympathy in "The Old Tory" section of "Old News," but in my view he underestimates Hawthorne's ironic distance from the "thorough-going democrat" who narrates the "Legends"; see "Thorough-Going Democrat," pp. 558–561.

44. For Hawthorne's "organic" sense of history, see Harry B. Henderson, "Hawthorne: The Limits of the Holist Imagination," *Versions of the Past* (New York: Oxford, 1974), pp. 91–126.

45. For the context of the Burke quotations, see the T. H. D. Mahoney edition of *Reflections on the Revolution in France* (Indianapolis: Bobbs Merrill, 1965), pp. 35, 108, 110. Hawthorne is known to have borrowed vol. I of an 1806 edition of Burke; see Marion L. Kesselring, *Hawthorne's Reading* (New York: New York Public Library, 1949), p. 45. That volume does not contain the *Reflections*, but it would be astonishing if, by 1838, Hawthorne had not read them somewhere.

46. For Lewis' formula, see *The American Adam* (Chicago: University of Chicago Press, 1953), p. 123. For Taylor's dictum, see *A Historian's Creed* (Cambridge: Harvard University Press, 1939), p. 31.

47. See *The Ancestral Footstep*, in *The American Claimant Manuscripts* (Columbus: Ohio State University Press, 1977), p. 38; and "The Old Manse," in *Mosses*. p. 26.

48. See Nelson, *American Tory*, p. 187.

49. Ibid., p. 188.

50. Bancroft was *like* the Tory historians in that he too "traced the origins of the Revolution to the very beginning of the colonies and to the irrepressible de-

sire for freedom"; see Greene, *Ambiguity*, p. 5. For Bancroft and Chalmers, see Nye, *Bancroft*, p. 94.

51. The political upshot of Hawthorne's own "unshakable" belief in Providence is the very opposite of latter-day Puritan ("post-millennialist") confidence in the efficiency of revolutionary effort. Not only are History's ultimate purposes inscrutable, but human efforts to aid them produce (at best) "incidental" advantages. According to the reactionary hyperbole of *The House of the Seven Gables*, Holgrave's great error lay in assuming "that it mattered anything to the great end in view whether he himself should contend for it or against it." And "The Old Manse" proposes, if only under erasure, that the one effective cure for a world "preternaturally wide-wake" to the prospect of apocalyptic change is "sleep."

52. The witchcraft-rebellion-frenzy connection could have come to Hawthorne through Daniel Leonard's *Massachusettensis;* see Nelson, *American Tory,* pp. 69–70. Oliver's more outrageous suggestions appear not only in his (then unpublished) *Origin and Progress* but also in the Boston *Weekly News-Letter* (11 January 1776), which I presume Hawthorne had read.

53. "The Contagion of Liberty" is the allusive title of the last chapter of Bailyn's *Ideological Origins.* The O'Sullivan quotation is from his editorial introduction to the *Democratic Review,* I (January 1838), 8–9.

54. Nelson, *American Tory,* p. 190.

55. Like Plumb, Hawthorne *begins* with history as criticism but does not end there. The worst state of all, apparently, is the one in which deconstructive criticism succeeds so well that historians flourish while everyone else loses "the sense of the past" altogether; see *Death of the Past,* pp. 102–108.

56. The Emerson judgments occur, respectively, in "The Young American" and "The Conservative."

57. See "Chiefly About War Matters," in *The Works of Nathaniel Hawthorne,* XII, 317.

PROBLEMATIC CONCLUSIONS

1. What I am resisting, most specifically, is the temptation to speculate about Hawthorne's "Theory of History." Doubtless he implies one. And, as Michael Bell has observed, his later works tend more and more to *express* one; see *Hawthorne and the Historical Romance of New England* (Princeton, N.J.: Princeton University Press, 1971), pp. 193–242. But, just as obviously, a full-scale investigation of this meta-subject lies well beyond the limits of the present, empirical study; moreover, I would argue, it would misrepresent the nature of Hawthorne's best "historicist" insights. For more or less apt speculations on the (bracketed) philosophical subject, see Gretchen Graf Jordan, "Hawthorne's 'Bell': Historical Evolution Through Symbol," *Nineteenth-Century Fiction,* 19 (1964), 123–140; Johannes Kjørven, "Hawthorne, and the Significance of History," in S. Skard and H. H. Wasser, ed., *Americana Norvegica* (Philadelphia: University of Pennsylvania Press, 1966), I,

110–160; Leo B. Levy, " 'Time's Portraiture': Hawthorne's Theory of History," *Nathaniel Hawthorne Journal*, 1 (1971), 192–200; Robert H. Fossum, *Hawthorne's Inviolable Circle: The Problem of Time* (Deland, Fla.: Everett/Edwards, 1972); Harry B. Henderson, *Versions of the Past* (New York: Oxford, 1974), pp. 91–126; and Paula K. White, "Puritan Theories of History in Hawthorne's Fiction," *Canadian Review of American Studies*, 9 (1978), 135–153.

2. Aside from the essays of Q. D. Leavis and Roy Harvey Pearce (cited ad hoc throughout this study), the best definition of Hawthorne's anti-idealist loyalty to real time is R. W. B. Lewis, *The American Adam* (Chicago: University of Chicago Press, 1955), pp. 110–126.

3. The best definition of the non-ideological character of Hawthorne's procedures as an historian remains Pearce's "Romance and the Study of History," in Roy Harvey Pearce, ed., *Hawthorne Centenary Essays* (Columbus: Ohio State University, 1964), pp. 221–244.

4. The editors of the "Ohio State" Hawthorne have reprinted sixty-seven tales and sketches published by Hawthorne between 1830 and 1840; for their chronological listing, see *The Snow-Image and Uncollected Tales* (Columbus: Ohio State University Press, 1974), pp. 484–487. Considering that the "break" in Hawthorne's "career" is marked by his employment in the Boston Custom House 1839–40), his residence at Brook Farm (1841), and his proximate plans for marriage (Winter/Spring, 1842); judging that "The Old Manse Period" begins, thematically, with "A Virtuoso's Collection" (May 1842); and including nine sketches excluded (so far) from the Ohio State Edition, but rejecting "The Haunted Quack" and "A Visit to the Clerk of the Weather," I count seventy-four published tales and sketches conceived (and largely written) in Hawthorne's "first period." Neal Frank Doubleday's study of this "clearly defined" period offers, as epitome, a source-oriented but essentially formalist analysis of twenty-three tales; see *Hawthorne's Early Tales* (Durham, N.C.: Duke University Press, 1974). A more inclusive and empirical (but less detailed) account has divided this period in two: see Nina Baym, *The Shape of Hawthorne's Career* (Ithaca, N.Y.: Cornell University Press, 1975), pp. 15–83.

5. "The Canterbury Pilgrims" (CP) first appeared in *The Token* for 1833, "The Shaker Bridal" (SB) in *The Token* for 1837; yet they may both have been written at the same time, shortly after Hawthorne's 1831 visit to a Shaker community. CP—which reminds readers of both "The May-Pole" and "The Great Carbuncle"—may well have been intended for "The Story Teller"; if so, it would have helped define a clear "marriage group" in that complex "pilgrimage" project. The deprivations of Martha Pierson are plainly supposed to recall those of Dorothy Pearson in "The Gentle Boy"; and the fanatical Old Quaker of GB reappears as the altogether childless Adam Colburn of SB. For a fairly recent summary of the available criticism, see L. B. V. Newman, *A Reader's Guide to the Short Stories of Nathaniel Hawthorne* (Boston: G. K. Hall, 1979), pp. 39–44, 287–289.

6. "The Ambitious Guest" (AG) first appeared in the *New England Magazine*

for June 1835; "The Great Carbuncle" (GCb—*Token,* 1837. Both were clearly intended for "The Story Teller"; see my own analysis in this discussion.

7. "The Duston Family" (DF), which Hawthorne wrote for the March 1836 issue of the *American Magazine of Useful and Entertaining Knowledge,* has its clear source in Mather's *Magnalia;* see B. Bernard Cohen, "The Composition of Hawthorne's DF," *New England Quarterly,* 21 (1948), 236-242; and Robert D. Arner, "The Story of Hannah Duston," *American Transcendental Quarterly,* 18 (1973), 19-23. As with Mather's "Life of Phips," Hawthorne's attitude is clearly ironic and revisionist. "A Bell's Biography" (BB), which first appeared in the *Knickerbocker Magazine* for March 1837, will shed light on Hawthorne's sense of New England's entire "provincial" phase and has been made the center of a study of his historical attitude in general; see Jordan, "Hawthorne's Bell." And "The Prophetic Pictures" (PP— *Token,* 1837), with its source in William Dunlap's *History of the Rise and Progress of the Arts of Design in the United States,* may yet tell us more about the status of art in the American provinces than in the haunted mind of Hawthorne; for a summary of available criticism, see Newman, *Reader's Guide,* pp. 243-247.

8. The discovery of sources for "The Wedding Knell" (WK—*Token,* 1836) in both Cotton Mather and Jeremy Taylor makes one suspect that more than a perfect gothic miniature may have been intended, especially as the tale may have been part of the "marriage-group" in "The Story Teller"; see John J. Homan, "Hawthorne's WK and Cotton Mather," *Emerson Society Quarterly,* 43 (1966), 66-67; and Frederick Asals, "Jeremy Taylor and Hawthorne's Early Tales," *American Transcendental Quarterly,* 14 (1972), 15-23. "Peter Goldthwaite's Treasure" (PGT—*Token,* 1838) naturally associates itself with *The House of the Seven Gables* which, in spite of its flagrantly gothic elements, remains one of Hawthorne's most relentlessly historical fictions; and, though we are not to suppose *roman à clef* in either case, Goldthwaite is, like Pyncheon, an aboriginal New England name. For the current state of criticism of PGT, see Newman, *Reader's Guide,* pp. 247-249. Even "John Inglefield's Thanksgiving" (JIT—*Democratic Review,* March 1840) might profit from some sort of redemptive source study; this would involve (at very least) "the many sermons and religious tracts that Hawthorne read between 1825 and 1839" (Newman, *Reader's Guide,* p. 170).

9. Though Doubleday argues for the inclusion of "Drowne's Wooden Image" in Hawthorne's "first period," his treatment of "Wakefield," "Fancy's Show Box," and "Dr. Heidegger's Experiment" makes it clear that his own interest is in Hawthorne's literary devices rather than in his historical vision.

10. The durability of the biographical "myth" of the "two Hawthornes" suggests some real basis in the raw evidence; see, for a most recent example, James R. Mellow, *Nathaniel Hawthorne in His Times* (Boston: Houghton Mifflin, 1980), pp. 48-59.

11. Mellow's analysis of the "solitary" Hawthorne slides with perfect ease from "The Haunted Mind" to "Young Goodman Brown"; see *Hawthorne,* pp. 57-60. Nina Baym shows no special discomfort in associating Hooper with

Swan, Etherege, and Fane; see *Shape*, p. 55. And Rita K. Gollin clearly offers "The Haunted Mind" as a sort of epitome of the Hawthorne tale "as dream"; see *Hawthorne and the Truth of Dreams* (Baton Rouge: University of Louisiana Press, 1979), esp. pp. 98-101.

12. The present chapter alludes, in its title, to Roy Harvey Pearce, "Robin Molineux on the Analyst's Couch," *Criticism*, 1 (1959), 83-90.

13. Surely it is no accident that Hawthorne has given us, as Gretchen Graf Jordan has well observed, "at least one tale" for each of the "generations" which preceded his own; see "Hawthorne's 'Bell,' " p. 124.

14. "The Haunted Mind" (HM) first appeared in *The Token* for 1835; for the text cited here, see *Twice-told Tales* (Columbus: Ohio State University Press, 1975), pp. 304-309. For "hypnagogic" (Jungean) analysis, see Barton Levi St. Armand, "Hawthorne's HM: A Subterranean Drama of the Self," *Criticism*, 13 (1971), 1-25.

15. Critics rarely fail to associate HM with "Fancy's Show Box" (FSB—*Token*, 1837). For the figure of Jeremy Taylor in that moralistic sketch, see Neal F. Doubleday "The Theme of Hawthorne's FSB," *American Literature*, 10 (1938), 341-343. Also relevant, I should imagine, is John Cotton's "esthetic" observation that a person sins "when he imagineth, deviseth, plotteth sin, as a Poet his Fictions"; see Norman Grabo, "John Cotton's Aesthetic," *Early American Literature*, 3 (1968), 8.

16. Mellow and Gollin (see note 11) are far from eccentric in treating HM as paradigm. Hyatt Waggoner proposes that it "forecasts most of what is best in the later works"; see *Hawthorne* (Cambridge: Harvard University Press, 1963), pp. 8-11. And Terrence Martin suggests that it "epitomizes essential features of Hawthorne's fiction"; see *Hawthorne* (New York: Twayne Publishers, 1965), pp. 45-47. Recent analysts follow the same line, fully confident that their analyses will be normative: see Norman H. Hostetler, "Imagination and Point of View in HM," *American Transcendental Quarterly*, 39 (1978), 263-267; and John E. Holsberry, "Hawthorne's HM, the Psychology of Dreams, Coleridge, and Keats," *Texas Studies in Literature and Language*, 21 (1979), 307-331.

17. Hawthorne's reliance (here and elsewhere) on his college training in the "associationism" of Locke and his Scottish ("common-sense") redactors was first established by Terrence Martin, *The Instructed Vision* (Bloomington: University of Indiana Press, 1961), esp, pp. 145-148; and it is fully presupposed by Gollin (note 11) and by Holsberry.

18. See *Hawthorne* (1965), pp. 34-38. Elsewhere Waggoner has made "Night Sketches" into a metaphor for Hawthorne's entire (not-quite-Melvillean) vision of "blackness"; see "Art and Belief," in Pearce, ed., *Centenary Essays*, pp. 179-187.

19. All quotations from "Night Sketches" (NS) are taken from *Twice-told Tales*. The sketch first appeared in *The Token* for 1838.

20. For Hawthorne's familiarity with and repeated "borrowings" from Charles Lamb, see Russell Noyes, "Hawthorne's Debt to Charles Lamb," *Charles Lamb Bulletin*, n.s., no. 4 (1973), 69-77. Taken together, Hawthorne's HM

and NS might be thought to provide an ironic gloss on Elia's suggestion—in "Witches, and Other Night Fears"—that "the degree of the soul's creativeness in sleep might furnish no whimsical criterion of poetical faculty in the same soul waking."

21. For the text of "Wakefield" (W)—first published in the *New England Magazine* for May 1835—see *Twice-told Tales*, pp. 130–140. For the tortured critical history of this brief tale (or is it a "sketch"?), which contains "the most quoted statement by Hawthorne on . . . the horror of isolating oneself from humanity," see Newman, *Reader's Guide*, pp. 311–317.

22. Austin Warren early noticed that Hawthorne's clearest "source"—Dr. William King's *Ancedotes of His Own Times* (1818)—itself contained the odd idea of motiveless non-malignity: after his return home, King's acquaintance "never would confess, even to his most intimate friends, what was the real cause of such singular conduct; apparently there was none"; see *Nathaniel Hawthorne* (New York: American Book Co., 1934), pp. 364–365. The connection of Wakefield with Rip Van Winkle has been widely noticed, and surely the Irvinesque word "whim-wham" points us in this direction. The link, in the other direction, to Melville's Bartleby would be the idea of "motivelessness," even as demolished by Jonathan Edwards: evidently nothing does follow from nothing.

23. See "The Christmas Banquet," in *Mosses from an Old Manse* (Columbus: Ohio State University Press, 1974), p. 305.

24. For "existentialist" readings, see Andrew Schiller, "The Moment and the Endless Voyage," *Diameter*, 1 (1951), 7–12; Robert E. Morsberger, "Wakefield in the Twilight Zone," *American Transcendentalist Quarterly*, 14 (1972), 6–8; and (most pretentiously) Jorge Luis Borges, "Nathaniel Hawthorne," in *Other Inquisitions*, R. L. C. Simms, trans. (Austin: University of Texas Press, 1964), pp. 47–65. For the more social emphasis, see John Gatta, " 'Busy and Selfish London': The Urban Figure in Hawthorne's W," *ESQ*, 23 (1977), 164–172.

25. Gatta has proposed the relevance of "one William Wake, whose attempt to live apart from his wife . . . brought him before the Salem Quarterly Court in 1651" ("Urban Figure," p. 170). More likely, I suppose, is the figure of Gilbert Wakefield, whose *Enquiry into the Expediency and Propriety of Public Worship* (London, 1792) essayed to "prove *public worship* to be unauthorized by Christianity" (p. 25). In King's original anecdote, the principal attends church every Sunday for the last seven years of his whim-wham, sitting where he can see his wife but not be seen (cf. Warren, *Hawthorne*, pp. 364–365). In Hawthorne's version it is never clear that the separated Wakefield ever gets into church at all.

26. Doubleday has warned against the tendency to treat "The Devil in Manuscript"—and the gerry-rigged text of "Fragments of the Journal of a Solitary Man"—as troubled self-revelation rather than as strategic point-of-view narrative (*Early Tales*, p. 11). And at least one of the new biographies take his warning to heart: the outlook of Oberon "is exaggerated so farcically in the early episodes and so whimsically throughout that he cannot be taken as a

spokesman for the author"; see Arlin Turner, *Nathaniel Hawthorne* (New York: Oxford, 1980), p. 75. Yet James R. Mellow continues to read "The Devil" in the old way and proceeds to elevate "Monsieur du Miroir" to the status of a major autobiographical metaphor; see *His Times*, pp. 44-46, 95-97.

27. For the text of "The Devil in Manuscript" (DM)—first published in the *New England Magazine* for November 1835—see *Snow-Image*, pp. 170-178. For the evidence concerning Hawthorne's own tale-burning, see Turner, *Hawthorne*, pp. 49-52.

28. Bridge marks Hawthorne's greatest literary dejection late in 1836, well after the publication of DM; see *Personal Recollections of Nathaniel Hawthorne* (New York: Harper and Brothers, 1893), pp. 70-76. And even here he may unconsciously overstate, to emphasize the "turning point" (p. 76) marked by his own sponsorship of the 1837 *Twice-told Tales*.

29. For the text of "Sunday at Home" (SH)—first published in *The Token* for 1837—see *Twice-told Tales*, pp. 19-26.

30. "Monsieur du Miroir," in *Mosses*, p. 168.

31. For the full text of "The Sabbath Bells," as reprinted by Hawthorne, see *American Magazine*, II (May 1836), 399.

32. Hawthorne's remarks on his own "negative capability" occur in the course of a letter to Sophia (27 February 1842), the more general subject of which is his inability to "gush" or "take [his] heart in [his] hand"; see *Love Letters of Nathaniel Hawthorne 1839–1863* (Chicago: Society of the Dofobs, 1907), pp. 77-81. Obviously Hawthorne protests too much. And doubtless no human utterance defies "analysis." Yet the simple point is worth emphasizing: Hawthorne insists that his stories were made to stand off, as far as possible, from his own self-baffling self.

33. Henry James, *Hawthorne* (Ithaca, N.Y.: Cornell University Press, 1956), p. 46. Neither Crews nor any modern biographer has sought to estimate the probable effect of Hawthorne's actual experience of available religious tradition: the proto-Unitarianism of the Hathorne and Manning families, the conservative apologetics of Bowdoin, and the counterpointed readings (after that) in all the major writers of Puritanism and the Enlightenment. Yet from all this some plausible inferences might still be derived.

34. See J. Donald Crowley, "The Unity of Hawthorne's *Twice-told Tales,*" *Studies in American Fiction*, 1 (1973), 35-61.

35. C. S. B. Swann has attempted, with the aid of the speculations of Walter Benjamin, to make the various early fragments of "The Story Teller" (along with, oddly, "Wakefield") yield up a sense of Hawthorne's most general literary situation and strategies; but his approach is altogether too athematic to be useful here; see "The Theory and Practice of Story Telling," *Journal of American Studies*, 12 (1978), 185-205. Otherwise, thematic criticism of "The Story Teller" has advanced only a little beyond the first reconstructive speculations offered by Nelson F. Adkins, "The Early Projected Works of Nathaniel Hawthorne," *Papers of the Bibliographical Society of America*, 39 (1945), 119-155. Seymour L. Gross has (to me, convincingly) added four

tales to Adkins' original table of contents; see "Four Possible Additions to Hawthorne's 'Story Teller,' " *Papers of the Bibliographical Society of America,* 51 (1957), 90–95. Nina Baym has considered it as evidence of Hawthorne's changing relation with his audience; see *Shape,* pp. 39–50. And the major effort of Alfred Weber, though it succeeds in emphasizing the importance of the narrative frame-story in Hawthorne's total *oeuvre,* is marred by the extreme sobriety of his biographical approach to the narrator as author-surrogate and *bildungsroman* protagonist; see *Die Entwicklung der Rahmen-erzählungen Nathaniel Hawthornes* (Berlin: Erich Schmidt Verlag, 1973), pp. 142–307.

36. Moncure Conway quotes Elizabeth Peabody's recollection that Hawthorne "cared very little for the stories afterwards, which had in their original place in *The Story Teller* a great degree of significance"; cited from Adkins, "Projected Works," p. 133.

37. Baym is certainly correct to stress the greater conventionality of *much* that followed after Hawthorne had written (and failed to "collect") his intensely historical "Provincial Tales." Yet the example of *Fanshawe* "versus" the "Seven Tales" may suggest that Hawthorne may have been quite *deliberate* in his later attempt to write what was wanted; see *Shape,* pp. 53–83.

38. Adkins believes that "The Seven Vagabonds" represented a first attempt "to write an introduction to his proposed volume" ("Projected Works," p. 134). Weber studies it, along with other early tales of "Vagabunden und Pilger" as but a "Vorstadium" of "The Story Teller" (*Die Entwicklung,* pp. 129–141). Yet the point of social-thematic departure is the same in either case, and indeed "Passages" makes explicit allusion to "Vagabonds."·

39. All citations of the text of "The Seven Vagabonds" (SV) refer to *Twice-told Tales.* The tale first appeared in *The Token* for 1833, along with "The Canterbury Pilgrims." And though this is prior to the famous breaking up of the proposed "Story Teller," both tales may yet have been destined for that ill-fated collection.

40. Quoted from James Duban, "The Triumph of Infidelity in Hawthorne's 'The Story Teller,' " *Studies in American Fiction,* 7 (1979), p. 53. Though I dissent from the "orthodoxy" of Duban's emphasis, yet I think his work marks a clear advance over that of Adkins, Weber, and Baym; as also over that of James G. Janssen, "Hawthorne's Seventh Vagabond: 'The Outsetting Bard,' " *Emerson Society Quarterly,* 62 (1971), 22–28.

41. Adkins finds the ending of SV "abrupt" and theorizes, consequently, that Hawthorne had already abandoned some original plan for another ("Projected Works," p. 134). Yet it is possible to see the conclusion as entirely strategic, whatever the bibliographical facts.

42. As Duban deftly observes, "Genesis iv:12 inspired seventeenth- and eighteenth-century ministers to refer more generally to those who had strayed from God's fold as vagabonds" ("Triumph of Infidelity," p. 58).

43. The precise state of neo-Puritanic prejudice against fiction in the New England of the 1820's and 1830's is yet to be sociologically certified. Yet something of its power may be inferred from Emerson's choice of the Unitar-

ian ministry as a "literary" vocation; see Lawrence Buell, *Literary Transcendentalism* (Ithaca, N.Y.: Cornell University Press, 1973), pp. 23–54. And also from the extreme piety exhibited by so many writers who did indeed turn to fiction; see David S. Reynolds, *Faith in Fiction* (Cambridge: Harvard University Press, 1981), esp. pp. 73–122.

44. Hawthorne's summer strolls around New England no doubt taught him all he needed to know about the indecorous tone of many a camp meeting. Or, if not, he had a full sense of the background from James Lackington, *Memoirs . . . Containing . . . a Succinct Account of the Watchnights, Classes, Bands, Love-Feasts, etc., of the Methodists* (New York, 1796), which he borrowed in February 1831; see Marion L. Kesselring, *Hawthorne's Reading 1828–1850* (New York: New York Public Library, 1949), p. 54.

45. Though it seems a bit "much" to regard Hawthorne *himself* as Walter Benjamin's "figure in which the righteous man encounters himself" (see Swann, "Theory of Storytelling," p. 185), it seems clear that the ironic intelligence behind the whole "Story Teller" project has thought more critically about the enterprise of fiction than any of his dramatized characters; and that his own progress is, if anything, away from the outrageous Byronism which characterizes the maudlin and self-indulgent figure of "Oberon" in the "Fragments from the Journal of a Solitary Man" toward which the Story Teller himself may somehow be tending.

46. The first three sections of what came, ruefully, to be called "Passages from a Relinquished Work" (PRW)—titled "At Home," "A Flight in the Fog," and "A Fellow-Traveller"—were published as "The Story Teller, No. 1" in the *New England Magazine* for November 1834. A clear fourth section—"The Village Theatre"—was published, together with "Mr. Higginbotham's Catastrophe" (MHC), in the same magazine for December 1834 as "The Story Teller, No. 2." Though Hawthorne published MHC by itself in the 1837 *Twice-told Tales,* and though he did not republish the "relinquished" portions until pressed (by James T. Fields) to do so for the 1854 *Mosses,* clearly the materials all belong together.

47. For the text of all four sections of PRW, see *Mosses.*

48. Since Adkins ("Projected Works," pp. 145–146), Irving's *Sketchbook* has been widely recognized as some sort of provocation for "The Story Teller"; see Newman, *Reader's Guide,* p. 244.

49. For a complete listing of all the various "American materials" possibly to have appeared in "The Story Teller," see Adkins, "Projected Works," pp. 138–142.

50. George Parsons Lathrop may well have overstated the case to claim that the Story Teller "was to relate in public, every afternoon, a story illustrating the text previously discoursed upon [that morning] by the preacher," but surely there was to be some relation between their differently motivated words; see his "Introductory Note" to *Twice-told Tales* (Boston: Houghton Mifflin, 1883), p. 9.

51. As Adkins could make no proper "thematic" sense of "Mr. Higginbotham's Catastrophe" (MHC), so most later critics have taken it (out of context) as all

but meaningless. Thomas H. Pauly ascribes its clear "failure" to Hawthorne's own misguided attempt to be popular rather than serious; see "The Story Teller's Disaster," *American Transcendental Quarterly*, 14 (1972), 22–27. Weber situates it in relation to the "Passages," but is entirely caught up in the plight of "Oberon"; see *Die Entwicklung*, pp. 183–192. Only James Duban can imagine a fully intellectual reading: from the title on ("catastrophe" is David Hume's word for death), we are involved in some parody of the case for and against historical Christianity; see "The Skeptical Context of Hawthorne's MHC," *American Literature*, 48 (1976), 292–301.

52. All citations of MHC refer to *Twice-told Tales*.

53. The probable sources of Hawthorne's apologetics (and his typology) are well summarized in Duban, "Skeptical Context," pp. 295–299. The quotation marks around the crucial formula of typology in the text itself clearly indicate that someone is aware of serious undertones.

54. Whether Duban is right or wrong about Hawthorne's quarrel with liberalism (see "Triumph of Infidelity"), there can be no mistake about close attention to New England's latter-day religious sociology.

55. Adkins wisely infers nothing from the order in which the fragmented elements of "The Story Teller" were published (in the *New England Magazine* and elsewhere) after the original installments of November / December 1834; what happens next is, he fears, an "insoluble problem" ("Projected Works," p. 138). Weber moves next to the White Mountain episodes (*Die Entwicklung*, pp. 192–208), but there is no sufficient reason to suppose those indeed came next.

56. Once we accept the premise of Hawthorne's genuine discouragement over the breakup of his most carefully designed collection, the popular and miscellaneous character of the *Twice-told Tales* is easier to accept: why bother? It may also follow that the record of subsequent republication may tell us very little about Hawthorne's own literary judgments—contra Neal Frank Doubleday, "Hawthorne's Estimate of his Early Work," *American Literature*, 37 (1966), 403–409.

57. Quoted from Edwin Gittleman, *Jones Very: The Effective Years* (New York: Columbia University Press, 1967), p. 283. The original reporter of Hawthorne's remark is Elizabeth Peabody.

58. For the figure of Jones Very (behind the character of Roderick Elliston), see Robert D. Arner, "Hawthorne and Jones Very," *New England Quarterly*, 42 (1967), 267–275.

59. Baym rejects Gross's tentative assignment of MBV to "The Story Teller" (*Shape*, p. 40); Weber allows the possibility, but discusses it elsewhere (*Die Entwicklung*, pp. 65–73, 362). Yet the connection between Abbott and Hooper (himself Hawthorne's most famous forestudy of Very-Elliston) makes the case for inclusion very strong indeed.

60. Parodied here, apparently, is a crucial text in the Old Testament's logic of "the covenant": "do two walk together, unless they have made an appointment?" (Amos 3:3). The answer here might be entirely less severe than in the case of Young Goodman Brown, which evidently came up along the way.

61. As with MBV, Weber regards MM as a *possible* item in "The Story Teller" but discusses it earlier, where it cannot complicate his Oberon-project; see *Die Entwicklung*, pp. 80–89, 362. Yet the case for its inclusion seems overwhelming, as its terms explicitly recapitulate those of SV and PRW.

62. Weber's association of "The Ambitious Guest" (AG) and "The Great Carbuncle" (GCb) with the sketches of the White Mountains (*Die Entwicklung*, pp. 192–208) is self-evidently correct, though it merely confirms the observations of Adkins ("Projected Works," pp. 140–141). His further speculations—as, for example, that YGB follows from a sketch called "A Night Scene"—seem merely fanciful; see *Die Entwicklung*, p. 363.

63. The two sketches of the White Mountains, "The Notch" and "Our Evening Party Among the Mountains," originally appeared in the *New England Magazine* for November 1835, under the encompassing title of "Sketches From Memory, By A Pedestrian, No. 1." All citations here refer to *Mosses*.

64. See Kenneth Walter Cameron, *Genesis of Hawthorne's AG* (Hartford, Conn.: Thistle Press, 1955); and Mario L. D'Avanzo, "The Ambitious Guest in the Hands of an Angry God," *English Language Notes*, 14 (1976), 38–42. The tale first appeared in the *New England Magazine* for June 1835.

65. The very first of the relinquished "Passages" ("At Home") promises us some "moral, which many a dreaming youth may profit by" (*Mosses*, p. 409); and the "Fragments of the Journal of a Solitary Man" (FJSM)—the putative conclusion of the entire project, first published in the *American Monthly Magazine* for July 1837—offers this gleaming gem of Puritanic wisdom: "the world is also a sad one for him who shrinks from its sober duties" (*Snow-Image*, p. 326). Unless we wish to praise Hawthorne for this utter parody of himself (see Weber, *Die Entwicklung*, pp. 276–283, 299–307), we had better admit that the ironic key has indeed been lost. It may even turn out that Park Benjamin and not Hawthorne himself wrote much of this "conclusion"; see David W. Pancost, "Evidence of Editorial Additions to Hawthorne's FJSM," *Nathaniel Hawthorne Journal*, 5 (1975), 210–226.

66. Adkins ("Projected Works," p. 142) and Weber (*Die Entwicklung*, p. 362) both regard the inclusion of GCb as merely probable. I regard its placement as certain, despite its later appearance, in *The Token* for 1837.

67. All citations of the text of GCb refer to *Twice-told Tales*. The evidence of "The Pine-Tree Shillings" chapter of *Grandfather's Chair* suggests that Hawthorne probably had in mind, as a model for Pigsnort, the inordinately wealthy Captain John Hull; see *True Stories from History and Biography* (Columbus: Ohio State University Press, 1972), pp. 35–39.

68. The fact that MA and GCb appeared together (in *The Token* for 1837) suggests some connection, as well as the possibility that "The Story Teller" may have been more inclusive than previously supposed. There is, after all, no reason to suppose that *all* its contents appeared at once, in Benjamin's *New England Magazine* and the *American Monthly Magazine;* and indeed it seems likely that, with Hawthorne first dispirited and then busy "concocting" material for the *American Magazine*, much of what appeared in the 1837 *Token* may have been left over.

69. Patrick Morrow proposes a "Pilgrimage Group" including "The Celestial Rail-road" and "The Christmas Banquet" along with GCb and CP from the early tales; see "A Writer's Workshop: Hawthorne's GCb," *Studies in Short Fiction*, 6 (1969), 157–164. More apt, perhaps, would be a study of the "pilgrim" couples of GCb, CP, and MM, along with certain figures from Asals' "Marriage Group," as expressing the (not too subtle) thematic mind of the (dramatized) Story Teller.

70. For the sense of a conventional opposition between adventure and domesticity in the early phase of American letters, see William R. Spengemann, *The Adventurous Muse* (New Haven, Conn.: Yale University Press, 1977), esp. pp. 6–118.

71. For the elements, at least, of a Biblical pattern in GCb—involving I Samuel and Matthew—see W. R. Thompson, "Theme and Method in Hawthorne's GCb," *South-Central Bulletin*, 21 (1961), 3–10.

72. The text is the "Our Evening Party" section of "Sketches from Memory" (*Mosses*). As if in despite of itself, Hawthorne's complex carbuncle-text advertises two of its own learned sources, both of which discover ironies that bend the mind. The Story Teller himself is constrained to notice the achievement of "the biographer of the Indian Chiefs" (SM, 429). Yet its single mention of the White Mountains merely quotes Joselyn's account (in *New England's Rarities*) of a mysterious "pond" to be found there, at a great height, and of "a vapor (like a great pillar) drawn up by the sun-beams out of a great lake, or pond, into the air, where it was formed into a cloud"; and this curious information is situated, oddly, in the midst of several poetic mis-accounts of Lovewell's Fight; see Samuel G. Drake, *The Book of the Indians; or, Biography and History of the Indians of North America* (Boston: Antiquarian Bookstore, 1841), bk. III, p. 131. Hawthorne is known to have borrowed the 1832 edition of this work in June 1837, but evidently he had seen it much earlier as well. The text of GCb itself begins with a footnote assuring us that "Sullivan, in his history of Maine, written since the Revolution, remarks, that even then, the existence of the Great Carbuncle was not entirely discredited" (149). Yet that author's scornful point is that "the Savages in North America, by their natural sagacity, discovered the leading passion of their visitors, and encouraged them in the fruitless pursuit . . . of mountains of ore which never existed" and of "a gem, of immense size and value" on a certain peak in the White Mountains; see James Sullivan, *History of the District of Maine* (Boston: I. T. and E. T. Andrews, 1795), p. 74. The man to work all this out, I suppose, will be John Seelye, who has already recognized that Hawthorne is deliberately conflating the White Mountain legend with John Winthrop's own aboriginal interest in some "Great Lake" which, however gem-like, would help him control the beaver trade; see *Prophetic Waters*, pp. 161–185. For the present it seems sufficient to recognize that the Story Teller's "gem" is really only a lake; and that, whether the transformation signifies lust for wealth or longing for spiritual empire, Hawthorne and the Indians know better.

73. Thompson correctly identifies Matthew 5:14–16 as the Biblical source for the

"light imagery" in GCb ("Theme and Method," p. 6). But surely this is the least part of Hawthorne's strategy in invoking a place as classic as the Sermon on the Mount: as the Story Teller's own mountain sermon applies the Matthean blessing on "the poor in spirit" (5:3) to the unsublime domesticity of the home and hearth of Matthew and Hannah, so the subtle invocation of "a city set on a hill" which "cannot be hid" (5:14) implicates the Winthrop-Mather-Bercovitch theory of an "American" Salvation: with or without Niagara and the Mountains, America itself embodies and exhausts the geographic sublime.

74. Thompson declares that "the transition from idea to event is too slight ("Theme and Method," p. 9), and Morrow pronounces that the real interest of this "remarkable piece of seminal fiction" is the opportunity it provides to watch Hawthorne "trying out ideas . . . for his future benefit" ("Workshop," p. 164). Leo B. Levy flirts with the religious implications of Hawthorne's manipulation of the "false" (merely geographic) sublime, both here and in "My Visit to Niagara"; see "Hawthorne and the Sublime," *American Literature*, 37 (1966), 391–402. And Weber takes up the topic (in both places) as an aspect of the spiritual autobiography of "Oberon" (*Die Entwicklung*, pp. 203–208, 237–240, 245–247). Only Duban thinks to relate the Yankee interest in sublimity to the displacement of the Edwardsean experience of God ("Triumph of Infidelity," p. 56). And nobody has bothered to imagine what orthodox sermons (of Eliakim Abbott) AG and GCb might echo or parody.

75. "Chiefly About War Matters," in G. P. Lathrop, ed., *Tales, Sketches and Other Papers* (Boston: Houghton Mifflin, 1883), p. 317.

76. Despite Mellow's sense of Hawthorne's "very real gifts as an observer of the social scene" (*His Times*, p. 51), and allowing for Hawthorne's own later admiration for Trollope's uncanny ability to hew "a great lump out of the earth and put it under a glass case," it seems clear that Hawthorne was doomed by his gifts to be an "allegorist." In this precise sense: his fiction is always more a repetition of past sayings than an imitation of present (or permanent) nature.

77. As Arthur Hobson Quinn ably demonstrated, the Reverend Rufus M. Griswold resorted to deliberate rumor-mongering and even to forgery in order to slander Poe's posthumous reputation; see *Edgar Allan Poe* (New York: Appleton-Century, 1941), pp. 662–681. All that the more amiable Benjamin did to Hawthorne—besides ripping off his stories at a few dollars apiece—was to anthologize those stories after his own, rather than Hawthorne's preferred plan, with the result that all future editors (including Hawthorne himself) would agree to the miscellaneous model of the *Twice-told Tales*.

78. The ultimate irony of Hawthorne's *actual* career with the critics may well reside in the fact that, lacking an available model or tradition of dramatic/thematic interpretation of the tales in question, the fullest attempt to reconstruct "The Story Teller" concludes its labor with a sober meditation on Oberon as "eine erfundene amerikanische Künstlergestalt"; see Weber, *Die Entwicklung*, pp. 299–307. Earnest misprision can go no further, I believe, in any language.

79. As I have briefly suggested elsewhere, against the athematic modernism of Kenneth Dauber, Hawthorne's personal invitations are a good deal less simple than they seem, including the most "hospitable" invitation into "the study" of the Old Manse: preventing Thoreau's famous insistence on "the first person," the writer asks the reader in only to *read* (if he cares to) a series of dramatic and very nearly "framed" tales which force him back out into the thematic world of "Consciousness in Concord"; see "Sense of an Author," *ESQ*, 27 (1981), 108–133.

80. See "Hawthorne and his Mosses," in Harrison Hayford and Herschel Parker, ed., *Moby-Dick* (New York: W. W. Norton, 1967), p. 540.

81. The well-made couplet of Richard Wilbur's "Epistemology, II" reads like an epigraph to Hawthorne's own analyses, in the tales of the 1840's, of the Cartesian schizophrenia of the American Transcendentalists; see *The Poems of Richard Wilbur* (New York: Harcourt, Brace and World, 1963), p. 121.

82. James's *Hawthorne* first appeared in 1879, several years before Lathrop's "Introductory Note" to the Riverside Edition first emphasized the significance of "The Story Teller" (see note 50). For his fullest answer to the solemnity of Lathrop (and the "pessimistic" interpretation of E. Emile Montegut), see *Hawthorne*, pp. 20–53. Though James imagines that Hawthorne "asked but little of his milieu" (p. 23), he also observes that the appearance of "Story Teller" pieces such as SV and GCb "must have been highly agreeable" (p. 44).

83. *Hawthorne*, p. 81.

84. "Hawthorne and His Mosses," p. 537.

85. At issue, perhaps, is Milton Stern's assertion that Melville stands alone as a mid-century precursor of American naturalism; see *The Fine Hammered Steel of Herman Melville* (Urbana: University of Illinois Press, 1957), pp. 1–28. In fact Hawthorne worked out the problem first, in an entirely historical way; and his "naturalistic" criticism of Transcendental idealism clearly "influenced" Melville in a powerful way.

86. Though Hawthorne specifically blamed Benjamin for cutting up "The Story Teller" (since it was he who reversed the earlier decision of Joseph Tinker Buckingham to publish the whole project serially in the *New England Magazine*), the larger problem may involve Samuel Griswold Goodrich as well. For that worthy had already declined the manuscript for book-length publication some time early in 1834; see Adkins, "Projected Works," p. 132; and cf. Turner, *Hawthorne*, pp. 72–73. Goodrich was always quite willing to publish a number of Hawthorne's individual pieces in *The Token*, so long as they were unsigned. Possibly Benjamin merely agreed that no magazine could risk publishing too much material that was *obviously* by a single author.

87. For an outline of the new paradigm, see Kenneth Dauber, *Rediscovering Hawthorne* (Princeton, N.J.: Princeton University Press, 1977), pp. 3–46. For approving reception, see the review by Nina Baym in *American Literature*, 49 (1978), 656–657. And for my own strictures against both, see "Sense of an Author," pp. 116–121.

88. A "second" volume of the present study (which I am inclined to let someone

else attempt) would argue that the tales of the "Old Manse Period" constitute in effect Hawthorne's (anti-Transcendental) "History of His Own Times." The "third" (which I may yet try to complete) would note that about 1849 Hawthorne's thematic "career" began to recapitulate itself, even as it braved the difficulties of fiction in its "specific continuous forms."

89. "Old News, No. 1," *Snow-Image*, p. 132. The "historicist" sentiment expressed here gains in both clarity and force when compared with the meditation on "old newspapers, and still older almanacs" in "The Old Manse" (*Mosses*, pp. 20–21).

90. Though the question of typology as a form of civil religion might well be folded into the historical recipe of R. W. B. Lewis, the result would scarcely change his admirable formula for the Hawthorne who discovered that the "visionary and impalpable Now" revealed itself, upon inspection, as "nothing": "He listened for echoes"; see *American Adam*, pp. 119–123.

91. *True Stories*, p. 209.

❧ INDEX ☙

663

Michael J. Colacurcio is Professor of English at
the University of California, Los Angeles. He is the
author of *New Essays on "The Scarlet Letter"* (1985).